RICHARD III

The Self-Made King

Michael Hicks

YALE UNIVERSITY PRESS
NEW HAVEN AND LONDON

For information about this and other Yale University Press publications, please contact:
U.S. Office: sales.press@yale.edu yalebooks.com
Europe Office: sales@yaleup.co.uk yalebooks.co.uk

Set in Baskerville by IDSUK (DataConnection) Ltd
Printed in Great Britain by Clays Ltd, Elcograf S.p.A

Library of Congress Control Number: 2019948596

ISBN 978-0-300-21429-1 (hbk)
ISBN 978-0-300-25918-6 (pbk)

A catalogue record for this book is available from the British Library.

10 9 8 7 6 5 4 3 2 1

RICHARD III

Michael Hicks is Emeritus Professor of Medieval History at the University of Winchester and has been described as 'the greatest living expert on Richard' by *BBC History Magazine*. His previous publications include *The War of the Roses*.

Further praise for *Richard III*:

'Hicks moves with assurance from matters of policy and patronage to Richard's piety and estate building. His nuanced judgements bring out the complexity of Richard's character . . . It stands as an impressive tribute to a scholar who, over a lifetime of research and writing, has substantially deepened our understanding of Richard III and late medieval England as a whole.' Michael Jones, *BBC History Magazine*

'Hicks anchors every known move in Richard's career to the (often conflicting) sources, making it easier for readers to form their own judgements.' John Guy, *London Review of Books*

'Who is ready to challenge the ruthless and driven Plantagenet drawn from the shadows? This Richard is not the creation of what followed his death, but the thirty-two years of life that preceded it. A meticulous and thrilling biography.' Leanda de Lisle, author of *Tudor*

'A tour de force, based upon a deep understanding of the vast and divergent secondary literature and a career spent among the archives of fifteenth-century England.' David Grummitt, author of *A Short History of the Wars of the Roses*

'An intricately detailed account of Richard's every recorded move on his journey from younger son of the powerful Duke of York to the last of England's medieval monarchs.' Mark Jones, *Albion Magazine*

'Michael Hicks's contribution on Richard III will prove to be a most significant and influential biography of this king since Charles Ross's volume in the same series almost forty years ago. It is a compelling, fascinating and revealing examination that challenges both Richard's admirers and detractors . . . Hicks has created a mesmerising portrait of a remarkable and complex man that cannot be ignored.' J. L. Laynesmith

Also in the Yale English Monarchs Series

* Available in the U.S. from University of California Press

CONTENTS

PREFACE

The 15th century, and especially the Wars of the Roses, is the era of Richard III and the focus of the author's career as a historian. It is almost 50 years since my MA dissertation on Henry Percy, 4th Earl of Northumberland (d. 1489), retainer and rival of Richard III, and only five fewer since my DPhil thesis on George, Duke of Clarence (d. 1478), Richard's brother and another rival. A succession of studies of other contemporaries culminated in 1991 in my *Rivals of Richard III*. I have written about the king's public image (1991, 2000), his father-in-law Warwick the Kingmaker (1998), his eldest brother Edward IV (2004), nephew Edward V (2003), consort Anne Neville (2005), and his whole family (2015). All interacted with Richard III and hence all contributed step by step to my understanding of the duke and king. Approaching him from so many directions has forced me to revise and correct earlier publications by myself and others and, I hope, to improve my understanding. Inevitably this book revisits many aspects and inevitably it supplements and corrects what I have written before. I have learnt a lot in the writing. I hope that this history is better too.

Three principles have shaped this book. First of all, Richard was a 15th-century nobleman (magnate) and needs to be treated as such, in the tradition of the great Oxford historian K.B. McFarlane (d. 1966). McFarlane taught his students to locate such men in the many contexts within which they were brought up: political, national and local, military, religious, and much else. Richard knew the standards shared by his peers and society more generally and catered for their expectations, albeit also often flouting them. Since such great men were landholders and dynasts, it is necessary to research and understand their estates, income and expenditure, public office, and retainers. It was by retaining men that magnates made themselves powerful: their power, known as bastard feudalism, could be abused. This book is therefore a biography of a great nobleman and indeed a royal prince who unexpectedly became a king and brought to this new role the outlook and experience of his former life. Henry IV and Edward IV are parallels. Richard sought advice and delegated to staff, but he was also, it seems to me, the author of his key decisions and actions.

Second, Richard lived for 32 years, only two of them as king. He had a career and personal life 30 years long before he became king. It was during those years that he grew up, absorbed beliefs, principles, values, morals, and prejudices, and shaped the outlook and conduct that he brought to monarchy. He was an aristocrat like the other aristocrats of his time, unusual because he had neither the inheritance of an heir nor the limited expectations of a younger son, and remarkable because of the strategic visions that he made into realities. A mature man does not change his whole character when he becomes king. Richard brought to his kingship the ideology, experiences, and modes of operation that he had developed as a duke, although now actuated by a heightened sense of dignity, an impatience of opposition, and a ruthlessness no longer fettered by others. This book therefore devotes exceptional space to Richard's life as duke and seeks to draw out the continuities in his behaviour before and after 1483.

Third, therefore, this is not a study of Richard's life and times, still less the comprehensive and rounded analysis of the reign that Charles Ross achieved, nor indeed a pre-history of the Tudors. It is an account of the formation and activities of Richard the man. It is a more direct biography that deploys all the evidence. That Richard's purported bones at Leicester reveal him to have been indeed a hunchback (a sufferer from scoliosis) has rehabilitated a key element of the Tudor legend. It enables this book to employ the testimony of such Tudor writers as the Crowland Continuator, Sir Thomas More, and Polydore Vergil that have been over-disparaged for so long: albeit critically and sceptically.

No biographies of medieval English kings are more indebted to the works of others than those of Richard III. My footsteps have been guided by my supervisors John Armstrong, who so splendidly edited Mancini's *Usurpation of Richard III*, T.B. Pugh, and Charles Ross and by their publications. I have often been grateful to such 19th- and early 20th-century historians as Sir Henry Ellis, James Gairdner, Charles Kingsford, James Raine the elder and younger, and Cora L. Scofield; to the excellent modern editions of sources by Armstrong, Lorraine Attreed, Joseph Bain, Barrie Dobson, Chris Given-Wilson, Peter Hammond, Rosemary Horrox, Nicholas Pronay, Anne Sutton, Richard Sylvester, and Livia Visser-Fuchs; to the ground-breaking studies of Alec Myers, Paul Murray Kendall, Ralph Griffiths, Horrox again, Louise Gill, and Tony Pollard; and to the literally hundreds of articles and notes published mainly in the *Ricardian*, the journal of the Richard III Society. Historians both professional and amateur have explored so many topics often overlooked, such as Richard's coronation and library, and have left every future biographer in their debt. A new generation of Ricardians has already emerged. My research students, especially Gordon McKelvie and Alex Brondarbit, have also played their part. There are too many historical and fictional works that touch on Richard III for anyone to read them all and to extract all the nuggets of originality that they contain. The foundation for modern study remains Charles Ross's *Richard III*, now almost 40 years old, but still fundamental and not superseded here. The present book does not engage in detail with Ross's work or strive to correct, applaud, or update everything he wrote. Crucial though the narrative sources are, this book makes much of the documents that record actions at the time and often enough those of Richard himself. The author gratefully acknowledges his debts to those before him who are too numerous to itemise individually.

Regrettably, historians of Richard III never secure everybody's approval and no doubt many unwitting contributors to this study will disavow the use made of their work. I thank them nevertheless, while acknowledging that I am personally responsible for my interpretations and for the errors that have inevitably crept in. My friends and colleagues, parents and children have always been supportive, but my greatest debt is to my long-suffering and ever-encouraging wife Cynthia with whom I discussed Richard III at that first party over the acupuncture clinic at Hornchurch in 1972. The book was overshadowed by the death of our son Ralph (1978–2015) to whose memory we dedicate it.

Documents in the National Archives, formerly the Public Record Office, are cited by their call number only.

MICHAEL HICKS

Taunton, August 2018

ILLUSTRATIONS

PLATES

8. Middleham Church, North Yorkshire. © Historic England Archive.

9. King Richard III and Queen Anne Neville as heirs of the earldom of Warwick from the *Rous Roll*.

10. Bisham Priory, Berkshire. Courtesy of the Roxburghe Club.

11. King Richard III and Queen Anne Neville in their coronation robes. Courtesy of the Roxburghe Club.

12. York Minster, 'the acropolis of the North', completed in 1472. Steve F-E-Cameron / CC-BY-SA-3.0.

13. The frontage of St William's College, York. Tim Green / CC-BY-SA-2.0.

14. The upper hall in St William's College, York. Mary Evans Picture Library / age fotostock.

15. Richard Duke of York and Edward V. With kind permission of the Chapter, Canterbury Cathedral.

16. Richard III's mandate to Lord Chancellor Russell for delivery of the great seal as he takes personal command against the rebellion of the duke of Buckingham in 1483.

17. Richard III: the image of a cunning and masterful king. From the misericord at Christchurch Priory (formerly Hampshire). © Christchurch Priory.

PEDIGREES

ABBREVIATIONS

Arrivall	*Historie of the Arrivall of Edward IV*, ed. J. Bruce (1838)
BIHR	*Bulletin of the Institute of Historical Research*
BL	British Library, London
CCR	*Calendar of the Close Rolls*
CDRS	*Calendar of Documents Relating to Scotland*, iv, ed. J. Bain (1888)
CFR	*Calendar of the Fine Rolls, 1461–1509*
CPL	*Calendar of the Papal Registers*
CPR	*Calendar of the Patent Rolls*
Crowland	*The Crowland Chronicle Continuations 1459–86*, eds N. Pronay and J. Cox (1986)
EHR	*English Historical Review*
'Financial Memoranda'	'Financial Memoranda of the Reign of Edward V', ed. R. Horrox (1987)
Foedera	T. Rymer, *Foedera, Conventiones, Literae, and cujuscunque generis Acta Publica*, eds J. Caley, et al. (1827)
GEC	G.E. Cokayne, *The Complete Peerage of England, Scotland, Ireland, Great Britain and the United Kingdom*, eds H.V. Gibbs, et al. (1910–59)

Gill, *Buckingham's Rebellion*	L. Gill, *Richard III and Buckingham's Rebellion* (1999)
H433	*British Library Harleian Manuscript 433*, eds P.W. Hammond and R.E. Horrox (1979–83)
Hall's Chronicle	*Hall's Chronicle*, ed. H. Ellis (1811)
Hanham, *Richard III*	A. Hanham, *Richard III and his Earlier Historians 1483–1535* (1975)
Hicks, *Clarence*	M. Hicks, *False, Fleeting, Perjur'd Clarence. George Duke of Clarence 1449–78* (1980)
Hicks, *Edward V*	M. Hicks, *Edward V: The Prince in the Tower* (2003)
Hicks, *Richard III*	M. Hicks, *Richard III* (2000)
Hicks, *Rivals*	M. Hicks, *Richard III and his Rivals. Magnates and their Motives during the Wars of the Roses* (1991)
Hicks, *Wars*	M. Hicks, *The Wars of the Roses* (2003)
Hicks, *Warwick*	M. Hicks, *Warwick the Kingmaker* (1998)
Horrox, *Richard III*	R.E. Horrox, *Richard III: A Study of Service* (1989)
HR	*Historical Research*
Lander, *Crown and Nobility*	J.R. Lander, *Crown and Nobility 1450–1509* (1976)
Mancini, *Richard III*	D. Mancini, *The Usurpation of Richard III*, ed. C.A.J. Armstrong (1969)
More, *Richard III*	T. More, *History of King Richard III*, ed. R.S. Sylvester (1963)
ODNB	*Oxford Dictionary of National Biography* (2004)
Paston L&P	*Paston Letters and Papers of the Fifteenth Century*, eds R. Beadle, N. Davis, and C. Richmond (2004–5)
Plumpton L &P	*The Plumpton Letters and Papers*, ed. Joan Kirby (1996)
Pollard, *NE England*	A.J. Pollard, *North-Eastern England during the Wars of the Roses. Lay Society, War, and Politics 1450–1500* (1990)

Pollard, *Princes*	A.J. Pollard, *Richard III and the Princes in the Tower* (1991)
PROME	*The Parliament Rolls of England 1275–1504*, ed. C. Given-Wilson (2005)
Ross, *Edward IV*	C.D. Ross, *Edward IV* (1974)
Ross, *Richard III*	C.D. Ross, *Richard III* (1981)
Somerville, *Lancaster*	R. Somerville, *History of the Duchy of Lancaster*, vol. 1 (1953)
TRHS	*Transactions of the Royal Historical Society*
Vergil, *English History*	*Three Books of Polydore Vergil's English History*, ed. H. Ellis (1844)

Pedigree 1: The Royal Line of Succession

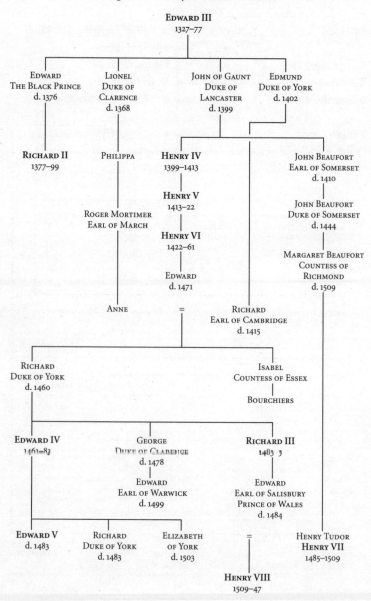

Pedigree 2: The House of York 1452–64

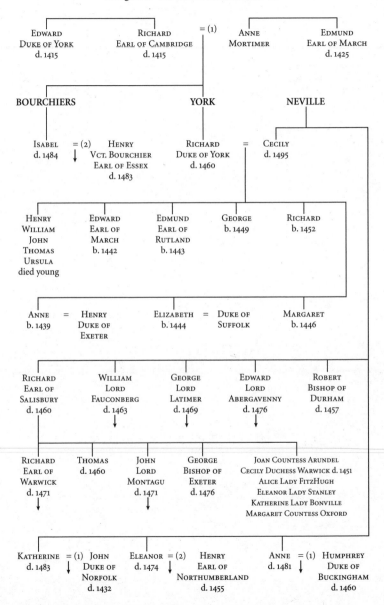

EDWARD
DUKE OF YORK
d. 1415

RICHARD
EARL OF CAMBRIDGE
d. 1415

= (1)

ANNE
MORTIMER

EDMUND
EARL OF MARCH
d. 1425

BOURCHIERS   **YORK**   **NEVILLE**

ISABEL
d. 1484

= (2)

HENRY
VCT. BOURCHIER
EARL OF ESSEX
d. 1483

RICHARD
DUKE OF YORK
d. 1460

=

CECILY
d. 1495

HENRY
WILLIAM
JOHN
THOMAS
URSULA
died young

EDWARD
EARL OF
MARCH
b. 1442

EDMUND
EARL OF
RUTLAND
b. 1443

GEORGE
b. 1449

RICHARD
b. 1452

ANNE
b. 1439

=

HENRY
DUKE OF
EXETER

ELIZABETH
b. 1444

=

DUKE OF
SUFFOLK

MARGARET
b. 1446

RICHARD
EARL OF
SALISBURY
d. 1460

WILLIAM
LORD
FAUCONBERG
d. 1463

GEORGE
LORD
LATIMER
d. 1469

EDWARD
LORD
ABERGAVENNY
d. 1476

ROBERT
BISHOP OF
DURHAM
d. 1457

RICHARD
EARL OF
WARWICK
d. 1471

THOMAS
d. 1460

JOHN
LORD
MONTAGU
d. 1471

GEORGE
BISHOP OF
EXETER
d. 1476

JOAN COUNTESS ARUNDEL
CECILY DUCHESS WARWICK d. 1451
ALICE LADY FITZHUGH
ELEANOR LADY STANLEY
KATHERINE LADY BONVILLE
MARGARET COUNTESS OXFORD

KATHERINE
d. 1483

= (1)

JOHN
DUKE OF
NORFOLK
d. 1432

ELEANOR
d. 1474

= (2)

HENRY
EARL OF
NORTHUMBERLAND
d. 1455

ANNE
d. 1481

= (1)

HUMPHREY
DUKE OF
BUCKINGHAM
d. 1460

Pedigree 3: The House of York 1461–83

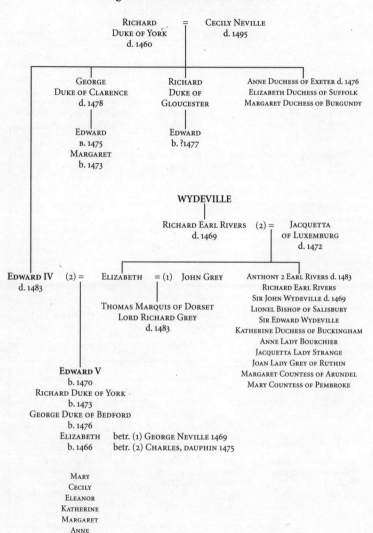

RICHARD
DUKE OF YORK
d. 1460
= CECILY NEVILLE
d. 1495

GEORGE
DUKE OF CLARENCE
d. 1478

RICHARD
DUKE OF
GLOUCESTER

ANNE DUCHESS OF EXETER d. 1476
ELIZABETH DUCHESS OF SUFFOLK
MARGARET DUCHESS OF BURGUNDY

EDWARD
B. 1475
MARGARET
b. 1473

EDWARD
b. ?1477

WYDEVILLE

RICHARD EARL RIVERS
d. 1469
(2) = JACQUETTA
OF LUXEMBURG
d. 1472

EDWARD IV   (2) =
d. 1483

ELIZABETH   = (1) JOHN GREY

THOMAS MARQUIS OF DORSET
LORD RICHARD GREY
d. 1483

ANTHONY 2 EARL RIVERS d. 1483
RICHARD EARL RIVERS
SIR JOHN WYDEVILLE d. 1469
LIONEL BISHOP OF SALISBURY
SIR EDWARD WYDEVILLE
KATHERINE DUCHESS OF BUCKINGHAM
ANNE LADY BOURCHIER
JACQUETTA LADY STRANGE
JOAN LADY GREY OF RUTHIN
MARGARET COUNTESS OF ARUNDEL
MARY COUNTESS OF PEMBROKE

EDWARD V
b. 1470
RICHARD DUKE OF YORK
b. 1473
GEORGE DUKE OF BEDFORD
b. 1476
ELIZABETH   betr. (1) GEORGE NEVILLE 1469
b. 1466   betr. (2) CHARLES, DAUPHIN 1475

MARY
CECILY
ELEANOR
KATHERINE
MARGARET
ANNE
BRIDGET

Pedigree 4: Richard III's Family 1483–5

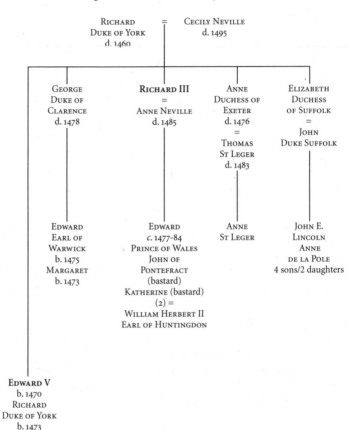

RICHARD = CECILY NEVILLE
DUKE OF YORK   d. 1495
d. 1460

GEORGE   **RICHARD III**   ANNE   ELIZABETH
DUKE OF   =   DUCHESS OF   DUCHESS
CLARENCE   ANNE NEVILLE   EXETER   OF SUFFOLK
d. 1478   d. 1485   d. 1476   =
   =   JOHN
   THOMAS   DUKE SUFFOLK
   ST LEGER
   d. 1483

EDWARD   EDWARD   ANNE   JOHN E.
EARL OF   c. 1477-84   ST LEGER   LINCOLN
WARWICK   PRINCE OF WALES   ANNE
b. 1475   JOHN OF   DE LA POLE
MARGARET   PONTEFRACT   4 sons/2 daughters
b. 1473   (bastard)
   KATHERINE (bastard)
   (2) =
   WILLIAM HERBERT II
   EARL OF HUNTINGDON

EDWARD V
b. 1470
RICHARD
DUKE OF YORK
b. 1473
ELIZABETH
b. 1466
CECILY = RALPH SCROPE
KATHERINE
ANNE
BRIDGET

Chapter One

MYTHS ANCIENT AND MODERN
THE SHAPING OF RICHARD III

I

It is half a millennium since Richard III (1483–5) was king. He is traditionally regarded as the last of England's medieval monarchs – 14th and last of the great house of Plantagenet (1154–1485) and third of the Yorkist kings (1461–85). He terminated both dynasties. He has been bracketed with King John as the worst of English medieval rulers. England's greatest playwright William Shakespeare depicted Richard III as an evil, power-crazed tyrant whose crimes fully justified the accession of the Tudors.[1] Certainly Richard was one of the most disastrous monarchs ever to occupy the throne of England. Not only had he one of the shortest of reigns – a mere 26 months – but it terminated in complete defeat, with his deposition and death on the battlefield of Bosworth in 1485. Bosworth was long accepted as the decisive moment that divided English medieval history from the modern history presided over by the Tudors (1485–1603), the Stuarts (1603–1714), the Hanoverians (1714–1837), and our own house of Windsor. That chronology no longer works. Centuries have passed since this divide was first acknowledged. It is no longer easy to lump Tudor England together with our own post-industrial, post-colonial, democratic, and digital age. 1500 no longer appears modern.

[1] W. Shakespeare, *Richard III*, ed. A. Hammond, Arden edn (Methuen, 1981).

1

Richard lived during the Wars of the Roses, three civil wars that lasted with decade-long breaks roughly from 1450 to 1500. It was an era of turbulence when the people and continental neighbours intervened repeatedly in English affairs and when all governments were weak. Civil war broke out when the ruling Lancastrian King Henry VI (1422–61) was challenged by the Yorkists, whose descent in the female line via the Mortimers from an elder son of Edward III (1327–77) was argued to be superior. The First War of 1459–61 brought Richard's eldest brother Edward IV (1461–83) to the throne. As the new king's youngest brother, Richard (b. 1452) was created duke of Gloucester. He engaged in politics from 1468–9. Actually King Edward reigned twice. His First Reign of 1461–70 was interrupted briefly by the Second War (1469–71) and the return of the defeated Henry VI (1470–1). This upheaval was orchestrated by Richard Neville, earl of Warwick and Salisbury (Warwick the Kingmaker, 1428–71), Queen Margaret of Anjou, and the French King Louis XI. The teenaged Richard featured prominently. Edward IV won again: his Second Reign of 1471–83 was more successful. Domestic politics was dominated by the titanic struggle of the two royal dukes, Gloucester and his elder brother George Duke of Clarence, which ended in 1478 with Clarence's execution. They contended over the great Warwick inheritance, to which their duchesses – Warwick's two daughters – were heiresses. Richard had married the younger sister Anne Neville, and on the strength of her inheritance he came to dominate northern England. He was 'Lord of the North'. The culmination of Richard's first 30 years was his victory against the Scots in 1480–3. While Duke Richard was undoubtedly as self-interested and ruthless as other great noblemen, he has been revealed as an effective operator who may have been genuinely popular in the North. He was destined nevertheless to feature only marginally in the history books.

All this changed in 1483, when Richard's eldest brother King Edward IV died a natural death (9 April 1483). At this point what is known of Richard moves from a couple of events or documents per year to almost a day-by-day narrative. Edward IV was succeeded by his underage son Edward, but only for 10 weeks. The boy's uncle Duke Richard made himself first Lord Protector and then king. Two coups d'état mark his advance to the throne: in his First Coup in early May he seized control of

Edward V and in his Second Coup (13 June) he eliminated the young king's most committed supporters. Richard III's accession followed on 26 June 1483. Richard argued that Edward V was illegitimate and therefore that he himself was rightful next heir, but his claim was not generally accepted. He aspired to be a good king who was devoted to the public good, but his accession brought not stability but division, the Third War of the Roses. Richard was strongly criticised and indeed reviled for his usurpation, for the disappearance and probable killing of Edward V and his brother (the Princes in the Tower), for the poisoning of his own queen in 1485, and for planning incestuously to marry his niece Elizabeth of York, eldest daughter of Edward IV and elder sister of Edward V. His two-year reign (1483–5) was coloured by attempts to depose him, unsuccessfully in 1483 (Buckingham's Rebellion), but ultimately successfully, when Richard was defeated and killed by Henry Tudor (Henry VII, 1485–1509) at the battle of Bosworth (22 August 1485). This was the end of Richard and of this book, but the Wars of the Roses puttered on with a series of other claimants into the reign of King Henry VIII (1509–47), in whose veins ran the blood of the warring houses.

The facts of the Third War after 1483 and Richard III's part in it are not disputed, but what it all means – how it is to be interpreted – is contested. This chapter looks first at the traditional Tudor orthodoxies, at the modern Ricardian counter-attack, at the enormous research effort of the past half century, and at the current news generated by archaeological and scientific investigation.

II

Should Richard be held at fault or were his actions justified? For five centuries, there was no contest. The victors of Bosworth, Richard's enemies, wrote Richard's history, and inevitably found against him. The victors always do write the history. Richard's reign, moreover, was so short that nobody had time to document it before it had ended. If history must always be written after the event, Richard was allowed only two years before the Tudor era, which inevitably asserted the righteousness of his enemies and denigrated the hopeless and deserved failure of Richard's own career. That Richard was wrongly a ruler and was an evil tyrant were the founding principles of the

Tudor regime. The victors made this into the historical orthodoxy, while the vanquished remained silent, self-effacing, anxious not to draw attention to themselves and their backing for the insupportable. It was Henry VII's men, not Richard's, who reported to Sir Thomas More and Polydore Vergil, who made convincing and connected history out of this partisan material. Tudor historians therefore accepted the charges against Richard III. Their version of events as set out by Sir Thomas More, publicised by Edward Hall and Raphael Holinshed, and dramatised by William Shakespeare held sway until the mid-20th century.[2] This was the accepted orthodoxy for James Gairdner's critical scientific history in 1898 and for A.L. Rowse in 1966.[3] New productions of Shakespeare's play repeat this message.

Although More was a mere child when Richard reigned and Polydore Vergil came across from Italy after his death, both had undertaken considerable research, talking in particular to those who had witnessed events. Thomas More was especially well informed. That he conformed to classical models and sometimes satirised them, cracked jokes and deliberately misled his readership is unfortunate as it makes it hard to distinguish his hard data from his literary and other devices.

More's analysis of Richard's character was immensely influential, but is often discounted today because it is so obviously biased against Richard. Readers were intended to take away the most violent, malign, and villainous impression of the king. Yet More's portrayal is not wholly hostile, no hatchet job. It is all three of the York brothers who, correctly, are declared 'statelye of stomacke, gredye and ambicious of authoritie, and impacient of parteners'. In comparison with his brothers King Edward and Clarence, that 'goodly noble prince', Richard was 'in witte and courage egall [equal] with either of them' – just as intelligent and just as brave. He was warlike and military-minded as princes ought to be, a good general, and 'free . . . of despence', generosity being a virtue highly prized in gentlemen and princes. Such positive characteristics, however, were deliberately lost in a morass of double negatives and all were qualified. Readers skate over the praise of Richard's wit and courage to the 'bodye and prowesse far vnder them

[2] More, *Richard III*; Vergil, *English History*; Shakespeare, *Richard III*, pp. 74–5.
[3] J. Gairdner, *History of the Life and Reign of Richard the Third* (Cambridge University Press, 1898); A.L. Rowse, *Bosworth Field and the Wars of the Roses* (Macmillan, 1966).

bothe', that was perhaps less true. To be 'little of stature' and 'hard fauoured of visage' as in his portraits is deployed against him. Always it is the unfavourable option or interpretation that More highlighted. The military service and military mindedness that were (and are) so desirable in a prince (states) become 'in other menne otherwise' – the mindless violence of the football hooligan. 'None euill captaine was hee in the warre' – a double negative obscuring what is actually praise of him as a good commander. To be generous is good; to be lavish beyond one's means is to be deplored as extravagance; even worse is when what is given away belongs to others. Never to fail either by 'hardinesse or polytique order' makes Richard's admirable audacity and foresight sound unattractive. Admittedly there are many nastier charges: 'not letting to kisse whom he thoughte to kyll' alludes unmistakeably to Judas Iscariot who betrayed Christ with a kiss. That Richard was 'dispitious and cruell' could be rendered almost pardonable by ill-will, yet it is exacerbated when motivated by 'ambicion . . . either for the suretie or encrease of his estate'. Richard was ruthless in eliminating any 'whose life withstoode his purpose'. If Richard did kill Henry VI with his own hands, he performed the 'boocherly office' in person 'without commaundemente or knoweledge of the king', because he wanted to wreak the slaughter himself. If he facilitated the death of his brother Clarence, he did it because 'hartely minded to his welth'. There is a consistency from Richard's unnatural birth to his usurpation of the throne that is sustained not by direct statements and proofs, but by allusion and argument secured by the keystone that 'hee [i.e. Potyer] was not likelye to speake it of noughte'.[4] Literary acrobatics carry the reader to the inevitable conclusion that Richard was irredeemably evil.

Yet More the Renaissance Man did not believe that an unnatural birth really determined personality, that Richard had killed Henry VI for pleasure, that he conspired Clarence's death 'whiche hee resisted openly', nor that Potyer's comment, if true, clinched the argument. When his portrayal is analysed, More's skill becomes even more apparent. The real Richard was indeed a small man, military-minded and ruthless, he did give

[4] More, *Richard III*, pp. 6–8. Potyer, mentioned by More as prophesying that Richard would be king, may have been the Richard Potyer recorded in Richard's service who was eventually appointed attorney of the Duchy of Lancaster in chancery.

away what had been confiscated, he did advance himself at the expense of others, he did dissimilate and betray. If the Leicester bones are genuine, More was right to mention Richard's deformity. It is easy to conjure up examples that illustrate More's points – to identify, for instance, Edward IV's three anonymous mistresses. Our problem is, however, that More was not an eyewitness and appears sometimes closer to a secondary source. The single illustration for each characteristic that occurs to historians may be the only one known to More also. Like any secondary writer, More was generalising about Richard's whole life and character on the basis of such single, isolated, and perhaps exceptional examples. Yet his portrait might be true. Historians constantly wrestle with their sources and are fortunately trained to do so, but there can be few sources like More's history that so deliberately and skilfully set out to deceive. More's characterisation therefore cannot be accepted as it stands, but neither can it be rejected out of hand.[5] It is not purely Tudor propaganda.

More supplied us with some background – Richard's unnatural birth, evil character, and earlier crimes – before focusing on the most detailed narrative of Richard's accession that continues today to form the core of any biography of the king. He also built up towards Buckingham's Rebellion as the origins of Henry VII's regime that, like Vergil's closely related account,[6] surely derives from Tudor sources and obscures what was initially not about Henry at all.[7] It is Vergil also who sets Richard into the providential framework (the Tudor myth) that was to be so much better presented by Edward Hall (d. 1547).[8] Not only was Richard a wrongful king, the beneficiary of the whole cycle of illicit usurpations since 1399, but he was not even the rightful Yorkist claimant. He was personally evil, guilty of great crimes, and a tyrant who deserved to lose his throne and who indeed was destined for hellfire. A portrait of Richard III was doctored to make him into the hunchback of legend.[9]

[5] This discussion is based on More, *Richard III*, pp. 5–10.

[6] Ibid. pp. 90–3; Vergil, *English History*, pp. 194–202.

[7] M.A. Hicks, 'Unweaving the Web: The Plot of July 1483 Against Richard III and its Wider Significance', *Ricardian*, 114 (1991), pp. 108–9; Hicks, *Richard III*, pp. 155–9.

[8] F.J. Levy, *Tudor Historical Thought* (Huntington Library, 1967), pp. 171–7.

[9] M.A. Hicks, *Richard III: The Man Behind the Myth* (Collins & Brown, 1991), p. 7.

III

No contemporary presented Richard's case. Surviving supporters had avoided sharing Richard's fate by concealing their participation in his regime and their alignment with the intolerable. To reveal their presence at Bosworth risked forfeiture of land or rights, or at least heavy fines and bonds that restricted their movements and liberty.[10] It is a sparse and unreliable smattering of snippets that are recorded. It was only when the Ricardian cause was no longer a live issue that anybody could safely take Richard's side, even then paradoxically defending the indefensible. When the first serious Ricardian historian Sir George Buck sought to take a more balanced view, he could find no pro-Ricardian portrait or narrative on which to build and scarcely any more records than we possess today. Forced to rely on the testimony of Richard's enemies, Buck was reduced to pointing out the inconsistencies and improbabilities of the traditional orthodoxy and to bemoan the erroneous criteria against which Richard was judged.[11] Richard's history and his appraisal therefore have to be reconstructed from the narratives and records of his enemies. This is not impossible: Buck, in 1619, and Horace Walpole, in 1759, have shown how much useful material for Richard's case can be extracted from Thomas More's hostile history.[12]

As Richard became more remote in time and his standing ever less important, it became easier to take a more favourable view. Was anybody ever so irredeemably wicked as Richard was portrayed? The times when he lived, so similar to the age of More and Shakespeare and even Buck, became alien and indeed unacceptable to later ages. The standards of political conduct current in Richard's own day have ceased to be appropriate or even worthy of mention. Buck showed that Richard's actions could be justified by *raison d'état* (national interest). Richard was being assessed more harshly than earlier rulers, both classical like Julius Caesar and medieval like England's other post-conquest kings.[13] Since then the

---

[10] William Catesby and the Brachers were executed. Henry had 23 attainted at his first parliament, *PROME*, vol. 15, p. 108. The earl of Westmorland had to surrender his heir and was enmeshed by bonds, *CCR 1485–1500*, no. 82.

[11] E.g. G. Buck, *History of King Richard III* (1619), ed. A.N. Kincaid (A. Sutton, 1979).

[12] E.g. Buck, *Richard III*, p. 26; H. Walpole, *Historic Doubts on the Life and Reign of Richard III*, ed. P.W. Hammond (A. Sutton, 1987), pp. 31, 36.

[13] Buck, *Richard III*, pp. 28–9.

Stuarts, like the Tudors, have passed away, monarchy had been succeeded by constitutional democracy, and governments have come to be assessed by their contribution to the wellbeing of the governed. Tudor writers took the battle of Bosworth as God's judgement on the wicked, which subsequent historians, from the 18th century on, no longer believed. Nobody since the 18th-century Enlightenment has accepted the roles attributed by Tudor historians to divine providence, the stars, and omens, or believed that character is betrayed at birth, in physical imperfections, or stamped upon one's face. Moreover, the overwhelming hostility of the key sources and of generations of English people proved, on closer examination, to be very insubstantially based. Whatever firsthand knowledge was cited by Richard's surviving contemporaries in the parliament of 1485 to dismiss his regime and to condemn the king himself, it never passed beyond the spoken word and is now irretrievably lost. As for the chronicles, not only is there often only one witness, frequently assertive or mere hearsay, but all such narratives were written after Richard's fall by those who were employed by his Tudor vanquishers or at least in their era when their rightfulness and the king's wrongfulness was unquestioned. The criteria by which Richard was historically judged has been decisively rejected by Richard's modern supporters (the Ricardians).

The official version was too absolute and unqualified to meet modern historical standards or indeed those of earlier critical historians. If Richard was so transparently wicked, how could he have reigned at all? Those sympathetic to King Richard exploited to the full the Tudor character of his critics. Two of his earliest historians, Bernard André and Polydore Vergil, respectively poet laureate and official historiographer, were commissioned by Henry VII. Sir Thomas More in other capacities worked for Henry VIII. Without exception all of the others – including the writer of the Crowland Chronicles and John Rous – became Tudor subjects and bowed to the verdict of Bosworth. All of them therefore were influenced by the Tudors and peddled Tudor propaganda. Their testimony was thus biased and tainted, the Ricardians argued, and should be rejected. This blanket rejection covered all their writings, including More's history that had been the main source hitherto. Not only did the Ricardians rebut Richard's reputed crimes, especially the murder of the princes, but also the story of his unnatural birth and his supposed deformity. The king's hunched back was also propaganda.[14]

A second string to the Ricardian case was that there was no definitive proof for the charges. None of the chroniclers were eyewitnesses to the murder of the princes and their testimony was mere hearsay. Nobody accused Richard of killing the princes at Henry VII's first parliament: or rather, there is no evidence that they did.[15] Strictly applied, these arguments rule out of consideration all the principal narratives. Only records will do. The Ricardians imply that histories written during Richard's reign, had they existed, would have been less hostile and indeed favourable to the king. Doubtless this is correct. There would have been the same pressure to be deferential among Richard's subjects during his reign as later under Henry VII and VIII.

Key works in developing a more favourable interpretation have been Josephine Tey's deservedly famous novel *The Daughter of Time* (first published 1951), Paul Murray Kendall's pioneering biography (1955), and Jeremy Potter's *Good King Richard?* (1985), each of which combines a commitment to Richard's reassessment with some original research and findings. In 1954 and later Professor Alec Myers carefully re-examined the evidence for the murders that More hinted that Richard had committed before his accession. Myers found the foundations to be inadequate and that the stories grew in the telling, after Richard's fall had marked him out as irredeemably wicked.[16] He deployed the more favourable assessments of the contemporaries Bishop Thomas Langton and Pietro Carmeliano.[17] However, the first historian to look beyond the Tudor narratives and beyond the traditional sources was the American Paul Murray Kendall. Although far from even-handed in his assessment – Professor Charles Ross characterised his work as 'the high-water mark of Ricardian apologia' – it was Kendall who first appreciated Richard's career as 'Lord of the North',

[14] J. Potter, *Good King Richard?* (Constable, 1985), pp. 136–7.

[15] Ibid., p. 131.

[16] A.R. Myers, 'The Character of Richard III' in *English Society and Government*, ed. C.M.D. Crowder (Oliver & Boyd, 1967); 'Richard III and the Historical Tradition', *History*, 53 (1968), pp. 182–3; see also *English Historical Documents*, iv, *1327–1485*, ed. A.R. Myers (Eyre & Spottiswood, 1969), pp. 314–15.

[17] Myers, 'The Character of Richard III', pp. 112–32, at pp. 116–17.

who first exploited the York civic records, Harleian MS 433, and other unused nuggets, and who made something of the reign itself. Kendall's biography was the first to cover the whole of Richard's career.[18] Although Kendall was a professor of English Literature rather than History and has seduced generations of undergraduates with his splendidly persuasive style, his work still contains much of merit and lasting value. None of these modern finds were known to Richard's earliest historians.

Such reassessments have reached a large non-academic audience, as have the debates they have stimulated. 'This house believes that Richard III was more sinned against than sinning' is now always a winning proposition before and after the debate, as in the celebrated 'Trial of Richard III' on Channel 4 in 1983.[19] By the time of his Quincentenary celebrations (1983–5), the Ricardians had successfully countered the traditional interpretation. They have made Richard III into a household name that is genuinely popular. The role of Tudor propaganda in destroying Richard's reputation is familiar to many people who know little else of his story. So is the argument that Richard had no motive for slaying the princes, since as bastards they had no rights to the crown, and that it was Henry Tudor or the duke of Buckingham who committed the bloody deed. Ricardians have embroidered hassocks for Ricardian churches, and have funded various appeals for Fotheringhay and Middleham churches, a public statue with many replacement swords at Leicester, and the king's monument in Leicester Cathedral. Literally thousands attended the week at Leicester in 2015 to celebrate the re-interment of Richard III's bones, headed by the Catholic Cardinal Vincent Nicholls and the Anglican Archbishop Justin Welby. The Richard III Society has made Richard really popular. The Society has gained hundreds of new members and Ricardian sites in Leicestershire attract a flood of tourists.

Within the Richard III Society and outside there are many enthusiasts who, among other things, buy these books, funded the Leicester friary excavations, and financed new editions of all the relevant chronicles and histories. Such notable Ricardians and quality historians as Peter Hammond, Anne Sutton, and Livia Visser-Fuchs have contributed

[18] P.M. Kendall, *Richard III* (W. W. Norton, 1955).
[19] R. Drewett and M. Redhead, *Trial of Richard III* (A. Sutton, 1984), p. 160.

substantially to historians' understanding of Richard III. The Society's journal *The Ricardian* contains much reputable research and findings. *The Ricardian* is an expression of the Richard III Society's view 'that many features of the traditional accounts of the character and career of Richard III are neither supported by sufficient evidence nor reasonably tenable'. More and better evidence is to Richard's advantage. Hence 'the Society aims to promote in every possible way research into the life and times of Richard III, and to secure a reassessment of the material relating to this period, and of the role in English history of this monarch'.[20] It is for this reason that the Society has funded editions of his coronation records, the York House Books, and of Richard III's signet letter book British Library Harleian Manuscript 433,[21] and that individual members have studied his books, his religion, and other relevant topics, both the highways and byways of his life, his times, and his career.[22] Several authors have told the gripping story of the location and identification of the king's bones,[23] and 16 distant relatives took to the courts, unsuccessfully, to secure his reburial at York. Philippa Gregory's novels,[24] and the TV series *The White Queen* (2015) are the most successful of the many popular biographies, plays, and novels published around this era of English history. Amazingly Richard has been transformed into a romantic figure, a young hero, whom some Ricardians venerate and even love.

IV

Modern debate has forced historians to interrogate the evidence more closely and to uncover inconsistencies in what appeared to be clear-cut

[20] Printed at the front of every edition of *The Ricardian*.

[21] *The Coronation of Richard III*, eds A.F. Sutton and P.W. Hammond (A. Sutton, 1983); *York House Books 1461–90*, ed. L.C. Attreed, 2 vols. (A. Sutton, 1991); *H433*.

[22] A.F. Sutton and L. Visser-Fuchs, *Hours of Richard III* (A. Sutton, 1990); *Richard III's Books* (A. Sutton, 1997).

[23] E.g. P. Langley and M. Jones, *The Search for Richard III: The King's Grave* (Hodder & Stoughton, 2013); Grey Friars Research Team, *The Bones of a King. Richard III Rediscovered* (Wiley, 2015); M. Morris and R. Buckley, *Richard III: The King Under the Car Park* (University of Leicester, 2014); *Finding Richard III: The Official Account*, ed. A.J. Carson (Imprimis Imprimatur, 2014); M. Pitts, *Digging for Richard III: How Archaeology Found the King* (Thames & Hudson, 2014); J. Ashdown-Hill, The *Last Days of Richard III* (The History Press, 2010).

[24] P. Gregory, *The White Queen* (Simon & Schuster, 2009); *The Kingmaker's Daughter* (Simon & Schuster, 2012).

evidence. Because Richard's earliest historians lived under his enemies the Tudors, accepted the legitimacy of the Tudor regime, and justified it, need not mean that they can safely be disregarded as Tudor propagandists.[25] Actually, of course, there is no such thing as contemporary history, in the sense of history that is written as it actually happens. Much history is written by contemporaries – that is, by people who lived at the time and who may well have lived through the events that they report. However, even such historians wrote later than the events they retold, whether by hours, months, years, or decades, for all history has inescapably to be written after it has happened. Anything else is prophecy or speculation. Normally indeed history is written after the event to be recorded has finished, when the whole story can be told, or after the subject under discussion has reached its natural conclusion. The chief narratives of the First War of the Roses were written after Edward IV's accession. The Italian Dominic Mancini penned his account of Richard's accession to the throne months after Richard had actually become king. He marshalled the events and devised the section headings (and perhaps rearranged them) to culminate at that point.[26] Inevitably such narratives build up to the known conclusion. Hindsight makes sense of the details and shapes a story that explains the result. Biographies too are normally written after the death of the subject, whether a saint or King Henry V. Such lives are compositions that construct pre-agreed interpretations for which the date, mode of death, and reputation are already known. They commonly take the form of eulogies or hagiographies. Modern biographies that are written mid-life or even earlier, like those of pop stars, footballers, and other ephemeral celebrities whose distinction arrives young, are a 20th-century innovation. The nearest 15th-century parallel to such 'kiss and tells' are the sketches of Richard in John Rous's rolls of the earls of Warwick.[27]

Only Richard's succession in 1483 was sufficiently sensational to demand a separate record. The usurpation was already complete when

[25] J. Tey, *The Daughter of Time* (Penguin, 1969), p. 76; Potter, *Good King Richard?*, pp. 3–4.

[26] D. Mancini, *The Usurpation of Richard III*, ed. C.A.J. Armstrong, 2nd edn (Oxford University Press, 1969), p. 16. Mancini may not have spoken English, but could communicate in Latin with the well-connected churchmen with whom he mixed.

[27] *The Rous Roll*, ed. W.H. Courthope (London, 1859).

Mancini first recounted it. He was Richard's exact contemporary who witnessed the events at first hand and wrote them up within a few months. Composed abroad, perhaps at Beaugency in northern central France, his history was compiled from memory and was not polluted by the hostile Tudor propaganda that arose later.[28] It is critical nevertheless and coloured by hindsight. Richard's reign and life were brief. Rather than unfolding and ending naturally, both terminated abruptly and prematurely. There was therefore insufficient time for any histories of Richard III to be written during the reign itself. Richard's suppression of Buckingham's Rebellion later in the same year was apparently not memorable enough to deserve an official history like the *Arrivall of Edward IV*. The historical significance of the rebellion was rather that it foreshadowed and prepared the way for Tudor rule. It features prominently in the Tudor works of Polydore Vergil and Thomas More. The Bosworth campaign itself could only be documented after Richard's demise. The histories that underpin our knowledge of Richard's character and career were therefore written during the Tudor regime: not just those officially Tudor by Bernard André and Polydore Vergil, but the annals of Tudor years by the London chronicles,[29] and even the Second Anonymous Crowland Continuation (henceforth Crowland) first penned in November 1485, and the history of Britain of John Rous, who died in 1491.[30] As early as November 1485 Crowland already accepted the justice of Richard's defeat and disgrace. Rous's condemnation follows within six years. Although both authors had lived through the Yorkist Age and should have known better, each was coloured by Tudor propaganda about Richard's last hours and birth,[31] that cannot have been current during the king's life. Both accepted that the whole era of civil war (the Wars of the Roses) had ended with the succession of the Tudors.[32] Henry VII was the 'angel sent from heaven through whom God deigned to visit

[28] Mancini, *Usurpation*, p. 104.

[29] B. André, *Historia Regis Henrici Septimi*, ed. J. Gairdner, Rolls Series (Longmans, 1858); Vergil, *English History*, pp. 232–8; *Chronicles of London*, ed. C.L. Kingsford (Clarendon Press, 1905), pp. 189–93.

[30] M.A. Hicks, 'The Second Anonymous Continuation of the Crowland Abbey Chronicles 1459–1486 Revisited', *EHR*, 122 (2007), pp. 351–70; A. Hanham, *Richard III and His Early Historians 1483–1535* (Clarendon Press, 1975), pp. 118–24.

[31] *Crowland*, p. 180.

[32] Hanham, *Richard III*, p. 124.

his people and to free them from the evils which had hitherto afflicted them beyond measure'.[33]

Even these most contemporary of surviving accounts can be shown to contain fictions. Crowland and Rous were the first historians to write of Richard after his fall. The writer of Crowland was a highly educated cleric who had worked in the central government machine throughout the Yorkist era and may indeed have risen to be clerk of the royal council.[34] His narrative of the Wars of the Roses is sober and factual. He is unlikely to have invented these fictions himself. Nearby but not actually at Richard's final battle, Crowland reported elaborately on the king's last hours, his guilty nightmare, his lack of breakfast and a chaplain to celebrate mass, and on his pale and deathly appearance, none of which he had observed himself.[35] This hearsay material, perhaps wholly apocryphal, was disseminated at once, most probably by Richard's Tudor vanquishers and thus picked up by Crowland at the time. Rous similarly reports on Richard's unnatural birth,[36] surely of no interest until the obscure baby became a king, and that Rous himself (a celibate male) cannot have perceived at first hand. He too is unlikely to have invented the story – although he did apply the astrological lessons[37] – and his history had too few readers to spread it much. Most likely Rous also assimilated rumours disseminated (and probably invented) by the victorious Tudors.

V

The Richard III Society has presumed that the more that is known of Richard III, the better his reputation will be. That has not proved to be the case. Although excellent research has added so much to historical knowledge and assessment of Richard it has not significantly improved his reputation. If the deaths of Henry VI, his son, and Clarence are no longer blamed on Richard, he did nevertheless dispossess the two countesses of Warwick and Oxford of their rightful inheritances and seems never to have

---

[33] *Crowland*, pp. 182–3.

[34] M.A. Hicks, 'Crowland's World: A Westminster View of the Yorkist Age', *History*, 90 (2005), pp. 172–90; 'Second Anonymous Continuation', pp. 362–70.

[35] *Crowland*, p. 180.

[36] Hanham, *Richard III*, p. 120.

[37] Ibid. However, Richard's star sign was not Scorpio but Libra.

legitimated his own marriage. Academic historians do not generally accept his case to become king and most attribute to him the deaths of the princes. It is not true that all Richard's subjects favoured Richard.

Careful reassessment has often resulted in academics, from Charles Ross on, confirming the old version of events. All the relevant biographers who discussed the fate of the princes in the *Oxford Dictionary of National Biography* (2004) maintained still that Richard was the guilty perpetrator.[38] If the quest for the defeated king's bones at Leicester in 2012 was apparently successful,[39] it has substantiated much Tudor testimony about the king's physique, health, appearance, and even temperament. If nobody now accepts the Tudor denigration of Richard III in its entirety, the divisions between critics and protagonists remain as sharp as ever. It is in this careful and critical tradition that Charles Ross, Rosemary Horrox, and Tony Pollard have written. Moreover, Hicks demonstrated in his 1991 book that Richard's own voice was not wholly obscured. Although Mancini did not believe such messages, he did report what Richard himself wrote, said, and circulated in the weeks before his own accession.[40] Richard himself was a propagandist who aimed to shape, to manipulate, and to mislead public opinion.

Horrox, Pollard, and Ross belong to the McFarlane school of history. The highly influential Oxford historian K.B. McFarlane (d. 1966) taught that medieval monarchs and nobles should be studied with reference to the standards current at the time, not those of today, by their actual actions, as far as possible from an understanding of their personal affairs – income, expenditure, interests, connections – and from the sources that they themselves had generated. McFarlane stressed the importance of their staff, their households, and retainers, together with the bastard feudal resources that enabled great men to exercise influence in peacetime and power in times of war.[41] All these historians appreciated that Richard owed his power especially to the estates and to the connection that his consort Anne Neville had inherited from her father Warwick the Kingmaker and his

[38] E.g. *ODNB* (60 vols, Oxford, 2004), vol. 17, p. 861; 46, p. 742.

[39] See, e.g., this casual assumption in *The Times*, 21 June 2016.

[40] M.A. Hicks, *Richard III: The Man Behind the Myth*, pp. 81–8.

[41] K.B. McFarlane, *The Nobility of Later Medieval England* (Clarendon Press, 1973); *England in the Fifteenth Century* (Bloomsbury, 1981).

Neville predecessors. Richard's key supporters in the North were identified by the fees he paid them from his lordship of Middleham in Yorkshire, by the indentures by which he retained them, and by the knighthoods he bestowed on his Scottish campaign. Such material was trawled and explained by Kendall, by Gladys M. Coles, by Ross, Hicks, Dockray, and especially Pollard, who set the Middleham/Richmondshire connection on the soundest historical footing.[42] Richard III's signet book enabled all these historians, and especially Rosemary Horrox, to study the continuance and vast expansion of his affinity as king.[43] This kind of prosopography (collective biography) could also be applied to Richard's enemies, as Horrox and Louise Gill have demonstrated. Detailed research has illuminated a range of other topics, such as Richard's reign, his library, and the development of the Tudor opposition. Short though Richard's reign was, the ranks of his supporters and opponents are better known than those of the monarchs who immediately preceded him and followed after.

Undoubtedly King Richard had enemies. There were opponents to Richard who appealed to public opinion during his reign, who sought to win it over to their point of view, and who endeavoured in particular to alienate Richard's subjects from the king. Tudor propaganda antedated the Tudor monarchy.[44] The principal charges against him circulated during his lifetime and reign. The key charges against Richard were known and indeed familiar even before the Bosworth campaign.

The simplest of Ricardian messages, that the narrative sources were Tudor propaganda because written after Richard's death and should therefore be rejected, is not tenable. They may be polemical and propagandist, but their message is contemporary, devised by contemporaries as part of the ideological struggle in Richard's own lifetime, and rightly therefore part of the original sources that demand critical appraisal by sceptical historians. We are not obliged to believe the charges. The best propaganda, however, is that which rings true to the audiences that it addresses. Note

---

[42] G.M. Coles, 'The Lordship of Middleham', unpublished MA thesis (Liverpool University, 1961), p. 18; A. Pollard, *North-Eastern England during the Wars of the Roses* (Clarendon Press, 1990); A.J. Pollard, *The Worlds of Richard III* (Tempus, 2001); Hicks, *Rivals*, chapters 21 and 13; Horrox, *Richard III*; Ross, *Richard III*.

[43] *H433*.

[44] As demonstrated by Hicks, *Richard III: The Man Behind the Myth*.

that most of this propaganda was accepted by many contemporaries at the time and has passed into the mainstream histories of Richard and his reign.

Ricardians point out that none of this has proved that Richard killed any of those debited to him as duke of Gloucester, or that he plotted to secure the throne, or that he invented the precontract story that justified the deposition of Edward V, or, most important, that he killed the princes. There are no explicit avowals of his intentions and none of our sources witnessed his supposed crimes. He would not be convicted on this evidence in a modern court of law. All of this is true. However, the standard of proof being applied is too high. Historians constantly work from inadequate sources and make deductions from actions. Undoubtedly witnesses and testimony that once existed have disappeared. There can be no access to what was *said* at the time or in Henry VII's parliament. The evidence really is overwhelming that Richard concurred in the death of his brother Clarence – which was not illegal – and almost all contemporary historians put the deaths of the princes down to Richard. What is certain, however, is that together the historians of Richard III – both critical academics and Ricardians – have enormously enriched our knowledge and understanding of Richard III as duke and king, to the enormous benefit of this book.

VI

A new dimension to knowledge and understanding of Richard III has been added by the application of archaeology and science, although the generation of such new material has not proceeded very far. Without doubt medieval people had more limited understanding of the world and of the forces that shaped natural events than is true nowadays. What could not be explained naturally was explained supernaturally. The five centuries since Richard died have witnessed enormous extensions of human knowledge and understanding of natural causation. Hence we understand some aspects very often better than he did. We are better informed on standards and values, beliefs and principles, prejudices and presumptions that underpinned past societies and shaped human motivations and actions.[45]

---

[45] E.g. M.A. Hicks, *English Political Culture in the Fifteenth* Century (Routledge, 2002); R.E. Horrox (ed.), *Fifteenth-Century Attitudes: Perceptions of Society in Late Medieval England* (Cambridge University Press, 1994).

Beyond such background context, historians have applied science to illuminate specific topics and problems of the age of Richard III. Most famous is the examination of the bones of participants in these events.

A cache of bones were found in the Tewkesbury Abbey tomb of Richard's brother George Duke of Clarence and his consort Isabel Neville. Studying these should have revealed their stature, health, and potentially the cause of their deaths, disproving perhaps that Clarence was drowned in malmsey wine. Unfortunately the bones proved to be of much older individuals much later in date, the remains of the 18th-century Hawley family who appropriated the vault for themselves.[46] Tewkesbury Abbey is full of tombs, including victims of the 1471 battle as well as the duke and duchess, but these cannot now be attributed to particular individuals. Over 500 years many corpses have been relocated and often separated from the monuments that once identified them. Queen Elizabeth II has declined to authorise the testing for DNA comparison of the royal bones interred at Windsor Castle. Investigation of the tomb of Richard's sister Margaret of York at Mechlen Cathedral failed to identify her precisely and did not produce DNA suitable for comparison with her relatives.[47] Conclusive identification, uncorrupted DNA, and suitable kinsfolk for comparison are three demanding prerequisites to be fulfilled to inform us today about particular individuals. The bones for comparison need not be contemporary – the brothers and sisters of Richard III, for instance. A brilliant alternative devised by the late John Ashdown-Hill is to extract relevant DNA for comparison from relatives living today. This technique was applied using both mitochondrial and Y chromosome DNA.[48]

Most famous until recently of the skeletal remains of this era are the bones of the two Little Princes in the Tower, Edward V and his brother Richard Duke of York. Found in the Tower of London in 1674, these bones were attributed to them at the time and reinterred at Westminster Abbey. They were forensically examined in the 1930s by the abbey

[46] Hicks, *Clarence*, pp. 200–4; M. Donmall and R.K. Morris, 'The Bones in the Clarence Vault', in *Tewkesbury Abbey: History, Art and Architecture*, eds R.K. Morris and R. Shoesmith (Logaston Press, 2003), pp. 31–40.

[47] Ashdown-Hill, *The Last Days of Richard III*, p. 123.

[48] M.A. Hicks, *The Family of Richard III* (Amberley Publishing, 2015), p. 182.

librarian Lawrence Tanner and the anatomist William Wright. Tanner and Wright found that these were indeed the bones of the princes, that they died in Richard III's reign, and that the causes of death were not apparent from the skeletal remains.[49] Their conclusions have been questioned. Tanner and Wright assumed rather than proved that the bones were from the right era and were of the right gender. Their analysis was defective and since then forensic science has advanced enormously.[50] Forty years ago Theya Molleson reassessed their report and uncovered physical peculiarities that indicated that the bones were of blood relations that shared an anomaly with the younger prince's wife Anne Mowbray, whose remains at the London Greyfriars have been firmly identified and forensically studied.[51] This condition was more common in earlier centuries. Molleson's paper provoked a storm of objections in the press and the Ricardian *Bulletin*. The bones might date from other periods, even perhaps from before the Tower of London was constructed. Anne Mowbray was related to the princes principally by marriage, not blood, and her rather distant blood relationship to the two princes came via two sisters, her great-grandmother Katherine Duchess of Norfolk and the princes' grandmother Cecily Duchess of York, two of the 25 children of Ralph Earl of Westmorland (d. 1425), whose genes had become widely disseminated amongst the aristocracy half a century later.[52] Molleson could not examine the bones or apply the carbon dating that might have identified the half century when the bones were alive. DNA fingerprinting had yet to be invented. The most circumstantial account of the fate of the princes is that of Sir Thomas More, not an eyewitness, who stated that the boys were smothered, a mode of death that ought to have left no marks on their bones, and that they were moved to an unknown location.[53] Ricardians of course reject the testimony

[49] L.E. Tanner and W. Wright, 'Recent Investigations Regarding the Fate of the Princes in the Tower', *Archaeologia*, 34 (1934), pp. 1–26.

[50] P.W. Hammond and W.J. White, 'The Sons of Edward IV: A Re-examination of the Evidence on their Deaths and on the Bones in Westminster Abbey', in Hammond, *Richard III: Loyalty, Lordship and Law* (Richard III and Yorkist History Trust, 1986), pp. 104–47.

[51] T. Molleson, 'Anne Mowbray and the Princes in the Tower', *London Archaeologist*, 5(10) (1987), pp. 258–62.

[52] Moreover, Earl Ralph's second countess Joan Beaufort had children by her first marriage.

[53] More, *Richard III*, pp. 83–7.

of More as Tudor propaganda and are disinclined to accept that the princes perished in the Tower, which points to their death at the hands of Richard (or Buckingham or Henry Tudor) rather than surviving beyond 1485, perhaps under the alias of Perkin Warbeck. Why these particular bones were hailed as those of the princes when discovered is unclear: another pair of skeletons was discovered in the 17th century and is now lost. If supporting material was found with them – writing, clothes, or jewellery perhaps – it was not recorded then and is now lost. If re-examined today, a few questions might be answered. Such reinvestigation has not been permitted and hence such tests have not been attempted.

The bones of the princes have been relegated in importance because of the supposed discovery of the bones of Richard III himself on the site of the former Greyfriars church in Leicester. The quest for Richard's remains by John Ashdown-Hill, Philippa Langley, Richard Buckley, and the Leicester University archaeological unit, and funded by Ricardians in and beyond the Richard III Society, is one of the most exciting of detective stories and a feat of forensic archaeology that attracted international acclaim. The bones were uncovered where they should have been if undisturbed, in the choir of Leicester's friary church, strangely undamaged by repeated demolitions and building, and still capable of DNA analysis. The bones belonged to a young man of slight build and modest height with a curvature of the spine (scoliosis), who died from a series of violent blows and who was interred in a rough grave. They have been radio-carbon dated within the right era and share mitochondrial DNA with descendants in the continuous female line from Richard's sister Anne.[54] No other descendants of Richard's grandmother Joan Beaufort and therefore sharing this DNA are known to have been killed in 1485 at the battle of Bosworth.[55] The identification of the bones with Richard have generally been accepted, both popularly and by the authoritative University of Leicester, Leicester

[54] See, e.g., Ashdown-Hill, *The Last Days*; Langley and Jones, *The Search for Richard III*; Pitts, *Digging for Richard III*; Morris and Buckley, *Richard III. The King under the Car Park*; Carson (ed.), *Finding Richard III*; T.E. King et al., 'Identification of the Remains of King Richard III', *New Communications*, 5 (2014), pp. 1–8.

[55] The tests sought to prove the bones were those of Richard III rather than being open-ended: the DNA tested was labelled Richard III and the date of death was assumed to be 1485.

Cathedral, and Leicester County Museums, and by the archbishops of Canterbury and Westminster.

Actually, however, the evidence is not conclusive. Others share the same mitochondrial DNA derived from Joan Beaufort's maternal ancestresses, still to be identified. The Y chromosome ought to have tallied with that of the Somersets, the only Plantagenets surviving today, but did not. Professor Martin Biddle has pointed to defects in the excavation – the severance of Richard's feet and the limited scale of the trenches – that cast doubt on the reliability of the finds.[56] The radio-carbon dating does not prove 1485 to have been the date of death. The wounds incurred and the nature of the tomb do not match the literary and record evidence. Moreover, some of the deductions from the bones about Richard's lifestyle do not fit what else is known about the king.[57] New myths are in the making. It would be very convenient to the present author if the bones were indeed those of Richard III and probably not particularly difficult (but costly) to settle the issue either way. This book presumes the identification and builds on it, albeit with fingers firmly crossed.

Before the discovery of the Leicester bones, it was already known that Richard III was killed on 22 August 1485 at the battle of Bosworth against the invading force of Henry Tudor, who by his victory became King Henry VII. Richard was known to have died fighting bravely, was stripped naked, and was interred in the choir of the Leicester Greyfriars. The excavation confirms this information. What happened to his body after death, the construction of a monument over it, the plan, architecture, and the re-use of the site after the dissolution of the friary in 1536, are issues not particularly relevant to this study of Richard's life and reign. What has been revealed by the excavation is, first of all, information on the corpse's physique. A whole battery of different kinds of scientists, second, have engaged in post-excavation analysis of the remains. The wounds have been expertly explained by the types of blows and the weapons used. Much the most interesting findings relate to his physique, his small size, slender and almost effeminate build, and his distorted spine, the result of scoliosis in adolescence. This finding has become essential to

---

[56] https://www.historyextra.com/period/medieval/was-the-skeleton-in-the-leicester-car-park-really-richard-iii/.

[57] These issues are discussed in Hicks, *Family of Richard III*, ch. 9.

prove the identity of the bones with Richard that Ricardians, who hitherto rejected the hunchback story as Tudor propaganda, now assert as proof of identity. Alterations to his portrait did not mislead therefore, but were designed to present a more faithful depiction. That this element of Tudor propaganda is now accepted by Ricardians strengthens the case for crediting other post-Bosworth testimony from Thomas More, John Rous, and Polydore Vergil. While accepting the scoliosis, which certainly made the shoulders uneven and caused him to stoop, some Ricardians who are upset by imperfection in their darling have argued that the deformity was not noticeable in life and was indeed only discovered when he was stripped after death. Rous, who knew Richard, might not have perceived his disability in life, but heard about it later, perhaps via Tudor propagandists. The reconstruction of the face working from the skull produced a result very similar to surviving portraits of Richard III, from which the hairstyle and colouring were 'borrowed', and the white drawn appearance to which Crowland referred.[58] Sir Thomas More records that Richard resembled his father Richard Duke of York rather than his fair-haired brother Edward IV.[59] Subsequent DNA analysis of the bones indicated a 70 per cent probability that Richard was fair-haired and blue-eyed, at least in youth, in contrast to the best known portraits of the king that are primary evidence dating from near his time. The research team have selected those portraits that fit these findings best. Other aspects supposedly illuminated are the king's domicile, movements, diet, internal parasites, and changes in diet over time. Some such details also do not conform to what is known from other sources. The research team presume that science cannot lie and therefore that their findings take precedence over the written sources. If such findings are to be accepted and applied, the bones must be firmly identified. Certainty rather than very high probability is essential.

Another new field of study is battlefield archaeology. Remarkably little is recorded about the battles of the Wars of the Roses.[60] In most cases the course of the battle was narrated and of course the results are known, but

[58] *Crowland*, p. 181.

[59] More, *Richard III*, p. 67.

[60] M.A. Hicks, 'The Sources', in *The Wars of the Roses*, ed. A. J. Pollard (Palgrave Macmillan, 1995), pp. 20–4.

often the site is not certain (e.g., the Battle of Barnet), the numbers of combatants and casualties on each side are obscure, and at most a few score of individuals are named. Battlefield archaeology, the study of the physical remains, can fill some of these gaps, although even landscapes can change (e.g., Tewkesbury). Scarcely any artefacts have escaped five centuries of rot and degradation, agriculture and plundering (e.g., Towton). The graves of very few combatants have been found or studied.[61] If musters were taken before the battles, if troops were paid and casualties recorded by the heralds, none of these records now survive. The Battle of Bosworth in 1485 was decisive and remains a household name, yet it is as little known as any. The precise site is not recorded – it has been difficult to locate the now vanished marsh and the battle certainly was not fought at Market Bosworth or on Ambion Hill where the Leicester County Council Bosworth Centre is located.[62] Particularly few combatants on either side are known for certainty: only 30 were attainted.[63] The list of those petitioning for Henry VII's favour or named in the Stanley ballads cannot be trusted.[64] It is suspected but not known that both armies were unusually small, that Richard's forces were the larger, and that a high proportion of the Tudor army were French and Scottish mercenaries. Michael K. Jones suggested that these professionals were equipped with 16-foot pikes on which Richard's charging force impaled themselves.[65] It is known that the earl of Northumberland's division of Richard's army did not engage and that the late intervention of Lord Stanley's men was decisive.[66] Amid so much confusion, a study of the locality could expect to yield results, but the conclusions of a large-scale archaeological investigation are disappointingly meagre. The survey of the battlefield was more successful as a landscape study invaluable to local historians than in adding to understanding of the battle. So thorough has the investigation of this empty landscape been that no archaeological

[61] For the lost sunken lanes at Tewkesbury, see *The Arrivall*, p. 29. Even the celebrated mass grave at Towton contains remains of only 37 individuals slaughtered in flight, none of them identifiable. Archaeology reveals more about the masses than individuals.

[62] G. Foard and A. Curry, *Bosworth 1485; A Battlefield Rediscovered* (Oxbow Books, 2013).

[63] *PROME*, vol. 15, pp. 107–8.

[64] C.F. Richmond, '1485 and All That, or What was Going on at the Battle of Bosworth?', in Hammond, *Richard III*, p. 173.

[65] M.K. Jones, *Bosworth 1485: Psychology of a Battle* (Tempus, 2002), pp. 162–4.

[66] Vergil, *English History*, pp. 224–5.

evidence is lost to redevelopment.[67] A scattering of minute artefacts of little individual importance marks where conflict and flight occurred and indicates the approximate site of the battle, although the main fighting seems to have taken place beyond the large area studied. Thirty-three projectiles of various sizes have been found, too few to have been decisive. Which army fired them is unclear. Not Bosworth, as asserted, but Castillon in 1453 was the first battle decided by artillery. No fragments of pikes have been identified. It is not obvious in what direction these two armies of indeterminate size were facing, how large they were, nor why the Tudor army won. No mass graves have been discovered.[68] New material has been discovered at great cost that could have been acquired by no other means, but it does not substantially alter or confirm what little was already known.

There can be no doubt therefore that archaeology and other sciences can add to the stock of primary sources available to the modern historians. At present the range of potential subjects seems small and the implications not at all significant. Differences between the disciplines should be noted. Whereas archaeologists study sites, historians are interested in how archaeology adds to the larger picture, in this case to explain what happened. Most scientists are content with Bayesian probability, but for the bones to be identified as Richard's their date has to be 1485. Even scientific evidence does not equate to fact. It is not the raw data but considered conclusions that were placed in the historical domain and such findings need to be weighed against other evidence and interpreted. This book, therefore, like all its predecessors, relies principally on the written sources, both narratives and records, to illuminate King Richard and his story.

[67] *The Times*, 28 August 2018.
[68] Foard and Curry, *Bosworth 1485*.

Chapter Two

FROM INFANCY TO ADOLESCENCE

FORMATIVE EXPERIENCES 1452–68

I

The future Richard III was born on 2 October 1452. He appears to have embarked on adult roles late in 1468, when he was 16, the same age that his elder brother George was allowed his majority. Late medieval noblemen normally came of age at 21. Edward IV wanted to make his brothers useful as soon as possible. They may have been mature for their age.[1] Obviously these first 16 years were of fundamental importance in the upbringing and formation of the future king, yet very little is known directly or can be established about Richard's infancy, childhood, adolescence, and even his adulthood up to the age of 19 in 1471. Yet Richard was not born in isolation. He had a context – indeed a whole series of contexts – and these contexts are known. He had a family, which evolved over the years into something considerably different. He was born into rank and wealth, into the lifestyle of conspicuous consumption that went with his class, all radically different from the counterparts of the baby of a peasant, an artisan, merchant, or a bastard born to a single mother. Surely he was brought up like other aristocrats, nobles, and princes. Richard was also immersed in and inescapably

[1] That Clarence made fun of Lord Mayor Oulegreve in 1468 when both were judicial commissioners suggests Edward's optimism was misplaced, *Great Chronicle of London*, eds A.H. Thomas and I.D. Thornley (Guildhall Library, 1938), p. 206. Edward also declared William Herbert II of age at 16.

adopted the attitudes characteristic of his class. He imbibed the assumptions, prejudices, superstitions, expectations, values and standards, ideals
and political principles of his age.[2] Few of these can be demonstrated in his
case, but they have to be presumed. They helped form the man who was to
be king. How Richard responded to each influence, each lesson, and each
stimulus is seldom apparent. Moreover, what little is recorded is cloaked
with myth and superstition, with deduction, and with hindsight.

Richard was born at Fotheringhay Castle in Northamptonshire to
Richard Duke of York and his duchess, Cecily Neville. He was the 11th of
12 children, the youngest of the seven offspring and of the four sons who
lived to adulthood.[3] Because he became king, stories were repeated about
his birth much later, and at least some of them were invented. All of them
were reported by men, who were never admitted to the birthing chamber
and who were absent on this particular occasion. The list of unnatural
circumstances listed by Rous and More include some that are actually
commonplace (but unfamiliar to men) and others that are incredible. That
Cecily's 11th labour was difficult is not surprising. An undated petition
from Cecily to Queen Margaret of Anjou makes reference to 'the disease
and infirmite that . . . hath growen and growith, uppon me' that caused
'th'encomerous labour, to me full paynfull and unesy', which Professor
Carole Rawcliffe identifies with the duchess's pregnancy with Richard.[4]
This, however, is not likely, as the suffering, which was still happening,
ended with Richard's birth not less than 10 months before Margaret's
bearing of Prince Edward, which cannot have been anticipated so early.
The two pregnancies cannot have coincided. That Richard's gestation
period was unusually protracted is credible, but not for the two years stated
by Rous, which is impossible both medically and because his short-lived
next brother Thomas was born some time then. Again Richard could have
been a breech birth and delivered by Caesarean or (more probably) by

[2] Hicks, *English Political Culture in the Fifteenth Century* (Routledge, 2002), esp. pp. 6–7. The
classic study of aristocratic education is N. Orme, *From Childhood to Chivalry. The Education of
English Kings and Aristocracy 1066–1530* (Routledge, 1984).

[3] For the table of births see M.A. Hicks, *The Family of Richard III* (Amberley Publishing, 2015),
p. 49. For the reports discussed below, see More, *Richard III*, p. 7; Hanham, *Richard III*, p. 120.

[4] C. Rawcliffe, 'Richard, Duke of York, "the King's Obeisant Liegeman": A New Source for
the Protectorates of 1454 and 1455', *HR*, 60(142) (1987), pp. 236–7; see also ibid. pp. 232–3.

cutting to enlarge the exit (an episiotomy). Neither procedure was unknown or necessarily lethal at this time. Conceivably Richard was born with some hair and some teeth, though certainly not the full complement of teeth or hair hanging to his shoulders reported by More and Rous. Richard was told his birthday, remembered it, and entered it 30 years later into the calendar of his book of hours. It was an occasion memorable to him and was commemorated. Was his birthday celebrated each year as a child and did he mark it then? Nobody it seems, not even Richard, made much of the fact that his birthday was also the festival of St Thomas Cantilupe.[5] He was baptised that day or the one following. Certainly his mother, still bed-bound, was absent. Whether the father was present or whether it was Duke Richard himself who bestowed his name (and his own father's name) on his youngest son cannot now be known. It is strange that other names were selected for his first seven sons.

Richard III lived in an era when virtually everyone was a Catholic, a devoted practitioner, and was conventionally pious. Everybody became Christian virtually at birth and piety was ingrained in Richard from the very beginning. Richard's baptism at Fotheringhay on the very day of his birth made him (in contemporary parlance) into a Christian, a full-member of the Church and thus capable of salvation, and supplied him with at least two godfathers and a godmother to insist on his knowledge, understanding, and commitment to the faith. We do not know who these were, perhaps because they had died before Richard started generating records himself. He was probably confirmed in infancy. His parents' household was shaped and time-tabled by religion.[6] Life was regulated by the Christian calendar, from Advent to Trinity, by such principal feasts as Christmas, Easter, and Whitsun, and by fasts, especially Fridays and the 40 days of Lent. The Church prescribed the liturgy (church services) for the whole year, varying them by the day with specific prayers and readings. Many of the other days were saints' days, eves of saints' days, or octaves of saints (the saints' day and the seven days that

[5] Rous was in error (probably deliberate) in dating Richard's birth to 21 October, the feast of 11,000 Virgins (victims as innocent as the princes), and under the star sign Scorpio that portended his subtle character, Hanham, *Richard III*, p. 120. St Ursula, whom Richard later venerated, was one of these virgins.

[6] For this topic see K. Mertes, *The English Noble Household 1250–1600* (Blackwell, 1988), ch. 5.

followed), again with their own observances. There were literally thousands of Christian saints, scores of them being specifically celebrated in any location. Richard knew all this by osmosis, from the church services he had to attend, but also from his diet, which varied from meat days to fish days, ale days and wine days, festival days. And on certain specific days the household commemorated the deaths of parents and ancestors whose anniversary it was. Every great household had a staff of chaplains who lived with them – often graduates with their own rectories – and even a choir of trebles and professional singers. His father employed an almoner and was licensed to choose a confessor for his whole household. Wherever young Richard resided, there was a chapel – sometimes several: at Fotheringhay there was both the castle chapel, formerly collegiate, and the parochial college of St Mary and All Saints. The 13th-century chapel at Ludlow Castle survives. Some such chapels had their own endowed clergy. All could be served anyway by the household chaplains, who held several services a day, one at least being mandatory for all household members including the boy Richard. On journeys York took a portable altar that enabled him to attend mass in-house wherever he was and even before daybreak.[7]

Even when on the move, Richard visited some of the 9,000 parishes, the chapels, the 900 religious houses and the uncountable shrines, often attending services and making offerings. The York estates were littered with family foundations like archaeological deposits that reminded of past pieties. Richard's ancestors had scattered their estates with their benefactions – abbeys like Wigmore, friaries like Clare and Little Walsingham in Norfolk, colleges like Fotheringhay and Stoke by Clare in Suffolk, chantries and hospitals. Dozens of ancient annuities and other pious concessions are recorded in York's estate accounts. Cantarists, almspeople, and anchorites throughout the estate were subsidised.[8]

Richard resided with his mother Duchess Cecily, who had her own self-sufficient household that sometimes merged with that of her husband Richard Duke of York. Slight evidence of their itineraries reveals the duke

[7] CPL 1431–47, pp. 259, 463, 486, 489; 1447–71, p. 92; 1455–64, p. 538; J.T. Rosenthal, 'Richard, Duke of York: A Fifteenth-Century Layman and the Church', *Catholic Historical Review*, 50(2) (1964), p. 182.

[8] See Rosenthal, 'York', pp. 171–87.

as frequently on the move, around his estates in England and Wales, attending parliaments and councils. Twice, in 1454–5 and 1455–6, York was Lord Protector, head of the government, and based principally in and around London.[9] Cecily, most probably, was more settled and sedentary. She was confined four times at Fotheringhay, once at Hatfield, and once at Neyte by Westminster.[10] Her twelve children had probably diminished to six by the time of Richard's birth and then briefly increased to eight on the birth in 1455 of Ursula. Richard may have remembered this youngest sister. He never lived with the eldest, Anne, born in 1438, who was married in 1447 to Henry Duke of Exeter, York's ward. Probably Anne resided with Exeter from 1450 when he had special livery of his lands without proof of age.[11] At some point before June 1454 the two eldest sons, Edward and Edmund, moved independently to Ludlow in Shropshire.[12] Edward, Edmund, and Anne had left Cecily's household before Richard's birth or very soon afterwards and were besides too much older for Richard to know well. The nursery he knew comprised two elder sisters Elizabeth (b. 1443) and Margaret (b. 1446), his elder brother George (b. 1449), and Richard himself. Elizabeth, who was married in 1458 to John Duke of Suffolk (d. 1491), had left the York household before it becomes documented.

Richard lived a life of the most conspicuous consumption in a great household and was to continue to do so all his life. He surely took such a lifestyle for granted. His mother Duchess Cecily was attended by well-born ladies, Duke Richard by gentry in his service. Duke and duchess dressed in the finest imported fabrics and furs, and their lives were regulated by etiquette that was detailed in courtesy books. There were literally scores of male menials engaged in departments devoted to the production of food

[9] Although not comprehensive, the duke's movements are charted by P.A. Johnson, *Duke Richard of York 1411–60* (Oxford University Press, 1988).

[10] 'Annales Rerum Anglicarum', in *Letters and Papers Illustrative of the Wars of the English in France*, ed. J. Stevenson, Rolls Series, vol. 2, part 2 (1864), pp. 762–5, 771.

[11] He was actually 20, GEC, vol. 5, pp. 212–13. For the marriage, see T.B. Pugh, 'The Magnates, Knights and Gentry', in Chrimes et al. (eds), *Fifteenth-century England, 1399–1509: Studies in Politics and Society* (Manchester University Press, 1972), p. 118n.11, which, however, miscalculates the dowry; see T.B. Pugh, 'Richard, Duke of York and the Rebellion of Henry Holland, Duke of Exeter, in May 1454', *HR*, 63 (1990), p. 249.

[12] C.L. Scofield, *The Life and Reign of Edward the Fourth*, 2 vols (Longmans Green, 1923), vol. 1, pp. 19–21.

(kitchen, bakery) and drink (cellars of wine and ale), manning the chapel and the stable, and so on. The Yorks and therefore young Richard ate well, consuming lots of red meat and fish, the more luxurious salmon and shellfish as well as the commonplace salt herrings and stockfish, and drank ale and wine. There were never shortages of food, drink, and clothing. They resided in a succession of well-appointed castles and houses, such as Fotheringhay, Ludlow, Clare and Baynard's Castle in London, splendidly caparisoned. Young Richard had a pony to ride and parks in which to hunt. Nothing was stinted in the York households, but everything was strictly regulated as in all such establishments, portions at meals being generous but never excessive,[13] and magnificence being tempered by economy and strict accountancy. All that was different in the York households was the scale, for York was the wealthiest of noblemen. His household was costing about £5,000 a year in 1450–1 and eventually probably matched the 120 staff in the upper household alone of his brother-in-law Buckingham. York possessed a jewelled collar worth 4,000 marks (£2,666 13s 4d) and two very rich brooches,[14] and paid annuities of £900 to his retainers. During the 1440s York certainly commissioned the most expensive outfit known (a jewel-encrusted state dress) for the Duchess Cecily that cost £688 and the largest marriage portion (£3,000) for his daughter Anne.[15] He secured dukes for his daughters and sought a princess for his son Edward. The duke's estates in Ireland, which Richard never visited, in Wales where York had 17 marcher lordships, and in England brought in revenues perhaps of £5,800 and certainly greater than any other noblemen. The duke's estate revenues were supplemented by his salaries as lieutenant of Ireland and Lord Protector. The profits from marcher lordships had crashed in about 1450 and much of his government salaries were in arrears, as much as £26,000 in 1444. York therefore strug-

---

[13] C. Woolgar, 'Fast and Feast: Conspicuous Consumption and the Diet of the Nobility in the Fifteenth Century', in *Revolution and Consumption in Late Medieval England*, ed. M. Hicks (Boydell Press, 2001), pp. 1–25, at p. 24.

[14] The mark was not used in coinage but just as a unit of account. The value of a mark was two-thirds of a pound sterling, so 100 marks was equivalent to £66 13s.4d.

[15] Hicks, *Clarence*, pp. 3–4; T.B. Pugh, 'The Estates, Finances and Regal Aspirations of Richard Plantagenet (1411–1460), Duke of York', in *Revolution and Consumption in Laye Medieval England*, ed. M. Hicks (Boydell Press, 2001), pp. 78–9; C. Rawcliffe, *The Staffords, Earls of Stafford and Dukes of Buckingham, 1394–1521* (Cambridge University Press, 1978), p. 69.

gled to make ends meet, selling some rights to his Welsh tenants and even some lands, and left a heap of debts at death that took 20 years to repay. His daughters' dowries were payable by instalments, which were delayed or went unpaid. York really needed the profits of high office from the crown. What the duke did not apparently do, however, was retrench: the conspicuous consumption continued unabated.[16] Young Richard of course was unaware of the debts. He witnessed only the splendour. He was to replicate it in his own household both as duke and king.

Richard's immediate context was his nuclear family, his parents and siblings. Cecily is known to have borne 12 children between 1438 and 1455. Four of her last six babies had died in infancy including her four sons Henry, William, John, and Thomas. George, born 1449, was apparently healthy, but Richard, the bones suggest, was undersized and slight in build. Not much was expected of him and a fourth son, anyway, was surplus to requirements. That in about 1455 Bokenham, the family chronicler, remarked merely that 'Richard liveth yet' need not be more than the convenient ending of a line of verse,[17] but in view of what is now known it may hint at ill-health and predict an early demise, which of course did not happen. These were the years when young Richard certainly learnt to read, was introduced to Latin, and learnt to ride. The fourth son even of a duke was not scheduled to inherit anything and had no future mapped out for him. As the highest nobility did not take up the law, the options open to a non-inheriting son like Richard were knightly, certainly demanding proficiency in arms, and ecclesiastical, certainly demanding a more bookish education and proficiency in Latin if the more dignified and lucrative ranks were to be attained. Probably the duke of York had made no decisions about his youngest son in the boy's first seven years, up to 1459. Richard is not known to have received any of the minor orders, which would probably not have been recorded anyway, nor indeed had he been presented to any church livings as some noble churchmen were even at such an early age.[18]

[16] Pugh, 'The Estates, Finances and Regal Aspirations', pp. 71–84; T.B. Pugh, 'Richard Plantagenet (1411–60), Duke of York, as the King's Lieutenant in France and Ireland', in *Aspects of Late Medieval Government and Society*, ed. J.G. Rowe (University of Toronto Press, 1986), p. 125.

[17] W. Dugdale, *Monasticon Anglicanum*, vol. 7, pp. 1600–2.

[18] For example, Richard's cousin George Neville, eventually archbishop of York.

Richard also learnt about his wider families, his ancestral lineages, and his living uncles, aunts, and cousins. It could hardly be otherwise. Not only were the hangings and vestments, the castles and churches adorned with the coats of arms and badges associated with the families, but he was constantly enjoined to pray for past members on their anniversaries and to make offerings at their tombs. At Fotheringhay, probably his principal residence, there was the brand new and as yet unfinished Fotheringhay College, where past dukes of York were interred in the most up-to-date splendour. He may not himself have perused any of the decorative pedigrees mass-produced at St Paul's churchyard, the Founders Chronicle of Wigmore Abbey, Bokenham's Clare Roll, and the Neville family chronicles, each of which traced particular lines of his family, but those around him knew the contents and surely imparted them to him. The Mortimers had accrued battle honours against the Welsh, the Nevilles against the Scots, and Richard's great-uncle Edward Duke of York had fallen at Agincourt. Not just lustre but shame was inherited: the treason of Richard's grandfather Richard Earl of Cambridge in the Southampton plot in 1415 supposedly corrupted the blood of his descendants.

What Richard certainly learnt – indeed surely took for granted – was that aristocrats such as the Yorks were created, enriched, and transmitted their titles, estates, and honours by inheritance. They were a hereditary caste. Primogeniture prevailed. The family titles and resources were not divided on the death of the current holder, but devolved instead on a single heir. While heiresses could occur, the senior male in the next generation took the whole inheritance. Where such an heir did not exist, the property could proceed through the female line. Most commonly the line ended with a daughter or daughters. Alternatively, when the line ran out, an heir had to be sought up and down the family tree among the issue of some past daughter. It was not uncommon for a lady to become an heiress after marrying or even after dying. Lands passed from one family to another through heiresses. Often enough marriages were arranged with this end in mind. A great inheritance like that of Richard Duke of York combined a clutch of smaller heritages inherited in the female line. Richard was made aware from whence came the titles, honours, estates, and wealth of the family. Even more certain he knew that his eldest brother Edward was his father's heir, that his other brothers Edmund and George were next in line of succession and his sisters nowhere, and that he, Richard himself, 'nakidly borne into this wretched world destitute of possessions, goods and enheretamentes',[19] could expect to inherit nothing. He was a non-inheriting son, bound to defer to his father and to his brothers, dependent on whatever largesse they extended or on what he could amass on a military career or by service to greater men. This was the system to which Richard belonged. These were the facts of his life. As a fourth son, moreover, Richard may already have realised that he was not to become a great nobleman. Only in 1461, when he became a royal duke with a lay career mapped out for him, his bookish education was curtailed to fit in more aristocratic training.

What he learnt furthermore was that there were several components to his family. On his father's side there were his grandfather Richard Earl of Cambridge (executed in 1415) and two earlier dukes of York, and only four generations back his great-great-grandfather King Edward III (1327–77). Thence the line of English monarchs led back to the first Plantagenet Henry II, the Norman William the Conqueror, Ethelred the Unready and early Anglo-Saxon kings, back eventually to Adam. Edward III had taken the title of King of France, to which Duke Richard had pretensions, and the first duchess of York Isabel had transmitted a claim to the kingdom of Castile. Duke Richard had his title to the crown of Castile investigated and written up. York's son Edward IV cherished his titles to all three crowns.[20] Young Richard's paternal grandmother Anne had a lengthy Mortimer lineage, much of it Welsh, but including descent in the female line from Edward III's second son Lionel Duke of Clarence (d. 1368) and from Edward I's daughter Joan of Acre. It was these lines together that had united Duke Richard's princely title of duke with the earldoms of March in Wales and of Ulster in Ireland and the vast estates that compensated for the more limited lands of the house of York. No additional property had been accrued via Richard's mother Cecily, the youngest of the 25 children of Ralph Earl of Westmorland (d. 1425), but her Neville lineage stretched

---

[19] 'The Statutes Ordained by Richard Duke of Gloucester, for the College of Middleham. Dated July 4, 18 Edw. IV, (1478)', ed. J. Raine, *Archaeological Journal*, 14 (1857), p. 160.

[20] M.A. Hicks, 'Edward IV's *Brief Treatise* and the Treaty of Picquigny of 1475', *HR*, 83 (2010), pp. 256–7.

back to the Norman Conquest and before and included all the principal
families of northern England. What had lifted the Nevilles from regional
magnates to an earldom was Earl Ralph's royal marriage to Joan Beaufort,
another granddaughter of Edward III via John of Gaunt, duke of Lancaster
(d. 1399), the forebear of the Lancastrian kings. It had been as a loyal
member of the house of Lancaster that Westmorland had secured the
custody of Richard Duke of York and had bestowed his hand on his
youngest daughter Cecily. All these blue-blooded and royal ancestors were
identifiable then and are known today bar only one great-grandmother,
also Geoffrey Chaucer's mother-in-law. The prolific Neville line supplied
an intricate cousinage to make up for the tiny house of York.

Richard Duke of York had only one sibling, his sister Isabel, who had
married Henry Bourchier, viscount Bourchier (1446) and in 1461 earl of
Essex, whom Richard must surely have encountered. Bourchier was royal
in his own right as a grandson of Edward III's youngest son Thomas of
Woodstock, duke of Gloucester (d. 1397). They had numerous offspring,
including five sons, all a decade older than Richard. Less familiar were
probably Bourchier's three brothers Thomas, from 1454 Archbishop of
Canterbury, William Lord FitzWarin (d. 1469), and John Lord Berners (d.
1474). There were also Beauchamp descendants of great-aunt Constance
Lady Despenser (d. 1416).[21] Cecily Neville, however, had numerous relatives – five full brothers, her sisters Anne Duchess of Buckingham and
Katherine Duchess of Norfolk, a host of their offspring, and her cousins. If
it is quite unclear which of these Richard knew at first hand, he cannot
have been unconscious of their existence and may have been able to place
them on his family tree(s).

The Yorks prided themselves as members of the royal families of
England, France, and Castile and indeed of the international nobility. York
tried to match his son with a daughter of King Charles VII of France. As
representative of the fourth son of Edward III, York took precedence after
the three Lancastrian royal dukes, but as these all died without legitimate
issue – Clarence in 1421, Bedford in 1435, and Gloucester in 1447 – York

---

[21] GEC, vol. 1, p. 341. Her daughter Isabel (d. 1439) was mother of Anne, Countess of
Warwick (d. 1492) and Elizabeth Lady Bergavenny (d. 1448).

came to be premier duke in 1447 and perhaps also male heir to King Henry VI. Henry VI recognised that York was special. He treated him with greater respect than other recalcitrant dukes. Not only was York's eldest son Edward allowed the courtesy earldom of March, as other ducal heirs were, but this privilege was extended to his second son Edmund, by courtesy earl of Rutland. Through two female descents (Philippa of Clarence and Anne Mortimer) York was also heir of Edward III's second son Lionel, elder brother of John of Gaunt. Applying the usual rules of inheritance (primogeniture), York's Clarence title was superior to that of the Lancastrian kings and he should have been king. The special circumstances of 1399 had resulted in the succession of the Lancastrian Henry IV. This was in accordance with the wishes of Edward III who had been anxious to prevent female inheritance, ruling out the female line in 1376–7 and by implication in 1362.[22] The dukedom of Clarence and its endowment had been entailed in the male line in 1362 and consequently reverted to the crown on Lionel's death in 1368. It was not therefore part of the inheritance of Richard Duke of York, who was not entitled to the arms or livery of Clarence that he usurped in 1460. To claim to be heir of Duke Lionel came very close to laying claim to the crown: potentially treasonable and too dangerous by far.[23] The Wigmore chronicler was well aware of York's claim and said so in his chronicle,[24] which York surely read. Whether young Richard knew of it or not, he moved among those who thought York's title at least arguable.

II

Richard is next glimpsed in 1459. This was the beginning of the Wars of the Roses: an era when the gravest economic crisis, the humiliation of defeat in the Hundred Years War, and the bankruptcy of the government enabled protesters to threaten and even displace ruling regimes. The First War lasted from 1459 to 1461. These two years of kaleidoscopic politics affected

[22] M. Bennett, 'Edward III's Entail and the Succession to the Crown', *EHR*, 113 (1998), 582–3.

[23] This may be what York implied when explaining why he did not use the arms of Clarence in 1460.

[24] C. Given-Wilson, 'Chronicles of the Mortimer Family, c. 1250–1450', in *Family and Dynasty in Late Medieval England*, eds R. Eales and S. Tyas (Harlaxton Symposium, 2003), p. 77.

Richard directly. He was with his parents at Ludlow in 1459 when the duke's latest coup d'état failed. The duke and his two elder sons fled into exile abroad: Duke Richard and Edmund to Ireland, Edward with the earl of Warwick to Calais. They were all attainted for treason by parliament and the family estates were confiscated. Duchess Cecily and her younger sons George and Richard were at Ludlow when it was sacked and were placed in the custody of Anne Duchess of Buckingham, Cecily's much older sister. Cecily may have moved to London, but was recorded at Coventry in December 1459. It was probably about this time that George and Richard were supported by their great-uncle Archbishop Bourchier.[25] We cannot know how much Richard knew or understood about his father's politics during the 1450s.

The Yorkists returned to England in 1460, slaying Buckingham at the battle of Northampton, and seized control of Henry VI's government. The death of her brother-in-law seems to have freed Duchess Cecily and her younger children, who leased the Duke of Norfolk's residence in London in mid-September. She was summoned by her husband on his return to England, departing on 17 September for Hereford, leaving George, Margaret, and Richard behind. They were visited daily by their brother Edward Earl of March who, it may be deduced, saw them as politically useful.[26] It was at this point that York laid claim to the crown and asserted the superiority of his title in the female line from Lionel Duke of Clarence over that of the king derived from John of Gaunt. The Accord of November 1460 that was concluded by York with Henry VI acknowledged the duke's title as rightful. They agreed that King Henry would reign for life and that York's line would succeed him. Specific provision was made for York's two elder sons Edward and Edmund, the next heirs apparent. George and Richard, his third and fourth sons, were not mentioned, but their futures were nevertheless set to be royal princes. Not everyone accepted the Accord. York proceeded northwards to enforce it to Wakefield, where on 30 December 1460 – only two months later – he was defeated and he and

---

[25] Scofield, *Edward IV*, vol. 1, p. 37n.; R.E. Horrox, 'Richard III' in *ODNB*, 46, p. 738. By placing traitors' women in custody, they were prevented from communicating with and supplying their menfolk.

[26] Horrox, 'Richard III' in *ODNB*, 46, p. 738; Scofield, *Edward IV*, vol. 1, p. 102.

his second son Edmund were killed. Although his youngest son Richard may have been scarcely acquainted with them, this was a shock, and one that he was anxious to commemorate from the mid-1470s.

York's eldest son and heir Edward determined to continue the struggle – to make himself king of England – took the title on Edward IV on 4 March and won the decisive battle at Towton on 29 March. These developments made the fatherless George and Richard much more politically important as the next heirs to the Yorkist cause. In February 1461 Cecily sent them abroad to safe-keeping in the Low Countries to Utrecht, where they were received by the prince bishop David of Burgundy. Once Edward had won, the boys were fêted by Philip the Good, Duke of Burgundy, before being returned to England via Canterbury, where they had a civic reception, and London.[27] This could have been a formative interlude – Richard's first sojourn abroad, his first exposure to Francophone, Flemish, and Burgundian mercantile culture and to shrines like that of St Ursula – but very little is known about it. Reportedly Richard was smaller than George.[28]

III

The accession of his elder brother as Edward IV fundamentally changed Richard's life. Now transformed into his sovereign, Edward's claim to Richard's allegiance and obedience became overriding. Henceforth George and Richard were state assets, whose futures Edward shaped. The two boys featured prominently in the inaugural ceremonies of the new regime. Both were knighted ahead of the coronation (26 June 1461): a process that ruled out an ecclesiastical career, committed each to an aristocratic and chivalric future, and that required appropriate upbringings. First George and then Richard became knights of the Garter. George was created a duke – with the highly symbolic title of Clarence – and then in the autumn on All Hallows Day (1 November 1461) Richard was created Duke of Gloucester and was elected knight of the Garter. He received his helmet,

---

[27] C. Weightman, *Margaret of York, Duchess of Burgundy, 1446–1503* (St Martin's Press, 1989), p. 19; L. Visser-Fuchs, 'Richard in Holland, 1461', *Ricardian*, 6 (1983), p. 185; Scofield, *Edward IV*, vol. 1, p. 178.

[28] Richard may already have suffered scoliosis, a condition that affects teenagers.

crest, and sword in February 1462 and took up his stall in St George's
Chapel in Windsor in 1466.[29] He bore the arms of England and France
quarterly with a label of three points that marked him as a younger son.
George and Richard were the first two English dukes who were not already
earls. They were also created premier dukes, with precedence over existing
dukes such as their brother-in-law Suffolk, husband of their sister Elizabeth,
Buckingham and Norfolk. Clarence was appointed steward of England to
organise the coronation.[30] Richard was appointed admiral of England on
12 October 1462: 'The kynges Highness grayntyth this for terme of his lyf',
wrote Edward.[31] It was George of course who was the elder, indeed heir
apparent until 1466, and who was to be preferentially treated until at least
1468. The two boys were destined to become the king's right-hand men but
they were still children of course. In the meantime their offices were exercised by deputies on their behalf.

This exaltation impressed the two boys. They certainly knew they were
royal and did not understate what that signified. Henceforth, they were
high and mighty princes and dukes (*prepotentes*), as others described them
and their formal instruments said,[32] an address comparable to the modern
'Your Royal Highness'. Their written style continued from their dukedom
with any supplementary notices that were appropriate: earldoms, principal
lordships (e.g., Glamorgan, Richmond),[33] and such honorary offices as
constable and admiral of England. The great chamberlainship may have
been honorary, but the dukes fought each other for the right to use it.[34] The
10-year-old Richard cannot have exercised the considerable responsibili-

[29] Hicks, *Clarence*, p. 18; Scofield, *Edward IV*, 1, p. 216. Gloucester first took his seat on 23
April 1466, C. Halstead, *Richard III as Duke of Gloucester and King of England*, 2 vols (Longman,
Brown, Green, 1844), vol. 1, p. 122.

[30] Hicks, *Clarence*, p. 17. But not to pronounce sentence on Henry VI in parliament, *CPR
1461–7*, p. 63.

[31] *CPR 1461–7*, p. 214; C81/1491/43; BL MS Cotton Julius BXII ff.117–18. A surviving
admiralty seal for the south and west and references to admiralty cases show that jurisdiction did not depend on an active adult admiral. The title had belonged to Richard's brother-
in-law Henry, the Lancastrian Duke of Exeter. Gloucester superseded Warwick's uncle
William Earl of Kent. Presumably Warwick, reappointed keeper of the seas 1462–4, aspired
to be admiral also, Hicks, *Warwick*, p. 257.

[32] E.g., C 81/1491/10.

[33] E.g., Raine, *Statutes*, p. 160.

[34] *CPR 1467–77*, pp. 262, 344.

ties, nor probably have received the emoluments.[35] There were local officers to exercise these functions without the need for the lord's initiative or intervention. Perhaps the other cathedrals, monasteries, and towns that they frequented treated them with reverence and ceremony comparable to that shown them at Canterbury. On the vigil of Trinity (30 May) 1461 when both dukes returned from overseas, they were received at Canterbury Cathedral with the utmost honour 'by the prior and convent in green copes with the response *Summe Trinitatis*. And that same day, they were present at vespers, and the following day [31 May, they were] in procession at High Mass, and at second vespers.' On their next visit with Archbishop Bourchier on 28 August 1463 they again had a procession at high mass. What impact this made on these boys, both in self-worth and arrogance, is shown by Clarence (not Gloucester), who had his sword borne point uppermost in procession in the cathedral and 'in other places'.[36] Later Gloucester described himself as called by God to his high rank and wealth.[37]

In the meantime, the boys were children, who needed looking after and bringing up. What befell them was determined by their eldest brother King Edward, who made a number of decisions about them. Perhaps these decisions were unconscious, as the young king simply took as his model his own experience in the 1450s as the son and heir of a great nobleman and destined to become the same himself. First of all, as we have seen, Edward bestowed on his brothers titles of nobility, knighthood, and great national offices. Second, he removed them from the nurture of their mother, the widowed Duchess Cecily, and gave them a separate establishment of their own. The youngest children, the king's brothers George and Richard and their elder sister Margaret, were settled instead in a tower at the newly constructed and state-of-the-art palace of Greenwich on the Thames within easy distance of London, Westminster, and the other royal residences where the king himself commonly dwelt. Their establishment was funded

[35] As supposed by A.F. Sutton, 'The Admiralty and Constableship of England in the Later Fifteenth Century: The Operation and Development of these Offices, 1462–85, under Richard Duke of Gloucester and King of England', in *The Courts of Chivalry and Admiralty in Late Medieval Europe*, eds A. Musson and N. Ramsay (Boydell Press, 2018), p. 188.
[36] *John Stone's Chronicle. Christ Church Priory, Canterbury, 1417–72*, ed. M. Connor (Medieval Institute Publications, 2010), pp. 108, 110–11.
[37] Raine, *Statutes*, p. 160.

through the royal household under the financial direction of a member, John Peke. Clarence had a chancellor in Dr John Tapton, dean of St Asaph, to manage his affairs, who conceivably may have acted for Gloucester too, or perhaps Gloucester already had a separate chancellor of his own. Tapton seems to have researched what the king had to give and organised the petitions that secured properties for his master Clarence. Fewer bills from Gloucester were approved, probably because less was requested. Apart from expensive fabrics and masses of fur to be made up into the most splendid attire, we know only that the dukes had henxmen, nameless boys of their own age to keep them company and to be educated with them.[38] Perhaps they were the young gentry who recur in their service, some of whom appear to be Gloucester's friends as well as his servants. Almost all our information at this stage comes from the expenses in setting up the Greenwich establishment.

Greenwich was bestowed on the new queen in 1465,[39] but the royal children may no longer have been living there. The two boys were apparently still there in 1463, when they were summoned to a great council at Leicester.[40] It may be that this was the moment when they moved on, Clarence perhaps to the custody of Archbishop Bourchier,[41] and Richard to that of the Earl of Warwick. The evidence in both cases is retrospective. In 1464–5 Warwick was granted the wardship and marriage of the important heir Francis Lord Lovell as compensation for the expenses already incurred and to be incurred in the future for Prince Richard.[42] Richard had no independent income – as yet no seisin (legal possession) of the lands granted to him by the king – but apart from his keep, on the model of other minors he probably required progressively more attendants, richer clothing, better horses, jewellery, and equipment year by year, which Warwick had to defray. The earl did arrange for Lovell to marry his niece Anne FitzHugh, daughter of his brother-in-law and trusted retainer Henry Lord FitzHugh, securing her rank, wealth, and security for the rest of her life. Surely her

[38] Hicks, *Clarence*, pp. 20–2.

[39] *CPR 1461–7*, pp. 433–4.

[40] Hicks, *Clarence*, p. 21.

[41] *CPR 1467–77*, p. 296; *John Stone's Chronicle*, p. 110. This may, however, have been in 1459–60, see Horrox, 'Richard III' in *ODNB*.

[42] Scofield, *Edward IV*, vol. 1, p. 216n.

father and Warwick himself were happy with their side of the bargain?[43] It was probably at this time that Lovell and Richard struck up the friendship that is implied much later by Lovell's appointment in 1483 as chamberlain of Richard III's household. Possibly Richard was living with Warwick as early as 1463 and up until his own majority in 1468. There is little direct evidence for this phase in Richard's adolescence. He accompanied the earl and countess to Warwick College in 1464 and to York in 1468–9, making offerings in each case, and was seated with the earl's daughters at Cawood Palace near York at the enthronement feast of Warwick's brother Archbishop George Neville in 1465.[44] He was later to marry the younger daughter Anne, but, in 1465, when she was aged nine and Richard was 13, their youth and the age gap makes unlikely the romantic attachment stated by the Burgundian chronicler Jehan Waurin.[45] It took until 1469 for Warwick to contrive the marriage of Isabel his eldest daughter to Richard's brother Clarence. If there was ever a scheme to wed Gloucester to Anne Neville, it was obviously incompatible with the alternate proposal of Princess Jeanne of France, a match that King Louis XI sugared with the additional incentive of three Burgundian provinces. Probably neither speculation came to Richard's attention.[46] Almost certainly Richard's 'sojourn in the household of Warwick the Kingmaker had a powerful influence on his later development, although we possess no corroborative details'.[47]

These sightings reveal the earl and countess of Warwick in company and that on such occasions Richard was with them, but this is unlikely often to have been the case. The countess and her daughters would not have accompanied the earl on campaigns in Northumberland, nor on diplomatic missions to Scotland, Burgundy, or France. It is safe to deduce that Richard was part of the earl's household. Whether he was part of the subgroup, the riding household, that escorted the earl on his ceaseless travels on horseback between Scotland and the continent, is much less certain. It cannot safely be

[43] GEC, vol. 8, p. 225.

[44] Hicks, *Warwick*, pp. 230, 253; Hicks, *Richard III: The Man Behind the Myth*, p. 50.

[45] J. Waurin, *Recueil des Croniques et Anciennes Istoires de la Grant Bretaigne*, eds W. and E.L.C.P. Hardy, Rolls Series 5 (London, 1891), pp. 458–9. No other proposal for Anne's marriage is known at this date.

[46] Scofield, *Edward IV*, vol. 1, p. 412.

[47] Ross, *Richard III*, p. 7.

presumed that Richard accompanied Warwick everywhere. His presence is never mentioned by the chroniclers or foreign diplomats, as it should have been, nor was he honoured by corporations or showered by them with gifts of wine, which are two revealing indicators of the movements of the great. His formal education surely required stability, daily access to schoolmasters, books, stables, and tiltyard, in one location. Where that was is not obvious. Probably it was not Cardiff, since Warwick scarcely appears in Wales in the 1460s, nor in Calais where the earl had resided in 1456–60. It is probably correct to suppose that Richard became acquainted with the earl's power-bases around Warwick, Hanley Castle in Worcestershire, and Tewkesbury Abbey in Gloucestershire, and in Yorkshire and the North-West, wherein lay the earl's castles of Barnard Castle in County Durham, Middleham in Richmondshire, Sheriff Hutton in Ryedale, and Penrith in Cumberland that later, unpredictably, were to become his own. It seems to have been Warwick who modernised the old castle of Middleham with a great chamber atop the keep. How familiar was Richard with Carlisle Castle and the West March towards Scotland where Warwick was warden or with Pontefract Castle in Yorkshire, Warwick's seat as chief steward of the duchy of Lancaster north of Trent? From 1464 informally and from 1465 formally England and Scotland were at peace. Was Richard acquainted with the northern nobility, all of them related to Warwick, and his principal retainers? Richard's later career suggests he knew about Warwick's affinity and what made it tick, which most probably he imbibed at this time. That 'he was not personally a stranger to this society . . . [nor] no unknown and alien southerner', observed Ross, may have eased his rule of the North in the 1470s.[48]

Richard's sojourn with Warwick may imply a life of provincial obscurity removed from the court, government, and public life. The young duke scarcely features in the chronicles or the public records as he should have done if he accompanied Warwick to the court, to great councils, to parliaments, or to the churching of the queen in February 1466. Like Warwick, Richard missed the coronation of the new queen on 26 May 1465. Like Warwick, who was negotiating abroad, Richard missed the tournament of the century at Smithfield in June 1467 between the queen's brother

[48] Ross, *Richard III*, p. 8.

Anthony Lord Scales and the Grand Bastard of Burgundy. In June 1468 he did join his elder brothers in escorting their sister Margaret through Kent to her embarkation at Margate en route to her marriage to Duke Charles of Burgundy. Warwick was also in attendance.[49] During these years Richard certainly observed how a great household was run. Warwick's hospitality was especially open-handed. Any visitor, it was later recalled, could take away as much meat as he could carry on the end of his knife. Warwick served 60 dishes to the French ambassadors, and his consumption was more conspicuous than anyone else's, probably including the king.[50] Somehow Richard also learnt the language of bastard feudalism, how to recruit and how to manage retainers, which he was shortly to undertake on his own behalf. There are so many possibilities, so many experiences and opportunities in these years, that cannot be confirmed or denied. Even by 15th-century criteria, Richard was underage, not to be consulted by the earl, still less to be his confidant. Nor did he become Warwick's political disciple. 'It is a sign of Richard's early independence of character', wrote Ross, 'that this close association with his overweening and overwhelming cousin of Warwick did not persuade him to follow his brother Clarence's example of supporting Warwick's factious opposition to Edward IV'.[51]

Presumably Richard was one of the staff of the earl's chamber attendant on the earl himself. His copy of the romance *Ipomedon* that lists the duties of a gentleman usher is conceivably in his own hand. He should perhaps be compared with the henxmen in the royal household, who were schooled in everything necessary for young aristocrats according to the *Black Book* of Edward IV's household.[52] Richard was not alone, merely the highest ranking of the group of adolescent aristocrats brought up in Warwick's household. While their names are not known, they may have included some of the Northerners who became his feoffees and who died in his service in 1471, towards whom he became a friend and developed a warm

[49] Weightman, *Margaret of York*, pp. 46–7.

[50] *Great Chronicle of London*, p. 207.

[51] Ross, *Richard III*, pp. 8–9.

[52] P. Tudor-Craig, *Richard III* (National Portrait Gallery, 1973), p. 63. For what follows, see A.R. Myers, *Household of Edward IV* (Manchester University Press, 1959), pp. 126–7. Hard evidence for this paragraph is scattered throughout this book.

affection.[53] His training included book learning in 'things of virtue that he shall be most apt to learn'. He had been taught to read using the Latin primer or book of hours, which also contained the cross row – the alphabet. Richard wrote with a neat and confident hand and had some Latin, familiarising him at the least with the Latin of church services.[54] Richard was in 'wit' – intelligence – as capable as his brothers Edward and George. It was surely at this stage that he learnt to master the technicalities and detail – religious, chivalric, or legal – to put a complex case, and to become a good administrator although, as yet, he had nothing to administer. The training of henxmen included urbanity – mixing in polite society, 'to have all courtesy in words, deeds, and degrees', in etiquette, precedence in processions and seating plans, and personal conduct in line with contemporary books of courtesy and chivalry. He should have developed such accomplishments as piping, singing, dancing, and harping.[55] Certainly Richard appreciated choral music.

This was the time when the young prince was civilised into the standards and values of the aristocracy. He should also have acquired the athletic skills expected of aristocrats: 'to ride cleanly and surely', to learn to wear his harness (armour), and to fight with lance, sword, and longbow. On 12 August 1468 King Edward himself funded archery equipment already 'delyvered by our commandement to our derrest brother'.[56] We cannot document the hunting that all aristocrats engaged in except perhaps indirectly – the new parks that he was to create at Middleham.[57] Anyway rather slight and slender, by this stage, Richard may have additionally suffered the scoliosis that was to distort him physically, that rendered him less physically adept than his peers, that denied him the strength to wield certain weapons, and that may have limited his stamina.

Evidence from his later life indicates that Richard was instructed about retaining, patronage, good lordship, and arbitration. It was now surely that he learnt to dance, but it is known that he became an accomplished rider,

[53] C. Ross, 'Some "Servants and Lovers" of Richard in his Youth', in *Richard III: Crown and People*, ed. J. Petre (Sutton, 1985), pp. 146–8.
[54] Sutton and Visser-Fuchs, *Richard III's Books*, p. 5.
[55] Myers, *Household*, pp. 126–7.
[56] E 404/74/1/60.
[57] Pollard, *NE England*, pp. 203–4.

accustomed to armour and competent in the use of swords and other hand weapons. To attain these skills if at all disabled was harder for him, though expected of a knight and royal duke, and implies the courage that was well attested at Bosworth, the determination to succeed that is such a striking feature of his subsequent career, and considerable practice in the use of weapons, probably more than his peers. His prowess may have remained far under that of his brothers, as More says,[58] though his aggression is not in question. The qualities required of a general go far beyond hand-to-hand combat and certainly he possessed these attributes. Like Warwick he became a master of the administrative side of warfare, a logistics man. His self-image may have been that of a soldier. Richard never engaged in the infrequent public jousts, now a specialist set of skills displayed by a few semi-professional contemporaries, such as the Wydevilles and Greys, but he did preside over them. His education, both formal and aristocratic, was completed by 1468, when he was 16.

The daily religious observance that was required by Edward IV's *Black Book of the Household* moved beyond the assumptions of Richard's childhood towards the more formal understanding that Richard took into his later life. Richard took his religion seriously. He understood the basics, the language of the Church and of administration, and the Latin that was the gate of all learning. Certainly he knew the Latin Lords Prayer (*Pater Noster*), Hail Mary (*Ave Maria*), and Creed. Whether his Latinity went beyond liturgical Latin cannot at present be judged. It is surely at this point that he developed the informed understanding of the Christian calendar, the different components of services and the role of music, and the personal preferences that he was later to apply. It was probably also at this time that he selected his favourite saints. He particularly favoured St Ninian, bishop of Whithorn in south-western Scotland, whom he encountered in the chronicle of John Brompton that he was lent or given by Henry Lord FitzHugh (d. 1472), Warwick's brother-in-law and lieutenant of the West March.[59] Richard took his personal devotions from the simple primer (book of hours) rather than the larger and more sophisticated breviary and missal used by

[58] More, *Richard III*, p. 7.
[59] Tudor-Craig, *Richard III*, p. 79.

professional clergy, although he adapted it with additional orisons to his own taste.[60]

Virtuous Christian conduct was also demanded. That included the sexual morality that gave way to the double standard of aristocratic sexuality. Richard was a sensual man. Like many aristocrats, perhaps most, he was to have a mistress and bastards. The education of the aristocracy included some study of the mirrors for princes, books of instruction that enjoined the pursuit of virtue and the avoidance of vice. Richard owned at least one such book, *Of the Rule of Princes*, by Giles of Rome,[61] and almost certainly encountered others. Such works taught their readers to practise the Christian virtues and to eschew vice: highly desirable messages conducive to the good of their souls and society, but less than realistic in a rough age where pragmatism and ruthlessness was essential for effective rule. Such books taught that government was God's creation for the benefit of human society (the commonwealth), kings being God's agents.

The nobility advised and assisted the king. They were his natural councillors. However inadequate a king was, like Henry VI, he was entitled to rule and to the deference and support of his subjects. Even the greatest of subjects, nobles and princes like Richard, owed allegiance to the king that took precedence over all other ties. These were constitutional principles that governed political conduct and that Richard cannot have overlooked. To rebel or to break one's allegiance was unacceptable, treason, a step that was taken only with the utmost reluctance.[62] It had taken 10 years to progress from Cade's Rebellion in 1450 to Richard Duke of York's bid for the crown in 1460. Yet young Richard was living with Warwick the Kingmaker, who had rebelled in 1459–61 and had argued that he was promoting the public good against Henry VI's evil councillors. At first, of course, Warwick had given his allegiance and obedience to Edward IV as rightful king and had indeed been his principal protagonist against pockets of Lancastrian resistance and in securing foreign recognition. Warwick had been right-hand man to King Edward – indeed the public face of the regime. He and his brothers George, the chancellor, and John, the field commander, had

[60] Sutton and Visser-Fuchs, *Hours of Richard III*.

[61] Tudor-Craig, *Richard III*, p. 65.

[62] Hicks, *English Political Culture*, pp. 31–4.

accrued almost all the key offices to the point where England in 1461–7 appeared to be ruled by the Nevilles.[63] Warwick made policy as well as executed it. Where better could Richard learn to live nobly and to serve the crown than in the household of his brother's greatest supporter and principal agent?

Gradually, however, Edward IV had grown up – he was only 19 years old at his accession – and took the reins of government into his own hands. Complete victory over the Lancastrians and international recognition removed his dependence on the Neville brothers. Rashly in 1464 Edward had married Elizabeth Grey (née Wydeville) in defiance of all advice and England's diplomatic interest. In 1467 he had replaced Warwick's brother, the long-serving Archbishop Neville, as chancellor. He had developed his own Burgundian foreign policy in preference to Warwick's Francophile stance and in 1468 he contracted an aggressive alliance with Burgundy against France. Edward recruited new councillors who balanced the power of the Nevilles and indeed eroded it. The new men were the queen's relatives the Wydevilles, headed by her father the treasurer and constable Earl Rivers and her brother Anthony Lord Scales; the Welshman William Herbert II, Lord Herbert from 1461 and in 1468 earl of Pembroke, whose aspirations in South Wales and marriage policy in the North directly threatened Warwick's own domains; and the youthful Humphrey Lord Stafford of Southwick (from 1469 earl of Devon), the king's man in the South-west. The king regarded the marriages of his siblings as diplomatic pawns. He did marry his sister Margaret to Duke Charles of Burgundy and vetoed the projected marriage of his brother George Duke of Clarence to Warwick's elder daughter and heiress Isabel Neville. Warwick found himself thwarted at many points and his plans for the future impeded. Of course King Edward was entitled to act as he did and Warwick should have deferred as befitted a subject, but he did not. He withdrew from court, railed against the king's new evil councillors, appeared to threaten coups d'états, and persisted with Isabel's marriage plans.[64] In 1469 he was to claim that he had consistently pursued the common good against evil rule,

---

[63] Hicks, *Warwick*, ch. 8.
[64] Ibid., pp. 264–70; 'Annales Rerum Anglicarum', pp. 786–9.

now represented by Edward IV and his evil councillors. It was a claim that many accepted. How much of this came to the ears of Richard Duke of Gloucester can only be guessed, but he was in Warwick's household when the earl distanced himself from court and the tensions rose. Warwick was no longer a good model for a royal prince.

What Richard thought at the time of the marriage of his brother Edward IV to the widow Elizabeth Grey (née Wydeville) is not known. Much later, in 1483, he claimed to have disapproved, but he had ulterior motives then for that stance and there is no direct evidence of his reaction from 1464 – not that the views of a 12-year-old brother would have influenced Edward IV then. Although Richard was living with Warwick, there is no evidence that he shared Warwick's political outlook. When civil war resumed in 1469, Richard backed his brother, not his former guardian. What this absence of evidence betokens is a matter for speculation.

By making his brothers into dukes, Edward IV had committed himself to endowing them sufficiently to support their new estate. The new king started granting them spare estates almost from the start of his reign. This was the most expensive option. Probably Edward was unaware that King Edward III had merely made earls of his sons, later marrying them to heiresses whose resources financed their promotion into dukes. Henry IV and Henry V had been very slow to raise Princes Thomas, John, and Humphrey to ducal status, and initially had endowed them only for life, thus leaving themselves the opportunity of restricting their promotion to life only and clawing back what they had been given. These princes received the minimum endowments for dukes of 2,000 marks (£1,333 13s. 4d.), much of it in annuities rather than lands, and much less also than the £5,000 accrued through inheritance by the dukes of Buckingham, Norfolk, and York. These Lancastrian princes were to be royal agents without independent regional power-bases merely for as long as they were useful to the crown. The lands of the crown itself were insufficient to support Henry VI's Tudor half-brothers at even the minimum rate for a duke, £1,333 6s. 8d., which was far short of Richard's father York or his mentor Warwick. Henry VI could make them only into the most marginal of earls (£666 13s.4d.), which was all that he could afford. Previous kings had granted annuities pending the substitution of lands that often never materialised.

Edward IV, however, was different. He started his reign with the most enormous fund of lands of any late medieval king. Not just those of the crown, the queen, and the prince of Wales that came with kingship, not just the duchy of Lancaster that he annexed to the crown and much of his own York/Mortimer estate, but also all the lands forfeited by the defeated Lancastrian nobility – Beauforts, Butlers, Cliffords, Courtenays, Percies, Tudors, Rooses, and Welles – and gentry. There are signs that Edward intended initially to retain some of these lands towards rebuilding the solvency of the crown – he had inherited enormous debts and much diminished ordinary revenues – but in practice he could not resist the demands from his supporters for patronage and had also to return some estates to those Lancastrians who had submitted to him and had made their peace.

Politics took precedence over budgeting. The earl of Warwick and his family the Nevilles added to what they had already been given. Because inquisitions were not automatically held on these forfeitures, Edward did not know precisely what he had to give. By 1464 nothing remained to give away. Grants were made to the king's brothers that were later rescinded: the honour of Richmond, for instance, first allocated in 1462 to Gloucester, was then redirected to Clarence. There is a suspicion that Gloucester resented this, if not at the time, then later. Neither prince, however, was of age and therefore neither had seisin of their estates and their revenues. It was only when they came of age that each duke had to be endowed properly. This was not at the modest level of the Lancastrian royal dukes, the brothers of Henry V. In 1467 Clarence was guaranteed lands worth 5,600 marks and reversions worth 1,000 marks (£666 13s.4d.) a year, totalling £4,400.[65] Presumably this was also the standard intended for Richard Duke of Gloucester. Each duke received several major estates and manors scattered across England. Edward's intention was apparently to make each of his brothers into a great regional magnate. He seems to have changed his mind several times. In 1461–2 he earmarked for Richard swathes of territory in three areas: Beaufort and Hungerford lands in central southern England, the de Vere lands of the earl of Oxford in Essex and East Anglia,

[65] *PROME*, vol. 13, p. 270.

and the honour of Bolingbroke in Lincolnshire.[66] The Beaufort lands were restored almost at once to Henry Duke of Somerset in 1462 and the De Vere lands were restored to John, the 13th earl in 1464. The grant of Bolingbroke was rescinded in 1465.[67] The doughty Margaret Lady Hungerford clung on to her estates and Kingston Lacy was reallocated to Edward's new queen.[68] Underage, Richard appears never to have seisin or other benefits from any of them. After further treasons, terminated this time with the execution of Henry Duke of Somerset, the Beaufort lands returned to him, but this paltry estate was apparently all. By 1464–8 Edward actually lacked the forfeitures to endow them and his queen and in each case had instead to carve a great estate from the Duchy of Lancaster. Clarence received the honours of Tutbury in Staffordshire and Duffield in Derbyshire, and on 7 May 1469 Gloucester secured the honours of Clitheroe in Lancashire and Halton in Cheshire.[69] By that time he had graduated from childhood into the political world of adults.

---

[66] CPR 1461–7, pp. 197, 228; Somerville, Lancaster, vol. 1, p. 257n.

[67] M.A. Hicks, 'Edward IV, the Duke of Somerset, and Lancastrian Loyalism in the North', in Rivals, pp. 150–3; J. Ross, John de Vere, Thirteenth Earl of Oxford, 1442–1513. 'The Foremost Man of the Kingdom' (Boydell Press, 2011), p. 50; Somerville, Lancaster, vol. 1, p. 257n.

[68] See below; DL 29/711/11465.

[69] Somerville, Lancaster, vol. 1, p. 257n. But he never apparently had seisin of any of them.

Chapter Three

THE YOUNG ADULT

THE SECOND WAR 1469–71

I

From October 1468, when he was 16, Richard entered public life and commenced his particular career, but he did not come formally of age.[1] No certificate of homage exists, like that of 1466 for Clarence, also aged 16. Most probably there was none. Surviving accounts demonstrate that he did not receive seisin of those Duchy of Lancaster lands granted to him by the king,[2] although very likely he did secure some Hungerford lands by negotiation. The re-grant of Alwerton, Tywarnail Tees in Cornwall and Wilmington in Kent explicitly included back revenues from 1461.[3] The king made grants to his brother without proof of age, yet withheld the livery of Duke Richard's lands.[4] This curious anomaly is perhaps to be explained by the unwillingness of King Edward to give up the Duchy revenues and/or to allow his youngest brother complete financial and hence political independence. Warwick's dissidence may have made the earl less suitable as a mentor for the king's

[1] This discussion corrects the assumption in Hicks, *Edward V*, p. 83.

[2] *CCR 1468–76*, nos 198, 409; BL MS Cotton Julius BXII f.122–3. None of the accounts reveal Richard as lord, DL 29/8/100–101; DL 29/17/240–2; DL 29/77/1520–2; DL 29/90/1650; DL 30/5/72. Evidently John Pilkington and John Parr were unable to fulfil Gloucester's order to take seisin, DL 37/38/7.

[3] *CPR 1467–77*, p. 179; C 81/828/2933.

[4] There seems to be a parallel here in the grant of office without proof of age to William Herbert II in 1471, C 81/836/3304.

brother, but it was the king's decision to employ his youngest brother underage that was the decisive factor. Richard received his first commission in February 1468, but did not act. That Richard did not join the powerful commission to try Sir Thomas Cook in June 1468, but did try Sir Thomas Hungerford and Henry Courtenay in October,[5] may bracket the moment when he achieved political maturity (and includes his 16th birthday on 2 October). Richard participated at the second trial. Courtenay and Hungerford were convicted of treason and executed at Salisbury in January 1470.[6] Richard was now old enough to be useful to the king – though Edward cannot have expected to impose such responsibilities on him so quickly. Richard's formal education now ended, but he lacked of course all the experience that he was going to need as a great magnate, a military commander, and a royal prince. He picked all these up in the next three tumultuous years.

Even at 16 Richard had potential uses for Edward. The birth of three royal princesses moved him further from the succession, but he was a visible embodiment of the house of York and was moving beyond being a mere symbol to become actually useful. There was no immediate plan to marry him off diplomatically. Only gradually did it emerge that there was potential conflict between serving the king's interests and his own aspirations.

II

If Richard was to become a great magnate, he had to start almost from scratch. He needed his own great seal, signet, badge, livery, and motto. Manors ran themselves – each had its own hierarchy of officers – and the admiralty had its own bureaucracy and procedures. There were established models for the estate management of receivers, auditors, surveyors, stewards, and supervisors and for households that needed to be replicated. Initially Richard had no household, no estate administration, relatively few estates, no furnished residences, and no retinue, all of which had to be created. Richard started with inadequate resources to fund the expected lifestyle of a duke, yet he was quickly given ducal responsibilities that required the rapid expansion and development of his household and retinue. Probably

---

[5] *CPR 1467–77*, pp. 69, 126.
[6] Scofield, *Life and Times of Edward IV*, vol. 1, pp. 480, 482.

Richard did already have a core (but unidentified) entourage of chancellor, secretary, chamberlain, attendants, grooms, and chaplains around which his new household was constructed. He needed besides (and perhaps shared) 'men to fetch and carry and run messages . . . musicians (whom he is known to have employed by 1465–6), [and] huntsmen'.[7] In the early 1460s King Edward had appointed some trusted Yorkists to his service, such as John Peke and the esquire John Skelton,[8] perhaps John Milewater who had served Edward as earl of March at Ludlow in 1454,[9] and probably also a chancellor, chamberlain, grooms, and chaplains who remain anonymous. Richard's personal entourage would have grown with his age. Most probably Warwick introduced the newcomers – an important element to his patronage – which may explain why two cadets of northern families, Thomas Parr and Thomas Huddleston of Millom, appear in Richard's service and perished there in battle in 1471. Two Parr brothers, Thomas and William, were implicated in the Lincolnshire Rebellion in 1470, when their father Sir William Parr was intermediary for Warwick with the king. They were all related to the earl. Parr was married to Elizabeth, daughter of Henry Lord FitzHugh by Warwick's aunt Alice Neville, and Huddleston's elder brother Sir Richard Huddleston was husband of Warwick's bastard daughter Margaret.[10] The Northerners John Pilkington and John Parr, already esquires of the body to the king and later king's knights, were selected – probably by Gloucester – to deliver him seisin of Halton and Clitheroe in 1469.[11] The service to the Nevilles of Pilkington and Sir John Huddleston dated back to their rebellion in 1459–60 and probably before. Both were gentry of substance. The 25 servants, splendid bed of arras and jewellery that Pilkington left indicate a lifestyle of considerable splendour. Pilkington

---

[7] A.F. Sutton, 'Richard of Gloucester 1461–70: Income, Lands and Associates. His Whereabouts and Responsibilities', *Ricardian*, 26 (2016), p. 43.

[8] Hicks, *Clarence*, pp. 20–1; *CPR 1461–7*, p. 52.

[9] Halstead, *Richard III as Duke of Gloucester and King of England*, vol. 1, p. 57.

[10] Ross, 'Servants & Lovers', in *Richard III: Crown and People*, ed. Petre, pp. 146–8. Parr acted for the duke in November 1469, *CCR 1468–76*, no. 409; 'Chronicle of the Rebellion in Lincolnshire 1470', ed. J.G. Nichols, *Camden Miscellany*, vol. 1 (1847), pp. 14–16. Hicks, *Warwick*, p. 234; *CPR 1467–77*, p. 218. Had Parr and Huddleston been brought up also in Warwick's household?

[11] DL 37/38/7.

was to become Richard's chamberlain.[12] In 1473 Pilkington, Sir John Huddleston himself, and William Hopton esquire were Richard's feoffees – among his most trusted men – and in 1477 they were designated benefici- aries of his prayers.[13] Pilkington and Milewater were already associated with Richard by January 1470.[14] Others killed by Richard's side in 1471 and remembered by him were Christopher Worsley esquire, marshal of the king's hall and three times sheriff of Somerset, and the administrator John Harper. Worsley may have had Hungerford antecedents and Harper may have been encountered in Wales.[15] Richard's commemoration reveals the warmth of their relationship, at least from his point of view. They remind us how geographically diverse may have been the connection that Richard had to construct so quickly. Edward gave him £433 towards his household expenses in November 1469.[16]

Another glimpse that is rather more revealing dates from June 1469 when Richard was on pilgrimage with the king in East Anglia and was possibly already planning to campaign with him against the Yorkshire rebel Robin of Redesdale. Perhaps in response to new restrictions on retaining non-residents in the 1468 statute of livery, John Duke of Norfolk had dropped John Paston III, Bernard, and Brome from his livery list, which by implication freed them to take service elsewhere. Bernard and Brome, together with Berney and Calthorpe 'ar sworn my lord of Glowcetyrs men'.[17] William Calthorpe (d.1494) of Burnham Thorpe and John Berney (d. 1471) of Great Witchingham were significant Norfolk gentry, but the others are obscure. Bound now to Gloucester by oath, at the very least they received

---

[12] *English Wills Proved in the Prerogative Court of York 1477–99*, and H. Falvey, L. Boatwright, and P. Hammond (Richard III Society, 2013), pp. 13–15; Hicks, 'The Last Days of Elizabeth Countess of Oxford', in *Rivals*, p. 310.

[13] North Yorkshire Record Office, ZRC 17503; W.G. Searle, *The History of the Queens' College of St Margaret and St Bernard, Cambridge* (Cambridge Antiquarian Society, 1867), p. 90. Hopton's early commitment to Richard certainly casts doubt on the political neutrality of his father John Hopton as argued in C.F. Richmond, *John Hopton: A Fifteenth Century Suffolk Gentleman* (Cambridge University Press, 1981), esp. p. 117.

[14] *CPR 1467–77*, p. 198.

[15] Ross, "Servants and Lovers", pp. 146–8; Horrox, *Richard III*, p. 37.

[16] Hicks, *Clarence*, p. 61. Presumably, however, the king funded Richard's whole establish- ment in some unrecorded manner, from the royal household or chamber.

[17] *Paston L & P*, vol. 1, p. 545. Calthorpe delivered seisin of Sudeley to Gloucester next November, *CCR 1468–76*, no. 409.

his livery, at most were bound to him in writing by indentures and were granted annual fees. These men were surely relieved to find a new niche and pleased to relocate so quickly to such a prestigious lord. Service to the duke and his livery gave them standing wherever they were and potentially (and notoriously) enabled them to bully those they encountered. Household membership itself remained legal, but is not demonstrated here. Short-term military contracts within England, like those suggested by Horrox for these men,[18] were not legal. Bernard, Berney, Brome, and Calthorpe are not known ever to have become ducal councillors or ducal officers. They seem unlikely to have been retained for life. Swearing a mere oath, receipt of livery, and perhaps a fee apparently committed them – John Paston III prided himself on being free of such obligations – but potentially only for six months, until they were dropped from the autumn livery roll. Such weak bonds and easy transfers from lord to lord were the sort of casual retaining that had been banned by the new statute of livery.[19] It was very common nevertheless:[20] John Paston III was offered such a deal by the queen's brother Anthony Lord Scales who at least was a Norfolk peer.[21] Acceptable on the fringes, to bulk up a retinue perhaps for instant use in civil war, such recruits were not a satisfactory foundation for a new connection. On this evidence, at this date Gloucester had no idea which locality he would come to rule.

It is significant that the duke's first extant signet letter of 24 June to Sir John Say begged for a £100 loan towards the costs of the king's counter-measures against the rebel Robin of Redesdale. Gloucester and Say already had a relationship in which Say sought some favour from the duke that was not yet concluded. The duke now requested 'such frendlynesse in the same as I may doo for your hereafter' and in his own hand begged Say by name not to fail him, promising 'that I schewe yow my goode lordshype in that

[18] Horrox, *Richard III*, p. 32.

[19] *PROME*, vol. 13, pp. 384–5; M.A. Hicks, 'The 1469 Statute of Livery', *HR*, 64 (1991), p. 17. While Ward suggests that their parting with Norfolk was in compliance with this new act – see M. Ward, *The Livery Collar in Late Medieval England and Wales: Politics, Identity and Affinity* (Boydell Press, 2016), p. 59 – their new connection with Gloucester seems similar.

[20] M.A. Hicks, 'Retainers, Monks and Wine: Three Insights into Everyday Life', in *The Later Medieval Inquisitions Post Mortem: Mapping the Medieval Countryside and Rural Society*, ed. M. Hicks (Boydell Press, 2016), p. 179.

[21] *Paston L & P*, vol. 1, p. 545.

matter that ye labure to me for' – that compliance would bring success in his
pre-existing suit. This is the authentic language of a good lord who already
was retaining gentry and backing one in his (un)just cause. Short though the
letter is, it reveals that Gloucester was already applying the documentary
format used by such other lords as Clarence and York and later indeed
Gloucester himself. Had his secretariat imported the forms and procedures
that they had practised elsewhere? Headed 'the Duc of Gloucestre' and
signed 'R. Gloucestre', his letter opens 'Right trusty and welbeloved' and sets
out the circumstances, need, and request briefly and directly. The only facet
from later letters that is missing is the signature of the scribe – perhaps John
Kendal was not yet his secretary?[22] Richard's signature is as yet immature,
but by August 1470 he had achieved an elegant proficiency.[23] Although a
chance survival, this letter was probably one of several, even many, of the
same date, to each of which the duke added a personalised postscript
addressed to the individual recipient and to his particular circumstances and
aspirations. Though inducements were offered, such letters also contain
veiled threats. If not compliant, might the correspondent next receive a letter
commencing 'We marvel that . . .'? It appears that the duke meant to accom-
pany the king to the Midlands, but did not.

　　Richard was a new duke who inherited nothing. He was therefore wholly
dependent on what his brother King Edward bestowed on him. Before
becoming Warwick's ward he had been funded from the royal household, by
the cofferer, and surely still needed household subventions at this time. These
could have been the 'dyvers materes' that he spoke of with John Lord
Howard, then treasurer of the royal household. Howard, of Stoke by Nayland
in Suffolk, was a substantial East Anglian landholder and cousin to John
Duke of Norfolk, who was his primary lord. Howard is perhaps the best
documented instance of someone who gave good service to the king and
several peers. He had remembered Norfolk to 'my lord a Glowseter', who
(he reported back) was 'as wel disposed to ward yow as any lord may be to a

　　[22] *Richard III: The Road to Bosworth Field*, eds P.W. Hammond and A.F. Sutton (Constable,
1985), pp. 34, 36; *Original Letters Illustrative of English History*, ed. H. Ellis, 2, 1 (Harding,
Triphook and Leonard, 1827), pp. 143–4.
　　[23] Ibid., p. 34; E 101/71/5/950.

noder'.[24] Can we see here the teenaged prince again playing the good lord and condescending to an older duke who was not in such favour at court?

What these fragments do reveal is that the young duke – remember, he was still only 16 years old – was handling his own finances and itinerary and had moved apparently effortlessly into the roles of good lord and patron both on paper, which could be shaped by his more experienced staff, and in interpersonal relations.

Assuming Richard was to be endowed on the same scale as his brother Clarence, his expectations were enormous and extremely difficult to satisfy. But Edward always had more pressing commitments, to reward existing supporters, to manage the regions, and to restore former enemies, all of which repeatedly took priority over the endowment of his youngest and politically active brother. It was on 4 April 1461 that Gloucester was granted out of the Duchy of Lancaster the honours of Bolingbroke in Lincolnshire and Pickering with Barnoldswick in Yorkshire, together worth £1,000 a year. On 12 August and 9 September 1462 King Edward had made a further major allocation to Richard of substantial lands scattered across England and Wales: the castle of Gloucester, the Beaufort castle of Corfe in Dorset, a swathe of estates in eastern England forfeited by John de Vere, 12th earl of Oxford (executed 1462), the honour of Pembroke forfeited by Henry VI's half-brother Jasper Tudor, the honour of Richmond held by Henry VI's other half-brother Edmund Tudor (d. 1456), and the extensive lands in central southern England of Robert Hungerford II, Lord Hungerford and Moleyns (executed 1464).[25] Together these may well have added up to the £4,400 a year that Edward seems to have had in mind. It was a miscellaneous conglomeration that did not indicate much regional planning and does not even hint at the rule of the North that Richard was later to exercise. Actually Richard did not have tenure of any of them and probably never did in the future. There is no record of a grant of the issues ahead of his majority like that for his brother Clarence.[26]

---

[24] Crawford dates the year to 1468, but Horrox's dating of 1469 is preferred, both because Gloucester was in East Anglia and because he was acting independently as of age, A. Crawford, *Yorkist Lord: John Howard, Duke of Norfolk, c.1425–1485* (Bloomsbury, 2010), p. 53; Horrox, *Richard III*, p. 32.

[25] Somerville, *Lancaster*, vol. 1, p. 257n; *CPR 1461–7*, 197, pp. 228, 292.

[26] *CPR 1461–7*, pp. 212–13. Both brothers had all royal patents and writs free of fees and fines, *CPR 1461–7*, p. 387. Several grants were not enrolled.

Despite the formal grants, Edward IV felt free to reallocate these estates as convenient and did so several times. The patent of 9 September 1462 was revoked next year.[27] Richmond honour was granted instead to Clarence on 20 September. The grants of Bolingbroke and Pickering were rescinded in 1465.[28] Gloucester Castle was back in the king's hands in 1465.[29] Corfe was restored to Henry Duke of Somerset when he made his peace with the king and on 20 February 1463, following his desertion, it was included among all his not very substantial lands bestowed anew on Richard.[30] The Hungerfords successfully demonstrated that their estates had not been held by the traitor Robert II Lord Hungerford and Moleyns and therefore, on 30 March 1463, Edward revoked Richard's title by word of mouth.[31] The king's title to the Hungerford lands was weak and most of them remained in practice with the two dowager Hungerford ladies Margaret and Eleanor. The De Vere estates were restored in 1464 to the next heir, John 13th Earl of Oxford, who had married Warwick's youngest sister, and Pembroke was to be granted to William Herbert on his creation as Earl of Pembroke in 1468. Corfe and Chirk aside, therefore, Richard retained scarcely anything in 1468. A trawl of the king's entitlements in August 1468 uncovered only the Beaufort manors of Alwarton and Tywarneil Tees in Cornwall and Bedminster south of Bristol that had reverted to the crown on the death of Eleanor Duchess of Somerset in 1467.[32] Only the Beaufort lands therefore passed to Richard: £500, the income estimated by Ross, may be a serious overestimate.[33]

[27] Ibid., p. 228.

[28] Somerville, *Lancaster*, vol. 1, p. 257n. Kingston Lacy in Dorset granted to him in tail in 1462 was cancelled by Chancellor Neville in 1465–7 by order of the king, ibid. p. 257n; BL MS Cotton Julius BXII f.111v.

[29] Somerville, *Lancaster*, p. 441.

[30] Ibid., pp. 197, 292. The grant did not include the annuities that funded his dukedom. Margaret, daughter of Duke John (d. 1444), not his nephews Dukes Henry and Edmund, were the heirs to the Holland estates of Margaret Duchess of Clarence (d. 1439) and widow of John Beaufort, 1st earl (d. 1410).

[31] Ibid., p. 228; Hicks, 'Piety and Lineage in the Wars of the Roses: The Hungerford Experience', in *Rivals*, pp. 170–1.

[32] *CPR 1467–77*, pp. 94,139; BL MS Cotton MS Julius BXII ff.113v–114v; see also 108–v. Her Roos children by her first marriage were the heirs to her Beauchamp and Lisle inheritances.

[33] Ross, *Richard III*, p. 10. Gloucester's resources are seriously overestimated in Sutton, 'Richard of Gloucester 1461–70', pp. 43–53.

Edward had no more old forfeitures to give away. He did try to endow
Richard properly with new forfeitures and out of the Duchy of Lancaster.
On 7 May 1469 he carved out of the duchy the two honours of Clitheroe
and Halton in Lancashire and Cheshire and indeed everything else he held
in these two palatine counties. With the castle, lordship, honour, manor
and hundred of Clitheroe in Lancashire went the forests of Amounderness,
Bleasdale, Blackburnshire and Bowland, Myerscough, Queensmore,
Penhill, Rossendale, West Derbyshire and Wyresdale, the manors of
Penwortham, Ulnes Walton, Toddington, Colne, Penhulton, Worton,
Chatburn, Accrington, Haslingden, Skelyon, Overton, Slyne, Rygby and
Raa, West Derby and Corby, the castle and lordship of Liverpool, and the
parks of Croxteth, Myrescogh, and Toxteth. With the castle, honour, lordship and manor of Halton went the manors of Runcorn, More, Widnes,
Whitleigh, and Congleton.[34] Valued at £1,169 a year above reprises in
1463–4,[35] they constituted a princely estate that placed the duke at the head
of landholders in that region. Royal power here was theoretically more
immediate because both Chester and Lancaster were palatine counties in
royal hands. In both cases, however, the last active lords, Henry V as Prince
of Wales and the first two Lancastrian kings, had ceased operating half a
century ago, and the power vacuum had been filled by the principal local
landholders, the Stanley family. Thomas Lord Stanley was lord of the Isle
of Man and had 'a powerful concentration of estates' in Flintshire, Cheshire,
and Lancashire. He and his brothers also held the key offices in the two
palatinates.[36] Potentially, therefore, Richard was intruding into the Stanleys'
hegemony in the North West. Lord Stanley had actually been steward of
Halton since 1460.[37] Richard also intruded into their sphere of influence in
North Wales when he was appointed chief justice of the northern principality. These grants therefore brought the duke into instant conflict with the
Stanleys. Not passive either as landholder or officeholder, Richard acted to
make reality of these assets and to substitute his own authority for that of the
Stanleys. Their resistance and obstruction can be glimpsed through the

[34] DL 37/38/7; Somerville, *Lancaster*, vol. 1, p. 257n,

[35] DL 43/15/15.

[36] M. Jones, 'Richard III and the Stanleys', in *Richard III and the North*, ed. R.E. Horrox
(Hull, 1986), pp. 27–30.

[37] Somerville, *Lancaster*, vol. 1, p. 511.

sharply worded writs of the king whose backing Richard invoked.[38] Unfortunately, moreover, the grant was not permanent, but during the king's pleasure.[39] It should have provided Richard with the income and local authority appropriate for a royal duke, but not the permanent endowment or the foundation for enduring power. The king's pleasure signified that Edward hoped at some future date to revoke the grant, perhaps when other properties escheated to him, yet the duke surely must have hoped to extend his tenure to inheritance. Anything less was too little for him to invest in developing the castles, parks, and other resources at his own costs.

Richard's actions in the Hornby Castle dispute indicate an interest in this region, but he does not actually seem to have secured seisin of the lands that Edward had given him. He is not mentioned in any of the comprehensive sets of accounts for this period for either honour or the other properties for 1469–71, which continued to be run by Thomas Lord Stanley as receiver and as steward and constable of Halton.[40] Possibly, as argued above, Edward did not take Richard's homage or grant seisin of his estates at this time, a considerable saving to the king, but, in that case, where did Richard secure the substantial sums he used for his household, day-to-day living, retaining, and security for loans that he is known to have incurred? There is no concrete answer at present.

Clitheroe and Halton were important additions to Richard's landholdings, but they were not enough. Gloucester had at most half the lands of his brother Clarence. The extra forfeitures arose from further Lancastrian treasons in which were implicated Ralph Lord Sudeley (d. 1473), and Sir Thomas Hungerford (executed 1469), son of Robert II Lord Hungerford and Moleyns (executed 1464), and heir presumptive additionally of the two Hungerford ladies. Although neither indicted nor attainted, Sudeley was induced on 23 February 1469 to convey his principal estate and splendid new castle of Sudeley in Gloucestershire to the king's feoffees who passed them to Gloucester on 14 November.[41] Apart from Thomas Hungerford's

---

[38] *CCR 1468–76*, no. 535.

[39] DL 37/38/7.

[40] DL 29/8/100–101; DL 29/17/240–2; DL29/77/1520–2; DL 29/90/1650; DL 30/5/72.

[41] *CCR 1468–76*, nos 198, 409; BL MS Cotton Julius BXII ff.122–3.

own property held jointly with his widow Anne Percy, his forfeiture handed potentially the three baronies of Botreaux, Hungerford, and Moleyns to the king and hence by his grant to Richard. One chronicler explained the trial and execution of Henry Courtenay, heir to the earldom of Devon, as a device to secure his estates for Humphrey Lord Stafford of Southwick, henceforth Earl of Devon.[42] If no such charge against Richard is recorded, Hungerford's death was certainly very convenient.

On 25 October 1468 Richard was granted the Hungerford estates of Farleigh Hungerford in Somerset, Heytesbury and Teffont Evias in Wiltshire and all other estates late of Robert II and forfeited by his attainder in 1461.[43] Robert II actually had seisin of none of the Hungerford estates, but Duke Richard really needed to make the most of his inheritances. Although never united, the three baronies of Botreaux, Hungerford, and Moleyns together constituted the largest estate in south central England and were worth about £2,000 a year altogether. They comprised the Hungerford lands, mainly in Somerset and Wiltshire, the Botreaux possessions mainly in Devon and Cornwall, and the Moleyns properties, mainly in Buckinghamshire and Oxfordshire. Unfortunately none of them had devolved on the traitor Robert Hungerford II, either by the time of his attainder in 1461 or by his death in 1464. Because Robert II had been captured by the French at Castillon in 1453 and had been ransomed for £6,000, almost the whole Hungerford estate of his father Robert I (d. 1459) and the whole Moleyns inheritance of his wife Eleanor Moleyns had been enfeoffed to use (effectively mortgaged) to repay his creditors, a process that was still ongoing and that was never completed. The third element, the Botreaux barony, was the heritage of Robert II's mother, the redoubtable but aged Margaret Lady Hungerford. Margaret had used the enfeoffments to keep control of the Hungerford and Botreaux estates and was determined to honour the trusts that governed them. Robert II had never held any of these in his own right. Duke Richard had no immediate legal rights to any of them, but only rights of reversion. So too with Robert II's

---

[42] *Death and Dissent. Two Fifteenth-Century Chronicles*, ed. L.M. Matheson (Boydell & Brewer, 1999), p. 98.

[43] *CPR 1467–77*, 139; BL MS Cotton Julius BXII f.111–v. These random estates were probably the most attractive.

son Sir Thomas Hungerford. In practice it was only to these reversionary
rights that Duke Richard could aspire. Moreover, the enfeoffments could
permit the estates to bypass the traitor Thomas to the benefit of Thomas's
brothers Walter and Leonard or Thomas's own daughter Mary. In 1469
Richard needed to extract something from the estate, to expedite the
devolution, and to maximise his own share.

Richard did have certain advantages in his dealings with the Hungerford
ladies. He was one of the commission that had sentenced Sir Thomas
Hungerford to death. Thomas's own lands and his hereditary expectations
were forfeit. His only issue was his baby daughter Mary Hungerford. For the
moment, most of the lands to which Thomas had been heir apparent were
held by his grandmother Margaret and his mother Eleanor, who wished for
inheritance by his next heirs, Thomas's baby daughter and his next brother
Walter. Richard had a royal grant and the rights to reversion, royal authority,
and could bring force to bear. Duke Richard could coerce, though these
ladies proved more resistant than Elizabeth Countess of Oxford in the 1470s.
He may have used the same tactics. As the mother and grandmother of traitors, Margaret had been placed three times in custody, latterly in the nunneries
of Amesbury in Wiltshire and Syon in Middlesex. Alternatively and in
conjunction, Richard could allure the two ladies by facilitating the results that
they wanted. Margaret wanted to pass most of the Hungerford and Botreaux
estates to her grandchildren, which was technically difficult, especially if
opposed by the king's brother. Additionally she wanted to found a chantry in
Salisbury Cathedral for her husband Robert I Lord Hungerford and to
complete the hospital at Heytesbury begun by her father-in-law Walter Lord
Hungerford (d. 1447). Both required licences to alienate in mortmain from
the king that she lacked the political clout to secure. Moreover, being very
old, she had not the luxury of time. Eleanor meanwhile had remarried to Sir
Oliver Manningham, who was another suspected Lancastrian conspirator.
She wanted to shrug off the mortgage obligations of her last husband Robert
II, to bilk his creditors, to preserve her new husband from the penalties of
treason, and to provide in the event of her death for her new husband. Duke
Richard could facilitate all these aspirations, albeit at a considerable price.

Richard's grant had given him leverage to treat with the two ladies.
It was probably he who had Margaret confined to Syon Abbey. Richard

secured at once from Margaret the lordship of Farleigh Hungerford in Somerset with its new castle. He did not get Heytesbury. Margaret and Eleanor were allowed to proceed with the devolution of their estates. In his indenture of 14 May 1469 the duke had to concede that Margaret and various groups of feoffees could retain uninterrupted a string of manors. He also promised Margaret that he would secure the two licences within 12 months. In return he did secure Farleigh Hungerford permanently and at once. Edward IV himself was to countersign: it cost him nothing. The king also indented with Eleanor and protected Manningham from the penalties of treason.[44] On certain issues Richard could mobilise the king's influence, though not necessarily at once. The two licences to alienate were implemented only in 1472.[45] Out of these negotiations Richard secured principally the two modern country houses of Farleigh Hungerford and Sudeley, which were far less than what he needed. Presumably it was Richard's adult advisers rather than the duke himself who devised these agreements, but they were useful preparation for the much tougher deals that he imposed in 1473–5 on the countesses of Oxford and Warwick. Richard was to return for more from the Hungerfords in 1473–4. He may have always intended to do so.

The second area where Richard was granted land was in the North-west, where on 7 May 1469 he received the two Duchy of Lancaster honours of Halton and Clitheroe, each with its small motte and bailey castle.[46] The Clitheroe honour was north of the River Ribble on the west of the Pennines and Halton in what is now Runcorn. It was 70 years since these passed to the crown, much longer since they had housed a resident lord, and they were certainly therefore out of date, probably out of repair, and ill-furnished. Although not altogether neglected – Clitheroe received a new chamber in 1425 and Halton a new gatehouse in the 1450s – much needed to be amended and much spent to bring them up to scratch. Richard was also appointed chief forester of Amounderness, Bowland, and Blackburn.[47]

[44] Hicks, 'Piety and Lineage', in *Rivals*, pp. 167–9, 177–9. Although Edward had no real title to Eleanor's estate, he did secure two manors by their indenture of 13 March 1469 in return for sparing Manningham, ibid. p. 177.

[45] *CPR 1467–77*, 306, 311.

[46] Somerville, *Lancaster*, vol. 1, p. 257n.

[47] Ibid., pp. 506–7. Edward's grant of Halton and Clitheroe proved abortive.

III

Richard still had minimal resources and retainers in June 1469 when England stumbled into the Second War of the Roses. In spite of Edward's opposition, Warwick had secured the necessary dispensation from the pope for the marriage of his daughter Isabel and Richard's brother Clarence, which was conducted at Calais (where Warwick was captain) on 11 July 1469 by his brother Archbishop Neville. Five knights of the Garter attended though it seems unlikely that Gloucester was among them. On 5–6 June he joined the king on his East Anglian pilgrimage and judicial progress via Walsingham to Norwich. On 24 June he was at Castle Rising in Norfolk, in attendance on the king, who was about to proceed northwards to suppress the second rebellion of Robin of Redesdale. Richard borrowed money and recruited retainers.[48] Redesdale's rebellion purported to be a popular uprising that Edward seems to have taken insufficiently seriously. Actually it cloaked a rising of Warwick's Richmondshire retinue, Robin himself being a relative of the steward Sir John Conyers, probably his brother William Conyers of Marske, Warwick's cousin Sir Henry Neville of Latimer being a leader, and Warwick's brother-in-law Lord FitzHugh probably being involved. Robin's rebellion appears in retrospect an element in a multipronged seizure of power organised by Warwick. Robin's rebellion was timed to coincide with Warwick's and Clarence's own invasion from Calais and with disturbances in the West Midlands. That Gloucester missed the wedding and was with the king indicates that he was no part of Warwick's coup d'état. Edward's new-found favourites Pembroke and Devon were defeated by the northerners at the battle of Edgecote on 24 July 1469 and both, together with the queen's father Earl Rivers, were slain. Archbishop Neville arrested the king at Olney in Buckinghamshire, where he was almost on his own. King Edward was confined first at Warwick, then at Middleham, while Clarence and the archbishop steered the royal council in London in Edward's name. Charges of sorcery were laid against the queen's mother Jacquetta Duchess of Bedford, apparently to discredit her granddaughters, the king's only children, and to restore Clarence as heir apparent. The parliament summoned to York that never

[48] *Paston L & P*, vol. 1, p. 545; Ellis, *Original Letters*, pp. 143–4.

met was presumably intended to revise the order of succession and to provide an enduring legal framework for Warwick's rule.[49] Aspects of this coup d'état are reminiscent of those of Richard Duke of York in 1455–6 and 1460, suggesting that Warwick was applying a tried and tested strategy that had worked before. They are echoed in Gloucester's own assumption of power in 1483. Duke Richard missed the battle of Edgecote and his company attracted no attention from the chroniclers. He seems not to have been at Olney with the king and was not among the royal council at Westminster. On 10 August he was sent his first individual writ of summons to a parliament to meet at York on 22 September, but this parliament was cancelled on 7 September.[50]

Warwick's rule ended when he proved unable to overcome another northern uprising, by the Lancastrian Sir Humphrey Neville of Brancepeth. Warwick was therefore obliged to release the king. Gloucester reappeared as one of those who turned out in force to escort the king into London.[51] On 23 October Gloucester witnessed Henry Percy's oath of allegiance on his release from the Tower of London.[52] Presumably the duke attended the great council at Westminster that met early in November – the first such meeting that he was to attend. Whether Richard was one of the hawks, who wanted to use force against Warwick, Clarence, and the archbishop, or whether he backed the peacemakers, we cannot tell. While Edward made his peace with Warwick, Clarence, and the archbishop, he conceded none of their demands. Archbishop Neville was dismissed as chancellor, Prior Langstrother as treasurer, and Warwick as chief justice of South Wales. The peerage was reshuffled to replace the three executed earls and significant responsibilities were given to the king's youngest brother Richard. Edward confirmed the worst fears of Warwick and Clarence that Henry Percy and Henry Tudor would be restored to their hereditary earldoms of Northumberland and Richmond and to the estates that had endowed them. Henceforth Percy could challenge Warwick's rule of the North. Although Henry Tudor was still a minor, representations were being made for his

---

[49] Hicks, *Warwick*, pp. 276–9; Hicks, *Wars*, 190–3.

[50] J.C. Wedgwood, *History of Parliament 1439–1509. Register of the Ministers and Members of Both Houses* (HMSO, 1938), 363; *CCR 1468–76*, nos 339, 460.

[51] Scofield, *Edward IV*, vol. 1, p. 503.

[52] *CCR 1468–76*, no. 403.

restoration, to the potential loss of both Warwick and Clarence. Warwick's nephew George Neville, the son of his brother John, was betrothed to the king's eldest daughter Elizabeth and created Duke of Bedford with precedence over all other dukes, including Clarence and Gloucester.[53] The message here that Elizabeth was heiress apparent to the throne disappointed Clarence and indeed Gloucester, who surely had no aspirations to the crown at this point. He may have regretted the loss of precedence that would be maximised even if King Edward fathered sons, as he intended.

On 17 October 1469, in the reallocation of offices of the deceased earls, Gloucester secured the highly prestigious title of constable of England, which had been held by Earl Rivers with reversion to his son Anthony, 2nd earl, whose expectations were snubbed.[54] While the constableship was no sinecure, involving the administration of military and chivalric law and the oversight of the heralds, it had its own courts, judges, and officials that in peacetime did not require much direction from the 16-year old constable. A sign of Richard's new standing is his appointment on 19 October by Anthony's sister Queen Elizabeth as steward of her estates in the East Midlands.[55] On 12 November a new office was created for him, approver and surveyor general of the Duchy of Lancaster on terms to be agreed with the king.[56]

Gloucester's part in this political reordering was to fill the gap in Wales left by William Herbert, Earl of Pembroke, whose son and heir William Herbert II was underage. From the ranks of the Welsh gentry and officers of such great lords as York and Warwick, Herbert had constructed an estate worth £2,500 a year centred on his new marcher lordship of Raglan and had come to dominate the southern marches and the southern principality of Wales.[57] Herbert had accumulated many of the key offices in the

---

[53] Hicks, *Clarence*, pp. 57–61, C53/195 m.2, *Report of the Lords' Committee on the Dignity of a Peer* (1820–9), vol. 5, p. 377.

[54] *CPR 1467–77*, vol. 19, p. 178; BL Cotton MS Julius BXII f.123. However, he was superseded on 14 March 1470, *CPR 1467–77*, p. 205.

[55] Beds., Bucks., Hunts., Northants., BL MS Cotton Julius BXII f.122v. In 1472 her fee was raised to £100, ibid., 123v.

[56] DL 37/ 28/12.

[57] T.B. Pugh, 'The Magnates, Knights and Gentry', in *Fifteenth-century England 1399–1509*, eds S.B. Chrimes, C.D. Ross, and R.A. Griffiths (Manchester University Press, 1972), p. 92; see also D.H. Thomas, *The Herberts of Raglan and the Battle of Edgecote 1469* (Freezywater Publications, 1994).

principality of Wales, some of them heritable. Herbert's rule had been relaxed – indeed many of his Welsh supporters had been killed at Edgecote – and on 17 August 1469 Warwick had himself appointed chief justice and chamberlain of South Wales.[58] Warwick was not in control. The castles of Carmarthen and Cardigan were occupied by the rebel gentlemen Morgan and Henry ap Thomas ap Gruffydd, grandsons of the notorious Gruffydd ap Nicholas, whose family (the house of Dinefwr) strove to rule western Wales in opposition to Lancastrians and Yorkists alike until at least the early 1470s. Perhaps both rebels counted at this point as adherents of the Lancastrian Jasper Tudor. They may have been fighting for him in 1468, when Harlech fell to the Yorkists, and certainly both were excluded from Edward IV's general pardon of 14 July 1468.[59] Perhaps Warwick had made them his officers. Alternatively they were acting on their own behalf. Edward IV removed Warwick and Hastings from their offices and substituted his younger brother Richard Duke of Gloucester in their places. This was a paper exercise, for Morgan and Henry ap Thomas remained nevertheless or inserted themselves.

Richard was commissioned to suppress the rebellion and to retake the castles.[60] On 29 October he and Walter Devereux, Lord Ferrers of Chartley, were commissioned to array the border counties of Shropshire (with Lord Dudley), Worcestershire, and Gloucestershire (with Lord Berkeley).[61] King Edward made a flurry of new appointments: John Donne as constable of Kidwelly; Dudley as steward of Monmouth, Piers House as constable of Grosmont, Skenfrith, and Whitecastle; and Sir Roger Vaughan as constable, steward, and receiver of Ogmore.[62] On 16 October Richard himself had been appointed chief justice of South Wales, chamberlain of South Wales, steward of Cantref Mawr and all the king's lordships and manors in the counties of Carmarthen and Cardigan during the young

[58] *CPR 1467–77*, p. 165. On the 12th his brother-in-law Lord Hastings became chamberlain of North Wales, ibid. Warwick mistakenly counted on Hastings' political backing.

[59] R.A. Griffiths, *Sir Rhys ap Thomas and his Family: A Study in the Wars of the Roses and Early Tudor Politics* (University of Wales Press, 1993), p. 30.

[60] *CPR, 1467–77*, pp. 180–1; BL MS Cotton Julius BXII f.120–v.

[61] *CPR 1467–77*, p. 195.

[62] DL 37/28/13, 14, pp. 16–18.

Herbert's minority. On 3 February 1470 he was also appointed in his own right for life to the chief justiciarship of North Wales that Pembroke had secured only in 1469. On 13 December he supplanted Dudley as steward of Monmouth. He was also appointed on 30 November chief steward, approver, and surveyor of the principality of Wales and the earldom of March at the king's pleasure. Although mostly exercised by deputy and therefore dependent on the capacity and trustworthiness of whoever Richard found to substitute, these appointments made him 'virtual Viceroy of the principality of Wales', for the moment.[63] Although no formal council was appointed for the duke, Lord Ferrers as brother-in-law of William Herbert I and uncle of William Herbert II, was the safe pair of hands needed to guide the young prince. As nothing more is heard of Carmarthen or Cardigan, it may be that Kendall was right to suppose that Gloucester regained possession for force or by dint of the pardons he was empowered to issue. The Welsh poet Lewis Glyn Cothi records a skirmish at Cefn Glasfryn near Abermarlais, Carmarthenshire, which was certainly not decisive. Richard had asserted control over Carmarthen at least by 18 June 1470 when he presided over the great sessions there.[64] Edward did not intend to supersede the Herberts. Although aged only 14, William Herbert II had married the queen's sister Mary. Meanwhile his role was to be performed by Richard under the guidance of Ferrers, who could draw on the dominant, but momentarily headless, Herbert connection. Richard's rule was always intended to be temporary.

On 6 January 1470 Edward issued commissions of oyer and terminer to the duke, William Herbert II, Lords Dudley, Ferrers, and Strange, Sir James Harrington, John Pilkington, John Milewater, other local gentry, and a judge to try offenders in South and North Wales.[65] Gloucester was not therefore required for the king's campaign against the rebels in Lincolnshire that left London on 4 March 1470. Disappointed by Edward's reconstruction of his

---

[63] *CPR 1467–77*, pp. 179–80, 185; Hicks, *Clarence*, p. 56; Kendall, *Richard III*, pp. 78–9; Somerville, *Lancaster*, vol. 1, p. 648; BL MS Cotton Julius BXII ff.119–20; C 81/828/ 2914 & 2937; C 81/830/3006. Richard, however, may have thought otherwise.

[64] Griffiths, *Rhys ap Thomas*, pp. 30–1; Griffiths, 'Gentlemen and Rebels in Later Medieval Cardiganshire', *Conquerors and Conquered in Medieval Wales* (Sutton, 1994), p. 61; Kendall, *Richard III*, p. 79.

[65] *CPR 1467–77*, p. 198.

regime, Warwick and Clarence tried to seize power again, this time to replace Edward as king by Clarence. They fomented what appeared to be a popular rebellion in Lincolnshire led by Sir Robert Welles as 'great captain' of the county while they themselves recruited in the West Midlands. Welles, however, proved to be no Robin of Redesdale, their own retainers refused to join what looked like a treasonable insurrection, and Edward reacted much more decisively. Welles was defeated at Empingham near Stamford on 12 March and the complicity of Warwick and Clarence was exposed. Far from giving up, they tried to bring together Warwick's other northern kin, retainers, and friends, unsuccessfully. They were still at Rotherham on 26 March. Failing to recruit enough of Warwick's Richmondshire affinity commanded by Warwick's brother-in-law Lord FitzHugh or, across the Pennines, those of another brother-in-law Lord Stanley, they sped south-westwards to Exeter, whence they fled into exile on 3 April.[66] As the scale of the rebellion emerged, Edward really needed Gloucester, first as constable to try and execute the rebels, then to distract Lord Stanley, and finally to intercept Warwick and Clarence on their flight southwards. However, Gloucester seems not to have been in Wales nor focused on the king's business. On 14 March at Stamford Edward appointed John Earl of Worcester as constable of England in lieu of Richard, for life not merely in an acting capacity, which surely indicates both Worcester's greater suitability – he had exercised the office before with a gusto that earned him (later?) the nickname of the Butcher of England – and dissatisfaction with Duke Richard's performance. It was Worcester who replaced Clarence as lieutenant of Ireland during pleasure – he had already served as deputy – and he became also Warwick's chamberlain of the exchequer.[67] Gloucester was superseded: his patent was not cancelled. It was Worcester who presided over the executions of the Lincolnshire captains at York and of Warwick's shipmen at Southampton. From York on 25 March Edward proclaimed that 'no man of whatsoever degree, under colour of any wrong done unto him for any manner of variaunce late fallen between his brother the duke of Gloucester and the lord Stanley, distress rob or despoil

[66] Hicks, *Clarence*, pp. 66–71.
[67] *CPR 1467–77*, pp. 205, 207. He may have exercised it earlier when married to Warwick's (twin?) sister Cecily dowager-duchess of Warwick in 1449–50.

any of his subjects'. Those aggrieved should seek remedy before the courts.[68] Such disorders must cease. Instead of doing the king's business therefore, Duke Richard had been pursuing his own private war in north Lancashire, which may incidentally have prevented Stanley from joining in Warwick's uprising. Instead it could have driven Stanley into the arms of Warwick. A gift to Gloucester intermixed with others to the king's secretary and chamberlain and exchequer clerks suggest that he had joined the king at York by 26 March.[69] It was on that day that Richard was commissioned by the king to array Gloucestershire and Herefordshire[70] – there is no record that he did – and he may well have participated in the later stages of the pursuit. There would otherwise have been no point in his inclusion in the commissions of array for Devon and Cornwall sealed at Exeter on 17 April.[71]

What distracted Richard from the king's business was his intervention in the Harrington inheritance dispute over the castle of Hornby in north Lancashire. When the Neville retainers Sir Thomas Harrington[72] and his eldest son Sir John perished on the Yorkist side at the battle of Wakefield in 1460, the direct heirs to Hornby by primogeniture were John's little daughters Anne and Elizabeth Harrington. Their custody was granted to Lord Stanley. Other parts of the estate may have been entailed and thus heritable by John's younger brothers Sir James and Sir Robert. The trust of 1458 in his own favour that Sir James pleaded was probably fraudulent.[73] That Sir James helped apprehend Henry VI in Lancashire in 1465 earned him the eternal favour of the king and some indulgence for his disobedience; he was also feed by Warwick from Middleham.[74] It was nevertheless Warwick as arbiter who ruled that Anne and Elizabeth were the rightful heiresses. In 1474 King Edward also awarded in their favour. Both were married off to Stanleys. Possession of Hornby Castle, however, was withheld by Sir James Harrington,

[68] CCR 1468–76, no.535.

[69] The king was in York on 22–26 March, D. Palliser, 'Richard III and York', in Richard III and the North, ed. R.E. Horrox (Hull University, 1986), p. 55; 'Chronicle of the Rebellion in Lincolnshire, 1470', p. 17.

[70] CPR 1467–77, 219. Obviously he could not have been simultaneously at York.

[71] CPR 1467–77, 219. As deduced by Ross, Richard III, p. 17.

[72] A.J. Pollard, 'The Northern Retainers of Richard Nevill, Earl of Salisbury', Northern History, 11 (1976), p. 67.

[73] John surely hoped to father sons of his own.

[74] CPR 1461–7, p. 460; G.M. Coles, 'The Lordship of Middleham', appendix B.

the heir male, who appealed for support from Duke Richard and apparently served him in South Wales. Richard's great castle of Clitheroe and his forests lay between the River Ribble and Hornby. Gloucester backed Sir James – indeed he was at Hornby Castle on 26 March 1470[75] – and was sucked into direct conflict with the Stanleys according to the highly unreliable legend reported in about 1562 by Bishop Stanley. This records a 'fond fray' between their tenants and more significant, a meeting at Ribble Bridge in or near Preston between the 'army bigge' of Gloucester (from the north?) who threatened murder and arson, and the pacific Thomas Lord Stanley (from the south?).[76] Certainly Richard did enter Hornby Castle, which remained in Sir James's hands. Third parties did suffer collateral damage. Richard's military action against the powerful Stanleys was both audacious and risky. In 1456 Henry VI's half-brother Edmund Tudor had been captured and killed in West Wales in similar circumstances. Gloucester may also have been discomfited, since Jack Morris of Wigan captured his banner and posted it in Wigan church.[77] One wonders where Richard found his troops, how many there were, and how reliable were such newcomers to his service.

Professor Pollard praises Gloucester for his good lordship. 'It was imperative . . . during this first test of his lordship, to be standing firm for his man . . . Gloucester had passed his test.'[78] A 'good lord' was meant, however, to support his retainers in their just causes, not when – like Sir James – they were in the wrong. The obduracy and defiance of Sir James did eventually secure him a better deal, but that is no justification for Gloucester's action. The duke should have exercised his authority to maintain order, to restrain the excesses of his retainers, and to encourage reconciliation rather than confronting other lords, precipitating self-help, and polarising connections as Gloucester evidently did. 'Clearly the occupation of his Lancashire estates and offices was the real reason for the conflict', writes Jones.[79] A relatively small

[75] When he granted a Welsh squire four marks a year from his marcher lordship of Chirk, 'Grant from Richard, Duke of Gloucester to Reginald Vaughan, 10 Edward IV', *Archaeologia Cambrensis*, 3rd ser, vol. 33 (1863), p. 55.

[76] *Palatine Anthology*, ed. J.O. Halliwell-Phillips (1850), pp. 233–5.

[77] *Ibid.*, p. 235.

[78] Pollard, *NE England*, pp. 325–6.

[79] Jones, 'Richard III and the Stanleys', pp. 35–40, at p. 36; see also Hicks, *Richard III*, 61–3.

private quarrel could have blown up into a major conflict between the principal local magnates. This was bastard feudal abuse: the sort of escalation of lordly conflict that contemporaries and modern historians have most deplored. It was not a good introduction to local politics by the teenaged duke.[80] Stanley tradition states that it was Lord Stanley who complained to the king, who took his side:

> Though he was his brother, he let him well knowe
> He should not by power his nobles overthrow.[81]

For the moment, Richard came to heel, but he was not silenced. Indeed he continued to back Harrington until the final settlement in 1474. The Harrington feud coincided moreover with the hiatus in royal authority that enabled the escalation into violence in the West Country, Norfolk and Lincolnshire.[82] The same aggressive assertiveness characterised Richard's power-building in the North-East in the early 1470s, when again he persisted in defiance of the rulings of both king and council. Now and later, Richard operated within the law and used legal means if possible, yet resorted to threats, force, or fraud when the law did not run his way.

The departure of Warwick and Clarence left many voids to fill. One was the defence of the Scottish borders west of the Pennines and the 'rule' of a region where uprisings by Lord FitzHugh in Richmondshire and Richard Salkeld in Carlisle and the West March had only just been suppressed.[83] It was filled on 26 August 1470 by the appointment of Gloucester as warden of the West March in succession to Warwick for one year at £1,250 in peace and £2,500 in war.[84] On 18th Duke Richard, the new earl of Northumberland and Lord Greystoke, and all the judges were

---

[80] That in 1468 Clarence was drawn into the Derbyshire gentry feuds suggests, unsurprisingly, that teenaged dukes were too young for responsible rule of the localities. But Edward repeated his error with William Herbert II.

[81] *Palatine Anthology*, p. 236.

[82] Hicks, *Wars*, pp. 193–4.

[83] A.J. Pollard, 'Lord FitzHugh's Rising in 1470', *BIHR*, 52 (1979), pp. 170–5.

[84] R.L. Storey, 'The Wardens of the Marches of England towards Scotland, 1377–1489', *EHR*, 72 (1957), p. 607; *Rotuli Scotiae*, eds D. MacPherson, J. Caley, and W. Illingworth, 2 vols (Record Commission, 1814–19), vol. 2, pp. 423–4; E101/71/5/950. Northumberland, warden of the larger east and middle marches, was paid 2,000 marks (£1333. 6s.8d.) in peace and £4,000 in war, *Rotuli Scotiae*, 2, p. 423.

commissioned to try all treasons in the border areas.[85] That Richard's military responsibilities now stretched from Carmarthen to Carlisle suggests that this was rather a desperate measure by a king who was running short of lieutenants. The Nevilles had underpinned the wardenship with their hereditary lands in Yorkshire and Penrith in Cumberland and with forfeitures – the cumulatively huge Percy honour of Cockermouth, Clifford, and Dacre lands. These Richard did not hold. Possibly Edward thought that Richard's lands in Lancashire and Cheshire would suffice. The king did not see this as a permanent solution. In 1471 he commissioned Gloucester for only another three years, whereas Henry Percy, earl of Northumberland was appointed to the more extensive East and Middle Marches for five years.[86] In any case Duke Richard had no more than six weeks to establish himself and probably therefore did not do so.

King Edward was unwilling to negotiate with Warwick and he took action to deny him Calais as a base. There was to be no repetition of the Yorkist planning and invasion from Calais in 1459–60. Denied his base, Warwick was pursued by the fleet of Edward's brother-in-law Charles the Bold, who kept reminding King Louis of his obligations under the Treaty of Péronne (1468). The rebels were able nevertheless to take refuge in Normandy and to compel King Louis XI to back them. They reconciled themselves to Queen Margaret's Lancastrian exiles, contracting Warwick's younger daughter Anne to Edward, the Lancastrian Prince of Wales. In October a combined force landed in the South-west – there were other uprisings led by FitzHugh in Richmondshire and in Kent – and swept the board. Henry VI was reinstated on his throne. His Second Reign was dubbed the Readeption. Richard was involved in almost none of this. From Exeter Richard proceeded to Carmarthen, where on 18 June he presided over the great sessions.[87] Commissions of array and oyer and terminer for Gloucestershire, Herefordshire, and Somerset dated 2 June, Lincolnshire (11 July), and 26 August for York perhaps indicate his itinerary to join the king in the North. Faced by overwhelming numbers, and betrayed by

[85] C 81/1381/33.
[86] Storey, 'Wardens', p. 615.
[87] R.A. Griffiths, *The Principality of Wales in the Later Middle Ages*, I, *South Wales 1277–1536* (University of Wales Press, 1977), p. 158.

Warwick's brother John, King Edward fled from King's Lynn to the Low
Countries, the king embarking on Richard's 18th birthday (2 October).[88]

IV

King Edward had evaded with difficulty interception at sea by the Hanseatic
fleet and landed near Alkmaar in the Low Countries, part of the domains
of Charles the Bold, duke of Burgundy, husband of Edward and Richard's
sister Margaret. Richard apparently stayed in England a little longer,
perhaps collecting other adherents, and came independently to Weilingen
in Zeeland and to Veere.[89] This was his second visit to Burgundy, his
second period of exile, although this time he joined his king, the queen's
brother Earl Rivers, Lord Hastings, and several other English notables.
On 13 October Richard was at Hesdin. About the same time he borrowed
money at Veere and was a guest of Louis Lord Gruthuyse at the Hague.
Early in January he arrived at Oostcamp near Bruges. He visited his sister
Duchess Margaret at Lille on 12 February.[90] Although formally received,
the fugitives were not very welcome. Duke Charles did not want a war with
England and her new ally France and was not therefore inclined to assist
an invasion of England. That mood changed when France and England
attacked him, Warwick launching an assault from Calais. Henceforth
Charles helped Edward prepare a small squadron of ships to carry 2,000
supporters to England. It is not known what part Gloucester played in the
logistics that presumably compared to those that are well-documented for
Warwick the previous year. Although admiral of England, Gloucester was
no mariner himself and was never to acquire shipping comparable with the
squadrons of Warwick and Lord Howard. The exile lasted five months,
from October 1470 to March 1471. Edward himself resided with Louis
Lord Gruthuyse, the great bibliophile whose splendid house still survives.
How Gloucester filled his time is not recorded.

  Embarking from Flushing on 2 March 1471, the squadron encountered
contrary winds, and had to make a new start on 11 March. Touching first at

[88] *CPR 1467–77*, pp. 220–1; Scofield, *Edward IV*, vol. 1, pp. 538–9.
[89] L. Visser-Fuchs, 'Richard was Late', *Ricardian*, 147 (1999), pp. 616–18; Horrox,
'Richard III', in *ODNB*, vol. 46, p. 739.
[90] L. Visser-Fuchs, 'Richard in Holland, 1461', *Ricardian*, 6 (1983), pp. 182–9.

Cromer in Norfolk, which was too strongly defended, it ran into a tempest that scattered them. All the invaders seem to have landed safely on the Yorkshire side of the Humber estuary, but piecemeal, the king and Hastings with 500 men at Ravenspur, Gloucester 'and, in his company, 300 men' four miles away, Rivers and another 200 men 14 miles away, and the remaining thousand 'where they myght best get land'. Reassembling on 15 March, they negotiated their way past much more formidable opposition into the Midlands, where they repelled a substantial force near Newark and then blockaded Warwick himself in Coventry. Edward was joined en route by 'some folks' at Wakefield, 'but not so many as he supposed wolde have comen'. At Nottingham he was reinforced by Sir William Parr and Sir James Harrington, 'two good knights, with two good bands of men, well arrayed, and habled for warr, [to] the nombar of 600 men'. Previously adherents of Warwick and members of the royal household, this North-western contingent can be credited here to Duke Richard. They were probably accompanied by their brothers and by the Westmorlanders Christopher Moresby and Thomas Strickland, all to be knighted at the battle of Tewkesbury. At Leicester King Edward was joined by another 3,000 men, all Lord Hastings' men, and then outside Coventry by George Duke of Clarence with another 4,000. Warwick's army was considerably larger, but he had avoided battle until joined by Clarence, whose additional numbers should have given him a decisive advantage. Clarence, however, had found the Readeption uncomfortable, the returning Lancastrians ungrateful allies, and had been suborned by his mother and three sisters, his Bourchier uncles Archbishop Thomas and Henry Earl of Essex, and by the former chancellor Bishop Robert Stillington together and separately who persuaded him that he should rejoin King Edward. 'A perfite accord' was achieved, so that when he approached from the south he joined not Warwick, but the king. Between their two armies the brothers met: Edward accompanied by Gloucester, Rivers, and Hastings met with Clarence 'with hym a fewe noble men', 'where was right kynde and loving langwage betwixt them twoo', as befitted 'two brethren of so grete nobley and astate'. Clarence and Gloucester also spoke together and were reconciled. The official Yorkist chronicle stresses the perfection of the agreement, the warmth and friendliness, and public joy, celebrated with the sounding of trumpets and the honouring of Clarence.[91] Proceeding southwards, on 10 April the combined army took London, which had been unwisely vacated by the Lancastrians, apprehending both King Henry and Archbishop Neville. The queen, Stillington, and various Bourchiers came out of sanctuary. Several fought for Edward in the ensuing battle. For the capture of king and capital city was not the end. The real leaders of the Readeption were Warwick himself as king's lieutenant, and Queen Margaret of Anjou and her son Prince Edward, who arrived from France on 14 April.

Warwick had counted on London being held against the invaders and on trapping them with his substantially larger force, which now included his brother John Marquis Montagu, the duke of Exeter and earl of Oxford. Edward emerged from London to confront him on a site near Barnet on Easter Day (14 March) 1471. Battle was joined in fog at dawn: circumstances that explain why the armies were not precisely aligned, for considerable confusion, and to some extent for the victory of the smaller Yorkist force. Warwick and Montagu were killed. Lords Say and Cromwell and the heirs of Lords Berners and Mountjoy fell on the Yorkist side. Although the decisive fighting took place on the flanks, the vanguard was heavily engaged. Duke Richard was stationed there. He may indeed have commanded the division,[92] not many of whom can have been his men.[93] Richard was in the thick of the fighting and was wounded:[94] not too severely, however, as he accompanied the king westwards a fortnight later and fought again at the battle of Tewkesbury.[95] If it was a flesh wound, there would have been no scar to be detected on his bones. Probably it was at Barnet that Richard's retainers Thomas Parr, John Milewater, Christopher Worsley, Thomas Huddleston, and John Harper were killed, to the duke's abiding sorrow. Six years later he commissioned prayers in their affectionate memory.[96] Perhaps his company was already identified by his badge of the white boar.

[91] *Arrivall*, pp. 1–11; Horrox. *Richard III*, p. 41.

[92] *Great Chronicle of London*, eds A.H. Thomas and I.D. Thornley (Guildhall Library, 1938), p. 216. This is a late source. *The Arrivall* does not specify who commanded each battle.

[93] On 26 April Gloucester was commissioned to array only in Gloucestershire, Herefordshire, and Shropshire, whereas Clarence officiated everywhere, *CPR 1467–77*, p. 284.

[94] Scofield, *Edward IV*, vol. 1, pp. 580–1; Pollard, *Princes*, p. 51; H. Kleineke, 'Gerhard von Wesel's Newsletter from England, 17 April 1471', *Ricardian*, 16 (2006), p. 81.

[95] P.W. Hammond, *The Battles of Barnet and Tewkesbury* (Sutton, 1990), p. 144n.23.

[96] Ross, "Servants & Lovers", pp. 146–8.

Even this triumph was not the end. After meeting Queen Margaret and Prince Edward, the Lancastrian Edmund Duke of Somerset and John Earl of Devon raised an army in the West Country and marched it up the Severn Valley to meet up with Jasper Tudor, earl of Pembroke, and the Welsh Lancastrians. Having refreshed his forces, King Edward strove to intercept the Lancastrians in a hectic and exhausting chase through the Cotswolds that ended on 7 May at Tewkesbury where he won the decisive battle. Richard definitely did have 'the rule' of the vanguard here. Showered with cannon balls and arrows, Somerset left his defensive position, engaged with King Edward's battle and the vanguard, and was outflanked and routed.[97] Many defeated Lancastrians who took sanctuary in the abbey (but perhaps not all) were pardoned. Even though Tewkesbury's privileges did not explicitly cover treason, the king promised them immunity on the holy sacrament. The more important ones captured on the field, in battle, or in the abbey were nevertheless tried for treason by Duke Richard, once again constable,[98] and John Duke of Norfolk, the Earl Marshal. They condemned all those before them to death 'notwythstondyng the kynges pardoun'. Among those convicted and executed on a scaffold in the town were Somerset, Prior Langstrother, Lord Wenlock, and other diehard Lancastrians. *The Arrivall* ignored Edward's perjury, but commended him for allowing those Lancastrians slain and executed to be buried in the abbey and spared dismembering and 'setting up' of such parts anywhere. They were conceded honourable Christian burials. Duke Richard seems to have been more respectful of sanctuary than his brother when king, but apparently Gloucester had no qualms in exterminating their Lancastrian enemies.[99] Perhaps Edward feared future opposition. A few were spared, such as the ancient Sir John Fortescue and the cleric John Morton, who later rendered good service to King Edward. There had been no such bloodbath after the battle of Barnet – presumably more of the defeated made good their escape and only local men were identified by local juries at the subsequent sessions. Richard

---

[97] *Arrivall*, pp. 27–9.

[98] The Earl of Worcester was executed by the Readeption regime. No new appointment for Gloucester is recorded: apparently he resumed office on the strength of his patent of 1469.

[99] *Arrivall*, pp. 30–1; *Death and Dissent*, p. 114. This is a first attempt to exclude treason from the protection of sanctuary.

led the ceremonial entry to London for which a celebratory poem was penned. One verse was in the honour of the young duke, who was compared to the Trojan hero Hector.[100]

Barnet and Tewkesbury were decisive. Meanwhile Warwick's sea commander Thomas Neville, Bastard of Fauconberg, had besieged London unsuccessfully. He submitted and so did other followers of Warwick in the Midlands. The king stayed only one night in London before marching to Canterbury 'with a great multitude of armed men' including Gloucester, three other dukes, five earls, barons, and esquires.[101] 'Wherefore the Kynge sent thethar his brothar Richard Duke of Gloucester, to receyve them [into his allegiance] in his name, and all the shipps; as he so dyd the xxvj. day of the same monithe [26 May].'[102] Most of the Kentishmen were indeed pardoned their lives. What the *Arrivall* omits is that most were fined and a few, notably Nicholas Faunt, Mayor of Canterbury, were executed.[103] Again it was the constable and marshal of England who held judicial sessions. Probably Duke Richard was not involved in the detail of who was pardoned, who was fined, and how much, which may well have been undertaken by King Edward himself, but he observed the process and probably later modelled his own treatment of Buckingham's rebels on it in 1483. Gloucester was at Norwich on 23 August[104] and then went northwards.

Pardoned by King Edward, the Bastard of Fauconberg was in his company. He was an illegitimate son of William Neville, earl of Kent and Lord Fauconberg, brother to Richard's own mother Cecily Duchess of York, and was thus Richard's first cousin. The Bastard was probably already the kingmaker's naval commander when he first encountered Warwick's ward Duke Richard. On 14 June 1471 Richard himself granted a protection to 'Thomas Fauconberge esquire *alias* gentleman'.[105] Once up

---

[100] *Political Poems and Songs*, ed. T Wright, Rolls Series, vol. 2 (Camden Society, 1861), p. 280.

[101] *John Stone's Chronicle: Christ Church Priory, Canterbury, 1417–1472*, ed. M. Connor (Medieval Institute Publications, 2010), p. 130.

[102] *Arrivall*, p. 39.

[103] C. Richmond, 'Fauconberg's Kentish Rising of May 1471', *EHR*, 85 (1970), pp. 682–9; S. Sweetinburgh, 'Those who Marched with Faunt: Reconstructing the Canterbury Rebels of 1471', *Southern History*, 39 (2017), pp. 36, 49–50, 54.

[104] A.F. Sutton, 'Richard of Gloucester Visits Norwich, August 1471', *Ricardian*, 95 (1986), p. 333.

[105] C 81/1310/4.

North, before 11 September, the Bastard committed some other offence
that is unrecorded and difficult to imagine. Back in Gloucester's custody by
15 September, he was executed by the duke: his head was posted on
London Bridge. At best the duke exacted the most rigorous justice. More
probably it was the ruthless elimination of a problem and tidying up of
a loose end.[106] That the Bastard was first cousin to the duke did not save
him. His fate foreshadowed King Richard's summary elimination of other
cousins and brothers in law.

V

Ricardians have made much of Richard's loyalty to Edward IV during this
Second War. He was consistently loyal, in contrast to the treachery of
Warwick, Clarence, and others. Leaving aside the justifications that the
latter offered for their actions – in Warwick's case, the public good, which
was widely accepted at the time – loyalty was not so much a virtue as an
obligation and expectation to be taken for granted. Moreover, Richard does
not seem to have had much choice. So far as we know, Warwick offered
him nothing at any juncture. Richard had no great following to offer
any contender. Perhaps the diminutive 17-year-old was considered of little
account. Richard was not in Warwick's confidence in the 1469 and 1470
rebellions. On both occasions he joined the king only after the rebels had
been bested. He was with King Edward when he took flight in 1470.
Whether Lancastrian forfeitures or severed from the Duchy of Lancaster,
all his lands were bound to be lost. In 1469–71, his whole future was therefore tied to the fortune of the king. Disloyalty was never a viable option.
Obedience to King Edward, compliance with Edward's policies, subjuga-
tion and his abandonment of those activities that the king disapproved,
were less in evidence.

Professor Kendall somewhat exaggerated Richard's contribution to the
Second War of the Roses. Certainly he was not 'the King's first general, the
chief prop of his throne, and his most trusted officer'.[107] King Edward was

---

[106] *Death and Dissent*, p. 115; Scofield, *Edward IV*, vol. 2, p. 20; M.A. Hicks, 'Neville
[Fauconberg], Thomas, [called the Bastard of Fauconberg] (d. 1471)', in *ODNB*, vol. 40,
p. 542.
[107] Kendall, *Richard III*, p. 104.

his own best general. It was unfortunate perhaps that Richard's political apprenticeship was of internecine strife that prioritised ruthlessness and violence, rather than the more normal peacetime discourse, especially as his own temperament inclined him in that direction. Certainly Richard observed the factionalism, bastard feudal abuses, and prioritisation of private issues over public business of 1470. He did not learn that such errors were to be avoided. No bodily weakness had deterred him from combat, nor had wounds stopped him from fighting again. The balance between the opposing sides was too narrowly poised for him to be protected, yet he had survived. The prestige and honour of such successful war service affected both his estimation of himself as a military man and the respect of others. Richard had delivered what was required, whether in battle, perhaps surprisingly, or in the judicial murder of opponents, with or without due process. He had been a princely figurehead in Wales and capable of leadership in battle. 'Victorius', 'that nobill prynce' had certainly not let himself down, and even at this young age he was compared by the official poet to Hector, the Trojan hero. Fortune and God also were on his side.[108]

While loyal himself, he had observed how Warwick staged coups d'état, the popular appeal that had made the earl so formidable and that he was to imitate himself. Richard leant that loyalty was not just obligatory: it brought dividends and should be stressed as publicly as possible. Several times in the future he was extremely obsequious in pledging his fidelity. Richard had also learnt something about campaigning, about military organisation and supply, of the logistics of invading, about bivouacking and billeting, about killing at a distance and the savage slaughter and maiming of hand-to-hand fighting, even at first hand about medical care in the field. While clemency and magnanimity earned praise and left people to nego-tiate with, executions and ruthlessness scotched opposition for good. Richard also grieved quite genuinely for those who perished in his service. It was aggressive strategies, prompt and decisive action that had enabled Edward IV to confound the odds and to defeat his more powerful oppo-nents. Consistently aggressive, Edward's direct action forced his enemies to

---

[108] *Political Poems*, vol. 2, p. 280.

stand and fight – a sudden death play-off. The battles of Barnet and Tewkesbury and the smaller scale engagements at Glasfryn and Hornby taught Richard nothing of the art of compromise. He never did learn. This was a weakness that his brother Edward IV recognised and sought to mitigate in the next phase of the duke's career. Undoubtedly it was a chain of formative experiences, that 'shaped the man he was to become'.[109]

[109] Pollard, *Princes*, p. 55.

Chapter Four

ADULT MATURITY

THE KING'S SERVANT 1471–5

I

Now 18 years old, Richard Duke of Gloucester was old enough and experienced enough to participate both in war and in politics and to be useful to his brother the king. He was the king's brother: third in precedence after Prince Edward and Clarence. All three royal brothers, Edward, Clarence, and Gloucester, wrote Thomas More, 'wer great states of birthe' (born unto the highest rank) 'soo wer they greate and statelye of stomach, gredye and ambicious of authoritie, and impacient of parteners',[1] as the following chapters will show. Duke Richard was a prince – 'a right high and mighty prince', as he wrote and those who addressed him said.[2] 'Youre highnesse' was how he was sometimes addressed.[3] Probably he wore the more splendid robes made of the rare and sumptuous fabrics that were to be restricted to royalty by the 1483 sumptuary law. Certainly he was entitled to wear a coronet even in the king's presence. It is hardly surprising therefore that he presumed his own superiority and authority whether specifically commissioned or not.

[1] More, *Richard III*, p. 6.
[2] BL Add. Ch. 67545; 'Private Indentures for Life Service in Peace and War', eds M. Jones and S. Walker, *Camden Miscellany*, 32 (1994), p. 176.
[3] BL Add. ch. 67545.

At both ends of Edward IV's Second Reign, in 1472 and in 1483, Richard was praised in parliament for his martial achievements.[4] None of the Yorkist nobility had much opportunity to distinguish themselves militarily at this time, but Richard seems to have regarded himself as a military man. His apprenticeship in 1469–71 had taught him much, not just about invasions, strategy, tactics, and open combat, but about defence, the management of public opinion, and the role of deceit and terror in power politics. When King Edward had returned to England in 1471, he was seriously outnumbered. He disarmed his opponents, like Henry IV, by declaring his sole objective to be his father's dukedom of York, which Yorkshiremen could not deny was his rightful inheritance. 'Neuer wuld [he] clayme no title nor take vppon hond to be kyng off Englond', he declared.[5] It was a ruse. King Edward perjured himself: excusably, Crowland opined, because it was 'necessary to disguise his intentions'.[6] Duke Richard also observed and approved the luring of the Lancastrian leadership out of sanctuary with promises of immunity and their subsequent despatch.[7] The two royal dukes of Clarence and Gloucester interceded for cities that had incurred the king's wrath, notably Bristol, Coventry, and York, and on behalf of retainers of Warwick, whose service they wanted for themselves. The constable and marshal presided over proceedings against the Kentish rebels and the Bastard of Fauconberg's shipmen, most of whom were hanged by the purse rather than the neck. Certainly Richard became accustomed to condemning traitors to death. In 1450–60 the Yorkists had made death into the most effective cure for opposition and even mere criticism. Was Fauconberg's execution an early instance of the ruthless and summary treatment of Richard's opponents, however closely related, and of the absence of compassion that he displayed later? Did it prefigure his later arrogance towards the non-royal and the baseborn?

At last the Lancastrian royal family were all gathered into Edward's hands. Queen Margaret and her ladies including Anne Neville were

[4] *PROME*, vol. 14, p. 412; C.L. Kingsford, *English Historical Literature in the Fifteenth Century* (Clarendon Press, 1913), p. 382.

[5] *Death and Dissent*, ed. L.M. Matheson (Boydell & Brewer, 1999), pp. 107–8; *Arrivall*, pp. 4–6.

[6] *Crowland*, pp. 122–3.

[7] *Arrivall*, 30–1.

arrested and spared, the queen languishing in prison until surrendered to the no more merciful custody of Louis XI. Both Henry VI and Prince Edward of Lancaster had perished: the blame later being ascribed to Duke Richard. Supposedly these were the first in the succession of Richard's crimes that cleared the way for his usurpation in 1483 and that foreshadowed the murder of the Princes in the Tower. Actually, as Myers showed, the stories grew in the telling, in the light of Richard's later career, and were not debited to Richard when they occurred. The official and strictly contemporary *Arrivall* records that Prince Edward of Lancaster was 'taken, fleinge to the towne wards, and slayne, in the fielde'. Pseudo-Warkworth also reports that the prince perished in battle, 'whiche cryed for socour to his brother-in-lawe the duke of Clarence'. It is the Tudor chronicler Edward Hall who first has the prince captured and brought before Edward IV, whose title he rejected boldly, and then cut down by those about the king, specifically Clarence, Gloucester, Dorset, and Hastings. Published as late as 1542, Hall's version has generally been rejected, but a copy of the *Short Arrivall* illustrated in the 1470s depicts this story.[8] Even if Hall's story was true, the killers acted with the approval and on the authority of the king. Prince Edward was too dangerous to let live, ever more dangerous as he matured.

On 11 May 1471, the very evening that King Edward arrived at the capital, his rival King Henry VI expired in the Tower. Supposedly it was a natural death. The official version was that he died of 'pure displeasure and melancholy'. As usual the corpse of the late king was exposed to public view to demonstrate (from in front at least) the absence of any wounds. It is highly unlikely that Henry's body bled on the pavement, but probably he did die violently. Murder, regicide, and martyricide were the most heinous crimes that were exacerbated in this case by the helplessness of a prisoner, yet they were nevertheless expedient and arguably in the interests of public peace. Duke Richard was certainly nearby. Rous says that 'he caused others to kill the holy man King Henry VI or, as many think, did so by his own hands'. Philippe de Commines, a contemporary Burgundian

---

[8] *English Historical Documents*, iv, *1327–1485*, pp. 313–15; *Arrivall*, 30; *Death and Dissent*, p. 113; Sutton and Visser-Fuchs, *Richard III's Books*, plate 9. The queen's son Thomas Grey not yet marquis of Dorset.

chronicler, says that Richard slew Henry himself or had him killed in his presence. Even worse was Thomas More's explanation of why Richard did it – though he does not actually state it but insinuates it. Richard killed King Henry with his own hands and from choice. Since, moreover, King Edward would have allocated the task to 'some other than his owne borne brother', More makes it appear that Richard liked killing people and insisted on committing the murder himself. Crowland condemned the perpetrator in typically ambiguous terms:

'May God have mercy upon and give time for repentance to him, whoever it might be, who dared to lay sacrilegious hands on the Lord's Anointed! And so let the doer merit the title of tyrant and the victim that of a glorious martyr!'[9]

Was Crowland referring to the killer or to whoever directed the killer? Who was the tyrant – Edward IV himself, whose peccadilloes Crowland constantly sought to excuse, or the future Richard III, whom he was to expose as tyrannical when king? Crowland was writing in 1485, after miracles had been worked at King Henry's tomb, after the translation of his remains to St George's Chapel at Windsor, by when he may have become regarded as a saint, which was not necessarily the case in 1471. Whoever despatched the former monarch, it was certainly Edward IV who approved it and the actual agent, somewhat humbler than a royal duke, acted on his orders. Again, the responsibility was not that of the killers, but that of King Edward. At this date Richard cannot conceivably have regarded these deaths as removing obstacles to his own succession. Not only had Edward's three daughters and Clarence better claims than Gloucester, but the monarch now had a son, another Edward Prince of Wales, as first in line.

II

The new prince had been born during the Readeption and was to succeed in due course in 1483 as King Edward V. On 3 July 1471 in the parliament

[9] Myers, *English Historical Documents*, p. 315; Hanham, *Richard III*, p. 121; *Arrivall*, p. 38; P. de Commines, *Mémoires*, eds J. Calmette and G. Durville, 3 vols (Paris, 1923–5), vol. 1, pp. 215–16; More, *Richard III*, pp. 7–8; *Crowland*, pp. 128–31; *Death and Dissent*, p. 116.

chamber at Westminster Richard joined with other notables to acknowledge and accept Prince Edward as 'undoubted heir' and to pledge his allegiance on the Gospels to him as 'very true and rightwise king of England'
after King Edward's death. Gloucester was to repeat the oath in 1477 and
at least three more times – at York, Stony Stratford, and Westminster – in
1483.[10] The king's two brothers Clarence and Gloucester were appointed
to Prince Edward's council, which they may occasionally have attended
when at Westminster, but could play no part in it after the prince's reloca-
tion to Wales in 1473.[11] As Edward IV's Second Reign progressed, the king
fathered other children. Briefly in 1477–9 Edward had three sons, two
outliving him, and altogether seven daughters, of whom five survived him.
Under primogeniture all took precedence in the line of succession over
Duke Richard, who ceased to count as a dynastic heir. If Richard ever had
any aspirations to the crown, his relegation to eighth in line for the throne
– or, more probably, tenth after Clarence's offspring – should have stilled
them. He was firmly reminded every time that he deferred to his nephew
Edward and when his other nephews Princes Richard and George were
created dukes with precedence ahead of him. Richard was indeed a royal
duke, a senior peer – indeed the most senior adult peer in the last five years
of his brother's reign – and occupant of three of the greatest offices. Yet he
did not matter diplomatically. King Edward was interested in marriage
alliances, but for his own children – starting with Cecily and Mary in 1474,
Elizabeth in 1475, and Anne in 1480. Edward actively opposed Clarence's
matches with foreign princesses in 1477. It suited him that his brother
Richard had made his own marriage and with it his own fortune, and
thereby saved himself the expense of endowing him.

Writing in 1483, Dominic Mancini portrays the duke as a critic of the
regime who absented himself from court,[12] which was a myth that Richard
himself found convenient at that time to disseminate though it was untrue.
In the early 1470s the duke was often in and around London, indeed
perhaps ordinarily resident there, although he had no house of his own that
satisfied him – perhaps none large enough for a ducal household or none up

---

[10] *CCR 1468–76*, no. 858; Hicks, *Edward V*, pp. 58–9; see below.
[11] Hicks, *Edward V*, pp. 93–7.
[12] Mancini, *Richard III*, pp. 62–3.

to date enough. He never resided at the earl of Oxford's place by London Wall, and Warwick's great house of le Erber in Thames Street was allotted to Clarence, apparently to Gloucester's displeasure. Instead he used a house at Stepney belonging to Sir Thomas Vaughan, treasurer of the king's chamber, another house there of one Chedworth, and a third house of his own at Walbrook in the City. In 1476 he was leasing a house called the Tower in the parish of St Thomas the Apostle in the City and in 1483 at Crosby Place in Bishopsgate Street. It was in London that he wooed Anne Neville, where he abducted her with her consent, and where he secured the approval of the king and royal council both for the match and for the division of Warwick's great inheritance. King, royal dukes, and council convened at Sheen Palace on 16 February 1472.[13] Gloucester attended the Garter chapter at Windsor on St George's Day (23 April 1472), was in London again on 31 July, and in North Yorkshire on 6 October.[14] The dispossession of the countess of Oxford, which demanded the duke's personal attention, took place from Christmas 1472 to Christmas 1473, and the well-documented Gregories manor dispute came irregularly to his attention between October 1472 and March 1473.[15] He attended Garter chapters at Windsor in 1472, 1473, and 1474.[16] He probably attended all seven sessions at Westminster of the parliament of 1472–5, which transacted much of his personal business. After that date, Gloucester did focus his activities on the North, where he was responsible for the defence of West March towards Scotland. He was commander-in-chief in the aggressive war against the Scots in 1480–3. He was excused attendance at nine Garter chapters because on royal business,[17] yet he was no exile from the South. He was at the Garter chapter on 4 November 1476 and shopped in London that winter (20 November–4 December). Perhaps spending Christmas and

[13] *Paston L & P*, vol. 1, p. 447; M.A. Hicks, 'The Last Days of Elizabeth Countess of Oxford', in *Rivals*, pp. 304, 310–13.

[14] C.L. Kingsford, *English Historical Literature in the Fifteenth Century*, p. 380; *A Descriptive Catalogue of Ancient Deeds*, vol. 4, A6298; KB 9/330/23.

[15] Hicks, 'Last Days', pp. 297–306; R. Horrox, 'An Invisible Man: John Prince and the Dispute over Gregories Manor', in *Much Heaving and Shoving*, eds M. Aston and R. Horrox (Aston & Horrox, 2005), pp. 67–85.

[16] *Register of the Most Noble Order of the Garter*, ed. J. Anstis, 2 vols (London, 1724), vol. 1, pp. 186, 187, 190; Kingsford, *English Historical Literature*, pp. 380–1.

[17] Anstis, *Register*, vol. 1, pp. 191–3, 197, 201, 203, 204, 208, 210, 212.

the New Year around London, he was at Stony Stratford (Bucks.) on the
Great North Road in 11 January 1477, perhaps on his way northwards,
back at Westminster on 8 March, and at Sheriff Hutton in Yorkshire on 1
April. Frequent and exhausting travel on the Great North Road was punctuated by occasional journeys further afield, to Swansea in September 1479
and to Southampton on 6 December 1477. Back at Westminster, he
attended the great council of November 1477, the parliament of January–
February 1478, and the great council of November 1479. He attended the
Garter chapter at Windsor on 10 February 1480, the council on 20 February
1481, and the Westminster parliament of January 1483.[18] He was present
occasionally at sessions of the royal council that were usually held in the
South.[19] *Pace* Mancini, Richard certainly did not absent himself from the
capital and was frequently in or around London.

III

Duke Richard was appointed to many offices, which he exercised normally
by deputy, and received a host of commissions – of array, oyer and terminer,
the peace, *de wallis et fossatis* – some of which he exercised in person. The
most prestigious of these commitments were the series of great offices to
which Edward appointed him. Richard was expected to do the king's
bidding. He was more than a figurehead. Already admiral of England
in 1462 – (not the same as the keeper of seas!) – Richard was appointed
constable of the realm in 1469, and great chamberlain in 1471.[20] These
were highly prestigious offices. In 1472 Richard titled himself 'the right
high and mighty prince Richard duke of Gloucestre, great chamberleyn,
constable, and admirall of England'.[21] Three great offices actually were too

[18] *PROME, vol.* 14, p. 349, 412; see above; Anstis, *Register*, vol. 1, pp. 196, 206; Hicks, *Clarence*, p. 145; Pollard, *Princes*, p. 189; Searle, *The History of the Queens' College of St Margaret and St Bernard at the University of Cambridge*, p. 87; *CCR 1476–85*, no. 473; *Glamorgan County History*, vol. 3, *The Middle Ages*, ed. T.B. Pugh (University of Wales Press, 1971), p. 201; *Ancient Kalendars and Inventories of Treasury of his Majesty's Exchequer*, ed. F.C. Palgrave, 3 vols (Record Commission, 1836), pp. 19–30; DL 29/639/10360d, 1d; DL 29/639/10386 m.1.

[19] E.g., *Paston L & P*, vol. 1, p. 447; *Crowland*, pp. 132–3.

[20] *CPR 1461–67*, p. 197; *1467–77*, pp. 178, 262, 307; *1476–85*, p. 67.

[21] *Documents relating to the Foundation and Antiquities of the Collegiate Church of Middleham*, ed. W. Atthill (Camden Society, 1847), pp. 84–6; Jones and Walker, 'Private Indentures', pp. 176–8; *York House Books 1461–1490*, vol. 1, p. 171; *Stonor Letters and Papers of the Fifteenth*

many. It was desirable politically to share such offices among the great. Richard was induced to give up the chamberlainship to his brother Clarence. He did not abandon it, however. Although cancelled, he had his original patent copied into his cartulary, and in 1478, following Clarence's fall, he secured his reappointment.[22] In 1473-7 he titled himself merely constable and admiral of England.[23]

The most important of these offices was the constableship of England. Gloucester was appointed constable in 1469 and resumed it in 1471 without a new patent. It may be, as Ramsay suggested, that Richard had urged his own appointment,[24] but at 17 years of age and still a minor his views are unlikely to have been decisive. Richard cannot have possessed yet the personal expertise needed to organise tournaments, to deploy armies, or to resolve disputes about coats of arms and between heralds. He was a figure-head: somebody else, unfortunately anonymous, guided him. The much more experienced former constable John Earl of Worcester had taken his place in the campaigns of 1470. It was Worcester who tried the rebels in Lincolnshire and at Southampton and who had them executed. Initially perhaps this was because Richard was elsewhere, though Worcester continued as constable after Richard's return, perhaps because the duke had acted inappropriately in the Stanley–Harrington dispute. Richard rated the office highly and often titled himself 'great constable'[25] – no doubt to distinguish himself from all the lesser constables, of single castles or even of manors. Heraldry must have been part of Richard's earlier education. Then or later he acquainted himself with the other functions of the office and with the officers at arms. He chose the white boar as his badge, appointed his own pursuivant Blanc Sanglier and his own Gloucester herald (Richard Champneys). He possessed two rolls of arms – Jenyns's Book (c.1410) by 1480-1 and St George's Roll (c. 1280) – that he probably

Century, ed. C.L. Kingsford (1924), vol. 2, p. 81. There are no minutes of council attendance at this time.

[22] BL MS Cotton Julius BXII f.123; *CPR 1467-77*, p. 262, 344; *1476-85*, p. 344; C266/63/24.

[23] BL MS Cotton Julius BXII ff. 224, 315-v.

[24] N. Ramsay, 'Richard III and the Office of Arms', in *The Yorkist Age*, eds H. Kleineke and C. Steer (Harlaxton Medieval Studies, 2013), p. 146.

[25] E.g., Attreed, *York House Books*, vol. 1, p. 8.

consigned to the custody of his officers of arms. Gloucester is recorded as settling two disputes in his role as 'ordinary judge' as provided by his ordinances. He also issued nine ordinances to regulate the officers of arms.[26] When king he was to incorporate them.

A chivalric education inevitably imparted a knowledge of genealogy and heraldry in noble boys like Richard. 'Heraldic science' and 'professional practice' in Richard's day had not yet attained their 'classic form' and fell far short of his clear vision of what ought to be and the orderly system that he sought to impose. Richard's ordinances for the officers of arms presumed his right and authority to impose reforms that must be obeyed. Evidently the officers of arms had developed piecemeal and independently. Pursuivants, heralds, and even kings of arms need not be qualified by their expertise. They need not have studied 'the Bokes of maner, eloquens, Cronicles, Actes and gests of honour, fetez of Armes' that should be their guides, nor need they have mastered 'the Foles and bestes, Signes and tokens in Armes', nor the heraldic significance of 'colours, herbes, and [precious] stones'. Duke Richard was at least acquainted with such things and expected expertise of the professionals. The English officers of arms had no code of conduct. They frequented dishonest places (pubs and brothels?), dishonest company, swore, and generally brought their office into disrepute. Each officer awarded arms independently. They trespassed on the jurisdictions of others, quarrelled among themselves, rejected 'vncurtesly and Irreuerently' the authority of their superiors, and failed to keep proper records. Were such complaints brought to Gloucester as constable or did they merely come to his notice? At some point therefore, Richard as 'grete Constable of Englonde' stepped in and imposed 'a reformacion of Abusions vsed' to 'the honour and pleasur' of the king and 'the worship of all estates nobles and gentilles of this Reaulme'. What he had in mind was a much tidier system, comprising a hierarchy of officers in each march or province under the relevant king of arms. Each king of arms would have authority over the lesser officers who would defer to him 'humbly and Beningnely' and show respect to their king of arms. Each king

[26] Ramsay, 'Richard III and the Office of Arms', pp. 142, 144–6, and for what follows, see pp. 142–63.

was to exercise disciplinary supervision over his heralds and pursuivants. In future only the kings of arms could validate any award of arms: heralds and pursuivants would operate under his licence. The kings of arms were to hold chapters whenever required: 'to thentent that more honour, Bettur Rewle and gouernaunce may be providede Amonge all thoffice of armes to ther Comfort and consolacion. Also to encresse of more Connynge [knowledge] amonge the same dayli to be hadd to the kinges pleasur and worship, Also for Correccion and punicion of the offenses and for dewe Reformacion to be hadd.' Henceforth kings of arms were to keep registers of new coats of arms and of decisions. The whole was to be enforced *sub pena*, by a series of penalties. So Richard decreed. He took his role as constable seriously.

While Richard must have been advised, most probably by Garter king of arms (John Writhe), he can be observed in action in January 1478, when four knights created at Prince Richard's wedding 'not counselled to their worshippe' refused to pay their dues: the heralds appealed to the Lord Chamberlain (presumably still Clarence?) who 'well-understoode the auncyent custume of chivalry' and referred the issue to 'the high and mighty prince' Gloucester as constable of England and 'Judge of the Office of Arms'. Richard took the heralds' side. In person and forthwith he commanded that the dues be paid and set the future rate at 20 shillings for a knight bachelor and 40 shillings for a baron (and banneret?).[27] Richard's ordinances date perhaps from about 1478, as they resemble some of his prescriptions developed for his college at Middleham and perhaps were modelled on them. They appear personal to him since he dominated.[28] There was as yet no chief officer comparable to the dean of Middleham or to Garter, who was the best paid from 1461 and to whom he awarded precedence once he was king. No register or chapter minutes survive, even in fragments or copies, and the system cannot have developed as Richard planned. Perhaps his solution was too advanced and too prescriptive for the handful of practising officers, most of whom were private appointments who depended financially on their grants of arms, and would have required

[27] Ibid., p. 147n. One such knight, Sir William Redman, was Gloucester's retainer.
[28] 'The Statutes Ordained by Richard Duke of Gloucester, for the College of Middleham. Dated July 4, 18 Edw. IV, (1478)', ed. J. Raine, *Archaeological Journal*, 14 (1857), pp. 160–70, esp. p. 169.

instead the premises, incorporation, and royal salaries that Richard was to provide as king.

These ordinances do reveal Richard as an orderly thinker and reformer, as an administrator and worker in detail, as the drafter of a formal document that covered every eventuality and that was to be enforced, and as an umpire willing to act as final resort in any disputes. He did not acquiesce with what he found, whether established institutions or estates that he had acquired, and sought constantly to improve on them or extend them. He codified, organised, and commanded. Such characteristics recur again and again in his career. Gloucester was impatient – it was *now* that he wanted his reforms – and something of a fantasist, since some of his ordinances were not capable of attainment. As befitted a successful good lord, he recognised the importance of common purpose and cohesion. He sought also the fraternal affection of 'Felough and Broder of armez', of the collegiality, in short of the body corporate that he was to establish as king.

Richard was also admiral of England almost throughout Edward IV's reign. This office exercised jurisdiction over the maritime affairs of the whole kingdom, including piracy, smuggling, and maritime warfare. Although the records are almost entirely lost, there was geographical devolution, with sub-admirals of the South-west, the Solent, and the North, for instance. The seal matrix of Richard as admiral of the West survives.[29] There was also a principal court of admiralty that sat at Westminster and that was presided over in 1478 by Master William Goodyear, doctor of laws. This system operated automatically, without much involvement of the admiral, but may have been profitable to him. In a case that went to appeal in 1478, Richard's share of the damages was £80. No central records survive, but a few admiralty cases were recorded in other records.[30] These were interventions by the king, to urge action – a second injunction in one instance – or to allow an appeal. Given also that the duke himself dabbled in piracy, it does not seem an area that Richard improved. The admiral did not command the fleet, nor whatever ships the crown possessed. In time

[29] J. Cherry, 'The Admiralty Seal of Richard, Duke of Gloucester', in *Tant D'Emprises – So Many Undertakings*, ed. L. Visser-Fuchs, *Ricardian* 13 (2003), pp. 114–20; Tudor-Craig, *Richard III*, no. 145.

[30] *CPR 1476–85*, pp. 23, 49, 78, 102.

of war the king indented with a keeper of the seas, like Warwick the Kingmaker in the 1450s and Lord Howard in the 1480s, who was not automatically the admiral and did not answer to the admiral. Richard was not so interested in maritime affairs as Warwick and Howard. Although he did possess ships, he did not acquire a squadron like Warwick, nor engage in large-scale piracy, nor take the tiller as Warwick had done. Richard did not ever take ship except for the invasion of France, and did not have significant trading interests.

It is not obvious what the functions of the great chamberlain were or what Richard made of this office.

IV

Much more time-consuming, responsible, and rewarding was the wardenship of the West Marches towards Scotland. This involved the military command of the Cumbrian borders, indeed government of the northwestern borders, and was salaried – £1,250 in times of peace or truce and £2,500 in times of war. Richard indented for three years from 1470, then for a further five from 18 August 1471 and again in 1475, and then for a further 10 years from 20 February 1480 at reduced rates, £1,000 in war and £800 in peace. These funds enabled the warden to recruit troops – northern gentry and their retainers – and to maintain the fortifications of Carlisle.[31] A handful of protections were issued to combatant gentry.[32] No warden, it appears, kept separate accounts – their expenditure was not audited by the crown – but instead they paid annuities from their estates, like those attributed to the duke's lordship of Middleham. The wardenship did not require Richard's continuous presence in the West Marches. Like his predecessor wardens, he employed deputies, both a lieutenant warden in the border, Humphrey Lord Dacre of Gilsland, and a constable of Carlisle, Sir William Parr, both receiving part of his fee. The duke resided generally in the rear, more probably at Middleham or Barnard Castle than at Penrith or Carlisle. Gloucester had to supply and munition his forces

---

[31] Storey, 'Wardens of the Marches', pp. 607–8, 615.
[32] The esquires Peter and Richard Bank of Allerton (Yorks.), Richard Forthey of Bristol esq., and Walter Pleasance of Selby gent., *Rotuli Scotiae*, vol. 1, p. 440; C 81/1310/4, 33; C 81/1311/28–9; C 81/1312/9.

and a score of protections were authorised by him to tradesmen (drapers, grocers, mercers, merchants, salters, skinners, and tailors), mainly from London. He had his own ordnance train, contributing two guns together with crossbows and £100 for repairs to the city of Carlisle in 1480.[33] Some defence works at Carlisle still exhibit the duke's boar badge. The drastic cut in salary in 1480 surely meant that he could afford less and may have left him out of pocket.

Warden of the West March was a role that suited Richard's temperament, although his first decade of tenure were years of peace. When Edward exterminated the northern Lancastrians in 1464, he recognised the recovery of Berwick to be beyond his immediate resources and left it in Scottish hands. In 1465 he had concluded a 14-year truce to last until 1479. Edward's invasion of France in 1475 presupposed secure Scottish borders. The truce was extended until 1519 and in 1474 the deal was sealed by the betrothal of the king's third daughter Cecily to the baby Prince James, eldest son and heir presumptive to King James III and from 1488 King James IV. The first instalment of 2,000 marks (£1,333 6s.8d.) of Cecily's dowry was paid at Edinburgh on 3 February 1475 in St Giles' church.[34] These negotiations took place at national level, above the heads of the wardens and the local populace, and Duke Richard was not involved. Macdougall opines that the nobility of southern Scotland disapproved of James's peace policy, both because the English were traditional enemies and because border raiding was profitable.[35] Although not substantiable, the same may be true of the Cumbrians and Northumbrians. What Edward expected of his warden was therefore defence, not aggression, the restraint of the English borderers, collaboration in peacekeeping with the Scottish warden, the holding of regular march days, the quelling of friction, and the correction of infractions of the truce. Guidelines were agreed by ambassa

[33] H. Summerson, 'Carlisle and the English West March in the Later Middle Ages', in *The North of England in the Age of Richard III*, ed. A.J. Pollard (Sutton, 1996), pp. 98–9.

[34] D. Dunlop, 'The "Redresses and Reparacons of Attemptates": Alexander Legh's Instructions from Edward IV, March–April 1475', *HR*, 63 (1990), pp. 341–53, at p. 342.

[35] N. Macdougall, 'Richard III and James III. Contemporary Monarchs, Parallel Mythologies', in *Richard III: Loyalty, Lordship and Law*, ed. P.W. Hammond (Richard III and Yorkist History Trust, 1986), p. 157.

dors of both sides on 1 May 1472.[36] This peacekeeping role did not apparently appeal to Richard. The new retainers that he indentured from his
Yorkshire lordships in 1471–4 were recruited with hostilities with the Scots
in mind.[37]

One area where the duke did not accrue experience was diplomacy.
Though warden, Gloucester was never commissioned to treat with the Scots,
perhaps because he was inflexibly aggressive and his hostility set him at odds
with Edward IV's more conciliatory policy of rapprochement. 'Richard was
almost as much of a handful as his brother George', writes Pollard.[38] 'The
traits that allowed him to act against his brother's wishes in the early 1470s
showed that his attitude to authority bordered on the irresponsible', writes
Booth.[39] It was reported in spring 1473 that neither the duke nor his counterpart on the east and middle Marches had been attending march days and
had missed in particular a meeting to resolve the long-running issue of fishgarths on the River Esk. In another capacity, as admiral, not only had he not
been keeping the peace, but it had been his ship the *Mary Flower* that had
plundered two Scottish ships. On 27 April 1474 an 'incummyn' by Gloucester
in the west and middle marches was predicted by the Scots and the western
Scottish warden Alexander Duke of Albany was alerted to resist.[40] Heightened
tensions were certainly not what Edward wanted. With his invasion of France
looming, Edward needed his rear protected from Scottish attack and his
peace policy towards Scotland to prevail. What Gloucester did on the borders
and what he saw as desirable failed, from Edward's point of view, to take
account of the wider picture and English foreign policy as a whole. Edward's
emissary Dr Alexander Legh was ordered to apologise to the Scots about
these deficiencies, which were insufficiently adverse to colour national relations, to assure the Scots that the march days would be held in future, and
to set up a diet of admirals at Alnwick on 8 May 1474. Gloucester and

[36] *CDRS*, vol. 4, pp. 285–6.

[37] Jones and Walker, 'Private Indentures', pp. 176–7; Sir John Savile's Household, http://
savilehousehold.co.uk/index.php/the-saviles/.

[38] Pollard, *Princes*, p. 74.

[39] P. Booth, 'Richard, Duke of Gloucester and the West March towards Scotland, 1470–
1483', *Northern History*, 36 (2000), p. 246.

[40] *Accounts of the Lord High Treasurer of Scotland, vol. I, 1473–98*, ed. R. Dickson (HM General
Register House, 1877), p. 49.

Northumberland were instructed to attend the diet in person or by deputy, to officiate with due diligence without fail, as it was 'the kynges pleasir', and to report back to King Edward on what was resolved. Gloucester as admiral was given quite detailed instructions. Edward relied on him, so Legh was to say, to 'sett a spedy sadd, and just direction therin, such as may be for the goode of peax and rest of thoo partyes in the kynges absence'. In September the ambassadors of both kings timetabled the next six march meetings for redress of grievances. Those relating to the *Salvator*, a Scottish ship that had been wrecked and plundered by the English, were to be settled by the lieutenants of 'my lord of Gloucester' and the Scottish admiral 'my lord of Albany'. A further embassy was commissioned on 22 February 1475 specifically to resolve the issue of the fishgarths on the River Esk.[41] About this time the duke was ordered to make restitution to the tenants of the Scot Sir John Carlill who had been robbed by Englishmen in defiance of the truce.[42] Presumably their deputies did continue to meet – the wardens themselves went to France – and in the absence of contrary evidence relations between the two realms are believed to have become cordial until war broke out in 1480. At national level certainly the annual instalments of the dowry were paid more or less on time, but, in 1477, at Scottish prompting, Edward had to direct Gloucester to remedy another English raid in his wardenship in 1477. A Percy retainer Robert Constable was summoned by the king to explain himself.[43] It is not obvious, writes Dunlop somewhat euphemistically, that Richard's management of the march was excellent.[44]

The war with Scotland in 1480–3 proved more to Richard's taste. It is significant perhaps that Edward never used Gloucester, unlike Warwick, for diplomacy. The duke did not agree with the king's peace policy. The northern bishops normally officiated. Henry Earl of Northumberland served. So did Lords Dacre, Greystoke, and Scrope of Bolton, Sir James Strangways, Sir William Parr, Sir John Conyers, and Thomas Witham, all

---

[41] Dunlop, 'Redresses and Reparacons', pp. 344–7; *Rotuli Scotiae*, vol. 2, pp. 450–1. Humphrey Lord Dacre represented Gloucester, who was not himself an ambassador, *Rotuli Scotiae*, vol. 2, p. 450.

[42] Summerson, 'Carlisle and the English West March', p. 98.

[43] *Letters of the Kings of England*, ed. J.O. Halliwell-Phillipps (H. Colburn, 1848), pp. 147–8; *Testamenta Eboracensia*, ed. J. Raine (Surtees Society, 1864), vol. 3, p. 306.

[44] Dunlop, 'Redresses and Reparacons', p. 348.

northern connections of Warwick, and all probably retainers of Gloucester too,[45] whose interests they could represent, and the Percy retainer Sir William Plumpton. The panels were completed by civil servants, usually doctors of law.

Scotland took second place in the early 1470s in Gloucester's thinking to his dispute with his brother Clarence over the Warwick inheritance of their two duchesses. Crowland rated this quarrel the main domestic issue of these years and the Pastons thought it likely to come to blows in 1473. The inheritance was partitioned in July 1474 and the settlement was facilitated and enforced by two acts of parliament. Also in 12 May 1473 the royal council imposed peace on the duke and the earl of Northumberland, whose sphere of influence Richard had invaded, which underpinned the settlement they agreed on 28 July 1474.[46] Simultaneously, as discussed in the next chapter, Gloucester was imposing his will on the countess of Oxford and Lady Hungerford. These were followed in February 1475 by the realignment of Richard's estates, from the eastern counties to the North, and his appointment as sheriff of Cumberland for life.

V

Scotland took second place in these years in the king's thinking too, second to his great enterprise against France. By backing Warwick and the Lancastrian Readeption, King Louis XI had reinforced Edward IV's enmity, and had given additional justification to the reconquest of France that Edward had previously projected in the late 1460s. Edward's earlier plans had been thwarted by the Treaty of Péronne that Louis had negotiated with Charles the Bold. This appears to have been a popular project, for which, however, English taxpayers were reluctant to pay. In the early 1470s Edward secured agreements with Burgundy, Brittany, and Scotland and levied the taxes to fund the full-scale invasion of France that eventually happened in August 1475. By English standards, Edward had prepared a

---

[45] *Rotuli Scotiae*, vol. 2, pp. 429–31, 437, 444–5, 451–2. Strangways (d. 1480) and Witham (d. 1481) died before concrete evidence of connection with Gloucester.

[46] BL Cotton Julius B XII ff.135v–6; Jones and Walker, 'Private Indentures', pp. 177–8; *Crowland*, p. 130–3; see the discussion 'Dynastic Change and Northern Society: The Fourth Earl of Northumberland, 1470–89', in *Rivals*, pp. 370–1.

huge, splendidly equipped, and state-of-the-art army, but it was small by
current European standards and ill-experienced to take on Louis's more
professional force. Edward managed to raise funds for wages only for six
months. This army was recruited by the traditional English indenture
system, with contingents from all the higher nobility. Largest were those of
the two royal dukes of Clarence and Gloucester, each of whom indented
for 1,110 troops comprising 10 knights (including themselves), 100 men-at-
arms, and 1,000 archers. Gloucester, the constable of England, brought
rather more, all of whom bore his badge of the white boar. Knights in
particular were not numerous at this time. The contingents of the royal
dukes dwarfed those of other magnates: the dukes of Norfolk and
Suffolk each recruited only two knights, 40 men-at-arms and 300 archers;
the duke of Buckingham four knights, 40 men-at-arms, and 300 archers;
and the earl of Northumberland 10 knights, 40 men-at-arms, and
200 archers.[47]

The names of very few of Gloucester's company are known for certain.
There were protections for one knight Ralph Ashton of Middleton
(Lancashire) and Fryton (Yorkshire), two esquires Thomas Fulthorp of
Witton (Yorkshire) and Auckland (Durham), and Thomas Greenfield
of Romsey (Hampshire), and two tradesmen, John Golande skinner of
London and Arthur Nele alias Neleson of London and Calais.[48] One
subcontract does survive, for the younger son Edmund Paston esquire, an
extraordinary hostilities-only retainer who was not so far as is known a
member of the duke's household or an officer on his estates. On 7 April
1475 Paston was 'reteyned and withholden with the sayd Duc to do him
seruice of werre with the Kyng our souuerayn lord now in his viage ouir the
see for an hol yere' with one man at arms (Paston himself) and three archers.
Paston was to be 'well and suffioyently horsed, armed and arrayed as it
apperteyneth to a man of armes' and his archers, also to be mounted, were
to be 'herneised, habilled, and arrayed as it apperteneth to archers'.[49]This

[47] F.P. Barnard, *Edward IV's French Expedition of 1475. The Leaders and their Badges* (Clarendon
Press, 1925).
[48] C 81/1312/9, 29, 31; C 81/1313/16, 25. For Greenfield see also Hicks, *Rivals*,
pp. 317–21.
[49] *Paston L & P*, vol. 1, pp. 636–8.

was a model indenture, into which the name of the retainer and the size of
his troop could be inserted, and was therefore probably one of 20 or more.
Some phrases were borrowed from Gloucester's indentures of retainer with
Burgh and Savile, but this contract is much longer and more elaborate
than other such indentures of war for 1475, such as those of Gloucester's
brother Clarence with James Hyde and William Floyer,[50] and perhaps
signals the detail and thoroughness that was the hallmark of the duke in
other contexts. Gloucester, who signed it, wanted everything stated explicitly and nothing left to be improvised or to chance. The indenture spelled
out when and where Paston should muster and what he was to be paid. He
'shal dvely and truly obeye al the Kynges proclamaciouns and ordinaunces'
and take his turn on guard duty. Other clauses specified the division of
ransoms and other profits of war, what should happen if Paston was
discharged, if his troop diminished, or even 'if the sayd Duc be takyn, hurt,
or diseased with in the sayd tyme'.[51] Duplicating all these indentures
must have taken Gloucester's clerks a considerable time. In anticipation
of genuine conflict, Gloucester was covering every eventuality. Four of
Gloucester's retainers indented separately with the king,[52] and for two of
these a subcontract survives. Richard's retainers of war identified themselves by wearing his badge of the white boar.[53]

However, there was to be no fighting. The campaign was abortive.
Paston was ordered to muster at Portsdown Hill above Portsmouth
Harbour on 24 May 1475,[54] but the fleet sailed for Calais only on 4 July
and the army moved on from there only on the 18th. Marching rather
slowly, the English captains were at Seyncre in Vermandois, still to the
south of Péronnne, on 13 August. Edward embarked too late in the season
for a full campaign. He found that the Burgundian Duke Charles the Bold
could not be relied upon for military support. Isolated, funded for only six
months, and with winter approaching, disaster threatened. Edward may
have realised all this even before departing, but had proceeded too far not

[50] See, e.g., J. Prince, *The Worthies of Devon* (Rees & Curtis, 1810), p. 373.
[51] *Paston L & P*, vol. 1, pp. 636–8.
[52] Ralph Ashton, James and Robert Harrington, Thomas Wortley.
[53] Barnard, *Edward IV's French Expedition*, p. 15.
[54] *Paston L & P*, vol. 1, p. 637.

to invade. He was quick, however, to agree terms for withdrawal with the French – good terms, that saved his face, but without honour. The French statesman Philippe de Commines attributed the first feelers to King Edward. Certainly the terms that Louis first offered were identical to those that were agreed.[55] This was at a council of war at Seyncre that rubber-stamped the agreement proposed by the king. The nobility backed the king – in some cases induced by French bribes – and ensured that the rest following the king's lead. Provision was made for the arbitration of the rival claims to the French crown, which never happened. A marriage was arranged between Princess Elizabeth and the dauphin Charles (the future Charles VIII). The French paid a lump sum and an annual pension, which Edward preferred to call tribute. To anticipate and forestall criticism back in England, the crucial council minute that had committed all the English commanders to the peace agreement was registered on the patent roll to demonstrate that responsibility was shared among them all.[56] Gloucester 'and some others' were discontented with this peace, reports Commines. 'None euill captaine was hee in the warre, as to whiche his disposition was more metely [suited] then for peace.'[57] As the constable of England, his view mattered, but he had to defer to the king. Soon after he met up at Amiens with King Louis, who softened the blow with splendid presents, both precious plate and well-accoutred horses.[58]

This campaign was a big opportunity for the young constable to demonstrate his organisational and disciplinary skills. He must, for instance, have issued ordinances for the conduct of the troops, but these, like every other instance of his constabulary authority, are unrecorded.

The Treaty of Picquigny proved not to be a stable settlement. Following Charles the Bold's death at Nancy on 5 January 1477, Louis XI attacked Burgundy, whose annexation or dismemberment was decidedly not in English interests. A great council was held to ensure the security of Calais and to decide on English foreign policy. John Paston II anticipated war. 'Wher-to I dowt nott ther shall be jn all haste both the Dukys off Clarance

[55] Hicks, 'Edward IV's *Brief Treatise* and the Treaty of Picquigny of 1475', p. 265.
[56] Ibid., pp. 262–5; *CPR 1467–77*, p. 583.
[57] More, *Richard III*, pp. 7–8.
[58] Commines, *Mémoires*, vol. 2, p. 67.

and Glowcestre, wheroff I wolde, that my brother E[dmund Paston] wyst.'[59] This was an opportunity for an aspirant soldier. But Paston was wrong: neither duke intervened. King and great council may have opted for neutrality.[60] In any case King Edward could not count on either duke backing his pusillanimous preference, to protect Calais and to preserve the Picquigny settlement and especially his French pension. Edward quickly rejected the proposal that Clarence should marry Mary of Burgundy and thus commit England to her side against the French. Gloucester, on previous evidence, probably favoured war and was anyway quite undiplomatic. Louis XI used Elizabeth's betrothal and his pension skilfully to string Edward along, so the English did not interfere in his aggression against Burgundy that gained the Somme towns and Artois permanently for France. In 1482 Louis dropped these Picquigny provisions and Edward was offered only war as an alternative to acquiescence, two unpalatable alternatives that he had not resolved before his death.

In 1475 Edward's failure to wage the war for which English taxpayers had paid was criticised at home and Edward took action to avert trouble,[61] which actually did not materialise. He did not levy the last instalment of taxes due. As he avoided paying the second instalment of wages to his troops, received a lump sum from Louis XI and a substantial annuity (which the English regarded as tribute), and significantly enlarged his crown estate, Edward was actually better off after the campaign. At last he paid off most of his inherited debts and indeed he accumulated some capital ahead of the Scottish war. He could now afford such kingly magnificence as his illuminated manuscripts and the massive redevelopment of St George's Chapel, Windsor.

VI

'He spent a great part' of his riches, reported Crowland, on the reinterment of the bones of his father Richard Duke of York and his brother Edmund Earl of Rutland, both slain in battle in 1460 at Wakefield, at the family mausoleum at Fotheringhay College in Northamptonshire.

---

[59] *Paston L & P*, vol. 1, 498.

[60] As argued in *The Calais Letterbook of William Lord Hastings (1477) and Late Medieval Crisis Diplomacy 1477–83*, ed. E.L. Meek (Richard III and Yorkist History Trust, 2017), pp. 18 ff.

[61] *Crowland*, pp. 136–7.

Originally they had been buried at the friary at Pontefract. Gloucester had the opportunity to visit their tombs several times when at Pontefract Castle. That he felt some affection for the locality is suggested by the elevation of Pontefract to a seignorial borough after his accession. The reburial process took 10 days (21–30 July 1476) and was led by Duke Richard himself as chief mourner: a substantial commitment of his time. Richard made offerings of the mass penny daily and at Fotheringhay five pieces of cloth of gold. The bodies rested each night on new hearses in churches en route where the funeral service and requiem masses were repeated. This involved a conspicuous display of heraldry: three kings of arms, five heralds, and four pursuivants were in attendance. The king, both royal dukes, the duke of Suffolk, five earls, and six barons attended the actual reinterments at Fotheringhay that were led by nine bishops. Following the ceremonies, there was a banquet attended, it was estimated, by more than 2,000 people. There are several accounts of these enormously grand ceremonies,[62] – Crowland thought them 'distinguished and wondrous'[63] – but nothing is recorded about the accommodation and feeding of everybody or the provision of hearses, hangings, liveries, and so forth that posed logistical challenges comparable to a small campaign. The surviving narratives are silent on how many of Richard's household attended him and where he stayed overnight. One wonders how involved in the preparations Gloucester as chief mourner and the head of the office of arms was. The whole sequence seems to have unfolded without a hitch.

This was the grandest of celebrations of the house of York and appears to have made a big impression on Duke Richard. He was only seven years of age when his father died, after a career often apart from his duchess and younger children, and apparently Edmund had lived at Ludlow before exile in Ireland in 1459–60. There is no evidence – why should there be any? – of Richard's sentiments about them until after the reinterments. In 1477, at Queens' College Cambridge and in 1478, at Middleham College, Richard made provision for the celebration of the obits and masses for the souls of his parents and those of his two elder siblings Edmund Earl of

[62] A.F. Sutton and L. Visser-Fuchs with P.W. Hammond (eds), *The Reburial of Richard Duke of York 21–30 July 1476* (Richard III Society, 1996).

[63] *Crowland*, pp. 138–9.

Rutland (d. 1460) and Anne Duchess of Exeter (d. 1476) who had achieved maturity. Gloucester did not commemorate by name any of his elder brothers (even Clarence), nor sisters Elizabeth and Margaret, nor even his youngest sister Ursula who had died in infancy. York and Rutland were also remembered at Richard's college at York and at many other private foundations when he was king.[64]

The dukes of York had intended Fotheringhay to be the resting place of the whole house of York, but Edward IV and his brothers thought otherwise. Clarence had to decide first: he interred his Duchess Isabel in her abbey at Tewkesbury among her ancestors and joined her a year later. King Edward rejected Fotheringhay and also the crowded east end of Westminster Abbey. Instead from 1471 he was appending to Edward III's existing Garter Chapel (now the Albert Memorial Chapel) at Windsor Castle the vast new state-of-the-art St George's Chapel. Only the east end had been finished when he himself was interred there in 1483, but he always intended that it would accommodate select kin and courtiers. Certainly places were reserved for William Lord Hastings, Walter Lord Ferrers of Chartley, and the king's late sister Anne Duchess of Exeter.[65] So perhaps were places reserved for those others who made benefactions, although they lie now elsewhere: John Duke of Suffolk and his duchess (the king's other sister Elizabeth) and his brother Richard Duke of Gloucester, who bestowed on Windsor College three East Anglian manors.[66] The chapter contracted for a chaplain to celebrate mass daily for 'the excellent prince' and his consort without specifying precisely whereabouts in the new chapel Richard's chantry was to be located. Richard indeed founded two colleges of his own, Middleham, where he did not intend to lie, and Barnard Castle, about which we know too little to be sure. It is striking, but not exceptional, how early these three brothers were choosing their mausolea and planning for the good of their souls.

[64] Searle, *Queens' College*, p. 90; Raine, 'Statutes', p. 160; see below.

[65] C. Wood, 'The Chantries and Chantry Chapels of St George's Chapel, Windsor Castle', *Southern History*, 31 (2010), pp. 51–4, 60–2, 72; *CPR 1476–85*, 242, pp. 269–70; *Register of John Blyth, Bishop of Salisbury, 1493–1499*, ed. D. Wright, Wiltshire Record Society 68 (2015), nos 348–9. Though now lost, the Ferrers chantry definitely operated. The other chantry chapels survive.

[66] *CPR 1476–85*, pp. 172, 219–20; St George's Chapel MSS, XI.P.11, 12; 4.16.

A second great celebration of the house of York was staged in January 1478 at Westminster. This was the child marriage of the king's second son and Richard's nephew Richard Duke of York to Anne Mowbray, the Norfolk heiress. Apart from the marriage itself in St Stephen's Chapel on 15 January, there was a banquet and a tournament (22 January). Gloucester did not joust, nor did he attend on the jousters, perhaps because as constable he presided over the whole. 'The high and mighty Prince the Duc of Gloucester' bore the gold basins of silver and gold that were cast among the people and led the bride from the chapel to the banquet.[67] The wedding was timed to coincide with parliament, itself a great logistical effort, to stress to the largest possible audience the unity of the house of York. The preliminaries to the jousting were in December 1477: the presentation of the articles to the king, Gloucester being present, the challenges, and their public posting. Even before then, in November, a great council had prepared for the marriage, the parliament that was to meet in January and February, and the trial of George Duke of Clarence that was its principal business. The juxtaposition of these events that guaranteed the maximum audience for the marriage and a display of unity for the ruling house thus helped to ensure that the judicial murder of a royal prince passed off without difficulty. The king himself led the prosecution and parliament was packed with supporters of the king's household and the queen's family.[68]

Perhaps Clarence's trial would not have been risked had it been opposed by the king's next brother Richard Duke of Gloucester. It was not. Formally he took the king's side: he was at the November council who first swore allegiance in the most abject way to the Prince of Wales (the future Edward V).[69] In 1483, however, Mancini reported, 'At that time Richard Duke of Gloucester was so overcome with grief for his brother, that he could not dissimilate so well, but that he was overheard to say that he would one day avenge his brother's death'. There was apprehension in 1483 that Richard would wreak this revenge, he adds. This is diametrically opposite to what

[67] 'Narrative of the Marriage of Richard Duke of York and Ann of Norfolk, the "Matrimonial Feast", and the Grand Justing', in *Illustrations of Ancient State and Chivalry*, ed. W.H. Black (Shakespeare Press, 1840), pp. 25–40, at p.30.

[68] Hicks, *Clarence*, ch. 4.

[69] Hicks, *Edward V*, p. 59.

More had to say. '[Regarding Richard Duke of Gloucester], somme wise menne also weene [think] that his drifte couertly conuayed, lacked not in helping furth his brother of Clarence to his death. Which hee resisted openly, howbeit somewhat (as menne demed [thought]) more faintly than he that was minded to [acquire] his welth.'[70] Neither Mancini nor More were eyewitnesses – each was writing years later – but both comment on Richard's ambiguous stance and his success in concealing his real feelings. Mancini was writing in 1483, when Richard did choose to express his disapproval of Clarence's fate, but More's account, that Richard backed Clarence's fall for personal gain, can be amply substantiated. The duke benefited in a dozen distinct ways, petitioned for four acts of parliament and eight royal grants, some initiated in January ahead of Clarence's conviction and forfeiture, or in November 1477 ahead even of his trial, or in one instance in the previous July.[71] This chronology demonstrates conclusively that Richard was exploiting Clarence's fall before his trial in ways that depended on his brother's dispossession and death. Richard's wish list is discussed in chapter 8. These were the king's rewards for Richard's support: perhaps the price that the duke exacted. While contemporaries deplored such fratricide, it was the king's decision and Gloucester was at one with everybody else in both houses of parliament who followed the king's lead. Gloucester acted as commanded. The responsibility and blame was King Edward's.

VII

Richard's public career at the centre of Yorkist affairs did not end in 1478. Increasingly he was based in the North. That explains why he missed such national events as the funerals at Windsor of Prince George in 1479, of Princess Mary in 1482, most Garter chapters, and the burial of Edward IV himself in 1483.[72] Yet Richard knew and was apparently on amicable terms with everyone who mattered: the queen who had feed him since 1469, her

[70] Mancini, *Richard III*, pp. 62–3, 70–1; More, *Richard III*, p. 8.

[71] Hicks, *Clarence*, p. 151 esp. notes; Searle, *Queens' College*, p. 90. The chancery warrants date before the patents, some before Clarence's death, C81/863/4658, 4665, 4669, 4670, 4671, 4687.

[72] As discussed in A.F. Sutton and L. Visser-Fuchs with R.A. Griffiths (eds), *The Royal Funerals of the House of York at Windsor* (Richard III Society, 2005).

brothers Anthony and Edward and her son the marquis of Dorset who had served with him in the Scottish war; the chief household officers Hastings and Stanley and Lord Chancellor Rotherham; Lord Howard, Lord Lovell, and of course the northern lords. His primary responsibility, however, was his conduct of the war against the Scots: his outstanding service to his brother. Following his triumphs in 1482–3, when he recaptured Berwick-upon-Tweed permanently, and briefly occupied Edinburgh, he was praised by parliament and received the signal honour of a new principality in the North. These topics are discussed in chapter 9.

Chapter Five

FORGING THE FUTURE 1471–83

I

'Yonge of age', Richard was still only nineteen years of age in 1471, the same age as Edward IV had been at his accession. He was no longer the immature and inexperienced figurehead that needed a guardian or mentor. Battle-hardened by at least four engagements, at Cefn Glasfryn, Ribble Bridge, Barnet, and Tewkesbury, and a successful invasion, the duke had shared in his brother's military triumph in 1471, and in 1483 he was to be publicly praised by parliament for his victorious campaigns in Scotland. These years spanned Edward IV's Second Reign and were when Richard forged his career as a mature adult. Happy to accept advancement and endowment by the king, he was willing to implement the king's commands when they coincided with what he saw as his own interests, but it is apparent that he was not content merely to be Edward's passive instrument. Richard had no intention of being just a figurehead, like the sons of Henry IV, or indeed many an HRH today. His target was to be a great magnate and a commander-in-chief, like his father Richard Duke of York and father-in-law Warwick the Kingmaker, and to establish a great noble dynasty of his own.

II

As will be demonstrated, Duke Richard was proud and ambitious, desirous
of wealth and power and responsibility, determined to marry well and to
establish his own dynasty, and was concerned also to ensure his own salvation after death. He wanted the biggest and the best of everything.
Everything was large in scale: the number and eminence of his honorary
offices (admiral, constable, and great chamberlain); his extensive estates
across at least 24 counties; his sphere of power, which came to transcend
the region assigned to him and eventually took in the kingdom itself; and
the number and splendour of his religious foundations and his building
works, which together may have outstripped the resources needed to fulfil
them. His interests and activities were extremely wide-ranging. He involved
himself in many events and disputes, in every region of England and in
many different projects, in ship-owning and mining, for instance. Personally
he took his own initiatives. The statutes of his college at Middleham, his
ordinances as constable of England, his indentures of war, and his cartulary
all betray his individual stamp. He was a man of dynamic energy and foresight and a master of detail, who was always in a hurry to achieve his ends.[1]
A younger son unfettered by nostalgia, he had strategic priorities that he
pursued single-mindedly, disposing of manors and lordships as well as
amassing them. He shaped his total estate and career in a manner that was
quite without parallel in his own day, but not uncommon a century later.[2]

To be fair, this was because his interests were promoted by King
Edward, who then tried to limit him, ineffectively. Edward wanted his
brother to be both a great nobleman and a reliable agent, to be subject to
his policies and at his beck and call. Richard did manage the West March
towards Scotland for Edward and indeed the whole Scottish war in 1480–3,
he did recruit the largest retinue for Edward's invasion of France in 1475,

---

[1] 'The Statutes Ordained by Richard Duke of Gloucester, for the College of Middleham.
Dated July 4, 18 Edw. IV, (1478)', ed. J. Raine, *Archaeological Journal*, 14 (1857), pp. 160–70;
Ramsay, 'Richard III and the Office of Arms', in *The Yorkist Age*, pp. 142–63; M.A. Hicks,
'Richard III as Duke of Gloucester: A Study in Character', in *Rivals*, pp. 251–2, 285 –9; see
above BL MS Cotton Julius BXII.
[2] N. Saul, *The Three Richards: Richard I, Richard II, and Richard III* (Hambledon Continuum,
2005), p. 72. Lawrence Stone identified such instances a century later, *Family and Fortune:
Studies in Aristocratic Finance in the Sixteenth and Seventeenth Century* (Clarendon Press, 1973).

he did take the lead as chief mourner in the reinterment of their father Richard Duke of York in 1476, and he did back the king's destruction of the duke of Clarence in 1478. Despite this, Edward actually got a great nobleman who devised his own priorities independently, who generally implemented royal wishes but sometimes subverted them, who apparently opposed the Scottish peace in the 1470s and the Treaty of Picquigny in 1475, who made more of what had been given than Edward had envisaged and who wrested yet more than the king had originally intended. Each concession was regarded by Richard not as the end, but as a stage in a process yet to be fulfilled. He did not accept that rebuffs by King Edward or the cancellation of royal grants were final. He did not write off grants that had been cancelled. They were copied into his cartulary Cotton Julius BXII. Some were exemplified in chancery (formally registered). In 1471 he had reactivated the constableship of England on the strength of the 1469 patent and in 1478 he secured anew the great chamberlainship of England and the Yorkshire castle of Richmond that earlier he had been obliged to disgorge.[3] Also in 1471 he had exemplified his 1469 patent of the justiciarship and chamberlainship of South Wales. That he seems to have hoped to make such grants good casts light on his sense of right title and entitlement and may also be relevant to his usurpation.[4] In 1477–8 Richard set the price – a very high price – for his compliance in the destruction of his brother Clarence.[5] These were the years when Richard learnt about peacetime politics, learnt to direct a great organisation, to wage war and to develop his own policies, and established firmly the character and characteristics that were to prevail for the rest of his short life. Precisely when each policy was developed and each trait was established is unclear. Was it in 1471? Perhaps. The trajectory on which he embarked, however, seems apparent by 1475. The culmination was his command of the English forces against Scotland and the creation of his principality in 1483.

[3] *CPR 1467–77*, 275; *1476–85*, pp. 67, 90.
[4] The holograph postscript to his warrant to Lord Chancellor Russell in 1483 indicates how strong was his sense of rightness, *Richard III. A Royal Enigma*, ed. S. Cunningham (National Archives, 2003), pp. 54–5.
[5] Hicks, *Clarence*, 150–1; see below p. 191–9.

The archive that Richard generated has almost entirely disappeared. Once there were literally thousands of minister's accounts, one per manor per year for 60 properties of his duchess's inheritance alone, annual accounts for at least a dozen receiverships and the ducal household, several registers of various types and hundreds of deeds, letters, leases, indentures, and so on. A handful of estate accounts and one cartulary (British Library MS Cotton Julius BXII) are the only chance survivors from his archive. A smattering of fragments of other transactions and counterparts retained by the other parties involved indicate the sheer range and hint at the quantity of the duke's other activities. His cartulary, probably commenced in 1472 and supplemented until 1483, casts some light on his actual possessions, on his aspirations and on disputes. It contains royal grants and acts of parliament relating to his principal properties, including those that Edward had taken back: presumably taken from the original documents, although only occasionally is the warranty noted at the foot. There are also documents relating to other properties such as the marcher lordship of Gower, Sherborne in Dorset and Trowbridge in Wiltshire, to which the duke had shadowy claims that evidently he hoped to make good, and details of the military service due to Gloucester and Richmond, honours that might in future be exploited financially. The Hungerford inquisitions post mortem for 1469 and 1473 justified additional acquisitions beyond those agreed with Margaret Lady Hungerford in 1469. Here were recorded his chancery suits with the countess of Oxford's feoffees and the countess of Warwick's pleas for her inheritance. At least two people went through the cartulary in Richard's own lifetime – and presumably on his orders – to note in the margins the places where the properties were located and the titles by which they were held – tail male, life or pleasure. Once only is the cancellation of a grant recorded.[6] Richard believed in research, to identify the full-range of rights and resources that previous lords and officers had enjoyed, and thus potentially to enable him to accrue them himself. Hence his historical investigations into the forest of Inglewood and in his exemplification in 1482 of the key document of 1312 that established the bounds of

---

[6] M.A. Hicks, 'Richard III's Cartulary in the British Library MS Cotton Julius BXII', in *Rivals*, pp. 281–90; 'Richard III as Duke of Gloucester', in *Rivals*, pp. 251–2.

Nidderdale Chase against the claims of neighbouring landholders.[7] Yet much is missing, relating to other manors that passed in and out of his hands, his compromises with Lancastrian traitors and his manoeuvres to win over the Neville heirs, his religious foundations, his retaining, wardenship, campaigning, and arbitrations, and his relations with the city of York, all of which generated documents signed with his own hand R.Gloucestre and many of which presumably were registered in other volumes that are now lost.

Had it survived, Richard's archive would certainly have documented how he established the luxurious and ostentatious lifestyle that was expected of so great a prince. 'Item I will that my lorde of Gloucestre shall have a emeraunt set in gold for which for said lorde would have geven me C mark.'[8] A hundred marks £66 13s.4d. was many times the income that justified the status of a gentleman. Sir John Pilkington's bequest reveals much about Richard's taste for jewellery, the prodigal expenditure, and the lavish lifestyle expected of a 'high and mighty prince'. Contemporaries wanted the nobility to live in noble style. Conspicuous consumption was an expectation and a necessity. Royal dukes came in and out of the king's chamber at will and wore coronets in the king's presence. Whenever at court, Richard dined with the king in his great chamber and dressed for the part. 'A duke in this courte', runs the *Black Book* of Edward IV's household, 'shall have etyng in the hall' for 'one knight, a chapleyn, three esquyers, and four yeomen', and was entitled at breakfast, supper, and night to ten loaves, four messes of great meat, four pitchers of wine, six gallons of ale, torches, candles, and faggots for fuel. Probably neither Richard nor any other English duke could afford the £4,000 a year estimated for a ducal household of chief officers, four knights, 60 esquires and gentlemen, 100 valets/yeomen in his chamber, chapel, menial, and outside offices (e.g., his stable), 30 grooms, and 24 pages, total 240. A duke's steward, treasurer, and controller were worth 40 marks a year and ranked with the barons.[9] In 1468 Clarence planned for a household numbering 399. Probably Gloucester employed fewer. Just to move

[7] *CPR 1476–85*, p. 318.

[8] *English Wills proved in the Prerogative Court of York 1477–1499*, eds H. Falvey, L. Boatwright, and P. Hammond (Richard III Society, 2013), p. 15.

[9] A.R. Myers, *Household of Edward IV* (Manchester University Press, 1959), pp. 94–5.

around, Duke Richard needed a train of horses with their harness, both for riding and for draught. At war Richard was paid at the daily wage of a duke, 13s.4d. a day; in church he gave the offerings of a duke, 6s.8d, £120 a year in all. What ought to have been the end result was set out in legislation about dress in the 1483 sumptuary act. Gloucester was one of the royal family permitted to wear the purple cloth of gold or silk that was prohibited to ordinary dukes and the cloth of gold of tissue forbidden to everybody below that rank. It was conventional each year to scatter New Year gifts among his family, friends, peers, and retainers that in 1482 included goldsmithery worth 200 marks.[10] Even the obscure London merchant George Cely possessed a jewel worth £100, once King Richard's.[11]

For all this Duke Richard needed money, a massive income constantly replenished, and a whole range of props that encompassed all aspects of life – from dwellings to dress, from horseflesh to parks, from banquets to piety. In January 1477 he paid for three horses bought for his use and for a ditch around the lodge of Hanslope Park in Buckinghamshire, just off the Great North Road via which he travelled from the North to London and back several times a year.[12] Richard was a man of his time, who seems to have shared all these tastes, and who was lavish, conspicuous, expensive, and extravagant. 'All avarice set a syde', wrote Rous.[13] Of such a man was expected open-handed generosity – the virtue of gentility, of a gentleman (in Latin *generosus*) without counting the cost, which Richard possessed in abundance. 'Free was hee called of dyspence, and sommewhat aboue hys power liberall.'[14] He paid numerous large fees to his retainers and was lavish in his religious benefactions.

There are mere hints of his moveable wealth and the lifestyle that he seems to have accrued during Edward IV's Second Reign. Returning to England in 1471, a teenager without heirlooms after a year's exile, Richard surely owned almost nothing. He may have garnered some booty after the

---

[10] On credit from Edmund Shaa of London and repaid only in 1484, *H433*, vol. 2, p. 88.

[11] S. Rose, *The Wealth of England* (Oxbow Books, 2018), p. 102. It is unknown how Cely acquired the gem.

[12] R.E. Horrox and A.F. Sutton, 'Some Expenses of Richard Duke of Gloucester 1475–7', *Ricardian* 83 (1983), p. 267.

[13] *The Rous Roll*, ed. W.H. Courthope (1859), no. 63.

[14] More, *Richard III*, p. 8.

battles of Barnet and Tewkesbury or from the castles of his foes, that of the earl of Oxford at Castle Hedingham in Essex and that of Warwick at Middleham and Sheriff Hutton, if they had not been pillaged ahead of his arrival. His contemporary Northumberland compensated the executours 'for ye stuff that I had of ye Marqueux Mountagugh at Wresill' with the derisory sum of £10.[15] Waste parchment from Warwick's estate accounts stiffened the binding of the cartulary of Richard Clervaux.[16] Richard's own household furnishings and chattels have long since worn out, become outdated and were discarded, his plate melted down and his jewels recycled. None of his coronets, his garter jewel, nor Pilkington's emerald brooch survive. Louis XI gave him plate in 1475. In 1474 Richard purchased jewels and silver vessels from the goldsmith Jacob Faslard valued at £274 that were charged to the receiver of Middleham. He had two covered spice plates of silver worth £90 11s.4d. that he pledged to Henry Ashbury.[17] His East Midlands receiver paid bills of £296 on luxuries: £50 for arras for wall-hangings and horse-harness from the previous year and the rest mainly furs, silks, velvets, and camlets bought for the duke and duchess from the best London tradesmen in 1476 in a pre-Christmas shopping spree.[18] Only a dozen badges of his emblem of the white boar survive in silver, pewter, or latten:[19] most of the 1,300 required for the Picquigny campaign were probably of cloth. Richard had his own herald, pursuivant, rolls of arms and his own minstrels. He had pronounced tastes both in the liturgy and in church music and could afford to commission them. If he cannot actually be observed at the chase, Richard possessed many hunting grounds, extended two parks at some cost at Middleham, and purchased hawks.[20] He certainly possessed weapons and armour and must also have practised using them. He admitted to enthusiasm for ordnance in 1480 and therefore presumably had some cannon, perhaps inherited from Warwick or the spoils of

[15] *Testamenta Eboracensia*, ed. J. Raine (Surtees Society, 1864), p. 306.

[16] Pollard, 'Northern Retainers of Richard Nevill', *Northern History*, vol. 11, pp. 53–5.

[17] PSO 1 2/1/43; E 404/80/ m 1d 43; Horrox and Sutton, 'Some Expenses', pp. 266–70.

[18] Pollard, *Princes*, p. 189; DL 29/648/10485 rot.14.

[19] E.g., Tudor-Craig, *Richard III* (National Portrait Gallery, 1973), pp. 136, 139–40; see also Pollard, *Princes*, pp. 86–9. Several more boar badges have been found since 1973.

[20] Pollard, *NE England*, p. 203; Ross, *Richard III*, p. 142.

civil war, and adapted the defences of Carlisle for artillery. A great
bombard was perceived as an appropriate gift for him.[21] He fantasised
about going on crusade. There survive a dozen books that passed through
his hands and that he may, indeed, have read.[22] He was a great builder: at
Carlisle and Barnard Castle, of defences and domestic quarters,[23] probably
the Mortham Tower and a new suite of rooms at Barnard. A stone boar on
an oriel window overlooking the River Tees marks his handiwork. Also at
Middleham, where his new works were erected above the ruins extant
today.[24]

His ceaseless rapid travels testify to his vigour and activity. Another
lifestyle choice was the extramarital sex to be expected of the aristocracy,
that produced two bastards, John of Pontefract and Katherine Plantagenet,
both probably born after his appointment as chief steward of the Duchy of
Lancaster in the north parts in 1471.[25]

Whatever Richard expected on his return from exile in 1471 was radically transformed. He was committed to a rank, responsibilities, and role
for which he lacked the necessary resources. His sojourn with Warwick and
his childhood in his parents' establishments set him the model that he
needed to attain. It is unclear quite how he financed the conspicuous
consumption expected of a royal duke. Perhaps he was able to appropriate
substantial wealth and chattels remaining in the castles of his defeated foes.
He certainly acquired some of Warwick's archives. Estate revenues took
time to materialise. There is piecemeal evidence of lands that he sold,[26]
marriages that he dealt in,[27] and traitors with whom he compounded.[28] He

[21] J. Calmette & G. Périnelle, *Louis XI et l'Angleterre 1461–83* (Auguste Picard, 1930),
p. 145; A.F. Sutton and L. Visser-Fuchs, 'Richard of Gloucester and *la grosse bombarde*',
Ricardian, 134 (1996), p. 461.

[22] Sutton and Visser-Fuchs, *Richard III's Books* (A. Sutton, 1997), pp. 279–93.

[23] A.J. Pollard, 'St Cuthbert and the Hog: Richard III and the County Palatine of Durham
1471–85', in *Kings and Nobles in the Later Middle Ages*, eds R.A. Griffiths and
J.W. Sherborne (A. Sutton, 1986), p. 113. Perhaps these works were unfinished.

[24] Pollard, *Princes*, p. 189.

[25] For their mother, see M.A. Hicks, *Anne Neville, Queen to Richard III* (History Press, 2005),
pp. 157–8.

[26] E.g., Hooton Pagnell, see J.A. Ross, 'Richard Duke of Gloucester and the Purchase and
Sale of Hooton Pagnell, Yorkshire, 1475–80', *Ricardian*, 22 (2012), pp. 47–54.

[27] E.g., *CPR 1467–77*, pp. 329, 338.

[28] Ibid. pp. 344–5; see below.

needed quickly to build and shape his resources and thus his future career. Most noblemen passively worked with what they had inherited. Richard too may have expected in 1471 merely to recover what he had formerly possessed. Instead he had to be more positive. What he already possessed and was allowed to retain was insufficient. King Edward's plans for him did not necessarily match the duke's needs and anyway were not commensurate with his ambitions. Highly unusually, Richard was able to mould his estates geographically to fit his strategic vision. On the positive side he enjoyed royal favour – King Edward at this juncture placed Richard's advancement high in his priorities – and he made the most of his own eligibility on the noble marriage market to wed the richest available heiress, Anne Neville, as discussed below.

III

Edward's victories meant that in late spring 1471 Duke Richard had recovered his estates and resumed the career that had been suspended the previous September. He had then been constable and admiral of England and on 18 May 1472 he became also great chamberlain of England, in which he took great pride.[29] Although cancelled, this patent was copied into his cartulary, and the office was recovered in 1478.[30] He had also been appointed to the new office of approver and surveyor of the Duchy of Lancaster that Edward created for him: neither the duties nor emoluments are known of what perhaps was a sinecure.[31] Now he also became chief steward of the North Parts of the Duchy of Lancaster, and on 18 May 1472 chief forester north of the Trent.[32] He was 'ruler' of western Wales and the West March towards Scotland, and a great landholder in Cheshire and Lancashire. Doubtless he expected to build on these and make his control a reality, but this was to be fulfilled only regarding the Scottish march.

His appointments in the southern principality of Wales were for the duration of the minority of William Herbert II, earl of Pembroke. Since Pembroke was aged only sixteen, Richard could expect to exercise his key

[29] BL MS Cotton Julius BXII ff.125v–6.
[30] *CPR 1467–77*, pp. 262, 344; *1476–85*, p. 67; BL MS Cotton Julius ff.125–6.
[31] Somerville, *Lancaster*, vol. 1, p. 257.
[32] Ibid., vol. 1, p. 422; *CPR 1467–77*, p. 338; BL MS Cotton Julius BXII ff.118, 125–6.

offices for another five years and might not unreasonably have hoped to make his tenure more permanent. But Edward thought otherwise. In 21 August 1471 without proof of age, William Herbert II was appointed to the chief justiciarship and chamberlainship of South Wales and all others to which he had rights of inheritance.[33] On 11 September 1471 Clarence's client John Earl of Shrewsbury was appointed chief justice of North Wales for life.[34] Gloucester understandably had not yet decided between Wales and the North-West – indeed he hoped to dominate both – but King Edward located him in the West March and wanted other magnates to run the principality for Prince Edward.

Gloucester's patents were not cancelled by the king, but superseded. He had to accept the king's decision, but he did not agree. On 26 August 1471 he secured exemplifications (*inspeximuses*) of those patents making him chief justice of North and South Wales, chamberlain of South Wales, and steward of Cantref Mawr, Cardigan, and Carmarthen. His letters patent of appointment had been lost during the upheavals of the previous two years, so his attorney Morgan Kidwelly swore.[35] Richard thus secured documentary proof of his former appointments through exemplification, a route that did not require the king's consent and that could perhaps enable him to regain possession at some future juncture.

Once again Edward had advanced the coming of age of a royal kinsman, for Pembroke was brother-in-law to Queen Elizabeth and her brother Earl Rivers. He may also have earned the king's favour by good service in the recent campaign.[36] Presumably the Herberts tested their muscle and proved at this stage to have more influence with the king than his youngest brother. In 1479 Pembroke in turn was to be supplanted by the council of the prince of Wales: again, perhaps, the queen and her family prevailed. In 1471 apparently Gloucester gave way to the earl, yet he did not accept his loss of

[33] This warrant was executed on 29 August, *CPR 1467–77*, p. 275; C 81/836/3304. The date of the warrant is closer to the date of the king's decision.

[34] *CPR 1467–77*, p. 277. He was to be hands on, see ibid. 293. When Shrewsbury died in 1473, presumably it was Prince Edward who made a new appointment.

[35] *CPR 1467–77*, p. 275.

[36] A.F. Sutton, L. Visser-Fuchs, and H. Kleineke, 'The Children in the Care of Richard III: New References. A Lawsuit between Peter Courteys, Keeper of Richard III's Great Wardrobe, and Thomas Lynom, Solicitor of Richard III, 1495–1501', *Ricardian*, 24 (2014), p. 37.

Welsh offices as final. Apart from his exemplification, in 1472 or soon after, he had the cancelled patents for his great Welsh offices copied into his cartulary.[37] Not only did Edward deploy Richard elsewhere, in the North, from 1471, but when Shrewsbury died in 1473 he was to make Wales the sphere of operation of Prince Edward and his council.

Richard's other power base had been in Lancashire and Cheshire, where he had been granted the two Duchy of Lancaster honours of Clitheroe and Halton during the king's pleasure. Evidently King Edward expected his victory to generate enough new forfeitures to replace his grants of these two honours to Gloucester. Revoking his pleasure unfortunately generated no record, but it had happened by 19 June 1471, when Thomas Lord Stanley was appointed steward of Toddington, Rochdale, and Penwortham and master forester of Penhull, Rossendale, and Trowden.[38] Richard objected. He secured contradictory appointments on 4 July not just to these offices, but also as steward of Clitheroe and Halton, as master forester of Amounderness, Blackburnshire, Blesdale, Bowland, Myrescogh, Queensmore, and Wyresdale, and in Yorkshire of supervisor of the manors, lordship, and forest of Galtres.[39] That the superseded patents for Halton and Clitheroe were copied into his cartulary indicates, once again, that Richard had not abandoned hope of making his title good.[40] The offices meant that Richard did retain some presence in Lancashire, though not Liverpool and not in Cheshire, and the rule of these areas, but of course only for life. With Gloucester's backing and in the teeth of the king's opposition, Sir James Harrington retained Hornby until about 1474.[41] Richard's intrusion into the two palatinates had disturbed the regional hegemony of the Stanley family, whose dominance in the North-West was also threatened by the more than nominal grant of the earldom of Chester to Edward's baby son, the new prince of Wales. All existing appointments were resumed into Prince Edward's hands, including the key ones held by the Stanleys and their men. Thomas Lord Stanley, however, now steward of the royal

[37] Hicks, *Rivals*, p. 254; C 81/836/3.
[38] DL 37/40/13.
[39] DL 37/40/28.
[40] BL MS Cotton Julius BXII f.123.
[41] M.K. Jones, 'Richard III and the Stanleys', in *Richard III and the North*, ed. R.E. Horrox (Hull University, 1986), p. 38.

household, also had the king's ear. The resumption of royal grants in the palatinate of Chester was revoked.[42] Effectively the crown conceded the dominance of Cheshire and Lancashire to the Stanleys. Lord Stanley's brother Sir William, a royal knight of the body, was building a power base in North-East Wales: the marcher lordship of Chirk became part of it when Gloucester surrendered it to him in 1475.[43]

In 1471 therefore Richard retained little more than the marcher lordship of Chirk on the Welsh borders and the scattered Beaufort and Hungerford estates in south central and south-western England. Their title deeds were copied into his cartulary. He had to start again, almost from scratch. But this time he was not restricted to the leavings of others. Reading between the lines, Edward was prepared to assign to Richard almost all the new forfeitures that he had accrued by his victories in the Second War.[44] Most important potentially were the estates of Warwick the Kingmaker, his brother John Marquis Montagu, and their principal supporters from the North, West Midlands, Kent, and Calais. King Edward may also have expected to attaint such Lancastrian traitors of 1468–9 as Ralph Lord Sudeley, Sir Thomas Hungerford, and Sir Humphrey Neville of Brancepeth; Robin of Redesdale and other victors from the Edgecote campaign (1469); Lord Welles, Sir Thomas Dymmock, Sir Thomas Delalande, and other Lincolnshiremen who had rebelled in 1470; Lords Sudeley (again) and Wenlock from the battle of Tewkesbury (1471); and Nicholas Faunt and the Bastard of Fauconberg from Kent and Calais. Many lesser men like John Paston III might have been drawn into the net. Yet there were to be no attainders of the lesser men on the wrong side at Barnet, even though some were to be indicted in 1472.[45] There is no complete record of all those potentially at risk and no inquisitions were held to reveal precisely what they had held. On 4 December 1471 Richard was granted in tail male all the lands of the earl of Oxford, Robert Harleston, Dymmock, Delalande, and John Darcy. Only Oxford and Delalande were among the 13 ultimately

---

[42] *PROME*, vol. 14, pp. 98–9.

[43] M.K. Jones, 'Sir William Stanley of Holt: Politics and Family Allegiance in the Late Fifteenth Century', *Welsh History Review* 14 (1988), pp. 6, 10; *CPR 1476–85*, p. 505.

[44] The Welles inheritance was a notable exception.

[45] KB 9/41.

to be attainted in 1475.[46] The Lancastrian dukes and other earls had been attainted before, so there was little new land forfeited to give away, and some moreover, like the Percies and Dacres, had been restored in blood and to their inheritances. Warwick and Montagu escaped forfeiture perhaps because most of their lands were in right of their wives and therefore not forfeitable, but principally because their forfeiture did not suit the two royal dukes of Clarence and Gloucester to whom these lands now passed.[47]

Edward's casual reversal of permanent grants in favour of others, as though they had never been given away, annoyed Clarence enough for him to request a formal guarantee by letter patent that this would not be repeated,[48] a promise that the king failed to honour, notably when he resumed Tutbury in Staffordshire and the rest of Clarence's North Midlands estate in 1473–4.[49] It should also have aggrieved Gloucester, who had suffered at least as much already, and was indeed to do so again and again. Arbitrarily in 1475 Edward took back much of the De Vere lands in eastern England to give to the queen, leaving Richard only those in Essex.[50] Presumably he felt that Gloucester's half share of the Warwick inheritance sufficed. Gloucester always submitted – which does not mean that he did not resent his kingly brother's action, but that he expressed his displeasure less violently and futilely. Gloucester recognised that Edward had the power and probably knew that he needed the king's good will too much in other areas to hazard good relations with him now. Both dukes were therefore agreed that they wanted to hold Warwick's lands by inheritance, by inalienable right and not by royal grants that were too easy to revise or reverse. Both dukes had inherited the service of some retainers of Warwick and neither wanted these new followers to be attainted for treason. Some of those liable to forfeiture compounded with the king or with Gloucester instead. And Gloucester sought to maximise what he held independently

[46] *CPR 1467–77*, p. 297; *PROME*, vol. 14, pp. 298–306.

[47] J.R. Lander, 'Attainder and Forfeiture 1461–1509', in *Crown and Nobility* (Hodder & Stoughton, 1976), p. 139n.

[48] *CPR 1467–77*, p. 330.

[49] Hicks, *Clarence*, pp. 122–5.

[50] See below Oxford; *CPR 1467–77*, pp. 560, 566–7. His intervention in Gloucester's dispute with Northumberland and reduction in his salary as warden of the West March are later instances.

of royal grant, by agreement – rather a euphemism – with Margaret Lady Hungerford and Elizabeth Countess of Oxford. Achieving these contradictory objectives took time, especially as Gloucester was determined to wrest much more from Clarence than his brother was willing to concede.

IV

Bereft of Halton and Clitheroe, Gloucester needed to maximise the potential of what was available if he was to build up the great estate to which he had aspired. That doughty dowager Margaret Lady Hungerford had muddled the titles to her various lands and had driven a hard bargain with the duke in 1469. Richard was determined not to permit such legalistic obstruction in the 1470s. He regarded the 1469 indenture as merely a starting point from which to secure further gains. Entered in his cartulary are evidence that Gloucester himself or his agents undertook the further research in the Hungerford estates lacking hitherto to clarify what the Hungerford estate comprised and the respective titles, and hence to establish what he was entitled to by the forfeitures of the two Hungerfords Robert II, Lord Hungerford and Moleyns (executed 1464) and his son Sir Thomas (executed 1469). Probably it was Richard who solicited writs from chancery and then directed the new inquisitions post mortem that were held in 1473. These were the basis in 1474 for the more precise grant of 12 manors and three hundreds immediately and the reversion of a further 13 manors on Margaret's death. Richard might perhaps have hoped for more, but he faced competition from two directions: from the king's chamberlain William Lord Hastings and from the male heir Walter Hungerford, second son to Moleyns and next brother to Thomas. Each had their own plans for the estate after Lady Margaret's death. Sir Thomas Hungerford had left a baby daughter Mary, whose wardship and marriage was secured by Hastings for his own son Edward. Hastings' indenture of 1472 with Lady Margaret secured the devolution to the young couple of Margaret's own Botreaux estates on her death. Margaret persuaded Hastings that Walter Hungerford should inherit the Heytesbury estate. Gloucester did add significantly to his previous gains,[51] but he had no great use for them beyond

[51] Hicks, 'Piety and Lineage in the Wars of the Roses: The Hungerford Experience', in *Rivals*, pp. 176–81.

their revenues. He did not intend to live in central southern England or to rule that region himself. These properties were useful pawns in the exchanges he made for lands in the North that he really did desire.

What was available to Gloucester comprised first of all the estates of the earldom of Oxford in eastern England forfeited by John de Vere, the 13th earl, and those of Oxford's retainers that were granted to him and the heirs male of his body. Altogether the De Vere estates were worth about £1,800,[52] but there were two dowagers, Earl John's wife Countess Margaret Neville (Warwick's sister) who was entitled to naught and received nothing, and his mother Dowager-Countess Elizabeth (née Howard), who had dower, jointure, and a substantial inheritance of her own. Elizabeth's entitlements were legally incontestable. Legally Gloucester had to wait for her death for her holdings to devolve on him in lieu of her attainted sons, although there was a risk that she might prevent this devolution and divert her own inheritance elsewhere. It was already in the hands of her trustees, who would execute her wishes both before and after her death. Her son the 13th earl, who had survived the 1471 campaign, was not reconciled to the Yorkist regime, and now continued to resist King Edward with French help. He landed in 1473 at St Osyth in Essex and then in Cornwall at St Michael's Mount, where he was captured in 1474 and consigned to imprisonment at Calais for the rest of Edward IV's reign. Oxford's next brothers and heirs were also attainted. These circumstances enabled Gloucester to dispossess the dowager-countess.

It was normal during the Wars of the Roses to prevent the wives and mothers of traitors from providing surreptitious help to their men by placing them and their resources in the hands of trusted custodians. Countess Elizabeth was first placed in custody at Stratford nunnery and then in December 1472, when it became apparent that Oxford himself was fighting on, on that of Duke Richard. Elizabeth herself was not accused of treason. Such custody should have been protective. It was Richard's opportunity. With considerable brutality, he seized her and her chattels and bore her away to Sir Thomas Vaughan's house at Stepney, east of London, where he was living, and then to Walbrook beside St Paul's Cathedral in

[52] J.A. Ross, *John de Vere* (Boydell Press, 2011), p. 111.

the City. She was made to walk the considerable distance from Stepney to Walbrook. Leading roles in the seizure of chattels and menacing of feoffees were played by John Lord Howard, Sir John Pilkington, Sir James Tyrell, and William Tunstall, all councillors of the duke. Gloucester subjected her also to emotional blackmail. He threatened the feeble old lady with removal to the frozen North, which she feared would be the death of her. She did indeed die on the last days of December 1474 and was buried at the London Austin friary. Both the duke and her cousin John Lord Howard attended her funeral.[53]

The countess had indeed surrendered her lands to Gloucester. He in turn claimed to have compensated her with an annuity of 500 marks, which predictably she did not live to enjoy, the repayment of her debts (unknown), most probably masses for the souls of herself and her late husband at Queens' College Cambridge, and certain other benefits for herself and her younger children. Her lands had actually been settled on her feoffees, who were directed to release them to Gloucester and were threatened with the direst consequences if they did not. 'Fals preeste and ypocrite!' shouted Howard at her confessor Piers Baxter. The duke ordered William Paston to seal the deed or 'hit shuld cost hym that he loved best'. The deeds were sealed. Gloucester took seisin of the lands on 22 February 1473, while the countess was still alive, but before some feoffees had given way and ahead also of a suit in chancery to compel them to do so. Such conveyances should have conferred a more secure title on the duke than any royal grant. As late as 1495 Oxford, by then restored, feared these concessions could not be impugned: by then the premature seisin and the antedating of the releases, both highly irregular, were almost forgotten.[54] In 1473–4 Gloucester's victory was complete. He had secured possession of all the countess's own estates.

Of course, what Richard had done was extremely high-handed. His own councillor William Tunstall refused any part in it. Rather chivalrously,

[53] Hicks, 'The Last Days of Elizabeth, Countess of Oxford', in *Rivals*, pp. 297–335, at pp. 310, 313. For an alternative interpretation, see A.F. Sutton, 'Richard of Gloucester's Lands in East Anglia', in *Richard III and East Anglia: Magnates, Gilds and Learned Men*, ed. L. Visser-Fuchs (Richard III Society, 2010), pp. 5–12. *Pace* D. Hipshon, *Richard III* (Routledge, 2011), p. 95, the Tudor depositions are substantiated at key points by contemporary evidence.

[54] Hicks, 'Last Days', pp. 297–301, 308–9; BL MS Cotton Julius BXII ff. 227v–28.

he advised the countess that it was incompatible with Gloucester's honour as 'a knyght and a kyngis' brother to dispossess her. Tunstall therefore deduced, wrongly, that 'he woll do her no wrong'. Actually what befell the countess was 'the mynde of the duke', who warned William Paston in person of the ominous consequences if he resisted. That the countess had been coerced made the transactions illegal. Edward IV himself admitted this, but he did nothing about it. The purchaser of any of her properties might not be able to retain what Gloucester had seized, he warned.[55] Obviously Gloucester was aware of this too, but he was rightly confident that he could keep hold of the lands in his lifetime and hoped that his heirs could maintain hold of them thereafter. Oxford and his brothers seemed highly unlikely to be restored. It took two dynastic revolutions and the succession of Henry Tudor to change that. In the circumstances of 1472–4, this was the safest of gambles for Gloucester. There is an obvious parallel in the Warwick inheritance, where there had been rival claims to all four components – the Beauchamp, Despenser, Montagu, and Neville lands – that the kingmaker had ignored and that the two royal dukes of Clarence and Gloucester were also to disregard.[56] They felt no need to compromise or back down in the face of disapproval of independent observers like Crowland and committed retainers such as Tunstall. The two dukes were too powerful to be held to account. The De Vere lands to which Richard was definitely entitled by the attainder of the earl and his heirs were a valuable source of income. Richard never intended keeping all of them. He had them conveyed not to him personally, but to his feoffees, whom he could direct in his lifetime and by his last will at death.[57] Some he sold, some he kept for their revenues, but from 1476 onward the bulk of the countess's own lands he earmarked as endowments to his religious foundations for the benefit of his own soul.[58] He gave them away.

As no inquisitions had been held, Edward did not know precisely what he was granting, nor its value. He expected Richard to add these

[55] Hicks, 'Last Days', pp. 309, 311.

[56] Hicks, *Warwick*, pp. 16–17, 225, 226. The claimants were the earl of Westmorland; Lord Lisle, the Rooses, Lady Latimer; George Neville of Bergavenny; and St Cross Hospital, Winchester. Ibid., p. 226.

[57] North Yorkshire Record Office ZRC 17503.

[58] See below.

miscellaneous estates to his own. Some of those on the wrong side in 1471 like John Paston III seem to have escaped detection, and others were not pursued. Perhaps they submitted quickly or paid fines. Yet others were deemed traitors and forfeited their lands, which were granted to Duke Richard. Besides the Oxford lands, Richard had been granted those of other traitors – Sir Thomas Dymmock and Sir Thomas Delalaunde, both Lincolnshire rebels of 1470, and of Lewis FitzJohn, Robert Harleston, and John Darcy, all East Anglians and probably clients of the earl of Oxford.[59]

Almost none of these properties, however, ended up in Richard's hands. They were all located in eastern England, not the English region of most interest to him, and they were encumbered by such rival tenants as the Hungerford dowagers. Some properties had been settled on feoffees, others as jointure for the offenders' widows, and there were underage heirs that contemporaries expected to be restored in due course. Hence Richard proved very willing to settle with the families. John Darcy, who had been indicted of treason, attainted, and outlawed and whose property of Tolleshunt Darcy in Essex had been granted to Richard, 'suyd unto the high and myghty prynce the duc of Gloucestre', who was 'pleased to departe from the said lyvelode', which was therefore restored by parliament.[60] Margaret, the widow of Thomas Dymmock, had remarried to Robert Radcliffe of Tattershall in Lincolnshire, an esquire of the king's body and one of Richard's estate stewards.[61] Richard remitted his rights. In 1472 they were granted custody of the lands, of the body of her son Robert Dymmock, and of his marriage.[62] Alice, the widow of Robert Harleston, remarried to the East Anglian knight John Heveningham. Together they petitioned for her jointure 'to the right high and mighty prynce my right good and gracious lord the Duke of Gloucestre'. Although set at 100 marks (£66 13s. 4d.) in her marriage agreement, her jointure had not been formally settled, but her husband when ill had assigned towards her jointure lands worth only £44 held by his trustees that now had been granted to 'youre highnesse . . . And

[59] CPR 1467–77, p. 297.

[60] CPR 1467–77, p. 297; PROME, vol. 14, pp. 271–2.

[61] DL 29/639/10386. He was not a relation of Sir Richard Ratcliffe.

[62] CPR 1467–77, pp. 336, 337. The Dymmocks of Scrivelsby were hereditary king's champions: ahead of his own coronation in 1483 therefore Richard knighted his champion Robert Dymmock, W.C. Metcalfe, Book of Knights (Mitchell & Hughes, 1885), p. 8.

also in consideracion of the true and feithfull service by the seid Sir John
Heueningham to the kynge and youre good lordship done [he asked] of
your goode grace, charite and Rightwysnesse' to have the lands for her
life.[63] In 1468–9 the lands of Sir John Marny of Mountnessing in Essex had
been mortgaged as security for a fine of £800 and were not therefore forfeitable for his further (and fatal) treasons in 1471. His feoffees paid a further
fine by the hands of Duke Richard for security of tenure. King Edward
granted the custody and marriage of the heir Henry Marny to Gloucester,
who sold them.[64] The property of Sir John Manningham of Old Ford,
Middlesex, was confirmed in 1474 to Anthony Lord Grey of Ruthin, who
reached an agreement that permitted Sir John to be restored in blood in
1475.[65] At least some of the forfeited lands of Sir Thomas Delalaunde
passed to the queen and those of John FitzLewis via the duke and queen to
Cardinal Bourchier.[66]

The problem was that royal grants had proved not to bestow sufficiently
secure titles. Often enough, such grants consisted of forfeitures, whose title
and extent had not been researched beforehand, and were therefore inac-
curate. Such grants were liable to be revoked when the traitors were
restored in blood. Whatever the king gave was liable to be resumed by act
of parliament, if not immediately then at some date in the future to the loss
of one's heirs, and the king also, as we have seen, was inclined to cancel his
patents and to reshuffle his patronage whenever it suited him. Recipients of
royal grants had no certain defence against any of these threats. It appeared
better to compound with the heirs for a secure title in some properties
rather than to rely on the forfeiture of the whole. Probably Richard
extracted good prices for his compliance and the families mortgaged their
estates to those who provided the monies to buy them back.

This was by no means the limit of the duke's land transactions. He helped
Robert Bolling achieve the reversal of his attainder of 1461.[67] At various

[63] BL Add. Ch. 67545.

[64] *CPR 1467–77*, pp. 329, 344–5; *A Descriptive Catalogue of Ancient Deeds* (HMSO, 1890–
1915), vol. 2, A6298.

[65] *CPR 1467–77*, pp. 485, 570.

[66] *Rolls of Parliament*, 6 vols (London, 1783), vol. 6, p. 127, *CCR 1468–76* no. 1428; *CPR
1467–77*, pp. 543, 560, 567.

[67] Horrox, *Richard III*, p. 44n, quoting SC 8/29/1426.

times he bought property at Hooton Pagnell (twice) and (for £431) at
Carlton-in-Craven (both in Yorkshire), the advowson of Seaham in County
Durham (£1250), and the manor of South Wells at Romsey in Hampshire.[68]
The Seaham property was given to Coverham Abbey, lands in Sutton on
Derwent to Wilberfosse nunnery, and South Wells passed to St George's
Chapel Windsor.[69] None of these were permanent additions to his estate.
They merely passed through his hands. The stories behind Hutton Pagnell
and South Wells in Romsey have been explored. Apart from Robert
Dymmock and Henry Marny, Gloucester was also guardian at various
times to William Waldegrave, George Neville son of Marquis Montagu, and
John son of Thomas Salvan.[70] When George Neville died in 1483, still
underage, Gloucester seems to have provided a stately tomb for him in
Sheriff Hutton church and was expected to arrange suitable marriages for
his two youngest sisters and heiresses.[71] Duke Richard had his fingers in
many pies.

V

Just as valuable as the Oxford estate but evidently much more highly
valued by the duke were the lands of Warwick the Kingmaker in the
North.[72] From 1470 Richard was warden of the West Marches, a military
role traditionally supported by the wardens' own estates. In the case of the
Nevilles as wardens of the West March these had comprised the lordships
of Penrith in Cumberland and the more distant lordships of Middleham
and Sheriff Hutton in Yorkshire. Past experience had shown that the
barons resident on the border itself, like the Lords Dacre, lacked the
resources required in times of conflict. Richard never had possession of any

---

[68] Ross, 'Hooton Pagnell', pp. 47–54; Hicks, 'Richard III and Romsey', in *Rivals*, p. 317;
CCR 1476–95, nos 500, 602; CP 25(1)/201/165/21/1, 9, 7, 14, Bodleian Ms Dodsworth
83 f.22–v.

[69] *CPR 1476–85*, 375; Hicks, *Rivals*, pp. 270n, 320.

[70] *CPR 1467–77*, 338; *1476–85*, pp. 117, 123, 449; BL MS Cotton Julius BXII ff. 166–v.

[71] W.E. Hampton, *Memorials of the Wars of the Roses* (Richard III Society, 1979), pp. 230–1;
Stonor L & P, vol. 2, p. 158.

[72] The ensuing account of the Warwick inheritance dispute is based on Hicks, *Clarence*,
ch. 3; Hicks, *Anne Neville* (History Press, 2005), ch. 4; Hicks, *Rivals*, chs 15, 18; Hicks,
'Descent, Partition and Extinction: The "Warwick Inheritance" ', in *Rivals*, pp. 323–35;
Hicks, *The Family of Richard III* (Amberley Publishing, 2015), pp. 95–101; *PROME*, vol. 14,
pp. 209–10, 257–60.

of these Percy and Clifford estates. In 1472 Richard leased additionally two duchy manors of Esingwold and Hoby (Cumbria) for 40 years.[73] Given that Warwick had died a traitor, Edward IV intended attainting him and confiscating his estates, and treated them as forfeit in 1471 ahead of the requisite act of attainder. When resuming the wardenship in 1471, Richard was granted the three key Neville lordships almost at once. He took over Warwick's northern retinue and afforced it immediately with new recruits. Richard's brother George Duke of Clarence, as son-in-law to Warwick and husband of his elder daughter Isabel, had taken possession of all her inheritance immediately after the battle of Barnet in April 1471. Someone, most likely a member of Warwick's northern administration, pointed out to Gloucester that the three key lordships – Middleham, Penrith, and Sheriff Hutton – had been entailed in the male line on Warwick's Neville forebears and were not therefore eligible for inheritance by his daughters. On 29 June 1471 these three northern lordships were granted to the duke. Following further research of precisely what they comprised, a more detailed patent was issued on 14 July 1471.[74] These Neville lands may have been worth as much as two thousand pounds a year, but Richard lacked (and was always to lack) the Percy forfeitures that Warwick had held in Yorkshire and especially in Cumberland (the honour of Cockermouth and lordship of Egremont especially). Initially also he lacked the lordship of Barnard Castle in County Durham and miscellaneous properties in Yorkshire that Warwick had inherited via other ancestresses.

Warwick's northern estates were no more than half of Richard's eventual share of the Warwick inheritance. The rest – the Beauchamp, Despenser, and Montagu/Salisbury/Holland lands – were heritable by females, Warwick's two daughters Isabel and Anne. Given his reconciliation with King Edward and good service at Barnet, Clarence could not be denied Isabel's inheritance from the traitor Warwick. While Clarence can only be proved to have possession of a few properties in 1471–4, he inherited Warwick's estate administration and records and therefore probably did

[73] BL MS Cotton Julius BXII ff.119v–20.
[74] *CPR 1467–77*, 260, 266. Also included were any other lands entailed on Warwick in tail: probably no more than Clavering in Essex and a house in London.

secure all these estates.[75] He took custody also of Warwick's second daughter Anne Neville, the 15-year-old widow of the Lancastrian Edward Prince of Wales, heiress presumptive to half the inheritance. Her late husband had left her nothing. Clarence certainly intended thwarting her remarriage and inheritance and the consequent partitioning of what he already held. There were plenty of precedents for this dispossession of unmarried child heiresses.[76] Clarence was content that Countess Anne Beauchamp, Warwick's widow, remained in sanctuary (custody?) at Beaulieu Abbey and thus denied herself the largest share of Warwick's estates, the Beauchamp and Despenser lands, that were her own heritage. Legally her two daughters could inherit these lands only on her death, but they were always entitled to Warwick's much less valuable Montagu/Salisbury/Holland lands located mainly in central southern England.

Clarence's title was therefore legally unsound, as Gloucester recognised. He calculated that much of the estate could be prised away from Clarence by marrying Anne Neville, whom he had known as a child in the 1460s, and claiming her inheritance. This was just as legally unsound as what Clarence intended, since it was the Countess Anne who was the rightful possessor, but both dukes (and their brother the king) colluded to override her title in defiance of the law. The two dukes were agreed that inheritance offered a much more secure title than forfeiture and royal grants, which could be overridden on second thoughts by the king and parliament. Ricardians like to think this was a love-match, which it could have been, but it is Gloucester's efforts to secure Anne's lands that are documented. Heiresses were attractive primarily because of the lifelong wealth they brought. Of noble birth, royal descent, and indeed a royal widow, Anne had as noble a lineage as Richard himself and had been brought up expecting to be married for her wealth. She was not the virgin that was expected for kings and no doubt royal dukes. In due course she delivered Richard the heir that he required.

---

[75] Hicks, *Rivals*, p. 327; *Clarence*, p. 121. The Neville lands in the North were not included.
[76] E.g., Mary Bohun, the younger of the Bohun heiresses, whom Thomas of Woodstock wanted to keep single, and the three nieces of William Earl of Suffolk (d. 1450).

Crowland records an unlikely legend that Clarence disguised his widowed 15-year-old sister-in-law Anne Neville as a kitchen maid.[77] Late in 1471, Anne Neville transferred herself to Gloucester's custody and agreed to marry him. Only in this way could she secure her entitlements – only the royal duke of Gloucester could stand up to the royal duke of Clarence – and of course the status, wealth, and other advantages of becoming a royal duchess. That was the most that Gloucester could offer anyone. For Gloucester it was the means of securing half the main Warwick inheritance.[78] Offered the choice of her hand in marriage instead of her estates, Gloucester declined. He insisted on her estates.[79] The issue was taken to the king and the royal council at Sheen in February 1472, where the two dukes in person argued their cases 'with the greatest acuteness', so 'that all who stood around, even those learned in the law, marvelled at the profusion of the arguments which the princes produced for their own cases'.[80] The conclusions reached to circumvent the normal application of the law were certainly ingenious. The two dukes paid retaining fees to judges and serjeants at law: in short the best legal advice. Crowland and More report on the ability of the three royal brothers.[81]

This may be the first instance of what were to prove characteristics of Duke Richard: his application and respect for the best expert advice (notably doctors of law), his own capacity to assimilate and master the technicalities of whatever topic that currently engaged him, and his debating skills.

In conclusion, King Edward decreed that Richard and Anne could marry and the whole estate (tail male and tail general) would be partitioned equally between the dukes. While the estates had to be valued and divided equally, Clarence – as husband of the senior daughter – was to retain the core lands in the West Midlands and the South and Gloucester those in the North and Wales. The geography of the division suited them both. Clarence's feelings were salved to some extent by his creation as Earl of Warwick and Salisbury, by the transfer to him from Gloucester of the office

---

[77] *Crowland*, pp. 132–3.
[78] Hicks, *Anne Neville*, pp. 109–11.
[79] *Paston L & P*, vol. 1, p. 447.
[80] Ibid.; *Crowland*, pp. 132–3.
[81] *Crowland*, pp. 132–3; More, *Richard III*, p. 7.

of great chamberlain of England, and by the inclusion in the deal of the
Neville lands in the North that Richard probably wanted to exclude. It is
known that Gloucester disliked surrendering the great chamberlainship
and probably also resented that Clarence obtained both earldoms, since in
1477–8 he petitioned for and acquired both the great chamberlainship and
the earldom of Salisbury.[82]

Agreement in principle, however, was not the same as implementation.
The final partition was agreed only in July 1474. In the interim, Clarence
obstructed the final settlement, and possibly the transfer of some lands to
Gloucester.[83] He threatened to 'dele wyth' Gloucester who, never willing to
back down or compromise, 'was constantly preparing for war with the
Duke of Clarence'.[84] King Edward brought Clarence to heel by denying
him exemption from the 1473 act of resumption. All Clarence's other
estates were resumed and could only be recovered by the division of the
Warwick inheritance. The two acts of parliament that legalised the settlement were passed in 1475.

Gloucester took the lead in this process. It was he who determined on
his marriage to Anne Neville and who confronted his brother – a confron-
tation that terminated the loving reconciliation achieved by the Yorkist
ladies in 1471 and that was now believed to threaten domestic peace.
Clarence did not back down, but when King Edward took Gloucester's
side, it was impossible for Clarence to persist.

All three brothers were complicit in this deal that overrode inheritance
law and the rights of others in their interests. The key point, as Crowland
recognised,[85] was that the royal dukes secured the whole inheritance and
that Gloucester wrested so much of it from his brother Clarence. However
good the legal advice they secured and however skilful their arguments, this
conclusion was extremely difficult to legalise and even harder to excuse. To
hold by royal grant would label the two dukes as intruders, as enemies who
had destroyed the much admired rightful lords, and therefore would have

---

[82] *CPR 1476–85*, p. 67; see below.

[83] The surviving partition (DL 26/69) covers only Gloucester's share of the tail general
estate, but both Clarence's share and the uneven division of the tail male estate, still to be
legalised, had been agreed, see BL MS Cotton Julius BXII f.135–6v.

[84] Hicks, *Clarence*, p. 117.

[85] *Crowland*, pp. 132–3

denied to them the automatic reversion of the loyalty and committed service that had distinguished Warwick's northern Richmondshire and West Midlands retainers and that they valued highly.

Attainder therefore was unacceptable.[86] Under normal circumstances that would have enabled Warwick's widow Countess Anne Beauchamp, his nephew George Neville, duke of Bedford, and Warwick's daughters to assert their rights. The two dukes wanted to hold the estates by inheritance, but neither daughter had any hereditary rights to the Neville lands, which were entailed on the male heirs, while most of the rest of the estate properly belonged to the Countess Anne, in her own right as the Beauchamp and Despenser heiress and as dowager of the Neville and Salisbury lands. She was to survive until 1492. Gloucester knew the countess well, having resided with her in the 1460s, but he seems to have made no concessions to her. The countess repeatedly petitioned for her rights, to no effect, ultimately in or after 1472 to parliament, but Richard did have her petition copied into his cartulary.[87] He did offer her shelter when she 'fled to him as her chief refuge', Rous wrote, 'and he locked her up for the duration of his life'.[88] Her rights were overridden just as brutally as those of Elizabeth Countess of Oxford.

An additional complicating factor was that Richard's marriage to Anne Neville, whenever it was contracted, was within the prohibited degrees and was never legalised. A dispensation was secured for impediments in the third and fourth degrees on 22 April 1472,[89] which enabled a form of marriage to be celebrated, but it did not dispense the closer relationships. No dispensation is known in the second degree to cover Richard and Anne's position as brother- and sister-in-law twice over. Undoubtedly Gloucester knew this, but he kept it secret and gambled that he could keep hold of her estate and perhaps, in due course, get his marriage validated. It is an unfounded assumption that 'the impediments of consanguinity had already been

[86] Lander, *Crown and Nobility*, p. 139n.

[87] BL Cotton Julius BXIIf.314–v partly printed in J. Gairdner, *History of the Life and Reign of Richard the Third* (Cambridge University Press, 1898), p. 22n.

[88] Hanham, *Richard III*, p. 121. She 'might also have her case for mistreatment challenged' strangely argues Hipshon, *Richard III*, p. 95.

[89] P.D. Clarke, 'English Royal Marriages and the Papal Penitentiary in the Fifteenth Century', *EHR*, 120 (2005), p. 1023.

absolved',[90] since a proviso to one act in 1474 revealed that no such authority had yet been secured and made provision for future nullification of Gloucester's marriage (in contemporary parlance, divorce).[91] This proviso may have been added by Clarence (if Richard did not contract a valid marriage, why should Richard secure Anne's inheritance?) but, since it reserved a life-estate on Richard, to which the duke had no legal entitlement, conceivably it was at his instance. To pass on Anne Neville's half share to their heirs required him to push further for a better dispensation that, so far as is known, he did not attempt.[92] Others had an interest too: notably Cardinal Bourchier, archbishop of Canterbury, guardian of the next heir Richard Lord Latimer,[93] yet he surely cannot have condoned the duke living indefinitely in sin. Richard raised the stakes in June 1473, when he had his trusted servant Sir James Tyrell fetch the Countess Anne from Beaulieu to the North. It was rumoured then that the king had restored her to her inheritance, so that she could grant it to Gloucester.[94] Whatever the duke promised to his mother-in-law was not honoured. That all three princes and both daughters consented cannot mitigate this ruthless expedient that was so cruel to her.

The eventual settlement was in two parts. First of all, the countess was treated as legally dead, thus allowing her daughters to anticipate their inheritance.[95] Second, the Neville lands were diverted to the two dukes for as long as the Marquis Montagu had male heirs living.[96] This preserved the rights of the next male heirs who had committed no offences.[97]

The settlement flouted the almost sacred rules of inheritance: rules moreover that generally prevailed through all the upheavals of the Wars of the Roses. Means had been found to circumvent both land law and canon

---

[90] M. Barnfield, 'Diriment Impediments, Dispensations and Divorce: Richard III and Matrimony', *Ricardian*, 17 (2007), p. 92.

[91] *PROME*, 14, p. 210.

[92] Hanham, *Richard III*, p. 121.

[93] The cardinal was a doctor of canon law. See below p. 366.

[94] Hicks, *Clarence*, p. 117.

[95] Should either die childless, the other would accrue the whole.

[96] Montagu's sole male heir was his son George Duke of Bedford (b. 1465). Should George die, it would devolve on his Neville cousin Richard Lord Latimer (b. 1469).

[97] These were descendants of the younger sons of Ralph Earl of Westmorland (d. 1425) by his second marriage to Joan Beaufort: Richard Neville, Lord Latimer, and George Neville of Abergavenny (d. 1492).

law. That Crowland, Rous, and other powerless onlookers were shocked, mattered not to two dukes who had obtained their objectives and had the power to fend off any challengers. The king's award also ignored other claims to these estates: of Anne Beauchamp's sisters to lands of the Beauchamp trust; of George Neville of Abergavenny, who was entitled to half the Despenser estate; and the Winchester hospital of St Cross, from which Warwick had wrested Cardinal Beaufort's endowment.[98] Nevertheless neither duke was satisfied. Clarence obviously lost the most, but Gloucester too had a long list of defects that he sought to remedy in 1477–8 and others that he was still pursuing into the 1480s.[99] As early as 1475 he was exchanging Bushey and Ware in Hertfordshire without the prior consent from Clarence that their agreement prescribed.[100] He cannot have wanted the two clauses allowing for the nullification of his own marriage and the succession to the Neville lands after George Duke of Bedford's death. The king had managed to provide nobly for both brothers at no cost to himself.

As the senior co-heir, Clarence plumped for the core lands of the Beauchamp earldom of Warwick in the West Midlands and was also awarded the earldom of Salisbury south of the Thames. The two dukes divided the miscellaneous properties in the East Midlands, which Richard did not value greatly; he was to dispose of the Hertfordshire properties. Gloucester also secured the Warwick chamberlainship of the exchequer, which he bestowed on his most trusted retainer Sir John Pilkington in 1477 and following his death in 1479 on Sir James Tyrell.[101] The other principal component of Gloucester's share consisted of Warwick's lordships in Wales. Certainly Clarence held the great lordship of Glamorgan with its capital at Cardiff in 1471 and probably therefore also the marcher lordships of Abergavenny and Elfael (Pain's Castle). They were transferred to Gloucester as Anne Neville's husband, but presumably only in July 1474, when the

---

[98] Hicks, *Rivals*, pp. 324, 343–4, 360–2.

[99] See below.

[100] *PROME*, vol. 14, pp. 260–2; *CPR 1467–77*, p. 507.

[101] A.B. Steel, *Receipt of the Exchequer 1377–1485* (Cambridge University Press, 1954), pp. 4, 425; E 159/254, recorda Easter 17 Edw. IV, m.3.Tyrell appointed Thomas Salle as his deputy, SP 46/139 (Black Book of the Exchequer) ff.46b, 167.

partition was agreed,[102] or later. Gloucester exchanged Elfael in 1477–8 for Ogmore, a Duchy of Lancaster enclave in Glamorgan.[103] He also held Chirk in north-east Wales.

Had he retained the Herbert offices in the principality in West Wales beyond 1471, Glamorgan might have been preferred as Gloucester's power base and Cardiff as his capital. Now, however, there was a prince of Wales, whose affairs were managed by a council, of which both royal dukes were members, that sat initially at Westminster. In 1473, prompted by the Commons, King Edward held an assembly of marcher lords at Shrewsbury, where he sought to establish order on the marches by regulating how the marcher lords managed their lordships. Henceforth marcher lords were committed by indenture to toeing the royal line. Also in 1473 the prince of Wales relocated to Ludlow in Shropshire, initially temporarily but then permanently, and his council based there became the devolved central government. Richard probably remained a councillor, albeit absentee, but it was the queen's brother Earl Rivers and her younger son Lord Richard Grey who were on the spot and managed the prince's affairs.[104] A key turning point came as early as 1475 when Richard chose to exchange his outlying lordship of Chirk with Sir William Stanley, who was building up his power in North Wales, in return for the forfeited Clifford lordship of Skipton in Craven in Yorkshire. Richard's notion of the boundaries of his northern hegemony were defined at the same time by his exchange with the king of the town of Chesterfield (Derbyshire), close to Sheffield and in most people's definition of the North, for the town of Scarborough on the North Yorkshire coast, and much of the lordship of Cottingham in South Yorkshire.[105]

Richard Duke of Gloucester did not lose interest in his Welsh estates – they were too large and valuable for that – but he seldom visited them. He was further west in 1479, at Swansea in the marcher lordship of Gower,[106] and indeed may have coveted it. He had copied into his cartulary a copy of

[102] BL MS Cotton Julius BXII f.204–5v.

[103] Hicks, *Clarence*, p. 151; DL 37/46/15.

[104] Hicks, *Edward V*, pp. 106–18.

[105] *CPR 1467–77*, pp. 507, 549: BL MS Cotton Julius BXII ff.246–52; *PROME*, vol. 14, pp. 211, 260–2.

[106] Pugh, *Glamorgan County History* (University of Wales Press), p. 201.

the Gower lawsuit of 1397 that had unfairly deprived his duchess's great-grandfather Thomas II, Earl of Warwick, of the lordship.[107] Richard's Welsh properties were also a valuable source of manpower and of patronage.

The division of the Warwick inheritance was implemented by two acts of parliament in 1474–5, which overrode the rights of the Countess Anne and Bedford.[108] Such acts could be reversed, and they were, by Henry VII in 1487, when it was Warwick's widow who surrendered her inheritance to the crown. Each title had other weaknesses.

As regards the tail general estate, Countess Anne survived until 1492 and outlived both her daughter Anne Duchess of Gloucester and her grandson Edward of Middleham. Had the 1474 act applied or indeed the normal rules of inheritance, the whole Beauchamp, Despenser, and Montagu/Salisbury/Holland estate should have devolved next on the issue of Isabel Duchess of Clarence, specifically Edward Earl of Warwick (d. 1499). Should the duchesses have died childless or had Richard's marriage been declared null, the 1474 act entitled both dukes to their estates for life.[109] Although the marriage of Anne and Richard was never validated, this defect seems not to have been publicly known and Richard counted on it being overlooked. Nullity, a divorce in 15th-century parlance, would have bastardised Gloucester's son and rendered him incapable of inheritance. It seems very careless of Richard not to block this loophole by securing another dispensation, but what he needed went beyond what popes normally granted and probably he realised that an application would proclaim that his marriage was invalid. Richard therefore did not seek a second dispensation. If he did not draw attention to it, he gambled that nobody would notice: rightly, for nobody did.

The 1475 act guaranteed the Neville lands to Richard for life, but to his line only for so long as the Marquis Montagu had male issue living. The marquis had one son, George Neville, titular Duke of Bedford and very

---

[107] BL MS Cotton Julius BXII f.181v; G.A. Holmes, *The Estates of the Higher Nobility in Fourteenth-Century England* (Cambridge University Press, 1957), p. 39; Hicks, 'Richard III as Duke of Gloucester', in *Rivals*, p. 236; Hicks, *Anne Neville*, p. 163. From 1478 Gower was held by the king's second son Richard and was controlled by the queen's family who also ruled Wales.

[108] *PROME*, vol. 14, pp. 209–10, 257–60.

[109] *PROME*, vol. 14, p. 210; see also Hicks, *Anne Neville*.

well connected, who was underage. To ensure possession by Richard's heirs, it was necessary to keep George alive, to marry him off, and for him to father a son(s) of his own. George also needed to be prevented from asserting his rights and recovering his inheritance, which was difficult to ensure since he had other expectations both actual (from his mother) and potential.[110] This was highly unsatisfactory for Gloucester, who had most of the Neville lands and hence most to lose. Evidently he expected to overcome the risks and may have calculated that, should the worst befall, he could persuade the king to adjust the partition of other Warwick estates in his favour. The first remedial action that Gloucester took was to remove young George Neville from parliament, which was achieved by having him degraded from the peerage in 1478. Next, in 1480, Richard managed to secure George's wardship, as heir to his late mother Isabel Marchioness Montagu (d. 1476).[111] This transgressed the convention that next beneficiaries should not have the guardianship of heirs. Gloucester never resolved his conundrum. Should George die, his heir was his cousin Richard Lord Latimer, also underage, who could only be induced to surrender his rights at his majority in 1490, if then. So it seems Gloucester thought. He secured quitclaims of doubtful value from Latimer's grandmother Elizabeth Lady Latimer and his aunt Katherine Radcliffe (previously Dudley),[112] who had no legal title to the estate. He did not manage to prise Latimer's custody from the boy's great-uncle Cardinal Bourchier, who did have Latimer's best interests in mind. Richard was still in this unfortunate limbo on 4 May 1483 when George Neville died and Richard's rights over the Neville lands were reduced to his own life.[113] This second gamble therefore failed.

VI

By 1475, therefore, Richard had a great estate that extended into almost every county. Too great. King Edward decided to take back a large proportion of the eastern counties estates, restricting Richard only to some

---

[110] Had he survived until 1484, he would have become earl of Worcester.

[111] Hicks, 'Richard III as Duke of Gloucester', pp. 273–4; *CPR 1476–85*, p. 192.

[112] Hicks, *Rivals*, p. 274; BL MS Cotton Julius BXII ff.291v–3v. Of course neither could ever be male heir.

[113] Hicks, *Rivals*, p. 275. In 1477 the rival Neville claimant accepted Anne's title, ibid., p. 373.

(perhaps a quarter) that were located in Essex by patent of 21 August 1475. His opportunity was provided by a petition from Gloucester that sought to clarify and maximise what he had been given in 1471. Because Gloucester needed a new and accurate patent as a title deed that stood up in law, King Edward had taken the opportunity to retrieve Earl's Colne and other properties. Presented thereafter with the fair copy petition, before signing Edward struck out Hedingham, Castle Hedingham, Lavenham, and Stansted Mountfichet on Essex, Sutton and Tydd St Mary (Lincolnshire) late of Sir Thomas Delalande, and the stewardship of the forest of Essex with the right to appoint a lieutenant and yeoman foresters.[114] Much of the rest was added to the queen's dower.[115] Edward felt able to take back and to reassign what he had given at will, as he had done before, without needing to resort to an act of resumption that revoked his patronage and that any parliament could be counted on to pass.[116] Richard bowed to the veiled threat, wisely recognising this as the price for the continued favour of his brother the king. Although Edward IV ultimately had the whip hand, he seldom exercised it, and acquiesced in the self-aggrandisement of his brother, of which he was only vaguely aware. Gone in particular were Hedingham Castle and Earl's Colne, the principal De Vere residences, that Edward retained for himself. Gone also therefore, if Richard had any such pretensions, the establishment of the duke as the (or a) leading magnate in East Anglia and the eastern counties. Certainly Richard spent much of the early 1470s in London and Essex and was wholly absent from Middleham in 1473–4. It may be therefore that Richard's focus on the North should be dated rather later than usually supposed, from 1475. The reallocation of the De Vere estates indicates that Edward had reached the limit of his generosity to his youngest brother. Richard did want and did indeed secure more lands in the North from the king, but he had to give up other properties in exchange and was unable to use Hedingham as part of the credit. Richard secured further favours from the king, but step by

<hr/>

[114] *CPR 1467–77*, 560; C 81/1511/1. The countess of Oxford's lands had not been forfeited and were therefore additional to whatever the king had bestowed on Gloucester.

[115] Sutton, 'Richard of Gloucester's Lands in East Anglia', p. 3.

[116] This new facet to royal coercion is explained in Hicks 'Attainder, Resumption and Coercion 1461–1529', in *Rivals*, pp. 71–7.

step and always at a price. The lands he wanted were obtained by exchange for properties that he held and that the king valued.[117]

The French campaign in 1475 forced Richard to reflect. His subcontract with Edmund Paston reveals him considering the possibility of early death, capture, and ransom.[118] The enfeoffment of his Oxford and Middleham estates gave him some control of them and their revenues after his death as prescribed by his last will, which no longer exist but that it would have been folly not to make. To encourage the nobility to hazard their lives abroad, King Edward had promised to honour such trusts and wills that safeguarded their heirs and estates from royal wardship. Richard had no legitimate offspring until 1476, but he was surely trying for one. If he had made his last will, as he probably did before embarking for France in 1475, it was to be superseded by subsequent will(s) and is now lost. Quite how he planned to use his new-found control after death at this early date is therefore uncertain.

[117] E.g., *CPR 1467–77*, pp. 505, 507, 549; *1476–85*, p. 90.
[118] *Paston L & P*, vol. 1, p. 638.

Chapter Six

LORD OF THE NORTH 1471–83

I

It was during Edward IV's Second Reign that Richard Duke of Gloucester made himself (in Paul Murray Kendall's words) 'Lord of the North' and the true successor to Warwick the Kingmaker in that region of England. Edward had not planned this, but rather the division of the greatest northern offices and estates between several magnates, of whom Gloucester was just the most important. Richard was not scheduled to become Lord of the North, but merely one leading lord among several. His wardenship of the West March was decidedly inferior to the East and Middle Marches held by Henry Percy, 4th Earl of Northumberland. Gloucester's standing and authority fell well short of a regional hegemony. Characteristically the duke declined to take 'no' for an answer – to acquiesce to the restrictions that Edward had in mind. Gloucester laboured to extend his possessions, his affinity, and his power nevertheless. That he came ultimately to dominate the whole region was largely because of his own vigorous initiatives. He exploited the king's favour, accruing more benefits step by step than Edward had initially intended. Ultimately he superseded or subsumed the spheres of power of the other northern magnates. In 1480 he became lieutenant of the North.

This story commenced in 1470, when Gloucester supplanted the traitor Warwick as Warden of the West March, which carried with it command of Carlisle and the borders. Next in 1471 he was granted the three Neville lordships of Middleham, Sheriff Hutton (Yorkshire), and Penrith (Cumberland) that had supplied the resources in men and manpower in the North to earlier generations of Neville lords: to Ralph Earl of Westmorland (d. 1425), to his son Richard Earl of Salisbury (executed 1460), and to Salisbury's son Richard Earl of Warwick and Salisbury (the Kingmaker, killed at the battle of Barnet in 1471). In Cumbria Gloucester held only the modest lordship of Penrith, worth £197, and its modern castle. Already approver and surveyor general of the whole Duchy of Lancaster in 1469, he became chief steward of the north parts of the duchy in 1471, and chief forester of England north of Trent in 1472.

Impressive though these offices were, Gloucester's power did not at first match that of Warwick. His offices were not underpinned as Warwick's had been by the enormous Percy and Clifford estates that Warwick had held,[1] nor were they complemented by the Percy holdings in Northumberland enjoyed by Warwick's brother Marquis Montagu as warden of the east and middle marches, and he had not succeeded to the Percy and Roos forfeitures in Yorkshire granted to the two Neville brothers. Briefly Warwick had been lieutenant of all the marches.[2] Nor at first did Gloucester command the royal castle of Bewcastle, nor the shrievalty of Cumberland. Indeed Edward had restored Henry Percy to the extensive Percy estates, earldom of Northumberland, and wardenship of the eastern and middle marches, had granted the Clifford castles to Sir William and Sir John Parr,[3] and had restored Humphrey Lord Dacre of the North to his Gilsland estates along the western border. Even within Gloucester's domain, the king had appointed Sir William Parr as deputy constable of Carlisle: a key post that was funded by deductions from Gloucester's salary.[4] Parr's command was independent of the duke, it has been suggested, and therefore a limitation to Gloucester's authority. It has been argued furthermore that Edward curtailed his brother by excluding any rights to high justice as warden that

[1] *CPR 1461–7*, pp. 186, 434–5.
[2] Hicks, *Warwick*, p. 221.
[3] *CPR 1467–77*, p. 264.
[4] Booth, 'Richard, Duke of Gloucester and the West March towards Scotland, 1470–1483', *Northern History*, 36 (2000), p. 238.

Warwick had enjoyed and by resuming the members appendant to Penrith.
Actually these suppositions are unlikely. The grant of the wardenship specifically included all rights exercised by Warwick or any predecessor. Parr had
served Warwick, was cousin-in-law to the duchess of Gloucester, was feed as
lieutenant of Carlisle from Gloucester's lordship of Middleham,[5] and served
under Duke Richard's military command. His brothers were Gloucester's
retainers. Moreover, Penrith was part of the Warwick inheritance, inherited
rather than a royal grant and not therefore Edward's to dismember, and was
allotted to Gloucester in the partition of the Warwick inheritance. Although
Penrith was merely listed in Edward IV's patent of 20 February 1475, the
act of parliament and its exemplification, yet 'youre moste humble subiecte
Richard Duc of Glocestre' certainly intended the inclusion of all its members
among the appurtenances, knights' fees, advowsons of churches and abbeys,
hospitals, chapels, and other religious houses, chases, warrens, franchises
and liberties, privileges, fairs and markets, hundreds, and all other conceivable emoluments whatsoever that he specified.[6]

The two principal Neville lordships were in Yorkshire, centred on
Middleham and Sheriff Hutton. Middleham town (now a village) lay south
of Richmond in Richmondshire in the north-west corner of Yorkshire that
bounded on County Durham to the north, Westmorland to the west, and
Lancashire to the south west. Sheriff Hutton was just north of York.
Middleham had many appurtenant estates, together yielding £1,200 a
year, but Sheriff Hutton was worth considerably less. Each featured
12th-century castles. Rebuilt on a new site to modern standards from 1382,
Sheriff Hutton Castle was a rectangle with lofty corner towers described in
the 1530s as 'very magnificent' by John Leland, who 'saw no house in the
north so much like the palace of a prince'.[7] At Middleham the courtyard
between the keep and curtain was narrow and pokey. On top of the keep,

[5] A.J. Pollard, *Worlds of Richard III* (Tempus Publishing, 2001), p. 148 n.29; A.F. Sutton,
'The Admiralty and Constableship of England in the Later Fifteenth Century: The
Operation and Development of these Offices, 1462–85, under Richard, Duke of Gloucester
and King of England', in *Courts of Chivalry and Admiralty*, eds Musson and Ramsay (Boydell
Press, 2018), p. 202.

[6] Ibid., pp. 233–4, 236; *CPR 1467–77*, p. 483, 486–7; *PROME*, vol. 14, pp. 257–9; C
81/1508/46.

[7] *John Leland's Itinerary*, ed. J. Chandler (Sutton, 1993), p. 550.

Warwick had erected an extra floor that provided the huge airy space and large windows that were fashionable in the 15th century and that may be seen today in the great towers at Raglan, Tattersall, and Warkworth castles. Middleham Castle was smaller than nearby Richmond, which the duke secured in 1478, and than Barnard Castle on the River Tees in County Durham, which was allotted to him in 1474 and may indeed have passed to him as early as 1472. Barnard Castle had been an outlying possession of the Beauchamp earls of Warwick that Richard Neville Earl of Salisbury had leased. Probably it had not been updated to modern 15th-century standards. This may be why Richard stayed on several occasions seven miles away at the castle of Raby in County Durham,[8] the principal seat of the senior house of Neville, of Ralph Earl of Westmorland (d. 1484) and his heir Gloucester's retainer Ralph Lord Neville. With three wards, Barnard was considerably larger than the duke's other castles and had therefore more palatial potential. At Barnard Richard is known to have engaged in extensive building works, both domestic and religious, and may possibly have designated it in the longer term as his principal seat. Apart from Barnard and Gainford Richard held no other lands in the Durham palatinate, but he did intervene in Tynemouth Priory north of the River Tyne in 1478.[9]

Warwick had numerous other Yorkshire properties, such as Bawtry, Cottingham on the outskirts of Hull, and Kimberworth, all allocated to Richard in 1474. To these the duke added Scarborough on the north-east coast (1474), Helmsley north of Sheriff Hutton (1478), Skipton-in-Craven (1475) in the far west, and Richmond in 1478. It has been speculated that Richard sometimes resided at Pontefract in South Yorkshire in his capacity as chief steward of the North Parts of the Duchy of Lancaster, but there seems no concrete evidence of this after the early 1470s.[10]

Richard's estates were concentrated in Yorkshire, especially the north-west, only crept over the Tees into south Durham, and in Cumbria consisted of little more than Penrith, but he strove to add depth to his holdings and to

[8] Pollard, *NE England*, p. 361.

[9] *History of Northumberland*, ed. E. Bateson and others, vol. 8 (A. Reid, 1904), p. 105.

[10] Horrox, *Richard III*, pp. 43–5. For documents dated there, see http://www.christies.com/lotfinder/ZoomImage.aspx?image=http://www.christies.com/lotfinderimages/d56242/d5624294&IntObjectID=5624294&lid=1

extend his power further. West of the Pennines he researched what else belonged to the crown, of which Edward may well have been unaware, requested these unconsidered trifles and accrued them all in several tranches. He had started on 20 June 1472 with a bundle of the king's miscellaneous rights in Cumberland: the subsidies and duties, except for woolfells (fleeces), wool and hides, in Cumberland and Carlisle, the royal sturgeon in the county, rights of pasture of oxen in Brademeadow, various other pastures, the fishery of the River Eden, all demesne lands in Carlisle, the sheriff's net in the fishery of Eden, and various enclosures in the forest of Inglewood, all for a rent of £46 17s. 8d. On 18 February 1475 he was appointed sheriff of Cumberland for life at a farm (rent) of £100 a year, and on 20 July following he expanded this grant to include all the issues of the sheriff's farm, the demesne lands of Carlisle Castle, the £40 fee farm of the city of Carlisle, the king's fisheries of the River Eden and elsewhere in the county, and 'all the other rents and farms rendered to the king within the county' for £100 a year, except the enclosures in Inglewood which he rented separately. Copies in his cartulary of an inquisition and a 14th-century perambulation of the forest suggest he had further aspirations hereabouts.[11] And finally in 1483 he mopped up the remnant of the king's rights when he was granted all the king's rights in Cumberland and the wardenship in heredity. When grants fell short of what he desired, he did not give up, returning repeatedly to the same topic, and in this case ultimately secured everything that the king had to bestow. This step-by-step approach can be paralleled elsewhere – in his relations with the earl of Northumberland, with the Neville heirs George and Richard, and with Thomas Lord Scrope of Masham.[12]

Richard dabbled repeatedly in the land market, acquiring Hooton Pagnell twice,[13] buying and alienating the advowsons of Seaham in Durham and Simonburn in Northumberland.[14] He was guardian to several wards,

[11] CFR 1471–85 (HMSO, 1949–63), no. 116; CPR 1467–77, pp. 485, 556; BL MS Cotton Julius BXII ff.211–17v, 222v–4; M.A. Hicks, 'Richard Duke of Gloucester and the North', in Richard III and the North, ed. R.E. Horrox (Hull University, 1986), p. 15.

[12] L.C. Attreed, 'An Indenture between Richard Duke of Gloucester and the Scrope Family of Masham, and Upsall', Speculum, 58 (1983), p. 1025.

[13] J. A. Ross, 'Richard Duke of Gloucester and the Purchase and Sale of Hooton Pagnell', pp. 47–50. See also E 159/262 recorda Hillary 1 Henry VII m. 23.

[14] C. Sharp, The Rising in the North: The 1569 Rebellion (Shotton, 1975), p. 369; Durham Priory Registrum IV ff.174v–5, 185v; CPR 1476–85, p. 260.

choosing to remain custodian and to marry off some, like George Neville
and his sisters, transferring others.[15] In Yorkshire he was constable and
steward of the honour of Knaresborough. In 1472, when Warwick's
brother Archbishop Neville was imprisoned and his temporalities were
seized by the crown, Gloucester was appointed steward of the archiepis-
copal estate at Ripon for as long as it remained in the king's hands.[16] Apart
from being the king's brother, he was first cousin of the archbishop, who
was uncle to his duchess. In November 1473 he was interceding with the
king for Archbishop Neville's release.[17] Perhaps it was for this reason that
the prior of Durham twice asked him to mediate for them with the archbishop. In return, he (and his duchess) expected a share of the priory livings
for their clients, not always successfully. Duchess Anne became a sister of
the priory in 1475.[18] Probably Gloucester was steward of other church
estates. In 1477 the tenants of the bishop of Durham were sworn to him
and placed under his military command.[19] And in Northumberland, where
he was otherwise unrepresented, he became dominant at Tynemouth, in
the extreme south-east of the county, retained the sheriff John Widdrington,
and in 1482 promoted many of the leading gentry to banneret.[20]

II

There was much to occupy Richard's energies and time at court and in the
eastern counties in the early 1470s, yet he was active also in the North and

[15] C 81/1638/73; *A Descriptive Catalogue of Ancient Deeds*, vol. 2, A6298.

[16] *CPR 1467–77*, p. 346.

[17] *Paston L & P*, vol. 1, p. 472. In 1475 the archbishop appointed Gloucester's chamberlain Sir John Pilkington steward of Sherburn in Elmet (Yorkshire), *Testamenta Eboracensia*, vol.
3, ed. J. Raine (Surtees Society, 1864), p. 239n. His trusted officer Edmund Chaderton
transferred to Gloucester's service, KB 9/41; see below p. 268.

[18] *Historia Dunelmensis Scriptores Tres*, ed. J. Raine (Surtees Society, 1839), pp. 356–9;
Pollard, *Princes*, p. 238.

[19] Durham University Library, Durham Halmote Court Records roll 1476–7; see also
A.J. Pollard, 'St Cuthbert and the Hog: Richard III and the County Palatine of Durham,
1471–85', in *Kings and Nobles in the Later Middle Ages*, eds R.A. Griffiths and J.W. Sherborne
(A. Sutton, 1986), pp. 116–17. A new bishop William Dudley had succeeded the more
independent Lawrence Bothe on his promotion to the archbishopric of York.

[20] Jones and Walker, 'Private Indentures', *Camden Miscellany*, 32 (1994), p. 178; *History of
Northumberland*, ed. E. Bateson, vol. 3, pp. 105–6; M.A. Hicks, 'Dynastic Change and
Northern Society: The Fourth Earl of Northumberland, 1470–89', in *Rivals* (1991), pp.
393–4.

may indeed already have regarded this as his primary focus. Most of his offices were inevitably discharged by deputies. Unfortunately only one major record remains of his administration, the sole set of accounts for the lordship of Middleham for 1473–4, a year when the duke did not visit Middleham.[21] It can be compared with an earlier set for Warwick's tenure in 1465–6 and fragments of an even earlier set of about 1458 for Warwick's father Salisbury.[22] The accounts reveal that most of the revenues were used to pay retainers, annuitants, and officers, especially of the families of Conyers and Metcalfe.[23] There was considerable overlap from one lord to the next: not unexpectedly, since fees and appointments were made for life, but surprising since Warwick's Richmondshire affinity had been the core of his army at Edgecote (1469), rebellions in 1470 and 1471,[24] and on the opposite side to Gloucester in the Second War. Admittedly some of Warwick's men had disappeared from the list: by death, like Robert Lord Ogle in 1469, Thomas Colt in 1467, Thomas Mountford in 1465, and Sir Henry Neville (killed at the battle of Edgecote 1469), but others who continued to serve Gloucester and were remunerated in other ways, like Sir James Harrington, Miles Metcalf, and Thomas Middleton. Ralph Lord Greystoke, first feed by Warwick's father Salisbury in 1447, remained councillor to Gloucester in 1475–6.[25] The nature of the reciprocal contracts, service in return for an annual fee and good lordship, scarcely altered. There was continuity in language too: whereas the indentures of Ralph Earl of Westmorland (d. 1425) were in French, those of his son Richard Earl of Salisbury (d. 1460), his grandson Richard Earl of Warwick (killed in battle in 1471), and Gloucester were in English, and the phraseology was only slightly tweaked across the generations.[26]

[21] DL 29/648/10485. I am indebted to Prof. Pollard for this insight.

[22] SC 6/1085/20; Pollard, 'Northern Retainers of Richard Nevill', *Northern History*, 11, pp. 66–8.

[23] Coles, 'Lordship of Middleham' (1961), appendix B.

[24] *Death and Dissent* (Boydell & Brewer, 1999), pp. 98–9; 'Chronicle of the Rebellion in Lincolnshire, 1470', ed. J.G. Nichols, *Camden Miscellany*, vol. 1 (1847), p. 12; A.J. Pollard, 'Lord FitzHugh's Rising in 1470', *BIHR*, 52 (1979), pp. 170–5.

[25] Jones and Walker, 'Private Indentures', pp. 157–8; *York City Chamberlains' Account Rolls 1396–1500*, ed. R.B. Dobson (Surtees Society, 1980), p. 152.

[26] Jones and Walker, 'Private Indentures', passim.

That Gloucester continued to employ these men and to pay their fees indicates that the duke wanted to take over the Richmond connection rather than to repress it. Its potential value to him rated more highly than any short-term treason against the king on behalf of an earl and a cause that had passed away. Although the Neville connection had been battered by its Pyrrhic victory at Edgecote in 1469, the uprisings of 1470 and 1471 and the bloody defeat at Barnet, it remained formidable and a highly desirable asset that Gloucester wished to revive. Three of these men – Sir John Conyers, Sir James Danby, and Sir James Strangways – joined the duke for quarter sessions at Bedale on 6 October 1472. Sir John Conyers of Hornby (Yorkshire) was father of John Conyers, the most probable candidate to have been Robin of Redesdale, the nominal leader of Warwick's rebels in 1469. Gloucester kept him on as steward of Middleham: indeed he increased his fee.[27] Those feed included two of Conyers' sons, his brother, three brothers-in-law, and a son-in-law. Pollard wondered whether it was Conyers himself who selected Gloucester's feed men.[28] There were good topographical and political reasons for the lord of Middleham to recruit a Burgh of Brough, Markenfield of Markenfield, and a Pudsey of Pudsey. Once Richard had married Warwick's daughter Anne Neville and had indeed fathered a son, Warwick's grandson, the duke could pose convincingly as Warwick's heir and was indeed accepted as such. Henceforth he could draw on the strong and traditional loyalty to the house of Neville of Warwick's erstwhile retainers. Many of the ministers, reeves and foresters, were minor Richmondshire gentry, the Metcalfes of Nappa being especially prominent.[29]

Professor Pollard has documented the tightly knit aristocratic network of Richmondshire that served the lords of Middleham. 'Sheer numbers and collective wealth' made for social cohesion. The local elite, comprising the barons Fauconberg, FitzHugh, Latimer, Scrope of Bolton and Scrope of Masham and leading gentry, were all feudal tenants of the honour of Richmond. They had intermarried over many generations. 'There was a

---

[27] This is based on the lists in Coles, 'Middleham', appendix B; KB 9/330/33.
[28] A.J. Pollard, 'The Richmondshire Community of Gentry during the Wars of the Roses', in *Patronage, Pedigree and Power in Later Medieval England*, ed. C.D. Ross (Sutton, 1979), p. 54.
[29] Metcalfe remains a common local surname.

marked tendency for the children of Richmondshire gentry to marry the children of other Richmondshire gentry'. They sponsored one another's offspring at the baptismal font, attended one another's marriages and funerals, interacted as feoffees and executors and witnessed one another's deeds, subscribed to the same guilds and hunted together, managed the estates for local monasteries and other lords and for the crown and Duchy of Lancaster, officiated as justices of the peace but more commonly as the officers of wapentakes, congregated at county election time and campaigned together against the Scots. Their families had served the lords of Middleham – the Nevilles of Raby, then the junior house of Neville, and now its heir, the duke of Gloucester – over the generations as estate officers and on the Scottish borders. They had constituted 'the engine room of Warwick's political power' and were to be the same for Richard.[30] All were under his sway and acknowledged his leadership.

Although less well recorded, much the same may apply to the gentry around Sheriff Hutton. What happened in Richmondshire was probably replicated around the less well-documented castles and lordships of Sheriff Hutton and Penrith and perhaps around Barnard Castle too. Pollard cites one-time Neville servants perhaps feed at Sheriff Hutton around this time.[31] Three founded chantries in the parish church. Dr Horrox has pieced together something of the Sheriff Hutton affinity that built upon the Withams of Cornborough, Gowers of Stittenham, Leptons of Terrington, and Hardgills of Lilling within a three-mile radius. Thomas Gower, Ralph Bigod of Settrington, and Ralph Bulmer of Bulmer were all knighted on campaign by Gloucester in 1482.[32]

The regional baronage and local gentry operated in the orbit of the lord-ships that King Edward had granted to the duke. Yet Richard was much more than an interloper because he had married Anne Neville, daughter and heiress of Warwick and earlier Nevilles. As heir to the junior house of Neville and specifically Warwick by marriage, Gloucester appropriated

[30] Pollard, 'Richmondshire Community', esp. pp. 42, 47, 49–50; Pollard, 'The Middleham Connection: Richard III and Richmondshire 1471–85', in *Worlds of Richard III* (Tempus Publishing, 2001), pp. 65–74; Pollard, *NE England*, chs 7, 8; C 219/17/2/1/18, 25, 27; 2/2/33.

[31] Pollard, *NE England*, pp. 323–5.

[32] R.E. Horrox, 'Richard III and the East Riding', in *Richard III and the North*, p. 3f8f.

these connections to himself. To the Nevilles – and therefore to Anne and
Richard – they were diffused by a tradition of dependence and loyalty to
the paramount family that imparted to the duke the committed service that
was truly exceptional. In 1485 Sir Richard Ratcliffe and William Catesby
reminded him that Anne's heritage was the origin and foundation of his
connection.[33]

Following the clearing up operation in Kent in May 1471 and the grant
of the Neville lands in June, Richard had set off for the North and began at
once to recruit new retainers. The indentures that he contracted with them
repeated word for word the terminology used by his predecessor Warwick.
William Burgh of Brough esquire had been retained in turn by Clarence
and Warwick's brother John when earl of Northumberland as successive
lords of Prudhoe before contracting on 4 October 1471 at Middleham with
the 'right high and mighty prince' for life 'with and towards the said duc
ayeinst alle persons' except the king. Because the contract was primarily
military, directed against the Scots, it specified precisely the division of
winnings of war and ransoms between the duke, Burgh, and the men that
Burgh brought with him. 'Wele and convenably horsed and harnessed
[William] shalbe redie to ride, come and goo, with, toward and for the said
duc aswel in tyme of peas as of werre at alle tymes and into alle places
uppon resonable warnyng.' Expenses were to be refunded and Burgh was
awarded an annual fee of 10 marks ($£6$ 13s.4d.) from the vaccary (cow
farm) at Sleightholme in the lordship of Middleham.[34] Gloucester had
retained Thomas Metcalfe on 20 August previously (10 marks), recruited
William Clonsett esquire (10 marks) on 4 October (the same day as Burgh),
two days later renewed Brian Metcalfe's fee ($£2$), four days later recruited
Robert Clifford (10 marks), on 26 October added Roland Pudsay ($£5$) and
in November both Thomas Tunstall (50 marks) and Thomas Talbot (10
marks), on 11 December Sir Thomas Markenfield ($£10$), on 12 August
Richard Conyers junior (10 marks), and on 31 January 1472 William
Conyers as bowbearer ($£2$). The dates recorded may record Richard's

[33] *Crowland*, pp. 174–5. The Catesbys were traditional Beauchamp retainers, but the
Ratcliffes of Derwentwater (Richard's father Thomas and brother Edward) were Percy
retainers.
[34] Jones and Walker, 'Private Indentures', p. 176n.

visits to the lordship. The variations in the sums indicate how attractive the duke found the service of each man and what he needed to pay to secure it. Note the numbers of the Conyers family and of Metcalfes who feature.[35]

The standard contract used departs only slightly from those of the two Richard Nevilles, Salisbury and Warwick.[36] Two later contracts, with Henry Denton (of Cardew, Cumberland) in 1473 and John Savile in 1474, are slightly more succinct and watertight. Allegiance was reserved to 'the kynges highness' (Edward IV). The principal retainers were to come accompanied and their response to a summons was specified to be without delay. Denton's fee of £5 was payable from the Forest of Inglewood, Savile's 10 marks (£6 13s. 4d.) from the lordship of Sheriff Hutton, and the £5 of Thomas Hutton of Hutton John (Cumb.) from Penrith.[37] Although unspecified, these subretinues could be substantial, although the esquire Walter Strickland's 290 archers and billmen in 1450 must always have been exceptional.[38] Other contracts recorded in the Middleham accounts and from other lordships that do not survive as originals almost certainly took the same form. What was expected in practice is shown by the frequent peremptory summons of the wardens of the other marches among the *Plumpton Correspondence*.[39] In the spring of 1473 Duke Richard granted annuities to the esquires John Redmayn (£5), Thomas Otter (£5), Richard Knaresborough (6 marks/£4), and William Clonsett (10 marks/£6 13s.4d.) and on 3 August to Thomas Blakeston (10 marks/£6 13s.4d.), on 3 September to Sir Roger Conyers (10 marks/£6 13s.4d.), and on 4 October to Robert Wyclif esquire (10 marks/£6 13s.4d.).[40] John Redmayn was kinsman and servant to the duke's councillor Sir William Redmayn (d. 1482) and the Otters, Warwick's

[35] Coles, 'Middleham', appendix B.

[36] Jones and Walker, 'Private Indentures', pp. 116–7, 120,–1, 126–8, 132, 138–40, 142–3, 147.

[37] Ibid. p. 177; C.H. Hunter Blair, 'Two Letters Patent from Hutton John near Penrith, Cumberland', *Archaeologia Aeliana*, 4th series, 39 (1961), pl. 35; http://savilehousehold. co.uk/index.php/the-saviles/..

[38] M.A. Hicks, *Bastard Feudalism* (Longman, 1995), 49; see also Jones and Walker, 'Private Indentures', pp. 158–9.

[39] E.g., *The Plumpton Letters and Papers*, ed. J. Kirby, Camden 5th series, 8 (1996), nos 33, 35.

[40] Coles, 'Middleham', appendix B. Again these may indicate Richard's presence: no fees were granted in 1473–4, when the accounts show Richard not to have been present.

men, were acting for Gloucester in 1483.[41] The surviving Middleham account shows that altogether Richard had granted 18 fees worth £140 by Michaelmas 1474.[42] Doubtless others were added in the following decade. The duke issued letters patent to recipients that were sufficient warrant for his ministers to make the actual payments.[43]

Unfortunately relatively few of the estate officers and annuitants of the duke attached to other estates and none of his household men are documented, but some insight into his principal retainers, who can be characterised as the lesser nobility and greater gentry of the North, and of the sway that Richard established in the North, is provided by the 31 knights that he dubbed and the 37 bannerets he created on the Scottish campaigns of 1481–2. Knighthood was one of the greatest and most recognisable rewards that Gloucester could bestow. It is striking how few of those heads of local families who had been feed by the duke from Middleham had been knights rather than esquires. To be an esquire was an honourable estate that recognised both wealth and gentility and was all that many of the MPs (knights of the shire), sheriffs, bearers of arms (armigerous), and coats of arms ever attained. Knighthood was also an obligation that brought financial burdens and expectations that 15th-century men were anxious to avoid. Commonly those eligible paid the fines instead. To be selected by the king for the order of the Garter or the Bath, on such notable occasions as a coronation or a royal wedding, was such a great honour that it had to be accepted. Among Gloucester's men very few had succumbed. To be knighted on the field of battle was also a distinction that had to be accepted: at Tewkesbury by Sir John Huddleston, Sir John Pilkington, Sir James Tyrell, and Sir William Parr. That so few northern gentry were knights in 1480 was because of the long peace with Scotland, the absence of northerners from the winning side in the Second War of the Roses, and the absence of any fighting in the Picquigny campaign in France. The northern gentry do appear to have welcomed their traditional role against the Scots when war resumed in 1480. The heads of many leading families turned out and many of them

[41] *York Chamberlains Accounts*, p. 164; *Testamenta Eboracensia*, vol. 3, p. 280; Hicks, *Warwick*, p. 286; E 405/71 m.1.

[42] Hicks, 'Dynastic Change', p. 369.

[43] Blair, 'Hutton John', pl. 35.

accepted the honour of knighthood on campaign from their commanders, the two wardens of the marches Gloucester and Northumberland. Both the duke and the earl knighted those men who campaigned with them in the eastern marches: retainers from west of the Pennines generally stayed to defend the West March and therefore went unknighted. The queen's brother Anthony Earl Rivers, Thomas Lord Stanley and Alexander Duke of Albany, the other principal commanders, also dubbed knights from Wales, north-western England, and Scotland respectively.[44] On his 1481 campaign Gloucester made knights of the Yorkshiremen William Beckwith of Clint, Ralph Bigod of Settrington, Ralph Bulmer of Bulmer, John Constable of Halsham, Richard Conyers of South Cowton, James Danby (d. 1497) of Leeds, William Darcy of Temple Hurst, John FitzRandolf of Spennythorne, Thomas Fitzwilliam of Aldwark, William Fitzwilliam of Spotborough, Thomas Malliverer of Allerton Mauleverer, John Melton of Kilham, Robert Middleton, John Neville of Thornton Bridge, John Savile of Thornhill (d. 1482), James Strangways of West Harlsey, Robert Waterton of Waterton, Thomas Wortley of Wortley, the Lancastrian Charles Pilkington (d. 1485) and the Durham man Ralph Bowes of Streatlam. In 1482 he knighted the Cumbrian Thomas Broughton, William Eure of Witton (Durham), Robert Harrington of Farleton (Lancashire), and the Yorkshiremen William Gascoigne of Gawkthorpe, Hugh Hastings of Fenwick and Lionel Percy. FitzRandolf, Harrington, Middleton, and Strangways were sons of men feed at Middleham in the 1450s and/or the 1460s; Malliverer was son of Sir John Malliverer, the right-hand man to the marquis Montagu.[45] The Yorkshiremen were leavened by a mere handful from Cumbria, County Durham, and Lancashire.

Relatively few of these are known from other sources to be Gloucester's men: Conyers and Savile were Gloucester's feed men, while Charles Pilkington was brother of his late chamberlain and Robert Harrington was son of his trusted retainer Sir James Harrington. There is independent evidence that most of those dubbed by Northumberland were indeed Percy

[44] W.C. Metcalfe, *Book of Knights* (Mitchell & Hughes, 1885), pp. 6–7. The following analysis is based on Hicks, 'Dynastic Change', pp. 390–4.

[45] Coles, 'Middleham', appx B; Pollard, 'The Northern Retainers', pp. 67–8; *Plumpton L & P*, pp. 43–4.

retainers.[46] Gloucester, moreover, and indeed Gloucester alone, as a high and mighty prince and the king's lieutenant, could elevate knights into bannerets. Bannerets bore banners rather than mere pennons and had knights under their command. Presumably the presence of bannerets in the army despatched to Scotland in 1482 interposed some intermediate structure between individual companies, numerous and tiny, and the three battles commanded by the senior peers. Gloucester knighted or made bannerets of several others who were not his retainers: several Scottish followers of the duke of Albany, his friend Francis Lord Lovell and John the future Lord Grey of Wilton, Edward Wydeville, brother of the queen, her cousin Richard Haute, Walter Herbert, brother of the earl of Huntingdon, Edward, son of Lord Stanley, and the treasurer of the king's household John Elrington. Nine men who had been knighted by Northumberland in 1481 were subsequently raised to banneret by the duke in 1482, who thereby created a direct connection and obligation with himself. Whereas Northumberland identified those retainers whom he deemed worthy of knighthood, he had to accept which of them Gloucester then chose to promote to bannerets. Some younger men like Richard Ratcliffe became knights while their fathers, perhaps too old to campaign, remained mere esquires. One sudden consequence was that the North was filled with knights and that these knights bulk disproportionately numerous among Richard's followers as king. Presuming £10 per fee, it is not wholly inconceivable that all those northerners knighted by Gloucester were retained directly as his officers, served in his household, or were in receipt of fees, total £310 or £680 if bannerets are included. The score of knights that Gloucester dubbed is better understood as a list of those in his circle or under his sway. The list of bannerets that he elevated as including beside some of his knights, others retained by the king and other peers, others with their own spheres of influence, yet all under his command in the campaigns of 1481-2. What this source cannot reveal is whether any served on this campaign who were already knights or bannerets.

[46] The Percy affinity is listed in M.A. Hicks, 'The Career of Henry Percy, Fourth Earl of Northumberland (c.1448–89), with special reference to his retinue', Southampton University MA thesis (1971), appendices II, III, which is based on printed sources only; Hicks, *Rivals*, ch. 21, which uses accounts of the Cockermouth, Northumberland, Petworth, and Yorkshire estates.

Richard enjoyed the service not just of those who served him directly or who indented with him in peace and war, but also of their own dependants, who could be numerous. Their local standing, authority, and spheres of influence extended his own, beyond his own estates and indeed into other shires. Many of them probably – and the gentry of Richmondshire and the West March certainly – had long traditions as warriors on the Scottish borders, of military exploits and profits of war, which an aggressive commander like Gloucester promised to provide into the future.

Gloucester also had a good deal of patronage and preferment to offer the gentry and lesser nobility of the North. His chamberlain Pilkington presided over his household, the membership of which unfortunately is unknown, Conyers over the lordship of Middleham, and a host of lesser men managed the manors and parks of his estates. The fees payable to stewards, constables, and master foresters, annuities of 10 marks, and 2d a day (60s. 8d.) for reeves and parkers were attractive supplementary incomes to knights, esquires, and gentlemen.[47] The posts themselves conferred local authority on recipients whose service to the duke and his livery carried status and standing. Moreover, the duke held many offices, of the crown, Duchy of Lancaster, archbishop, and other lords, that were exercised by his deputies, who enjoyed thereby part of his fees, the authority over lesser officers and tenants who were attendant on them, and local standing. From 1471 Sir James Harrington was his deputy as master forester of Bowland and steward of Pontefract. Pilkington deputised for him as steward of Bradford. In 1472 Pilkington and Thomas Everingham were assigned payments due to the duke from the exchequer.[48] Some sense of what this devolved authority could mean is revealed by the sway that Sir William Plumpton had been exercising over lesser men.[49] Horrox opines that the chief stewardship of the North Parts of the Duchy of Lancaster enabled Gloucester to appoint to the lesser posts and to grant leases on the northern honours of this vast estate.[50] The duke also solicited advancement for his men, notably clerics, from Durham

[47] Coles, 'Middleham', appx. B.

[48] Somerville, *Lancaster*, vol. 1, pp. 508, 522, 514.; E 405/85 rot.1.

[49] Hicks, *English Political Culture in the Fifteenth Century* (Routledge, 2002), pp. 155–6.

[50] Horrox, *Richard III*, pp. 44–5. *Pace* Horrox, it is not proven that 'The duke's influence is clear', ibid., p. 45.

Cathedral priory.[51] Richard had some influence moreover in appointments to local government and could offer access to royal patronage.

Day-to-day authority in the West Marches was exercised by the principal landholder on the border, Richard's lieutenant Humphrey Lord Dacre of Gilsland, whose income may well have been doubled. Although Sir William Parr, the principal landholder in Westmorland, owed his appointment at Carlisle to the king, he nevertheless deferred to the duke.[52] The elevation in 1478 of Richard Bell, prior of Durham, to the bishopric of Carlisle gave Richard another important ally in the West March. He backed Bishop Bell, albeit unsuccessfully, in his attempt to hold onto the priory in commendam.[53] In County Durham the principal rulers under the bishop were the Nevilles of Raby – Ralph Earl of Westmorland and his nephew Ralph Lord Neville[54] – but they set aside their disagreements with the junior house of Neville that Gloucester represented,[55] bowed to him, and indeed entered his service. Gloucester's councillors met at Raby Castle,[56] seven miles from his own Barnard Castle. In 1476 Gloucester even arbitrated a dispute between Westmorland's tenants.[57] Sir George Lumley, heir to the other palatinate peer and sheriff of the county, was a retainer.[58]

Moreover, other northern peers also entered his service: the Duchess Anne's cousin Richard Lord FitzHugh of Ravensworth in Richmondshire, John Lord Scrope of Bolton, and Ralph Lord Greystoke. Gloucester contracted with Elizabeth Dowager-Lady Scrope of Masham for the wardship of her son Thomas, whom he married in 1477 to Elizabeth, a daughter of the marquis Montagu and sister of his ward George Neville.[59] In 1483 Thomas was on good enough terms with the duke 'to cause my lord of

[51] E.g., Pollard, *Princes*, p. 238.

[52] See above p. 93.

[53] H. Summerson, *Medieval Carlisle*, vol. 2 (Cumberland & Westmorland Antiquarian & Archaeological Society, 1993), p. 463; R.B. Dobson, 'Richard Bell, Prior of Durham (1464–78) and Bishop of Carlisle (1478–95)', in *Church and Society in Northern England* (Continuum, 1996), pp. 154–6.

[54] *Historia Dunelmensis Scriptores Tres*, pp. 261–9.

[55] CP 25(1)/281/164/32.

[56] Pollard, *Princes*, p. 232.

[57] Christies sale catalogue, sale 5960, lot 47.

[58] Hicks, 'Dynastic Change', p. 373.

[59] Hicks, *Rivals*, p. 376; GEC, vol. 11, p. 570; *York City Chamberlains' Rolls*, p. 152; Attreed, 'An Indenture', pp. 1018–25.

Gloucestre ... to be contributorie to your charge'.[60] Among those Gloucester knighted in 1481were the barons FitzHugh and Scrope of Masham and Robert Greystoke, Lord Greystoke's heir.[61]

Gloucester provided the leadership against the Scots that his retainers expected. It offered them employment, promotion, potentially renown, profit, and good lordship. He used appointments and leases of the Duchy of Lancaster to patronise such trusted retainers as the Pilkingtons, Huddlestons, and Ralph Ashton.[62] Almost all the nobility and gentry of northern England served under his command in the Scottish war of 1480–3, either directly in his retinue or indirectly under other peers and captains. They were paid, had plenty of opportunity to pillage, and probably ransomed those Scots that they captured. Duke Richard chose to reside principally in the North, within striking distance of the Scottish borders, although day-to-day oversight was delegated to Dacre as lieutenant of the marches and Parr at Carlisle. In peacetime, moreover, he maintained some state, principally at Middleham and Sheriff Hutton or perhaps Barnard Castle. Northerners served in his household as estate officers or drew annuities. Gloucester thus fulfilled traditional expectations. Indeed he was fortunate that his wife Anne had brought him not just a hereditary estate, but the hereditary connection discussed below.

III

In 1471 Richard was not yet the king's lieutenant in the North, nor was he designated as Lord of the North by his brother the king. Edward's plans for the region assigned the West March to Richard and the East and Middle Marches to Henry Percy, earl of Northumberland, who had been restored in 1470 as counterweight to the Nevilles and who recovered the great Percy estates in Northumberland, where they had no rivals, in Cumberland and in Yorkshire (Topcliffe near Thirsk, Seamer near Scarborough, Spofford, Leconfield and Wressle in the East Riding). The Percies and Nevilles normally rated as equals and rivals: Edward considered there was room for

---

[60] This related to his sisters-in-law on the death of his wife's brother George Neville, *Stonor L & P*, vol. 2, p. 158.

[61] Hicks, 'Dynastic Change', p. 392.

[62] Horrox, *Richard III*, pp. 44–5.

both. The Percy and Neville connections were each somewhat shattered in 1470–1: the Percies by defeats in 1461–4 and a decade of forfeiture and the Nevilles by the defeat and deaths of Warwick and his brother Montagu in 1471. Surviving retainers, even those who had been attainted like the Northumbrians Gawen Lampleugh and Robert Thomlinson, were re-employed.[63] Yet it was not enough for Gloucester and Northumberland peacefully to resume the leadership of their family retainers. Both had rebuilding to undertake and both therefore set about the rapid reconstruction of their family retinues. Northumberland's recruitment in Cumberland, Northumberland, and the East Riding is actually the better documented. In 1470 Northumberland retained Christopher Curwen of Workington and John Pennington of Muncaster (Cumberland) and by Michaelmas he had burdened his Northumberland estates with fees: 27 per cent of his revenues were spent on extraordinary fees alone.[64] Beyond Richard's estates there were local gentry who sought his lordship. He offered more employment and potentially access to royal patronage than can be documented. The duke's influence spread into the East Riding of Yorkshire 'where his direct authority (as defined by land and office) was negligible'.[65]

Gloucester moved aggressively beyond his own territory into areas that the earl of Northumberland regarded as his preserve. Apparently he sought from the king and other lords the transfer of offices held by the earl. Furthermore he interrupted the earl and his servants in the execution of these offices and he drew into his service Percy retainers 'of fee, clothing, or promise'. On 18 May 1472 the duke had replaced the earl as chief justice of the forests north of the Trent.[66] Whether other offices changed hands later is not known: none of the crown or the Duchy of Lancaster are known to have passed from the earl to the duke, but possibly the stewardship of the archbishop's estate at Ripon fell into this category. Archbishop Neville, though disgraced, found support from the duke.

[63] Ibid., p. 369.

[64] Ibid., p. 368; J.M.W. Bean, *The Estates of the Percy Family 1416–1537* (Oxford University Press, 1958), p. 130. The Curwen indenture is again wrongly dated to 1469 in Jones and Walker, 'Private Indentures', no. 151.

[65] Horrox, 'Richard III and the East Riding', p. 89.

[66] Hicks, 'Dynastic Change', p. 370. The transcript in Jones and Walker, 'Private Indentures', p. 178, misdates the council act to 1474.

One retainer whom Gloucester had poached is known: John Widdrington, a member of the Northumberland family of Widdrington of Widdrington, who was actually the earl's master forester at Alnwick and was shortly to be his undersheriff of Northumberland. To recruit the earl's right-hand man in the government of his home county was aggressive indeed. It upset the natural order and equilibrium whereby the two wardens and the leading magnates 'ruled' their own home areas, coexisting and cooperating with each other. Richard was again a disruptive intruder. Private war loomed. The expansion of the duke's authority into what the earl surely regarded as his private domain threatened conflict, potentially violent. Certainly the earl complained to the king about the duke's encroachments. The matter was discussed at the great council held at Nottingham, one of a series of assemblies in the Midlands and Welsh marches that also treated the feud of Gloucester and Clarence and disorders in Wales. The great council upheld the separation and autonomy of the two noble spheres of influence. The 'appointment' of the king and 'the lords of his council' on 13 May 1473 decreed – and Gloucester had to accept – that the duke should seek no more offices held by the earl and his men, nor retain any of his men, Widdrington being the single exception.[67] The duke had suffered a humiliating check, but it appears that he was allowed to keep what he had already won.

The great council's award should have halted Richard's advance and relegated him once again to merely one of the northern nobility. Instead Richard made it the foundation for extending his supremacy and regional sway. Whatever the duke had promised, this ruling failed to resolve the dispute. Here can be perceived the duke observed elsewhere, the Duke Richard who, for instance, contradicted the king's peace policy with Scotland. Gloucester was not the man to back away from conflict or to compromise. He did not bow to restrictions even from the king, but worked away to achieve his objectives, perhaps by another route. The gains that he had secured became the basis on which he built. Most likely Gloucester continued to encroach on Northumberland's country (or sphere of influence) and to erode his authority, securing more offices and attracting more Percy retainers into his service. Very probably it was the retainers themselves who solicited Gloucester's good lordship rather than the duke himself who sought their service. Northumberland did not choose to fight back or could not resist the duke and next year, on 28 July 1474, he conceded Gloucester's superiority and submitted to his lordship. He 'promits and graunts unto the said duc to be his faithfull servaunt, the said duc being his good and faithful lorde, and the said Erle to do service unto the said duc at all tymes lawfull and convenient whan he therunto by the said duc shal be lawfully required', except against the king, queen, prince, and other royal issue. In return, Richard promised once more not to seek the earl's offices, to interrupt his performance of them, or to recruit his men as set out in the council's decree.[68] The second greatest magnate in the North forgave the hereditary rivalries with Richard's Neville forebears that had been sealed with the blood of his four predecessors and of his three uncles. Moreover, this agreement ranged Northumberland on Gloucester's side should the latter's feud with his brother Clarence turn violent.

It was a massive concession by the earl and protected his authority within his home counties: Richard's communication with the men of Northumberland and other Percy men would henceforth be via the earl. Whereas King Edward had intended the duke and earl to be equals, partners in the marches, and to offer different channels to his royal favour, Gloucester now had the rule, direct and indirect, over the whole North. Northumberland, Westmorland, Dacre, FitzHugh, Greystoke, Lumley, and the two lords Scrope all came to be his men. They acknowledged his political and social superiority, regarded service to him and knighthood by him as both an honour and a distinction, and like Lady Scrope of Masham offered him the service and faithful attendance of their sons and their servants and tenants.[69] Bishop Dudley of Durham and successive archbishops also deferred to him.

Each warden nevertheless reigned supreme in his own marches until, in 1480, Gloucester was appointed the king's lieutenant-general against the

---

[68] Ibid., p. 370; quotations from Jones and Walker, 'Private Indentures', p. 178.
[69] Pollard, *NE England*, p. 329.

Scots and thus became commander-in-chief in the east as well as the west.[70]
Rather limited evidence indicates that the earl kept the rule of the shire
that bore his name (Northumberland) and the East Riding, and that
Gloucester dominated Cumberland, the North Riding, and County
Durham. The earl retained the constableship of the two royal castles of
Bamburgh and Dunstanburgh, adding in 1483 the portership of Bamburgh
Castle for his cousin Sir Henry Percy, and dominated North Durham – the
bishopric liberties of Holy Island and Norhamshire north of the Tyne –
where his retainer Roger Heron became constable and steward.[71] In
Yorkshire the earl remained as constable and steward of the honour of
Knaresborough.[72] From 1476, when Lawrence Bothe was translated from
Durham to York, his successor Bishop Dudley proved more deferential to
Gloucester. The duke was added to the commission of the peace in County
Durham along with his retainers Thomas and Miles Metcalf and John
Vavasour. Another retainer Ralph Bowes was sheriff of the palatinate,
Thomas Middleton chief steward, and Richard Pigot steward of the North
Yorkshire liberty of Allertonshire. The duke received command of the
bishop's tenants.[73] Richard settled disputes within the palatinate as though
he was its lord.[74]

Northumberland yielded ground most obviously in Cumberland where
he was the greatest landholder, but Gloucester ruled. The annuitants that
Northumberland had inherited had almost all died by 1479 and very few
were replaced. Similarly in Westmorland, where Gloucester had no land
and few retainers, any influence operated via the sheriff-for-life Sir William
Parr. The duke and earl shared the leadership of Yorkshire, where sheriffs,
JPs, and county MPs seem to emanate from both connections. They and
their men served together on royal commissions of all kinds – of oyer and
terminer, the peace, array, and sewers (de wallis et fossatis) – and collaborated
to resolve the troublesome issue of fishgarths. In 1474–5 they went into

[70] CPR 1476–85, p. 205.

[71] Hicks, 'Dynastic Change', pp. 371–2n; Thirty-Fifth Report of the Deputy Keeper of the
Public Record Office (HMSO, 1874), pp. 100, 141; Somerville, Lancaster, vol. 1, p. 538;
CPR 1467–77, p. 258; 1476–85, p. 346.

[72] Somerville, Lancaster, vol. 1, pp. 524–5.

[73] Durham Halmote court roll 1476–7; see also 35th Report, pp. 102, 136, 138, 142.

[74] See below.

business together to exploit silver mines at Alston (Durham), Blanchland (Northumberland), and Keswick (Cumberland) and a copper mine at Richmond (Yorkshire). They arbitrated jointly several disputes involving their retainers.[75] And they seem to have cooperated amicably in the Scottish campaigns of 1481–2, when Gloucester as lieutenant-general led campaigns in Northumberland's eastern marches with the earl under his command, and promoted Percy retainers from knights to bannerets. Thus, Percy men became the duke's men. From this the earl had his reward. He emerged with the plum appointment of captain of the fortress of Berwick,[76] second only to the captaincy of Calais.

How delicate was their relationship is shown by the famous letter to Sir William Plumpton of Plumpton from his man of business in London, Godfrey Greene. Plumpton was a veteran Percy retainer who fell within the earl of Northumberland's sphere of influence in the Harrogate area, and was steward of his lordship of Spofforth. He should therefore have looked to the patronage of the earl and deferred to him. Increasingly, however, Plumpton was eclipsed by the earl's much younger brother-in-law William Gascoigne of Gawkthorpe, whom the earl had made his deputy as constable and steward of the Duchy of Lancaster honour of Knaresborough, in preference to Plumpton. Plumpton wanted to be a JP, to oust Gascoigne, and to have what he perceived as Gascoigne's misgovernances curbed. Rather than working through the earl and presumably uncertain of his support, Plumpton went to the top, over Northumberland's head. He sought the intercession of Lord Hastings, the king's chamberlain, to be JP; that of Sir John Pilkington to get his master Gloucester to pressurise his retainer the earl; and to the royal council regarding Gascoigne's misdeeds. Greene refused to act. Where the earl had chief rule, however, it was his goodwill – not that of Hastings – that counted. Going straight to the royal council was 'disworship' – disrespectful to the earl – and likely therefore to be ineffective. As for invoking Gloucester's authority over the earl, this was bound to fail. 'As long as my lord of Northumberland's patent therof stands good, as long will he haue no deputie but such as shall please him and kan him

---

[75] Hicks, 'Dynastic Change', 373–5; *CPR 1467–77*, pp. 319, 464, 505–6; see also below.
[76] See below.

thank for the gift thereof and no man els, and also doe him servise next the king.' A defiant and angry 'No' was to be expected. Only if Northumberland himself was removed from office could Plumpton succeed. 'Sir', wrote Greene, 'I took that for a watch word for medling betwixt lords'. However grateful Plumpton might be, it was insufficient grounds for the duke to imperil his whole relationship with the earl. Actually Northumberland was good lord to this troublesome retainer. He kept Plumpton as bailiff of Knaresborough, secured his promotion to JP, and in Plumpton's differ-ences with Gascoigne promised to 'see such a direction . . . as shalbe to your harts ease and worship' – a just solution, not necessarily the victory that Plumpton would have preferred.[77] The earl jealously patrolled his bounda-ries, disciplined his own retainers, and arbitrated their disputes, just as the duke managed his own. Gloucester was careful to consider the earl's wishes as his equal. Just as with the Duchess Cecily in the Gregories manor dispute, the two lords jointly arbitrated cross-retinue disputes.[78]

Their relations with the city of York are particularly well documented. York was special. It was one of the principal towns in England and certainly the largest town in the North and moreover a county in its own right. It was the economic hub of Yorkshire and engaged in international trade, but unfortunately was also in economic decline. York was a walled town with a castle. It was the religious capital of the North – the seat of the northern province's only archbishop, possessed in the newly completed York Minster 'the acropolis of the North' (Dobson), and a host of religious houses, hospi-tals, parishes, and chantries. It was the cultural centre too. Citizens were acutely conscious and protective of the city's status and liberties, but not strong enough to exclude the influence or even dominance of the local nobility. Lying between the estates of the Nevilles, at Sheriff Hutton and Middleham, and the Percies, at Leconfield and Wressle, York had been drawn into the violent Percy–Neville feud of the 1450s and its management was of great concern in the next generation to Richard Duke of Gloucester and the Earl of Northumberland. The people of York did not agree on how the city should be governed and the annual mayoral election on St Blaise's

---

[77] *Plumpton L & P*, pp. 51–2.
[78] See below p. 180.

Day was often riotously contested. What happened in the capital of the
North was of acute interest to the king, central government, and to the
leading northern magnates.

Following the defeat of the Lancastrian Percies in 1461, York was over-
seen by the Neville brothers: Warwick, who founded St William's College
for the Minster's chantry priests; John, who had the Percy estates in
Northumberland; and George, who became archbishop. Richard Duke of
Gloucester certainly knew the city. Initially in Warwick's custody he had
attended the archbishop's enthronement feast in 1465, made offerings at the
Minster, and mattered sufficiently in 1468–9 to receive his first gift (4⅜
gallons of red wine) from the city. Since York had refused Edward IV admis-
sion on his return from exile in 1471, it may have suffered suspension of its
liberties, and like Bristol and Coventry had cause to thank those who interceded for them with the king. Whether this included Gloucester or was
Gloucester himself is not recorded.

When the minute books commence in 1476, Gloucester was already in
close and amicable contact with York. He visited the city at least three times
that year and not infrequently thereafter, often receiving further gifts or being
greeted by a formal civic reception. He corresponded regularly with the
corporation. So did Northumberland, though less frequently and on more
equal terms. In the king's name as warden Gloucester requested and secured
the city's military support. They sent him a thief taken in their franchises.
Duke, earl, other nobles, and gentry to the number of 5,000 visited the city
on 13 March 1476 to urge that order be kept. Their presence was exploited
by the city, which enlisted the support of both magnates over the weirs (fishgarths) that interrupted their trade. Richard peremptorily ordered their
destruction on 22 March 1476. In November 1477 he took the matter to the
king and the Westminster great council and secured royal authority to sort
them out. Duke and earl each nominated two commissioners on another
occasion. After the city had dismissed its common clerk for misconduct,
it dared not make a new appointment without royal approval. They
approached the duke, who asked the king's chamberlain Lord Hastings and
his steward Lord Stanley to seek the king's permission to appoint whoever
they chose. It was most probably this successful mediation that brought the
corporation's thanks 'for his grete labour . . . for the conservacion of the liber-

ties of this cite' and their gift of six swans and six pikes. They communicated with Gloucester regularly and he in turn kept them informed, about the king's will and the Scottish war, for instance. However, the duke's influence went further than this. It is not at all clear what Holy Trinity Priory wanted when they sought his 'abundant grace and reformacion'. After some citizens had rung the bells – the signal for everyone to turn out fully armed for defence of the city – and the offenders had been incarcerated, the mayor lacked confidence in his own decision making and asked the duke what should be done. Release them, retorted the duke: whether considering it merely a prank or supposing the culprits sufficiently punished. In 1482 the corporation even sought the duke's approval of their peaceful mayoral election. The corporation abased itself to the 'high and mighty prince', 'his grace', and sought to know 'his gracious pleasure'. When at war with Scotland, the corporation voted him troops and staged a grand civic reception for him and the Scottish duke of Albany. The duke had his own candidate for the mayoralty, Thomas Wrangwish, who reputedly 'is the man that my lord of Gloucester will do for', but who was not elected. Evidently there were those who disagreed with Gloucester and even resented his intrusion.[79] Gradually the duke did come to dominate York, but he was never able to take its compliance for granted.

IV

The Neville lords were integrated into northern society. They had impacted on regional history repeatedly in the wars against the Scots. It was at the battle of Neville's Cross (1346) that the Scottish King David II was defeated and captured. Neville ancestors had founded the abbey of Coverham near Middleham, the Neville chantry in Durham Cathedral, St William's College at York Minster, Staindrop College and Well Hospital, and continued as patrons. Family tombs were located in all these places: younger sons were interred in Barnard Castle chapel, Middleham church, and at Sheriff Hutton church where an unidentified tomb survives.[80] Coverham Abbey saw itself as custodian of the family's memory, maintaining and updating

[79] Palliser, 'Richard III and York', in *Richard III and the North*, ed. R.E. Horrox, pp. 55–63; *York Chamberlains' Rolls*, pp. 126, 137, 152, 163–4; *York House Books*, vol. I, passim.

[80] Perhaps of Montagu's son George Neville (d. 1483), see W.E. Hampton, *Memorials of the Wars of the Roses* (Richard III Society, 1979), pp. 382–3.

the family chronicle.[81] Gloucester himself patronised Coverham and Jervaulx abbeys and founded his two colleges at Middleham and Barnard Castle. Alongside their own tombs and commemorations there were two chantries in the castle chapel at Barnard Castle founded by clients. Sheriff Hutton church contains the chantry and burial place of Thomas Witham, councillor in turn of the Neville earls of Salisbury (and executor), of Warwick, and then of Gloucester. At Middleham their chaplain John Cartmel founded a chantry in 1470. 'King Richard's chantry' was founded at Riccall by James Charlton. and other chantries were founded by William Chamberlain of Bugthorpe and the Gowers of Stittenham. Cartmel's chantry – and the Salisbury chantry at York Minster that he also founded – commemorated the duchess's grandparents Richard and Alice, earl and countess of Salisbury. All these men/and families were probably Gloucester's retainers:[82] In 1477 the duke and duchess of Gloucester joined the Corpus Christi guild at York alongside 55 other Yorkshire families and also on 10 April 1474 the fraternity of Durham Cathedral priory, the same day as Lord Scrope of Bolton.[83] The duke venerated such local saints as St William of York, St Cuthbert, and St Ninian and appears indeed to have popularised St Ninian's cult. He knew Middleham at first hand, taking an interest in the minutiae of the estate, exchanges of plots of land with the church and such issues as the tithes of hay. Gloucester established two fairs at Middleham in an effort to develop his town, as lords were expected to do, and enlarged both Cotescue and Sunscue parks.[84] He interceded for his townsmen, tenants, and retainers with King Edward, and when he himself became king the new county of Scarborough and the new borough of Pontefract were beneficiaries.[85]

[81] M.A. Hicks, 'English Monasteries as Repositories of Ancestral Memory', in *Monuments and Monumentality Across Medieval and Early Modern Europe*, ed. M. Penman (Shaun Tyas, 2013), p. 230.

[82] *CPR 1467–77*, pp. 185, 340; Hampton, *Memorials*, pp. 382, 384; Falvey, Boatwright and Hammond, *English Wills* (Richard III Society, 2013), p. 115; Horrox, 'Richard III and the East Riding', pp. 83–4.

[83] *Register of the Guild of Corpus Christi in the City of York*, ed. R.H. Scaife (Surtees Society, 1872), p. 101; Durham Cathedral archives, Registrum parvum 3, f.214; Pollard, *NE England*, p. 189.

[84] *Documents Relating to the Foundation and Antiquities of the Collegiate Church of Middleham*, ed. W. Atthill (Camden Society, 1847), pp. 84–7; *CPR 1476–85*, p. 154; Pollard, *NE England*, p. 203.

[85] Ross, *Richard III*, p. 58; *Calendar of the Charter Rolls 1427–1516* (HMSO, 1927), pp. 262–5; Somerville, *Lancaster*, vol. 1, p. 262n. Pontefract Priory contained the tombs of Richard's father and brother Edmund.

Richard took pride in Anne Neville's noble lineage, the benefits and obligations arising from them, and the local connections that she brought him and that he strove to continue and to protect. She fitted into the intermarried social network, related in varying degrees to much of high society, and Gloucester indeed contributed to this. The Nevilles had been remarkably prolific: Ralph Earl of Westmorland had 25 children and his son Salisbury fathered six daughters. Salisbury's brother and Anne Neville's great-uncle William Lord Fauconberg had three coheiresses, one of whom, Alice, had married John Conyers, son of Sir John, steward of Middleham to Warwick and Gloucester, and father of the future first Lord Conyers; another Elizabeth, who had married Sir Richard Strangways, son of her grandfather Salisbury's retainer Sir James and father of another James, whom Gloucester knighted in 1481.[86] The daughters of Henry Lord FitzHugh (d. 1472) and Salisbury's daughter Alice married respectively Gloucester's childhood friend Francis Lord Lovell (Anne), his lieutenant Sir William Parr (Elizabeth), and Sir Marmaduke Constable (Margaret).[87] In his capacity as guardian of the marquis Montagu's heiresses, Gloucester matched Elizabeth with his retainer Thomas Lord Scrope of Masham, Isabel with William Huddleston, another younger son of his retainer Sir John of Millom, and Lucy with Thomas Fitzwilliam of Aldwark, whom he had knighted on campaign in 1481.[88] Warwick's bastard daughter Margaret had married Sir Richard Huddleston, the eldest son.[89] It was apparently from this circle that Richard himself fathered two bastards, John of Pontefract and Katherine, perhaps brother and sister, perhaps about 1474 by Alice Burgh, gentlewoman, who may have belonged to the Knaresborough family and been connected to Henry Burgh and his wife Isabel, wetnurse to Richard's legitimate son Edward.[90] Even the relatively minor gentleman Richard Clervaux of Croft prided himself on his second cousinhood via the Nevilles of Middleham to Edward IV and Richard III.[91]

[86] 'Jones and Walker, 'Private Indentures', pp. 156–7; J.S. Roskell, *Parliament and Politics in Late Medieval England*, 3 vols (Hambledon Press, 1981–3), vol. 2, p. 305.

[87] GEC, vol. 8, p. 225; J.C. Wedgwood, *History of Parliament, 1439–1509. Biographies* (HMSO, 1936), p. 663; J.W. Clay, *Extinct and Dormant Peerages of the Northern Counties of England* (J. Nisbet, 1913), p. 75.

[88] GEC, vol. 9, pp. 93n–94n; *Stonor L & P*, vol. 2, p. 158; Pollard, *NE England*, p. 130.

[89] Hicks, *Warwick*, p. 234.

[90] Hicks, *Anne Neville*, pp. 157–8.

[91] Pollard, *NE England*, p. 110.

Gloucester acted frequently as a feoffee. He was executor to his chamberlain Sir John Pilkington, who confided his son Edward to him and Lord Hastings, and was supervisor of the will of his duchess's great-aunt Lady Latimer.[92] Richard may not have been born or brought up a northerner nor in Richmondshire, but he conformed very well to the model set out by Westmorland, Salisbury, and Warwick. Their Richmondshire affinity that backed them politically in 1455, 1459, 1469, 1470, and 1471 turned out for him in the Scottish war and again in the northern army that overawed London in 1483. Gloucester repaired, harnessed, and strengthened the Neville connection. His own direction was important, but secondary to the connection that he had inherited.

[92] Falvey, Boatwight, and Hammond, *English Wills*, pp. 14–15; *Testamenta Vetusta*, ed. N.H. Nicolas (London, 1826), p. 361.

Chapter Seven

RICHARD AS 'GOOD LORD'

I

Duke Richard resided in a great household where he ate, slept, worshipped, and took his recreations. His ducal household was the focus and power-house of a wide-flung estate. If the *Black Book* of Edward IV's household is to be taken literally, the status of a duke demanded a domestic establish-ment 240-strong and should have cost £4,000 a year.[1] This huge sum might have absorbed his whole income in the early 1470s and probably therefore exaggerates Gloucester's situation. Even at the end of Edward IV's Second Reign, such an establishment would have absorbed half the duke's revenues. There can unfortunately be no certainty, for none of its numerous accounts survive, there is no ordinance akin to Clarence's, no membership list nor any livery rolls. Noble households were modelled on that of the crown. Richard certainly employed a chamberlain, a steward, and a treasurer of his household, very likely a controller and a cofferer too, but who held which of these key offices in rarely recorded. Similarly, of Clarence's chief domestic officers, it is only John Delves, treasurer, and John Penne, controller, that have been identified. Already long in Gloucester's service in 1477, the duke's chancellor was Dr Thomas Barrow. Gloucester's secretary John Kendal was signing the duke's letters from

[1] Myers, *Household of Edward IV* (Manchester University Press, 1959), pp. 94–6.

1474.[2] Sir John Pilkington was chamberlain until his death in 1479, but his successor is not recorded. Robert Brackenbury was treasurer of the household by 1479; he was part of the Barnard Castle connection.[3] A handful of other household men are identified, such as John Green, who was a yeoman of the ducal chamber in Michaelmas 1474.[4] Sixteen household men accompanied the duke to Stepney to arrest the countess of Oxford and 20 wearing his livery under the command of the esquire Thomas de la Lande overawed John Prince at West Thorndon. Warned that they were acting without the duke's sanction, Lande retorted, 'We be servauntes to my lord of Gloucester and he woll mayntene his servauntes'.[5] But only Lande is named in the document.

It was difficult for Gloucester to know what was done by his men in his name and to keep control of them. The duke was a monarch in miniature – not much in miniature either – who had his own court and courtiers who interposed between him and the wider world. He dined in state, held formal audiences, and interacted informally with his chamber staff who shared his daily life. Duke Richard seems also to have devoted time to business. He read up and researched his responsibilities and devised detailed ordinances, statutes, and indentures of war. Sidelights to his management of his affairs are provided by his treatment of the countess of Oxford and his involvement in the Gregories manor dispute and in incidental remarks in the Paston letters. Although much older than Richard, John Lord Howard, treasurer of the royal household, deputy of Calais to Lord Hastings, and himself a baron, was also Gloucester's client. He waited on the duke and spoke with him daily, reported to him, and referred Gloucester's replies back to those soliciting his intervention. A decade earlier Howard was serving the duke of Norfolk in a similar way. Performing comparable functions were Gloucester's chamberlain Pilkington and Sir John Huddleston.

[2] Ramsay, 'Richard III and the Office of Arms', in *The Yorkist Age*, eds H. Kleineke and C. Steer (Harlaxton Medieval Studies, 2013), p. 143n; C.H. Hunter Blair, 'Two Letters Patent', *Archaeologia Aeliana*, 4th series, 39 (1961), pl. 35.

[3] DL 29/639/10387; Pollard, *NE England*, p. 324.

[4] E 405/58 m.4.

[5] Horrox, 'An Invisible Man', in *Much Heaving and Shoving*, eds M. Aston and R. Horrox (Aston & Horrox, 2005), p. 70; Hicks, 'The Last Days of Elizabeth, Countess of Oxford', in *Rivals*, p. 311.

Gloucester knew his own mind. It was he in person who seized the countess, threatened her feoffees, and rebuked those of whom he disapproved. However, he also referred the detail and matters of no direct interest to his legal counsel and council. Any ultimate decisions were made by him, but he was guided – and perhaps managed – by those around him.[6]

The household was the nerve centre and the principal expense of a great estate. Duke Richard held lands in 25 counties in England and in southern and east Wales. In most counties he was neither the principal nor indeed a significant landholder. In every case there were ministers – such as bailiffs, reeves, and stewards – who ran the property for him, rendered accounts and so on as had been done for generations. These isolated properties were not at risk of loss from powerful neighbours as sometimes supposed, or from encroachments, because they were protected by English property law and the courts and because the ministers were men of local substance who had been selected for that reason. Perhaps such offices added to their local standing. It is seldom apparent whether the duke's officers wore the duke's livery when on duty. In some areas, however, the duke was a leading landholder, even the principal or dominant landholder. Yorkshire is the best documented example.

Another such region where Duke Richard really mattered in the early 1470s comprised Essex, East Anglia, and the eastern counties, where the forfeited properties of the earl of Oxford and those adherents defeated at Barnet were concentrated. Initially King Edward may have intended to attaint those who had fought against him in 1470–1, but both royal dukes opposed this, hoping instead to secure for themselves the service of those who had been valued by their predecessors. While very few of the former De Vere retainers backed the earl of Oxford when he landed at St Osyth in 1473, the remainder are unlikely to have transferred their committed loyalty to the duke who had defeated him and who now occupied the family estate. Accounts for these lands during Gloucester's tenure record the orderly receipt of rents collected by local ministers and the payment of a handful of annuities granted by the countess to James Alabaster, John Power, and

[6] Based on Horrox, 'Invisible Man', pp. 67–75 esp. pp. 73–5; Hicks, 'Last Days', pp. 309–16.

Elizabeth Wychingham.[7] This was the usual pattern everywhere outside the North. The massive burden of fees payable at Middleham and on the Percy estates was not the norm in other regions. Richard certainly indented for service with the leading northern gentry, most of whom probably resided in their own houses or castles on their own estates. He paid them fees as his estate officers (constables, stewards), or retained their services with annuities from Middleham, Sheriff Hutton, Penrith, Barnard Castle, and probably his other northern lordships too. The large retinues that Oxford and other noblemen could deploy in crises were not made up principally of such annuitants, who cost more than could be afforded,[8] but rather of members of their households and tenants of their estates. Gloucester had both categories of follower: also whatever household servants and tenantry that his retainers brought with them. There are glimpses of Gloucester's household and council at work in his dealings with the countess of Oxford and over Gregories manor in Theydon Bois (Essex).

All Gloucester's officers and retainers were loyal subjects and some were explicitly employed by the king. It was the duke who nominated his own chamberlain to be Warwick chamberlain of the exchequer in 1477, but Pilkington was already a king's knight from 1471 and before that, from 1461, an esquire of the body.[9] That such offices could be combined together and with the officer's own interests demonstrates that some sort of rota system of on- and off-duty operated both at court and in the duke's own household. It was to Gloucester's advantage that Pilkington (and others) could put his case to the king. It was also in the king's interest that he had trusted servants in key offices around the duke. Such service was compatible – new duties were accepted because they could be accommodated with existing obligations – and it was only occasionally, in the direst of crises, that retainers had to choose between them. King or lord? Richard employed Tyrell to whisk the Countess of Warwick from Beaulieu Abbey on the south coast to the North. His retainers were men of substance, in the same category as Howard and Parr, who combined service for both king and duke.

[7] DL 29/295/4848 m.2d. In 1495 Power testified about Gloucester's maltreatment of the Countess of Oxford, Hicks, 'Last Days', pp. 315–16.

[8] Hicks, *Bastard Feudalism* (Longman, 1995), pp. 71–2.

[9] SP 46/139 f.166; *CPR 1461–7*, p. 17; *1467–77*, p. 279.

Superior to the ministers were the stewards, who held the manorial courts; the receivers, who collected the issues of each accounting unit; and the auditors, who vetted the accounts each autumn. Some of these men are known by name. On the duke's East Anglian estate Richard Radcliffe of Tattershall (Lincolnshire) was steward, Richard Spert was receiver, and John Luthington was auditor and receiver also of other estates and of other lords.[10] The duke's estates were gathered together into receiverships, each with a receiver and auditors. Most probably there were separate receiverships for each marcher lordship, each northern lordship, the two eastern groups of property, and perhaps other units too.

In theory the duke held all the strings and made all the decisions, but much was decided by his council. Owning land inevitably embroiled land-holders in disputes of title, about boundaries, rights of way and watercourses, access to commons and woodland, the calendar of sowing and harvesting, rights to game and poaching, to labour services, and much more. Again, no record of Richard's council survive, but this institution undoubtedly advised the duke on many topics, handled much of the basic estate management and made decisions on such topics as the granting of leases and prosecution of debtors and poachers in the duke's name. It was the council that disciplined defaulting officers and handled disputes between the duke's servants, between others who looked up to him, and between his men and the servants and retainers of other lords. Membership of the council was fluid. There were officials, leading retainers, and learned legal counsel. Attendance varied. Some sessions were calendared, but they were geographically so widespread – from London to Durham and Raby – that one suspects there were actually several councils operating in different localities. The councillors were those whom the duke trusted and whose advice he valued. The council certainly encompassed the key officers of his household and estates. Also included were northern barons and the leading gentry among his retainers.

His feoffees were prominent for Gloucester, unusually, appointed no honorary but inactive figureheads to hold his lands in trust. For both the Oxford and Middleham estates there was a core of active retainers who were feoffees: Barrow, Pilkington, Huddleston, Tyrell, Tunstall, and William

[10] DL 29/639/10382. Luthington served both Clarence and the king.

Hopton of Swillington (Yorkshire), who was Gloucester's esquire in 1475 and one of his receivers-general in 1480–1.[11] Pilkington and Huddleston had been with the Yorkist earls in 1459–60 and were most probably retainers of both the Neville earls of Salisbury and Warwick. After 1461 both served in the royal household. The Hoptons had a tradition of serving the earls of Salisbury, Montagus and Nevilles.[12] Tyrell hailed from Essex and Hopton from Suffolk, but the others were Northerners. So were the newcomers added about 1475: Robert Brackenbury, treasurer of the household, Geoffrey Frank, the receiver of Middleham, Richard Middleton (*domicellus* in Gloucester's household in 1480)[13], and Thomas Middleton, and Richard Ratcliffe, a Cumbrian younger son and constable of Barnard Castle by 1476[14]). Thomas Witham was a particularly long-standing Neville retainer.[15] Also named as councillors at various times were Sir Ralph Ashton, Ralph Lord Greystoke, Sir William Redmayn, and Edmund (rather than Edward) Hastings.[16] Probably the list should include Sir John Conyers, constable and steward of Middleham, and Sir James Harrington, who was a knight of the body and steward of Pontefract, who deputised for the duke (with Parr and Tyrell) as vice-constable of England in 1482.[17] Pilkington, Redmayn, and Witham had died by 1483 and Hopton in 1484, but Brackenbury and Ratcliffe had distinguished if brief careers under King Richard.

There was a warmth to these connections. Gloucester's feoffees were included in the prayers he commissioned from Queens' College Cambridge in 1477.[18] In his will of 1478 Sir John Pilkington asked Gloucester

[11] North Yorkshire Record Office ZRC 17503; Atthill, *Documents Relating to the Foundation and Antiquities of the Collegiate Church of Middleham* (Camden Society, 1847), p. 84; DL 29/295/4648. m 2d; DL 29/639/10382; DL 29/295/4648; R.E. Horrox, 'Richard III and London', *Ricardian*, 85 (1984), p. 323. Was this the William Hopton senior who was feed in 1473? See J.A. Ross, 'Richard, Duke of Gloucester and the De Vere estates', *Ricardian*, 15 (2005), pp. 31–2. For what follows, see Atthill, *Church of Middleham*, pp. 84–5.

[12] Although Hopton's father 'cannot by any stretch be said to have a political career', Richmond, *John Hopton* (Cambridge University Press, 1981), p. 110, see also pp. 104–7, this is contradicted by his service in Henry VI's household.

[13] *Testamenta Eboracensia*, 3, ed. J. Raine (Surtees Society, 1864), p. 344.

[14] Pollard, *NE England*, p. 324; Atthill, *Middleham*, pp. 84–5.

[15] *York City Chamberlains' Rolls*, ed. R.B. Dobson (Surtees Society, 1980), p. 152.

[16] Ibid. pp. 152, 164; *York House Books 1476–90*, ed. L.C. Attreed (A. Sutton, 1991), p. 255.

[17] Somerville, *Lancaster*, vol. 1, pp. 514; SC1/44/60; *CPR 1476–85*, p. 317.

[18] Searle, *History of Queens' College Cambridge* (Cambridge Antiquarian Society, 1867), pp. 86–92.

to intercede with the king to secure the grant of the wardship and marriage of his son Edward for his executors, to arrange for the boy to be placed in the household of Lord Hastings, and to assist in his marriage to an heiress. Gloucester and Hastings were appointed executors, although only the duke took on the administration, and Sir John bequeathed him an emerald set in gold that the duke had coveted and had been prepared to purchase for 100 marks (£66 13s.4d.).[19]

Much less is known about Richard's other lordships and their connections and there are huge chasms in what is known, most obviously about his Welsh lordships. Horrox filled some gaps, in the East Riding and elsewhere, by identifying individuals associated with Gloucester and their interactions,[20] but such data inevitably falls short of the concrete proof that indentures of retainer, payment of fees, or household membership could provide. Gloucester probably could not afford fees everywhere on the scale of his Middleham estate.

The reduction in his salary as warden in 1480 by £400 in time of peace and a massive £1,500 in time of war was a serious blow. That he renewed his contract on these less favourable terms, however, shows how important the wardenship was to him.[21] It is difficult to disagree with Pollard that 'by the end of the decade Gloucester had established a personal hegemony in northern England', although it is unlikely that it 'eclipsed even the might of Richard Neville [Warwick the Kingmaker] at the height of his power'.[22] King Edward had not intended this result. In 1473 he sought to divide and rule, but the council's decision was not enforced and Richard was able to make himself dominant directly or indirectly throughout the North. He amassed and distributed much of the regional patronage of the crown and the Duchy of Lancaster. Edward accepted the consequences. Indeed it was greatly to his advantage – and may indeed have made for greater unity and

[19] Falvey, Boatwright and Hammond, *English Wills* (Richard III Society, 2013), pp. 14–15.

[20] Horrox, *Richard III*, pp. 50–1; Horrox, 'Richard III and the East Riding', in *Richard III and the North* (Hull University, 1986), pp. 82–107.

[21] In the mid-1430s the Nevilles had briefly surrendered the West March, Storey, 'Wardens of the Marches', *EHR*, 72 (1957), pp. 613–14; R.W. Dunning, 'Thomas, Lord Dacre and the West March Towards Scotland? 1435', *BIHR*, 41 (1968), pp. 95–9.

[22] Pollard, *NE England*, p. 316.

better order in the North – provided of course that the duke and other peers saw eye to eye and worked to common ends. Richard's hegemony was subsidiary to the royal affinity and contained within it. Key retainers like Harrington and Pilkington were knights of the royal body and all prioritised their allegiance to the king. So did Northumberland: 'the duetie of the alegiaunce of the said Erle to the kinges highnes, the Quene, his service and promise to Prince Edward, thair first begotten son, and all the kinges issue begoten and to be begotten, first at all tymes reserved and hadd'.[23] Gloucester's retinue was at the service of the crown and did serve it during the Scottish war. Of course king and duke worked together and therefore their retainers too. They never came to blows. The question of who should prevail if they clashed should never have been posed, and was not until 1483.

II

Duke Richard could afford the best legal advice. He retained a string of lawyers and made use of them all at different times. The Welshman Morgan Kidwelly, who had been appointed receiver of Kidwelly when Gloucester became steward in 1469, was the duke's principal legal adviser. The Yorkshireman Miles Metcalf was his attorney-general by 1473. Thomas Witham and Richard Pigot had been veteran legal advisers to the Nevilles. In 1474 the duke expected the former chief justice Sir John Fortescue (Lord Fortescue) to act for him. Others who were paid retaining fees were Chief Justice Sir Robert Danby, the serjeants at law and future judges William Jenney (d. 1483), John Sulyard (d. 1488), and John Vavasour of Spaldington, Yorkshire (d. 1505) from 1473 to 1474, William Husy (king's attorney 1476–7 and future chief justice), and Thomas Lynom (from 1480), who was his solicitor general as king.[24] Gloucester needed them to handle not just his own

[23] Jones and Walker, 'Private Indentures', *Camden Miscellany*, 32 (1994), p. 178.
[24] BL MS Cotton Julius BXII ff.118–19; *CFR 1471–85*, no.116; DL 37/38/13, 19; DL 29/295/4648 m 1; DL 29/637/10360A; DL 29/639/10387; C81/1640/41; E 401/939; Somerville, *Lancaster*, vol. 1, p. 642; Ross, 'Richard Duke of Gloucester and the Purchase and Sale of Hooton Pagnell, Yorkshire, 1475–80', *Ricardian*, 22 (2012), p. 49; Horrox, 'Invisible Man', p. 74; Pollard, *NE England*, p. 324; *CFR 1471–85*, 26; *Historia Dunelmensis Scriptores Tres* (1839), 340; Pollard, *NE England*, p. 324; G.M. Coles, 'Lordship of Middleham' (1961), appx. B.

business, but whatever his retainers referred to him. Robert Portington of Skelton, Yorkshire was his attorney at the exchequer, from 1476 to 1477.[25] William Catesby esquire was somehow in the duke's service and in his trust before his accession. He was the eldest son and nephew of two judges and heir to a prominent Northamptonshire family traditionally dependent on the earls of Warwick and therefore on their heir George Duke of Clarence. A letter of 1480 reveals that the duke's learned counsel held prearranged sessions according to a timetable at particular locations, Raby and Durham, where they reviewed the evidence of contending parties and decided between them. Since their communications were written and signed by the duke,[26] he operated to the same calendar. Perhaps John Kendal, like a modern secretary, kept his master's diary.

Most of the hundreds of men who served Richard directly and the thousands who were his tenants or neighbours had interests that potentially clashed and raised issues of right and legality. This was a law-abiding yet litigious society in which the law was supplemented by violence (e.g., forcible entries) and corruption. Some of these cases came before the hierarchy of local and national courts. Many others, perhaps many more, were resolved locally by the mediation, pressurising, or arbitration of friends, neighbours, JPs out of session, or lords. The *Plumpton Letters* reveal that dozens of cases involving superiors, equals and inferiors, lords, monasteries, tenants, and widows touched on Sir William and Sir Robert Plumpton in many different capacities.[27] Most were resolved peacefully and without resort to the courts or to their lords. Yet the literally hundreds of men who served Duke Richard in many different ways expected his good lordship. They served him because it benefited them.

At the simplest level, his household men secured wages, keep and livery, while his officers and annuitants were paid retaining fees annually. To serve the duke brought status, distinction, local authority, preferment from others, and – the recipients hoped – more favourable treatment before the law. Beyond this Gloucester's retainers expected the duke actively to exercise his good lordship. He promised to be the 'good and faithful lorde' of

[25] BL MS Cotton Julius BXII f.224.
[26] Pollard, *Princes*, p. 237.
[27] Hicks, *English Political Culture in the Fifteenth Century* (Routledge, 2002), pp. 155–8.

the earl of Northumberland; to Lady Scrope of Masham and her family he promised 'to be good and loving lord to all of them', explicitly to 'support, succour and assist at all times'.[28] All lords were expected to be good lords to their dependants, to seek their advancement and to support them in their quarrels. Richard's surviving indentures do not specify the good lordship that was understood to be included.

Good lordship might involve lords in backing their retainers' causes, just or unjust, maintaining their quarrels and even joining in them, and protecting them from justice for their misdeeds. These abuses were publicly deplored, but they were what every retainer hoped for. Indeed such good lordship might be the primary motivation. Accused of murdering Richard Williamson of Riccall, in Yorkshire, the three brothers Robert, Richard, and John Farnell alias Forster, yeomen of Newsholme, and their father Thomas who harboured them, sought to take service with 'the right high and myghty prynce and full honorable lord Richard, duk of Gloucestre' with the intention that they 'shuld have been supported in their horrible felonye, murther and robbery'. They were successful. The father Thomas Farnell alias Forster called himself 'servaunt to the said duc' and wore his livery. On the other hand, lords could not afford to get embroiled in all the quarrels of all their retainers. They needed to keep the peace and maintain discipline within their connections and indeed foster amicable relations with their peers. When better informed, Richard consigned Thomas Farnell to York prison, pending trial, and left his offending servants in the Gregories case to the royal courts.[29] Lords might limit their obligation of good lordship to the retainers' just causes, and indeed interpret their role as the mediation, arbitration, and the peaceful resolution of disputes, in the teeth of retainers who naturally wanted to win. Northumberland promised 'he shall see such a direction , , , as shalbe to your harts ease & worship',[30] not necessarily a favourable one.

Richard can be observed in all these roles. He had an enormous range of his own interests, that he pursued in court, council, the law courts, and parliament. He was active on the land market, treated with traitors and the

[28] Jones and Walker, 'Private Indentures', p. 178; Pollard, *NE England*, p. 329.
[29] *PROME*, 14, pp. 83–5, 111–2; Horrox, 'Invisible Man', p. 71.
[30] *Plumpton L & P*, p. 52.

heirs of traitors, with minors, and took on as matter of course the role of trustee (feoffee). He could not engage with every case and relied on much to be handled by his council. That was why he employed such a train of the best qualified professionals.

Some lords sometimes did back their retainers in their unjust causes. Thus, Gloucester maintained Sir James Harrington in defiance of the superior title of his Stanley nieces and through all setbacks. Harrington did not want justice so much as favour. Similarly John Prince's lawyer did not allow the duke to delegate his cause to his legal counsel, who would treat both parties even-handedly, and thus forsake the advantage that he had already, his occupation of the estate. What Prince wanted was the duke's support to achieve victory.[31] Harrington did manage to suck Gloucester into his dispute, even apparently engaging the Stanleys by force, and he enjoyed the duke's backing in the face of contrary judgements until 1474 and even beyond.[32] Harrington was Gloucester's trusted retainer as duke and king and indeed afterwards. Thomas de la Lande, as already shown, counted on the duke's protection when misbehaving.[33]

Probably Richard's council handled many such cases that are wholly unrecorded. Even those known are poorly or partially documented. There is no archive for Duke Richard's council, nor any other noble council. A few random survivals in other people's archives illuminate aspects of certain disputes. Most common are those that reveal the duke as a trustee and the bonds or recognisances for debt that parties to arbitration sealed and that were registered on the government's close rolls or other courts of record. 'The most excellent prince' was often persuaded to become a feoffee to deter any potential rivals, often by relatively obscure gentleman like Thomas Caister,[34] whose title was suspect and open to challenge. Gloucester was among a panel of nine enfeoffed with six messuages in York that were disseised (dispossessed) in 1474.[35] It was a poor title to Gregories manor that the London goldsmith William Flour sought to assert in 1472

[31] Horrox, 'Invisible Man', p. 75
[32] M.K. Jones, 'Richard III and the Stanleys', in *Richard III and the North*, ed. R.E. Horrox, pp. 38–40.
[33] Horrox, 'Invisible Man', p. 70.
[34] Northamptonshire Record Office F(M) Charter/ 567.
[35] *York Memorandum Book*, 3, ed. J.W. Percy (Surtees Society, 1973),176, pp. 129–30.

when nominating the duke among his feoffees.[36] As King Edward observed, so great a man as the duke could defend a bad title that was beyond the power of lesser men.[37]

The next stage in Richard's involvement was receipt of a complaint or petition, oral or written. It is a reasonable presumption that it was normally the weaker party who invoked the duke's good lordship in a quarrel that the plaintiff could not settle himself. Often enough, as in chancery cases, the plaintiff pleaded that he could obtain no justice through the courts because of the local standing, maintenance, or corruption of his opponent. This was certainly the case with Gerald Salvan, a minor gentleman who complained to the duke about Thomas Fishburn's forcible entry into his manor house at Croxdale in County Durham and his attempted murder. He hoped that the duke would provide a remedy.[38] Christopher Stansfield complained that cattle stolen from him and impounded at Spofford had not been returned to him.[39] The 'pitueuse complaint' of the agriculturalist John Randson was that Sir Robert Claxton interrupted his tenure.[40] If the duke's attention was secured, he was persuaded to despatch a letter to the rival claimant that aped those under the king's privy seal and signet. Commencing 'Right trustie and Welbeloued', it was sealed with his signet and bore his signature (R. Gloucestre). The duke wrote to the steward of Spofford instructing him to release the cattle.[41] In the Gregories case John Prince was summoned to appear before the duke's council.[42] So too was Claxton or his legal counsel. Claxton, however, did not obey. Moreover, he fobbed off Randson with excuses and delays. Hence he received a second letter: we 'merveille gretly ... ye have not' and was summoned to another council session with his evidence. 'And so demeane you herin that we have no cause to

---

[36] Horrox, 'Invisible Man', p. 68.

[37] Hicks, 'Last Days', p. 309.

[38] R. Surtees, *History and Antiquities of the County of Durham*, 4 vols (1816–40), vol. 4, pp. 14–15. What followed is not known, nor whether the duke took Salvan on as a feed retainer as he hoped.

[39] *Plumpton L & P*, p. 46.

[40] Pollard, *Princes*, p. 237.

[41] *Plumpton L & P*, p. 46; 'we marveille' parallel Nottingham University Library MS Mi5b.

[42] Essex Record Office D/DQ/4/24/3/32; Horrox, 'Invisible Man', p. 74.

provide his lawfull remedy in this behalve.'[43] Somehow the brother of Sir William Stonor (maybe Thomas Stonor) offended the duke and had to be taught to perform his duty, following which the duke became again his good lord conditional on good behaviour: a result (wrote Tyrell) 'bettyr than he cowed persayve in the begynyng'.[44] Such letters repeat the case set out by the complainant, but do not prejudge the issue. Stansfield's replevin (or legal remedy) was 'as the law will' and he was to be bound over to sue his case in court.[45] The evidence of Claxton and Randson was to be examined so the truth of their titles might be ascertained and 'right woll shalbe duly mynystered'.[46] As none of these cases involved Gloucester's men or his estates, the duke lacked the jurisdiction or capacity to decide, calculating instead that the legality of his proposals or (as he wrote to the Spofford steward)[47] deference to his high rank would cause the parties to submit to his authority. John Prince declined. Moreover, he took the case elsewhere, to the mother of the duke (and indeed the king) Cecily Duchess of York, who wrote her own 'right trusty and right enterely welbiloved son etc' letter to the duke. Far from fighting it out, they agreed to act together to resolve the dispute peacefully, each nominating two members to an arbitration panel of four. Neither party could withstand such a combination – each, most probably, bound themselves to abide (accept) the award – and the panel almost certainly found for Prince and against Flour.[48] Violent misconduct took the matter to the royal council and thus out of Gloucester's hands.[49]

Arbitration was the most formal route to settlement out of court. Both parties had to agree to arbitration and generally both guaranteed compliance by binding themselves by a bond (recognisance of debt) to abide his award. Such bonds stated that the writer owed a huge sum, a penalty to be exacted if the conditions were not met, but cancelled if the award was

[43] Pollard, *Princes*, 237. For a parallel, see Clarence's letter to Lawrence Lowe, Hicks, *Clarence*, p. 181.

[44] *Stonor L & P*, vol. 2, p. 116.

[45] *Plumpton L & P*, p. 46.

[46] Pollard, *Princes*, p. 237.

[47] *Plumpton L & P*, p. 46.

[48] Horrox, 'Invisible Man', pp. 70–1, 74–5.

[49] A.F. Sutton, 'Richard of Gloucester's Lands in East Anglia', in *Richard III and East Anglia*, ed. L. Visser-Fuchs (Richard III Society, 2010), p. 17.

accepted and implemented. Each party agreed on a single arbiter or more commonly each nominated two or four to a panel, sometimes with final resort to an umpire. The parties pleaded to the panel, supporting their case with evidence, and the result was an arbitration award that resolved the issues, usually with an element of compromise. Dissatisfied suitors should have submitted, since otherwise the penalty in their recognisance for debts could be exacted by the royal courts. On occasion nevertheless the award was rejected, as Sir James Harrington resisted the first award in his Hornby Castle case.[50] The contending parties in two surviving awards had voluntarily submitted to Gloucester's arbitration. Richard Clervaux of Croft and Roland Place of Halnaby, two esquires and parishioners of Croft in dispute about their boundaries and stray beasts, church pews and hunting rights, bound themselves in £100 each to abide the award of Duke Richard, who duly ruled on 12 April 1478. On 15 March 1481 he also settled the dispute between Selby Abbey and the parishioners of Snaith disputing who paid for what in Snaith church. Both were cases where demarcation lines were drawn, not where one party won and the other lost.[51] Another case, between Thomas Ashton and Robert Hesketh, was apparently delegated to the duke's legal counsel Richard Pigot, Miles Metcalfe, and Thomas Ash.[52] The dominance that Richard established everywhere did not mean conflict ceased: it meant that all irreconcilable differences were contained within his affinity, and made him responsible for keeping the peace and settling them.

Where cases spanned Gloucester's and Northumberland's affinities, the two magnates left it to their retainers, as in the first Plumpton panel in 1480, or agreed to arbitrate together (with eight others), as in the second Plumpton panel in 1482. In 1474 in the dispute between John Pennington of Muncaster (Northumberland's man) and John Huddleston of Millom (Gloucester's), these two leading Cumbrian gentry bound themselves in 500 marks each conditional on implementing the award of four of their peers, failing which the duke and earl would arbitrate.[53] It was standard practice

---

[50] Jones, 'Stanleys', pp. 37–8.;

[51] Pollard, *Princes*, pp. 234–6; *Register of Archbishop Rotherham*, vol. 1, ed. E.E. Barker, Canterbury and York Society, 69 (1976), pp. 194–5.

[52] Pollard, *NE England*, p. 119.

[53] *Plumpton L & P*, p. 267; *The Plumpton Correspondence*, ed. T. Stapleton (Camden Society, 1839), p. 89; *CCR 1468–76*, no. 1317; Historic Manuscripts Commission, *10th Report*, iv.228.

that all existing suits were dropped. As there was no central archive like those of the central courts, and the constituent documents went out of date, there were certainly more cases than surviving awards.[54]

Such out-of-court settlements served the public interest by ending conflict: 'we the saide duc tendiryng the peas and welle of the contre where the saide parties doue inhabite and also gladly willyng gode concorde, rest and frendly unite ... fro hensfurth betwene the sayde partes'.[55] Pollard argues for Gloucester's neutrality between the humble and the well-connected − the Claxton whom he addressed so sharply had a bastard who served the duke and a daughter married to a ducal retainer − but the situation cannot be quite so clear-cut as it is not known who was victorious. In the Gregories case − and perhaps the others too − Gloucester was quite uninterested in the facts or the result. Twice he sought resolution in accordance with the king's laws. He saw no reason why the matter should not be resolved by his learned counsel. What was important to him was that disputes were referred to him, whether by his retainers seeking good lordship or by neighbours who volunteered into his jurisdiction, and that the quality of justice he offered was perceived as good. 'The duke's council had already begun to act as a court of poor requests in the north', writes Pollard, 'bypassing if necessary the usual channels'.[56] Gloucester's role here should not be exaggerated. Only four cases that he arbitrated are known, only half the numbers known to have been handled by his brother Clarence.[57] The duke also took the lead in more formal peacekeeping, as the senior commissioner for oyer and terminer in Yorkshire in 1478.[58] He presided at quarter sessions at Nottingham on 1 July 1473 and in Yorkshire at Bedale (North Riding) on 6 October 1472 and at Wakefield on 15 September 1479.[59] Maybe, reading between the lines, he regarded the council of the North that he set up as king to be continuing the peacekeeping that he and his council had undertaken as duke.

[54] Hicks, 'Restraint, Mediation and Private Justice: George Duke of Clarence as "Good Lord" ', in *Rivals*, pp. 145–7.

[55] Pollard, *Princes*, p. 234.

[56] Pollard, *NE England*, p. 336.

[57] Christies sale catalogue, sale 5960, lot 47; compare Hicks, 'Clarence as "Good Lord" ', pp. 141–5.

[58] *CPR 1476–85*, 144, 148; KB 9/349.

[59] KB 9/334/66; KB 9/351/77; KB 9/352/60.

Chapter Eight

STRATEGIC FORESIGHT I

GLOUCESTER'S WISH LIST 1477–8

I

Richard Duke of Gloucester had amassed a huge estate and a constellation of great offices that rivalled those of his brother Clarence and even Warwick the Kingmaker. Most noblemen, with family estates or expectations of inheritances, lived with any geographical or other inconveniences that came with them and were content to maintain their estates as they were or somewhat to augment them. They did not seek to change them or exchange them or to reshape their holdings according to some strategic plan. Duke Richard did. In this way he appears exceptional. Moreover, he was an active man, not content to keep things as they were, but open to change and anxious to reform. He decreed new ordinances for the heralds. He was a worker in detail, concerned to master his briefs, to dot every 'i' and cross every 't', his indentures of war being an instance. Of course he sought out the best advice and must have delegated much of the actual drafting to his lawyers and secretariat, but it was the duke's own authority that was invoked and it was he who made the key decisions. These were character-istics that he brought in 1483 to his kingship. The rewards he received from King Edward for his part in the destruction of their brother Clarence offer a window into his strategies for the future. Gloucester had asked for these favours. They should be regarded as a wish list of his aspirations for the future. Needless to say, he did not in 1477–8 expect or hope to become king.

Richard was already looking beyond his own life. He was concerned to endow his dynasty, as yet unborn, as well as himself. Some choices he had already made – inklings of the strategy he was pursuing – as he distinguished between properties to be retained, those to be conceded, and those that were to be devoted to pious purposes. He had concentrated his lands in the North by exchange with others in the South, East Midlands, and north-western Wales. On 19 February 1474 the properties that he wrested from the countess of Oxford were settled on his chosen feoffees,[1] and could thus be devised by his will. One such estate, Wivenhoe in Essex, was sold.[2] Most if not all the others were earmarked as endowments for his religious foundations: the manor and advowson of Fulmer, Cambridgeshire to Queens' College Cambridge; 200 marks-worth actually conveyed to Middleham College; probably another 400 marks-worth were intended for Barnard Castle College.[3] Having secured his share of the Warwick inheritance, Middleham too had been settled on feoffees and perhaps the rest of his northern estates as well.[4] Most probably Richard was taking advantage of the king's concession that participants in the Picquigny expedition could enfeoff all their lands, thus evading wardship and conferring greater freedom of disposition. He did not have his enfeoffments enrolled on the close rolls, but as the authority was parliamentary this was not required.[5] In the absence of a male heir, such property could be passed to a daughter, or otherwise assigned by his will. Richard cannot have worked all this out in his twenties, but what these provisions demonstrate is his early preparation for the future, his flexibility, and his openness to alternative possibilities.

II

These features emerge most clearly in 1477–8, when he exploited Clarence's fall to secure at least a dozen favours across the whole spectrum

[1] North Yorkshire Record Office ZRC 17503.

[2] A. Crawford, *Yorkist Lord* (Bloomsbury, 2010), p. 91.

[3] *CPR 1476–85*, 34; 67; North Yorkshire RO ZRC 17503.

[4] W. Atthill, *Church of Middleham* (London, 1847), p. 84; BL MS Cotton Julius BXII f.246v; North Yorkshire RO ZRL.

[5] *PROME*, vol. 14, pp. 335–6. This provision did not cover royal grants.

of his interests. These included the aspirations of his retainers. Gloucester's support was essential to the king: nobody else benefited as much. Most of his gains took the form of royal grants that originated in surviving petitions: the rest probably did also. Edward conceded what he requested, but the duke was careful not to ask for any grants that cost the king anything. Greater freedom with his own possessions and exchanges of property, not gifts, were what Edward was willing to concede. Parliament had closed on 21 February 1478. Gloucester's favour with King Edward can be traced through the dates of his grants, for which the chancery warrants are the most accurate guide. Not all were executed simultaneously and not all were enrolled, so the concentration in time does not appear from the published patent rolls. There may indeed have been some other favours for his clients, such grants seldom naming the sponsor: his servant, Richard ap Robert ap Ivan Vaughan, for whom he secured a grant on 20 February,[6] is unlikely to have been the only one. It is unknown whether any other requests were declined. Four acts of parliament recorded other concessions.[7] On 18 February Gloucester once again took the office of great chamberlain of England that his brother Clarence had held for life:[8] henceforth he was once again 'the Right high and myghty Prince Richard Duke of Gloucester, great Chamberleyn, Constable, and Admirall of England'.[9] Richard valued such titles. He had resented being obliged to surrender the great chamberlainship, and had continued to covet it. In 1479 he secured a re-grant for himself alone, the exceptional exemption from fees and fines for chancery documents that had been awarded to him and his brother Clarence in 1465.[10]

On 13 February 1478 Gloucester's son and heir Edward of Middleham was created earl of Salisbury.[11] This had been a title of Warwick the Kingmaker that had been assigned to Clarence by charter on 25 March

---

[6] Hicks, *Clarence*, pp. 150–1.

[7] *PROME*, vol. 14, pp. 355–6, 359–61; *Rolls of Parliament* (London, 1783), vol. 6, pp 70–1.

[8] Hicks, *Clarence*, p. 151; *CPR 1476–85*, p. 67; C 81/863/4665.

[9] North Yorkshire RO ZRC/17478; St George's Chapel Windsor MS XI.P.11.

[10] BL MS Cotton Julius BXII f. 226. Presumably Clarence retained the original: hence Gloucester's re-grant, *CPR 1461–7*, p. 387; *1476–85*, p. 166.

[11] *CPR 1476–85*, pp. 67–8.

1472.[12] 'The right high & mightie prince the duke of Clarence' started calling himself 'The duke of Clarence Erle of Warwik & Sarum & great chamberlain of England'.[13] Another charter had also made Clarence into earl of Warwick,[14] which title was inherited in his death by Clarence's son Edward. The Salisbury title seems, however, to have been regarded as forfeit. Indeed Richard had described his son as earl of Salisbury on 17 July 1477,[15] previous to Clarence's trial and forfeiture. This is evidence either that Edward had already decided to destroy Clarence and had assigned this title to Edward of Middleham, or that Gloucester already aspired to a title that belonged to Clarence. In 1472 surely one earldom each should have been allocated to each duke? Most probably Edward IV was godfather to Richard's son Edward of Middleham and gave him his name. In 1467 he had created John de la Pole, eldest son of his sister Elizabeth and his eldest nephew, earl of Lincoln.[16]

One of these acts of the 1478 parliament degraded George Neville, duke of Bedford, nephew of the Kingmaker and heir of John Marquis Montagu from his dukedom, his father's marquisate and barony, and indeed from the peerage altogether.[17] Obviously the marriage with Princess Elizabeth that had justified George's elevation would not now happen, especially as she had been betrothed since to the future Charles VIII of France. The principal reason for George's demotion was that he was rightful heir to Warwick's Neville lordships in the North. When parliament resettled the Warwick inheritance in 1474–5, George had been disabled from inheriting any of the Neville patrimony. This had been mainly to the advantage of Gloucester. However, George was still a great heir through his mother, whose case could well be advanced in future, and would indeed have succeeded as earl of Worcester in 1484. If he were to die childless, parliament had protected the rights of the next male heirs (in particular his cousin Richard Lord Latimer). When George came of age in 1486, he could take his seat in the Lords and press his case in person. Gloucester

[12] *Calendar of the Charter Rolls 1427–1516*, p. 239.
[13] E.g., J. Prince, *The Worthies of Devon* (Rees & Curtis, 1810), p. 373.
[14] *Calendar of Charter Rolls 1427–1516*, p. 240.
[15] Cambridge, Queens' College, charter 6.
[16] GEC, vol. 7, p. 688.
[17] *PROME*, vol. 14, p. 361.

foresaw this and needed to sideline him. A first step was this act, which denied George a forum where his complaints could be heard. Its contention, that he lacked the resources to support any estate, was patently untrue. Later Gloucester was to acquire his wardship and he sought, unsuccessfully, to secure that of Latimer as well.[18]

Richard focused his power in northern England, especially Yorkshire, and consolidated them by two grants of key holdings that had belonged to Clarence, Richmond castle and fee farm – the centre of Richmondshire, where Middleham was located – and the reversion of the castle, lordship, and manor of Helmsley on the death of Marjorie Dowager-Lady Roos.[19]

This grant of Richmond and its castle, which the Neville earls of Warwick and Westmorland had held, rounded off Gloucester's principal concentration of estates. The leading landowners of Richmond honour, such as Lords FitzHugh and Scrope of Masham, nominally owed castleguard to their feudal lord and now therefore to Richard.[20] If he wanted the honour of Richmond too, from which most of his Richmondshire retainers held their lands, he was not awarded it, but he nevertheless searched out its records. Anxious to maximise his estate and not to overlook any potential rights, he had copied into his cartulary the charter of Richmond honour and a list of its knights fees, the inquisitions post mortem of John of Brittany, earl of Richmond (d. 1334), and of three successive lords of Middleham: John Lord Neville of Raby (d. 1388), Ralph Earl of Westmorland (d. 1425), and his countess Joan (d. 1441).[21] Richard reinforced his local sway by the two colleges that he founded at Middleham and Barnard Castle in 1478 and the two fairs at Middleham that he had licensed in 1479. The colleges and fairs gave spiritual and economic dimensions to his local dominance, although ultimately all four failed.[22] Most probably he prevailed against

[18] M.A. Hicks, 'What Might Have Been: George Neville, Duke of Bedford, 1465–83: His Identity and Significance', in *Rivals*, pp. 291–6; see also M.A. Hicks, 'Richard Lord Latimer, Richard III, and the "Warwick Inheritance" ', *Ricardian* 154 (2001), pp. 314–20.

[19] *CPR 1476–85*, p. 90. Whether Clarence's held Richmond Castle has been disputed, but he definitely did, M.A. Hicks, 'The Career of George Plantagenet, Duke of Clarence, 1449–78' (D.Phil. thesis, Oxford University, 1975), p. 222. The reversion materialised immediately with the death on 20 April 1478 of the aged Marjorie Lady Roos, GEC, vol. 11, p. 104.

[20] As depicted in BL Faustina BVII f. 85; Hicks, *Warwick*, pl. 3.

[21] BL MS Cotton Julius BXII ff. 130–4, 256–59v, 262–4v, 269–89, 295–7.

[22] *CPR 1476–85*, pp. 67, 154.

Henry Tudor, earl of Richmond by right, who attended the marriage banquet of Edward's second son Richard Duke of York at this crucial time. Certainly Tudor wanted to recover his earldom – at some date his mother had Earl Edmund's original 1452 grant copied on the back of a draft pardon for Henry Tudor[23] – but nothing came of it. While Gloucester certainly wanted Richmond Castle, King Edward kept hold of the more lucrative demesne of Richmond honour in Cambridgeshire, Lincolnshire, and Norfolk. These were indeed almost the only parts of the crown estate that the king retained as income.

The grant of the forfeited lordship of Helmsley, like Scarborough and Skipton, strengthened him where he was already strong. Helmsley gave Richard reason to resist any restoration of the Roos family, its former holders.[24] He had a mid-fourteenth-century inquisition for Helmsley copied into his cartulary.

Whereas parliament in 1474 had barred the two dukes from alienating any part of the Warwick inheritance, in 1475 it permitted Richard to obtain another part of the lordship of Cottingham and the borough of Scarborough in return for Bushey and Ware (Hertfordshire) and Chesterfield.[25] Richard was strengthening his landholdings in the North. It is less clear why King Edward wanted these properties or indeed the castles of Corfe in Dorset, Sudeley in Gloucestershire, and Farleigh Hungerford in Wiltshire that he took in exchange for Clarence's lordships in 1478.[26] If anything, Edward gained more than what he relinquished: Farleigh Hungerford and Sudeley were brand new modern residences. Perhaps Richard had no use for them. Certainly he prioritised the consolidation of his estates and therefore his power in Yorkshire. His Yorkshire estates were valuable in themselves. They also underpinned the wardenship of the West March that he had renewed in 1480.

A second focus of his power was in Wales, where he also took the opportunity to consolidate his estate. It comprised two major marcher lordships

---

[23] Westminster Abbey MS 32378. I am indebted to the abbey librarian for a photocopy of this document.

[24] The Rooses were not included in the chancery suit over the Beauchamp Trust, National Archives C 1/66/376.

[25] *PROME* xiv. 126; *CPR 1467–77*, 507.

[26] *CPR 1476–85*, p. 90.

in South Wales, Abergavenny and Glamorgan, the greatest of them all, and two on the English border, Chirk and Elfael/Elvell (Pain's Castle). He had swapped Chirk for Skipton in 1475,[27] and now in 1477–8 he exchanged Elfael for the Duchy of Lancaster lordship of Ogmore, which was an enclave in Glamorgan,[28] thus consolidating his holdings in this second area of great strength. If, as stated previously, Gloucester also wanted the neighbouring lordship of Gower, including Swansea, his aspirations went unfulfilled.[29]

III

Richard's priorities extended beyond material wealth, political power, and his own lifetime. Although aged only 25, Richard was already making lavish provision for his immortal soul. The Duchess Anne was patroness of several religious houses that had been established by her forebears and in particular was foundress of the Augustinian priory of Bisham in Berkshire, the mausoleum of the earls of Salisbury where the two Richard Nevilles, her father and grandfather, had been laid to rest. Tewkesbury Abbey, Warwick College, and Durham Cathedral were three other grand places of burial and intercession for her ancestors. Gloucester rejected these potential objects of his patronage: perhaps Bisham, Tewkesbury, and Warwick were too far south for a northern magnate? New foundations were extremely expensive and approval was not guaranteed for the alienation in mortmain of endowments to them. Edward IV was disinclined to license such alienations to the Church and normally exacted substantial fines when he did.[30] Richard's plans required such licences and he wanted to avoid paying fines.[31] An earlier licence of 10 April 1477 had allowed him to endow Queens' College, Cambridge to pray for his soul and the souls of his consort, his son and the De Veres, to which on 17 July he had added the king and

---

[27] *CPR 1467–77*, pp. 505, 556–7; BL MS Cotton Julius BXII ff. 209–10v, 246–52.

[28] Ogmore was granted to him in November 1477, DL 37/46/15, and confirmed by act of parliament in 1478, *PROME*, vol. 14, pp. 355–6; BL MS Cotton Julius BXII ff.204–5v.

[29] See above ch. 5.

[30] S. Raban, *Mortmain Legislation and the English Church 1279–1500* (Cambridge University Press, 1982), p. 63 (graph 5); Hicks, 'Chantries, Obits and Almshouses: The Hungerford Foundations 1325–1478', in *Rivals*, pp. 88, pp. 94–6.

[31] *CPR 1476–85*, p. 166.

queen, Richard Duke of York and his brother Edmund who had a special obit, his other brothers, sisters, and any other children to be born to himself. Four extra fellows were funded.[32] About the same time he also licensed as feudal lord the endowment and steered the creation of John Skrene's new chantry in the college.[33] Also in 1476 the advowson of Seaham in County Durham that he had bought for £100 from Ralph Bowes esquire was conferred on and appropriated to the abbey of Coverham near Middleham.[34]

On 8–9 February 1478 he secured two further licences to found two new colleges: that dedicated to Christ, the Blessed Virgin and St Alkilda (the parish dedication) at Middleham and the second to Christ, the Virgin, St Ninian and St Margaret (the existing dedicatee) in the castle chapel at Barnard Castle. Middleham College absorbed the existing parish church and its rectory, which was appropriated as part of the college endowment. Middleham College was to consist of a dean, six chaplains, four clerks and six choristers. The larger Barnard Castle College consisted of a dean, 12 chaplains, 10 clerks, six choristers, and another clerk.[35] Both of course were chantry colleges that were intended to pray for his good estate in life and to speed him, his immediate family, and others named by them through Purgatory after his death. The De Veres were omitted. To his parents and siblings were added specifically his eldest sister Anne Duchess of Exeter (d. 1476), but not his late brother George. His statutes for Middleham do not suggest he intended burial there, but this may have been planned for the larger and grander establishment at Barnard Castle. Together worth £400 a year, these two colleges were the largest and wealthiest such establishments in northern England. Each dwarfed Staindrop College nearby, the relatively new foundation of the senior house of Neville.

Considerable planning had already gone into these prospective establishments. Richard had decided on the locations, dedications, numbers of

[32] Ibid., p. 34; Searle, *History of Queens' College* (Cambridge Antiquarian Society, 1867), pp. 87–92.

[33] A.F. Sutton, 'Sir John Skrene, Richard of Gloucester, and Queens' College, Cambridge', *Ricardian*, 21 (2011), pp. 38–45.

[34] Sharp, *The Rising in the North. The 1569 Rebellion* (Shotton, 1975), p. 369; *VCH Yorkshire*, 52, p. 244; Durham Priory Register, iv ff. 174v–175, 185v; Surtees, *History and Antiquities of the County of Durham* (1816), vol. 1, pp. 299–300.

[35] *CPR 1476–85*, p. 67; W. Dugdale, *Monasticon Anglicanum*, eds J. Caley et al. (1846), vol. 6, p. 1440.

chaplains, clerks, and choristers, and incomes of each establishment that, in Middleham's case, he subsequently elaborated in his statutes. Beyond these licences he secured from parliament permission to appropriate six rectories of the Warwick inheritance towards Barnard Castle College.[36] Such appropriations would enable him to divert spiritual income that he could not otherwise access from these parishes to his chosen purposes. The Church approved such asset-stripping because they increased divine worship. Such endowments cost him nothing in monetary terms, though he did sacrifice some ecclesiastical patronage thereby, but they could take effect only when the livings were vacated by death or resignation. Resignation involved buying out the incumbent. This complication and the consequent expense may explain why these appropriations had not happened by his death. Several of the churches indeed were diverted elsewhere, to St George's Chapel at Windsor and Queens' College, Cambridge.[37] That the licence specified Barnard College was a technicality that the duke ignored. His feoffees actually did convey to Middleham College lands worth 200 marks (£133 6s. 8d.) a year that he had extracted by duress from the countess of Oxford.[38] Her estate may also have been the intended source of the endowment for Barnard Castle, although in the absence of documentation this cannot be proved. It seems anyway unlikely to have been endowed. Richard intended these endowments to be permanent, but was prepared to give them away for the benefit of his soul, while yielding nothing of the Warwick and De Vere inheritances to the rightful heirs. He was not a compromiser.

Maybe the implementation of the college at Barnard Castle in the now vanished castle chapel was delayed, although some building was undertaken, but the mere absence of evidence for the foundation, staffing, and endowment does not prove these did not happen, since the same conclusion could have been reached about Middleham had the church archives remarkably not survived. Although Middleham College was never

[36] *PROME*, vol. 14, p. 360.

[37] *CPR 1476–85*, p. 255; St George's Chapel, Windsor MSS XI.P.7, P 9; XI.P.11, 12; *VCH Berkshire*, vol. 4, p. 484; Ross, 'Richard, Duke of Gloucester and the De Vere estates', *Ricardian*, 15 (2005), p. 26. The chapter had to pay £100 for Olney, but the grant was not effective, *VCH Bucks*, vol. 4, p. 438.

[38] North Yorkshire RO ZRC 17503.

completed and died with King Richard, new choir stalls had been constructed, the rectory house was adapted, the parochial living was appropriated, a spiritual peculiar was created, the dean and chaplains were named, the clerks and choristers were appointed, and the whole endowment was conveyed to the new college. Gloucester had renounced 200 marks a year to the college and was spending besides substantial sums each year on new buildings. He wanted his colleges big, he wanted them quickly, and he wanted them exactly as he had determined. There are striking parallels here with the two other colleges he established as king, of 100 priests at York and of a dean and six canons at Barking, whom he also appointed, endowed, and set in motion ahead of the buildings even though Middleham and Barnard Castle were still unfinished.[39]

Richard's deeds reveal an intimate knowledge of the town of Middleham and concern for his new college. He conveyed certain plots of land for particular purposes and allotted specific tithes. His knowledge emerges from his statutes of 4 July 1478 that show the college to be up and running, even if as yet in provisional premises.[40] Founders could shape such freestanding colleges much more freely as they wished than they could through new monasteries within the older religious orders that had prescriptive rules, or through chantries within existing cathedrals or colleges that operated by permission and under restrictions set by the church authorities. There was no external authority at Middleham. Aspects of Richard's foundations were borrowed from other colleges that he knew. Apart from Fotheringhay College, Richard was familiar with the colleges of Stoke by Clare in Suffolk, founded by his great-uncle Edmund, last Mortimer earl of March, with St Stephen's College at Westminster, and with his brothers' two colleges at Warwick and at Windsor. None of these operated exactly like his own, but he melded together from such existing establishments his provisions for financial management (e.g., chest with multiple keys), for the conduct and discipline of the clergy, the custody of the church's treasure, and the tuition of the choristers, and also, because Middleham remained

[39] See below.

[40] Raine, 'The Statutes Ordained by Richard Duke of Gloucester, for the College of Middleham', *Archaeological Journal*, 14 (1857), pp. 160–70. This is the principal source for the following three paragraphs.

parochial, for the cure of souls. Middleham was reconstituted an ecclesiastical peculiar, exempt from the authority of the archdeacon and archbishop, and Richard insisted on its autonomy directly under the authority of the dean. The liturgical provisions, which prescribed the Use of Sarum even in northern England, designated particular masses and prayers, commemoration of benefactors and obits that paralleled practice elsewhere, albeit with Richard's own particular preferences.

It is these individual features that step beyond any known models and whatever guidance that was provided by the learned clerics who surely drafted many of the statutes. These characteristics give insight into Richard's personal piety, into his knowledge and understanding of the liturgy, and his religious tastes. Richard thought big. He wanted maximum value for his money. The income was fully committed: there was no spare income, no hedge against the inflation that was to prevail in the Tudor century. The duke wanted a splendid choral and musical display.[41] There was an organ and an organist, who acted as choir master, and the most up-to-date church music: 'playne song, priked song, faburdon, counter, and descant of all measures used in any cathedral church or college'. Four saints – George, Ninian, Cuthbert, and Anthony – were allotted principal feasts, celebrations comparable in scope and elaboration to Christmas and Easter, and another 38 favourite saints were designated double feast days, each of which necessitated nine proper (special, specific) lessons and anthems on the feast day itself and observances for the following eight days (the octave). Since almost every day of the year had become special, Richard was expecting of his clergy, clerks, and choristers an unremitting and exhausting round of sung celebrations. Besides the primary dedications (see above), the dean and chaplains occupied in order of priority choir stalls dedicated to the Blessed Virgin, St George, St Katherine, St Ninian, St Cuthbert, St Anthony, and St Barbara. Most of his saints were biblical and antique and drawn from the calendar of Sarum, a couple from York alone (e.g., St William of York), yet others from neither, and most did not

[41] This most probably mirrored what happened in the roving chapel of his own household under its dean reported by Nicholas von Poppelau, L. Visser-Fuchs, 'What Niclas von Popplau Really Wrote About Richard III', *Ricardian* 145 (1999), p. 527; Raine, 'Statutes', p. 163.

feature in either the *Golden Legend* or Osbert Bokenham's *Legend of Holy Women* on which the duke clearly relied. This applied most obviously to St Ninian, the sixth-century apostle to the Picts and of the West March, whom the duke particularly venerated. Recognising that Ninian and others might lack the necessary services, Richard ordered 'that then the dean for the tyme being during my liffe shal take in this partie with myne adviace such good direccion as shalbe thought most according to theffect of this myne ordinance, which direccion so to be take, I wol be observid after my decese for ever'. He reserved to himself for life the resolution of any points of doubt and any further ordinances. To produce such a coherent set of statutes that fulfilled his personal religious aspirations certainly demanded careful composition and attention to detail from the founder. Richard committed himself to intervene and resolve in future.

Presumably the same was also true of the larger Barnard Castle College, if its statutes were finalised as conceivably they may have been. What necessitated such detailed statutes so early at Middleham was that the staff had already been appointed and the college was in operation. It is not known whether this applied also to Barnard Castle. The same sort of concentrated drafting and decisive direction is apparent in his ordinances for the office of arms that he devised as constable and in the reforms he implemented as king.

On 6 November 1478 Richard also founded a chantry of a single priest within his brother's new college at Windsor that he endowed with another three manors wrested from the Countess Elizabeth.[42]

IV

Richard's wish list of 1476–8 reveal a great nobleman with an excellent grasp of his own affairs, with a whole series of unsatisfied aspirations for his titles, status, estates, and foundations, that were underpinned by his strategic visions of the future for himself and his family both in this world and the next. Richard was a farsighted administrator, who looked ahead and liked working out details in advance of need. He was a man of independent and decided opinions who was not afraid to depart from the norm, who

[42] St George's Chapel MS XI.P.11, 12.

was determined to have things his way, yet who was prepared to adapt to
circumstances, to take what he could get now in the expectation of further
opportunities. The Middleham statutes commence with Richard's assessment of where he stood – quite remarkable, both because of its clear-eyed
frankness and because it was directed to a tiny audience, the staff of
Middleham College. This autobiographical statement thankfully attributes
to God his extraordinary transformation from a youngest son 'nakidly
borne into this wretched world destitute of possessions, goods and enheretamentes' into 'the grete astate, honor and dignite that he haith called me
now unto, to be named, knowed, reputed and called Richard Duc of
Gloucestre', and to great possessions, and his preservation from great jeop-
ardies (the Second War of the Roses). Such benefits went beyond his
deserts. Therefore, the duke explained, he was earmarking 'part of such
goods as He haith sent me . . . to do divyne service ther daily [and] to pray
for the good astates . . . and for the soules [of the king and his family] . . . in
part of satisfaccion of suche things as at the dredfull day of dome I shal
answere for'.[43] He was a sinner, repentant but answerable to God for his
sins at the Last Judgement, and he invoked Christ's 'blissed moder . . .
socour and refuge of all synners repentant'.[44] There is no inkling here of
any particular guilt, such as the murders ascribed to him of Henry VI,
Edward of Lancaster, or his brother Clarence, or his mistreatment of the
countesses of Oxford and Warwick and Lady Hungerford. He was utterly
conventional in his acceptance of the existence of Purgatory, when his soul
would be purged of sin by suffering in the aeons between his death and the
Last Judgement. He believed also in the mitigation of such suffering by the
masses in which he invested so heavily and that he was, moreover, to
commission in even larger numbers as king. Richard took it for granted
that he was entitled to what he held, no matter how obtained. He gave
away the countess's lands because he had acquired them personally and
there were no limits to his title, not because he feared to lose them. They
were after all his investment for his immortal soul. The overall impression
is of satisfaction at his lot, indeed astonished contentment, and the absence

---

[43] Raine, 'Statutes', pp. 160–70. 'ye' and 'yt', properly thorns, have been rendered as 'th'.
It is likely that a similar statement preceded statutes for Barnard Castle College.
[44] Ibid.

of further aspirations. Certainly on 4 July 1478 he had no ambitions for the rule of southern Scotland or the throne.

This does not mean that the duke would not develop further desires or grasp new aspirations. He was, after all, only 25 years of age. He hoped for other children: 'such other issue as shal pleas God to send me'. There was more business to be done. His two colleges alone needed to be constructed, endowed, and completed. He needed to assure his hold – and that of his heirs – on the Neville inheritance. It is impossible to gauge how seriously he aspired to possess those other estates held by Anne's ancestors that feature in his cartulary. There were other properties that he coveted to round off his estates and/or to which he nursed what he regarded as legitimate claims. Lincolnshire and Rutland do not appear an important area for him, but surviving accounts reveal that he now seized additional property, at Essendine and Shillingthorpe.[45] Additionally he thought the great mansion of Coldharbour (le Erber) in London should have been allotted to him rather than Clarence.[46]

Richard also sought a share of the lands of the Beauchamp Trust. These were lands in the West Midlands that were worth £323 in 1482. They had been assigned to the fulfilment of the will of Richard Beauchamp, earl of Warwick (d. 1439), the most notable purpose being the establishment of the earl's chantry in the Beauchamp Chapel at Warwick College. By 1475 the earl's instructions had been performed and arguably the lands should have devolved on the heirs, either his daughter the Countess Anne or the lines of all four of his daughters, whose dispute about the main Beauchamp estate had been settled in Anne's favour by 1467. These lands were not included in 1474–5 in the partition of the Warwick inheritance between Clarence and Warwick, as perhaps they should have been, and Gloucester had no share of them. In practice John Hugford, the sole surviving feoffee, held them to Clarence's use, but Elizabeth, the youngest and last survivor of the daughters, considered herself entitled to an allocation. Following Clarence's death, the coheirs petitioned for termination of the trust and the division of the estate. Those petitioning were Edward Grey of Astley, Lord

45 M.A. Hicks, 'Descent, Partition and Extinction: The "Warwick Inheritance" ', in *Rivals*, p. 331.
46 See below p. 346.

Lisle, representative of the senior line; Elizabeth Lady Latimer, third daughter; and Clarence's son Edward Earl of Warwick and Richard Duke of Gloucester, rather than the legally dead Anne Countess of Warwick, for the fourth line. The petition failed, perhaps because the second line was unrepresented, because Thomas Lord Roos had been attainted, and/or because the three-year-old Edward Earl of Warwick could not sue at law. Young Warwick would have been the principal loser – of seven-eighths of the properties or £280 a year. To secure at most one-eighth of the estate, £40 a year, in an area of no particular importance to himself, Duke Richard was seeking to dispossess his nephew of seven-eighths. Evidently he resented his exclusion and asserted his right, collaborating with any allies he could find. The other coheirs were to try twice more.[47] All they achieved, it seems, was to expose the trust to the attention of King Edward, who seized possession, perhaps under the guise of part of the inheritance of the king's ward Warwick.[48] Once king, Richard no longer cared.

In 1478, although appreciative of his unforeseen advancement, Duke Richard did not restrict himself to the limits set by the king, within the scope of his estates and offices, or within the traditions that he had inherited. He looked ahead, to the potential for further development and self-aggrandisement, and proceeded rapidly to action. His plans involved substantial capital expenditure. He gave away much that he had acquired by his own efforts and later, as king, he was to alienate lands of his duchess's inheritance that prudence demanded that he retained when duke. His projects, moreover, were based on careful research, on detailed planning that would take years to fulfil, and on implementation that began at once. Undoubtedly Richard had good advice from the best experts, but he himself was the guiding mind and often indeed the codifier. His statutes reveal how far ahead and how thorough he was and how distinctive were the personal tastes to which his foundations gave expression.

---

[47] C 1/66/376; C 1/58/156, C 1/77/30; M.A. Hicks, 'The Beauchamp Trust 1439–87', in *Rivals*, pp. 337–52 at 343, 347.

[48] *H433*, vol. 2, p. 57. An estate account survives in the royal archive, DL 29/645/10464.

V

Richard's wish list of 1477–8 demonstrates just how wide-ranging was the duke's grasp of his own affairs, how comprehensive and many-sided were his ambitions, how unsentimental he was in what he alienated and exchanged, and how astute and multifaceted were his tactics. Ruthless self-aggrandisement was coupled with a distinctive, well-informed, and highly expensive piety. While always respectful to Edward IV and Prince Edward, Gloucester exploited the king's need for his backing to extract the maximum advantage from Clarence's destruction. While accepting the king's lead and obeying his commands, Gloucester managed both the king and parliament, and concealed from everyone his real feelings, whatever they were, of Clarence's fall and the king's Wydeville relatives. Such presentational skills were to be useful again in 1483. Richard did not obtain everything he wanted and was indeed to return for more. The Scottish war was to give him the military command he craved and from there emerged new opportunities – the dominance of Cumbria and a Scottish principality for himself and his heirs – that he cannot seriously have aspired to in 1478. What Richard had secured became, once again, the basis for further appointments, grants, and even more elaborate schemes. Of course Clarence's death did ease Richard's path to the crown, but there is no contemporary evidence of any such fantasy at this early date.

Chapter Nine

CAREER CULMINATION

THE SCOTTISH WAR 1480–3

I

Richard's career as duke of Gloucester and as warden of the marches culminated in the Scottish war of 1480–4. He was king's lieutenant of the North – commander in chief – with royal authority over all the marches and in particular over the earl of Northumberland. This was what he and the people of the North had been preparing: strengthening defences, amassing ordnance, and recruiting retainers. His lieutenancy gave him overall command over the more important Eastern Marches, whence he launched at least three offensives. Henry Earl of Northumberland, who accompanied him, was treated sensitively and indeed given the place of honour. It was the fulfilment of Richard's ducal career. He achieved the renown he craved and the praise of parliament. Moreover, it set his career on a new trajectory, beyond mere dominance of the north of his brother's kingdom, to the unchecked authority of a principality created in south-west Scotland. What made it possible was that this was a role to which King Edward had aspired for himself. The king viewed war with Scotland as an opportunity for renown, to enhance his reputation, possibly to erase memories of his inglorious Picquigny campaign. He spent lavishly on it, financing the largest of armies and complementary naval forces, and equipping the army with a modern ordnance train led by professional gunners. It was the expectation of a glorious campaign under the king's personal command that caused everybody who mattered in northern England to participate, as well as a good many peers and other gentry from further south. They did recognise an element of risk. Actually the king did not campaign. He found once again, as in the 1460s, that he had other pressing concerns that kept him at headquarters. He had to delegate the responsibility and the honours to his brother. The disarray of the Scots limited what could be achieved. Success had to be hyped, rather than being self-evident, as in the next century after Flodden, Solway Moss, and Pinkie.

This war terminated a long period of amity between England and Scotland. The long truce of 1465 had been prolonged in 1474 and should have endured until 1519. The border town of Berwick on the North Sea coast, which had been surrendered to the Scots in 1460–1 by Queen Margaret of Anjou, remained in Scottish hands. In 1465 King Edward had accepted that he lacked the resources to recover Berwick. To recapture it would have required him to wage an expensive war on the extreme periphery of his kingdom. The abandonment of Berwick was a conspicuous blot on Edward's reputation. The town's loss and recovery symbolised much more to him than its actual military value. So, too, its retention by the Scottish King James III, who valued the town much more than the Scottish parliament.

Later, in 1474, English relations with Scotland took second place to Edward's invasion of France. Indeed the two kings agreed to marry Edward IV's third daughter Cecily (b. 1469) to the Scottish heir, the future James IV (b. 1473). Of course the two children were too young to cohabit or to consummate their union, but King Edward scrupulously paid instalments of Cecily's dowry each year.[1] Subsequently it was also agreed that King James's young sister Margaret would marry King Edward's brother-in-law Anthony Earl Rivers. Though both were old enough to proceed, the implementation of the marriage treaty of 1478 was repeatedly delayed. A whole series of safe conducts for her free passage to England went unused: she did not come. The financial weakness of the Scots was at the root of all delays. James III could not raise the money even for Margaret's dowry – the 4,000 marks

[1] Ross, *Edward IV*, p. 278.

(£2,666 6s. 8d.) due, so vast to the Scots, was trivial to the English – or indeed for her to travel in sufficient state to Nottingham where she was to be married.[2]

It was the responsibility of the wardens of the marches both in England and in Scotland to maintain the peace, to prevent breaches of the truce, and to arrange reparations. This role was not particularly attractive to the wardens or to the local populations, for whom warfare offered opportunities for distinction and perhaps for profit. There seem to have been more infractions of the truce – or perhaps more serious ones – towards the end of the 1470s. In 1477 King Edward had addressed two such infractions. Gloucester's retainer Robert Constable was commanded to make restitution to the Scot Thomas Yare and then, when he defaulted, the king summoned him in person to explain himself. King Edward directed Gloucester as warden to ensure 'due reformacion to be had' according to marcher law and custom to the robbed tenants of the Scottish Sir John Carlile.[3] In another such outrage, at a day of truce and with at least the acquiescence of the Scottish lieutenant, the Percy retainer Robert Lisle was murdered and Northumberland's cousin and lieutenant Henry Percy was captured.[4] In 1479 therefore James III had indicted of treason the warden, his brother Alexander Duke of Albany.[5] The English suspected that such infractions were fomented by the French, as Louis XI sought to distract Edward from intervention in his war with Burgundy by reviving the Auld Alliance, which was popular in Scotland,[6] but there is no hard evidence for this. Differences of this type, given the will, could be easily reconciled through the normal mechanisms of diets and days of the march. However all parties seem to have become irritated by the status quo.

Professor Macdougall considered that Edward had grounds for dissatisfaction, since he had paid much of the dowry without the marriage being

---

[2] N. Macdougall, *James III. A Political Study* (John Donald, 1982), pp. 141–2.

[3] Ellis, *Original Letters* (Harding, Triphook and Leonard, 1822–46), vol. 1, I, 17.

[4] *CDRS*, vol. 4, p. 414. Not Northumberland himself as in S. Cunningham, 'The Yorkists at War: Military Leadership in the English War with Scotland 1480–82', in *The Yorkist Age*, eds H. Kleineke and C. Steer (Shaun Tyas, 2013), p. 186. For the date, see Macdougall, *James III*, pp. 143, 156 n 22.

[5] A. Grant, 'Richard III and Scotland', in *The North of England in the Age of Richard III*, ed. A.J. Pollard (Sutton, 1996), p. 121.

[6] For some evidence here, see Macdougall, *James III*, p. 144.

effected,[7] but this seems premature, since Cecily was still only ten years old and James was a mere six. What is certain is that Edward felt much stronger than previously, that he now had the financial and other resources (e.g., cannon) to wage war at a distance from his base, and that he thought that he could recover Berwick without jeopardising his daughter's marriage. Probably he supposed the Scots were in no financial state to resist. The economic depression was particularly deep in Scotland and there was a great shortage of victuals. The Scottish parliament voted only enough money for 600 men for three months, and all James's other expedients to raise money, including a drastic debasement of the coinage, did not suffice. Edward proceeded very rapidly to threats of 'cruel and rigorous war' if reparations were not made and early in 1480 to an ultimatum. His four principal demands were the immediate marriage of James and Cecily; the handover of Berwick, Coldingham, Roxburgh, and other towns now in Scotland that at some dates had been held by the English; the homage of King of Scots in acknowledgement of English overlordship over Scotland; and the restoration of the exiled Earl Douglas to his offices and estates.[8] Perhaps Edward half recalled the English claims to Scotland that the forger John Hardyng had urged on him in his First Reign. Certainly on 20 February 1481 he looked out the record of the homage and fealty of King David II.[9] Princess Margaret's marriage was forgotten: by October 1480, her fiancé Earl Rivers had married Mary Lewis and the princess herself had lapsed into a dubious liaison with Lord Crichton, by whom she had a bastard daughter.[10] The subjection of Scotland was the least attainable of these demands – King James alone could not concede it and the Scots were proudly independent – and the restoration of Earl Douglas the easiest, though Edward clearly rated it least as it quickly disappeared from his demands. War could be averted, Edward declared, if Prince James was handed over immediately and if Berwick was surrendered. Offers to negotiate by the Scots were rudely brushed aside. Since the royal marriage was

---

[7] Ibid., p. 143.

[8] Ross, *Edward IV*, p. 279; Macdougall, *James III*, p. 144; *CDRS*, vol. 4, pp. 412–14.

[9] *Antient Kalendars and Inventories of Treasury of his Majesty's Exchequer*, ed. F.C. Palgrave (Record Commission, 1836), vol. 1, pp. 19–30.

[10] GEC, vol. 11, p. 24; Macdougall, *James III*, p. 198.

already agreed, it appears that what Edward wanted most was Berwick, which was unfinished business from his First Reign and that was a continuous stain on his honour. Berwick was his initial war aim. He presented the war fallaciously as a war of defence against Scottish aggression.[11] Presumably Edward hoped that the Scots would comply or at least expected some concessions. He miscalculated.

This obscure war is remembered for two reasons. It was the war that restored the border town of Berwick permanently to the English crown. Secondly and principally it is because the English commander was Richard Duke of Gloucester, who was offered an easy opportunity to accrue renown against a feeble, leaderless, and bankrupt foe. Martial and aggressive in temperament and expert in such attributes as heraldry and ordnance, Duke Richard had hitherto been denied the battleground he sought, but now had the chance for military distinction. To be warden of the lesser part of the most distant border in time of peace required policing minor raids, a role that the duke delegated as a matter of course to his lieutenant. In wartime the raids were bigger and more frequent, both by the English into Scotland and the Scots into England, and they affected more than the borderers. The whole northern aristocracy, as far south as Yorkshire and Lancashire, were expected to engage in combat. If he carried on southwards and did not join in, observed Richard's friend Lord Lovell, it 'wold be said I withdrew me for [from] the said warre',[12] a shameful act of cowardice that made his participation in the campaign imperative. Fighting the Scots was the raison d'être for the northern aristocracy, many of whom joined in the campaigns, some several times.

Unique insights are provided by three letters from the earl of Northumberland as warden of the Eastern Marches to his retainer Robert Plumpton, esquire and in 1482 knighted in Scotland by the earl. 'Right welbeloued frinde', he wrote briefly and to the point, 'I will & charge you on the kings our soueraigne lords behalf, and also on myne, that ye, with all such persones as ye may make defensibly arrayed, be redy to attend vpon

[11] Ross, *Edward IV*, pp. 278–9; *Coventry Leet Book*, ed. M.D. Harris, Early English Text Society 134–5, 138, 146 (Kegan Paul, 1907–13), pp. 475–6; H. Hatcher, *History of Modern Wiltshire: Old and New Sarum*, ed. R.C. Hoare (J. Nichols, 1822–44), p. 199.

[12] *Stono L & P*, vol. 2, p. 150.

the kings highness & me, vpon our warnyng, as ye loue me, and will answere to the king at your perill'. Each retainer brought his own household – and sometimes tenants too – horsed and harnessed for the fray. Notice was short, usually a muster being set a couple of days away, 'not failing hereof, as ye will answere to the kings highness and to me at your perill'. A similar letter of about 1487 tersely commanded 11 such knights and esquires 'to be ready vpon an ower warning'.[13] Planning such raids may have taken time, but lightning speed was required from Yorkshiremen to intercept Scottish reivers 50 miles away. No equivalent letters from Gloucester as warden of the West March and lieutenant-general survive, but they certainly existed.

Nothing is known specifically of the skirmishes, sieges, pillaging, and other atrocities that surely took place. There must have been casualties on both sides. Besides the raids and counter-raids, both sides raised bigger forces with ordnance and other paraphernalia for longer and more consid-ered invasions. Since King Edward was meant to take command in person, English armies were properly resourced. Edward spent the surplus remaining from the Picquigny campaign, levied the final instalment of tax voted for the French war, and extracted forced loans (benevolences) from the mercantile elite. He deployed the modern but so far unused artillery train created for the French war and the navy that he had been developing. The king's own household treasurer, Sir John Elrington, handled the logistics as treasurer of war. These raids and campaigns reminded the northern aristocracy that they were a military caste with a mission to fight the barbarous Scots and a series of apparently unchallenged successes gave them a taste for campaigning against these traditional enemies. Yet the war lingered on longer than it should have done. This was Edward's own fault – his unwillingness to give it first place in his own time. One campaign should have been enough, but three were required. Both in 1481 and in 1482 the attack was delayed until Edward arrived, but on neither occasion did he materialise.

---

[13] The quotations blend three letters that cannot be dated with any certainty, *Plumpton L & P*, pp. 55–7, 68.

II

What happened in the war is poorly documented. Facing rising tensions, Edward IV assigned £100 to repair the walls of Carlisle in 1479 and Gloucester supplied the city with two great guns, four barrels of gunpowder, two crossbows, 100 longbows, and 400 sheaves of arrows.[14] A deadline of 1 May 1480 was set by the English for the handover of Prince James to the earl of Northumberland.[15] The deadline passed. As early as 12 May, when it had not happened, Richard Duke of Gloucester was appointed lieutenant-general of all the northern marches with power to array the adjoining counties. The patent states explicitly that he had authority over the other warden, but does not specify for how long, just that it was in the absence of the king. The actual commissions of array, for Cumberland, Northumberland, Westmorland, and all three ridings of Yorkshire, were dated 20 June. Gloucester and Northumberland were appointed to every commission: the five other peers, five knights, and Robert Greystoke in the North Riding, served the duke in the 1481–2 campaigns as did most of the commissioners in the West Riding.[16] Bishop Dudley copied the commissions for County Durham and the Durham liberties in Northumberland (North Durham). The earl of Northumberland himself was at Alnwick on 28 June 1480,[17] but not apparently in sufficient strength to confront the 'gret power of Scottis' that Archibald Earl of Angus brought to Bamburgh, where he stayed a symbolic three days and three nights. The undefended village of Bamburgh was burnt and other places nearby spoiled.[18] Bamburgh Castle itself was impregnable and was not attacked. Gloucester was at Barnard Castle on 12 August, next stop Durham,[19] where in mid-September he was mustering troops against three hosts of Scots that were expected shortly.[20] The earl of Northumberland's own records show that he responded with an expedition

[14] H. Summerson, *Medieval Carlisle*, vol. 2 (Cumberland & Westmorland Antiquarian & Archaeological Society, 1993), p. 464.

[15] *CDRS*, vol. 4, p. 413.

[16] *CPR 1476–85*, pp. 205, 213–14; *Foedera*, vol. 12, pp. 115–18.

[17] *York Memorandum Book*, vol. 2, ed. M. Sellars (Surtees Society, 1914), p. 274.

[18] Macdougall, *James III*, p. 311; *CPR 1476–85*, p. 213.

[19] Pollard, *Princes*, p. 237.

[20] Pollard, 'St Cuthbert and the Hog', in Griffiths and Sherborne, *Kings and Nobles in the Later Middle Ages* (Gloucester, A. Sutton, 1986), p. 118.

1. King Richard III: a self-image of sober splendour. The king as he chose to present himself.

2. The execution of Edmund Duke of Somerset after the battle of Tewkesbury in 1471. It was Richard Duke of Gloucester as the constable of England who judged the Lancastrian leaders and carried out the verdicts.

3. The matrix of the seal of Richard III when Duke of Gloucester, as Admiral of England.

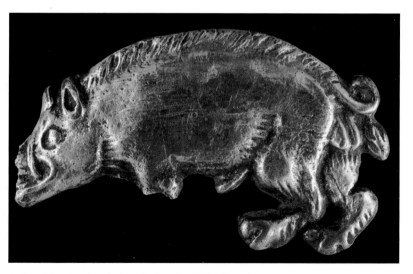

4. One of the white boar badges distributed to Richard's retainers.

5. One of the indentures of war used to recruit Gloucester's retinue of war in the Picquigny campaign. The captain was Edmund Paston. Gloucester's exhaustive contract was signed by the duke here (R. Gloucestre).

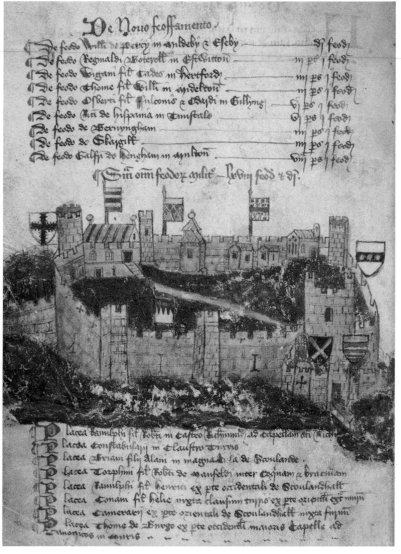

6. Richmond Castle, Yorkshire. The centre of the Richmondshire connection and Neville power and of Gloucester's military might. The principal tenants were responsible for the defences marked by their banners.

7 and 8. Two of the centres of Gloucester's estates and the locations of the colleges that focused on the new dynasty: Barnard Castle, County Durham towers above the trees (top) and Middleham Church, North Yorkshire, from the west (bottom).

9. King Richard III and Queen Anne Neville as heirs of the earldom of Warwick from the *Rous Roll*. John Rous may have devised the roll and presented it to them at Warwick Castle in 1483.

10. Bisham Priory, Berkshire: the mausoleum of the earls of Salisbury, including Anne Neville's father Warwick the Kingmaker, and where Richard chose not to be interred.

11. King Richard III and Queen Anne Neville in their coronation robes: the culmination of the second *Salisbury Roll*, which was probably updated for Richard and Anne in 1483.

2. York Minster, 'the acropolis of the North', completed in 1472. Here Richard tendered oaths to the gentry to Edward V, presided at the investiture of the prince of Wales, his son Edward of Middleham, and founded his college of a Hundred Priests.

13 and 14. St William's College, York: the magnificent half-timbered and jettied frontage of the new college of chantry priests of York Minster (top) and the upper hall (bottom). The whole quadrangle seems to have been reconfigured several times. Although founded by the Nevilles in the 1460s, the buildings may have been implemented by King Richard and may have also accommodated his Hundred Priests.

rilus dur Eboraci secundus
s Edwardi quarti

Edwardus princeps Wallie
primus filius Edwardi quarti

15. Richard Duke of York (left) and Edward V (right), sons of Edward IV, who became the Princes in the Tower.

16. Richard III's mandate to Lord Chancellor Russell for delivery of the great seal as he takes personal command against the rebellion of the duke of Buckingham in 1483. Richard writes angrily that never was 'the false traitor better provided for'. Buckingham was duly executed.

17. Richard III: the image of a cunning and masterful king. From the misericord at Christchurch Priory (formerly Hampshire), another monastery of the earldom of Salisbury, where Clarence's daughter and Richard's niece Margaret Pole, the last countess of Salisbury, founded the chantry.

from Alnwick as far as Jedburgh in August and September. The earl hired seven wagons and Percy tenants from Bilton, Denwick, Houghton, Lesbury, Rugley and Shilbottle were paid for carting 'arms and habiliments of war and victuals and other of the lord's stuff'. A French gunner 'greatly injured in his face and body' by fire at Jedburgh received medical care and a new outfit.[21] This was probably the 'Rode & recountre' into Scotland at the end of the summer that was made by the duke and earl, 'in myghty & noble apparell', with 'the nobles and Commons of the north parties of oure land'.[22] Although the Scots wisely avoided battle – or to English eyes 'shamefully . . . durst not defende their bordures ayenst the seid armee', they may have retaliated to the English foray with three other raids that wreaked 'great burning, hardship and destruction'.[23] There was a contingent from York that had returned home by 30 August.[24] Northumberland withdrew from Alnwick to the East Riding: he was at Wressle by 7 September.[25] He was expecting another incursion on 13 October,[26] which may not, however, have happened. Victuals, including 80 butts of malmsey, were sent from the south to the army and navy, and £100 to Duke Richard for repair to the city defences of Carlisle.[27] King Edward forecast a full-scale attack by the Scots in summer 1481.[28]

III

Both sides decided that in 1481 the war would continue on a larger and more organised scale. Edward IV set out his plans in the great council held at Westminster in November 1480. He was to take command himself,[29]

---

[21] Bateson et al., *History of Northumberland* (A. Reid, 1893–1940), vol. 5, p. 50; *Transactions of the Cumberland and Westmorland Archaeological Society* Tract series (1887), pp. 178–9. This may have been the counter-raid deduced by Ross, *Edward IV*, p. 282n. The earl took 15 wagons, a French gunner, and probably 'lez guncart', and bowyers made 104 bows at Alnwick Castle up to 7 November, *History of Northumberland*, vol. 5, pp. 50, 304.

[22] Ross, *Edward IV*, p. 282; *Coventry Leet Book*, pp. 475–6.

[23] *York House Books*, ed. L.C. Attreed (A. Sutton,1991), vol. 2, p. 700; *Coventry Leet Book*, pp. 475–6.

[24] *York House Books*, vol. 1, p. 221.

[25] *Plumpton L & P*, pp. 55–6 cannot relate to 1480.

[26] *York House Books*, vol. 2, p. 700.

[27] *Issues of the Exchequer*, ed. F. Devon (J. Murray, 1837), pp. 500–1.

[28] *Coventry Leet Book*, p. 476.

[29] Hatcher, *History of Modern Wiltshire: Old and New Sarum*, p. 184.

and therefore planned as impressive an expedition as possible 'to the well, surety and honour of him and his land', 'to the honour of him [and] the suerte of his subiettes', and invincible to his enemies. Spies were to be deployed in Scotland continually to report on Scottish military preparations. 'Articles of credence' directed to Gloucester and Northumberland among the York records reveal how comprehensive were the plans for recruitment and logistics and the king's desire that suppliers were duly paid at fair prices and reimbursed for any losses of war. Gloucester and Northumberland were ordered to convoke 'to their parties . . . their servauntes and inhabitauntes' to ascertain how many men the king could count on from every gentleman and township, and to nominate 'the wisest ande moste discret and best willing persones'. All troops were to wear white jackets bearing the cross of St George, if also desired worn with their lord's 'particular bagge', but not with his livery.[30] The duke and earl were to report to the king in person, which Gloucester apparently did. The king himself would bring his own troops and artillery from the south, much of it by sea.

On 12 December 1480 a practical seaman Thomas Rogers was appointed keeper of the king's ships.[31] It was Rogers who leased the ships to carry supplies and munitions northwards and also prepared the fleet that was to campaign by sea. The walls and ditches of Carlisle were to be upgraded with £100 paid by the king: there survives an indented bill dated at London on 14 December 1480 between Duke Richard and Mayor Denton recording the duke's transfer to them of 50 marks in part payment and four kildekins of gunpowder, and 400 sheaves of arrows of 'the kings stuff'.[32] Victuals were ordered in every town north of the Trent and also victuallers, who would be properly paid. Carts in the Newcastle area were to be purchased to carry victuals and a further 500 carts were to follow the host with supplies. A total of 10,000 quarters of wheat were to be conveyed from the South to Newcastle and there baked. The bakers of York, Durham,

[30] *York House Books*, vol. 2, pp. 694–5.

[31] *CPR 1476–85*, p. 242. Rogers had captained one of Warwick's ships.

[32] Cumbria Record Office, D/Lons uncatalogued. Gloucester had retained Henry Denton, son and heir of John Denton esquire, on 3 September 1473, M. Jones and S. Walker, 'Private Indentures', *Camden Miscellany*, 32 (1994), p. 173.

and Newcastle were to be ready to sell further flour as required.[33] In February 1481 11 ships were commissioned for six months. Edward IV commissioned Lords Howard and Cobham as commanders of his main North Sea fleet ('an armée roiall') with 3,500 crew victualled and furnished for 20 weeks.[34] Sir Thomas Fulford was to lead the more modest western squadron with 300 crew. These flotillas were intended to clear the seas of Scottish shipping, not to supply or support the English army.

Apart from the wardens and their retinues, the king's brother-in-law Earl Rivers was to bring 1,000 men, his stepson the teenaged marquis of Dorset 600 men from Warwickshire, and the king's steward Stanley 3,000 archers from Lancashire and Cheshire, 6,600 in all. For the militaristically minded Dorset, a champion jouster who aspired to military command, this was an opportunity to obtain experience and perhaps to add some lustre to his reputation. This time Edward was unable to suborn the Lord of the Isles. The Scots meanwhile strengthened their border garrisons. 'It is important to realize', wrote Ross, 'that by the early summer of 1481 England's resources were fully committed to war with Scotland.'[35] It is important because the campaign did not go to plan.

On 20 February 1481 Gloucester was one of the magnates of the royal council who was consulting records of the subjection of Scotland in the exchequer at Westminster. He left London by 16 April 1481,[36] presumably for the North. Howard and Fulford sailed in May 1481 and wrought havoc in the Firth of Forth. Howard captured eight ships at Leith, Kinghorn, and Pittenweem, destroyed others, burnt Blackness, and seized another large ship before returning home. Apparently he raided again, less effectively, returning to Harwich by 17 August.[37] That was before the land operation had even commenced, in late August, and well before Edward decided not to come, in October. Meantime Gloucester and Northumberland organised

---

[33] *York House Books*, vol. 2, p. 695,

[34] S. Cunningham, 'Yorkists at War', p. 187. *York House Books*, vol. 2, p. 695. Note that they answered to the king, not Gloucester as Admiral of England.

[35] Ross, *Edward IV*, p. 281; C.L. Scofield, *Edward IV* (Longmans, Green, 1923), vol. 2, p. 316.

[36] Palgrave, *Kalendars*, vol. 1, pp. 19–30; *Stonor L & P*, vol. 2, p. 124.

[37] Ross, *Edward IV*, p. 282, 17 August, Scofield, *Edward IV*, vol. 2, p. 318n; Macdougall, *James III*, p. 145.

a double-pronged raid from Northumberland. Both forces seem to have mustered separately on a prearranged date, Tuesday 22 August 1481, when they created 45 knights and bannerets. Elevations on campaign were distinctions and highly honourable rewards for service. Gloucester invaded Scotland from the East March. On 22 August his force was at Hutton Field near Berwick. Northumberland took the Middle March and mustered that same day at Cessford (the main of Sefford), between Jedburgh, Kelso, and Kirk Yetholm just over the Scottish border, very close to the final destination of his 1480 raid. Of course some retainers who may or may not have been present were already knights – Conyers, Harrington, Pilkington, and Tyrell, for instance – but these 45 names cast some light on the substantial size and composition of the English forces. The earl was qualified to create knights, it seems, who displayed a pennon, but not bannerets, a superior order, who displayed banners and probably constituted intermediate commanders. Northumberland knighted 18 men, almost all of them documented from other sources as Percy retainers. Apart from the Cumbrians Christopher Curwen and Christopher Ward, five were Northumbrians – Thomas Grey of Wark, Ralph Harbottle, Roger Heron, Roger Thornton, and Ralph Widdrington – and the other 11 were Yorkshiremen. Gloucester was accompanied by other peers, his cousins Lords Lovell, FitzHugh, and Scrope of Masham, by Sir George Lumley, heir to Lord Lumley, and Sir Robert Greystoke, the heir to his veteran councillor Ralph Lord Greystoke. Gloucester knighted the three peers, Greystoke and Robert Middleton of Belsay, Northumberland, and a dozen Yorkshiremen. He raised Lumley and two others, already knights, to the rank of banneret and made another seven both knights and banneret. Two came from south Durham, but none from west of the Pennines. Presumably his Cumbrian retainers were needed to defend the West March.[38]

It was an impressive array that Richard commanded – an army fully worthy of the king who was expected to take command and whose anticipated presence may have prompted the peers to serve. Of course there was nowhere else in the whole kingdom at this time where military experience

[38] M.A. Hicks, 'Dynastic Change and Northern Society', *Northern History*, 14 (1978), pp. 78–107; W.C. Metcalfe, *Book of Knights* (Mitchell & Hughes, 1885), pp. 5–7.

and renown could be acquired. Dubbing by the duke created a connection and an obligation between these peers and the duke. Perhaps these musters and knighting just over the border was all that the army did, since on 7 September both duke and earl were back in Yorkshire, summoning Sir Robert Plumpton and troops from York to counter a new Scottish threat.[39] On 22 August Gloucester and Douglas had been commissioned to receive Scottish deserters into English allegiance: only three are known to have done so, Alexander Jardine (who served with the English on the 1482 campaign), Master Patrick Haliburton, and Sir Richard Holland.[40] Meanwhile James III had raised a great host from the whole of Scotland, but he was apparently persuaded to disband it without fighting.[41] Gloucester may have come to Nottingham to confer again with the king about 20 October, when Edward handed over command and withdrew southwards.[42] Rivers, Dorset, and Stanley arrived, too late in the campaigning season, perhaps for the ineffectual attack on Berwick that apparently took place.[43] On 23 November Gloucester joined with Savile, Gascoigne, Redmayn and Wortley, all newly knighted, for a land transaction, probably in Nottinghamshire.[44]

Evidently Edward stepped up the publicity for his 1482 campaign. Three historians – Crowland, Vergil, and Hall – presented the war as the fault of the Scots and recalled only what happened in 1482.[45] Edward's plans for 1482 were initially to repeat those for 1481, probably with the same logistical backup, but to execute them better. 'Al the winter season', wrote Hall, 'he mustred his souldiers, prepared his ordinance, rigged his shippes, and left nothing apperteignyng to the warre, vnpurueyed or vnloked for . . . Al thinges wer prepared and nothyng was missed'.[46] Several

[39] *Plumpton L & P*, p. 56; York House *Books*, vol. 1, p. 244; Macdougall, *James III*, pp. 146–7.

[40] *CDRS*, vol. 4, p. 300; Macdougall, *James III*, p. 156n.34.

[41] Macdougall, *James III*, pp. 146–7.

[42] Scofield, *Edward IV*, vol. 2, p. 320. Cunningham deduces that some southern lords and the royal household attendant on the king missed the campaign, Cunningham 'Yorkists at War', p. 190.

[43] Macdougall, *James III*, p. 146.

[44] Nottingham Archives, DD/RS/1/20/2.

[45] *Crowland*, pp. 146–7; Vergil, *English History*, pp. 169–70; *Hall's Chronicle*, pp. 330–5.

[46] *Hall's Chronicle*, p. 331.

extra ships were added to the fleet, the *Mary of Greenwich* being completely refitted with new canvas, cables, bowstrings, and 400 gunstones. Coastal crayers from the Cinque Ports and carvels from Dartmouth were chartered to carry supplies northwards.[47] These preparations were just as well, as Scotland was suffering from a deep economic depression. There was a serious shortage of food, almost a famine, which was exacerbated by James's drastic debasement of the coinage. Unrecorded Scottish raids wasted the estates of Carlisle Priory and of Lord Dacre, notably Burgh-on-the-Sands on the Solway Firth west of Carlisle.[48] Even victualling the existing English garrisons was difficult. Hence on 24 February 1482 Gloucester was licensed to purchase 2,000 quarters of wheat and 1,000 quarters of other grains, beans, and peas wherever he could find them.[49] Five hundred carts had been ordered in 1481. Any English army would find it difficult to live off the country and especially the huge force of 20,000 men that Edward had commissioned. Twenty years earlier Warwick the Kingmaker had refused reinforcements because he was struggling to maintain those he already had.[50] The fleet was commanded on this occasion by the Lincolnshire knight of the body Sir Robert Radcliffe. It does not appear that the English ships were intended to supply the land force by sea and probably it was not originally planned that the English army would march deep into the interior of Scotland or along the coast road past Dunbar. No indentures of war or subcontracts survive for this campaign, but since this was a royal army organised by the king's treasurer of war, and all troops were paid wages at standard rates, it seems to have been recruited in this way. Moreover, the king hired 1,800 Swiss and German mercenaries in companies complete with drummers and standard-bearers and clad in uniforms bearing the cross of St George. There were also gunners and artillerymen.[51]

On a more positive note, however, the English appeared to have secured a new ally who might make it possible to achieve all their war aims. This was

[47] Cunningham, 'Yorkists at War', p. 187.

[48] Summerson, *Medieval Carlisle*, vol. 2, p. 464.

[49] *CPR 1476–85*, 254. Edward ordered the payment or assignment of 10,000 marks to Gloucester on 20 February 1482, E 404/77/3/67.

[50] *The Politics of Fifteenth Century England: John Vale's Book*, eds M.L. Kekewich, C. Richmond, A.F. Sutton, L. Visser-Fuchs and J.L. Watts (A. Sutton, 1995), pp. 171–2.

[51] Cunningham, 'Yorkists at War', pp. 188–9.

Alexander Stewart, duke of Albany, the exiled brother of King James III, to whom alliance with the English offered hope at least of restoration and perhaps the crown itself. Making Albany into king of Scotland could secure all England's war aims neatly and economically. The need to reach an agreement with Albany held Edward up and delayed the campaign. On 3 June at Fotheringhay King Edward and Albany formally agreed that, as king, Albany (Alexander IV) would surrender Berwick, do homage to Edward for Scotland, and would break the Auld Alliance with France that had showed signs of reviving. He would also give up the Debatable Lands of Liddesdale, Eskdale, Ewesdale, Annandale, and the castle of Lochmaben in the West March. He, rather than Prince James, would marry Cecily if he could do so canonically – which was hardly practical, as he had a French wife already and indeed also a son and heir. Edward expected to find considerable support for Albany in Scotland. The aim of the 1482 campaign was therefore now to place Albany on the Scottish throne. This treaty with Albany apparently diverted the northern peers from campaigns that were already in train.

Meanwhile, Gloucester 'the right high and myghti prince' was expected at York about 16 March 1482; he remained close by for several weeks, and then planned on 22 May 'brefly in hys owen person to entre Scotland . . . in subduyng the kynges greit enemye the kyng of Scottes and his adherentes'.[52] His objective was the West March. Next year it was reported to parliament that Richard Duke of Gloucester in his capacity as warden of the West March 'late by his manyfold and diligent labours and devoirs hath subdued grete part of the west bordures of Scotlande adjoynyng to Englond by the space of 30 miles & more, therby at this tyme not enhabite with Scots', and brought it under the allegiance of the king to 'grete reste and ease of thinhabitauntes' of the West March and to 'the grete suerty and ease of the north parties of Englond'.[53] A semicircle 30 miles into Scotland, to north-west, north and north-east, takes in most of these places, the town of Dumfries, the key castles of Annan, Hermitage and Lochmaben, and Annandale, Eskdale, Ewesdale, Liddesdale, Wauchopdale, and Clydesdale. The York contingent had indeed reached Dumfries.[54]

---

[52] *York House Books*, vol. 1, pp. 250, 256; vol. 2, pp. 702–3.
[53] *PROME*, vol. 14, p. 425. Presumably this was what Gloucester himself claimed.
[54] *York House Books*, vol. 2, p. 729.

In March 1482 the Scottish parliament had funded garrisons at Lochmaben Castle (100 men), Hermitage Castle (100 men), Castelmilk Castle near Glasgow, Annan Castle on the coast, and Bell's Tower (100 altogether) with effect from 1 May. The Scots were not merely victims: the damage they wreaked on Bewcastle was so extensive as almost to amount to demolition.[55] While Gloucester's achievements must surely be exaggerated – could the English conceivably have ethnically cleansed this whole area of Scots? – it must be essentially true, since king and parliament accepted Gloucester's claim, even though there is no recorded evidence to confirm the details. Did Richard really capture the formidable and well-garrisoned castles of Hermitage and Lochmaben? Surely he had not occupied Clydesdale? Albany conceded all these Debatable Lands in his treaty on 11 June – Lochmaben and Annandale were actually his own – and it was therefore in implementation of this concession that in July or possibly late June 1482 44 towns and villages in Scotland including Dumfries were burnt 'and many lordys takyn and slayne'.[56] No names are recorded. Rapine, wounding, and maiming are implied. The Scots may well have taken to the hills or the castles, but only temporarily. As Gloucester was elsewhere, this was surely the work of his lieutenant, Humphrey Lord Dacre. Most probably the raid was over by 24 June when Lord Lovell was near Durham on his way southwards and was diverted to the main campaign.[57] Gloucester remained in possession in January/February 1483, when King Edward agreed to grant this territory to the duke, who 'moche more therof he entendith and with Goddis grace is like to gete and subdue hereafter'.[58]

Gloucester was absent because he was recalled to Fotheringhay early in June 1482 to join in the discussions with Albany. The treaty with Albany was concluded on 11 June. Edward decided at once not to lead the expedition himself, and on 12 June Gloucester was reappointed lieutenant-general in command during the king's absence. Edward IV paid the enormous sum of £200 for transport of his ordnance, £100 for 120 draught horses, and

[55] E404/77/3/86.
[56] *Cely Letters 1472–88*, ed. A. Hanham (Early English Text Society, 1975), p. 164.
[57] *Stonor L & P*, vol. 2, p. 150.
[58] *PROME*, vol. 16, p. 425.

200 marks for 2,000 sheaves of arrows.[59] The scanty exchequer records indicate that Edward envisaged deploying a very large force for a very short period – 20,000 men for only four weeks from mid-July to be paid until 11 August: a further £595 was allocated to pay 1,700 of these recruited by Gloucester for a final fortnight.[60] Edward did not want his troops living off *his* country. York corporation were instructed to supply as many carts to transport foodstuffs and as much victuals as (in their judgement) sufficed to feed the host.[61] Four weeks was far too little for much in the way of conquest, but enough perhaps for a brief invasion to pressurise better terms from the Scots. The total cost including transport, munitions, and supplies surely exceeded this, but was probably defrayed from the king's chamber, whose treasurer Sir John Elrington was seconded as treasurer of wars. Elaborate and expensive provision was needed in time of dearth simply to feed 20,000 men for a month at Alnwick and another six weeks on campaign about which we know nothing. King Edward was anxious to keep a personal grasp of events and on any diplomacy, so he established an express courier service to carry messages: this, however, can only have extended to Newcastle (according to Armstrong) or possibly Berwick (Ross),[62] not to Edinburgh.

About 17 June Gloucester and Albany entered York, where the corporation staged an impressive civic reception.[63] Ahead of the campaign Sir William Gascoigne, Sir Piers Middleton, and Sir Thomas Malliverer were still at North Deighton near Leeds in 6 May.[64] Lovell was at Tanfield, west of Chester-le-Street on 24 June and Northumberland was at Wressle in the East Riding on 2 July. Lovell expected to join Gloucester, 'my brother Parr and suche other folk of worship as hath eny reule in the said northe parties'.[65] Almost certainly Sir William Parr, sheriff of Westmorland, constable of Carlisle, and also indeed by this time controller of the king's household,

[59] *Foedera*, vol. 12, p. 158.

[60] Ross, *Edward IV*, p. 288; Devon, *Issues of the Exchequer*, p. 501.

[61] *York House Books*, vol. 2, p. 697.

[62] Scofield, *Edward IV*, vol. 2, pp. 339–40; Ross, *Edward IV*, p. 288; C.A.J. Armstrong, 'Some Examples of the Distribution and Speed of News at the Time of the Wars of the Roses', in *England, France and Burgundy in the Fifteenth Century* (Hambledon Press, 1983), p. 107.

[63] *York House Books*, vol. 1, p. 259.

[64] West Yorkshire Archives, Leeds, TL 230/148.

[65] *Stonor L & P*, vol. 2, p. 150.

shared in Gloucester's raid on the West March before joining the duke's much bigger campaign in the east. The 'valiant captains' of the main force and the artillery set forward in May and assembled ahead of them at Alnwick in Northumberland. They waited there for several weeks. It was therefore at Alnwick that two of those Yorkshiremen promoted or to be promoted by Gloucester, in anticipation of a serious campaign in which they might be slain, made their wills. These were Sir Hugh Hastings of Fenwick (knighted 1482) on 20 June and Sir John Constable of Halsham (knighted and bannereted 1481) on 7 July. Each was 'entending and purposing under the protection and grace of almighty God to passe towards the Scottes the kinges en[e]myes' (and therefore were not on the Dumfries campaign). Hastings made provision for any persons 'beying with me and doing me service havyng my connysaunce (badge) this said jorney ayenst the Scottes [who] be hurte or maymed'. Hastings' will was witnessed by Sir Piers Middleton, knighted by Northumberland in 1481 and to be bannereted by Gloucester the next August, by the Percy retainer William Eland, and by Richard Bosville and Thomas Abney, also therefore campaigners.[66]

The force assembled and was arrayed at Alnwick 'about the beginning of July'.[67] The year 1482, unlike 1481, featured a single united army, but one divided into several battles and that was deployed as separate forces by the duke, the earl, Earl Rivers, and Lord Stanley, the principal commanders. It was on 24 July that the 'Englishmen's camp' was marshalled outside Berwick: it was probably there that the banner of St Cuthbert, released by Durham Cathedral priory, was hoisted over the host.[68] Here also Gloucester made 27 bannerets and seven knights, Northumberland dubbed three knights, Albany four, and Stanley 16. Presumably all these knights and bannerets brought other men with them, the bannerets significant numbers, but unfortunately there are no contracts or other sources to illuminate the make-up in more detail. Altogether 19,000 strong, the army was indeed a 'royall armie'. George Cely reports improbably that there were 60,000 men in three battles.

---

[66] Falvey, Boatwright, and Hammond, *English Wills* (Richard III Society, 2013), pp. 57, 62, 78.

[67] *Hall's Chronicle*, p. 331. Record evidence suggests that the duke and earl arrived a little later.

[68] Pollard, 'St Cuthbert and the Hog', p. 118. For the next sentence, see Metcalfe, *Book of Knights*, p. 7.

The army was 'very sizeable' by the standards of the time and 'exceeded all other English forces for over eighty years'.[69] Hall reports that Northumberland commanded the vanguard – the place of honour – with 6,700 men including, besides his own retainers, Lord Scrope of Bolton, Sir John Middleton of Belsay (Northumberland), and Sir John Ditchfield, two veterans of the Franco-Burgundian wars.[70] Gloucester himself, Albany, Lovell, Greystoke, and Sir Edward Wydeville were in the centre with 5,000 men, Lord Neville commanded the rearguard of 3,000 (perhaps from County Durham), Lord Stanley was on the right wing with 4,000 men from Lancashire and Cheshire, and Lord FitzHugh, Sir William Parr, and Sir James Harrington comprised the left wing with 2,000: perhaps the Cumbrian contingent that they had brought to Edward IV in 1471. Another thousand attended the ordnance.[71] Three men later prominent in Richard's service as king, Ralph Ashton, Richard Ratcliffe, and James Tyrell, were promoted from knights to bannerets. Also raised to banneret were the queen's brother Edward Wydeville and her cousin Richard Haute, controller of Prince Edward's household, Northumberland's cousin Henry Percy, the Scotsmen Alexander Baynham and Alexander Jardine, Edward Stanley (a younger son of Lord Stanley), Sir John Grey (heir apparent to Lord Grey of Wilton), Walter Herbert (brother of the earl of Huntingdon) and John Elrington, the treasurer of war, besides such prominent retainers of his own as Tyrell, Redmayn, and Ratcliffe. Apart from Albany, earl Rivers and Lord Stanley, each with their own companies, the army was probably comprised overwhelmingly of northerners. The gentry who were knights hailed predominantly from Yorkshire and Northumberland. The rank and file were probably tenants of the duke and earl, of the crown, of the baronage and gentry, and of the various ecclesiastical estates of which such men were officers. Middleton, for instance, was sheriff of North Durham, Norhamshire, and Elandshire and Roger Heron was constable of Norham Castle. Gloucester could not have asked to command a larger and more distinguished force and was surely

[69] Vergil, *English History*, p. 70; *Hall's Chronicle*, p. 331; *Cely Letters*, p. 164; Macdougall, *James III*, p. 154; Ross, *Edward IV*, p. 288. The knightings refer to the vanguard and were therefore probably in Hall's heraldic source.

[70] E. Meek, 'The Career of Sir Thomas Everingham, "Knight of the North" in the Service of Maximilian, Duke of Austria 1477–81', *HR*, 74 (2001), p. 247.

[71] *Hall's Chronicle*, p. 331.

gratified to honour and oblige those whom he created knights and bannerets
in campaign.

The town of Berwick surrendered at once and thus escaped the sack, but
not the castle, which was commanded by Sir Patrick Hepburn (later Lord
Bothwell) and had been garrisoned with 500 men by King James.[72] Hepburn
'would in no wise deliuer it, neither for flattering wordes, nor for menacinge
bragges', so the invaders 'planted a strong siege and enuironed it rounde
aboute'. Leaving a force of 4,000 under Stanley, Elrington, and Parr to
blockade Berwick, Richard proceeded to Edinburgh, arriving by 31 July.[73] It
was bold so to dash through the territory of an undefeated enemy, but justified by his overwhelming superiority in numbers and equipment. He
encountered no significant opposition. Yet it is unlikely that this was his
original plan. Duke Richard 'wastyd and burnyd all over the countrie',
reported Vergil.[74] Hall listed 62 places that the English army burnt and
several bastle houses that they won. Some apparently were wasted by Adam
Nisbet of that Ilk and other Scottish followers of Albany.[75] The earl of
Northumberland wasted 52 of these places, apparently raiding 25 miles
south-westwards along the border, as far as Morebattle, devastating Kelso,
Coldstream, and Old Roxburgh en route. Ten bastles were won: Lowhouses,
Brome Hill, Morebattle, Linton, Craylam, Ednam, Mickle and Little
Swinton, Cosmaynes and Weddon. It is possible that Northumberland also
took several of the castles garrisoned by the Scots, such as the great house
and tower at Blackadder near Duns and Cocklaw at Moorbattle, but others
were apparently bypassed.[76] The earl may have found victuals in short

[72] Macdougall, *James III*, p. 155.

[73] This is deduced from the proclamation on his arrival that gave James until 1 August to
comply, *Hall's Chronicle*, p. 332.

[74] Vergil, *English History*, p. 170.

[75] *Hall's Chronicle*, p. 332; A. Goodman, 'The Impact of Warfare on the Scottish Marches,
c.1481–c.1513', in ed. L. Clark, *The Fifteenth Century VII* (Boydell, 2007), p. 202. Bastle
houses [bastilles] were small, defensible, stone-built, two-storey structures, the bottom floor
for beasts and the upper storey accessed by external stairs for living accommodation.

[76] Goodman considers the damage rather mild, 'Impact of Warfare', p. 202. The castles
garrisoned by the Scottish parliament were Blackadder (20 men), Wedderburn near Duns
(20), Hume (60) under the earl of Buchan, Cessford near Yetholm (60), Ormistone (20), and
Egarstone (20) under the laird of Edmonstone; Jedburgh (60), Cocklaw in Morebattle (20),
and Dolphinstoun in Jedburgh(20) under the laird of Cranstoun, Macdougall, *James III*,
p. 150.

supply in a district that he had raided in 1480 and 1481. Gloucester by contrast burnt and pillaged only 10 places within a few miles of Berwick, none further north than Preston: Edington, Croffirge and Whitside, Paxton, Lishewike, Edingham, Whitmere, Brandike, Newtown Boswells near Melrose and Hutton. Their troops may have needed to forage. This sort of frightfulness accorded with the laws of war and was accepted by the standards of the time. Carrying the war to civilians was the way in which late medieval invaders – like Edward III's chevauchées in France – impaired the economy of their adversaries and temporarily destroyed the capacity of their foes to support themselves and to counter-attack against the English borders. Gloucester's strategy was either to force the Scots to the negotiating table or to the open battlefield. The latter stood some chance of success, as King James had brought 'the power of Scotland' down what is now the A68 to Lauder, 35 miles west of Berwick. A full-scale battle might have ensued, which the much larger English army ought to have won: unless of course it was dispersed to pillage or forage.

Instead on 22 July, two days before the English knightings, the Scottish 'lords of the council' staged a coup d'état. King James was arrested, his ministers dismissed, two were executed, and he himself was imprisoned at Edinburgh Castle. Perhaps it was on receipt of this news and knowing that no organised opposition was to be expected that Duke Richard changed his plans and marched directly to Edinburgh. *Hall's Chronicle* suggests that he knew the king to be there, but not apparently under what circumstances. Probably he took the coast road via Dunbar, since the royal granges there were wasted, though this could have happened on the return journey. Richard had occupied Edinburgh by 31 July, which he spared 'from fier, bloud and spoyle' at the instance of the duke of Albany. To sack it, as Crowland wished, would have alienated any potential support for Albany.[77] Northumberland had joined them by 2 August, possibly via another inland route. Richard should have been able to impose terms – to achieve his war aims – but this proved to be impossible. There was nobody to fight and nobody legitimate with whom to negotiate. The king was incommunicado

and hors de combat in an impregnable castle that Richard lacked the time
and probably the ordnance to besiege. Neither by force nor by diplomacy
could the duke substitute Albany for James as king. Hall reports that at the
high cross in Edinburgh market place the English herald Garter king of
arms called on King James to observe all his agreements with England and
to recompense the English for Scottish depredations against them, to the
deadline of 1 August, and to restore his brother Albany to his lands and
offices. Or else 'the high and valiaunte prince Rychard duke of Glocester,
leuetenaunt generall, and chiefetayne for the kyng of England, was redy
at hand to destroy him, his people and country with slaughter, flame &
famyn'. To which 'Kyng James would make no aunswere', Hall writes,
'knowing that his power now fayled, either to performe the request
demaunded, or to defend his countrey with such a puissant army invaded'.[78]
Of course James could not. He was not a free agent and he was probably
ignorant of the English demands. Did the English understand what had
happened at Lauder? Garter's proclamation was at best propaganda that
showed the Edinburgh burgesses how reasonable were the English terms.
By the end of July the plan to make Albany king had already been shelved.
It was apparent that neither the old regime, nor the new 'lords of the
council', nor indeed any other Scottish faction, backed Albany's elevation
to the crown.

Richard had no instructions covering this situation or indicating to him
what to do. He had progressed beyond the reach of Edward's courier
system. In retrospect, perhaps, his decision to press on to Edinburgh
appeared a mistake. He was deep in hostile territory, with long lines of
communication and supply, probably desperately short of victuals, and his
men were paid for only another fortnight and probably wanted to return
home. There is no evidence that the English fleet brought supplies by sea.
Hall reports that the Scottish 'lords of the council' had assembled an army,
improbably estimated at 50,000 strong in one source. The Scots barred the
way south at Haddington, 15 miles to the east of Edinburgh on the main
road to the south, although evidently they declined to risk a battle and in
the event let the English pass. Even if 'nocht sufficient to resist the army of

[78] *Hall's Chronicle*, p. 333.

England',[79] it was a significant threat to Richard and a reason not to disperse his force for foraging. Instead of seeking out the enemy, Richard avoided the battle that might have decided the war. This contrasted with the English Wars of the Roses, when battles were repeatedly forced on weaker forces as at the first battle of St Albans (1455), Blore Heath (1459), Northampton and Wakefield (1460), and especially Tewkesbury in 1471. Richard was cautious, did not hazard his army, and declined to force the Scots into a battle that his superior force should have won. Clearly he knew how much he stood to lose. One wonders whether Edward IV would have been any bolder or whether he would have replicated the slow movements and cautious avoidance of the enemy that characterised his Picquigny campaign. When Gloucester did withdraw southwards, he passed within a few miles of the Scottish forces. Permanent conquests were impractical in the limited time that was available to him. Richard has been criticised for not extracting more concessions while Edinburgh was at his mercy,[80] but it is not obvious what these could have been or who was in a position to concede them.

Gloucester had never been commissioned to treat with the Scots by King Edward, who had nominated Northumberland, Scrope of Bolton, and Parr as negotiators,[81] but in this scenario, the latter two being at Berwick, the duke was in charge. Northumberland was involved on 2–4 August and later. Stanley was also there. There are two versions of the negotiations that followed.

There survive in the English National Archives the records of two agreements that Gloucester reached on 2 and 4 August. The first on 2 August was with Archbishop Shreves, the ex-chancellor of Scotland, and others ousted by the coup at Lauder, who committed themselves to persuading King James, insofar as they and he were able, to restore Albany to his lands and offices. At Albany's prompting, second, the corporation of Edinburgh bound themselves on 4 August to reimburse Cecily's dowry if the marriage did not take place, leaving the decision whether to proceed to King Edward. Cecily's marriage portion amounted to 8,000 English marks ($£5,333$),[82] a

[79] Macdougall, *James III*, p. 167.

[80] Ross, *Edward IV*, pp. 289–90.

[81] *Rotuli Scotiae*, eds D. MacPherson, J. Caley and W. Illingworth, (Record Commission, 1814–19), vol. 2, p. 458.

[82] *CDRS*, vol. 4, pp. 303–4; Ross, *Edward IV*, p. 289.

very large sum by Scottish standards and substantially more than what King James had been unable to raise for his sister's dowry. It was effectively the ransom that kept Edinburgh safe. With nothing more to gain, Gloucester might have withdrawn at this point.

A much more elaborate tale is told by the chronicler Hall, who appears to have had access to a detailed English account of the diplomatic exchanges down to October. It includes verbatim copies of the two agreements mentioned above that survive independently in the National Archives and was perhaps the work of Garter king of arms (John Writhe, 1478–1504). Certain misunderstandings of the Scottish situation make sense in an English report. Vagueness in dating the assembly at Alnwick suggests that the account was written somewhat later. That Sir Patrick Hepburn is titled Lord Bothwell suggests a date of composition after his elevation in 1488. The Scottish 'lords of the council' agreed to Albany's restoration, naming him indeed as lieutenant of Scotland, and he therefore deserted the English army to join them. This was, after all, one of the English war aims. Before his departure, according to Hall, Albany promised again on 3 August to adhere to the agreement reached at Fotheringhay. If true, Albany was keeping all his options open.

Hall recites a series of messages over several weeks that were exchanged between Richard and the 'lords of the council', the new regime that controlled King James, exchanges that failed to produce an agreement. First of all the Scottish lords asked for peace – specifically to retain Berwick Castle, to allure Albany back to his allegiance, and to proceed with the marriage alliance. Duke Richard replied that he did not know the king's pleasure about the marriage. He requested repayment of the dowry and the surrender of Berwick Castle or, at least, no interference with the siege. A delegation of 'the lords, prelates, barons and estates of Scotland' refused immediate payment – the dowry of course had been spent and the original contract had set no date for repayment – but they did agree to future reimbursement 'according to reason'. They firmly refused to surrender Berwick Castle, which was part of the old inheritance of the Scottish kings and stood on Scottish ground. The surrender of Berwick Castle was essential, Richard retorted. The lords urged Albany now to relieve the siege of Berwick Castle. Gloucester wrote to Albany, advising him that this was neither honourable nor commendable and to act in this way was ungrateful to Edward considering the help that he had provided in the duke's necessity. Richard 'assured him in the woord of a Prince, that if he [Albany] & all the power of Scotland attempted to come to rayse the siege, planted before the Castell of Berwyke, that he hym selfe [Gloucester] with his armye would defende the besiegers, or els dye in the quarrel'.[83] Gloucester's resolve was not tested, for his brinkmanship worked yet again. The Scottish lords of the council declined to risk a battle and offered concessions. Through the Scottish Lyon king of arms they offered either to level the fortifications and thus to decommission militarily the town and castle of Berwick or alternatively the status quo, whereby the Scots retained the castle and the English the town. They wanted a truce during which discussions could be held concerning 'the welthes of both kingdomes'. Gloucester rejected both options. Given the expenditure of so much English treasure and effort, he insisted on the surrender of the castle of Berwick, whether by agreement or force, and refused a truce until this was achieved or, strangely, until he was vanquished.

On balance, the Scots decided that Berwick was not worth the risk of a serious defeat. Whatever attempts the English had made to storm Berwick Castle or to batter it into submission, they had been repelled, Crowland reports, with 'slaughter and bloodshed', though not of many men.[84] On 24 August the Scottish lords offered a short truce, from 8 September to 4 November, which Gloucester conceded. They also agreed to surrender Berwick: indeed they may have had no choice, since a garrison of 500 must quickly have exhausted its victuals. A great deal of damage seems to have been done to the fortifications, presumably by the formidable English artillery train.[85] There seem to have been no casualties among those of rank on the English side. Berwick Castle surrendered 'to the lord Stanley, and other thereto appoynted, whiche therein put bothe Englishmen and artilerie, sufficiente for the defence [defiance?] of all Scotland for. vi. monethes'.[86] Had Stanley retained this command, it would have been a major

[83] *Hall's Chronicle*, p. 334 This was a defensive gesture.

[84] *Crowland*, pp. 148–9. Probably the English ordnance wreaked the damage that Edward in due course had to repair.

[85] £293 and £216, E 405/71 mm.1s, 3d. Works continued into Edward V's reign, 'Financial Memoranda', pp. 218, 225.

[86] *Hall's Chronicle*, p. 333.

infringement of the earl of Northumberland's authority as warden of the East March. However, very soon Northumberland took over. He agreed the appointment at £438 per month for the safe custody of town and castle. Several payments recorded on the tellers' rolls suggest that his cousin Sir Henry Percy deputised.[87] Elrington meanwhile had to spend heavily on victuals for the garrison. The Scots still wanted Berwick and all other Debatable Lands to remain as they were at the last truce, but this Gloucester refused pending further instructions from King Edward.

By this date Gloucester must have withdrawn from Edinburgh to Berwick. He may have disbanded his army when its wages were spent, but the only evidence for this is the length of service that the exchequer paid for in advance. His troops could have been unfunded – ignorant that their employment had actually ceased – or were paid from other sources.[88] Given the dearth, it was difficult to keep them fed. The countryside around had probably been laid waste and his men could not be allowed to ravage it further once hostilities had ceased. The change of couriers, five in number, now extended to Berwick. The English had withdrawn over the border by 29 August.[89] Gloucester himself retreated first to Northumberland's castle at Alnwick, presumably with the earl. On 9 November he was at Newcastle upon Tyne, thence withdrew to Sheriff Hutton in Yorkshire 'and there abode'.[90] Meanwhile King Edward had decided by 27 October to drop Cecily's marriage and take instead the repayments of the dowry, which the provost and burghers of Edinburgh agreed to collect and remit.[91] About Michaelmas (29 September) King James was released by Albany from incarceration.[92] He recovered control of his seals about 19 October but does not seem to have been truly in control until the New Year.

[87] E 405/71 m.1. This seems to precede the payment for December noted in ibid., m.5.

[88] From May payments for Berwick were hand to mouth, from whatever came to hand (see 'Financial Memoranda', passim), and may have been so earlier.

[89] R. Pitcairn, *Ancient Criminal Trials in Scotland* (Bannatyne Club, 1833), vol. 1, pt. 1, pp. 16–18.

[90] *Hall's Chronicle*, p. 333.

[91] Ross *Edward IV*, p. 290; *Hall's Chronicle*, p. 334.

[92] Macdougall, *James III*, p. 171.

IV

King Edward was exultant at the success of the campaign, and maximised the publicity value of the capture of Berwick. Gloucester's triumph was so great, he told Pope Sixtus IV, that the duke 'alone would suffice to chastise the whole kingdom of Scotland'.[93] It was a national victory to be celebrated by a beleaguered government that otherwise had only bad news to report. From an English angle it appears almost bloodless, with no significant casualties. The one possible exception was the duke's councillor Sir William Redmayn, who died at Heversham in Westmorland, probably specifically Levens, on 11–12 September 1482.[94] A funeral lament for Edward IV singled out the defeat of the Scots and the recovery of Berwick as notable achievements. On 18 February 1483 Parliament commended 'the prepotent prince' Richard Duke of Gloucester, also the earl of Northumberland, Lord Stanley, 'and certain other barons and knights for their noble deeds and acts and for their services done and to be done for the aforesaid lord king in defence of the realm in the war recently fought with Scotland'.[95] Gloucester made the most of his success. Mancini in 1483 took his martial prowess for granted. 'Such was his renown in warfare that whenever a difficult and dangerous policy had to be undertaken, it would be entrusted to his discretion and generalship.' In 1484 the Scottish envoy Archibald Whitelaw called him 'the embodiment of military skill [and] prowess'. Gloucester, he declared, possessed such other military qualities 'to be sought in the best military leader [as] hard work in administration, bravery in the face of danger, application in developing a position, speed in execution, and care in forward planning'. The Scottish campaign marked him out as general, on the biggest available stage. 'Sundrye victories hadde hee, and sommetime ouerthrowes', wrote More, 'but neuer in default of his own person, either of hardinesse [courage] or polytyke order [generalship]'.[96] Circumstances, Scottish weakness, a lack of scrutiny, and

[93] *Calendar of State Papers Relating to English Affairs in the Archives of Venice*, ed. R. Brown (HMSO, 1864), vol. I, no. 483.

[94] Redmayne could have died of wounds or disease arising from the war, *Testamenta Eboracensia*, vol. 3, pp. 280–1.

[95] A.F. Sutton and L. Visser-Fuchs, 'Laments for the Death of Edward IV', *Ricardian*, 145 (1999), p. 516; *PROME*, vol. 14, p. 412.

[96] Mancini, *Richard III*, p. 79; More, *Richard III*, p. 8; Grant, 'Richard III and Scotland', p. 195.

the dynastic crisis that overshadowed the 1482 campaign somewhat exaggerated what had been achieved, but left Richard nevertheless with a substantial military reputation in England.

Certainly the duke had done well. It was no small achievement to recover the fortress of Berwick that had been 20 years in Scottish hands and that the Scots had striven not to lose. England's principal war aim had been achieved. The duke had secured repayment of Cecily's dowry. Alexander Duke of Albany had been restored to his lands and offices. Moreover, Gloucester had extricated his army safely from a perilous situation. Although at a loss for what to do when there was nobody to negotiate with, Gloucester seems to have handled the diplomatic exchanges skilfully and decisively, and to have set out clearly what he was prepared to accept. If he did not seek a full-scale battle – as happened repeatedly in the Wars of the Roses in England – he was prepared for one if necessary. Of course it helped that his army was so much stronger than its counterpart.

But the results were not permanent. Twice Gloucester had pledged his word as a prince. Albany had not become king of Scotland. The Scots had not abandoned their claim to Berwick. They had not surrendered Coldingham, Roxburgh, or any of the other Debatable Lands. King James had not done homage to King Edward and the kingdom of Scotland had not been subjected to the crown of England. Nor had Earl Douglas been restored. King Edward surely agreed with Crowland that he had suffered great expense. The three years of the Scottish war had cost Edward almost all the treasure that he had amassed in the French war. He cannot have been unaware, like Crowland, of the cost of fortifying, garrisoning, and munitioning Berwick. From 1 May, when Northumberland indented as captain to garrison Berwick with 600 men, it cost £438 a month, total £5,140 per year. Although far short of the £100,000 estimated by Crowland, it was a significant additional burden on a cash-strapped regime. A prodigious amount of victuals had to be imported for town and castle. On 16 November 1482 the clerk of the larder was ordered to commandeer 5,000 quarters of corn, 500 quarters of malt, 500 quarters of barley, 300 quarters of beans, 20 lasts of herring, and 40 weys of cheese in Lincolnshire, Norfolk, and Suffolk and to ship it northwards to supply the castle and town of Berwick. Edward authorised expenditure of £1,000 on repairs to the walls of town and castle, the erection of a new castle hall, and even construction of 120 new town-houses for £1,600.[97] Edward intended a prosperous future for a considerably larger fortress town. He may indeed have wondered whether it was a 'trifling gain, or more accurately, loss'. Crowland reports that the king 'was grieved at the frivolous expenditure of so much money although the recapture of Berwick alleviated his grief for a time'.[98] As a royal councillor Crowland must have been party to the struggles of the government to match income and expenditure week by week and to pay each bill as it became due. More might have been achieved in 1482 had Edward financed his army for a more realistic period, but it was crucial that the Scots were unwilling to risk a battle, that there was nobody on the Scottish side who was authorised to make real concessions, and in time of dearth so large an army could not be maintained for long.

Nor was the war finished. James III, it seems, had not abandoned Berwick and diplomacy had not achieved any permanent concessions. There had been no treaty by which the Scots, at the least, conceded Berwick to England permanently. By November 1482 Edward seems to have decided on a further campaign in 1483. His war aims are obscure. Was the subjection of Scotland to English overlordship, the conquest of further Debatable Lands in the West March, and the restoration of Earl Douglas sufficient justification? Did one take priority over the others? The parliament that was summoned on 15 November 1482 was probably always intended to vote taxes and the single 15th and 10th voted was perhaps sufficient for the short sharp sort of campaign conducted in 1482.[99] In the autumn of 1482 Gloucester and indeed King Edward seem to have expected further efforts to secure the Debatable Lands. Hostilities continued both on land and sea. Gloucester himself was paid £428 and on 4 March 1483 the second instalment of 200 marks (£133 6s. 8d.) for repairs to his castle of Bewcastle in the West March.[100] On 15 February King Edward,

[97] H433, vol. 3, pp. 13–14; Rotuli Scotiae, vol. 2, p. 458; 'Financial Memoranda', pp. 214–15, 225; Crowland, pp. 148–9.

[98] Crowland, pp. 148–9.

[99] PROME, vol. 14, pp. 411ff; M. Jurkowski, C.L. Smith, and D. Crook, Lay Taxes in England and Wales 1188–1688 (Public Record Office, 1998), p. 120.

[100] E 404/77/3/86. So large a sum surely betrays massive damage to the fortress wreaked by the Scots.

authorised payment of £1,455 to Sir John Middleton, Sir Thomas Everingham, and other captains and soldiers for safeguarding the East Marches. Unlike Calais, where the French inhabitants had been replaced by an English colony, Edward determined to retain the residents of Berwick and to persuade them to become his loyal subjects. Hence the charters of Berwick were confirmed in February.[101] The *Anthony* of Topsham was hired for two months to keep the western seas, at a cost of £40.[102]

A series of unforeseen events transformed England's relations with her international neighbours. In December 1482 Louis XI and Archduke Maximilian terminated the Franco-Burgundian War with the Treaty of Arras. Thereupon Edward's foreign policy since the Treaty of Picquigny collapsed. The marriage of Princess Elizabeth to the Dauphin Charles and the pension from Louis XI on which Edward had founded his international stance were both cancelled.[103] Edward wanted revenge. He was again considering war with France, for which he was quite unprepared. Next the reconciliation of James III and Albany broke down, the duke was detected plotting against the king, and in February Albany renewed his agreement with England. In return for English backing for his usurpation of the Scottish crown, Albany would recognise English suzerainty, surrender the Debatable Lands, and marry a daughter of King Edward. On 19 March, however, he and King James were reconciled.[104] And on 9 April Edward himself died. The war continued.

Edward was preparing his 1483 campaign in February and March 1483. He supplied Gloucester with 1,000 bows and 500 sheaves of arrows from the Tower. The parliament that met from 16 January to 26 February approved a far-reaching act in favour of Richard Duke of Gloucester.[105] The act made three grants to him. First of all, he was granted the warden-ship of the West March by hereditary right, to himself and the heirs male of his body, 'with all libertees, fraunchises, and other profites and commod-itees to the same apperteynyng' as any warden in the past. Second, to

[101] *Rotuli Scotiae*, vol. 2, pp. 458–60.

[102] E 404/77/2/64; /3/86.

[103] Ross, *Edward IV*, pp. 290n, 292.

[104] Macdougall, *James III*, p. 185. On 9 February 1483 Northumberland, Scrope, and Parr were appointed negotiators, *Rotuli Scotiae*, vol. 2, p. 458.

[105] *PROME*, vol. 14, pp. 425–8. This is the source of this paragraph.

support this office, Gloucester was no longer to receive a salary, but was granted instead everything that the king possessed in Cumberland, again to himself and the heirs male of his body. Third, he was granted all those Debatable Lands 'in the same dales and bordures', namely Liddlesdale, Eskdale, Ewedale, Annandale, Warcopdale, and Clydesdale that he had conquered and any others that 'with Goddes grace' he was to conquer in the future, in fee simple, that means to himself, to his heirs male and female, and to his assigns.[106] These concessions, the act explains, ensured that the West March was 'the more suerly to be defended and kept ayenst the Scottes' in future. Between the duke's lost petition for all this and the act there was an indenture of agreement, which unfortunately does not survive, to keep the West Marches towards Scotland between the two brothers.[107]

The marginal rubric to the parliament roll reads 'for the duke of Gloucester' (*pro duce Glouc*). Certainly Richard was the principal beneficiary. What Gloucester was granted was the city, town, land, and fee farm of Carlisle, hitherto held by Sir William Parr for life, the castle and manor of Bewcastle and the forest of Nichol that Richard held for life, and everything else 'to which the Kyngs grace hath or of right ought to have in any wise within the seid countee of Cumberland'. Duke Richard already held most of the king's known property in Cumberland, which amounted to less than his annual salary as warden. The pitiless detail is characteristic of the duke. Gloucester did not know that these other rights existed – certainly there were no hundreds nor ringildries – or how much they were worth, but certainly he planned to investigate what previous kings enjoyed and to revive lost rights, reckoning probably correctly that sustained attention could make more of them than was currently the case. Duke Richard could charge for licences to enfeoff lands and fines for unlicensed alienations that the king did not usually exact.

Actually Edward restricted what he gave. At an earlier stage he probably struck out certain items or inserted exclusions. Gloucester was already

<hr>

[106] Why the titles differed is unclear. The Scottish conquests were not viable without the rest.

[107] E 404/77/3/87. The 10,000 marks was payable in instalments, 2000 marks due at midsummer 1483 being compounded into bows (6 March) and arrows (21 March), E 404/77/3/ 87, 89. What the other instalments were, when due and whether paid is not recorded.

sheriff of Cumberland for life. Now he held this office in tail male and also
the escheatry, with the right to appoint to them 'fro yere to yere and fro
tyme to tyme'. Yet sheriff and escheator remained the king's officers, subject
to the royal exchequer and the courts, and it was the king who appointed to
the commission of the peace that reported to the king's court of king's
bench. Cumberland, moreover, was riven by franchises from which the
king's officers (and therefore Gloucester) were excluded.[108] Edward's grant
did not amount to the creation of a fourth palatine county in England, as
this writer has mistakenly supposed, not a palatinate of Cumberland, but a
palatinate or principality in territory annexed from Scotland.[109] The
Debatable Lands in Scotland were indeed granted with full palatine powers,
the model being the rights of the bishop of Durham within the bishopric of
Durham (County Durham and its franchises), with the single exception of
forfeitures by high treason. King, bishop, and the lord of Barnard Castle,
now Gloucester, were in regular dispute about that. No name was ever
assigned to Richard's new Scottish palatinate and no institutional structures, so far as is known, were ever created for it. Henceforth Richard could
admit aliens to English allegiance; seize the chattels of felons, fugitive, and
traitors; have right of wreck and treasure trove, and to a long list of fines for
various purposes and amercements from various courts. His powers were
not to include custody of the temporalities or other profits or commodities
of the bishopric of Carlisle during vacancies. They were not to include
forfeitures for high treason: most of the major lordships of the Percies,
Clifford, and Dacres had been forfeit during his First Reign. Rights of wardship that Richard now acquired were only to his own lands and those specifically granted to him in Cumberland: not any elsewhere, not the wardship
and marriage of the bodies of feudal heirs, not the crown's precedence over
other feudal lords (prerogative lordship), nor any rights over lords of parliament. And not, the catch-all, any other prerogative rights. Gloucester's new
domain was part of the kingdom of England and subordinate to it. Should
Gloucester leave an underage heir, the king could fill the wardenship. Such
details betray the give and take of detailed negotiations between king and

---

[108] Booth, 'Richard, Duke of Gloucester and the West March', *Northern History*, 36 (2000),
pp. 243–4.

[109] E.g., Hicks, *Richard III*, p. 60.

duke. The result created the sort of relationship that Edward was striving to achieve in his overlordship over Scotland.

Why did Edward make such wide-ranging concessions? He had no first-hand knowledge of what he was giving away, because he had never, so far as we know, visited either the West March or Scotland. It was another distinction that he bestowed on his brother. It was Gloucester indeed who most likely proposed the deal: he was (so Grant argues) 'surely a more innovative thinker than his brother' the king.[110] Edward was temperamentally inclined to agree to grants that were requested and that cost him nothing. Indeed he hoped that it would save him money. He wanted to cut the cost of the defence of the North and had therefore in 1480 reduced the salaries of the wardens. Ironically thereby he had transferred to the crown almost all the costs of the late war. Defraying the costs of the northern borders from local sources, which did not affect King Edward directly, made good sense and was indeed what Richard managed as king and what Henry VII was to develop further in the future. Actually the new arrangement was not cost-free. Edward agreed to pay Gloucester 10,000 marks (£6,666 13s.4d.), which evidently he regarded as a price worth paying to get rid of a problem. Perhaps it indicates that Richard took some persuading. A thousand bows and 500 sheaves of arrows that were set against the 10,000 marks indicate both that Richard intended another campaign and also his doubts that Edward could come up with the cash.[111]

Historians have differed considerably on the interpretation of this agreement. The act stands alone – it cannot be supplemented by any other record – and the intentions cannot be inferred from what happened later since it was never implemented.

Gloucester took a direct interest in his wardenship of the West March – witness his enhancement of the fortifications of Carlisle – and accepted the reduction in his salary in 1480, yet the Scottish war demonstrated the greater importance of the Middle and Eastern Marches. The West March was one of many interests, not the greatest or the focus of his future. Edward's massive and unparalleled concessions changed all that. They became the

[110] Grant, 'Richard III and Scotland', p. 126.
[111] E 404/77/3/87, 90.

logical next step to Richard's decade of aggrandisement during King
Edward's Second Reign and the culmination of his career. His own palatinate was an extraordinary distinction. There were only three palatinates in
England – Chester, Durham, and Lancaster – and Lancaster, the last, had
been created long ago by Edward III. It was temporary and made permanent only for John of Gaunt, indisputably the greatest English nobleman
since the Norman Conquest. Next best to the self-governing appanages
bestowed on the brothers and sons of kings of the French, Gloucester's new
palatinate resembled elevation to an independent monarchy. It gave the
duke the undisputed rule of a corner of the expanded English kingdom, with
superiority over the greatest families of the region. It substantially enhanced
his resources, albeit with new commitments. A palatine county was a great
distinction – the greatest regality in a region of liberties – and outshone any
mere nobles elsewhere. Gloucester was already Lord of Glamorgan, the
greatest of Welsh marcher lordships, where he appointed his own sheriff
and exercised regalian rights, yet he was shackled there by King Edward's new
indentures of the marches.[112] His Scottish palatinate placed him beyond the
authority of his brother the king. It was an appanage that compared with
those of French princes and an opportunity truly worthy of a high and
mighty prince. And it had the potential to be extended, both geographically
into Scotland and dynastically. It may have been what Gloucester had been
seeking.[113] It set him on a new trajectory. His future lay beyond England's
northernmost frontier, in Scotland.

Moreover, Gloucester was receiving 10,000 marks, a whole year's revenues and a sum that equated with the costs of the huge army of 1482 for four
weeks. On 20 February Edward ordered payment without delay.[114] This
sum could have funded a smaller force for a shorter period, probably veterans
of his successful campaign willing to serve him again. So Gloucester may
have felt. He possessed in his great English estates both considerable revenues – probably greater than the Scottish crown or any particular Scottish
magnate – and a well-established source of manpower. At 30 years of age, he

[112] Hicks, *Edward V*, p. 107.

[113] Grant, 'Richard III and Scotland', p. 125.

[114] E 404/77/2/67. Admittedly the bows and arrows supplied from the Tower were set
against this sum, E 404/77/3/87, 90.

was in his prime, with all the necessary experience in team building, warfare, and government, and remarkable vigour and energy that negated any physical weakness and deformity. If he already occupied most of the Debatable Lands or thought he did, his challenge was merely to hold on to them and to recolonise them. Gloucester's experience the previous year had revealed how weak financially, politically, and militarily the Scots were and may have given him the impression that they were easy to defeat. Did he hold any castles in Scotland and how prepared was he for the guerrilla-style warfare of the border reivers? Perhaps he counted on Albany's support as Alexander IV, King of Scots. Having said all that, this was an act of supreme optimism and another great gamble that realistically was more likely to fail – to wither away – than to succeed. Although the Scottish parliament cared little about the protection of Berwick, which they left to King James, they did care about the borders and were more likely to unite in their defence than concede them permanently to the English. Richard's own limited resources could be expected to run out and his failure would commit King Edward to a ruinous and unwinnable war. 'Richard . . . was proposing to bite off more than he could chew.'[115]

One wonders how much Richard knew about the task he had set himself. He had been warden of the Western Marches for a dozen years, the Cumbrian countryside and climate comparing well with the Scottish borders, the reiver mentality and dialect of the far North of England also akin to that of the Scottish borderers, and his raids over the past three years had acquainted him directly with the marches, the Debatable Lands, and as far into Scotland as Dumfries, Dunbar, and Edinburgh. The duke of Albany and Earl Douglas had spent several months in his company when they could have imparted useful information. Yet Richard was obviously an outsider to Scotland and his intended role was that of a conqueror, not the legitimate heir that he posed to be in northern England. The recognition of Duke Alexander carried little weight. What was needed was recognition by King Alexander. And that proved impossible to obtain.

[115] Grant, 'Richard III and Scotland', p. 126.

V

Of course Gloucester's new future never materialised. Within a month Albany had abandoned his usurpation plans and his alliance with England, so the prospect of Scottish support for Gloucester's Scottish palatinate was not to be expected. Within three months, the great northern estate that underpinned Gloucester's dominance in the North and on the borders had become a temporary resource. Gloucester had always appreciated the fragility of his tenure of the Neville lordships, which he held only for as long as John Marquis Montagu had male heirs living. In 1480 Gloucester obtained custody of the marquis's son George Neville, now aged 18. He needed to marry him off to some obscure lady who lacked the connections to threaten the duke's tenure and was fertile enough to bear him the sons that would prolong the hold of Gloucester and his heir on the Neville lordships. Richard never resolved this conundrum. No such match was concluded. Simultaneously he pursued an alternative strategy, to secure the rights of the next heir, Richard Neville, Lord Latimer. He strove to obtain possession of him unsuccessfully. Even his influence at court could not prevail against that of the cardinal-archbishop, uncle both to himself and the king. The releases he had secured from Latimer's grandmother Elizabeth Lady Latimer (d. 1481) and his aunt Katherine Radcliffe were insufficient. As both George and Richard Neville were minors, they could not quitclaim their rights anyway until they came of age, which was in 1486 in George's case and in 1490 for Latimer.[116] Cardinal Bourchier was old and died in 1486: perhaps Gloucester hoped to secure Latimer's wardship on his death. But George Neville died on 4 May 1483 leaving behind only five sisters. Richard was involved at once in marrying off the last two of these heiresses.[117] George had no younger brother to take over as male heir of the marquis Montagu. At this point, under the terms of the act of 1475, Gloucester's estate in the northern Neville lands was reduced to life only. His son Edward Earl of Salisbury was no longer the heir. The heir on Gloucester's death became Richard Lord Latimer. The act of 1475 had left

[116] Hicks, *Rivals*, chs 13, 15; Hicks, 'Richard Lord Latimer, Richard III, and the "Warwick Inheritance" ', *Ricardian* 154 (2001), p. 316.

[117] GEC, vol. 9, p. 93n; *Stonor L & P*, vol. 2, p. 158.

the duke secure in his tenure – he held by courtesy – but his claim on the loyalty of the family retainers was bound to erode over time to the reversioner. Young Edward could keep the wardenship, Cumbrian lands, and palatinate, but underpinning them were no longer the great Neville estate and connection, merely the admittedly substantial but scattered lordships of Barnard Castle, Cottingham, Helmsley, Richmond, Scarborough, and Skipton. In the longer term it was in the interests of Richard's heir to arrange a new partition of the Warwick inheritance, to substitute other property assigned to the duchess of Clarence in compensation for what was lost. Whether this was in Gloucester's interest is less obvious: even a life estate in the Middleham, Sheriff Hutton, and Penrith served him better.[118]

The Scottish war was the highest point in Richard's career so far. It was not yet over. There is no evidence that Edward IV had actually paid the 10,000 marks before he died. And his death imposed other responsibilities on the duke who was never to establish the Scottish principality authorised by the 1483 parliament. There unrolled other opportunities that Gloucester preferred.

[118] To repartition would presumably deprive Gloucester of the Neville lands that he would rather keep.

Chapter Ten

CHANGING TRAJECTORIES

THE ROAD TO THE CROWN 1483

I

The death of King Edward IV on 9 April 1483 sharply changed Richard's life and career. Richard mapped out his future. He had focused his career – dynastic, political, and spiritual – on the North of England where he had made himself dominant. There was still a war to fight with Scotland. He was licensed to expand into Scotland and to make a personal principality of the Debatable Lands that would require all his energy and resources in the immediate future. The future was rosy, if challenging. Richard's plans, however, were overtaken by Edward's death, which set him on a quite different (and ultimately disastrous) trajectory that took precedence over everything else. Ruling England became his immediate priority. During the next 13 weeks he made himself first Lord Protector, then king. He was the prime mover and kept his intentions concealed. Only the queen-dowager discerned that the crown was already his objective, perhaps prematurely. It could have been 12 weeks into Edward V's minority that usurpation of the throne became his objective.

II

On 9 April Duke Richard's whereabouts are unrecorded. Most likely he had remained in London some time beyond the dissolution of parliament

234

on 18 February to prepare for his next campaign. He then returned to his northern estates, certainly to Yorkshire, perhaps to the West March. His top priorities surely were to prepare his next campaign and to implement the creation of his principality. Probably he meant to miss the Garter Chapter at Windsor on 23 April. Once back in the North, of course, Duke Richard was far removed from the key events in the capital and the decisions that were taken there and that were designed to minimise his role. They may well have happened even before he knew of his brother's death. Edward Prince of Wales succeeded at once as Edward V, but – aged 12 – he was unquestionably too young to govern. Richard's status as the new king's sole uncle of the blood royal – his only paternal uncle – could not be denied, but his claim to rule was rejected. Richard could have accepted this decision, cooperated on (and indeed presided over) a minority council, and continued his regional rule undisturbed. That he declined to do so brought him to the crown, but also opened the way to his death at the disaster of Bosworth only 26 months later.

At various stages Richard deceived the Wydevilles and Hastings, with fatal consequences, as well as Cardinal Bourchier, the royal council and corporation of London, and many others besides. So effectively did Richard conceal his real intentions that these are difficult to divine today. Modern historians reject as implausible, impractical, and therefore inconceivable the long-term plot dating back to 1471 presented by More, and/or from 1478 in which all superior heirs were systematically eliminated. It is impossible to say how far ahead Richard peered in April 1483. Did he always intend to take the throne, as his first historians in retrospect came to believe? Was he persuaded only on 20–25 June, as he himself claimed? Or was it a step-by-step process, as each stage in his accretion of power drew him forward and made it essential for him to retain control against the new enemies he had made? These are questions that cannot now be conclusively answered and for which conclusive evidence is unlikely ever to be found. The actions of the earl of Northumberland in executing Edward V's uncle and brother do suggest that Richard envisaged usurping the throne before his first coup d'état on 1 May.

III

Edward IV's death was premature and unexpected, but not altogether unforeseen or unprepared for. The king himself had guarded against the worst eventualities by securing his throne, restoring his finances, bearing a son, and reigning for a further 12 years of stability. Whatever the nature of his last illness, Edward retained the use of his faculties and sought to guide what was to happen after his death.[1] The queen and her family (the Wydevilles) had managed the prince and his affairs for the last few years.[2] They intended now to take the dominant role in his regime as king and to be its principal beneficiaries. The queen's two elder sons, the new king's half-brothers, Thomas Marquis of Dorset and Lord Richard Grey, surely aspired to a dukedom and an earldom respectively. They had shared out the Exeter inheritance. Dorset had the custody and marriage of Clarence's son Edward Earl of Warwick and Grey had the marcher lordship of Kidwelly in South Wales.[3] The advancement of the Wydevilles in Wales had been at the expense of other powerful figures, such as William Herbert II, earl of Huntingdon, and Henry Duke of Buckingham,[4] who may have wished to overturn these arrangements. Equally aggrieved surely were John Lord Howard and William Viscount Berkeley, next heirs to the great Norfolk inheritance, whose rights had been sidelined to the benefit of Edward IV's younger son Richard Duke of York and Norfolk, whose affairs were also run by the Wydevilles.[5] Whether or not Clarence ever made plans to seize the throne should King Edward die, as the queen herself and Thomas More appear to have supposed,[6] his own death put a stop to them. The next brother Richard Duke of Gloucester cannot realistically have planned usurpation either in 1471 or 1478. In 1483 Richard claimed to

---

[1] Probably he nominated Richard as Lord Protector and certainly he sought to reconcile his household and the Wydevilles, see Mancini, *Richard III*, pp. 60–1, 78–71; Hanham, *Richard III*, p. 119; More, *Richard III*, pp. 10ff.

[2] Hicks, *Edward V*, ch. 4.

[3] *CPR 1476–85*, p. 212; Hicks, *Edward V*, p. 134.

[4] Hicks, *Edward V*, p. 113, 120. An indenture regulating Buckingham's rule of his marcher lordships survives, Hicks, *Edward V*, pp. 107–8; E 315/40/75. The queen may not have been aware of any hostility.

[5] From 1478 York was married to the child Anne Mowbray (d. 1481), Hicks, *Edward V*, pp. 128–30; *Clarence*, pp. 143–5.

[6] More, *Richard III*, pp. 7–12; Mancini, *Richard III*, pp. 62–3; Hicks, *Clarence*, pp. 146–7.

have disapproved of his brother's marriage and to have suffered at the hands of the Wydevilles,[7] but the record evidence speaks otherwise. The queen had made him steward of her Bedfordshire estate in 1469, increased his fee in 1473, and apparently backed him against Clarence over the Warwick inheritance.[8] They had collaborated in Clarence's destruction. Richard had cooperated amicably enough with the queen and her family up to now. In 1481 her eldest son Thomas Marquis of Dorset and her brother Earl Rivers had served under his command against the Scots, in 1482 he had raised another brother Edward Wydeville to banneret, and in late March 1483 Rivers had trusted the duke enough to nominate him arbiter in one of his disputes.[9] There is no contemporary evidence to substantiate that (as More states) 'the Queene and the Lordes of her bloode whiche highlye maligned the kynges kinred (as women commonly not of malice but of nature hate them whome theire housbandes loue)', nor of the jealousy at which Mancini hints.[10] Before 1483, when Richard declared his antipathy, there are no indicators that Richard hated the Wydevilles. It seems that the Wydevilles themselves were unaware that he was their enemy. Elizabeth may have wished to sideline Richard, but she did not fear him.

King Edward had prepared for the future by bearing a son and heir, whose right to succeed as King Edward V was unquestioned, and a second spare son, Richard Duke of York, who was next in line. Everybody who mattered had sworn allegiance to the young prince, most like Gloucester several times. The Yorkist dynasty was secure. King Edward had also made his last will.[11] Unfortunately it is lost, but most of the contents can be deduced. Edward had prepared for his funeral and burial in his new St George's Chapel at Windsor. Not everything was in place for the future, however, and he left behind considerable disarray for those left behind to

---

[7] Mancini, *Richard III*, pp. 60–1; More, *Richard III*, p. 9.

[8] BL MS Cotton Julius BXII ff.121v, 126v–7 as interpreted by Hicks, *Clarence*, p. 116.

[9] C. Moreton, 'A Local Dispute and the Politics of 1483: Roger Townshend, Earl Rivers and the Duke of Gloucester', *Ricardian*, 107 (1989), p. 305; see above, ch. 9.

[10] More, *Richard III*, p. 7; Mancini, *Richard III*, pp. 64–5.

[11] Administration was declined by the executors, who differed from those nominated in the extant but superseded will of 1475, *Excerpta Historica*, ed. S. Bentley (1831), pp. 366–79; *Registrum Thome Bourgchier Cantuaroensis Archiepiscopi AD 1454–86*, ed. F.R.H. Du Boulay, Canterbury and York Society, vol. 54 (Oxford University Press, 1957), pp. 52–3.

resolve. Four aspects demand preliminary attention: international relations, the royal finances, factionalism at court, and the form that the government of Edward V was to take. It did not help that the economy was in deep depression and the populace therefore susceptible to rabble-rousers.

Edward left a perilous international situation in which war threatened with both France and Scotland and both on land and sea. The capture of Berwick had not ended the Scottish war. Edward had renewed his alliance with the duke of Albany, who recanted once again in March 1483. Moreover, the Treaty of Arras of December 1482 that had brought peace between France and Burgundy also terminated Edward's Picquigny settlement with France. Calais, now an enclave within French Artois, was threatened. Louis XI's admiral, Philippe de Crèvecoeur, called Lord Cordes by the English, waged an aggressive campaign against English shipping in the Channel.[12] At first Edward IV considered a new war with France – in February he offered 4,000 archers to Brittany for use against the French – but in March he was again anxious to preserve the truce with France.[13]

It is not clear whether it was Edward or his successors who ordered military and naval countermeasures. The 300 extra troops from Derbyshire, presumably Hastings' men, had to be conveyed to Calais, paid, and victualled. Dorset was commissioned to keep the sea with 1,000 men costing 4,480 marks (£3,600), his uncle Sir Edward Wydeville as 'grete capeteyne of his navy' commanded 2,000 men (£3,280), and a carrack captained by Sir Roger Cotton was munitioned and crewed at a cost of £251 13s 8d.[14] For Berwick the government had to pay £438 a month in wages alone, to victual and equip the garrison, to repair the defences, and to develop the town. Edward had ordered the immediate payment of £10,000 due to Gloucester. Although no payments or assignments are known, it seems likely this charge was disbursed in Edward's lifetime as it does not recur in the financial memoranda of May and June.[15] It may be what enabled Gloucester to subsidise the minority government.

[12] Ross, *Richard III*, p. 66.

[13] Ross, *Edward IV*, p. 292.

[14] 'Financial Memoranda', pp. 215–6, 218, 220. These commissions were only for a few months each.

[15] Was this how Richard raised £800 he paid for the household? 'Financial Memoranda', p. 218.

A surviving book of financial memoranda reveals just how difficult the regime found it to meet these obligations and how hand-to-mouth were the expedients that Edward V's officers employed to defray each cost month by month. Edward IV had only £1,200 in cash at his death.[16] It is unknown what was spent on Edward V's abortive coronation on 4 May, which must surely have been much less grand than Richard III's, nor how it was funded. Not only had the costs of the regime increased, but the revenues available had collapsed. Only in February parliament had assigned £11,000 to fund the household, but £5,933 of this had come from the tonnage and poundage (customs) that Edward had held only for life and another £2,400 from the Duchy of Lancaster.[17] Merchants now refused to pay customs, winning the legal arguments on 3 June.[18] No wonder the royal council had struggled to locate £58 8s 8d in cash for wages due before Easter, £230 for 'fresshe accates' (purchases) for two weeks, and new accates worth 50 marks a week up to the opening of parliament.[19] Customs revenue from other ports also ceased.[20] So too of course had Edward's French pension. Edward IV's landed estate comprised little more than a few Clarence lands beyond £2,074 assigned to the household and a few southern manors.[21] The South Parts of the Duchy of Lancaster were included in the queen's dower. In 1475 Edward IV had enfeoffed almost all the North Parts of the duchy, worth about £7,000, to the use of his will, which automatically devolved at his death on his executors.[22] They could draw on this for as long as it took to carry out Edward's intentions: the king certainly did not die intestate. Since the executors started with at least £5,000, the feoffees had probably retained the half-year instalment of rents due on Lady Day 1483. Edward's final will probably updated that of

[16] Ibid., p. 219. But he also possessed quantities of jewellery, plate, weapons, horses, furniture, books, vestments, and much else.

[17] *PROME*, vol. 14, pp. 414–15; 'Financial Memoranda', p. 212.

[18] *Acts of Court of the Mercers' Company 1453–1527*, eds L. Lyell and C.D. Watney (Cambridge University Press, 1936), pp. 152–3; 'Financial Memoranda', p. 231.

[19] 'Financial Memoranda', pp. 217, 221. Does this mean Edward IV's household remained in being until parliament?

[20] Ibid., p. 217.

[21] Ibid., p. 222; *PROME*, vol. 14, p. 415.

[22] Somerville, *Lancaster*, vol. 1, pp. 238–9.

1475,[23] which had committed these revenues to raising dowries of 10,000 marks per daughter, to be paid from this trust. Probably in 1483 he earmarked four such dowries totalling 40,000 marks (£26,000 13s. 4d) for the four daughters destined to marry (Elizabeth, Cecily, Katherine, and Anne – Bridget was to become a nun), and sufficient revenues as long as needed to complete the construction of his new foundation of St George's Chapel Windsor, at a cost of several tens of thousand of pounds. In the context of 1483 what matters is that this duchy income was lost semi-permanently to the crown. Admittedly £5,554 was borrowed from Edward's executors, but this would have to be repaid. Reimbursement was also needed of another £800 advanced by Gloucester, who was also due his salary (whatever it was) as lord protector, and his expenses as protec-tor.[24] On 23 May Cardinal Bourchier authorised the sale of the late king's chattels to the value of £1,496 17s 2d to cover the costs of his funeral that remained unpaid.[25] Edward V's finances were in a parlous state.

The political elite that Edward had bequeathed to his son was riven by faction. England was a mixed monarchy, in which power was shared by the king and his greater subjects, most of whom in practice resided in the prov-inces. King Edward ruled by patronage rather than coercion. He did not compel obedience, but instead allured and rewarded service. His suitors arrayed in factions jostled and competed for the offices and other kinds of grants that came available for the king to bestow. Day-by-day politics there-fore revolved around the court, normally located in the Thames Valley, where the king, queen, and court determined policy and in particular the distribution of royal patronage that was to be decided. Edward allocated his patronage himself, so access to the king was therefore crucial. Such govern-ment ministers as the chancellor, the queen, and the royal family (e.g., Edward's uncle Essex), and the greatest magnates had rights of access to the king. Others had access via intermediaries, the most important being the chamberlain of the household, William Lord Hastings. Such favoured indi-

---

[23] *Excerpta Historica*, p. 336. There was no longer any need to endow his second son Richard. Cecily's received dowry for 8,000 mark for the abortive Scottish match.

[24] 'Financial Memoranda', p. 218.

[25] Ibid., p. 221; *Registrum Bourgchier*, pp. 54–5. This was properly the first call on the king's estate and essential for the good of his soul.

viduals channelled the petitions and representations of suitors that invoked their intercession with the king.[26] The principal court factions in Edward IV's last years were first his own household and Yorkist affinity led by Hastings and Stanley, as chamberlain and steward of his household, and, second, the circle of Queen Elizabeth, her brothers, and son Dorset (the Wydevilles). All such court factions sought to maximise their rewards, to determine policy, and even to 'rule the very king himself', as Mancini says. Actually Edward played them off against one another and kept the control in his own hands. Other notables, such as Cardinal Bourchier and Richard Duke of Gloucester, also secured royal favours. Edward 'loved each of them', but they detested one another. Edward was unconcerned by their competitions – he could control such rivals himself – but factional strife might rage unchecked and destructively after his death. In his last days therefore he strove to reconcile the queen's son Dorset with Hastings. In Edward's presence Hastings and Dorset formally forgave each other and shook hands, but, More opines, 'their herts wer far a sonder'. 'There still survived a latent jealousy', wrote Mancini. Hastings 'was afraid', wrote Crowland, 'that if supreme power fell into the hands of the queen's relatives, they would then sharply avenge the alleged injuries done to them by that lord'. Hastings thought himself at risk,[27] although actually the Wydevilles took no such actions and may have felt it unnecessary once Hastings ceased to be chamberlain and no longer controlled access to the king.

Hastings was distantly related to the queen. Long ago in 1464, when the widowed Elizabeth had besought from her kinsman Lord Chamberlain Hastings access to the king to secure her jointure from her first marriage, Hastings had driven the hardest of bargains for his services, which, however, lapsed when she became queen. Since then he and the Wydevilles had clashed on numerous occasions. It was Hastings, not the queen's brother Rivers, who became captain of Calais. When in 1474 the queen's son Thomas Grey, marquis of Dorset, bid for the hand of Hastings'

[26] The Yorkist system is convincingly analysed in A. Brondarbit, 'The Allocation of Power: The Ruling Elite of Edward IV, 1461–1483', PhD thesis (Winchester University, 2015).

[27] Mancini, *Richard III*, pp. 64–5, 68–9, 73; More, *Richard III*, pp. 10–16; Crowland, pp. 154–5.

stepdaughter Cecily Bonville, a royal ward, Hastings resisted but was overruled. Since then Hastings and his son-in-law Dorset had shared in the
king's debaucheries that the queen deplored. Hastings and the Wydevilles
feuded at court and used dirty tricks to discredit each other – 'the suborned
informers of each had threatened a capital charge against the other'.[28]
Nevertheless Hastings retained his chamberlainship and credit with King
Edward right up to the king's death. Although the marriages of the queen's
sisters had integrated the Wydevilles into the nobility, they may have been
unpopular,[29] and in Edward's final years had certainly secured the largest
rewards that he had to bestow, at the expense of other long-serving
Yorkists.[30] Although Rivers and Dorset dominated no regions from their
own estates, the Wydevilles commanded huge resources of the crown.
Rivers and her second son Lord Richard Grey had come to dominate the
household and estates of Prince Edward and therefore the whole principality and marches of Wales whence Rivers, for instance, had led a thousand men against Scotland in 1481. They also managed the huge estate of
the king's second son Richard as duke of Norfolk. As queen, Elizabeth
personally deserved respect, thought Crowland,[31] who was less deferential
towards her family. Lord Chancellor Rotherham thought so too and surrendered the great seal to her on Richard's First Coup.[32] Whatever Edward
planned, however, carried limited weight after his death. No dead king
could bind his successors. The Wydevilles had planned not just for the
succession but for the future several stages ahead.

How was England to be governed in the absence of an adult king? Only
40 years old at his death, Edward IV had not prepared for dying so early.

[28] Mancini, *Richard III*, pp. 68–9. A hint at what was involved emerges from John Edward's
confession, multiple copies of which survive among the papers of Earl Rivers' legal counsel,
E.W. Ives, 'Andrew Dymmock and the Papers of Antony Earl Rivers 1482–3', *BIHR*, 41
(1968), pp. 216–29; E 315/486.

[29] So says Mancini (Mancini, *Richard III*, pp. 68–9), but both he and More perhaps were
influenced by Gloucester's propaganda in 1483, Hicks, *Richard III*, pp. 121–3. They
blamed them for the death of Clarence (Mancini, *Richard III*, pp. 68–9), in which everyone
(including the king) had shared.

[30] Hicks, *Edward V*, ch. 5. There is some truth in Mancini's statement that 'the queen
ennobled many of her family', Mancini, *Richard III*, pp 64–5.

[31] *Crowland*, pp. 152–3, 158–9.,

[32] More, *Richard III*, p. 122. It was a misjudgement that he quickly corrected. He was
replaced as chancellor.

Even by fifteenth-century standards his 12-year-old son Prince Edward
was too young to rule. For about three years some interim arrangement
was needed. For his absence in France in 1475, Edward had nominated his
son as keeper of the realm, confided him to the care of the queen, and had
appointed a council of 20 to do the governing. Queens could exert great
influence, but there was no precedent in England for the French fashion of
queens regent. Most probably Edward expected his brother Richard to
direct the regime as Lord Protector, on the model of Henry VI's uncles in
the 1420s and Richard Duke of York in the 1450s. If correct, Edward
evidently trusted his brother in this matter, and did not see Richard as
posing any threat to his son. He may have designated Gloucester as Lord
Protector, as Rous, Mancini, Bernard André, and Polydore Vergil all
explicitly state,[33] and may even have notified the duke of his intention in his
last days. This appointment may have been the subject of one of the lost
codicils that he added to his will on his deathbed.[34]

A Lord Protector had far less power than a king or indeed the Regent
Bedford in Lancastrian France. His role was to protect the person of the
king and the kingdom and to lead a council that made decisions.[35] However,
one of the first actions of Edward V's minority council was to rule out a
protectorate.

IV

On 10 April, the day after Edward IV's death, the royal council met at
Westminster to acknowledge Edward V as the new king. Presumably the
meeting constituted those ministers, prelates, peers, and other notables who
happened to be in London at the time. Queen Elizabeth was present. Two
striking absentees and elder statesmen, it seems, were two of the king's great-
uncles, Lord Treasurer Essex who had predeceased the king by four days
(5 April) and his brother Cardinal Bourchier, Archbishop of Canterbury.
Two contemporaries, Dominic Mancini and the councillor Crowland, and

---

[33] Hanham, *Richard III*, p. 118; Mancini, *Richard III*, pp. 61, 107n, 108.

[34] *Crowland*, pp. 152–3.

[35] J.S. Roskell, 'The Office and Dignity of Lord Protector of England, with Special
Reference to its Origins', *EHR*, 68 (1953), pp. 193–233; R.A. Griffiths, 'The Minority of
Henry VI, King of England and of France', in *The Royal Minorities of Medieval and Early
Modern England*, ed. C. Beem (Palgrave Macmillan, 2008), pp. 170–2.

the later writer Thomas More report in very similar terms the issues and differences of view that were aired in council and the key decisions that were taken. They all described the Westminster scene. How things looked and what was happening at Ludlow, in the North, and everywhere else is unknown, murky, or has to be guessed. The impression the chroniclers give of Westminster politics is that all this decision making took some time, but actually it happened almost at once. A letter from Edward V to King's Lynn dated 16 April builds on instructions from court received on the 14th that therefore cannot have been despatched to Ludlow later than the 12th.[36] Some actions obviously had to be taken at once, perhaps on 10 April itself: about the late king's funeral, the reappointment of the chancellor and judges (their patents were dated 21 April),[37] the conduct of the Scottish war, the defence of Calais and the keeping of the sea, about foreign affairs and royal finances, all themes touched on above. The king's body lay in state at St Stephen's Chapel from 10 April and then progressed slowly from 17 April to the funeral at Windsor on 19 April. Perhaps this timetable was too rapid for many senior peers to attend and most indeed missed the occasion. The late king's nephew John Earl of Lincoln was the chief mourner. Lord Howard bore the late king's banner.[38] The new king needed to return from his residence at Ludlow in the Welsh marches to the capital and seat of government.

Decisions about the future shape of that government could and should have been deferred until the young king himself, his uncles, and the other dukes and earls had arrived. Gloucester's right to be consulted was asserted at the council, 'because Edward in his will had so directed'. Crowland states that 'the more foresighted members of the Council' (among whom he numbered himself) 'thought that the uncles and brothers on the mother's side should be absolutely forbidden to have control of the person of the young man until he came of age'.[39] For the moment, however, power rested

[36] Historic Manuscripts Commission, *11th Report Appendix III, MSS of the Corporations of Southampton and King's Lynn* (1887), p. 170; M.A. Hicks, 'A Story of Failure: The Minority of Edward V', in *Royal Minorities*, ed. Beem, pp. 198–9.

[37] *CPR 1476–85*, pp. 350–1.

[38] Sutton and Visser-Fuchs, *The Royal Funerals of the House of York at Windsor*, eds A.F. Sutton and L. Visser-Fuchs with R.A. Griffiths (London, Richard III Society, 2005), pp. 7–46.

[39] Mancini, *Richard III*, pp. 70–1; *Crowland*, pp. 152–3. Mancini adds 'by law the government ought to devolve upon him' without further explanation.

with them. Not prostrated by grief, Edward's widowed queen attended this council session and everybody deferred to her eminence. Gloucester's claims to become protector were disregarded. The council would rule, among whom Gloucester 'should be accounted the chief . . . and given due honour'. The queen's son Dorset stated that 'we are so important, that even without the king's uncle [Gloucester] we can make and enforce these decisions'. A vote was taken. 'All who favoured the queen's family voted for this proposal.'[40] Hastings, the household, and the traditional Yorkists were defeated, although Hastings himself, as captain of Calais, still carried weight. The Wydevilles seized control. This was a Wydeville coup d'état. There are no surviving records of the activities of this three-week Wydeville regime.

The most important decision reached was that Edward V was to be crowned at once.[41] Modern historians have deduced, on the precedent of 1429, that coronation would declare Edward V to be of age and would thus obviate the need for a protectorate or for rule by a formal royal council. Obviously so young a king required support and advice that could be expected to emanate from his mother, half-brothers, and maternal uncles. This decision therefore excluded from formal power the king's sole paternal uncle Richard Duke of Gloucester – the only adult member of the Yorkist blood royal – with effect from the coronation in only four weeks' time. The late king's household was already excluded, because dissolved by his death. At Edward IV's interment the chief officers were to cast their staves of office into Edward's grave,[42] thus signifying that their appointments had ceased.

The coronation date was set for 4 May, less than a month away. The new king was recalled to London under the guidance of his governor Earl Rivers. The council debated about the size of his escort: should it be an army capable of overawing everybody or merely 2,000-strong? Hastings urged the latter. Indeed Crowland reports that he threatened to flee (to Calais?) if the king's escort was larger than that. Limiting the size of his

[40] Mancini, *Richard III*, pp. 70–5. Mancini suggests they were fearful of being blamed by Gloucester for Clarence's death.

[41] *Crowland*, pp. 152–3.

[42] Sutton and Visser-Fuchs, *Royal Funerals*, p. 31. Funding for a royal household continued.

entourage was the queen's only concession.[43] Although conceded, the decisions were not agreed. Hastings at least hoped that this Wydeville coup d'état could be overturned and kept Gloucester informed through a series of communications.[44]

Gloucester wrote pleasant letters of condolence to the queen and council and pledged his fealty. He pointed out that he was loyal, that he was entitled to a role in new regime, and was also reasonable and respectful to the council's decisions.[45] He did not threaten or even hint that he would resort to force. Reassured, the Wydevilles did not anticipate any resistance or violence from Richard. They underestimated him. To send Dorset off to command the seas against French privateers – a command he certainly desired and a major new expense (£3,670) – deprived the Wydevilles of the military leadership that they were to require. Richard had always deferred to the king and now to the queen, so perhaps the Wydeville factions was unaware how formidable he was, how vigorous, intense, egotistical, ambitious, aggressive, ruthless, and uncompromising he had been away from court. They failed to appreciate how capable, cunning, and dangerous he was. And such a skilful propagandist too.

V

Edward V was at Ludlow when Edward IV died. 'His father's friends flocked to him', reports Rous,[46] and presumably, alongside Rivers, Grey, and the prince's household, they swore obedience to him as King Edward V. The new king wrote on 16 May to King's Lynn urging attendance at the coronation in what is presumably the sole survivor of many others letters despatched to English towns.[47] There was probably much correspondence to and fro with the government in London and with many others, including Richard Duke of Gloucester. This year the king held the Garter Chapter on St George's Day (23 April) at Ludlow, both the religious services and the banquet, and next day with his escort he set off for London.[48] Probably they

[43] Mancini, *Richard III*, pp. 70–3; *Crowland*, pp. 153–5; More, *Richard III*, pp. 16–17.

[44] Mancini, *Richard III*, p. 70–3.

[45] Ibid., pp. 72–73; More, *Richard III*, p. 17; *Crowland*, p. 155.

[46] Hanham, *Richard III*, p. 118.

[47] Historic Manuscripts Commission, *11th Report*, vol. 3, p. 170.

[48] Hanham, *Richard III*, p. 118. No record of this chapter was entered in the Garter register.

were all attired for riding, not harnessed nor armed against an unknown threat, and their armour and weapons followed in carts. Since the Ludlow establishment was closing down and the prince's household was moving permanently to Westminster, the baggage train may have been both large and slow-moving. Included were the armaments amassed for Rivers' contingent in the Scottish war. The council had instructed them to arrive three days before the coronation on 4 May. Instead of travelling down the Severn to Gloucester and along the Thames Valley (the southern route), they proceeded through the North Midlands to the Great North Road and overnighted on 30 April/1 May at Grafton Regis in Northamptonshire. The journey took seven days. Rivers may have wished to exhibit his royal nephew at his principal country seat.

Gloucester missed all the council meetings that took the key decisions in London. He made no effort to attend his brother's funeral, but he did plan to attend the coronation. Crowland reports that he proceeded to York 'with an appropriate company, all dressed in mourning, and held a solemn funeral ceremony [in York Minster] for the king, full of tears. He bound, by oath, all the nobility of these parts in fealty to the king's son; he himself swore first of all.'[49] By letter he pressed his own right to rule, unsuccessfully and almost certainly too late, but appeared to bow to the *fait accompli*.[50] It may be, however, that it was the rejection of his claims that were the 'insult' perpetrated 'by the ignoble family of the queen' of which he later complained,[51] but any such sentiments were surely concealed at the time. Once again Richard seemed to submit while planning to circumvent the decision. Actually he intended making himself Lord Protector and taking up the direction of the kingdom.

Duke Richard arranged with Rivers that they should meet up en route, thus making the entry of the new king into his capital more impressive. With this in mind Rivers may indeed have been persuaded to take the northern route rather than proceed via the Thames Valley. Indeed he

---

[49] *Crowland*, pp. 154–5. To clothe his whole household in mourning surely took both time and money.
[50] Mancini, *Richard III*, pp. 72–3,
[51] Ibid., pp. 74–5.

turned back from Grafton to meet Gloucester. Henry Duke of Buckingham joined them with a thousand men.[52] Buckingham was vitriolic in his hostility to the queen's family, to which his own duchess belonged, and was impatient for preferment in areas where they ruled. Gloucester, Buckingham, and Rivers met up on 30 April 1483 at Stony Stratford, about five miles from Grafton Regis, where they spent a convivial evening,[53] and then next morning (1 May) the two dukes staged Richard's First Coup d'état. According to More, the two dukes had conferred for much of the night. At dawn the following morning, they confined Rivers, and accompanied by their households armed and armoured they seized the person of the king, whose entourage had been preparing to travel but not to fight. The rest of Edward V's escort and most of his household were disbanded and disarmed.[54] The two dukes pledged their loyalty to King Edward V with due reverence – 'bared head, bent knee, and any other posture', 'with kisses and embraces' wrote Rous – and explained that Rivers, Grey, and Vaughan were not faithful or trustworthy subjects. They were not actuated by the honour and safety of the king as the two dukes were. Moreover, they had plotted the destruction of Duke Richard: an assertion that cannot now be substantiated and that is usually judged to be untrue. The young king objected. Rivers and the others had been appointed by his father Edward IV, whose judgement he trusted, and had committed no proven offence. He vouched for them. His expressions of devotion were overridden as the two dukes substituted themselves as his advisers.[55]

Earl Rivers had not recognised Richard as his enemy and had placed himself and the king in the duke's power. This First Coup transferred control from the Wydevilles to Duke Richard. The king, dukes, and probably other nobles formally processed into London. They were scheduled to meet the mayor and corporation of London clad in scarlet with 410 liverymen in

[52] C. Rawcliffe, *The Staffords, Earls of Stafford and Dukes of Buckingham, 1394–1521* (Cambridge University Press, 1978), p. 29.

[53] Mancini, *Richard III*, pp. 74–5.

[54] Mancini, *Richard III*, pp. 78–9, 126n85. Some remained: e.g., William Aubrey, the cofferer, and John Argentine, the physician, ibid., pp. 92–3; 'Financial Memoranda', pp. 229, 231.

[55] Hanham, *Richard III*, p. 118; Crowland, pp. 156–7; Mancini, pp. 76–7; More, *Richard III*, pp. 18–20.

murray at Hornsey Park.[56] The king arrived in London on 4 May, the date set for the coronation, which was therefore postponed.

Of course Richard's First Coup was planned, so secretly that the extent of the conspiracy cannot easily be gauged. It is not particularly surprising that Buckingham's rift with the Wydevilles was unknown, whether or not because he felt disparaged by his marriage to Katherine Wydeville as was alleged,[57] but Gloucester knew of it and negotiated in advance both his meeting with Buckingham and the coup that they jointly staged. Most likely Richard wrote to other potential allies: to Lord Howard perhaps. He may have already agreed on rewards for Buckingham and on delivery to Lords Howard and Berkeley of their shares to the Mowbray inheritance that Edward IV had denied them.[58] Howard's promotion to duke of Norfolk and Berkeley's to earl of Nottingham were dated 28 June, beyond Edward V's accession. Is it indicative that so few senior peers joined in Edward IV's funeral? Surely the earl of Northumberland, who should have borne the sword *Curtana* at the coronation, the earl of Westmorland, and Lord Neville knew there was to be no coronation on 4 May and hence stayed in the North? Perhaps Northumberland knew more than that, since he took command of the northern army that Richard summoned on 10–11 June and was the 'chief judge' over the trials and executions of Rivers, Grey, Vaughan, and Haute.[59] To execute the king's brother and uncle were not actions to be undertaken with impunity and without guarantees against reprisals. The coup may indeed have been the idea of Lord Hastings, as he apparently said, again surely after the event. Certainly it was Hastings who insisted on limiting the king's escort. He was confident that the dukes would bring more men. His recommendation that Richard seize the king cannot have been revealed at the time to the queen and would have failed if publicly known. Perhaps Hastings disclosed it later when claiming credit

[56] 'Financial Memoranda', p. 229; *The Coronation of Richard III: The Extant Documents*, eds A.F. Sutton and P.W. Hammond (A. Sutton, 1983), pp. 15–16. There is no narrative or record of such an event.

[57] Mancini, *Richard III*, pp. 74–5.

[58] Rightfully Anne Mowbray's, it had been retained by her husband Prince Richard on her death, Hicks, *Edward V*, p. 129. For the next sentence, see GEC, vol. 9, p. 611, vol. 8, p. 782.

[59] Hanham, *Richard III*, p. 119.

for the success of an almost bloodless coup.[60] Everybody still recognised
Edward V as king.

Possession of Edward V was Richard's first step towards taking over the
government. The queen suspected at once, perhaps correctly, that it was the
first step towards seizing the throne, but had her perception been shared,
Richard's usurpation would have been impossible. Had Richard deposed
Edward V at this point, all parties – Wydevilles and Hastings alike – would
have combined to thwart him. Richard did his best to indicate that this was
not his intention. He managed public opinion skilfully.[61] He declared his
loyalty to the young king in the reassuring letters that he sent to the royal
council and corporation of London. Like his earlier correspondence, these
were open letters that were widely distributed and approved. Edward V's
strongest supporters, such as Hastings and Crowland, praised Richard's
actions. The queen tried to stage a counter-revolution, but found it impossible to raise enough support. She therefore took her second son Richard
Duke of York and her daughters into sanctuary at Westminster Abbey.[62] On
4 May Gloucester and Buckingham therefore entered London unopposed
with their modest escorts and 'othir noble lordes' unnamed[63] – the only
armed force there was – and lodged the young king in the palace of the
bishop of London near St Paul's.

Most of the political elite, it seems, viewed the Wydeville coup as an
abuse of power and were convinced by Richard's expressions of loyalty and
service both before and after his own First Coup. Duke Richard presented
himself in the right light both to the royal council and the people. He
treated Edward V with great public respect, swore fealty to him, and
induced everyone else to do likewise. The oath 'was performed with joy
and pride by all because this promised best for future prosperity'. The king
was housed where he was visible and could be visited. That the royal
council accepted Richard as Lord Protector, an office carrying limited
powers on the model of Humphrey Duke of Gloucester (d. 1447), was
probably because new dates were fixed for the coronation (24 June) and a

[60] *Crowland*, pp. 158–9.
[61] Hicks, *Richard III*, ch. 3. This is the source for the next three paragraphs.
[62] *Crowland*, pp. 156–7.
[63] 'Financial Memoranda', p. 229.

new parliament (25 June) that limited his protectorate to a mere seven weeks. There is no surviving patent that defines Richard's powers, term of office, or salary. 'Everyone looked forward to the eagerly desired coronation day of the new king.' Richard 'exercised this authority with the consent and goodwill of the lords'. However, as Crowland remarked, he ruled like a king.[64] He courted popularity by riding around and showing himself. While these measures should have reassured everyone, Crowland reports growing anxiety (among the loyal uncommitted?), both because Rivers and Grey were kept in prison and because insufficient respect was shown to the queen.[65]

At this stage Richard constructed a new image for himself and destroyed the reputation of the Wydevilles. He had written openly to the queen, council, corporation of London, and the populace. Now he revealed that he personally had disapproved of King Edward's marriage in 1464 and had likewise regretted the destruction of his brother Clarence in 1478, both of which he blamed on the Wydevilles. It was the rule of the Wydevilles that had caused him to exile himself from court like previous popular idols, his father Richard Duke of York, and cousin/father-in-law Warwick the Kingmaker. The Wydevilles had seized Edward IV's treasure and they had intended ambushing him on the way southwards – witness the four cartloads of weapons bearing their arms and devices that he publicly exhibited.[66] Hence he sought the execution of Rivers, Grey, and Vaughan for treason.

With the exception of his attitude to the Wydeville marriage all these 'facts' have been proven to originate from Richard and to be false. Richard participated fully in Clarence's trial, did not exile himself from court, Edward left no treasure, and it is surely inconceivable that the ambushers were themselves ambushed. Yet Richard's claims were disseminated and believed, so that they became imbedded as fact in the chronicles. Richard also condemned the sexual immorality of the Wydevilles, especially Dorset

[64] *Crowland*, pp. 156–7.

[65] Ibid., pp. 158–9.

[66] These could legitimately have accompanied them from Wales. Mancini reports that they were left over from the Scottish war and stashed locally, Mancini, *Richard III*, pp. 70–1, 82–3.

with Elizabeth Shore, who had also shared her favours with Edward IV
and Hastings.

VI

What use did Richard make of power in the first five weeks of his protectorate? First of all, he reshuffled the ministers and filled vacant posts. Thus
Archbishop Rotherham, chancellor since 1475, who had overcommitted
himself to the queen, was superseded by John Russell, bishop of Lincoln,
and Dean John Gunthorpe became keeper of the Privy Seal. These were
unexceptional appointments of the type of well-qualified churchmen-
bureaucrats that normally staffed such posts. Hastings was retained as Lord
Chamberlain. The offices of the late earl of Essex were filled: the obscure
bureaucrat John Wood became Lord Treasurer, the earl of Arundel keeper
of southern forests, and Lord Howard Chief Steward of the South Parts of
the Duchy of Lancaster. Buckingham replaced the council of Wales. On 16
May he became chief justice and chamberlain of North and South Wales,
steward and constable throughout the principality and marcher lordships of
the crown and duchy, and thus by far the most powerful figure ever in
Wales. A total of £1,000 was found for him to sort things out in Wales.
William Catesby became chancellor of the earldom of March and chancellor of the exchequer. Morgan Kidwelly became attorney general. Nor
did it stop there. Earl Rivers was replaced as chief butler by Gloucester's
friend Lord Lovell and Dorset's northern lands were taken into royal hands,
as though he was a traitor. Several lesser men were already replaced.[67]

Second, Richard completed the defeat of the Wydevilles. At Stony
Stratford and Grafton Regis the two dukes had arrested four key men: Earl
Rivers, the young king's half-brother Lord Richard Grey, Sir Thomas
Vaughan (chamberlain of the prince's household), and Sir Richard Haute
(controller of his household). Richard had them imprisoned in his northern
castles: Rivers at Sheriff Hutton in the custody of Sir Thomas Gower and
Grey at Middleham. Such gentlemanly house-arrest was not uncommon to
cool off misbehaving noblemen and need not have betokened further
punishment, but in these instances Gloucester had determined on the

[67] *H433*, vol. 1, pp. 6–15, 29, 40, 65, 79; *CPR 1476–85*, pp. 349–50, 360, 363, 365, 474.

death penalty. He had made his captives into enemies. They were bound to be released when his protectorate ended and their influence with the new king might be dangerous to him. The answer was to eliminate them: dead men could pose no threat, as his father York, Warwick the Kingmaker, and other Yorkists had found. Here he was thwarted by the royal council, which may not have been persuaded that these men had plotted against the duke. Certainly the council denied that any plotting before Gloucester was even protector could constitute treason.[68] Richard decided on their elimination anyway. The seizure of their lands and chattels suggests that he wanted the next parliament to attaint them. However, he did not wait so long. By 23 June Rivers knew he was doomed. This was ahead of whatever form of trial that was organised at Pontefract. All four were condemned and on 25 June executed.[69]

The queen's eldest son, Thomas Marquis of Dorset, and her brother Sir Edward Wydeville had been appointed to the command of the fleet that the minority council had funded. Directed against foreign pirates, it could have been redeployed in English politics. Richard persuaded the council to disown it, and suborned the crews with promises of payment. Almost all deserted to him. This was a tactical triumph.[70] The queen meanwhile remained in sanctuary with her second son Richard and all five daughters. She should have been reassured by the oaths that Richard, the two archbishops, and diverse other lords were prepared to take and publicised. The draft oath was read to the common council of the City on 23 May.[71] Elizabeth resisted all inducements to come out of sanctuary, most unreasonably according to Simon Stallworth.[72] Greatly weakened, the Wydevilles were not destroyed, and looked forward to their revival at Edward V's majority.

Third, Richard tackled the financial shortfall. The government had already spent £5,524 2s. 11d that was properly part of Edward IV's personal

---

[68] Mancini, *Richard III*, pp. 84–5.

[69] Ibid., p. 125n.85; *H433*, vol. 2, p. 25. It is not known where Vaughan was placed, but all were moved to Pontefract on 23–5 June.

[70] Mancini, *Richard III*, pp. 84–7.

[71] Greater London Record Office, Corporation of London Journal, 9 f.23. Unfortunately the text was not copied into the minute-book.

[72] *Stonor L & P*, vol. 2, p. 160.

estate. Richard contributed £800 himself and at least temporarily deferred his emoluments as protector. Edward IV's funeral expenses were defrayed by sale of the late king's chattels.[73] On 7 May all of Edward IV's executors declined to act, effectively rendering him intestate and imperilling his soul, in sharp contrast to the determined efforts over the decades of the executors of the first two Lancastrian kings to fulfil their masters' last wishes.[74] Edward's moveables were sequestered by the cardinal, for distribution for the good of his soul. More significantly, the enfeoffments to fulfil Edward's will were terminated. The renunciation of administration was decided at the Duchess Cecily's house at Paul's Wharf in the presence of eight bishops, Gloucester, Buckingham, Arundel, Hastings, and Stanley.[75] The needs of the government now took precedence over Edward's testamentary dispositions – in particular over his daughters' dowries and St George's Chapel. Gloucester was probably behind this sensible retrieval of royal estates and income as Crowland, disapprovingly, reports.[76] A little later, on 23 May, he secured a share of Edward's chattels, perhaps the lion's share, towards the funeral.[77] The custody of the queen's estates was another asset.

A major blow to Richard personally was the death on 4 May 1483 of George Neville, late duke of Bedford and rightful heir to Richard's Neville estate. Richard had never resolved the quandary of how to keep him alive, to marry him off and yet keep him powerless. Gloucester had tried but not yet succeeded in wresting the next heir Richard Lord Latimer from Cardinal Bourchier's custody. All that he had feared therefore came to pass. Richard's tenure of Middleham, Sheriff Hutton, and Penrith was reduced to a life estate, Latimer becoming heir.[78] While the 30-year old Gloucester might have held on for a few further decades, he could no longer make permanent decisions and was confronted by reversionary

[73] 'Financial Memoranda', pp. 218, 221; *Registrum Bourchier*, p. 54.

[74] Their reluctance to take on the fourfold repayment of anybody that Edward had wronged 'through any contract, fraud, extortion or for any other reason' is understandable, see *Crowland*, pp. 150–3.

[75] *Registrum Bourgchier*, p. 52.

[76] *Crowland*, pp. 160–3.

[77] *Registrum Bourgchier*, p. 54.

[78] M.A. Hicks, 'What Might Have Been. George Neville, Duke of Bedford, 1465–83. His Identity and Significance', in *Rivals*, p. 296; 'Richard Lord Latimer, Richard III and the Warwick Inheritance', *Ricardian*, 154 (2001), p. 318.

interests that would become stronger as the years passed. The core of his northern power base was anyway lost to his son Edward, including presumably the Richmondshire connection. Richard could seek compensation by adjusting the partition of the Warwick inheritance, but that would deprive him of these Neville estates.[79] Moreover, it would be opposed by Dorset as custodian of the other half and probably back in favour with the adult king and might well require another act of parliament. To resolve the quandary Richard needed to be in power. George Neville had five sisters, heiresses to the rest of his property and expectations, at least two unmarried and in Richard's custody. By 17 May Thomas Lord Scrope of Masham, husband to Elizabeth, had agreed to pay his share of the costs of securing the inheritance and 'also cause my lord of Gloucestre . . . to be contributorie to your charge'.[80]

Richard was allied with several of the other greatest magnates – Buckingham, Hastings, most probably Arundel and Howard. A great council of lords temporal and spiritual met on 9 June. It helped plan the coronation, the transfer of the king to the Tower of London, and presumably the new parliament too (25 June),[81] when Richard's protectorate would cease. Richard cannot have viewed his removal with equanimity. Was not Edward V likely, once declared of age, to recall his mother, half-brothers, and Wydeville uncles to power? Had Duke Richard not made them his enemies by his First Coup? Would not they wish to hold him accountable? He had to fear their revenge. At the least, his capacity to repartition the Warwick Inheritance to his advantage would be more difficult. Chancellor Russell had written his speech for the opening of parliament: it foresaw some scheme to keep Gloucester in power beyond the king's majority.[82]

VII

The political trajectory was abruptly changed by Richard's Second Coup. The great council on 9 June apparently received no hint of the forthcoming

[79] A parallel is the repartition of the Bohun estate in 1421, Somerville, *Lancaster*, vol. 1, pp. 178–80.

[80] *Stonor L & P*, vol. 2, p. 158.

[81] Ibid., pp. 159–60.

[82] S.B. Chrimes, *English Constitutional Ideas in the Fifteenth Century* (Cambridge University Press, 1936), p. 177.

crisis. Yet next day, on 10 June, Richard reported to the York corporation another Wydeville plot, comprising the queen, her kindred, and her adherents, who intended the murder and destruction of himself, Buckingham, 'the old royall blode of this realme' whoever they were, by force and by sorcery, and (somewhat fancifully) 'the finall destruccion and disheryson [disinheritance] of you . . . and men of haner [honour] . . . of the north parties' of England.[83] No reference here to Lord Hastings, yet it was he whom Richard seized at a meeting of the royal council at the Tower on Friday 13 June and ruthlessly (and illegally) executed without any form of trial. The charge was treason, apparently treason in collusion with the queen.[84] This appears highly improbable. Crowland thought that Hastings 'serve[d] these dukes in every way and . . . deserved favour of them' and was exultant at the bloodless triumph of the First Coup, 'without any killing and with only so much bloodshed as might have come from a cut finger'.[85] The destruction of the North was fanciful. Only foreknowledge that Richard intended deposing Edward V could have driven Hastings and the queen together. There is no evidence for this and they seem poles apart as late as the great council on 9 June. Richard's two letters to the North suggest an element of preplanning for the coup. So too do the proclamations available at once and in multiple copies. Surely Sir Richard Ratcliffe had prior knowledge of the coup before he bore Richard's instructions to York and to Lord Neville? Surely Northumberland had prior warning of the army that he was to command only one week later? Thomas More reports that Richard had sounded out Hastings' loyalty through the lawyer William Catesby, whom Hastings wrongly supposed was committed to his service.[86] Had Richard's charges been true, the supposed plotters should not have been taken so completely by surprise.

Hastings was beheaded. Summary execution conclusively removed dangerous foes, as the Yorkists had shown several times. Lord Stanley (who was wounded), Archbishop Rotherham, Lord Stanley, and Bishop Morton

[83] *York House Books*, ed. L.C. Attreed (A. Sutton, 1991), vol. 2, pp. 713–14.

[84] Mancini, *Richard III*, pp. 90–1; More, *Richard III*, p. 48.

[85] *Crowland*, pp. 158–9.

[86] More, *Richard* III, p. 45. With hindsight More thought this a preliminary to Richard's coup and usurpation of the throne.

were arrested and incarcerated, the churchmen in different castles in Wales.[87] Those who seized them were led by Richard's northern retainers Sir Charles Pilkington and Sir Robert Harrington and, highly significantly, by Thomas Howard, son and heir of Lord Howard.[88] This was Richard's second coup d'état. Not+ only was he the prime mover, personally directing both the arrests and sentence, but it is to Richard that all our knowledge us due. It is Richard's charges that all the chronicles report, though they no longer believed them, and it was Richard who was the author of the sheaf of letters dated 10–11 June that were carried by Sir Richard Ratcliffe to the North. Two survive. Ratcliffe also carried oral messages: that to the York corporation was copied into the city minute book. The recipients were asked to despatch their men defensibly arrayed to London. The earl of Northumberland was to muster these forces at Pontefract on 18 June,[89] too late for the Second Coup, but in time for the opening of parliament and coronation or, as it turned out, Richard's usurpation. Which had Richard in mind? With this Second Coup, Richard disarmed the second of the principal factions, Edward IV's household and adherents of the house of York, to whom Hastings and Stanley had been leaders. They had been his own supporters too, but Richard nevertheless hoped to retain the support of the Yorkist affinity. He failed.

Proclamations in London reported both the plot and its suppression. The city was in crisis and torn with rumours. At first, however, people believed in the plot. Planning for the coronation, for Edward V's majority, and for parliament proceeded for a few days. The protectorate continued. Very reasonably, Richard asked that Edward V's younger brother Richard should leave sanctuary in order to attend the coronation. The boy's great-uncle Cardinal Bourchier removed him on 16 June. Even after Hastings' fall, therefore, the cardinal perceived no threat to the boy's life or liberty from the Lord Protector.[90] Prince Richard joined his brother at the Tower, the palace from which all coronation processions departed.

[87] *Crowland*, pp. 158–9; Hanham, *Richard III*, p. 121. Morton was imprisoned in Buckingham's castle at Brecon.

[88] Hanham, *Richard III*, p. 167.

[89] *York House Books*, vol. 2, p. 714.

[90] *Crowland*, pp. 158–9.

That same day, however, parliament was postponed.[91] This was a marked change of direction, that perhaps anticipated a change in trajectory from Edward V's coronation to Richard's usurpation of his crown. That is what came to be believed in retrospect by the chroniclers, who reinterpreted Gloucester's praiseworthy actions in April and May as preliminary stages to the usurpation. In this scenario, Hastings' death was a pre-emptive strike, as he would not have consented to Edward V's removal. Supposedly Catesby revealed Hastings to be immovably loyal to Edward V and therefore an obstacle to Richard's usurpation. Therefore the chamberlain was expunged.

Richard had now scotched both the warring factions that had dominated Edward IV's court. He had powerful allies in the duke of Buckingham, Lord Howard, and Viscount Berkeley, to all of whom he may have promised the rewards that they accrued on his accession. He had a substantial armed force to hand, the northerners summoned on 10–11 June and commanded by Northumberland, and Welshmen too, perhaps Buckingham's men.[92] Other peers had been told to bring only small companies. Richard was in control. Rivers, Grey, and Vaughan were executed. 'This was the second shedding of innocent blood', wrote Crowland.[93]

VIII

A fortnight after Hastings' death Richard was king. On 20 June Dr Ralph Shaa preached at St Paul's Cross advocating Richard's title to the crown and on 25 June an assembly met at the Guildhall to approve his title on the model of 1399 and 1461. Not a parliament, it consisted of the London corporation, those who had already arrived for the cancelled parliament, and Richard's troops. Together they represented the estates of the realm. They were presented with *Titulus Regius*, an elaborate justification of Richard's title to the crown.[94] Chaired by Buckingham, the assembly elected Richard as king. After an appropriate show of reluctance, Richard

[91] J.C. Wedgwood, *History of Parliament, 1439–1509, Register* (HMSO, 1938), p. 465.

[92] *Crowland*, pp. 158–9.

[93] Ibid., pp. 160–1; Hanham, *Richard III*, p. 119.

[94] *PROME*, vol. 15, pp.13–17. Although this dates from 1484, its claim to date from 1483 is confirmed by its presentation to the Calais garrison, Hicks, *Richard III*, pp. 103–4. *Titulus Regius* is the source of the next paragraph.

accepted the crown, and on 6 July he was crowned. Although constitutional convention demanded that Richard was offered the crown and accepted it reluctantly,[95] there can be little doubt that Richard himself was the prime mover.

Richard's succession was justified by the disqualification of all other candidates. Although he was Richard Duke of York's youngest son, there was no doubt about his parentage and legitimacy and he was born in England, unlike his brothers. Those born abroad had no rights of inheritance in England except royal princes: did Edward and Clarence, sons of a duke who should have been a king, qualify for this exemption? More seriously Edward IV and his offspring were disqualified on two grounds. First the king himself was illegitimate, the product of a liaison by the Duchess Cecily, an old story that was feasible but improbable.[96] Supposedly but improbably Richard's mother Cecily said so, even though it made her an adulteress. Rightful or not, Edward IV was indisputably king. Second, and more important, the validity of Edward's clandestine marriage to the queen was disputed because he had already betrothed himself to another lady, the widow Eleanor Butler. If so, his marriage to his queen was invalid, and their offspring illegitimate and incapable of inheriting the crown or anything else. Certainly Edward had sexual relations with several ladies and may well have promised marriage to get them to bed.[97] Lady Eleanor Butler did exist and had needed King Edward's favour. Richard stated that he had proof that he would publish. He is not known to have done so and certainly it does not survive. Of course the validity of marriages and legitimacy were matters for the Church, not parliament or public opinion, but such a technicality may not have weighed much with Englishmen, who took bastardy much more seriously than the Church or any other realm,[98] and needed to decide at once. It is not possible to confirm whether the story of Eleanor Butler's

[95] C.A.J. Armstrong, 'The Inauguration Ceremonies of the Yorkist Kings and their Title to the Crown', in *England, France and Burgundy in the Fifteenth Century* (Hambledon Press, 1983), p. 76.

[96] M.K. Jones, *Bosworth 1485* (Tempus, 2002), pp. 65–71.

[97] Hicks, *Edward V*, pp. 31–43.

[98] See Hicks, 'The Royal Bastards of Late Medieval England', in *La Bâtardise et l'Exercice du Pouvoir en Europe du XIIIe au début du XVIe siècle*, eds E. Bousmar, A. Marchandisse, C. Masson and B. Schnerb (Université Lille, 2015), p. 371.

precontract of marriage was new to Richard, whether it emanated from the Yorkshireman Bishop Stillington who had been keeper of the privy seal at the time,[99] or whether Richard believed it. What is certain is that, once king, Richard was convinced of the righteousness of his title.

The process that converted Richard from the unchallenged Lord Protector to the king is obscure. He took the crown because he could. He was already in charge, ruling like another king, and was obviously the man most capable and suited to rule. He had the necessary power and his rivals had not. It was a process, not a revolution, that made the protector into a king. It is easy to read his First cand Second Coups as parts of a predetermined plan, as the chroniclers did in retrospect. Must not the elimination of Rivers and Grey, the recruitment of the northern army, and the preliminaries of his own coronation have been preplanned as part of his bid for the throne? So it appears, yet there is no concrete evidence for any of it. The duke was secretive and concealed at least some of his intentions. He had committed nothing irrevocable and might indeed have withdrawn from the brink until the last days of Edward V's reign. There is no independent record that either the Wydevilles or Hastings were plotting against him. The precontract story has the appearance of a justification for a decision to usurp that had already been taken: a reconsideration, the first thought being to rely on Edward IV's bastardy. That his inauguration ceremonies follow earlier precedents and constitutional conventions suggest prior planning.[100]

[99] *Crowland*, pp. 160–1, states merely that everybody knew the identity of the author who was in London at the time.

[100] Armstrong, 'Inauguration Ceremonies', pp. 89–90,

Chapter Eleven

RICHARD III

THE CONSOLIDATION OF THE REGIME

I

Richard III had made himself king. Although greatly assisted by Buckingham, Richard was his own kingmaker. He planned his own accession and carried it through. It was a usurpation, as he displaced the existing sovereign Edward V, whose right to reign as son and heir of Edward IV had been one of the certainties of the past dozen years. Richard's accession was achieved by a combination of secretive planning, skilful publicity, surgical violence, and the momentary deployment of overwhelming force. Only Richard himself can have planned it all, timed his coups, provided the necessary leadership and decision making, and authorised if not created his own publicity and propaganda. Only Richard had dared to raise the political temperature and to up the political risks by stepping firmly from the shadows beyond the conventions that applied even during the Wars of the Roses. Richard alone had resorted to violence and bloodshed. Only he had eliminated those who stood in his way.

Now Richard was king, his intentions could no longer be concealed. While there was still a place for violence against rivals, Richard could no longer count on secrecy and surprise. Lord Lisle, brother-in-law to the former queen, who was one of those who had taken sanctuary, cannot have been alone in fearing the new king and in anticipating violence where none was intended. Richard needed to make himself attractive to those who were not already his men. To keep his throne demanded persuasion: not just the negative propaganda that had so successfully denigrated his Wydeville opponents, but the presentation of himself and his regime in the most positive light, both at home and abroad. Richard needed to convert himself from the *de facto* to the *de jure* king and to reveal himself in the process as the worthy protagonist of the common weal, the generous patron of the politically important, and the worthy recipient of national allegiance and service. He needed to assert his right to rule and his entitlement to the obedience and allegiance of his new subjects. In the summer of 1483 he had yet to persuade them.

Already Lord Protector and effectively in control, unquestionably Richard became a king, indeed *the* king. He was acknowledged and acclaimed, titled, anointed, and crowned. His coronation was a supreme display of monarchy and royal magnificence and was recorded as such. It was the first double coronation of king and queen and thus differed from whatever was planned for Edward V. Some preparation, such as the court of claims, may have remained relevant. Precedents had been researched and some changes were made. Symbolism really mattered. The ampulla of holy oil was confided to Westminster Abbey. Richard was the first to take his coronation oaths in English. Several times afterwards he alludes to what he had vowed to his people. On formal occasions he wore his crown. He gave instructions to his judges. Everybody of note, moreover, had acclaimed him, swore allegiance to him, and bowed to his commands.[1] Set aside from his greatest subjects, Richard expected them to defer and obey.

Richard lacked the personal attributes of his brother Edward IV, who had been thought so handsome by the standards of the time, and so tall and imposing a figure that he towered over most of his leading subjects. From his great height, Edward could browbeat even the greatest in the land, which was the more terrifying because he did it so seldom. Edward had a memory for faces and could place everyone in context. He had recognised everyone of significance wherever and however encountered and he could

---

[1] *The Coronation of Richard III: The Extant Documents*, eds A.F. Sutton and P.W. Hammond (A. Sutton, 1983), esp. pp. 4–8.

conjure up their interests, contexts, services, offences, and deserts. King Edward charmed men and women of very different ranks and circumstances. He maximised the panoply of his kingship, and cultivated magnificence in dress, in household, and ceremonial.[2]

Richard, in contrast, was less physically impressive. He was a small man – if the Leicester bones are his, merely medium in height and rather slight – and perhaps also somewhat deformed. His portraits reveal him as dark-haired with white drawn features – 'hard fauoured of visage' wrote More, 'short and sowre [in] cowntenance' said Vergil, who perceived in his features the 'savor of mischief . . . craft and deceyt'. In retrospect: neither More nor Vergil ever met him: certainly they had sought out the testimony of those who had and perhaps also they had seen his portrait. Reportedly Richard was a fidgety man: when 'thinking of any mater, he did contynually byte his nether lyppe . . . Also he was woont to be ever with his right hand pulling [his dagger halfway] out of the sheath . . . and putting [it] in agane'.[3] Like his unnatural birth, his features and mannerisms must have reflected his deficient character and were supposed with hindsight to betray the wickedness within. Intensity, passion, and calculation seem faithful to the original. Sheer force of personality, hard work and physical vigour, determination, good research and a mastery of detail filled some of the gaps. Richard did recognise many individuals by sight and name, perhaps mainly his Northerners, whom he genuinely cared for. He had his own affairs at his fingertips. He too cultivated magnificence: in dress – witness the attire for his coronation[4] – in diet, in celebrations, and in open-handed generosity. His noble upbringing had imparted his taste for hunting, choral music, building, heraldry, and jewellery that he shared with aristocrats everywhere.

Certainly Richard considered himself the man best equipped to rule, by birth and ability, by inheritance, by acclamation and by leadership of the government (conquest). His belief in his rightful rule is best demonstrated by his angry postscript in his own hand about Buckingham's betrayal that

[2] *Crowland*, pp. 146–7, 150–3; see also J.R. Lander, 'Edward IV: The Modern Legend and a Revision', in *Crown and Nobility 1450–1509* (Hodder & Stoughton, 1976), pp. 159–70.
[3] More, *Richard III*, p. 7; Vergil, *English History*, pp. 226–7.
[4] Ross, *Richard III*, p. 140.

he penned in October to Lord Chancellor Russell.[5] Richard was convinced
by his own arguments. Everyone else had to be persuaded of his right and
authority. Actually almost everyone who was anyone did indeed acknowledge his title, did swear allegiance to him, and thereby did submit to
his authority. Probably allegiance was sworn throughout the country. On
20 July 1483 the king personally commanded JPs in 33 counties to minister
the oath of fealty to the king.[6] Even the garrison of Calais bereft of their
captain, collectively and as individuals, accepted him as monarch. Richard
was therefore surprised, deeply offended, and indeed livid at the rebellion
of those who owed allegiance to him.

The Calais garrison did, however, raise the issue of how this new oath
was to be reconciled with the preceding oath that they had all been made
to swear to Edward V. Richard's response was to send them a copy of
Titulus Regius, which was not just an explanation of how and why Edward
V was disqualified and supplanted by Richard, but also a formal act that
had been approved by the three estates of the realm outside parliament.
Previous oaths to Edward V had been based on a misunderstanding, he
explained, that Edward V had been legitimate and was thus entitled to
reign. *Titulus Regius* demonstrated this assumption to be erroneous. The
oath was therefore invalid.[7] Likewise in 1460, it was as misunderstandings
that the oaths sworn by Richard Duke of York (the new king's father) and
everyone else to Henry VI had been set aside. York had given priority to
natural and divine law. Like his father York then, so now King Richard
was convinced by his own argument, and therefore expected the Calais
garrison to accept it too. Apparently they did, for they transferred themselves into his service and to his allegiance.

II

Any king *de facto* was entitled to the overriding allegiance, obedience, and
service of all his subjects. Additionally, Richard presented himself as king
de jure (by right): the just heir to the rightful ruling house of York, to his

[5] *Richard III: A Royal Enigma*, ed. S. Cunningham (National Archives, 2003), no. 9.
[6] *CPR 1476–85*, p. 370. Significantly perhaps in view of Buckingham's Rebellion,
Cornwall, Devon, and Somerset were not included.
[7] *H433*, vol. 3, p. 29.

father Richard Duke of York the 'verrey and rightfull heire to the corones, roiall estate, dignitie and lordship',[8] and to his brother and the first Yorkist king Edward IV, to whom he was next surviving brother. The legitimate birth of King Richard was never in question. Richard's accession corrected the brief reign of Edward V, which had been a mistake. The accession of Richard III therefore did not interrupt the royal line, but instead restored its continuity. Richard wanted to take over Edward's regime and the Yorkist affinity as a going concern just as he had earlier substituted himself for Warwick the Kingmaker as the heir to the house of Neville. In June/July 1483 his northern army and his predominantly northern councillors and household gave him momentarily the military and political clout to take the throne. It was also such retainers as Tyrell, Ratcliffe, and Brackenbury whom he trusted with any delicate and contentious tasks that demanded unambiguous commitment. Yet such existing adherents consti-tuted merely a powerful faction of the political nation, not the majority or a consensus. His part-time army especially could not be maintained at arms indefinitely and he needed to remain in charge once it had disbanded. To rule effectively and permanently, Richard needed to take over the Yorkist establishment. Thus he could become king of the whole nation as Edward IV had been.

Of course the apolitical administrators and clerks of the central govern-ment departments and law courts under Edward IV continued in the service of Edward V and Richard III. Bishop Russell remained as chancellor, John Wood as treasurer, and Dr John Gunthorpe as keeper of the privy seal. Even the disapproving Crowland stayed in government. A smattering of official documents acknowledge that Edward V was indeed a bastard.[9] Across two decades Edward IV had melded together peers and gentry of different generations and loyalties. Whereas Hastings had served as cham-berlain of the household from 1461 to 1483, actually very few of Richard Duke of York's original retainers survived until 1483. Much of York's estate was in the hands of the Dowager-Duchess Cecily and the authority in his

---

[8] *PROME*, vol. 12, p. 523, vol. 15, p. 16.
[9] G. McKelvie, 'The Bastardy of Edward V in 1484: New Evidence of its Reception in the Inquisitions Post Mortem of William, Lord Hastings', *Royal Studies Journal*, 3(1) (2017), pp. 71–7.

earldom of March in Wales had been transferred to the council of his grandson, the future Edward V. It was to Buckingham that direction of the Welsh affinity was now assigned. But neither the York nor Mortimer affinities were prominent in Edward IV's final household, which was headed by knights and esquires of those gentry families drawn from every corner of the realm who were accustomed to exercise local rule. No less than half the knights and esquires of his body were southerners from outside Edward's original range. They were selected from the leading county gentry, from those most landed, from the wealthiest, the best born and the best connected. Behind them lay generations of honourable service as sheriffs, knights of the shire, and justices of the peace.[10] Nobody was closer to a king than his household. His household were his most intimate connection, akin in contemporary parlance to the sons of their father the king, those most committed to the king and his heir. Membership of Henry VI's household and loyalty to him had excused the resistance of Sir Thomas Tresham to Edward IV at the battle of Towton.[11] Serving in rotation, alternatively at court and at home in the provinces, the knights and esquires of the body and yeomen of the crown were Edward's 'most faithful servants' and had been 'distributed all over the kingdom as keepers of castles, manors, forests and parks', reported Crowland. '[Hence] no attempt could be made however stealthily by any man, whatsoever his distinction, without his being immediately faced by it.'[12] If Crowland exaggerated somewhat here, for their monopoly of patronage and office was far from complete, the chronicler does identify the core of the Yorkist regime that Richard most needed to bind to himself and whose service he most desired. Many of them hailed from the many counties, especially in southern England, where the lordship of the duke of Gloucester had scarcely featured at all.

A new reign offered scope for a radical revision of royal patronage and especially of household personnel, most of whom served at the king's pleasure or on appointment by the chief officers, but Richard seems scarcely to have availed himself of this opportunity. There was no resumption of

[10] Gill, *Buckingham's Rebellion*, p. 87.

[11] He had been controller of the household, D.A.L. Morgan, 'The King's Affinity in the Polity of Yorkist England', *TRHS*, 5th ser. 23 (1973), p. 7.

[12] *Crowland*, pp. 146–7.

royal grants and no act of resumption at Richard's only parliament. In theory Edward IV's household died with him. His death and funeral terminated the appointments of his chief officers, his chamberlain and steward, and all other members of his household should have expected their appointments to be terminated also. But actually Hastings and Stanley stayed on for Edward V and Stanley thereafter for Richard III. So, strikingly, did the formidable Ralph Hastings, esquire of the body, brother of the executed Lord Hastings, who secured confirmation of most of his offices and the lands granted him by Edward IV, a general pardon and reimbursement of expenses. He was required only to yield up the command of Guines Castle by Calais that he held during the king's pleasure, and that in retrospect temporarily.[13] Probably most other household men remained in situ. No domestic records survive, but 'continuity even at the upper level of the household seems to have been almost complete in 1483'.[14] A handful were removed,[15] but most remained. It was household men that Lord Protector Gloucester commissioned to counter Sir Edward Wydeville's fleet. Wydeville adherents retained their local and other offices and even stepped into the gaps. Of Edward IV's known household knights, 24 out of 29 seem to have persisted into Richard's service.[16] At the very least they were expected to acquiesce in the new regime. Not to do so threatened worse penalties for them than mere loss of office. So much continuity was there indeed that 'it becomes more appropriate to think of Richard III putting himself at the head of his brother's household, and augmenting it with some of his own subjects', writes Horrox, 'than to envisage him taking selected servants of his brother into his own retinue'.[17] Richard valued the service of his brother's men more than rewarding and promoting his committed supporters. He counted on taking over a going concern.

[13] E.C. and P. Hairsine, 'The Chancellor's File', in *Richard III: Crown and People*, ed. J. Petre (Sutton, 1985), pp. 413–4; C 81/1392/2; C81/1529/24–26, 28; *H433*, vol. 3, p. 31, 38–9; *CPR 1476–85*, p. 365.

[14] Horrox, *Richard III*, p. 146. Did his household join Edward V at the bishop of London's palace and the Tower of London?

[15] Sir Thomas St Leger, widower of Richard's sister Anne, Sir Robert Radcliffe, John Cheyne, Robert Poyntz, Piers Curteys, and George Lovekyn, Horrox, *Richard III*, pp. 141–2; Gill, *Buckingham's Rebellion*, p. 61.

[16] Horrox *Richard III*, pp. 142, 146.

[17] Ibid., p. 146.

There were exceptions of course. Richard's uncle Essex and several lesser men had died. Bar Edward V's physician Dr John Argentine,[18] almost all Edward V's household as prince of Wales were dismissed rather than joining his royal household as king. Admittedly Richard withdrew the compliment of promotion to the order of the Bath from 46 of the well-born youths singled out for knighting by Edward V and knighted only 18.[19] It is more likely that the household of Queen Elizabeth was dispersed than that they transferred into the service of Richard's queen Anne Neville. It is unclear what befell the household of Lord Protector Gloucester. Where there were vacancies, it was men known to Richard who filled the gaps: clerks, lawyers, and retainers who had served him as duke. Some of Richard's intimates did transfer directly to King Richard's household. Tyrell became a knight of the body and Catesby, Geoffrey Franke, and John Huddleston became esquires of the body. Whereas Lord Stanley continued as steward of the household, Francis Lord Lovell (now Chief Butler of England) became the new Lord Chamberlain and constable of Wallingford. William Hopton, separately knighted on 28 June, became treasurer of the king's household, and Robert Percy of Scotton, Yorkshire, controller of the household. John Kendal continued as Richard's secretary. Dr Thomas Barrow, the ducal chancellor, became master of the rolls. Twice in times of crisis he was to step up to keep the seal himself. Master Edmund Chaderton became keeper of the hanaper in chancery and later also treasurer of the king's chamber. Dr William Beverley, dean of Middleham, became additionally dean of the Chapel Royal, dean of Wimborne Minster, dean of Windsor College, and precentor of York. Sir Roger Bigod of Settrington, Yorkshire, became master of the ordnance. On 30 June William Catesby was appointed chancellor and chamberlain of the exchequer and chancellor of the earldom of March.[20] None of these roles conferred the access to the king's innermost counsels that Catesby nevertheless enjoyed and that explain the numerous annuities that others paid for his intercession that

[18] Mancini, *Richard III*, pp. 92–3.

[19] Compare *H433*, vol. 3, pp. 11–12; W.A. Shaw, *The Knights of England* (Sherratt and Hughes, 1906), vol. 1; Ellis, *Original Letters* (Harding, Triphook and Leonard, 1822–46), vol. 1, p. 147.

[20] *CPR 1476–85*, pp. 210, 219–22; 259–60, 360–1, 474; *H433*, vol. 1, pp. 3, 62, 65, 78–9, 100, 102, 181, 189, 190, vol. 2, p. 86; Myers, *Household of Edward IV* (Manchester University Press, 1959), pp. 288–9, 294; E 401/950 m 2.

are the best evidence for the exceptional influence with Richard that Crowland reported.[21] It was understandable and indeed inevitable that Richard promoted those that he knew and trusted. Such key appointments reinforced rather than supplanted or swamped those inherited from Edward IV. For Edward IV's affinity, the mere continuance of existing offices (and fees and annuities) was a positive form of patronage. That all these men swore allegiance to Richard, thus committing themselves to him utterly, seemed to signal Richard's success in taking over his brother's affinity. Honour bound them into his service and his personal connection: or should have done.

Richard could count on his own men, of course, and other Northerners, although the reliability of his northern army was never tested. He added some particular allies among the nobility. Top of the list was Henry Duke of Buckingham, by a long way the greatest of contemporary magnates, both royal in descent and massively landed. Buckingham was appointed to two of the great offices that Richard now relinquished, as constable and great chamberlain of England. Although not made steward of England – an office that he had briefly held in 1478 and to which he also had claims – he did preside over the new king's coronation. Buckingham succeeded the prince's council as ruler of Wales – even York and William Herbert I never held so much – and in the traditional Stafford domain of the North Midlands, where first Clarence and then Hastings had held sway. Many of Hastings' men apparently transferred to his service. So many Stafford knots were distributed that the duke boasted that his retainers matched those of Warwick the Kingmaker, but actually, wrote Rous who had known Warwick, they were far fewer.[22] The duke also secured the other half of the Bohun earldoms of Essex, Hereford, and Northampton worth a thousand pounds a year that rightly descended to him, after the extinction of the house of Lancaster.[23] Perhaps, however, recognition by Richard was

[21] *Great Chronicle of London*, ed. A.H. Thomas and I.D. Thornley (Guildhall Library, 1938), p. 236; *Crowland*, pp. 174–5.

[22] *CPR 1476–85*, pp. 349, 361, 363; Somerville, *Lancaster*, vol. 1, passim; *Stonor L & P*, vol. 2, p. 161; Hanham, *Richard III*, p. 122. But many of his Welsh offices were reversions, effective when vacancies materialised, which did not happen in the duke's lifetime.

[23] Horrox, *Richard III*, p. 165. The Bohuns had ended with coheiresses, Buckingham's ancestress Eleanor and the Lancastrian ancestress Mary. The lands were handed over to Buckingham but an act of parliament was needed to complete the process.

reluctant and anyway confirmation depended on the new act of parliament requisite to sever them from the Duchy of Lancaster. Perversely Buckingham may not have prepared to wait.

Second was the veteran John Lord Howard, who had known Duke Richard ever since he was treasurer of Edward IV's household (1467–74), who had acted for him in the countess of Oxford and Gregories disputes in 1472–4, who had commanded the fleet in the Scottish war, and who was one of those deputed to offer Richard the crown. Duke Richard entrusted the arrest of Lord Hastings to Howard's son Thomas and two Northerners.[24] Howard's substantial East Anglian estates sufficed to support the barony to which he had been promoted in 1470 and he should have inherited half of the huge Mowbray dukedom of Norfolk on the death of the child Anne Mowbray in 1481. Although so stalwart and trusted a servant of Edward IV, Howard's legitimate expectations were thwarted by that avaricious monarch, who instead contrived the retention of that whole inheritance by his younger son Richard. Now at last Howard was allowed his half share of his Mowbray heritage. He became duke of Norfolk and his son Thomas Earl of Surrey (another Mowbray title), with 1,000 marks a year during his father's lifetime, while another coheir William Berkeley took the title of earl of Nottingham.[25] A share of the Arundel estates were allowed to devolve on Stanley and Sir John Wingfield. Howard was also granted the Scales properties in Norfolk that Anthony Earl Rivers had retained after his wife's death and those Hungerford estates in south central England that Richard himself had secured. Howard was recognised as earl marshal and succeeded Richard himself as admiral of England, thus holding two of the greatest honorary offices, and was appointed steward of England for the coronation. It was he who succeeded the earl of Essex as chief steward of the South Parts of the Duchy of Lancaster. His appointment on 16 July as sole commissioner to supervise and array the counties of Bedfordshire, Berkshire, Buckinghamshire, Cambridgeshire, Essex, Hertfordshire, Huntingdonshire, Kent, Middlesex, Norfolk, Suffolk, Surrey, and Sussex, the whole region of 13 counties of the

[24] Hanham, *Richard III*, p. 167; Ross, *Richard III*, p. 87n.
[25] GEC, vol. 9, pp. 611–13, 782.

South-East, East Anglia, and East Midlands, shows how confident in him and reliant on him was the new king.[26]

Richard also secured the backing of William Herbert II, earl of Huntingdon, who married Richard's bastard daughter Katherine in mid-1484.[27] William Earl of Arundel, already constable of Dover and warden of the Cinque Ports, became chief justice of the southern forests, and may have been another ally. Despite his Wydeville wife, Arundel's son Thomas Lord Maltravers became a royal councillor and received an annuity of 300 marks (£200) for life.[28] The queen's cousin and Warwick retainer Edward Grey, Lord Lisle was promoted viscount and secured fragments of the Astley inheritance that he coveted.[29] John Lord Scrope of Bolton supplanted the Fogges as chamberlain of the Duchy of Lancaster.[30] John Grey of Wilton, heir to Baron Reynold Grey, became master of the king's mews.[31] Lord Dynham became governor of Calais and received numerous preferments in the West Country.[32] Less prominent were Lords Cobham and Zouche. King Richard intervened decisively, not necessarily justly, to award Lisle, Bergavenny, and Northumberland lands that they claimed from the Despenser, Beauchamp, and Brian inheritances.[33] The dalesman Thomas Metcalf became chancellor of the Duchy and County Palatine of Lancaster and Robert Brackenbury, lately treasurer of the ducal household, became constable of the Tower, master of the mint and keeper of the royal menagerie (lions, lionesses, and leopards) housed there.[34] Richard's Northerners retained their northern preferments and, as the reign progressed, filled many posts also in the South, the Midlands, and in Wales.

[26] *CPR 1476–85*, pp. 358, 360, 362; Somerville, *Lancaster*, vol. 1, p. 429; *H433*, vol. 1, pp. 73, 80–2, 117.

[27] Sutton, Visser-Fuchs and Kleineke, 'Children in the Care of Richard III', *Ricardian*, 24 (2014), p. 35; *CPR 1476–85*, p. 538.

[28] *CPR 1476–85*, pp. 358m, 431; *H433*, vol. 1, p. 165.

[29] Forfeited by his nephew the marquis of Dorset, H433, vol. 1, pp. 76, 152.

[30] *H433*, vol. 1, p. 74; Somerville, *Lancaster*, vol. 1, p. 418. He also received Martock and other Somerset properties.

[31] *H433*, vol. 1, p. 158.

[32] Ibid., p. 161.

[33] M.A. Hicks, *The Family of Richard III* (Amberley Publishing, 2015), pp. 149, 150; J.M.W. Bean, *The Estates of the Percy Family 1416–1537* (Oxford University Press, 1958), p. 122.

[34] *CPR 1476–85*, pp. 405, 418, 463; *H433*, vol. 1, pp. 68–9.

III

Richard tried hard to persuade everyone of his legitimacy. He made the most of solemn ceremonial, magnificence, and display. His title was approved by the city of London and the estates of the realm and was sealed by his coronation, which came only 10 days after his formal accession. Somebody had researched into the precedents, the inauguration ceremonies of the usurpers Henry IV and Edward IV,[35] and Richard's coronation must also have been informed by the earlier preparation for the abortive crowning of Edward V. Obviously the coronation of a child was much less complex than this first double coronation of a king and queen. Was it possible, indeed, for the planning to have commenced after his accession, a bare 10 days earlier? Richard took seriously the oaths that he swore at his coronation and cited them at least twice to justify his subsequent actions.[36] Apart from a display of ordered magnificence in which so many participated,[37] his coronation was extremely well-attended, by almost all the peerage, by the royal household, and by many other members of the elite, all of whom did homage, swore fealty, or otherwise pledged themselves to the new king. The king and queen in their coronation robes was the culminating image of the final version of the *Salisbury Roll*.[38] The coronation was preceded on 28 June by the creation of 18 knights of the Bath – a careful selection of the noblest youths that required some preparation. They included several sons of peers and some leading provincial gentry, notably Edward Courtenay of Bocannoc in Cornwall, Thomas Arundell of Lanherne (Cornwall), and William Uvedale of Wickham (Hampshire),[39] all of whom were shortly to rebel.

This ceremony at Westminster was followed by the unprecedented investiture at York on the feast of the Nativity of the Virgin (8 September)

[35] See C.A.J. Armstrong, 'The Inauguration Ceremonies of the Yorkist Kings and their Title to the Crown', in *England, France and Burgundy in the Fifteenth Century* (Hambledon Press, 1983).

[36] A.F. Sutton, ' "The Administration of Justice Whereunto We Be Professed" ', in *Richard III*, ed. Petre, p. 359.

[37] As demonstrated in Sutton and Hammond, *Coronation of Richard III*.

[38] *Medieval Pageant. Writhe's Garter Book*, eds A.R. Wagner, N. Barker, and A. Payne (Roxburghe Club, 1993), pl. 75; see plate 11. Presumably Richard confided the roll to the Garter King of Arms John Writhe.

[39] Sutton and Hammond, *Coronation of Richard III*.

of Richard's heir, Edward of Middleham, prince of Wales, at York Minster. The prince was invested with a golden wand and a wreath upon his head. King, queen, and prince sat crowned for four hours in what Crowland called a second coronation. The succession was assured. Richard staged 'splendid and highly expensive feasts and entertainments to attract to himself the affections of many people'. What the royal family would wear was planned in great detail – a 'doublet of purpille satyne lined with holand cloth and entrrelyned with busk [linen]', for instance – and massive quantities of cloth were ordered from the great wardrobe (such as 740 pensels [pennons] of buckram, 350 pensels of tartarin [silk cloth]). Banners of the Holy Trinity, St George, St Edward the Confessor, and St Cuthbert were requisitioned.[40] Supposedly England's second city, York was the capital of the North where Richard had held sway, and the celebrations there were especially gratifying to Northerners. Richard maximised their enthusiasm to impress outsiders. Those at parliament the following January at Westminster also swore allegiance to the heir to the throne.[41] In April Richard's title was again recited at Westminster to the London ironmongers and most probably to representatives of all the London livery companies. While this may indicate that the message had not caught on,[42] it was a further guarantee of compliance with the king's title.

The ceremonies at York were stage-managed as a display of loyalty to the new king by his closest adherents to impress the southerners in his entourage – certainly southern peers and southern members of his household – 'which will mark greatly your receiving of their graces'.[43] It was the culmination of a formal progress that Richard made immediately after his coronation through the Thames Valley and the Midlands to the capital of the North (York) that courted local elites and promoted the new king and his praiseworthy actions. From York he proceeded to Lincoln, where his progress was interrupted. Where was he going next? Richard had realised

<hr/>

[40] Ibid., p. 139; F. Harrison, *Life in a Medieval College* (John Murray, 1952), pp. 111–2; *Richard III: The Road to Bosworth Field*, eds P.W. Hammond and A.F. Sutton (Constable, 1985), pp. 140–1; *Crowland*, pp. 160–1.

[41] *Crowland*, pp. 170–1. As on several occasions to the future Edward V.

[42] A.F. Sutton, 'Richard III's "Tytylle and Right": A New Discovery', in *Richard III*, ed. Petre, p. 57; Pollard, *Princes*, p. 154.

[43] Hicks, *Richard III*, pp. 148–9.

that mere acquiescence was insufficient. Subjects everywhere needed to be persuaded that he was worthy to be king. His entourage was impressive. The king personally attended academic disputations in Latin at Oxford University and plays were laid on for him at Coventry and York. He stopped off at Tewkesbury, location of the battle that had confirmed the rule of the Yorkists in 1471, and visited the Benedictine abbey, wherein lay Queen Anne's first husband Prince Edward of Lancaster and the other Lancastrian leaders that Richard as constable had condemned to death. The queen's Despenser ancestors were interred there too – her grand-mother Isabel Countess of Warwick and Worcester in particular – and there was a splendid new tomb for her sister and Richard's brother, the duke and duchess of Clarence. Richard and Anne stayed for a week at Warwick, which was familiar to both as the principal seat of Anne's father Warwick the Kingmaker. Both had worshipped at St Mary's church in 1464–5. The queen's grandfather Earl Richard Beauchamp was buried in the lavish new Beauchamp Chapel: their cousins Sir Henry Neville and Oliver Dudley had been added in 1469. Earl Richard Beauchamp was a chivalric hero whose life was newly recounted in the splendid *Beauchamp Pageant* that may have been presented to the royal couple on this occasion. So too may the earliest version of the *Rous Roll*, newly created by the local cantarist John Rous, that celebrate the queen's Warwick ancestry. King Richard deferred to local legend and harnessed it in his own support. Rous credits Richard with some building there:[44] quite what is unclear.

Richard made the most of his consort's ancestral renown and of the northern support that he had built up as duke. Pontefract, where the king's father and brother Edmund had originally been buried, was another staging post, where 70 local gentry were summoned to reinforce his proces-sion into York that was impressive enough anyway: five bishops, three earls, and six barons. Bishops Langton, Redman, and Stillington were all Northerners. Richard stayed for three weeks at the archbishop's palace: Archbishop Rotherham himself was still incarcerated in Wales. Apart from his son's investiture and banquet and the performance of the Creed play, Richard's visit was distinguished by his foundation in York Minster of the

---

[44] Hanham, *Richard III*, p. 121. Richard never held Warwick and and it was Clarence who funded building there that the Kingmaker had left unfinished, Hicks, *Clarence*, p. 196.

greatest chantry of them all, for a hundred priests. Quite possibly, given the lack of space at Westminster Abbey, York Minster was intended for Richard's mausoleum. Moreover, Richard confirmed the privileges of St William's College east of York Minster, which the queen's father Warwick and uncle Archbishop Neville had incorporated for the Minster chantry priests and of which Queen Anne was patroness. The city fee farm was reduced. Much of the fee farm of Newcastle was assigned towards the construction of a new bridge across the River Tyne. The 13,000 white boar badges Richard had made and distributed exceeded the whole population of York. 'All northerners must have appeared to be Richard's men.'[45]

Richard did care about the North and about Northerners: witness his stream of charters, privileges, and other gifts to the towns, monasteries, and other churches, and his promotions of Northerner peers, gentry, and churchmen.

The king scattered other favours on his route. 'He contents the people where he goes best that ever did prince', wrote the Northerner Bishop Langton, 'for many a poor man that hath suffered wrong many days have be relieved and helped by him and his commands now in his progress'. It was 'by popular request' that he disafforested much country, on the border of Oxfordshire and Worcestershire, that Edward IV had drawn into Wychwood and subjected to forest law. To the town of Gloucester – whence Richard took his ducal title – and to Pontefract he granted new charters that allowed them to appoint mayors and aldermen. Little Scarborough was raised to a county and a clutch of monasteries – Tewkesbury, Coverham, and Wilberfosse – were patronised. It was customary on such occasions for town corporations such as London, Oxford, and Worcester to make large cash donations to the king, but Richard declined them all 'with thanks, affirming that he would have their love than their treasure'. 'On my trothe', wrote Langton, who accompanied him throughout. 'I liked never the conditions of any prince so well as his: God hath sent him to us for the weal of us all.'[46]

[45] Hicks, *Richard III*, pp. 144–9; Hanham, *Richard III*, p. 121; Hammond & Sutton, *Richard III: The Road to Bosworth Field*, p. 140; *H433*, vol. 1, pp. 93, 99, 120; but see L. C. Attreed, 'The King's Interest: York's Fee Farm and the Central Government, 1482–92', *Northern History*, 17 (1981), pp. 24–33.

[46] *Christ Church Letters*, ed. J.B. Sheppard (Camden Society, 1877), vol. 19, p. 46; Hicks, *Richard III*, pp. 146–50.

IV

While Richard sought acceptance as his brother's rightful successor, he promised additionally to be a better ruler than Edward IV, whose rule he implied had not been distinguished as it should have been by good counsel, morality, and equity, the rule of law and repression of crime, the defeat of foreigners, and the promotion of trade and employment. Considering the new king to be 'more naturally enclyned to the prosperite and comen wele', the three estates looked to him to deliver 'the peas, tranquillite and wele publique of this lande'.[47] These aspirations were given some concrete form. He denounced the sexual immorality of Jane Shore (Mrs Elizabeth Shore) and all her extramarital partners – Edward IV, Hastings, and Dorset.

In particular Richard took seriously his promise at his coronation oath to administer 'egall and rightfull justice', 'whereunto we be professed'. From his throne in Westminster Hall the new king commanded the judges to do justice without delay or favour and after his coronation he commanded the departing lords to ensure there were no extortions in their countries. Twice his proclamations urged those with grievances against royal officers or other persons to bring their complaints to him for remedy.[48] A complaint by Richard Bostock against Roger Sharp caused the latter to be summoned to appear before the king at Warwick on 9 August 1483.[49] This was given formal expression in Richard's creation of what became the Tudor court of Requests, which was to take third place behind the other prerogative courts of chancery and the Star Chamber. Richard's contribution was to appoint and fee at £20 a year a new post, the first holder John Harrington being a Northerner, probably the notary and from 1484 common clerk of the city of York. Harrington rates as the first master of Requests. He was already servicing the Lords and the council in 1483 and 'especially in the custody, registration, and expedition of bills, requests and supplications'.[50]

[47] *PROME*, vol. 15, pp. 13–17, at p. 16.

[48] Sutton and Hammond, *Coronation of Richard III*, p. 220; Sutton, 'Administration of Justice', pp. 359–61, 363; Ross, *Richard III*, pp. 172–3.

[49] Pollard, *Princes*, p. 154.

[50] *York House Books*, vol. 1, pp. 159, 307, 346; *CPR 1476–85*, p. 413. Harrington must have moved south with Richard and his role cannot therefore be pushed back to Edward IV's reign.

Unfortunately no archive for Requests (or indeed) the council survives from Richard's reign, so it is not possible to illuminate what this first master actually did. Richard expected his local rulers to remedy local complaints and directed his commissioners to still any local quarrels that might obstruct recruitment.[51]

Unlike most kings, Richard had first-hand acquaintance with enfeoff-ments to uses and fines and with some of their technical deficiencies, which he clarified in consultation with the judges. He deferred to their legal expertise: 'And this is the king's will to wit. To say "by his justices" and "by his law" is to say one and the same thing.' His bowing to the judges recalls his deference to those other experts, the heralds. Minor legal reforms approved by his parliament may have been official measures. He was not a major lawgiver and there are no hints that he planned to become one in the future. 'The king's "main preoccupation seems to have need to draw atten-tion to, if not to remedy, obvious defects in the administration of the laws".'[52] The coronation oath bound Richard also to be merciful: actually he was prepared to pardon most traitors and was susceptible to appeals from 'sorowfull and repentaunt' offenders for his 'princely pite'.[53] Richard promised to eschew extortion and his parliament did indeed abolish benev-olences, the forced gifts that Edward IV had used to raise money.[54] Much of the good rule he sought – an end to civil war, greater respect from foreigners, and the recovery of the economy – unfortunately proved beyond his power in the short time available.

The foreign relations that Richard sought are somewhat obscure. Like any usurping monarch, he needed international recognition and to avert foreign intervention on behalf of a rival. King Edward IV's reign had ended at risk of war with France as well as Scotland, but that danger was allayed by the death in August 1483 of King Louis XI and the succession in Charles VIII of an underage heir. Did Richard III want to resume the

[51] E.g., *Letters and Papers*, ed. J. Gairdner, Rolls Series (Longman, Green, 1861), vol. 1, p. 80; Sutton, 'Administration of Justice', pp. 360–1.

[52] Sutton, 'Administration of Justice', pp. 361–70, at p. 363.

[53] Richmond, '1485 And All That, or What was Going on at the Battle of Bosworth', in *Richard III: Loyalty, Lordship and Law*, ed. P.W. Hammond (Richard III and Yorkist History Trust, 1986), p. 198.

[54] *PROME*, vol. 15, p. 58.

Hundred Years War? Certainly he took a more aggressive line in foreign policy, asserting his overlordship over Scotland and encouraging piracy against the Bretons, who were harbouring Sir Edward Wydeville with two ships, the attainted Jasper Tudor, earl of Pembroke, and his nephew Henry Tudor. It seems that Richard viewed Henry as a threat from the start, quite rightly since Brittany funded five ships and 325 men for his intervention in Buckingham's Rebellion. Although that expedition failed, Duke Francis received the English exiles back and subsidised them.[55] Richard found, moreover, that kings have to make compromises, financial and diplomatic, that as a mere duke he had not had to do.

Richard's coronation followed too closely on his accession for a new parliament to be summoned. About 22 September writs were issued for a new session of parliament to meet on 6 November, close to the date to which Edward V's abortive parliament had been postponed.[56]

Certainly there were good financial reasons for such an assembly. However, Richard may have had more resources than Edward V possessed. Since Edward IV's executors refused to act, Richard may have taken over his brother's moveables for day-to-day housekeeping: he certainly pledged some of them. Edward's enfeoffments of parts of the Duchy of Lancaster took no effect and the new king added the estates of the ex-queen and prince of Wales to his own. Richard still lacked the usual customs revenue (tonnage and poundage). He may also have envisaged an act of resumption. Presumably he intended the November parliament to confirm his title (*Titulus Regius*) and to attaint the July plotters. Buckingham's title to the Bohun lands needed parliamentary confirmation and the sparse legislative programme of the January 1484 session was probably already projected. Buckingham's Rebellion caused the session to be cancelled on 2 November. A replacement parliament was summoned on 9 December and duly met from 23 January 1484.[57] It did not vote any taxes. However, the convocation of the clergy that met on 3 February 1484 did vote a clerical tenth.[58]

[55] Ross, *Richard III*, pp. 192–6. Foreign policy is discussed more fully below, ch. 14.
[56] *PROME*, vol. 15, p. 3.
[57] *PROME*, vol. 15, pp. 3–4.
[58] E 159/261 recorda Easter 1 Richard III m. 9.

V

Finally any potential rivals needed to be scotched. The most obvious of these were the deposed king Edward V, his brother Richard, and his sisters, all children of Edward IV and his queen. The two princes Edward (aged 12) and Richard (aged nine or ten) were lodged in the Tower of London, where they could be visited. They were observed playing in the gardens.[59] All five princesses were in comfortable sanctuary with their mother at Westminster Abbey. No longer queen, she was described as mere Dame Elizabeth Grey. Richard had bastardised her offspring by Edward IV, thus depriving them of their royal status and titles to the throne, but only, as Richard realised, in the eyes of those persuaded by his arguments. Inevitably there were some who were not convinced: 'especially', wrote Crowland who named no names, 'those people who, because of fear, were scattered throughout franchises and sanctuaries',[60] where they were beyond Richard's reach. The princes and princesses therefore threatened Richard's position. They were destined to become ever more dangerous as they grew up, when the former princes could take command rather than featuring merely as figureheads for any opposition and the former princesses could confer royalty on whoever they married. The boys were too threatening to let live. Mancini realised this even before Richard's coronation and so too, he tells us, did Edward V himself.

The two princes were shut away in the Tower, 'with a specially appointed guard', wrote Crowland. If Mancini did not know of their deaths around 1 July, he did not know either if they still lived.[61] A plot to spring them in late July led by an officer in the Tower implies that some in a position to know believed them to be still alive then.[62] A second plot to restore Edward V (Buckingham's Rebellion) was scheduled for 18 October, but at some point before 3 November (perhaps as early as 25 September) it became believed that the princes were dead and alternative claimants were

[59] *Great Chronicle of London*, p. 234.

[60] *Crowland*, pp. 162–3.

[61] Mancini, *Richard III*, p. 22.

[62] Horrox, *Richard III*, pp. 149, 151. As indeed the Elizabethan John Stow wrote, *Summarie of the Chronicles of England*, ed. B.L. Beer (Mellen, 2007), p. 226n.

sought.[63] If their mother the late queen supported Henry Tudor's claim to the throne, which is not quite certain, it indicates that 'she [too] had given up all her hope that her sons were still alive'.[64] Politics moved forward on that presumption. The two boys were never seen again. They had become politically dead.

Only on 15 January 1484 is there any explicit statement – by Chancellor Guillaume de Rochefort of France to the French Estates General – that they had murdered.[65] De Rochefort was a responsible figure who may have had access to special information. As chancellor he had no axe to grind other than his desire to spare the young Charles VIII a similar fate. On grounds that are unknown, the Polish chronicler Caspar Weinreich dates Richard's murder firmly to the summer.[66] All the other narratives locate the deaths within Richard's reign and most of them in 1483 and at his hands. Even if Buckingham were responsible, as several continental chronicles state,[67] the deaths of the princes must have preceded Buckingham's own execution (2 November 1483), must have occurred when they were in Richard's custody and care, surely (at least retrospectively) with his knowledge, and most probably at his command. Who would dare to kill a former king without authorisation?

The most detailed account of what happened dates from 30 years later. Sir Thomas More certainly elaborated on his source: perhaps a lost confession by Sir James Tyrell, that was also mentioned by the *Great Chronicle of London*.[68] More reports that King Richard commanded Sir Robert Brackenbury to kill the princes, which Brackenbury refused, remaining however a trusted adherent, and then directed Tyrell, who commissioned

---

[63] *PROME*, vol. 15, p. 24 identifies 24 September and 18 October as key dates (which, however, seem too soon); see also *Crowland*, pp. 162–3. For 3 November, see I. Arthurson and N. Kingwell, 'The Proclamation of Henry Tudor as King of England, 3 November 1483', *HR*, 63 (1990), pp. 104–5.

[64] As stated by K. Dockray, *Richard III: A Source Book* (Sutton, 1997), p. 76. However, Buckingham may have rebelled on their behalf, the Tudor narrators perhaps antedate her complicity and October 1483 is anyway too early for Tudor's candidacy.

[65] Mancini, *Richard III*, p. 62.

[66] Dockray, *Richard III*, p. 77.

[67] Ibid., pp. 77–9. An anonymous London chronicle ('Historical Notes') is too late and too ambiguous to be of use.

[68] Even if the confession existed, it need not be authentic.

lesser men to perform the actual deed.[69] Tyrell was a man to whom King Richard had entrusted important tasks and might well have confided this one. Miles Forest and John Dighton, his supposed assistants, also existed, but nothing about their own careers points to appropriate rewards or punishment. In the absence of better data, More's version is the hypothesis to substantiate or to disprove.

Additionally, of course, there is the evidence of the bones discovered in the Tower in 1674 and safely preserved since then at Westminster Abbey. Even modern forensic re-examination cannot carry debate far enough to resolve all the questions. Comparison of their DNA with that of relatives (contemporary or modern, using Ashdown-Hill's technique) could at least establish if the remains are male and whether they are those of the princes. Modern anatomical science can establish the genders and ages at death and hence the approximate year of the two deaths. Radio-carbon dating brackets the date, but is too imprecise for this purpose. While the mode of death might also be uncovered, Tanner and Wright found nothing of relevance here. What the bones alone cannot reveal conclusively, however, is the identity of the killer.

There is actually no mystery about what befell the princes. If the questions to be answered are how they died, where they died, why they died, and when they died, the 'when' is much the easiest to establish and the other answers follow from it. Nothing subsequent indicates that they were still living after their final disappearance. That date, autumn 1483, is the key that unlocks their fate.[70] At Richard's command the two boys perished violently in the Tower of London in the late summer/autumn of 1483.

The demise of the princes was leaked, as it had to be to deter those rebelling in their favour, and became public knowledge. Realising what bad publicity their deaths might generate, Richard (guilty or not) concealed what exactly had befallen them. Their deaths protected him from his most eligible rivals and was an act of self-preservation. To a king who believed in his title, the elimination of the princes could be argued to be in the public interest, just as the deaths of Edward II, Richard II, and Henry VI, all

[69] More, *Richard III*, pp. 84–6. The best modern analysis is Hicks, *Edward V*, pp. 176–81. For a full survey of the evidence, see Pollard, *Princes*, pp. 115–39.
[70] As demonstrated in Hicks, *Edward V*, pp. 176–81.

deposed kings, had been. It removed King Richard's most obviously credible rivals.

The next in the male line, Edward Earl of Warwick, was also in Richard's power, and Edward IV's daughters, the former princesses, were blockaded at Westminster Abbey. His own son Edward of Middleham, earl of Salisbury and now prince of Wales, promised to continue Richard's line. His senior nephew John de la Pole, earl of Lincoln, his bastard son John of Pontefract, and his bastard daughter Katherine Plantagenet, were pressed into service as the wider royal family. Already and rightfully king, Richard was secure.

When the princes disappeared, Henry Tudor became a possible alternative. He had resided in Brittany since 1471, aged 14, with his uncle Jasper Tudor, the attainted earl of Pembroke. Henry Tudor was the posthumous son of Henry VI's senior half-brother Edmund Earl of Richmond (d. 1456) by Lady Margaret Beaufort, sole heiress of John Beaufort, Duke of Somerset: heir presumptive therefore to Somerset's substantial estates mainly in the West Country and Westmorland (but not to Somerset's dukedom or endowments as duke).[71] The duke's widow survived until 1482 and Lady Margaret outlived her son Henry (Tudor/Henry VII), who never therefore enjoyed any of his maternal inheritance. Although the titles and associated endowments were exempt from resumption in 1461, Richmond honour had been nevertheless granted to Edward IV's brother Clarence in 1462 and Richmond town and castle to Gloucester in 1478. Henry still titled himself earl of Richmond. He claimed his paternal inheritance in 1470–1 and probably again in 1478.[72] He had a very slight Lancastrian claim to the crown, through a female (Lady Margaret) to the heirs male (the legitimated bastards the Beauforts) of John of Gaunt, third son of Edward III. But who after 1471 cared about Lancastrian claims? Margaret wanted Henry back and enabled to inherit her estates. She negotiated a deal with Edward IV in 1482,[73] but it had not been implemented when Richard III acceded to the

---

[71] *Calendar of Inquisitions Post Mortem* (Boydell, 1906), vol. 26, pp. 178–94.

[72] Hicks, *Clarence*, pp. 97, 99; see above p. 186–7.

[73] M.K. Jones and M.G. Underwood, *The King's Mother. Lady Margaret Beaufort, Countess of Richmond and Derby* (Cambridge University Press, 1992), p. 60; M.K. Jones, 'Richard III and Margaret Beaufort: A Re-assessment', in *Richard III*, ed. Hammond, pp. 29–30.

crown. Either Richard repudiated the arrangement or the Tudors doubted his approval. Still in Brittany, Henry joined in Buckingham's Rebellion, first as a leader and then as candidate for the throne. In Henry's favour was his undoubted noble and royal descent, that he was old enough both to command and rule, that nobody knew him, and hence there was no stain on his reputation. All Richard could find against him was that he was of bastard lineage on both sides. Henry had been too young in the Second War to commit any offence and indeed the blood of neither he nor his father had been corrupted by treason. He was unmarried and capable therefore of marrying Princess Elizabeth. Perhaps he brought Lancastrian supporters with him – the Courtenays of Bocannoc and the Hungerfords had been attainted in 1461 – but can the descendants of supporters of a line apparently extinguished a decade earlier really be regarded as Lancastrian in 1483? Hungerford, at least, belongs to the Yorkist establishment. What mattered in 1483 was the Yorkist affinity loyal to Princess Elizabeth. Tudor's own title was of little more than antiquarian interest.

Tudor's claims were magnified by the disappearance of Richard's own family. He had cut back on it himself by bastardising Edward IV's children and by the execution of Sir Thomas St Leger, widower to Richard's eldest sister Anne, and by the disinheritance of their daughter Anne. He had reduced the royal family to the king, queen, and their son Edward. Then as now royal princes and princesses had values as office-holders, in ceremonial roles, and for marriage alliances. Richard turned therefore to the numerous offspring of his elder sister Elizabeth, Duchess of Suffolk: in particular to her eldest son John Earl of Lincoln, born in 1467, and her second daughter Anne de la Pole. The paucity of royals was one reason why Richard acknowledged and indeed promoted his two bastards, Katherine Plantagenet, who was old enough to wed William Herbert, earl of Huntingdon, and John of Pontefract. Affection, no doubt, was another. These supplementary kin were elevated in importance when Richard's only legitimate son Edward died in April 1484. The succession was in doubt. Initially, Rous reports, Richard favoured his nephew Edward Earl of Warwick, son of his own brother Clarence and the queen's sister Isabel, but his candidacy had the severe disadvantage that but for his father's attainder, his title was superior to the king's. Apparently thereafter Richard preferred

Lincoln.[74] Better by far would be to father another son himself, which Richard tried to do. His queen, however, never apparently healthy, ailed and on 16 March 1485 died. From Christmas 1484, when that sad event was anticipated, there was speculation and even planning for Richard to remarry. That opened the prospect of a new, more fertile, queen, who could bear further children to the king, but there was not time for Richard either to remarry or to father new heirs before the battle of Bosworth.

[74] Hanham, *Richard III*, p. 123.

Chapter Twelve

THE CREATION OF AN OPPOSITION
BUCKINGHAM'S REBELLION 1483

I

On 26 June 1483 Richard surely fulfilled his most extravagant aspirations. His future was as golden as it could possibly be. Unfortunately things did not work out like that.

For all his life, up until his accession, Richard had operated within the framework of the standards and expectations of the political elite and under the direction of Kings Henry VI, Edward IV, and Edward V. He had committed himself publicly to Edward V before and after the boy king's accession. In June 1483 Richard moved beyond this. Throughout his adult career, it appears, it was he who took the initiative, he who maximised his own interests, and he who pressed the limits of what was attainable and permissible. Those he interacted with, his siblings, peers, and rivals, had always responded to him, resisted him, or more often retreated and submitted. Richard was not a compromiser but a gambler, who pushed his claims to the utmost, never accepted setbacks as permanent, and counted on his opponents giving way. When forced to compromise, temporarily, Richard always planned to build on what he had gained. His brother Clarence, the earl of Northumberland, and the countess of Oxford all succumbed. Even his brother King Edward accepted what Richard had grabbed, let him gradually accrue royal rights (Cumbria), allowed him to

oppress the two countesses of Oxford and Warwick, and declined to
confront him. Only the Stanleys in the North-West seem to have been
adamant. The summer of 1483 was the point that the initiative passed from
Richard to his critics and that he encountered enemies who refused to bow
to his wishes, who declined to submit to his demands, or to back down
without a fight. Some hazarded their lives, incurred forfeiture and exile,
and proved irreconcilable. Even some who had submitted were nevertheless to defect to his enemies. Henceforth the key decisions were taken by
others and it was Richard who was on the defensive, he who resisted, retaliated, or at least responded to the actions of others. Despite being king, he
was no longer in control.

There were those who feared Richard, who identified themselves as his
enemies, and opposed him from the start. Hence he had removed Rivers,
Grey, Vaughan, and Haute in the preemptive strike that was his First Coup.
Other kinsmen and servants of Edward V were also detained.[1] Early in May
1483 Queen Elizabeth was the first of those to reject his rule. Precisely who
accompanied her into Westminster Abbey and stayed with her there is not
recorded. Initially her son Dorset was among them, but he had left by 9
June, when Richard was seeking out his chattels and her brother Bishop
Lionel Wydeville had joined her. Richard wanted to arrest Dorset and
presumably others unknown. Edward Grey, Lord Lisle, paternal uncle to
the queen's sons, took sanctuary too.[2] Actually he was more closely affiliated
to Warwick the Kingmaker and Clarence. Any misunderstanding had been
clarified by 28 June, when Richard promoted him viscount. Lisle bore the
rod with the dove at the coronation and was allowed to grab two manors
from the Beauchamp trust.[3] Another with better reason to take sanctuary
'for fere of hym' was Edward IV's long-serving keeper of the wardrobe Sir
John Fogge, 'long deadly hated' by Richard and now ostentatiously reconciled to the king who 'tooke him by the hand'.[4] Apart from Hastings, who
was executed, the Second Coup had involved the arrest of Archbishop
Rotherham, Bishop Morton, and Dr Oliver King, the king's secretary.

---

[1] *Crowland*, pp. 158–9.
[2] *Stonor Letters & Papers*, vol. 2, p. 159; Hanham, *Richard III*, p. 119.
[3] GEC, vol. 8, p. 60; Hicks, 'The Beauchamp Trust 1439–87', in *Rivals*, p. 347.
[4] More, *Richard III*, pp. 81–2.

Their ecclesiastical status spared them from more drastic punishment.[5] The arrest of John Forster, the queen's receiver-general, is known only because he had dealings with the letter-writer Sir William Stonor, who may have had no connections with any others and anyway did not mention them in his letter.[6] Forster's office had required him to travel far and wide and offered him a network of contacts around the whole of the queen's southern estates. Other unnamed dissidents took refuge in franchises and sanctuaries, of which there were many in and around London, and remained there. There is no list or survey of them comparable to Gerhard von Wesel's newsletter of 1470. Richard respected sanctuary and commanded that such sanctuary men should not be molested ahead of his coronation (6 July).[7] It is not known at what stage such men first took refuge, after Richard's First Coup, Second Coup, or his accession, but apparently some remained there throughout the summer of 1483.[8]

Also unknown is whether their fears was justified. Nobody else is known to have been imprisoned and none were executed in these months. Hastings was the first to die on 13 June 1483 and Rivers, Grey, Haute, and Vaughan perished 12 days later at Pontefract. Whatever summary tribunal condemned them cannot have been legal.[9] Their deaths must have been on the instructions of the Lord Protector,[10] who hoped that this semblance of justice and sheer terror would impress the northern army he had assembled at Pontefract and cow potential opponents into compliance. It was overdone somewhat since, so Crowland reports, 'all the rest of his faithful men expected something similar'.[11] That Hastings – apparently Richard's friend and ally – had been despatched so suddenly was a dreadful warning to all. If the king deferred to sanctuary and spared churchmen, he disregarded ties of blood, the deference due to women, and even the respect due to the queen. It was insufficient to know that no offence had been

---

[5] *Crowland*, pp. 158–9.
[6] *Stonor L & P*, vol. 2, p. 161.
[7] *H433*, vol. 3, p. 31.
[8] *Crowland*, pp. 162–3.
[9] *Pace* Sutton, 'The Admiralty and Constableship of England in the Later Fifteenth Century', in *Courts of Chivalry and Admiralty*, eds Musson and Ramsay (Boydell Press, 2018), p. 205.
[10] As stated by Mancini, *Richard III*, pp. 92–3.
[11] *Crowland*, pp. 158–9.

committed. A handful of men are known to have been dismissed, superseded, or dropped from office, the household, or commissions of the peace. Among them was Lord Hastings' brother Sir Ralph Hastings, lieutenant of Guines Castle at Calais, Sir Robert Radcliffe and Robert Poyntz, and the Wydeville kinsman Sir William Haute.[12] Evidently such refugees were able to enter and leave their sanctuaries and to communicate, although at some point Richard had Westminster Abbey blockaded by his northern esquire John Nesfield.[13] While Westminster Abbey and the college of St Martin le Grand were only two among many sanctuaries in and around London, they had the most ample franchises of any. Conceivably it was the former queen and others in sanctuary who planned and coordinated Buckingham's rebellion in the late summer.

Richard's accession did not dispossess the Yorkist establishment either of their household offices or rule of their local communities. The exceptions were the queen's eldest son Thomas Grey, marquis of Dorset and Sir Thomas St Leger, widower of Edward IV's elder sister Anne Duchess of Exeter. Dorset had expected advancement from his younger brother's accession and had indeed already planned to become the leading magnate in the West Country. By themselves his three baronies in the North (Harrington), the East Midlands (Ferrers of Groby), and the South-West (Bonville) scarcely justified his marquisate. Edward IV had allowed him a share of the Exeter inheritance and the rest was assigned to Thomas's son by his betrothal to Anne St Leger, daughter of Edward's sister Anne by Sir Thomas St Leger. By cancelling this deal and seizing possession of 'the duchess of Exeter',[14] Richard was thwarting the aspirations of Dorset and St Leger, two men with most vested interests in Edward IV's and Edward V's regime: justification enough for them to rebel. No such motive existed for other Yorkists for whom, as Ross argues, 'rebellion was a direct result of the outrage and resentment felt by Edward's loyal servants of Richard's treatment of his heirs'.[15] Richard had overstepped the invisible line between conduct that was acceptable and what was not.

---

[12] Horrox, *Richard III*, pp. 141–2.
[13] *Crowland*, pp. 162–3. This cannot be dated.
[14] Hicks, *Edward V*, pp. 132–3, 157–8.
[15] Ross, *Richard III*, p. 112

For Richard's claim to the crown was not universally accepted. Restating 'his tytylle and right' to parliamentarians and London craftsmen may have convinced some, but indicates, as Pollard observed, 'a credibility problem'.[16] Some contemporaries, like Crowland, may have questioned abstractly whether secular assemblies could adjudicate on the validity of marriage,[17] or whether bastardy could retrospectively dethrone an acknowledged king. Others may have doubted the truth of the precontract story. It is not recorded whether Richard ever did exhibit the proofs as promised, nor what constituted his evidence. The case was never tried. None of the chroniclers credited the story. In the light of Richard's usurpation, all the contemporary historians (from Mancini on) came to believe that Richard had always intended to usurp the throne, that the whole chain of events had skilfully implemented a preconceived plan, and that the precontract therefore was invented to justify a decision already made. Yet others may have put their prior oaths first – as indeed did many in 1460 who opposed Richard Duke of York. Crowland cannot have been alone in dissenting silently and remaining in his job. Presumably those who swore allegiance to Richard III while remaining loyal to Edward V did not regard themselves as perjuring or dishonouring themselves. Their earlier oath took priority. Even Fogge, so ostentatiously reconciled with the king, was to rebel again in the autumn. If asked, would such dissidents have pleaded that the oath to King Richard was exacted under duress? Many in these categories came to dislike Richard so much that displacing him became their priority and came to matter more than who replaced him, even Henry Tudor once Edward V was believed to be dead. Tudor had at best a feeble case to be a Lancastrian claimant to the crown, but he was a useful tool, first of Brittany and then of France, in their diplomatic relations with England. Each in turn was willing to resource his raids on England, much more generously indeed than in earlier stages of the Wars of the Roses. Their support made him into a serious contender.

This new pretender gave the defeated rebels both a reason for prolonging their rebellion and the resources essential to do so. How the new candidate was agreed, how the news was disseminated, how quickly, and how widely,

[16] Pollard, *Princes*, p. 154.
[17] *Crowland*, pp. 168–71.

are all unknown. The rebels do not seem to have regarded Richard's usurpation as an error to be corrected, but as treason, the most shameful and damnable of crimes, and its perpetrator as a traitor. 'Yorkist sensibilities had been outraged by the circumstances of Richard's accession.'[18] At some point, perhaps later, Richard was blamed for the elimination of the princes – was indeed presumed to have murdered them – and the heinousness of their deaths was developed into an act of *infanticide* against *innocent* children comparable to the slaughter of the Holy Innocents by the wicked King Herod in the Bible. This became the staple of Tudor propaganda in the letters that Henry Tudor sent to his adherents in England during Richard's own lifetime and ever since Richard's death.[19]

Richard was ruthless in his elimination of Hastings, Rivers and Grey, Buckingham and St Leger, all of them his friends and/or kinsmen. Executing them brought an end to their affinities and had no obvious adverse repercussions, in the short run at least. But the princes were different. Their disappearance did not destroy their cause or put an end to conspiracies as Richard, allegedly the killer, presumably calculated. Their sisters, Edward IV's daughters and former princesses, moved up the succession to become next in line. Although useless as military commanders or rulers, the girls could qualify whoever they married as such. Perhaps they might have been smuggled abroad, beyond the king's reach, like Clarence and Gloucester in 1460–1 and as was suggested for Clarence's son Warwick in 1477.[20] Perhaps they might have been married off to dissident noblemen who would thereby be elevated into royalty and become potential claimants to the throne. King Richard respected sanctuary. He did not wrest the princesses from Westminster Abbey, but blockaded it like an armed camp so that they could not escape. Perhaps he thought sanctuary breaking too damaging for his reputation. The Tudor story that Lady Margaret Beaufort proposed the marriage of her son Henry Tudor to Princess Elizabeth as early as July 1483 hardly seems credible:[21] supposedly her brothers, whose titles were

[18] Horrox, *Richard III*, p. 171.

[19] Hicks, *Richard III*, p. 178.

[20] Hicks, *Clarence*, p. 166.

[21] Jones and Underwood, *The King's Mother* (Cambridge University Press, 1992), p. 62, which does, however, indicate the king's backing over the Orleans ransom.

superior and took precedence, were still living at that date. Following rumours of their deaths, the marriage of Princess Elizabeth to Henry Tudor was indeed mooted. That was obviously in autumn 1483 as stated by Crowland.[22] Whether Queen Elizabeth or the princess herself knew of the proposal and consented to it is unclear. There are no contemporary records to substantiate the pro-Tudor accounts of Thomas More and Polydore Vergil. Yet on Christmas Day 1483 in Rennes Cathedral the exiled rebels did indeed acknowledge Henry Tudor as their king on condition that he married Elizabeth of York.[23] What Richard eventually agreed was to marry his nieces safely to trusted gentry, but only one such match was arranged in his reign.

Those people fearful of Richard and those disapproving of his title already existed at the time of his usurpation (26 June) and coronation (6 July), but they offered no stronger resistance then than retreating into sanctuary and (if More is to be believed) keeping silent at Buckingham's public meetings where Richard was to be acclaimed. Perhaps Richard was too well protected by committed adherents to be vulnerable to assassination. Most of the leading dissidents duly attended Richard's coronation, acknowledged him as king, and swore the oath of allegiance to the new king that was required of them. Although Richard himself had gone back on his oaths to Edward V, he seems to have believed that others committed themselves when they swore oaths, to himself as king and to his son as prince of Wales, when soliciting pardons. He required Kentish dissidents to swear allegiance in the spring of 1484. In July 1483 Richard supposed that he had secured the Yorkist establishment and therefore that objectors and conspirators were a small minority that needed watching rather than fearing.

In late June and early July it was King Richard who had the power. Besides his own entourage, which he had inflated while restricting those of others, the new king had the backing of his northern army. After the coronation, however – after the troops had returned home and after the king had departed to the Midlands and the North – southern malcontents made contact with one another and became organised into an opposition. These

[22] *Crowland*, pp. 162–3.
[23] R.A. Griffiths and R.S. Thomas, *The Making of the Tudor Dynasty* (History Press, 1985), pp. 104–5.

manoeuvres are hidden from the view of modern historians. The former queen at Westminster Abbey, her eldest son and other sanctuary men, and members of Edward IV's household who had been committed to Edward V may have formed the leadership. Messages were exchanged by the conspirators both at home and abroad. What matters, however, is that the summer of 1483, from July onwards, witnessed the creation of an opposition movement that was to last for the rest of Richard III's reign.

It is a modern argument that Richard had nothing to fear from the princes because they were bastards, since Richard was well aware that not everyone accepted his claim and argument. He always appreciated that Edward's children were dangerous, but not perhaps how dangerous, nor how their potential could be exploited. The princes were despatched, but the princesses were left in sanctuary. Only later did he question the credentials of some sanctuaries: Beaulieu Abbey, for instance.[24]

Such sanctuary men may have orchestrated the first known conspiracy, which was revealed as early as July 1483, only a month after Richard's accession. It was intended to release the princes from confinement. The Tower of London was too great a fortress and too well guarded for a handful of plotters to storm, so fires were to be set in the City to distract the garrison. The principal plotters were in custody by 29 July. This plot ('fact of an enterprise' as Richard called it in a letter to Lord Chancellor Russell) was scotched. A commission tried the offenders who were duly executed. Four men were taken from Westminster to the Tower and there executed: Robert Russe, serjeant of London; William Davy of Hounslow, a pardoner; John Smith, groom of the stirrup to Edward IV; and Stephen Ireland, officer of the wardrobe in the Tower. That two household men, an official within the Tower, and 50 Londoners were implicated were all causes of alarm for Richard.[25] Clearly, however, these small fry were merely the tips of the iceberg of a much more extensive but secret conspiracy for which the princes were to be the figureheads and that was to be led by people of much higher rank and resources. The Elizabethan chronicler John Stow reports that the insurgents sought the support of the titular earls of Pembroke and

[24] Gill, *Buckingham's Rebellion*, p. 86; *H433*, vol. 2, p. 59.

[25] P. Tudor Craig, *Richard III* (National Portrait Gallery, 1973), p. 98; Horrox, *Richard III*, p. 149; Stow, *Summarie of Chronicles*, ed. B.L. Beer (Mellen, 2007), p. 226.

Richmond, Jasper and Henry Tudor, exiles in Brittany, who had no time to do anything before the plot was foiled. If Edward V was to resume his reign, all the Tudors can have hoped for was to return home and recover their earldoms. If the Tudor earls were seriously involved (rather than merely part of the conspirators' wish list), their participation implicates Lady Margaret Beaufort, countess of Richmond and Derby and consort of Lord Stanley, steward of the king's household. Had the lost indictment said this,[26] however, then Lady Margaret should at the least have been arrested, which she was not. On 13 August her half-brother John Welles was declared a rebel and his lands seized. Another hint at the extent and make-up of conspiracy was the seizure of the temporalities of Lionel Wydeville, bishop of Salisbury on 23 September, one day after he is recorded at Buckingham's residence at Thornbury in Gloucestershire,[27] but a fortnight before Buckingham's own collusion was exposed.

II

A major movement against the king was the so-called Buckingham's Rebellion, an insurrection across the whole of southern England that may have been timed for when King Richard was absent in the North, supposedly for 18 October,[28] and that was designed initially to put Edward V back on his throne. The candidacy of the former king gave prestige and legitimacy to the project and was a cause behind which all the insurgents could unite. Crowland exaggerates how much Richard's spies revealed before the plot exploded.[29] They had not discovered Buckingham's involvement in advance and did not learn enough for other leaders to be arrested before they rose. Perhaps it was after the first plot that the princes were eliminated, perhaps after this second movement was uncovered. Certainly it was at this point that rumours of their deaths were leaked. For Richard, who believed in his title, the princes were threats to himself and to the public good, and were also bastards who counted for nothing. Killing them

[26] Jones and Underwood, *King's Mother*, p. 62.

[27] Horrox, *Richard III*, pp. 150–1; J.A.F. Thomson, 'Bishop Lionel Woodville and Richard III', *BIHR*, 59 (1986), pp. 132–3.

[28] *PROME*, vol. 15, pp. 24–34. The precise chronology is confused, especially when Tudor became first involved and when he became a claimant to the crown.

[29] *Crowland*, pp. 162–3.

meant that Edward V could not be restored to the throne, denied the rebels their figurehead, and thus removed the justification for their rebellion. So presumably Richard reasoned.

However, Richard miscalculated. Many of the rebels, it seemed, still wanted Richard removed and were prepared to risk everything, death and forfeiture, in that cause. They had accepted Richard as Lord Protector and worked with him, but rejected him as king, for reasons that are obscure and may have boiled down to personality and trust. Richard had flouted normal constitutional conventions by usurping the throne, normal familial expectations in many ways, and normal conduct if he indeed slew the princes, yet he was still male heir of the house of York and indeed of Edward IV himself. The rebels were prepared even to back instead the improbable candidacy of Henry Tudor, whom – they decided – should marry Elizabeth of York, the eldest daughter of Edward IV and now heiress presumptive of his line. That proposal could have been scotched if Richard had exhibited the princes alive, as Henry VII did with the earl of Warwick in 1487 to discredit the pseudo-Warwick, Lambert Simnel. But Richard did not do this, either because he could not – the princes being dead – or because to do so would merely strengthen an opposition for which Edward V was clearly a candidate preferable to Henry Tudor. The death of the princes that Richard had intended to conceal became public (though possibly mistaken). Somebody among the opposition realised the potential propaganda value of their murders that in Richard's lifetime and ever since has sullied his name.[30]

It was on 10–12 October that Richard first became aware of the insurrection that historians have named Buckingham's Rebellion. Unfortunately there survive no manifestos to explain its objectives or leadership and no intervening records to pin down the chronology of events. Historians are reliant on three unsatisfactory and retrospective overviews. Most trustworthy is the cursory summary of Crowland, who was at least a contemporary, although writing after the Tudor triumph in 1485 and inspired by it. Fullest is the act of attainder of 1484 against the rebels, which gives dates and lists 104 participants, but rationalises and reconstructs what the government knew and deduced rather than what the rebels planned or achieved. It is an

---

[30] For their use as propaganda in Richard's reign, see Hicks, *Richard III*, p. 178.

outside story. Perhaps it records the findings of commissioners at Maidstone, Newbury, Salisbury, and Exeter rather than the organisation of the rebellion around these centres. The rebels in each county, however, must have been given local musterpoints, for they could not all assemble at the same location. The third overview, the Tudor version, written down much later by Thomas More and Polydore Vergil, probably gives too large a role to Henry Tudor, antedates his leadership, and allows later Tudor stalwarts to enhance their contribution to these events. The Tudor version credits the Tudors with the organisational roles in the summer in contradiction to Crowland, who also seems to be influenced by the later Tudor version. Since Henry Tudor, his mother Margaret Beaufort and Cardinal Morton cannot have been the prime movers, the essentially Tudor interpretation of the rebellion must have developed retrospectively,[31] apparently before Henry's accession. It is not obvious precisely when Henry Tudor became the candidate, who backed him, how his candidacy spread, or how widespread his cause became. Professor Griffiths tries to reconcile these incompatibilities by postulating two independent uprisings – a Buckingham/Tudor one and a Yorkist Edward V one – which merged after the death of the princes.[32] There can have been no conference or other open discussion of Tudor's case during the actual rebellion, when even communication between the disparate uprisings must have been difficult. Gill has composed a narrative of best guesses that charts how the insurrection unfolded.[33]

There were three principal elements to the revolt. First of all, in timing and scale, was a rising of the whole of southern England, from Kent to Cornwall, which was probably organised from London by the former queen and the Wydevilles from sanctuary.[34] Essex and even East Anglia were involved. This uprising involved many of the southern nobility and leading gentry, sheriffs, JPs, and other leaders of the shire communities, frequently also members of the royal household. Prominent here were the

[31] The problems of the narratives are explored in Hicks, *Richard III*, pp. 155–9.
[32] Griffiths and Thomas, *Tudor Dynasty*, pp. 89–91.
[33] Gill, *Buckingham's Rebellion*, pp. 71–4.
[34] Although Edward IV's household and county elites were prominent, Kendall was probably right that the queen and Wydevilles were the organisers, P.M. Kendall, *Richard III* (W.W. Norton, 1955), pp. 260–1; but see Ross, *Richard III*, p. 105; Gill, *Buckingham's Rebellion*, pp. 92–3.

queen's son Dorset, her brother Lionel Bishop of Salisbury, and her chamberlain Richard Lord Dacre of the South; Piers Courtenay, the bishop of Exeter; Sir John Fogge, John Cheyne, master of the horse to Edward IV, and many other courtiers. The Wydevilles were what connected the Kentish rebels. Many of the insurgents were substantial landholders: Sir George Browne, Sir John Guildford in the Weald, the Leukenors in Sussex and Berkeleys of Beverstone; William Uvedale in Hampshire; Walter Hungerford, Clarence's former right-hand man Sir Roger Tocotes of Bromham, his stepson Richard Lord Beauchamp of St Amand, and John Cheyne of Falstone Cheyne in Wiltshire; some of the Courtenays of Powderham and Bocannoc; and Thomas Arundell of Lanherne in the far west. Many had connections with the Wydevilles, the late queen, and with one another. The known rebels, principally those who were attainted in January 1484, were men of rank, wealth, and royal office whose estates, appointments, and kindred are well documented. Their antecedents have been investigated by a whole series of historians, most fully by Dr Rosemary Horrox and Dr Louise Gill, to whose work this discussion is particularly indebted. They included 32 JPs.[35] The whole list is most impressive. Those attainted were the tip of a larger iceberg. Sir Thomas Bourchier of West Horsley in Surrey, son to the king's cousin Lord Berners, Thomas Butler heir to the Irish earldom of Ormond, and even Cardinal Bourchier seem to have been suspected.[36] Others were implicated or suspected and relieved of their commissions, notably Lords Audley and Delawarr.[37] The extensive Bourchier cousinage so important to Edward IV seem to have deserted Richard III without actually rebelling. Double the number of gentry rebels were uncovered by two inquiries in the far west and this may have been replicated across the South. Richard's act of attainder reports 'grete nowmbre of people': there were 500 insurgents in Cornwall and 5,000 in Kent,[38] where the insurrection persisted for two months.

---

[35] *PROME*, vol. 15, pp. 24–34. Participants are exhaustively analysed by Horrox, *Richard III*, ch. 3, and Gill, *Buckingham's Rebellion*, ch. 5.

[36] Their special pardons are entered in *H433*, vol. 1, pp. 98, 103, 274; *CPR 1476–85*, pp. 307, 373, 375.

[37] However, Lord Audley later became Richard's Lord Treasurer.

[38] Arthurson and Kingwell, 'Proclamation of Henry Tudor', *HR*, 63 (1990), p. 105; Devon Heritage Centre, ECA 51, p. 321; Horrox quoting Stow.

These defections demonstrate how completely Richard had failed to take over Edward IV's southern affinity. It was indeed a rebellion of the Yorkist establishment. It was not the rebels, but Richard's backers who were the faction. Furthermore, the rebels included three who had just been made knights of the Bath by the new king – William Uvedale of Wickham (Hampshire), William Berkeley of Beverstone (Hampshire), and William Knyvet of Buckenham Castle (Norfolk) – whom Edward V had made constables of castles in lieu of the Wydevilles. They included almost all the maritime commanders deployed against Sir Edward Wydeville.[39] This was decisive testimony both that the rebels were not all Wydeville clients and that being anti-Wydeville did not make them protagonists of Richard. No wonder Richard seems no longer to have trusted any southerners. But there were exceptions. That the earl of Arundel and his son Maltravers and the southern barons Bergavenny, Cobham, Audley, and Dynham backed Richard was a serious weakness in the rebellion. It was a minority of the justices of the peace who defected and only five out of Edward IV's 29 king's knights that rebelled. To combine elements from the South-East, Wessex, and the far west into one movement, moreover, was decidedly optimistic. While demanding multiple responses from the king, it was only when fully mustered that they could unite against him, and that they were never able to do. The Cornishmen in particular seem to have risen after even the Wiltshiremen had been quelled. Probably the Cornishmen presumed the death of the princes when they proclaimed a new king at Bodmin on 3 November:[40] too late, surely, for this heinous crime to aid their recruitment and to deter Richard's. It had taken Richard two months to suppress the rebellion when, on 9 December, he summoned the parliament that was to attaint the rebels. Two months was a long campaign in the Wars of the Roses.

The second element in the uprising centred on Henry Duke of Buckingham at Brecon Castle. His defection remains as much a mystery today as it apparently was in 1483. Quite why did Richard's own king-maker defect? If Buckingham was offended by Richard and aggrieved by

[39] *H433*, vol. 3, pp. 1–5.
[40] Arthurson and Kingwell, 'Proclamation of Henry Tudor', pp. 104ff.

the denial to him of the Bohun inheritance, he should have been appeased both by the grant of these estates, by his appointment to the two great offices of constable and great chamberlain, and by the virtual viceroyalty conceded to him in Wales. What more could any subject expect? No issues of principle are known to have divided the regime.[41] If Buckingham truly aspired to the crown himself, as heir to Edward III's youngest son Thomas of Woodstock, why did he apparently plot first to make Richard king, then to restore Edward V, and finally in favour of Henry Tudor (if he did)? Tudor historians say that he was persuaded by the former Lancastrian Bishop Morton and by Lady Margaret Beaufort, mother of Henry Tudor, who may have linked the various components together. Both were condemned in Richard III's parliament.[42] While Buckingham was a great magnate in terms both of his own resources and the offices that Richard had bestowed on him, his uprising never got off the ground. If, however, he had enlisted the Talbots and Stanleys on his side, as Horrox suggests he tried,[43] he might have been more formidable. But he did not. In retrospect, Stanley always delayed committing himself until he knew who was winning, which in 1483 was King Richard.

The third element was the Tudors: Jasper Tudor, earl of Pembroke, half-brother of the Lancastrian King Henry VI and his nephew Henry Tudor, titular earl of Richmond, who was also a blood relative of Henry VI via the Beaufort line. At the age of 14 Henry had been carried abroad to Brittany in 1471 by his uncle Jasper. Jasper was irreconcilable, and probably neither Edward IV nor Richard III were interested in pacifying him. Young Henry Tudor, however, had committed no offence and was heir to important English possessions and titles, both in right of his mother Margaret Beaufort, daughter of John Beaufort, duke of Somerset (d. 1444), married thirdly to Lord Stanley, and to the honour of Richmond that had belonged to his father. She wanted her son repatriated, pardoned, and restored to his hereditary rights and in 1482 seems to have secured Edward IV's agreement – but not apparently Richard's.

[41] Unless, which seems unlikely, Buckingham opposed killing the princes or placed the return of Henry Tudor as a top priority.

[42] *PROME*, vol. 15, pp. 34–6.

[43] Horrox, *Richard III*, p. 164.

The July plotters may have sought the support of the Tudor earls: presumably, as Horrox suggested, at Lady Margaret's prompting.[44] Buckingham was Tudor's cousin and had known him as a child: almost the only person who had. Richard's act of attainder credits Buckingham with summoning Henry Tudor from Brittany on 24 September.[45] This date allowed Henry little time to organise his expedition – had he also begun to prepare in response to the July invitation? – but surely was before the princes were known to have died. Presumably Tudor's incentive was that any vanquisher of Richard would restore him to his rights. On the other hand, Polydore Vergil credits the summons to Lady Margaret, who was in constant communication with France and sent her chaplain Lewis Caerleon to her son. She sent him 'greate sommes of money' raised in London and elsewhere (which her act of condemnation confirms) and 'messages, writynges and tokens . . . desiryng, procuryng, and stirrynge hym . . . to come into this roialme'. Richard's act of attainder states that Margaret supported Buckingham's treason. Vergil also has her agreeing with Queen Elizabeth over Tudor's marriage to Elizabeth of York.[46] This story therefore implies that the princes were known to be dead and that Henry Tudor was a claimant. Surely therefore it dates somewhat later than September, if true at all.

Whatever money Lady Margaret sent Tudor was not enough to fund the ships and troops that he hired abroad. It was the Bretons who financed the earl to destabilise the new regime just as Louis XI had backed Pembroke in the 1460s and Oxford early in the 1470s. Henry's expeditionary force was substantial: seven ships and 515 men.[47] Unfortunately they did not arrive together and Henry's landfall near Plymouth in early November came too late, after the other elements in the rebellion had been defeated and when Richard's south-western resources were already deployed.

[44] Ibid., p. 150.
[45] *PROME*, vol. 15, pp. 24–5.
[46] Vergil, *English History*, pp. 195–7; Jones and Underwood, *Kings Mother*, pp. 62–3; *PROME*, vol. 15, p. 36.
[47] Griffiths and Thomas, *Tudor Dynasty*, p. 102.

There was no battle in autumn 1483 and hence no list of casualties. Apart from Buckingham, Dorset, and Richmond, of the 104 who were attainted, there were 20 knights, 25 esquires (also yeomen of the crown), and 24 gentlemen. Measured another way, six out of 24 of Edward IV's knights of the body and 11 out of 40 esquires of the body were actually attainted, 25 per cent in all or half of those based in the South;[48] others may have been sympathetic or undetected.

During the Wars of the Roses the women of defeated aristocrats remained at home, secure in their own inheritances and jointures and sometimes in their dowers, and were consequently suspected by the victors of funding their exiled menfolk. Often they and their resources were consigned to trusted custodians, normally less brutal than Richard had been to the countess of Oxford, but only one, Alice Countess of Salisbury in 1459, had ever been attainted. In 1470–1 it had been the king's mother, queen, and sisters who had contacted Clarence across the seas and who had lured him back to his Yorkist allegiance. Queen Elizabeth and Countess Margaret helped organise Buckingham's Rebellion: Margaret was attainted, but as a woman she was spared from death, imprisonment, and even forfeiture as her husband Lord Stanley was made custodian of her and her lands. Stanley had been loyal and was too important for Richard to alienate. Appointment as constable of England and custodian of a dozen estates besides those of his countess rewarded his loyalty.[49] Queen Elizabeth and Princess Elizabeth, who had presumably approved her Tudor spouse, were not attainted.

This was therefore a very wide-ranging insurrection with at least three prongs to it: the Welsh marches, southern England – south-east, south-central, and south-west – and a foreign invasion of the south west from across the Channel. It was also strong in depth. It involved 32 JPs and leading landowners in every constituent county. In total there were enough insurgents to win had they been combined,[50] but not the massive numbers of commoners that swept away governments in 1460 and 1470. Of course the rebellion failed. A range of factors may have contributed.

[48] Gill, *Buckingham's Rebellion*, p. 87.
[49] *PROME*, vol. 15, p. 36; *H433*, vol. 1, p. 94; *CPR 1476–85*, p. 367.
[50] This corrects my assessment in *Wars*, pp. 225–6.

III

Demagoguery was a skill that few magnates in the Wars of the Roses mastered. What was the right message to appeal to the commons?[51] In 1483 the populace may also have been less discontented than on previous occasions. The worst of the Great Slump of *c.*1440–80 had passed. Perhaps also the people were deterred by Richard's anti-Wydeville propaganda both in the spring and in his latest proclamation. Richard chose not to justify his usurpation, but sought instead to disarm his opponents, by blackening their characters and suborning their troops. Thomas Marquis of Dorset, Richard proclaimed on 23 October, 'hath many and sundry maydes, wydowes and wifes damnably and without shame devoured, defloured and defouled'. Such character assassination, Richard apparently calculated, would discredit the rebel leadership and deny them the military backing of those who agreed with them politically. However good the cause, the respectable would not join such villains. Just as earlier he had suborned the fleet, so now Richard promised immunity to any yeomen or commoners deceived, 'abused and blynded by thes tratours, adult[e]re[r]s and bawedes', who deserted to him. He offered rewards for the capture of the ringleaders – Buckingham (£1,000), Dorset (1,000 marks/£666 13s.4d.), and the knights William Norris, William Knyvet, Thomas Bourchier, and George Browne (500 marks/£333 6s.8d.) in cash or the equivalent in land. Lesser men Richard was prepared to forgive – immunity was offered from punishment to yeomen and below, which certainly made it easier for them to redefect and submit. In his benignity many were pardoned.[52] Richard evidently thought this strategy, first deployed with Sir Edward Wydeville's shipmen, to be effective, since he repeated the offers in 1485. Of the ringleaders, Buckingham, St Leger, and Thomas Rameney were indeed surrendered to him, but apparently nobody else. Ralph Banaster collected the bounty on Buckingham's head and did indeed receive Buckingham's forfeited manor of Yalding, valued at £50.[53] If the princes were rumoured to be dead, what was the point in rebelling? 'The

[51] It is not known what message the rebels promulgated.
[52] *Foedera*, vol. 12, p. 204; *PROME*, vol. 15, pp. 23–4.
[53] *H433*, vol. 1, pp. 118, 206; vol. 3, pp. 58–9, 144; *Foedera*, vol. 12, p. 204.

more party of the Gentilmen of England were so dismayed', wrote a Londoner, 'that they knewe nat which party to take but at aventure'.[54]

It was always difficult to coordinate and combine uprisings that were geographically separate. Moreover, the rebels rose in staccato fashion – the Weald of Kent in early October and Cornwall only on 3 November – and the weather intervened, the Severn in spate to confine Buckingham to Wales and the winds in the English Channel to delay Tudor's arrival until after Richard had already won. Credit should be given to his decisive actions that thwarted the rebels and to his well-targeted propaganda that perhaps deterred potential recruits, but it was primarily the problems in timing and coordinating the different components and the unfavourable weather that prevented the rebels from maximising their resources. Richard never had to confront the rebel forces as a whole.

Richard was at Lincoln when the rebellion broke. The Kentishmen rose first. It was their task to seize London, a key target in earlier campaigns, but John Howard, duke of Norfolk declared his intention to prevent them. Suppression took considerably longer than originally expected, in Essex as well as Kent, but the duke nevertheless achieved it. The Kentish rising was known on 10 October. Already Richard had learnt of the complicity of Buckingham: 'the most untrewe creatur lyvyng'. He demanded the despatch of his great seal from Lord Chancellor Russell on 12 October. A scrawled postscript in his own hand reveals both his sense of personal betrayal and his desire for vengeance. 'We wyll be in that parties & subdewe his malys', he wrote. 'We assure you ther never was falss traytor better provayde for.'[55] Richard took personal direction both of the government and of the campaign. He intended to lead from the front. Although ultimately justified, Richard may have been overconfident, for at this stage he cannot have known the sheer scale and extent of the southern rebellion that was to unfold.

Some troops were summoned even before the king's proclamation on 14 October. As in the Bosworth campaign, Richard had selected Leicester

[54] *Chronicles of London*, ed. C.L. Kingsford (Clarendon Press, 1905), p. 192.
[55] *Richard III: A Royal Enigma*, ed. S. Cunningham (National Archives, 2003), no. 9. On arrival on 24 October it was probably kept by the trusted Thomas Barrow, keeper of the chancery rolls and Richard's chancellor as duke.

as the rendezvous for the assembly of his army. 21 October was the date for
the muster. Here he could receive his northern supporters,[56] and contingents from the whole of the Midlands. Troops from Coventry and York
were summoned. At this stage presumably Richard invoked the allegiance
due from every adult male to his king. At Lincoln on 11 October, Lord
Chamberlain Lovell summoned his adherents to meet at Banbury on 18
October and Leicester two days later. Richard commissioned Lovell by
word of mouth on 23 October to array the South.[57] The king had been
joined by Henry Percy, earl of Northumberland and William Herbert II,
earl of Huntingdon, by 19 October, when both peers and his household
steward Thomas Lord Stanley witnessed the delivery of the great seal in the
king's chamber at the Angel Inn at Grantham in Lincolnshire.[58] Richard's
army was eventually very large: Ross suggests it also included Lords Lovell,
Scrope of Bolton and Zouche.[59] It was easier to recruit to a winning side as
Henry VI had found in 1459 and Edward IV in 1470. From the central
midlands, Richard was well placed to move against the Welsh, against the
southerners, and on London. If Richard's first intention was to strike
directly and in person at Buckingham, this proved unnecessary. The duke
never emerged from Wales into England. Attacked from the rear by the
Vaughans of Tretower, blocked from crossing the Severn by Humphrey
Stafford of Grafton, and impeded by the flooding of the Severn, Buckingham
was deserted by his own men and arrested almost alone. John Howard,
duke of Norfolk took charge in the south-east, blocking the crossings over
the River Thames, so that the Kentish rebels never reached London, the
normal objective of rebels during the Wars of the Roses. On 8 November
at Exeter Richard commissioned Norfolk's son Thomas Earl of Surrey,
Lord Cobham, and others to raise troops to besiege remaining rebels in

[56] *York House Books*, vol. 1, p. 296; Hull Bench Book 3A f.135d.

[57] *CPR 1476–85*, p. 370; *Stonor L & P*, vol. 2, pp. 162–3. Notoriously Sir William Stonor,
recipient of Lovell's summons, rebelled.

[58] *CCR 1476–85*, no. 1171; *Foedera*, vol. 12, p. 293. Also present were Bishops Alcock
(Worcester), Dudley (Durham), Langton (St David's), and Redman (St Asaph).

[59] Ross, *Richard III*, pp. 117–18. This is also indicated by commissions dated at Exeter on
13 November: certainly the four commissioners for Kent and Cornwall were active on 3
December, *CPR 1476–85*, p. 371; Arthurson and Kingwell, 'Proclamation of Henry Tudor',
p. 104.

Bodiam Castle in Sussex.[60] The new Fiennes castle of Herstmonceux may also have been besieged. Lord Dacre of the South died on 25 November, perhaps by violence, and Sir George Browne and a handful of others were captured and executed in London.

While mustering his army, Richard had learnt how geographically extensive the rebellion was. He must have been shocked. Buckingham and indeed London became side issues that were left to others to solve. The southerners became recognised as the main enemies. Richard's proclamation of 23 October had focused on Dorset's sexual immorality and sought to cut off the leadership and suborn the rank and file. Aware that the Welsh and Londoners had already been neutralised, Richard himself diverted to Salisbury, the regional capital of central southern England, where he presided over the trials and executions of Buckingham and St Leger. With the defection of Buckingham, he needed a new constable to try to despatch the traitors. At Coventry on 24 October by word of mouth he had appointed Sir Ralph Ashton as vice-constable 'to proceed against certain persons guilty of lèse majesté' and then at Salisbury on 18 November he appointed Lord Stanley for life as constable of England.[61] It was at Salisbury, on 2 November, when it was apparent that the campaign continued further west, that he cancelled the parliament convened for 6 November at Westminster.[62] No Devonians or Cornishmen had been denounced in his earlier proclamation. The Cornish rebels assembled at Bodmin only on 3 November: they had raised the banner for a new king,[63] most probably Henry Tudor, but just possibly Buckingham, whose execution the previous day may not have been known. Tudor had yet to arrive and in fact never disembarked. He may have been expected in Wales: at Bridport (Dorset) on 5 November, again orally, Richard commissioned Huntingdon and Tyrell to array the Welsh.[64] From Salisbury the king proceeded westwards to Exeter, 'with a great army' according to Crowland. 'Overcome by fear at this terrible arrival', wrote Crowland, 'the bishop of Exeter Piers Courtenay

[60] By word of mouth, *CPR 1476–85*, p. 370.

[61] *CPR 1476–85*, pp. 367, 368.

[62] *PROME*, vol. 15, p. 3.

[63] Arthurson and Kingwell, 'Proclamation of Henry Tudor', pp. 104–5.

[64] *CPR 1476–85*, p. 370.

as well as Thomas Marquis of Dorset and various other nobles of neighbouring districts . . . or as many who could find ships in readiness took to
the sea and finally landed on the desired shores of Brittany'. Others took
shelter with friends and then took sanctuary: Bishop Wydeville at Beaulieu
Abbey in Hampshire. By 25 November Richard was back in London. On
the 26th he restored the great seal to Bishop Russell. On the 30th he
appointed Northumberland to the other great office that Buckingham had
held in succession to himself, the great chamberlainship of England.[65]

IV

Richard's victory appeared complete. The former queen and princesses in
sanctuary, key figureheads for any future usurper, remained effectively in
his protective custody. Commissions sat locally to identify those who were
involved. Those leaders who fell into Richard's hands were executed. The
landed estates and chattels of the traitors were regarded as forfeit and were
seized into the king's hands. These decisions were confirmed by the act of
attainder passed by parliament in January 1484: 104 rebels were attainted.
Apart from treason, Dorset and others were again charged with gross
sexual immorality as in Richard's proclamation, and were smeared also
with the misgovernance of Edward IV's last years. That parliament not
only confirmed *Titulus Regius*, but also witnessed formal oaths of allegiance
of its members to Prince Edward as Richard's heir to the throne.[66]
Parliament was thus an instrument to disseminate throughout county and
urban elites both Richard's just title and the sinfulness of his opponents.
Richard may have believed his own propaganda that lesser men had been
deceived into rebellion. On 16 January 1484 he appointed eight groups of
commissioners to take the oaths of allegiance to himself on all men aged
16–60 throughout Kent.[67]

So complete indeed did Richard's victory seem and so hopelessly
lost did the cause of Edward IV's children appear that Queen Elizabeth

---

[65] Ross, *Richard III*, p. 117; *Foedera*, vol. 12, p. 293; *CCR 1476–85*, no. 1171; *CPR 1476–85*,
p. 367.

[66] *Crowland*, pp. 170–1.

[67] *H433*, vol. 2, pp. 75–6. Gill assembles the scanty evidence for Richard's peacekeeping,
Gill, *Richard III*, pp. 78–9.

abandoned the proposed match between Elizabeth of York and Henry Tudor, if indeed she had ever subscribed to it, and made terms with the king for herself and her daughters to leave sanctuary. Given that the princes were dead, which she seems to have accepted, and that her daughters were no longer princesses, the girls could not remain in sanctuary indefinitely and needed to be properly provided for. Elizabeth agreed with the king on 1 March 1484 for their emergence from sanctuary into his custody, to 'be guyded, Ruled and demeaned after me [Richard]'. The king promised them their lives, freedom from 'ravishment or other harm against their wills' and from imprisonment, accommodation in 'honest places of good name and fame', and keep as befitted the king's kinswomen. When old enough, he promised to marry them to 'gentlemen born' – no disparagement therefore – and to endow each for life with 200 marks a year. He did not trust the former queen mother, who was granted 700 marks a year to be administered by John Nesfield, a guarantee that it would not be used to support the king's enemies. This did not mean that Elizabeth trusted Richard. Indeed the agreement was quite humiliating to him, since it guarded against any change of mind or breach of faith on his part and had to be declared publicly to the corporation of London.[68] But it was a major victory for Richard nevertheless, that removed the most dangerous internal focus of rebellion and rivalry for the crown, checkmated Henry's match with Elizabeth of York, and might have delivered him those Yorkists devoted to Edward IV and his children. The dispensation to wed Elizabeth of York that Henry Tudor had just secured on 27 March, probably without her consent or even knowledge,[69] seemed destined to be abortive. This deal offered Richard, through marriage, a solution to the problem of the princesses. The king had several years to find suitably well-born and trusty husbands who would pose no threat to him. In that respect they should have been less difficult to dispose of than George Neville Duke of Bedford had been. Even better, the queen's son Dorset was included in the arrangement and was permitted to return to England in safety.

[68] *H433*, vol. 3, p. 190.
[69] P. D. Clarke, 'English Royal Marriages and the Papal Penitentiary in the Fifteenth Century', *EHR*, 120 (2005), pp. 1024–5. It was defective in other ways and had to be supplemented by several other dispensations.

If Richard failed to convince the Yorkist establishment and to secure their adherence, he had by the spring of 1484 confirmed his hold on the throne in the face of strenuous and formidable opposition. All his enemies had been routed. Parliament had confirmed both for his own title and for the succession of his heir. He was reconciled with the queen and the Wydevilles and had relegated Henry Tudor once more into a foreign exile. This surely was the high point of Richard's reign.

However, Richard failed to exploit his advantage. Of Edward IV's daughters, only Cecily was married off before Bosworth, to Ralph Scrope, a safe loyalist. The most dangerous princess, because the eldest and most adult, Elizabeth of York remained unmarried at Bosworth, thus allowing Henry's supporters to hope that her Tudor match could yet materialise and enabling Henry to retain the support of diehard Yorkists. This was a serious miscalculation by Richard, although for six months from Christmas 1484 to June 1485 he apparently hoped to marry her himself. Not only would that match have deprived Henry Tudor of many such allies, but it should have greatly enhanced Richard's claims to the Yorkist establishment, even perhaps in battle. Dorset, moreover, never actually arrived.[70]

[70] Polydore Vergil explains why, *English History*, pp. 210, 213.

Chapter Thirteen

COUNTERATTACK

REBUILDING THE REGIME 1483–5

I

Richard must have been chastened by the extent of the rebellion and by his failure to take over the household of his brother and indeed the whole Yorkist establishment. Three bishops joined the rebels: John Morton (Ely), keeper of the privy seal to the exiled Henry VI and councillor to Edward IV; Piers Courtenay (Exeter), secretary to Clarence and to Henry VI during the Readeption; and Lionel Wydeville (Salisbury), the former queen's brother. Several other senior churchmen were implicated, notably the future bishop John Arundel, dean of Exeter and David Hopton, the archdeacon of Exeter. Even Cardinal Bourchier required a pardon on 13 December 1483.[1] Richard had bastardised Edward IV's children, he had made enemies of the Wydevilles, and he had lost the committed support of Edward IV's extensive network of in-laws. Even though he prevailed in this particular contest, many opponents did not trust him enough to submit to him and apparently preferred anyone else instead. Additionally he had lost Buckingham, the front-rank magnate who had helped make him king and a cousin several times over, and his brother-in-law – the widower of his sister Anne – Sir Thomas St Leger. His eldest nephew John de la Pole, earl of Lincoln, son of his sister Elizabeth, became more important.

[1] *CPR 1476–85*, p. 373.

Moreover, his principal rivals escaped. There was no battle, so few of the rebels were killed. As in 1460 and 1470, the discomfited side were not destroyed but had escaped abroad, where the rebels were enabled to plan their return and to prepare to fight another day. As many as 500 joined the two Tudor earls in Brittany. They were useful diplomatically to the Bretons and French. With foreign subsidies, in turn from the duke of Brittany and the French regency, they were able to subsist and to hire the ships and mercenaries with which they invaded in 1485. This was a recurring pattern during the Wars of the Roses, which featured numerous attacks across the sea: three of these invasions of exiles, in 1460, 1470, and 1471, had already succeeded. The Bosworth campaign was a fourth. The standing of the exiles in their home countries endured. Their shires were potential sources of manpower should they invade. While Richard was prepared to receive the submission of the exiles, to receive them back into his allegiance, and to restore their possessions, his reign was too short for much pacification to be completed. Defeat of the invaders in 1485 and sheer desperation should have forced any remaining dissidents to submit.

It is important to remember that Richard's reign lasted only two years and ended in ruin. Hindsight can be helpful. Historians generally look into Richard's deficiencies to help explain his final disaster. But his reign was too short a period to allow for fair assessment of Richard's security measures. How Richard reacted to Buckingham's Rebellion, notably the confiscation of the rebels' possessions, the substitution of trusted outsiders for the natural rulers of the South, and his tyrannical imposition of northerners, was condemned by Crowland at the time and has been criticised by many modern historians since. Yet Crowland was a hostile source, who did not disapprove of such punishment of Lancastrians and northerners by Edward IV, but deplored the very similar measures against recalcitrant Yorkists and southerners taken by King Richard as unprecedented and tyrannical. Moreover, it is not clear that Richard's policies failed. It was not inevitable in 1485 that Richard would be overthrown. It was not in the South that Richard lost the War. It was not the southerners who vanquished his northerners, nor indeed the northerners who were defeated. That it was not a southern army that prevailed at Bosworth can be read as a tribute to the success of Richard's reactions and to his defence measures.

II

Richard acted decisively against the rebels. He took direct hold of the reins of government and instructed his secretariat by word of mouth. In his company were Dr Thomas Barrow, his chancellor as duke, then keeper of the chancery rolls, who took custody of the great seal, and Dr John Gunthorpe, keeper of his privy seal. The king's commands were issued with the highest authority immediately. Richard summoned the army that he was to lead into battle and intended to tackle Buckingham in person. He delegated authority in each sector to men on the spot, to Norfolk and selected commissioners. He put prices on the heads of the rebel leaders. Browne was executed but Knyvet and Bourchier submitted. These measures sufficed. Richard was not needed to quell the Welsh revolt, nor the south-eastern sector, and his foes melted away ahead of him as he advanced into the West Country.

Yet thousands of people rebelled. What was to be done about them?

III

There were plenty of precedents to guide the king. The Yorkists were notorious for killing their principal opponents, most infamously the remnants of the house of Lancaster in 1471. No traitor was more effectively scotched than one who was executed. Dead men do not fight again. So it appears that Richard believed. Targeted ruthlessness had disproportionately large effects in deterring others and was probably intended to do so. Actually there was no bloodbath. Probably Richard desired 'the great fear amongst the most steadfast' reported by Crowland, that he achieved by a mere handful of executions.[2] While Richard had eliminated only five men up to his accession – Rivers, Grey, Hastings, Haute, and Vaughan – the impact was maximised by the abruptness and unexpectedness of their seizure, and by the summary nature of their despatch. At least those plotters executed in London in August and autumn 1483 were subjected to some form of trial.[3] Richard himself oversaw the execution at Salisbury of Buckingham and at Exeter of St Leger. Again, no account was taken of the high birth of those punished. Buckingham

---

[2] *Crowland*, pp. 170–1.
[3] Tudor-Craig, *Richard III* (National Portrait Gallery, 1973), p. 98.

after all was a prince of the blood royal, a cousin, and indeed brother-in-law of King Richard, and should have accrued considerable credit for securing the king's usurpation. Had Henry VI treated Richard's father Richard Duke of York so cursorily, that duke's career would have ended in 1452. Sir Thomas St Leger was another of Richard's brothers-in-law – the widower of his eldest sister Anne. He begged for mercy and offered a large sum for his life,[4] to no avail. These surely were cases where justice needed tempering by mercy. Also beheaded were Sir George Browne of Becheworth (Surrey) and the wholly obscure Thomas Rameney. A trickle of other traitors were caught, tried, and executed as the reign progressed: William Collingbourne, Wiltshire squire, and author of the famous derogatory couplet, is the best known.[5] Negotiation with the captives might also have brought dividends for Richard. Other men, less important perhaps, agreed deals with the king or with his most influential adherents.

The deterrent effect has to be balanced against the loss of service of so many local notables and experienced officers. In practice Richard realised that he could not afford to lose the service of all these influential individuals and did indeed pardon a considerable number.[6] Many, however, did not trust him. They were so alarmed by Richard's unpredictable ruthlessness that they sheltered beyond his reach. Richard's leniency to lesser men does not seem to have earned him much credit and did not rub off on the leaders. Arbitrary and summary executions frightened even those who were loyal and whose rank required them to engage in politics. Taking sides was dangerous, John Lord Mountjoy warned his heir, and should be avoided.[7]

For those who were executed, and especially perhaps those who escaped, the penalty was forfeiture of their chattels and their lands. Their property was seized, depriving them and their families of the resources to continue the fight. This happened first in the autumn of 1483. Richard's parliament

---

[4] *Crowland*, 164–5.

[5] Horrox, *Richard III*, p. 276; KB 29/115 Hil. 2 Ric.III rot.16; see e.g. KB 29/115 Easter 2 Ric. III rot.23v; see below ch. 15 p. 371 for Collingbourne's couplet.

[6] Horrox, *Richard III*, p. 274.

[7] *The Logge Register of Prerogative Court of Canterbury Wills 1479–1486*, eds L Boatwright, M. Habberham and P. Hammond (Richard III Society, 2008), vol. 2, p. 448; K.B. McFarlane, 'The Wars of the Roses', in *England in the Fifteenth Century* (Bloomsbury, 1981), p. 60.

in January 1484 passed an act of attainder proscribing 104 of the leading rebels. Attainder corrupted their blood. It was not just the offenders who suffered forfeiture, but their heirs. Richard seized their property, collected their rents, appointed estate officers, and granted their estates to his adherents without waiting for the return of inquisitions clarifying what lands were forfeited, their value, and others with title to it. For this he has been criticised: for instance, by Ross, who condemned his 'flagrant indifference to the established rules of law and rights of property'.[8] But Richard was not exceptional here. No inquisitions post mortem were automatically triggered when the holders were still living, as most of Buckingham's rebels were, and the precise title, identity, and age of the heir were of purely academic interest for property that was forfeited anyway. The commissions of inquiry that Richard did appoint did not ask all these routine questions. It had taken Edward IV half a decade both in his First and Second Reigns to clarify such matters and to admit all the mothers, joint tenants, creditors, and others to their rights. Undoubtedly there were innocent victims of every crisis.

Four of the most important traitors escaped attainder. Most important perhaps was Henry Tudor's mother Margaret Beaufort, whose husband Thomas Lord Stanley had remained loyal and indeed had offered good service. Mindful of this, the king forbore to attaint her. She was to be neutralised by the forfeiture of her lands, which were then passed to her husband for life, who therefore suffered no immediate financial loss. He had no hereditary entitlement anyway. However, Richard granted the reversion of much of her property to his trusted followers, who received annuities in the interim. The creation of such reversionary rights, of course, reduced the political value and loyalty of the estates for Stanley.[9]

Likewise Piers Courtenay, John Morton, and Lionel Wydeville, bishops respectively of Exeter, Ely, and Salisbury, who 'of their pretenced malices and traitour[ou]s entent' had conspired with Buckingham and Dorset and levied war against the king, 'deserved to lese lyf, londes and goodes by the lawe of this londe'. Whereas Henry VIII did indeed have Bishop Fisher

---

[8] Ross, *Richard III*, p. 120.

[9] *PROME*, vol. 15, pp. 36–7; *H433*, vol. 1, pp. 134, 173, 178, 186. Richard also superseded Stanley's jurisdiction as constable of England.

and various abbots executed, Richard did not. In respect to their clerical status, 'preferryng mercy and pitee before rigour', and at the prayer of the lords spiritual in parliament, Richard spared their lives, confiscated their temporalities only for their lives – the next bishops would have them back – and forfeited to himself any other lands and moveables that they possessed. Property that they had held jointly, as feoffees or executors, was henceforth held by their co-feoffees and co-executors 'as though the same bisshopes were dede':[10] an expedient reminiscent of the treatment in 1474 of the countess of Warwick. Bishops Courtenay and Morton fled abroad, whereas Wydeville took sanctuary at Beaulieu (where Richard probably encountered him) and died in 1484. Morton apparently returned and submitted before Bosworth. He was pardoned and recovered his temporalities back on 12 August 1485.[11] Lesser churchmen, such as Arundel and Hopton, respectively dean and archdeacon of Exeter, were pardoned their lives and apparently retained their livings.[12]

Most of the attainted were those with property enough to be worth confiscating and who had not yet made their peace. There were a few other lesser men, such as five of Falstone in Wiltshire who were brothers and servants of John Cheyne, and the four servants of Sir Giles Daubeney of Barrington, Somerset who fled abroad with him. Richard categorised lesser offenders, 'yeomen and commoners', as misled rather than malicious, 'abused and blynded', and offered them immunity 'in their bodies and goodes' if they withdrew from the revolt,[13] which did indeed ebb away. Some may have silently disappeared, but many apparently formally submitted. The act of attainder reports that Richard, aware 'of the abusioun and desceit of the said multitude' had mercifully 'graunted to dyverse persones culpable in the said offenses his grace and pardoune'.[14] Regrettably no pardon roll covering the offenders exists for the first eight months of Richard's reign. Mercy was a cherished and highly personal prerogative of kingship that Richard took

[10] *PROME*, vol. 15, pp. 34–5. Note the treatment is the same as that of the countess of Warwick in 1474.

[11] C 81/898/ 656; *H433*, vol. 1, p. 243. *Pace* C. Harper-Bill, 'Morton, John (d. 1500), administrator and archbishop of Canterbury', in *ODNB*, vol. 39, p. 422.

[12] *H433*, vol. 1, pp. 98, 113; *CPR 1476–85*, pp. 37, 381; C 66/553 m.14; C 67/51 m.20.

[13] *Foedera*, vol. 12, p. 204.

[14] *PROME*, vol. 15, pp. 23–4.

seriously and did not delegate. Of the 963 pardons on Richard's 1484 pardon roll 712 were warranted by the king himself (*per ipsum regum*), those that were not perhaps being scribal oversights, and the king himself therefore probably authorised, even if perfunctorily, every single one, even those whose surviving warrant was a list or a scrap of parchment like that exonerating the priest William Wode.[15] Did those submitting really escape wholly scot-free, without even the mass fines exacted in 1471 and 1497, or were they obliged to take out recognisances for their good behaviour secured by monetary penalties or sureties? Adult males in Kent and Lancashire were required to swear oaths of allegiance. Those indicted at Bodmin included the minor gentry Geoffrey Beauchamp, Ralph Densell, John Rosygon, and Ralph Arundell, all of whom were omitted from the act of attainder. That they acted by compulsion of the duke of Buckingham and Sir Thomas Arundell, as the indictment alleges,[16] may have contributed to their escape. None were attainted. Very likely they submitted and suffered lesser punishments. Some more substantial figures compounded for their offences and or made their peace: Sir Thomas Bourchier of Barnes (Surrey), Sir John Donne, Sir John Enderby, and John Redenes, who may have proved his innocence, and Sir William Knyvet of Buckenham Castle in Norfolk, a principal conspirator who paid 800 marks in fines and surrendered some of his lands to avoid attainder. Others surrendered properties to Brackenbury, Edward Redmayn, and Tyrell, who were influential enough with the king to mitigate their sentences. John Wingfield senior abandoned his claim to part of the Arundel (not Mowbray) inheritance, to the benefit of the duke of Norfolk and Lord Stanley. This was not corruption, as Gill supposes,[17] not at the public expense. King Richard was well aware of what was happening.

Richard was a man of foresight who looked several stages ahead even in the direst crisis of his reign. Well before the rising was suppressed, he was assuring himself of the assets and revenues of the principal rebels. As early as 23 September 1483 he ordered the seizure of the temporalities of Lionel Wydeville's bishopric of Salisbury and about a week later the entry into the

---

[15] C 67/51; C 81/1531/end. The general pardon was for offences committed before 21 February: almost none were for known rebels.

[16] Arthurson and Kingwell, 'Proclamation of Henry Tudor', *HR*, 63 (1990), p. 105.

[17] This is fully documented and discussed in Gill, *Buckingham's Rebellion*, pp. 95–9.

lands of Walter Hungerford at Heytesbury and the seizure of any goods there. On 2 November, at Salisbury, Richard had ordered Thomas Fowler, usher of his chamber, to seize the lands, revenues, and chattels of the rebels in Bedfordshire and Buckinghamshire, outside the area of the actual revolt, and to pay his receipts over to him. The traitors' officers were directed to pay their revenues to Fowler without delay on peril of the king's grievous displeasure. Commissioners were ordered to seize the lands and chattels of Buckingham '& othere traitors' in Wales and of 17 named ringleaders 'and alle other gentre and houshold servauntes within Wiltshire & Hampshire'. The moveables of John Redenes of Hailsham in Sussex were to be seized. On 5 January 1484 Richard ordered his commissioners in Somerset and Dorset to hand over all of the sheep, horses, cows, oxen, swine, and other chattels, hay, corn, and grain that they had seized.[18] By 6 November, at Beaulieu Abbey, the king had already divided the ringleaders (including those still in rebellion) into those eligible for pardon and those not, and had entered their names into the *Boke of Excepcion* that he had personally marked with his 'owen gracious hand'.[19] On 13 November, at Exeter, he issued four commissions for eight south-central and south-western counties to arrest the rebels, to seize their lands and chattels, to inquire into the value of such estates and to receive the issues, all to be reported back to king and council.[20]

Already, therefore, well before the rebellion was quelled, Richard was planning the next stage – pacification, the fates of the offenders, and the management of the forfeitures. Initially his commissioners accounted to Sir John Elrington, Edward IV's household treasurer, but then to Edmund Chaderton following Elrington's death in December 1483. It was also at this time that many new sheriffs were appointed, not in chancery, as was normal, but by the king under the privy seal, who conceded favourable terms in some cases. Sir Thomas Wortley, for instance, was released from exchequer audit.[21] Richard's nominees were given the rule over particular estates, with

[18] B.P. Wolffe, *The Crown Lands 1461–1536* (George Allen & Unwin, 1970), p. 121; *H433*, vol. 2, pp. 23–4, 31–4, 68–9.

[19] Richmond, '1485 And All That', in *Richard III: Loyalty, Lordship and Law*', ed. P.W. Hammond (Richard III Society and Yorkist History Trust, 1986), p. 198.

[20] *CPR 1476–85*, p. 371. Regrettably no such returns survive.

[21] *CFR 1471–85*, pp. 763–4, 799; *H433*, vol. 2, p. 96; C 60/293 mm.12, 17; E 404/78/2/1, 5, 7, 8, 11, 13, 22; PSO1/56/2877, 2906.

power to appoint and dismiss officers. All inhabitants were required to swear allegiance and were forbidden to be retained by anyone else. In some cases those directed to be attendant upon Richard's officers were told to regard them as the owners.[22] The well-known instructions to Sir Marmaduke Constable for the Stafford estates in Kent and Tutbury (Staffordshire) are the most explicit but possibly merely the only ones written down. Other instances are Elrington's 'rule, keping & oversighte' of the Lewknor lands in Sussex, Lord Grey of Codnor's rule of Oakham (Rutland), and John Hutton's rule at Bisterne (Hampshire) with 'the making, advoiding or continuyng of the officers'.[23] None of their appointments of these subordinates feature on the patent roll.

Noblemen and gentry who had not submitted by January 1484 were duly attainted by act of parliament. Crowland was appalled: 'so many great lords, nobles, magnates, and commoners, and even three bishops, were attainted that we nowhere read of the like even under the triumvirate of Octavian, Anthony, and Lepidus'.[24] It was only after that date that Richard starting granting away forfeited estates, at values commensurate with the rank of the recipients, almost always in tail male, and with rents reserved to the crown. Considerable research and forethought went into these grants that are listed in British Library Harleian Manuscript 433. However, attainder and alienation were not final. It was still possible for offenders to be pardoned and to be restored to their estates, although no absolute reversals of attainders were possible between parliaments. Some, like Sir Thomas Lewknor, had featured in Richard's *Boke of Exceptions*, which (Lewknor explained) indicated eligibility for pardon, yet still required the king's explicit sanction in every case. In April 1484 Lewknor appealed to Richard's 'princely pite' for himself and a group of others who were now 'sorowfull and repentaunt'. Although the list once attached has been lost, those on it were grouped together in Richard's signet book: John and Nicholas Gaynsford of Carshalton (Surrey), John Harcourt of Stanton Harcourt (Oxfordshire), Walter Hungerford of Heytesbury (Wiltshire),

---

[22] *H433*, vol. 2, p. 125; *Letters and Papers*, ed. J. Gairdner, Rolls Series (Longman, Green, 1861–3), vol. 1, pp. 79–81.

[23] *H433*, vol. 2, pp. 33, 35, 52, 58, 59, 81, vol. 3, pp. 116–8.

[24] *Crowland*, pp. 170–1.

Roger Kelsale of Southampton, Sir Nicholas Latimer of Duntish in Buckland (Dorset), Sir William Norris of Yattendon (Berkshire), Thomas Rither of London and Rither (Yorkshire), Sir John St Lo of Chew Episcopi (Somerset), John Trenchard of Hordhill (Hampshire), and William Uvedale of Wickham (Hampshire).[25] They all had to swear allegiance to King Richard. At least six of these were bound over on their own recognisance and sureties to be 'of good abearing to the king' and to serve him militarily when commanded. Sir William Berkeley of Beverstone was another. Additionally Lewknor was required to reside with the Lord Treasurer and Nicholas Gaynsford outside Kent.[26]

Most if not all of those pardoned were required to seal bonds and to find sureties. These bonds recognised a substantial debt to be owed, 2,000 marks in Berkeley's case but more commonly 1,000 marks. Such debts would be cancelled if the conditions were fulfilled, but forfeited if the parties committed further treasons, were suspected of such, broke the conditions, or merely misbehaved. Their sureties guaranteed compliance on financial penalties payable by themselves that were exacted if their principal defected. John Lord Stourton, for instance, had to pay £500 in final payment when William Berkeley fled abroad and Sir Edward Berkeley paid his £200 in three instalments.[27] It was not only the principals who were threatened with financial ruin, but their sureties, who had strong reasons to ensure their principals kept faith. Although only a handful of such bonds were registered on the close roll, it may be that as complex a net of bonds enmeshed offenders, kin, and friends into obedience as in the better recorded system constructed by Henry VII. Richard here probably developed the more selective experimenting of Henry VI and Edward IV.[28]

[25] Richmond, '1485 And All That', p. 198; *H433*, vol. 1, pp. 181, 190, 195.

[26] *CCR 1476–85*, nos 1242–5, 1258–9. Such bonds could not bind those prepared to risk everything.

[27] *CCR 1476–85*, nos 1393, 1412; Gill, *Buckingham's Rebellion*, p. 98. Stourton was a stepson of John Cheyne.

[28] P.M Barnes, 'The Chancery *corpus cum causa* Files', in *Medieval Legal Records*, ed. R.F. Hunnisett and J.B. Post (HMSO, 1978), pp. 430, 435–40; Hicks, *Wars*, p. 99; J.R. Lander, 'Bonds, Coercion and Fear: Henry VII and the Peerage', in *Crown and Nobility* (Hodder & Stoughton, 1976), pp. 267–300; S. Cunningham, 'Loyalty and the Usurper: Recognizances, the Council, and Allegiance under Henry VII', in *Who was Henry VII?*, ed. M.R. Horowitz, *Historical Research* Special Issue (Institute of Historical Research, 2009), pp. 459–81. More systematic records survive for Henry VII.

There may have been scores of erstwhile offenders and potentially hundreds of guarantors exposed to financial hurt or even ruin. Such threats were designed to prevent further offences. Such bonds, in short, should have committed local society to King Richard and stopped even the preliminary sounding out of potential conspirators. The downside was that any committed traitor, who was prepared to hazard his own life, his inheritance, his wife, and children, was not further deterred by such additional threats of financial ruin.

Not all the pardons were approved at once and the terms varied, reflecting both the different terms of what each petitioner requested and what Richard was prepared to grant. Their petitions are highly individual: some spelled out in painstaking detail what others presumed and the most elaborate are more than double the length of the most cursory. Lewknor's pardon was relatively brief. It pardoned the full range of offences, all kinds of sentences, the death penalties, outlawry, loss of his goods and chattels, but not, significantly, the forfeiture of his lands. Petitioners were expected to submit to the king in person – there survives a safe conduct of 10 February 1484 for John Norris[29] – to declare themselves sorrowful and repentant, and to discuss their case with him before being pardoned and readmitted to their allegiance. This has been doubted, because John Harcourt apparently died abroad, but Horrox has exposed this as an error.[30] Richard had the initiative in such discussions, but not always. Some more generous pardons, especially the very special one to Thomas Lovel,[31] indicate people whom the king most wanted back. Only these politically significant pardons that demanded the king's more careful scrutiny, 95 in total and 17 explicitly sparing the lives of the recipients, were included in Richard's signet book, warranted under the privy seal, and enrolled on the patent roll rather than the pardon roll.[32] That a third of those attainted were pardoned does not mean they were wholly rehabilitated: none for instance were restored to the commission of the peace before the end of the reign.[33]

[29] H433, vol. 2, p. 91.
[30] Horrox, Richard III, p. 273n.
[31] C 81/1531/81.
[32] Based on analysis of H433, vol. 1, passim; CPR 1476–85 passim; C 66/ 553–558.
[33] Ross, Richard III, pp. 118–19.

To take out a general pardon like that effective from 21 February 1484 was to secure forgiveness for a wide range of offences not normally including treason or debts to the crown. Traitors in contrast needed explicit forgiveness for treason, the remission of punishments, especially the death penalty, and the cancellation of outlawry, allowing them to receive shelter and victuals and to plead at law. Ideally offenders wanted back their chattels (if they could be found) and lands that were not necessarily covered by the earlier clauses. Despite what Lewknor wrote, there was no template for these special pardons, which varied considerably in detail. All were effective from the date when the king assented. It was also the king who decided when to pardon offenders: St Lo, Hungerford, and Latimer almost at once, Lewknor after one month, Rither after two, the Gaynsfords after three, and Uvedale after nine.[34] Others had to wait a year or more. A pardon for all offences and punishments, one might think, meant that those pardoned recovered their goods and chattels and especially their lands, but apparently this was not the case. Michael Skilling was pardoned on 11 January 1485, the same day that his lands were granted to the esquires John and Richard Pole and their assigns.[35] The pardons of Richard Edgecumbe, Sir William Berkeley, and Sir Roger Tocotes did explicitly restore their goods and chattels[36] – those that could be found, of course, not least because Richard seized all grain and livestock before Christmas 1483. Others got their lands back – or some of their lands. Nicholas Gaynsford secured the income of one of his estates.[37] The veteran Yorkist administrator Sir John Fogge recovered two manors.[38] Most generously, Thomas Lovel, later treasurer and steward of the Tudor household, obtained a pardon that restored his moveables, all his lands, and also the revenues due since the previous Michaelmas.[39]

IV

Conceivably Richard would have preferred to manage these forfeitures himself, to enhance his income, but security took precedence over revenue

[34] *CPR 1476–85*, pp. 435–6, 478, 504.
[35] C 66/558 m.16.
[36] C 66/ 556 m.15; C 66/558/m.12; C 81/1530/27.
[37] C 66/557 m.11.
[38] C 66/558 m.7.
[39] C 81/1531/81.

raising. Instead he had to disgorge many of these lands at once, both to endow the new rulers he appointed and to reward his backers. In explanation Richard normally cited good service done and to be done, not only favouring himself 'and our right and title of us and our heirs kings of England', and also 'for the defence of us' against traitors, enemies, and rebels and for repressing the late rebellion.[40] Whereas hitherto he had little to give to his own retainers and few opportunities to reward them, the forfeited estates of a hundred southern aristocrats enabled him to advance many of his supporters on a lavish scale.

There can be no doubt that Richard handled his own patronage. It is striking how many people were advanced by Richard, who clearly shared Edward IV's encyclopaedic memory for individuals, how their promotions to offices were coordinated with grants of land that underpinned them, and how comprehensive were the signet office lists that he used to track his patronage. Some grants were huge. Lords Neville and Scrope of Bolton were each granted forfeitures worth more than £200 a year and Sir Thomas Malliverer £120 per annum. Northumberland received Buckingham's huge lordship of Holderness in Yorkshire valued at 1,000 marks (£633 6s. 8d.), which was entailed jointly on himself and his second son Alan, and the Poynings and Brian estates in the southern counties worth £278 a year of which he was legally only a coheir. Most politically significant was the patrimony of the Courtenay earls of Devon, worth £616 13s.4d., which had been passed in succession to Humphrey Stafford of Southwick, the marquis Montagu, and the duke of Clarence, and that Richard now bestowed on Sir Richard Ratcliffe,[41] who could expect an earldom (perhaps of Devon) in due course. The properties Richard granted out were often much more lucrative indeed than many front rank estates in the North whence the recipients came. If £50 a year made Richard Clervaux into one of the leading gentry of Yorkshire, how attractive must have been the £66 13s.4d. (100 marks) a year granted to the second-rank Durham gentleman John Hutton?[42] Some grants endowed younger sons (Robert Brackenbury, John Musgrave,

---

[40] C 81/891/274d

[41] Ross, *Richard III*, p. 120; *H433*, vol. 3, pp. 146, 152.

[42] Pollard, 'Richard Clervaux of Croft', in *Worlds of Richard III* (Tempus Publishing, 2001), p. 104; *H433*, vol. 3, p. 149.

Thomas Stafford) who otherwise had virtually nothing. The household men/ local rulers, now exiles, had almost monopolised the constableships of castles, the stewardships, bailiwicks, and parkerships on the estates of crown, the duchies of Lancaster and Cornwall, and the queen's lands in the South, all of which carried annual fees for life and needed now to be refilled. Grants of lands in fee tail that endowed the recipients and their heirs forever were highly attractive incentives for service.

Defeating the rebels had proved relatively easy. Much more challenging was to fill the political vacuum that their defections and departures had created in southern England.[43] Buckingham's Rebellion had spanned 13 shires, all those south of the Thames plus Gloucestershire, Oxfordshire, Berkshire, and Essex, more than a third of the total. Admittedly town councils were little affected. Not all the local nobility, county gentry, and county officers of the affected areas had rebelled. Those that did rise and flee constituted a high proportion of the most influential and active of the elite. 'The rebels far outdistanced their loyal colleagues in terms of wealth, power and position', writes Gill. 'As regional powers with a tradition of service, the rebels' exodus from public life deprived the crown of local knowledge and expertise acquired not simply in a lifetime but over the generations, and impossible to replace.'[44]

Normal management of the counties by sheriffs, escheators, JPs, and hundred officials, their enforcement of law and order, the military defence of the coastline, and the mustering of local manpower by commissioners of array all required that replacements were found. These officeholders were meant to implement the government's commands and were the channel for petitions, information, and remonstrances from the localities to the centre. Richard had to find new sheriffs and JPs for 40 per cent of the posts vacated. He did continue such commissioners as had not rebelled, but he does not seem to have promoted loyal gentry from the insurgent localities, lesser men or younger sons, with whom he had no prior contacts. The exception who proves the rule is the obscure but conspicuously loyal Somerset squire William Bracher, a yeoman of the crown, who was granted

---

[43] The following discussion is especially indebted to the research of Horrox, *Richard III*, ch. 4, and Gill, *Buckingham's Rebellion*, ch. 6.
[44] Gill, *Buckingham's Rebellion*, pp. 87, 89.

the manors of Cheddar, Barrow Gurney, and Tykenham, appointed keeper of the parks of Okehampton (Devon) and Barrington (Somerset), and who accrued various other favours.[45] Nor did Richard immediately confer local offices on those rebels that he pardoned: a third of the total. Richard was willing to pardon those who submitted and restore them to their estates. He may have hoped in time, when Henry Tudor was defeated, to restore them all and might then have felt able to trust them. But the two years of his reign was too short for that.

In the interim Richard decided that Edward IV's Yorkist establishment could not be trusted. He relied ever more heavily on his northern supporters – especially those Neville retainers tied to him through his queen. This too was a radical change in policy that was forced upon him. He had no other choice. That was why Richard did not create the new peerages that Horrox expected of him.[46] Of course he continued to govern the North through traditional northern rulers, but additionally he employed northerners everywhere, in chancery (Barrow, Chaderton), in Calais (Sir Richard Tunstall, Sir Thomas Everingham), Wales (Sir Richard Huddleston, Thomas Tunstall),[47] and above all in the South. Richard's signet letter book records the promotions, responsibilities, and rewards of dozens of them. Some were very substantial. Prominent on the list were Lords FitzHugh and Scrope, Sir Ralph Ashton, Sir Robert Brackenbury, Sir Marmaduke Constable, Harringtons, Malliverers, Markenfields, Metcalfes, Musgraves, Redmayns, Ratcliffes, Savages, and Stanleys. One wonders whether recipients realised that their preferments were only temporary and how (or if) that realisation affected their commitment and actions.

If Richard henceforth distrusted the southern aristocracy, he seems to have been absolutely confident of his northerners, whether his retainers or not, and was convinced of their loyalty and committed service. The core were members of his consort's Warwick connection, whose crucial importance to him Ratcliffe and Catesby memorably reminded him. Even their

---

[45] Horrox, *Richard III*, p. 261; *CPR 1476–85*, pp. 366, 373, 390. The Brachers father and son were hanged after Bosworth, *Crowland*, pp. 182–3.

[46] Horrox, *Richard III*, p. 202. He reigned for two years and should have had plenty of time for new creations.

[47] *H433*, vol. 1, pp. 95, 96, 102, 126, 138.

loyalty was not unconditional.[48] Many others had personal connections, having served in his household (e.g., Geoffrey Franke), as his feoffees (e.g., John Huddleston), as his estate officers (e.g., Sir Robert Brackenbury, Thomas Metcalf), as his lawyers (Morgan Kidwelly, Miles Metcalf), and as his retainers. Those who served Northumberland, Neville, Scrope, and the other northern lords that he had retained qualified as members of his wider affinity. Like Sir John Conyers and Sir James Harrington, most remained in the North, but two Yorkshiremen knighted by Northumberland in 1481 were substantially promoted in the South. Sir Marmaduke Constable of Flamborough became steward of Tonbridge, Tutbury and sheriff of Staffordshire. Sir Christopher Ward of Givendale near Ripon became master of the harthounds, ranger of the forest of Wolmer and master of game at Alice Holt (both in Hampshire), steward of Witley and Worplesdon (both in Surrey), receiver of these and other manors, JP in Sussex and Surrey, and commissioner of array in Sussex and Hampshire.[49] Sir Gervase Clifton, Sir Marmaduke Constable, Sir William Eure, Sir Thomas Everingham, Sir Thomas Grey of Horton, Sir Hugh Hastings, Sir Robert Manners, Sir Henry Percy, and Sir Christopher Ward, nine of the earl's knights, and John Cartington, John Hastings, George Percy, Thomas Radcliffe of Derwentwater, father of Sir Richard, and Thomas Strother, five of his esquires, were patronised by King Richard.[50] Such connections had been reinforced on campaign in 1481–2, when Duke Richard had made knights and bannerets of many northerners including those whose primary ties were with Northumberland and others. Obviously many other lesser men who were not knighted had also served in his forces in Scotland. Richard exploited the useful southern connections of such men as Sir Ralph Ashton, husband of Elizabeth Kyriel (née Chichele), whom he made vice-constable of England, Sir Richard Ratcliffe as consort of Anne Arundell of Lanherne (Cornwall), and Halnath Malliverer, already settled in the West Country, but they were exceptional.

---

[48] *Crowland*, p. 175.

[49] W.C. Metcalfe, *Book of Knights* (Mitchell & Hughes, 1885), p. 6; *H433*, vol. 1, pp. 127, 147, 149; *CPR 1476–85*, pp. 397, 399, 572, 574; Wolffe, *Crown Lands*, pp, 61–2, 126.

[50] Hicks, 'Career of Henry Percy, (c.1448–89), with special reference to his retinue', MA thesis (Southampton University, 1971), p. 60n.47; *H433*, vol. 1, p. 196.

All these categories of Northerners were employed by the king. The fortunes of Lord Scrope of Bolton were transformed. He became constable of Exeter, was feed to the tune of £437 a year, and received Martock in Somerset and other properties in the three most south-western counties.[51] Brackenbury, already constable of the Tower, was made a leader in Kentish society. Edward Redmayn of Harewood (Yorkshire) and Levens (Cumbria) based himself at the Edgecumbe seat of Cotehele in Devon. Richard's indentured retainer Sir John Savile was appointed captain of the Isle of Wight, with a fee of £200 a year, and commissioner of array and of the peace for Hampshire. John Hutton of Dunwick (Durham) moved to the forfeited Berkeley seat of Bisterne and was appointed constable of Southampton and Christchurch. John Nesfield, the blockader of Westminster Abbey, appointed esquire of the body and constable of Hertford Castle, was granted the plum Hungerford estate of Heytesbury in Wiltshire.[52] Brackenbury, Ratcliffe, and Redmayn were all younger sons, as were such lesser luminaries such as John Musgrave and Thomas Stafford. William Malliverer, cadet of the knightly family from Allerton Mauleverer, replaced the Fogges as Richard's man around Ashford in Kent.[53] Tyrell and Catesby are rare instances of those few of southern and Midland origins, but most of them – more than 40 in all – were northerners on whom Richard felt he could rely. These were what Gill called parvenus.[54]

Their responsibility for ruling the South emerges most strikingly in appointments to the key offices in local government. Two-thirds of the sheriffs appointed to counties south of the Thames–Severn line in 1484 were northerners. Shrievalties demanded personal attention; so too did escheatries – William Malliverer convened several inquisitions in Kent.[55] These northerners were expected also to officiate as JPs, in and outside sessions, to array the militia and fulfil other commissions. Others may have been absentees. Richard Lord FitzHugh surely treated his keeping of the

[51] H433, vol. 1, p. 149.

[52] Pollard, Princes, pp. 145–6; Horrox, Richard III, pp. 188–9, 196; CPR 1476–85, pp. 399, 410, 572; H433, vol. 1, pp. 87, 113, 121,143, 152–3, 166–7.

[53] Hicks, Richard III, pp. 169–70.

[54] Gill, Buckingham's Rebellion, p. 89.

[55] Calendar of Inquisitions Miscellaneous 1422–85 (Woodbridge Press, 2003), vol. 1, pp. 480, 503.

forest of Hay and North Petherton (Somerset) as a sinecure,[56] the performance of which was delegated to deputies. Heads of Northumberland families
such as Sir Robert Manners of Etal, John Cartington of Cartington, and
Thomas Strother more probably used their new manors in Somerset,
Devon, and Cornwall for income rather than as homes.[57] A younger son like
Gilbert Manners, who was granted Cornish manors worth £19, is more
likely to have changed his domicile.[58] Seldom can it be demonstrated in such
a short period that these northerners took up residence in the South – but
some definitely did. They had been granted the lands forfeited by attainted
rebels that were necessary to give such outsiders the local presence, the
standing, and the wealth that enabled them to rule locally. They could now
afford to staff their households and to live in some style, as heads of groups
rather than isolated individuals. When Sir Marmaduke Constable of
Flamborough was appointed to be steward of Buckingham's lordship of
Tonbridge, Richard directed that he should 'make his abode amonges you
and . . . have the Rule'; as steward of Tutbury Constable received model
instructions that required assiduous personal supervision of the subordinate
officers and tenantry.[59] This was probably also what Richard expected of the
others for whom such explicit instructions are lacking. They were the king's
agents in the localities, expected to channel the commands of the government into the shires and to intercede for natives with the centre – although
few of them were figures of real substance in the new regime – and to activate local administrations in which they were always in the minority. Pollard
rightly says that they were much more important than their relatively small
numbers suggest,[60] but there are actually few sources to indicate what they
actually did. Also unrecorded is what use they made of their new-found
wealth and responsibilities. John Hutton placed his retainers in inferior
offices in the New Forest and was courted by the corporation of
Southampton.[61] John Musgrave, a Cumbrian squire, was elected MP for

[56] *H 433*, vol. 1, p. 109.
[57] Ibid., pp. 134, 196; *CPR 1476–85*, pp. 483, 516. Cartington and Manners were JPs only
in Northumberland, *CPR 1476–85*, p. 568.
[58] *H433*, vol. 1, p. 201.
[59] *H433*, vol. 2, p. 81, vol. 3, pp. 116–18.
[60] A.J. Pollard, 'The Tyranny of Richard III', in *Worlds of Richard III*, p. 30.
[61] Pollard, *Princes*, pp. 145–6.

Salisbury. Three northerners also of Cotehele acted for Edward Redmayn in Devon. In Dorset, where Redmayn administered forfeitures, his agents included Henry Haggerston and Philip Thirlwall, both Northumbrian cadets like him of Percy families.[62] Richard's northerners, numerous enough in themselves, headed groups – households and affinities – and do indeed constitute the invasion that Crowland deplored and Ross confirmed. They constituted, wrote Ross (himself a Yorkshireman), 'nothing less than a veritable invasion of northerners into the landed society and administration of the southern shires'.[63] They were intended to integrate themselves into and to head local society.

The Westminster civil servant Crowland reports that their impact was indeed disproportionate. He found the newcomers appallingly alien. 'The northerners whom he [Richard] had planted in every part of his dominions [were] to the shame of all the southern people who murmured ceaselessly and longed more each day for the return of their old lords in place of the tyranny of the present ones.'[64] In two short years, this horde of northerners could not be assimilated. Their distinctive dialects, attire, and manners, we can deduce, made them stand out. It is difficult to confirm Crowland's Westminster perspective and his southern bias with concrete evidence from the southern shires. A rare example is the Kentish carol 'The Briar and the Periwinkle' that lamented the oppressive rule of the alien William Malliverer and that looked forward to his destruction.[65] How widely was this northern invasion viewed as tyranny? What was offensive to Crowland and the Yorkist establishment among whom he moved was that southerners like them were on the receiving end of practices that they found acceptable when applied to others, such as Northerners.

Modern historians have accepted Crowland's judgement, have substantiated the invasion of northerners, and have regarded it as a failed policy. But what else could Richard have done? These men had rebelled and needed to be punished, to deter others. Could Richard have disciplined

---

[62] *Calendar of Inquisition Miscellaneous*, vol. 1, p. 264; see also Horrox, *Richard III*, p. 196.

[63] Ross, *Richard III*, p. 119.

[64] *Crowland*, pp. 170–1.

[65] Hicks, *Richard III*, pp. 169–70. Richard gave Malliverer a diamond ring, A.F. Sutton, 'The Court and its Culture in the Reign of Richard III', in Gillingham, *Richard III* (Collins & Brown, 1993), p. 81.

them in other ways, by imprisoning or fining them perhaps? They did offer him that opportunity, by remaining at hand, surrendering to him, or submitting. The evidence seems to be that in the short term the southern rebels were irreconcilable and no more lenient policy could have worked. Nor is it obvious that Richard's policy failed. The risk that so many traditional rulers might return posed a constant threat to Richard's security, drained his resources, and forced the king to remain mobilised for two whole years. In the last resort, however, Henry Tudor chose not to invade on the south coast and thus failed to exploit this apparent advantage. Tudor's southerners were not leaders of the whole population, but acted as mere individuals on the Bosworth campaign.

The Northerners themselves were few in number, but they did enforce order and activate the home guard. Richard made the most of the obligation of defence owed by all adults to maximise the numbers and organisation of the militia and especially coastal defences. The king appointed commissioners of array in every county in December 1484. Characteristically he issued them with detailed instructions that may have been novel – none are recorded before – and that presumably tightened up the rules. Already it seems the constables and bailiffs of towns, townships, villages, and hundreds had established 'the nombre of persones suffisauntly horsed, harneysed, and arrayed' and had somehow gathered money to pay them. Now these new commissioners were commanded to muster and review these forces, to check that they were able-bodied, properly equipped, and 'noo rascal', to augment their numbers if possible, and to chase up the money-raising needed to pay them. The troops were commanded to attend upon captains appointed by the king and those gentry able 'to doo the kinges grace service' were commanded to make ready for when they were warned.[66] Amended instructions on 22 June 1485 presumed that these directions had been fulfilled and indeed thanked all involved for their good demeanour, raised the level of readiness to an hour's warning, and threatened defaulting gentry with forfeiture of their 'lyfes, landes & goodes'.[67] This could have been mere rhetoric or indicative of unwillingness to support King Richard.

---

[66] *Letters and Papers*, ed. Gairdner, vol. 1, pp. 85–7
[67] *H433*, vol. 2, p. 229.

If implemented, such comprehensive measures were grounds enough to
deter any landing along the coast of England. A landing at Milford in
Hampshire was indeed feared[68] – was this misinformation a feint designed
to commit Richard's resources far from the action? – but the threat never
materialised. Was this because the plantation of northerners in the South
had achieved its objectives and any landing where Richard was best
prepared was ill-advised? In 1471, likewise, the earl of Oxford's defence of
East Anglia had deflected Edward IV to land in Yorkshire. Henry chose
instead to land in Wales where such measures did not apply and moreover
in a part of Wales where Richard's defences were less organised.

Though the allegiance due to the king should have sufficed to mobilise
the militia, yet Richard reinforced it with organisation, discipline, a high
degree of readiness and penalties for default that should have sufficed.
Undoubtedly such levies were poorly equipped and trained in arms, inferior in effectiveness and enthusiasm to noble households and retinues,
however numerous they may have been. Richard was also concerned to
maximise the force of well-equipped troops that his trusted retainers
brought to his ranks and had apparently agreed the numbers with each
leader. Norfolk listed 1,000 men 'that my lord hath granted to the king'.
Henry Vernon of Netherhaddon (Derbyshire), esquire of the body and
bailiff of the liberty of High Peak, was instructed to bring 'such number as
ye have promised us sufficiently horsed and harnessed 'for the Bosworth
campaign, 'without failing, all manner excuses set apart', and on pain of
forfeiture.[69] While no such agreements or other summonses survive, this
is probably representative of many such arrangements, especially with
northerners.

On the other hand, Richard's 'radical policy' to deploy many of his trusted
northerners in the South denied him their services elsewhere. Of Richard's
northern peers, neither the Lords Scrope, the earls of Northumberland
nor Westmorland (Neville), FitzHugh nor Greystoke, nor more than half a
dozen northern gentry were attainted for service at the battle of Bosworth.
Constable, Tyrell, Malliverer, and Ward were all conspicuously absent.

[68] *Crowland*, pp. 176–7.

[69] A. Goodman, *The Wars of the Roses: Military Activity and English Society, 1452–97* (Routledge
& Kegan Paul, 1981), p. 134.

Brackenbury failed to arrive in time. A contributory factor may have been that such Northerners were absent, guarding the South. Some of Richard's most trusted servants moreover were overstretched. Sir Marmaduke Constable of Flamborough, for instance, was not at Bosworth: his custodies both of Tutbury Castle and honour, each with the obligation of continuous residence, obviously could not be reconciled. He also belonged to the king's household, as knight of the body. Richard Lloyd served both in the Calais garrison and as bailiff of East and West Budleigh in Devon.[70] Tyrell was simultaneously Richard's master of the horse at court, chamberlain of the exchequer at Westminster, supervisor of Guines in Calais, constable of Cardiff and sheriff of Glamorgan, and steward of the Duchy of Cornwall.[71] Richard recognised the problem, to some extent at least. Even though the king 'sendethe him to Guysnes', the lieutenant and other officers of Glamorgan were commanded nevertheless to accept Tyrell as their governor and leader and to hold themselves 'redy with horses and harneys and money for men t[o] attend upon his deputies to doo the kinges service when they shalbe called'.[72] Whichever duty he was performing on 22 August 1485, Tyrell was not at Bosworth. Ratcliffe, who was slain at Bosworth, the absentee landholder of his huge West Country estate, was a knight of the body and royal councillor, deputy warden of the West March and sheriff of Westmorland for life,[73] and surely normally absent from all his provincial responsibilities. The continental veteran Sir Thomas Everingham became lieutenant of Rysbank Tower at Calais and a naval commander against the Scots who captured him, yet was rewarded with grants of Barnstaple and Torrington in Devon.[74] Catesby cannot have given priority to all his royal offices. The southerners did not rebel in 1485, but neither were they present in large numbers at Bosworth. If they absented themselves, it may be that their northern replacements were too busy to be there as well. Perhaps Bosworth marks the moment when Richard's overstretched right-hand men found that all 'his wishes could not be met'.[75]

---

[70] Horrox, *Richard III*, p. 189.

[71] *H433*, vol. 1, pp. 125, 255, vol. 2, p.197; C 76/169 m.6.

[72] *H433*, vol. 2, p. 197

[73] *H433*, vol. 1, p. 141.

[74] C 81/890/231; C 81/891/256; *Crowland*, pp. 172–3.

[75] The quotation is from R.E. Horrox, 'The Government of Richard III', in Gillingham, *Richard III*, p. 68.

V

Richard sought also to maximise his power in other ways. Crowland credited him with a network of spies, so that he knew in advance of Buckingham's plot and something of Tudor's planning abroad, and also the maintenance of Edward IV's pony express to bring him news as rapidly as possible.[76]

Five centuries ago Sir George Buck argued that Richard's fault was not that he was tyrannical, but that he was too merciful to his enemies. The king could have 'preserved his fortunes and his crown', Buck contended, if he had dealt properly with Bishops Morton and Courtenay, the marquis of Dorset, earls of Richmond, Pembroke, Oxford, and Northumberland, 'the principal gentlemen' Hungerford, Bourchier, Digby, Savage, Talbot, Mortimer, Rice, Blount, Bray, Poins, Sanford, young Stanley, Fortescue, and the doctors Morgan, Lewis, and Urswick.[77] Perhaps so. But he quailed at such slaughter. He had very few offenders executed. Short of a bloodbath, he tried his utmost in his last 20 months to bolster his regime. It is not obvious what more he could have done.

[76] *Crowland*, pp. 162–3, 172–3.
[77] Buck, *Richard III*, ed. A.N. Kincaid (A. Sutton, 1979), p. 29

Chapter Fourteen

STRATEGIC FORESIGHT II

SO MANY ENTERPRISES

I

The principal functions of English governments were the conduct of foreign relations, the waging of war and defence of the realm, justice and the main-tenance of law. 'Lo! To judge and to fight is the office of a king', declared Richard's contemporary Chief Justice Fortescue.[1] King Richard stepped naturally into these roles. He took them seriously and can be shown to have been active in all three areas. How he sought justice for all and his applica-tion of his prerogative of mercy have already been discussed. Not much more was expected. Government as a reforming institution – government on behalf of the Commonwealth and committed to the reshaping and improvement of society – was a notion first coined by Thomas More 30 years into the future and implemented by the Commonwealth men 70 years into the Tudor age. The late medieval English central government machine made decisions – the functions of king and council – and imple-mented and communicated the king's will. The royal household and exchequer provided the domestic environment for government and resourced it financially. Smaller agencies handled such subcategories as works, the navy and ordnance, the great wardrobe and the chapel royal.

---

[1] S.B. Chrimes, *English Constitutional Ideas in the Fifteenth Century* (Cambridge University Press, 1936), p. 14.

Networks of local government reaching from shire down to tithing acted on commands from the centre. These systems were wedded to routine, keeping things going, and punctuated by occasional troubleshooting when things went adrift. The major government departments of chancery, exchequer and privy seal, the central courts, and local officers operated almost on autopilot, with whatever initiative coming from the king or his reaction to external factors. Such structures and rhythms evolved only very gradually over the centuries. This was not therefore a situation where change or reform was perceived to be normal or even desirable. Kings did not need to be reformers and rarely acted to change things. Ministers and indeed the government seldom had the legislative programmes that are expected today.

Buckingham's Rebellion, its aftermath, and the constant external threat posed by Henry Tudor and his foreign backers raised defence of the realm and of his own crown to the top of Richard's agenda. Moreover, a reign of a mere 26 months was too brief for the achievement of the radical reforms that nowadays some anachronistically expect of King Richard III. Professor Ross wrote: 'Richard III's reign was too short to allow him to make much significant change in the ways in which his realm was governed, even had he wished to do so.'[2] Yet, surprisingly and almost out of period, King Richard was different. He did want change in many different areas. He launched major projects across the whole range of government activity. Characteristically they were as big and as lavish as possible and were to be fulfilled as rapidly as possible. Richard was not the man to postpone action or wait decades saving up or deferring results. His signet letter book *Harleian Manuscript 433* hints at this. It contains many grants and actions that he initiated, though certainly not all of them, and a few, but definitely not all, of his finished state papers. Duke Richard brought to his kingship a list of aspirations, an urge to codify them and to work them out in detail, and a willingness to invest lavishly that he could fortunately afford. Every 'i' was dotted and every 't' crossed. Even while systematising and creating rules and conduct for others, he himself was impatient of impediments, strict law, and procedures. How often, for instance, did he declare his signet and sign manual to

[2] Ross, *Richard III*, p. 170.

be sufficient warrant?[3] Not all his officers agreed and sometimes they had to be overridden.[4] Richard told the treasurer of his chamber and the keeper of his great seal what to do, his oral command being enough authority, he declared.[5] Of course his projects were those expected of a fifteenth-century king: not the national health, social care, education, or transport to be expected today, but the castle-building and new colleges that were approved by even such a hostile contemporary as John Rous.[6] Upgrading the militia and appointing a master of requests were other examples.

Richard was an extremely active king who worked hard and played hard. Unlike his brother, who almost confined himself to the Thames Valley, King Richard travelled energetically around his kingdom, as far west as Exeter, as far north as Newcastle upon Tyne (1484) and Scarborough (1483), and resided for extended periods at his castles of Pontefract in Yorkshire and Nottingham in the East Midlands. An itinerary so different from that of Edward IV and Henry VI demanded the upgrading to contemporary requirements of such castles as Kenilworth and Nottingham where he resided. Nottingham, which he called his 'Castle of Care', was a useful military base to overview his kingdom. Richard stayed there several times for months at a time. On the north side of the castle King Edward IV had commissioned a great polygonal tower extending from the outer ward and containing 'ornate and beautiful' apartments, no doubt spacious and state of the art. Richard supplemented them with an extra upper storey for his own use.[7] He commissioned another such tower at Sandal Castle (Yorkshire), the seat of the earl of Lincoln and council of the North. He reserved nearby Pontefract for his own visits. Rous credits him with new building at other castles, but the great towers at Warwick and Tutbury (Staffordshire) are more probably the work of his father-in-law the Kingmaker and his own brother Clarence.[8] Richard did reside frequently at the Tower of London,

[3] B.P. Wolffe, *The Crown Lands* (George Allen & Unwin, 1970), pp. 120, 127; *H433*, vol. 2, pp. 18–19, 22.

[4] See, e.g., below note 107.

[5] Wolffe, *Crown Lands*, p. 119; *CPR 1476–85*, p. 370.

[6] Hanham, *Richard III*, p. 121.

[7] *John Leland's Itinerary*, ed. J. Chandler (Sutton, 1993), pp. 355–6.

[8] Hanham, *Richard III*, p. 121; *The Rous Roll*, ed. W.H. Courthope (London, 1869), no. 59; Hicks, *Clarence*, 195–6.

Westminster and Windsor, and sometimes at Greenwich and Woodstock, but he is not recorded at the palaces of Clarendon (Wiltshire), Eltham (Kent), King's Langley (Hertfordshire), or Sheen (Surrey). He cultivated magnificence in dress, in his household, in music, in ceremonial and court entertainments. Hunting and hawking were passions. It is no accident that he was staying at the hunting lodge of Beskwood, rather than in the nearby castle of Nottingham, when he heard of Tudor's landing. He also built up his ordnance, acquiring another 20 guns and two serpentines in March 1484, and employed five foreign experts to manufacture and deploy them.[9] Richard brought to the throne many relevant experiences, as a northern warden, as constable of England, as a landholder, and as a founder of religious institutions. So had other kings who succeeded as adults, such as Henry V and Edward IV, but they did not apply their earlier experiences as Richard did to change and ideally improve the operation of government.

II

Richard already had much practical experience in military matters, as both constable and admiral of England, and as warden of the West March, and the king's lieutenant in the North. He appears to have been a critic of the conciliatory and somewhat timorous foreign policy of Edward IV's last post-Picquigny years that had seen England maintaining peaceful relations with both the warring powers of France and Burgundy. West Country seamen treated Edward's death as ending the peace and apparently stepped up piracy in the Channel. At first Richard reacted favourably to foreign complaints, but then took a more aggressive stance.[10] He hoped thereby to bring Brittany to heel, to winkle out Edward Wydeville, and, after Buckingham's Rebellion, Henry Tudor. He evaded Scottish overtures for peace and continued the war against Scotland, finding, however, that it was not easy to bring about a successful conclusion and managing inadvertently on 13 March 1484 to revive the Auld Alliance of Scotland and France against

[9] C. Skidmore, *Bosworth. The Birth of the Tudors* (Weidenfeld & Nicolson, 2013), pp. 172–3.

[10] A. Grant, 'Richard III and Scotland', in *The North of England in the Age of Richard III*, ed. A.J. Pollard (Sutton, 1996), pp. 127, 129.

himself.[11] Painfully he learnt that what appeared desirable to the duke required compromise from the king. Foreign powers could not be commanded as subjects were.

Richard's earliest actions indicate his dissatisfaction with the military organisation of his realm, his readiness to make changes, and in particular to bring England's armed forces directly under his control. There was no standing army, each new force being recruited afresh, and the king remained dependent on three traditional sources of manpower: the royal household; the obligation of all males between 15 and 60 to bear arms; and those retained by the nobility, of which he had so recently been one. There were additionally two major garrisons of professional mercenaries funded by the crown, at Berwick and Calais, but recruited and commanded by noble captains and capable of redeployment in English politics, even against the king, as Warwick the Kingmaker most famously had done. Richard had to maintain these and had also to delegate command, but evidently he had no intention of allowing them to be privatised or directed against himself.

Obviously Richard ceased to be warden of the West March on his accession, but he remained interested in it. He patronised Carlisle and Carlisle Priory, to which he allocated two tuns of wine a year and revenues from Hull and Penrith. He contributed to the glazing of Carlisle Cathedral in return for prayers for the good estate of himself and his queen and their souls after death.[12] The hereditary wardenship and principality created for him as duke of Gloucester in the West March was quietly abandoned now he was king. The next warden might reasonably have been the earl of Northumberland, the principal Cumbrian landholder, becoming thereby warden of all three marches. Actually Richard retained direct control of the West March, his deputy Humphrey Lord Dacre of the North remaining lieutenant at a salary of a mere £200 even in war, and after his death Sir Richard Ratcliffe.[13] Northumberland's new enhanced title of warden general applied only to the east and middle marches. The earl's annual

---

[11] Macdougall, *James III* (John Donald, 1982), pp. 210–11.
[12] H. Summerson, *Medieval Carlisle* (Cumberland & Westmorland Antiquarian & Archaeological Society, 1993), vol. 2, pp. 465–6.
[13] Ibid., vol. 2, p. 465.

contract at £1,250 moreover was extended only for one year from 24 July 1483 and then prolonged only for a further five months to December 1484.[14] Records fail thereafter. No indentures nor commissions survive, but that does not mean that none ever existed. Actually Northumberland did continue to sanction protections as 'warden of the East and Middle Marches towards Scotland and as captain of the town and castle of Berwick for the victualling, safeguarding, and defence of the same' until at least 4 June 1485,[15] and probably therefore for the rest of the reign. As in the past, the earl probably contracted for five or more years. If Richard III did not actually abolish the wardenship, as Grant surmised,[16] these military commands had been made very much less lucrative and independent. The £438 a month payable for Berwick covered the wages of the garrison and no more.[17] There is no record of who commanded the coastal fortress of Dunbar, surrendered by the duke of Albany to the English. Dunbar was under siege from the Scots in September 1483. The Percy retainer Thomas Elrington was renewing the fortifications.[18] Neither exchequer nor signet records reveal how the eastern warden, his troops, and the Berwick and Dunbar garrison were paid no less than £6,482 a year, but presumably it was by assignment from nearby estates. Master Alexander Lee, long a specialist in Scottish affairs, was chamberlain of Berwick at least from 13 March 1485.[19]

Similarly the fortress and garrison of Calais had been commanded by a great nobleman as captain, Warwick officiating from 1456–71 and Hastings from 1471–83. In 1479 Hastings had contracted for a further 10 years.[20] Hastings' death had created a vacancy that was initially filled by John Lord Dynham, but during pleasure, not for life or a fixed term and with the lesser title of warden and governor (*custos et gubernator*). Richard firmly

[14] *Rotuli Scotiae*, eds D. MacPherson, J. Caley, and W. Illingworth (Record Commission, 1814–19), vol. 2, pp. 463–4; Grant, 'Richard III and Scotland', p. 144.

[15] C 81/1327/3, 4, 8, 9,11, 12, 15, 16, 19, 39, 54–5, 57, 63; *Rotuli Scotiae*, vol. 2, p. 468.

[16] Grant, 'Richard III and Scotland', p. 144.

[17] This was misunderstood by Ross, *Richard III*, p. 168.

[18] *Christ Church Letters*, ed. J.B. Sheppard (Camden Society, 1877), p. 46; *H433*, vol. 2, pp. 101–2.

[19] *Rotuli Scotiae*, vol. 2, p. 467.

[20] D. Grummitt, 'William, Lord Hastings, the Calais Garrison, and the Politics of Yorkist England', *Ricardian*, 12 (2001), p. 268.

crossed out the sentence in Dynham's petition that stated he should have the same powers as previous captains and lieutenants.[21] On 14 January 1484 Dynham was calling himself lieutenant general of the town, castle, and marches of Calais.[22] It was not Dynham who appointed the lesser commanders, of Hammes and Rysbank, but the king himself. Richard substituted Lord Mountjoy for Hastings' brother Ralph Hastings at Guines. On 11 September 1483, as an economy measure and 'considering . . . how the season of any gret daungere of adversaries is of likelyhode over past for this yere' – tension had been reduced by the death on 30 August 1483 of King Louis XI – he laid off the emergency crew recruited by Edward V's council.[23] He had to reinstate the crew later. Moreover, Richard intervened directly in the running of Calais by confirming on 'the advice of our council' the ordinances for its government first promulgated by Warwick in 1465,[24] when he had been in Warwick's household. Perhaps he remembered Warwick issuing these ordinances. It is interesting that he chose to confirm them rather than to reshape them into his own. On 11 March 1485 he appointed his young bastard son John of Pontefract (the Lord Bastard) as captain of Calais: a royal figurehead,[25] to whom the lieutenants of the component fortresses were advisers, Dynham being the senior. One such, Sir James Blount, was suborned about October 1484 by his captive the earl of Oxford,[26] but the garrison itself was Richard's resource, no longer that of a noble captain.

Richard had been warden of the Western Marches and lieutenant of the North and was critical of the system of defence. When warden he had seldom visited the border, delegating direct responsibility to Dacre as lieutenant and to Parr at Carlisle at lesser rates of pay. He knew therefore that economies were feasible, admittedly at some risk to security. Richard was poacher turned gamekeeper. Six weeks of warfare was all that he expected

[21] C 81/1529/18; C 76/168 m.11.

[22] C 81/1327/21.

[23] *H433*, vol. 2, pp. 14–15.

[24] C 76/168 m 4; C 81/1530/43; Hicks, *Warwick*, p. 249; D. Grummitt, *The Calais Garrison. War and Military Service in England, 1436–1558* (Boydell & Brewer, 2008), pp. 63–4. Richard confirmed Warwick's ordinances, not Edward IV's *inspeximus* of them, see C 76/149 m.14; C 76/168 m.4.

[25] Grummitt, *Calais Garrison*, p. 70n; *H433*, vol. 1, p. 271; C 76/169 m.5.

[26] J.A. Ross, *John de Vere* (Boydell Press, 2011), p. 82.

of Northumberland before the earl was permitted to withdraw and the crown would take over.[27] The savings in wardens' wages achieved by Edward IV and Richard III equated with the £5,300 (at £438 per month) that the Berwick garrison cost.[28] Of course Richard was aware of the other resources that northern magnates could bring to the borders from their estates in County Durham and Yorkshire. He visited the city of York six times as king, and Durham and Newcastle upon Tyne in June 1484.[29] A forward policy on the borders against Scotland offered opportunities to Northerners and was presumably popular in the region. One key figure was Ratcliffe, a younger son of the Derwentwater family, whom Richard made sheriff of Westmorland for life on Parr's death and lieutenant and lead conservator of the Western Marches.[30] Scarcely anything is known of the personnel involved on the borders or the course of events. Cutting down the responsibilities and emoluments of the wardens may have weakened border defences, but made royal authority more immediate. Richard, it seems, intended to rule the marches more directly than Edward IV had found desirable or feasible.

The northern commands need to be considered in the broader context of the Scottish war, which was a continuous drain on resources. Initially Richard did not see it this way. James III sought peace at once, but Richard was evasive and indeed downright misleading in his responses. The excuses he made for not agreeing a truce have been shown to be disingenuous.[31] Richard wanted to win the war and therefore prolonged it. He intended on 18 February 1484 to lead a full-scale campaign in person the following May.[32] His objectives are uncertain. He was determined to retain Berwick

[27] C 01/1529/29.

[28] If Richard dispensed with wardens altogether. The wardens' fees were cut in 1463–83 from £3,000 in peace or £6,000 in war to £1,333 6s.8d./£1,066 13s.4d. for the East and Middle Marches and £1,250 in peace/£2,500 in war to £120 for the West March, R.L. Storey, 'Wardens of the Marches', *EHR*, 72 (1957), pp. 608, 615n; 'Financial Memoranda', p. 214; *H433*, vol. 3, pp. 12–14.

[29] He bestowed his parliament robe of blue velvet at St Cuthbert's shrine, A.J. Pollard, 'St Cuthbert and the Hog', in *King's and Nobles in the Later Middle Ages*, eds R.A. Griffiths and J.W. Sherborne (Sutton, 1986), p. 118.

[30] Grant, 'Richard III and Scotland', p. 144; *H433*, vol. 1, p. 141. Ratcliffe must have delegated the shrievalty and lieutenancy.

[31] Macdougall, *James III*, pp. 208–9; Grant, 'Richard III and Scotland', pp. 128–9.

[32] Grant, 'Richard III and Scotland', p. 131.

and whatever Debatable Lands he occupied,[33] but perhaps less so Dunbar, which was an important base for campaigns further north, but also an expensive liability, which had to be garrisoned and supplied by sea. Richard wanted to establish his overlordship of Scotland, perhaps also to make Albany into king, both of which he thought attainable, but probably no longer to conquer the Debatable Lands. The Scots wanted peace, but on the status quo of 1482, which would have nullified Richard's achievements in 1480–3 and that required the return of Berwick and Dunbar.

The year 1484 was scheduled for a trial of strength between the two kingdoms. King Richard intended to campaign in person in the summer 'both by sea and land'.[34] The Scottish parliament voted funds for the siege of Dunbar, which was in train in March.[35] Also in March the Scots renewed their Auld Alliance with the French: an unfortunate consequence of Richard's aggression and one that he had apparently not foreseen. These circumstances caused Richard to reconsider: 'Richard, for the first time, seems on the defensive towards Scotland.'[36] On 13 April Richard was considering a cessation of hostilities until 31 October.[37] He was up north from late April to mid-July, basing himself from 27 June to 11 July at Scarborough Castle, whence he could direct a fleet commanded by Lord Scrope of Bolton.[38] It had not been Richard but Howard who had commanded the fleet in 1482–3. The 1484 campaign is not as well documented as those of 1481–3. There survives no heraldic narrative. Finance emanated not from the exchequer, but from the royal chamber, directly under the king's control. The Scottish siege of Dunbar failed, the garrison perhaps being relieved by sea. Sir Thomas Everingham and John Nesfield, two English maritime commanders, were captured by the Scots, but an obscure naval victory rated as significant by Crowland was achieved.[39]

---

[33] *Letters and Papers*, ed. Gairdner (London, 1861–3), vol. 1, p. 56.

[34] D.M. Yorath, ' "There and Back Again":The Career of John Ramsay of Terrenzeane (c. 1464–1513)', *Northern History*, vol 55 (2018), p. 143.

[35] Grant, 'Richard III and Scotland', p. 131.

[36] Ibid., p. 133.

[37] Ibid. However, Richard campaigned and failed rather than he defaulted as suggested by Yorath, 'There and Here Again', p. 143.

[38] Captain '*classis nostre super mare*', C 81/1327/30.

[39] *Crowland*, pp. 172–3. This episode is overlooked by Meek, 'The Career of Sir Thomas Everingham', *HR*, 74 (2001), p. 247.

Richard dropped his proposed campaign. Apparently there was no invasion by land in the eastern marches, but in the west Richard unleashed the exiled earl of Douglas with some English troops in support of the duke of Albany. They were conclusively defeated on 22 July at Lochmaben near Dumfries. Albany escaped, but Douglas at last fell into Scottish hands. The Disinherited were finally quashed.[40] It was Richard's success at sea that Crowland supposed brought the Scots to the negotiating table as petitioners, but it is more likely that the defeat at Lochmaben showed him that victory was not to be achieved easily.

Both sides therefore had failed in their objectives when their negotiators met at Nottingham in September 1484. In this impasse both kings had to accept less than they wanted and to defer the implementation of their policies. The Scot Archibald Whitelaw spoke at length in favour of the *status quo ante*, the return of Berwick and Dunbar in return for lasting peace, but this did not suit King Richard, who joined in person in the early negotiations that proceeded, so Crowland claimed, as the king desired. There was no treaty, merely a three-year truce from Michaelmas 1484 until Michaelmas 1487 and a marriage agreement. For three years Berwick was to remain in English hands, but it was not resigned by the Scots, as Richard surely wished. Richard cannot have been pleased either that the truce covered Dunbar only for six months and then only if ratified by James III: thereafter it could be besieged without impelling full-scale war. Presumably James chose not to object. The future James IV was betrothed to Richard's niece Anne de la Pole, eldest unmarried daughter of his sister Elizabeth Duchess of Suffolk.[41] No dower was agreed. It is unclear why these terms suited Richard. Once the outlines were agreed, Richard handed over to 'his Chancellor and other his Commissaries . . . [to] passe, conclude, write, endent and seel' the details in conjunction with Scottish envoys, his signet and sign manual providing sufficient authority.[42] He had retained Berwick, but Dunbar eventually fell to the Scots in 1485–6. A truce rather than a

[40] *Crowland*, pp. 172–3; Macdougall, *James III*, p. 211.

[41] *Foedera*, vol. 12, pp. 235–47; *Rotuli Scotiae*, vol. 2, pp. 464–6; *Crowland*, pp. 172–3; Grant, 'Richard III and Scotland', pp. 136–41, 193–200. Katherine de la Pole, later Lady Stourton, may have been older and already married.

[42] C 81/1531/11.

treaty allowed the Scots to despatch Sir Alexander Bruce of Earlshall and troops to France that were to fight with Henry Tudor at Bosworth. 'It can scarcely be said that Richard III conducted his relations with Scotland with much ability or discretion', observed Ross.[43] Perhaps, however, this is to take too short a time span. It was in character for Richard to keep his options open to pursue his objectives further in the future. Truces suspended hostilities only briefly.

Moreover, the truce agreement placed on paper comprehensive arrangements for cross-border management. Most of the dozen clauses had antecedents dating to the 1450s, but they had apparently never been treated as a code before. Two provisions were wholly new: that wardens warring during peace were traitors – like Albany and indeed Gloucester – and that there would be regular meetings of commissioners to settle the inevitable breaches of truce. The first four appointments for commissioners to meet were timetabled into the agreement. Northumberland's men were commissioned in the east and Richard's exclusively in the west, where Sir Richard Ratcliffe was the most prominent.[44] 'A joint Anglo-Scottish Council of the Marches' may have been implied, but was not formally established, nor could it be without the commitment of the Scottish king.[45] The English wardens were not abolished, but it was the commissioners who kept the peace in the marches. Such comprehensive regulations recall Richard's urge to codify heraldic practices and the rule of Calais and therefore probably reflect (as Grant suggests) his hand and his initiative. Again Richard's past experiences informed decisions that he might have opposed when duke.

III

Richard did not wish to delegate his power base in the North, nor indeed to transfer his only professional force to a potential rival. Though his son remained in the North as a figurehead to his affinity there, there was no formal transfer of powers, but Prince Edward's death forced a change of plan. By

[43] Ross, *Richard III*, p. 194.
[44] *Foedera*, vol. 12, pp. 246–7: Sir Robert Constable, Sir William Gascoigne, Sir Henry Percy, John Cartington, and Robert Collingwood were Percy retainers; Dacre, Ratcliffe, Richard Salkeld, and William Musgrave were Richard's men.
[45] Grant, 'Richard III and Scotland', pp. 141–4.

rejecting Edward IV's children and his in-laws, Clarence's son Warwick (too close to the throne), and his brother-in-law St Leger, Richard found himself short of royal relatives whom he could trust. John Duke of Suffolk, husband to his sister Elizabeth, never featured in his plans, but roles were found for Suffolk's eldest son John Earl of Lincoln and his daughter Anne. Edward de la Pole was scheduled for the Church: Edward IV and then Richard III had authority from the pope for him to administer a diocese until he was old enough to become bishop.[46] The other brothers (at least three) and sisters might have proved useful in time. Perhaps this paucity of kin was a reason why Richard's bastards were acknowledged and given public roles.

Richard settled Lincoln in the North with a substantial household funded by the crown and with the support of a council, as the focus of devolved royal authority. The model for a council with a royal figurehead had evolved during Edward IV's second reign in Wales. An experiment had then been made to devolve central government in Wales, where Prince Edward and his council had been settled at Ludlow, given control of the principality, county of Chester, all royal, Mortimer, and Lancaster marcher lordships, and oversight of the marcher lordships held by others through indentures of the marches contracted with their lords.[47] Although a member of the prince's council, Duke Richard rarely or never attended meetings at Ludlow and abandoned the Welsh conciliar experiment as king, though bestowing the key offices on Buckingham in the principality and marches (that is, everywhere) whatever their origins and constitutional status. Apparently lessons were learnt from the devolved council experiment by the king himself or by his advisers that were applicable to the North and Calais. Again Northumberland may have expected to succeed Gloucester as lieutenant of the North, but he had instead to be *primus inter pares*, the only man commissioned throughout the North. Lincoln had served against Buckingham's rebels and in April/May 1484, though only 17, he was granted forfeitures and appointed a commissioner of array.[48]

There is no evidence as to whether Prince Edward of Middleham had any function in maintaining Richard's affinity or the informal peacekeeping

[46] He was aged 15 in 1484, *CPL 1471–84*, 13, no. 1, 274. No suitable vacancy arose.
[47] Hicks, *Edward V*, pp. 106–12.
[48] *CPR 1476–85*, pp. 386, 387, 399, 400.

of the ducal council in the year up to his death in spring 1484. Thereafter Richard seems to have determined on more formal arrangements for the governance of the North. Three ordinances effective from 24 July 1484 are contained in Richard's signet book.

The first was a set of 'articles ... ordeyned and Stablisshed by the kinges grace to be used & executed by my lord of Lincolne and the lordes and other of his Counselle in the North parties for his suertie & welthe of thenhabitauntes of the same'. The council's principal function was apparently peacekeeping: to deal with (and indeed pre-empt) riots, assemblies and gatherings, forcible entries, distraints, variances, debates, and 'other mysbehavors ayenst oure lawes and peas' and to hear, examine, and order all 'billes of compleyntes'. It thus combined the roles of the prerogative court of Star Chamber, not yet formally constituted, and of arbitration, criminal and civil justice combined. It was to hold formal sessions quarterly at York and less formal meetings in between. It had no jurisdiction over landed title unless, as in arbitration, both parties submitted themselves to its authority. If sessions coincided with quarter sessions, presumably the sheriff could service them both. The council could subpoena individuals and its correspondence was to be warranted 'by the council of the king' (*per consilium regis*) and the signatures of the councillors. Their authority apparently derived from the commission of the peace, the king's command, and the obedience due from royal officers, both estate and local government. There were rules to ensure the impartiality of councillors. The king's castles would serve as gaols. Lawyers were to attend on the rotation. Although the ordinance is dated, there are blanks in the regulations where the names of the councillors and quorum were to be inserted, which Richard had yet to specify, so the surviving text is a draft. No records of its actions survive.

The second ordnance regulated aspects of Lincoln's household at Sandal Castle, an estate of the Duchy of York south-west of Wakefield and York. Sandal seems a strange choice for a royal household to be preferred to the queen's Neville castles or such Duchy of Lancaster castles as Pontefract where Richard often resided. Sandal's shell keep was small, it was an underfrequented residence, and short of facilities. A new brewhouse and new bakehouse had to be constructed. Henry Lord Morley, a teenaged cousin of Lord Lovell and brother-in-law to Lincoln, headed the king's northern wards living in the household.

The third ordnance assigned revenues worth £1,344 to the household, smallish for a royal household, but larger than most other noble establishments.

Although effective from 24 July 1484, the rules seem underdeveloped, by comparison within the cross-border arrangements devised a couple of months later, and were surely still bedding in a year later at Bosworth. The only officer of the household recorded is John Dawney, the treasurer. The household included Clarence's two children, Edward Earl of Warwick and Margaret.[49] Such northern barons as FitzHugh, Greystoke, Scrope of Bolton, and Scrope of Masham, such leading gentry as Sir John Conyers, such justices and lawyers as Sir James Danby and Miles Metcalfe, as Ross suggests, may have been councillors.[50] A quorum was required for any 'mater of gret weghte or substaunce' comprising Lincoln and two commissioners of the peace 'throughout those parties'. It was Northumberland or Lincoln to whom the City of York were referred in October 1484, though the king still served as backstop.[51] Northumberland's countries, the East Riding and Northumberland, seem likely to have been omitted. The geography of jurisdiction is unclear. Presumably the council did not rule the palatinates of Lancaster and Durham or the other liberties. After an interval, it was revived and developed by the Tudors.[52]

IV

King Richard was also a past constable of England and remained interested in some of its roles even after the appointments in turn of Buckingham and Stanley. He appointed his own man, the Northerner Sir Ralph Ashton, as vice-constable to try Buckingham's rebels.[53] Hence William Worcester

[49] Sutton, Visser-Fuchs and Kleineke, 'Children in the Care of Richard III', *Ricardian*, 24 (2014), p. 32.

[50] Ross, *Richard III*, p. 182. Alternatives or additions were Lords Dacre and Neville, Chief Justice Fairfax or Serjeant Richard Pigot, Archdeacon Poteman and Treasurer Portington.

[51] *York House Books*, vol. 1, pp. 335–7, 341.

[52] *H433*, vol. 3, pp. 107–8, 114–15, vol. 2, p. 168; see also R.R. Reid, *The King's Council in the North* (Longman, 1921).

[53] *CPR 1476–85*, p. 368.

presented the king with his *Boke of Noblesse* and William Caxton presented him with Ramon Lull's chivalric manual. Both men lamented the decline of chivalry. Caxton wanted Richard to institute training jousts.[54] Sympathetic or not, Richard did not do so, perhaps due to the shortness of the reign. To say that Richard brought 'the role of the Constable to an end' is to exaggerate, for the constable's court continued to operate on autopilot, but he certainly circumscribed it by intervening directly in treason trials and incorporating the heralds.[55] Richard III cannot have known that his constable, Lord Stanley, was to be the last to hold the office for life.

Another aspect where there was progress was the reorganisation of the heralds. Richard's ordinances as duke had sought to create and formalise order and a hierarchy of command subordinate to the sovereign where hitherto there was none. As monarch Richard created a fourth king of arms, Gloucester, his former herald Richard Champneys, with responsibility specifically for Wales, who received an annual fee of £20 and livery as in the days of Edward III. King Edward IV had feed only the three kings of arms: Garter, by 1461 his principal herald (£40), Clarencieux for the South (£30, 1476), and Norroy for the North (£20). Richard feed additionally Chester, Windsor, and York heralds (£20), Faucon herald (£40), and the pursuivants Berwick (£10) and Bluemantle. They cost in total about £200 a year.[56] The heraldic establishment was nationalised and became a recurrent charge on the king. There were other heralds like Northumberland's Esperaunce pursuivant that were not paid by the crown. All royal officers of arms received livery as in the time of Edward III. Richard allocated £100 for their largesse at the coronation and granted them freedom from fees and fines at the hanaper.[57]

Richard's reorganisation also incorporated what later became the college of heralds and assigned them premises where they could work, hold meetings, worship, and house their books and records. Richard never

[54] Pollard, *NE England*, p. 214.

[55] A.F. Sutton, 'Admiralty and Constableship of England in the Later Fifteenth Century', in *Courts of Chivalry and Admiralty*, eds Musson and Ramsay (Boydell Press, 2018), pp. 187, 213–4.

[56] *CPR 1461–7*, p. 72; *1476–85*, pp. 389, 415, 465, 482, 522; *H433*, vol. 1, pp. 103. 116, 218; DL 42/20 f. 12v.

[57] *H433*, vol. 1, pp. 68, 157.

visited Paris, but his model could have been nevertheless the chapel in the church beside the Hôtel of St Pol that Charles VI of France had founded for his kings of arms and heralds in 1407.[58] Richard's patent of 2 March 1484 was the culmination of his favour and his earlier ordinances. All the heralds – the kings of arms, heralds and pursuivants – were created a permanent corporate body with its own seal, able to plead and implead. Queen Anne's noble messuage of Coldharbour (le Erber) in the City of London (89 Thames Street) was granted to the 12 principal heralds. This palatial mansion could house the heralds, their libraries and archives,[59] and also presumably the chapter meetings that Richard had already ordained. Of course there was a chapel too. Additionally the heralds were licensed to acquire further property in mortmain worth £20 to endow a priest offering masses for the good estate of the king, queen, and prince, benefactors of the heralds, and their souls after death.[60] Richard did not supply the endowment, which indeed was never acquired. Though highly original, this privilege was thus couched in terms of an alienation in mortmain, and should have created a chantry for King Richard. A college of heralds and premises to house it still exists today.

V

Another structural change may have been in the funding of the royal family. Edward IV's queen had been assigned dowerlands worth £4,300 above reprises a year.[61] Prince Edward was allowed the income of about £4,500 from the principality of Wales, duchy of Cornwall and county Chester – the traditional endowment of princes of Wales – and also of the earldom of March and other marcher lordships in Wales.[62] King Richard made no

---

[58] R. Barber, 'Heralds and the Court of Chivalry: From Collective Memory to Formal Institutions', in Musson and Ramsay, *Courts of Chivalry and Admiralty*, p. 25.

[59] N. Ramsay, 'Richard III and the Office of Arms', in *The Yorkist Age*, eds H. Kleineke and C. Steer (Harlaxton Medieval Studies, 2013), pp. 148–9. Presumably he gave them his two rolls of arms, Sutton, 'Admiralty and Constableship of England', p. 213. Actually le Erber was not Richard's to give as it had been allotted to Clarence in the partition of the Warwick inheritance in 1474–5, *PROME*, vol. 14, p. 359.

[60] *CPR 1476–85*, p. 422; C 66/554 m.5; *Foedera*, vol. 12, p. 215.

[61] A.R. Myers, 'The Household of Queen Elizabeth Woodville, 1466–7', in *Crown, Household and Parliament in Fifteenth Century England*, ed. C.H. Clough (Hambledon Press, 1985), p. 254.

[62] Hicks, *Edward V*, pp. 83–5.

grants at all to his queen and did not concede to his son the revenues from his appanage. Queen Anne did not automatically take over Queen Elizabeth's dower – indeed six receivers of lands late of Dame Elizabeth Grey were accountable to the king on 6 January 1484[63] – and could not have secured obedience from the officers without formal patents. Similarly much of Anne's own inheritance (Barnard Castle, Bawtry, Abergavenny, and Glamorgan) was deployed freely by the king.[64] Presumably she was funded by the treasurer of the chamber and probably at a lower figure.[65] Richard's rearrangements did not endure. Henry VII's and Henry VIII's queens were to have dowerlands of the traditional type. Outgoings were substantially reduced following the deaths of Prince Edward (April 1484) and Queen Anne (March 1485). After the prince's death, the earl of Lincoln's household in the North was assigned approximately 2,000 marks a year from northern estates: much less than the prince's appanage was worth. The line was drawn quite strictly between expenses incurred in the king's service, which were allowable, and his own expenditure, which was not.[66]

The hostile Crowland Continuator was critical of Richard's expenditure, both extraordinary on warfare and everyday on magnificence, of his lavish patronage and on his revenue-raising, but he does not seem to have understood the whole picture and is not perhaps the best guide. Richard seems to have taken over Edward's moveables, his treasure. Richard certainly took possession of some of it and dipped into it, selling some plate and pledging other items.[67] Compensation promised by Edward IV to Breton victims of English piracy must come from this source, Richard declared in July 1483, 'whereof as yet no man hath takyn adminystracion',[68] and indeed, so far as is known, nobody ever did. The repression of Buckingham's Rebellion may have forced Richard to dissipate Edward IV's rich treasure, as Crowland observed. Defensive measures in the South against Henry Tudor thereafter were also costly, but need to be balanced against the resultant enhancement

[63] Wolffe, *Crown Lands*, p. 125.
[64] Ibid., pp. 62, 122, 125, 131.
[65] This deduction corrects that in Hicks, *Anne Neville* (History Press, 2005), p. 188.
[66] *H433*, vol. 3, p. 114.
[67] *H433*, vol. 2, pp. 66–7; *Crowland*, pp. 160–3.
[68] *Letters & Papers*, ed. Gairdner, vol. 1, p. 23.

of royal revenues.[69] Crowland took no account of Edward's enfeoffments. To the income enjoyed by Edward IV, King Richard added most of the revenues of queen and prince, and the estates of himself and his consort, worth somewhere between £8,000 and £10,000 a year, of the Welsh marcher lordships, and the forfeited revenues of Buckingham and other rebels. These forfeitures were the source of the alienations worth £13,500 a year that he granted to his most trusted supporters and religious foundations, the lavish gifts that both Crowland and More condemned, yet substantial amounts remained in hand.[70] For the year 1484–5 Richard assigned £10,674 to his household, almost the same as £11,000 assigned to Edward IV's household in 1483, but made up almost entirely from his land revenues, whereas Edward had drawn £6,000 from the customs, alien subsidy, and other miscellaneous sources,[71] which Richard therefore had uncommitted. Wolffe surely underestimates Richard's land revenues at £22–£25,000.[72] On 4 February 1485 Richard appropriated to the castle of Windsor the lordships and manors of Amersham, Chesham, Datchet, Langley Mareys, Wendover, Wyrardisbury (Wraysbury) in Buckinghamshire; Swallowfield, New Windsor borough, the manors and seven hundreds of Cookham and Bray (Berkshire); and lands in Cleygate, Pirbright, Cold Kennington, Worplesdon (Surrey), and St Margaret's Stratton in Wiltshire.[73] Richard therefore enjoyed an income somewhat greater than his brother, which funded his massive patronage and magnificent lifestyle, but he did need to resort to forced loans in February 1485. Earlier loans from the exchequer, such as the 100 marks each from Kidwelly and Brackenbury at Michaelmas 1484, or the £100 each advanced by Shaa and four monastic superiors on 1 June 1484,[74] probably aided cashflow and were repaid. Unlike his brother's unpopular benevolences, which had been abolished by act of parliament early in 1484, these were not permanent gifts, but loans with dates set (that we do not know) for repayment that fell due after Bosworth.

[69] *Crowland*, pp. 172–3, 184–5.
[70] Wolffe, *Crown Lands*, pp. 61–5.
[71] *PROME*, vol. 14, pp. 414–15; *H433*, vol. 3, pp. 155–8.
[72] Wolffe, *Crown Lands*, p. 64.
[73] *H433*, vol. 2, pp. 197, 223. No assignment for Berwick is recorded.
[74] E 401/950 m. 2; E405/73.

VI

Most kings rewarded their servants 'for service done and to be done' with appointments to offices for life and grants of land in inheritance that the recipients enjoyed – or their heirs held – without further monitoring or regard to the cost. Acts of resumption enabled the review of such patronage and the cancellation of grants that were no longer justifiable. Full-scale resumptions in 1461, 1465, 1467, and 1473 and partial resumptions more frequently enabled Edward IV to claw back lands and offices that were no longer serviceable.[75] Resumption was a facet of the management of the royal demesne. B.P. Wolffe highlighted the expansion of the Yorkist crown estate and improvements in its management: in particular its removal from the tortuous course of the exchequer – henceforth the exchequer was merely briefed on what the king thought it need to know – and its administration by the treasurer of the chamber Thomas Vaughan.[76] Chamber land administration may have been busy early in Edward IV's reign, when the king acquired vast forfeited estates from the defeated Lancastrians, but wholesale grants and numerous restorations of Lancastrians later diminished the crown estate to little more than the Clarence lands – what his brother duke had held in his own right, which was forfeited Lancastrian property, and on behalf of his underage son. Much crown property was exploited instead by the queen and prince. Acts of resumption added remarkably little to the crown's resources, many grants being exempted and offices needing to be renewed, and were perhaps more important as instruments of political control than revenue raising. This decline in the Yorkist estate administration may be symbolised by the appointment of Vaughan simultaneously as treasurer of the prince's household and his consequent residence in Wales.[77] There was not much crown estate to be managed.

Richard started with more lands than his brother – besides the queen's lands and prince's lands, he cancelled Edward IV's enfeoffments – and he added substantial new forfeitures to them. Richard retained existing

[75] Hicks, 'Attainder, Resumption, and Coercion, 1461–1529', in *Rivals*, pp. 71–5.
[76] Wolffe, *Crown Lands*, pp. 51–65.
[77] Hicks, *Edward V*, pp. 93, 95.

administrative structures and officers as far as possible. He grouped his lands into receiverships by county, and authorised those given the rule at particular places to continue, dismiss, and replace officeholders as appropriate. A remembrance on land management survives among his records: not a repetitive reminder or mere continuation of Edward's policy, but a memorandum that systematised and standardised the system that Richard now reinvigorated. Edmund Chaderton, treasurer of Richard's chamber, 'our dearest councillor and chaplain', was charged with implementing it. The tellers' accounts often record cash received by the king himself in his chamber by Chaderton's hand.[78] Chaderton received directly the revenues of 20 receiverships and undertook much of the expenditure. Richard 'revived the chamber system of finance and ran it effectively'. He did much more than transmit Yorkist practice to Henry VII who brought it to fulfilment.[79]

Richard's signet book contains lists of estate revenues, offices, and officeholders, as well as annuities that show that he kept track of his lavish patronage. The forfeitures of Buckingham's rebels meant the king could well afford what he gave away. Moreover, he reserved rents from his donations at the rate of 1 shilling in the mark or 7½ per cent, totalling £700 a year that represented a new and permanent stream of income for the future.[80] Reserved rents were an innovation that was later adopted by Henry VIII when alienating monastic lands. Such rents reminded recipients to whom they owed their estates. It may not have been immediately apparent to Northerners granted lands in tail male that these were subject to review – Richard would surely have secured acts of resumption had he ruled longer – and that their continued tenure would be balanced against the benefits of restoration of repentant rebels and subjected to oversight by the exchequer. Richard was happy for the exchequer to chase up arrears in reserved rents and supplied it with a tabulated list. Chaderton and the chamber were to focus on revenue raising and spending, leaving the exchequer to tackle the laborious and tiresome process of audit.[81]

[78] Wolffe, *Crown Lands*, pp. 119, 132–7; H433, vol. 3, pp. 118–20; C 81/896/513; E 405/72.
[79] The evidence is surveyed by E.J. Bolden, 'Richard III: Central Government and Administration', *Ricardian*, 149 (2000), pp. 75–6; Horrox, *Richard III*, pp. 236–7.
[80] SC 11/ 827.
[81] SC 11/827.

VII

Although reigning for only two years, 'this King Richard', Rous reports, acted as was expected of the best of kings. He 'was praiseworthy for his building, as at Westminster, Nottingham, Warwick, York, and Middleham', and for his religious foundations at Cambridge, Middleham, York, and All Hallows, Barking.[82] While Rous as a cleric approved of religious benefactions, laymen likewise expected conspicuous consumption, piety, and patronage of the Church from their kings. Religion mattered to Richard. He corresponded with the pope. He exercised the extensive ecclesiastical patronage of the crown to favour learned men, especially from the North and Cambridge University: Beverley, Chaderton, Langton, and Redman. Most probably it was at Nottingham that he met the Oxford theologian Dr John Roby, prior of the local Franciscan friary, whom he appointed his confessor in 1485.[83] Richard respected both sanctuary and benefit of clergy, albeit to his own disadvantage. When congratulating the Hungarian visitor Niclas von Popplau on the discomfiture of the Turks, he fantasised about defeating them himself, a conventional aspiration hardly likely to be fulfilled.[84]

Although conventionally pious, Duke Richard had been exceptionally demonstrative and generous in his religious practice. While still a duke he had been an outstanding patron of the Church. Barnard Castle College, Coverham Abbey, Middleham College, and St George's Chapel Windsor were all endowed. He joined Corpus Christi Guild in York and his duchess had become a sister of Durham Cathedral priory. They gave a bell to the shipman's fraternity at Hull and contributed to the glazing of Great Malvern priory. Richard was well versed in the liturgy and enthusiastic about holy music. Already he had developed the distinctive religious preferences that he developed as king, when he had much more to give. The prayers that Richard added to his book of hours present the same picture of a man of conventional piety, acutely conscious of sin, confident of God's

---

[82] Hanham, *Richard III*, p. 121. Not Barnard Castle: evidence perhaps that Barnard Castle College never operated.

[83] *CPR 1476–85*, p. 506; A.B. Emden, *Biographical Register of the University of Oxford to AD 1500*, vol. 3 (Clarendon Press, 1959), p. 1580.

[84] Visser-Fuchs, 'What Niclas von Popplau Really Wrote About Richard III', *Ricardian*, 145 (1999), p. 528.

mercy, and anxious to mitigate his sufferings in purgatory. He asked God to release him from the affliction, temptation, grief, sickness, and danger 'in which I stand'. This was not, however, the self-torture of a man bedevilled by his mortal sins.[85] Richard appears to have attended a mass every day and his progresses took him via many cathedrals and abbeys where he became acquainted with local saints, shrines, and other works deserving of his patronage, and where at the least he made offerings.

Richard was just as concerned as king with the spiritual health of himself, his parents, consort, and son. Additionally his coronation oath committed him to cherish the Church. He routinely received requests to license alienations in mortmain. These had diminished almost to nothing as kings approved ever fewer, as the fines that they levied became prohibitive, and as potential founders, of whom there were still many, enfeoffed their endowments instead, permanently and illegally, and counted on their unlicensed alienations escaping detection and punishment. In his short reign Richard approved 13 licences. The resultant masses benefited the souls not just of the principal benefactors, but invariably also the good estate of the king, queen, and prince while living and their souls after death. These were not Richard's own foundations, although two of them – at the chapel of Hedistaston near Wem in Shropshire and at Riccall in Yorkshire – were each titled the chantry of Richard III.[86] He patronised religious houses wherever he went. He repaid the outstanding costs (£300) of Clarence's tomb to Tewkesbury Abbey, granted a meadow by Worcester castle to the Worcester Franciscans rent free during his pleasure, directed the forfeited revenues of a prebend 'towardes the making of Sainct Osmondes Shryne' in Salisbury Cathedral, and forfeitures worth £3 a year to the maison dieu at Dover.[87] Most of those institutions that he favoured were in the North, which he knew at first hand, such as Coverham Abbey, Monkbretton Priory, and Wilberfosse Priory. He gave five marks a year to the Austin friars of Tickhill in Yorkshire in honour of St Ninian (to whom he had a special devotion), £2 a year to the anchoress at St Helen's church at Pontefract, and £5 towards the cost of a window in

[85] Sutton and Visser-*Fuchs, Hours of Richard III* (A. Sutton, 1990), pp. 77, 83.
[86] *CPR 1476–85*, pp. 385–6, 464, 473, 496, 498, 505, 510, 525; DL 42/20 f.30v; *pace* M.E. Williams, 'Richard III: Chantry Founder', *Notes and Queries*, 167 (1934), pp. 23–5.
[87] *H433*, vol. 1, pp. 88, 152, vol. 2, pp. 7, 214.

Carlisle Cathedral.[88] Just as he had endowed masses at Cambridge as duke for the souls of those in his company slain at Barnet and Tewkesbury in 1471, so now, as king, he gave £5 a year to the Dominicans of Pontefract to keep the obit of his father Richard Duke of York, slain at Wakefield in 1460, contributed £40 to the building and edifying of the large but never finished chapel on the battlefield of Towton (1461), and another seven marks a year to the chaplain celebrating mass there to the souls of the fallen, the good estate in life and souls after death of himself as king and his queen, and to all faithful departed.[89] Most striking perhaps was his munificence to the church of York, which justified Archbishop Rotherham, no longer incarcerated, to title him 'the most Christian prince King Richard III'.[90]

Richard continued with the works on St George's Chapel and the new vicars' lodgings at Windsor commissioned by his brother, though certainly rather more slowly than King Edward had intended. He allocated 250 marks a year for that purpose.[91] Edward IV had wanted to revise and update the chapel statutes and had secured papal authority for the bishop of Salisbury to draft them. Although particularly qualified as prelate of the Garter, this bishop was the diocesan from whose authority the chapel was exempted, and its chapter feared therefore that their exemption from the diocesan might be breached and that his authority would be exercised in future not in accordance with their wishes. That Bishop Richard Beauchamp had been succeeded by Lionel Wydeville may have contributed to Richard's willingness to apply to the pope for this role to be passed to the bishops of London, Lincoln and/or Rochester, then Thomas Kemp, John Russell, and Edmund Audley.[92] Richard also translated the miracle-working remains of King Henry VI from Chertsey Abbey to Windsor, where his shrine on

---

[88] *H433*, vol. 1, pp. 88, 89, 103, 119, vol. 2, p. 28; *CPR 1476–85*, pp. 375, 377, 388, 505–6.

[89] C.D. Ross, 'Some "Servants and Lovers" of Richard in his Youth', in *Richard III: Crown and People*, ed. J. Petre (Sutton, 1985), pp. 146–7; *CPR 1476–85*, DL 42/20 ff.8–9, 12; C 81/893/370; DL 42/20 f. 12v.

[90] See below; Borthwick Institute of Historical Research, archbishops' registers 23 f.99v; 24 f.4; *H433*, vol. 1, p. 88. Unfortunately the published calendar omits such details, *Register of Thomas Rotherham, Archbishop of York, 1480–1500*, i, ed. E.E. Barker, Canterbury and York Society, 69 (1976), 782, p. 96.

[91] *H433*, vol. 1, pp. 204–5, vol. 2, p. 131.

[92] *CPL*, vol. 15, no. 3.

the south side of the high altar, opposite the tomb of Edward IV, became an object of pilgrimage and a source of revenue to the building project.[93]

Richard's own religious foundations as duke were not yet finished. Building work continued on the construction of his two northern colleges at Middleham and Barnard Castle, now retitled as colleges of King Richard III rather than of Richard Duke of Gloucester. The manor of Wiggenhall worth £73 was earmarked for Middleham.[94] That William Beverley, dean of Middleham, was now also dean of the chapel royal may have caused the latter to align its orisons with Richard's own taste.[95] Certainly the music did: in 1484 John Melyonek was authorised to press-gang for the chapel royal all singing men and boys skilled in the science of music – that is, polyphony.[96] This was altogether a distinguished and costly record.

Richard also made three wholly new foundations of his own at Cambridge, York and London. Each was comparable in scale and cost to Henry VI's Eton College and King's College in Cambridge and to Edward IV's St George's Chapel at Windsor, all of which had strained the finances of the founders and had remained unfinished at their deaths. Richard, in comparison, was interested less in splendid architecture than in results, in the multiplication of prayers for his soul. Priests and their masses were funded straight away from income ahead of the endowments and building works.

Back in 1477 Richard had endowed four new fellows and prayers at Queens' College Cambridge. This old endowment (*antiqua dotatio*) was dwarfed by a much larger new endowment (*nova dotatio*) made by him as king. On 25 March 1484, following King Richard's visit to Cambridge University, Master Andrew Doket, the president, and the fellows were licensed to acquire advowsons and lands in mortmain worth 700 marks, above reprises. In fulfilment the king further licensed on 5 July the alienation to the college of lands and fee farms (£170) totalling £329 3s.8d. a year from the inheritance of Queen Anne, at whose request the licence was granted. Several subsequent transactions reveal the college to be in possession.

[93] Hanham, *Richard III*, p. 123.

[94] *H433*, vol. 3, p. 143.

[95] *H433*, vol. 1, pp. 100, 189, 190.

[96] J. Hughes, ' "True Ornaments to Know a Holy Man": Northern Religious Life and the Piety of Richard III', in *The North of England in the Age of Richard III*, ed. A.J. Pollard (Sutton, 1996), pp. 157–8; *H433*, vol. 2, p. 163.

Perhaps the king expected to find the extra £170 later. It seems this new endowment was to fund 33 extra fellows (at approximately £10 each). They would pray for the good estate in life and souls after death of King Richard and Queen Anne and the souls of their fathers, not just his father Richard Duke of York, but her father Warwick the Kingmaker. King Richard intervened four times further to smooth away administrative hurdles: to prevent the hanaper from charging a fine, perhaps at five year's purchase or more than £2,000; to forgive the £20 fee for concord of queen and college in the court of common pleas; to jog the bailiff of Covesgave (Northamptonshire) into paying his arrears for 1484–5 to the college; and to remit a theoretical £7,480 arrears in the fee farm of Aylesbury.[97] Considerable administrative costs were incurred by the college, which may have adopted new arms incorporating Richard's white boar. It was destined to receive new statutes. It was to be retitled as the College of Queen Anne, Saint Margaret and Saint Bernard, thus airbrushing out the former queens and foundresses Margaret of Anjou and Elizabeth Wydeville.[98] This new endowment transformed the fortunes of Queens' College, which should have dwarfed in wealth and numbers King's Hall, Henry VI's Kings College or any other Cambridge institution at this time.

Richard singled out York Minster, the metropolitan cathedral for the North, for especial favour. He presented it with 12 silver gilt statuettes of the apostles and later with a jewelled calvary containing relics of St Peter, its patron saint.[99] York Minster was the location for another major project, his 'noble chantry for a hundred priests in the Cathedral of York'.[100] This new

[97] *H433*, vol. 1, pp. 171, 192, vol. 2, pp 201–2, vol. 3, p. 155; *CPR 1476–85*, pp. 423, 477; C 81/1530/33; E 159/261 brevia Hilary 2 Ric.III m 12; Searle, *History of Queens' College Cambridge* (Cambridge Antiquarian Society, 1867), pp. 95–100, 107–9, 112. See also S. Raban, *Mortmain Legislation and the English Church* (Cambridge University Press, 1982), p. 69; A.B. Cobban, *The King's Hall Within the University of Cambridge in the Later Middle Ages* (Cambridge University Press, 1969), table 4 & appendix.

[98] A.F. Sutton and L. Visser-Fuchs, ' "As dear to him as the Trojans were to Hector": Richard III and the University of Cambridge', in *Richard III and East Anglia: Magnates, Gilds and Learned Men*, ed. L. Visser-Fuchs (Richard III Society, 2010), pp. 126–9 & corrigenda.

[99] Hicks, *Anne Neville*, p. 179; A.F. Sutton, ' "A Curious Searcher for our Weal Public": Richard III, Piety, Chivalry and the Concept of the "Good Prince" ', in *Richard III: Loyalty, Lordship and Law*, ed. P.W. Hammond (Richard III and Yorkist History Trust, 1986), p. 65.

[100] Hanham, *Richard III*, p. 121. Even Polydore Vergil rated this favourably, *English History*, p. 192.

college was the largest chantry foundation in northern England or indeed anywhere. The huge York Minster, only completed in 1472, was seriously understaffed by comparison with the cathedrals of Lincoln, Salisbury and Wells. There were a mere 36 dignitaries and canons, of whom no more than four were actually in residence, and significantly less than the statutory number of 37 vicars choral of the Bedern college could be afforded. These deficiencies may have been partly mitigated by the participation in the main services of the cathedral of the 20 parsons or cantarists. These parsons had been incorporated in 1461 into the new college of St William founded by the Northerners Warwick the Kingmaker and his brother George Neville, then Bishop of Exeter and not yet archbishop. Apart from a site for the college, Edward IV's licence had permitted the acquisition in mortmain of lands worth £100 a year (not 100s. as in Dugdale's *Monasticon*).[101] Warwick's daughter Anne Neville, Richard's queen, was therefore the patron. On his first visit to the North as king in August 1483, Richard had determined to remedy these defects and was credited by Archbishop Rotherham with the improvements. King Richard confirmed the foundation of St William's College on 1 October 1483,[102] but did not apparently endow it. He was also behind the enhancement of two of the minster's dignitaries, the precentor and chancellor, by annexing wealthy prebends to their offices. He restored the vicars choral to their proper numbers by granting them the wealthy rectory of Cottingham, part of his consort's Holland/Salisbury inheritance that had originally been designated in 1478 for Barnard Castle College. Archbishop Rotherham finalised its appropriation on 28 June 1485.[103]

Finally Richard added the college of one hundred priests, dedicated to God and Richard's favourite saints Mary, George, and Ninian. The priests prayed especially for the good estate of himself and his immediate family in life and their souls after death.[104] Undoubtedly the priests shared also in the mainstream minster services. Receivers' accounts prove that the hundred

---

[101] Dugdale, *Monasticon Anglicanum* (1846), vol. 6 (3), pp. 184–5 (a partial transcript of C 66/493 m.17); R.B. Dobson, 'Richard III and the Church of York', *Kings and Nobles in the Later Middle Ages*, eds R.A. Griffiths and J.W. Sherborne (Sutton, 1986), p. 132.

[102] C 81/884/45.

[103] Dobson, 'Richard III and the Church of York', p. 132; F. Harrison, *Life in a Medieval College* (John Murray, 1952), pp. 109–11, *PROME*, vol. 14, p. 360.

[104] Dobson, 'Richard III and the Church of York', pp. 145–6.

priests were in post and paid from Easter 1484.[105] They were not ordained specifically to these chaplaincies, but were drawn instead from the huge floating population of the unbeneficed. They were ecclesiastical foot soldiers, mere chaplains, a grade below the cantarists at Middleham and at least two grades below the highly qualified graduates who became canons at All Hallows Barking. They were paid at most a modest £5 10s. a head. There was considerable scope for extra masses at existing altars in the cathedral, but the fabric accounts reveal the construction of six new altars within the Minster, two begun in the financial year 1483–4 and all completed in 1484–5 at the very modest cost of £13 19s.6d. Eighty-two wainscots, perhaps decorated planking attached to timber frames, were constructed somewhere in the cathedral by seven carpenters over 315 days. They were used to create wooden structures within the Minster,[106] perhaps creating a series of chapels separated by parvis screens, alternatively in the retrochoir/ Lady Chapel, in a transept, or even maybe in the crypt. One of these may have been the altar of St Ninian, Richard's favoured saint, first recorded at this time. Even if the priests celebrated mass on a timeshare basis, six altars alone cannot have sufficed for 100 masses a day, and other existing altars must have been pressed into use. More than six masses were said almost every daylight hour. Apart from the minimum of six clerks needed to say the responses, the new college acquired chalices, vestments, and other paraphernalia that Archbishop Rotherham described as splendid.

Work was also undertaken to create their accommodation, conceivably at St William's College. When St William's was originally founded, no site had been selected, but subsequently that college took over the prebendal house of the prior of Hexham to the east of the cathedral, where a splendid timber range was erected fronting the street and a quadrangle behind. The £19 19s.0¼d clear income in 1546 conferred only the most modest living on the 24 parsons for 'theire lodgynges and commons all together in one house called the College'.[107] The premises have been so much altered

[105] DL 42/20 f. 67A.

[106] *The Fabric Rolls of York Minster*, ed. J. Raine (Surtees Society, 1859), p. 87. The financial year ran from 28 November.

[107] *The Certificate of the Commissioners Appointed to Survey the Chantries, Guilds, Hospitals etc in the County of York*, I, ed. W. Page (Surtees Society, 1894), pp. 7–8.

that it is not apparent today how large was the original hall, nor how numerous were the lodgings. Could it have been completion of this extensive building to accommodate his hundred priests that Richard was funding? Dendrochronological research might answer that question. No head priest for the new college is recorded. It was subordinate to the cathedral chapter and its affairs were managed as proctors, commissioners, and attorneys by the four canons residentiary who were rewarded by Richard with exemption from spiritual taxation.[108] The four canons levied revenues of approximately £472 a year assigned from five Duchy of Lancaster honours in northern England for the wages of hundred priests. There is no record of where other funds for building and equipment came from and what was to be the long-term endowment. All five duchy receivers ignored Richard's first privy seal warrants of 23 September 1484, but did act on reminders correctly made under the duchy seal (2 March 1485), 'we nat willing oure said prestes to be vnpaid of their wages seeing that by their praiers we trust to be made the more acceptable to god and his saints'.[109] Such other necessary documentation as the licence incorporating the cantarists or any statutes are unfortunately lost.[110]

Richard undertook a third major foundation that was wholly new, the erection into a college of the royal chapel of St Mary Barking. This was located north of the parish church of All Hallows Barking (All Hallows by the Tower) in the large churchyard that has since been much reduced by redevelopment and road-widening on every side. Wrongly believed to house the heart of King Richard I, the great crusader, this chapel was distinguished by an image of the Blessed Virgin that commemorated a vision of Mary that appeared to Edward I that had inspired him and future kings of England to victory over the Welsh, the Scots (a cause close to Richard's heart), and indeed the Jews. This image was the object of public veneration and offerings and benefited from a fraudulent indulgence offering 40-days remission from purgatory from visitors who made offerings

[108] Dean Robert Bothe, Treasurer Thomas Portington, Archdeacon William Poteman and Canon John Hert, *H433*, vol. 1, pp. 242, 267; E 159/261 brevia Trinity 2 Ric. III m. 6d; C 81/894/390.

[109] DL 42/20 ff.67A–v; DL 29/263/4126 m 3, 482/7778 m.4, /7779 m. 3d, 500/8103 m.3d; 526/8391 m.4d, /8392 m.6; /554/8784 m.3d

[110] The scheme was committed to parchment, 'vt patet in bulla', *H433*, vol. 1, p. 201.

there. An existing fraternity was chartered in 1442 and acquired statutes in 1470. In 1465 Edward IV made St Mary's into a chapel royal and endowed within it a chantry of two chaplains to celebrate for the good estate of himself, his mother Duchess Cecily, and his brothers the two royal dukes, for their souls after death, and the souls also of his father Richard Duke of York, his brother Edmund Earl of Rutland, 'and especially those who shed their blood for his right'. Edward endowed his chantry from the alien priory of Ogbourne with the manor of Tooting Bec and rectory of Streatham.[111] Since it was so close to the Tower, it is conceivable that King Edward and King Richard did indeed visit the shrine five times a year, as instructed by the legend. Richard's itinerary took him there three times in the summer of 1483.[112] Both kings preferred to develop the chapel, which was immediately to the west of the Tower itself and thus convenient for worship whenever the king was resident, in preference to the chapel of St John the Baptist in the White Tower or St Peter ad Vincula in the outer ward. There were thus several good reasons why Barking chapel should attract the attention of a king hostile to the Scots and already commemorated there. Richard passed it whenever he rode between Westminster and the Tower.

In 1484 King Richard elevated this royal chapel into a college of a dean and six canons, drew up foundation deeds and/or statutes, and conveyed an endowment sufficient to pay each canon about £40 a year, much more than mere chantry priests and at a rate comparable to the larger royal colleges of St Stephen's Westminster (dean and 12 canons, £38 each) and St George's Windsor (dean and 12 canons, £51).[113] The dean and canons cannot have been intended to become mere mass priests. Evidently Richard wanted more such non-resident opportunities in London and in particular to reward his seven chosen graduates instantly. The master of the chapel

---

[111] *CPR 1461–7*, p. 428; E 36/110; *The Religious Houses of London and Middlesex*, eds C.M. Barron and M. Davies (Institute of Historical Research, 2007), p. 227; R.E. Horrox, 'Richard III and All Hallows Barking by the Tower', *Ricardian*, 77 (1982), pp. 38–40. The endowment was conveyed, *H433*, vol. 1, p. 281. Perhaps the grant to the college took priority over that to Sir Thomas Montgomery, Horrox, 'All Hallows', p. 40n.

[112] Lord Chamberlain Lovell paid £1 in offerings, for three days at 6s.8d. each, *H433*, vol. 2, p. 8.

[113] *Valor Ecclesiasticus*, eds J. Caley et al., 7 vols (Record Commission, 1810–34), vol. 2, pp. 153, 430; *London and Middlesex Chantry Certificate 1548*, ed. C.J. Kitching (London Record Society, 1980), no. 190.

had been Master Richard Baldry, whom on 5 March 1484 Richard appointed to a prebend in Tamworth College.[114] Richard's treasurer of the chamber Edmund Chaderton was admitted dean and another six university masters, Baldry being one, were designated as canons. All beneficed elsewhere, they were surely not to officiate in person: vicars choral and clerks are implied. The existing chapel was large enough. It already contained two table tombs and eventually five chantries, but it was demolished on dissolution in 1548. Nothing remains of the fabric and its scale is unknown. Surely therefore some expansion was needed to accommodate the stalls of the chapter and doubtless other chaplains and clerks that Richard needed. The endowments that Richard assigned from forfeited Vere and Stafford lands, worth £492 4s.3d. a year, plus the £15 annuity, totalling £507, outstripped his gifts to all his northern colleges. Barking Abbey surrendered the rectory (advowson) to Dr William Talbot, briefly rector, being compensated with an annuity of £15, and All Hallows parish church was appropriated to the new college. Talbot received Chaderton's former canonry at Southwell Minster.[115] There was a foundation document, perhaps including statutes,[116] which surely explained the purpose of the college and most probably prescribed the liturgy, but this is regrettably lost.

Repeatedly Richard commissioned masses for the estate of his consort, son, and himself in life and for their souls after death. His son Prince Edward died in spring 1484 and was buried locally, probably at Middleham College. His queen Anne Neville died on 16 March 1485 and was interred in Westminster Abbey 'with honours no less than befitted the burial of a queen'. Unfortunately no heraldic account of her funeral survives. Although Rous reports that she was buried in front of the high altar, it seems more likely that it was 'by the south door that leads into St Edward's Chapel'. This should probably be viewed as a temporary resting place, ahead of a worthier tomb for both her and King Richard. Whether Richard planned this to be at Westminster Abbey, which was short of suitable space, at

[114] C 81/895/357.

[115] *Register of Archbishop Rotherham* ed. E.E. Barker, Canterbury and York Society, 69 (1976), vol. 1, p. 95 (no 771–2); *CPR 1476–85*, 470. In March 1484 Richard had also granted him a prebend at Salisbury, C 81/892/338.

[116] *H433*, vol. 1, pp. 279, 281, 286, vol. 2, p. 8, vol. 3, pp 144–5.

Windsor with Edward IV or in York Minster, is not known.[117] Middleham, Barnard Castle, and All Hallows Barking all appear insufficiently grand. Where Richard himself was to be buried was surely specified in his lost will.

VIII

In the two years that were all he was allowed, Richard was extraordinarily active. He wanted to change his military and financial arrangements. He had so many ambitious projects that he wished to fulfil, not some time in the future, but now. All of the king's 'proposed practices . . . straightway to coom to naught', as Polydore Vergil unkindly remarks, but not (in these cases) because Richard was 'sommehat aboue hys power liberall', as More also wrote.[118] Richard set his colleges in operation, funded them, and started the buildings. They failed because his reign ended and he was not able to continue funding them from income. They failed also because the endowments were wrested away, not just those based on forfeitures that were inevitably reversed by his vanquisher, as with the two northern colleges and All Hallows Barking, but because the endowments from Anne's inheritance to Queens' College and the York vicars choral were seized back although they had been donated perfectly legitimately and with proper licences. Within a fortnight of his accession King Henry had wrested Coldharbour from the heralds and transferred it to his mother Margaret Beaufort, whose principal London residence it became.[119] These were vindictive actions by Henry VII that do not detract from Richard's seriousness of purpose. It is testimony to the value of Richard's reforms that several were continued or revived: the court of requests, the council of the North, and the college of heralds.

[117] Hicks, *Anne Neville*, pp. 212–3; *Crowland*, pp. 174–5.

[118] Vergil, *English History*, p. 192; More, *Richard III*, p. 8.

[119] M. Condon, 'Bosworth Field: A Footnote to a Controversy', *Ricardian*, 96 (1987), p. 364.

Chapter Fifteen

SETBACKS AND ADVERSITY 1483–5

I

Richard III was never stronger than in February 1484. Parliament had approved his title, the succession was established, and his enemies routed and attainted. Yet only 18 months later, on 22 August 1485, he was defeated and killed at the battle of Bosworth, and all his plans came to naught. His honeymoon period was very brief. Buckingham's Rebellion, only three months into his reign, has been regarded as the turning point, although Richard's parliament was when he was at his most ascendant. Henceforth the king was always on the defensive. After Buckingham's Rebellion failed, Richard strove to rebuild his regime: to re-establish control over his whole kingdom, to replace the rulers of the South, to destroy his rivals, to achieve international recognition, and to extradite Henry Tudor. Had he been successful – had Henry Tudor been prevented from launching his invasion – Richard might have retained his throne. This chapter considers what else went wrong from Richard's point of view. That his immediate family died, that he lost the propaganda war, and that his foes were able to prepare a formidable invading force were three factors that weakened his hold on power. Surviving evidence does not permit the judgement that Tudor's invasion was bound to succeed.

II

Richard lacked one key source of strength for English medieval kings. This was a royal family that gave substance to his court, that assured him the succession, that constituted the top rank of society, that deputised for him in the components of his kingdom and the great honorary offices, that bound his greatest subjects to him and his cause, and that could bind foreign powers to England by marriage. This was very largely his own fault. King Richard had disqualified Edward IV's queen, sons, and daughters from royalty, and hence those Wydeville in-laws who had tied the noble families of Stafford, Bourchier, and Grey of Ruthin to the crown. He had disparaged the offspring of his brother Clarence and his sister Anne Duchess of Exeter and had even executed St Leger, her widower, and his brother-in-law. He had his cousin the Duke of Buckingham beheaded. Only the de la Poles, the family of his sister Elizabeth, her husband John Duke of Suffolk, and their numerous progeny remained royal. The oldest of his de la Pole nephews and nieces were teenagers just mature enough to become useful, but they did not add anything to his political or military strength. Admittedly Richard did acknowledge two bastards. Richard's nuclear family was exceptionally small, comprising only his queen and son, and diminished over time.

Edward of Middleham remained in the North during the first year of Richard's reign. His investiture as Prince of Wales in August 1483 and the oaths tendered to him as heir apparent in February 1484 reveal him as Richard's hope for the future, the destiny of the new dynasty, and what alone gave his regime a future beyond Richard's own lifespan. Not merely a political symbol, Edward was apparently the cherished only child of his parents, the king and queen, father and mother, who suffered perfectly natural distress when he died suddenly in April 1484.[1] Prince Edward's death made a key political issue of the succession. John Rous reports that Richard turned first as heir apparent to Edward Earl of Warwick, son of his late brother Clarence, but dropped him as a potential successor. Instead he elevated to next in line his senior nephew, John de la Pole, Earl of Lincoln,

---

[1] 'Almost out of their minds for a long time when faced with sudden grief', *Crowland*, pp. 170–1.

born in 1467, whose family pedigree roll proudly boasted his new status.[2] Of course these expedients were meant to be temporary. Richard did not intend dying any time soon and did not plan on his demise that either Warwick or Lincoln would succeed him, for he had every intention of marrying again and fathering further sons of his own. While he had plenty of time physiologically, politically he needed further offspring quickly.

Richard also acknowledged publicly his two bastards Katherine Plantagenet and John of Pontefract, and accepted responsibility for them. Moreover, extramarital sex is implied in September 1483 by the 'sensual pleasure' that Bishop Langton deplored and perhaps even by the excessive attention to singing and dancing at Christmas 1484 that Crowland lamented.[3] Richard perceived none of the incompatibility or hypocrisy that modern historians have remarked in denouncing the infidelities of his brother, the Greys and the Wydevilles, and yet fathering and advancing his own bastards. He even pressed his bastards into public service.

Richard had time to father further legitimate children who would be his heirs. Since he himself was aged only 31 and his queen was aged only 28, they had many years of potential propagation ahead of them. They were still sleeping together but no pregnancies resulted. There can be little doubt that it was Queen Anne, who had borne only one live child during a dozen years of marriage, and that eight years previously, whose fertility was at fault. She was in bad health. Royal doctors recommended abstention from intercourse, so Richard gave up trying about Christmas 1484.[4] The easy solution adopted by King John and some preconquest monarchs, to set the queen aside and substitute a newer model better able to bear children, was no longer canonically acceptable. It was to take Henry VIII longer than Richard's whole reign to replace Queen Catherine of Aragon with Anne Boleyn. For Richard, however, there was an easier option, since his marriage was never valid and the necessity to persist with it had passed. It had never been feasible for Richard to reveal that he was related to Anne twice over

[2] P. Morgan, ' "Those Were the Days": A Yorkist Pedigree Roll', in *Estrangement, Enterprise and Education in Fifteenth Century England*, eds S. Michalove and A. Compton Reeves (Sutton, 1998), p. 114 & pl.1.

[3] Hanham, *Richard III*, p. 50; *Crowland*, pp. 174–5.

[4] *Crowland*, pp. 174–5.

in the second degree of consanguinity and that this impediment had not been adequately dispensed, because then his only son Prince Edward would have been bastardised. The prince's death removed that obstacle. By simply revealing the undispensed impediment, King Richard could rid himself of his queen and free himself to marry again. This course of action did carry disadvantages: the revelation that the king had lived in sin for a dozen years, the loss of his right to Anne's inheritance, and potentially the loss also of the loyalty of those whose devotion was primarily to the Warwick inheritance that Anne encapsulated. Yet Richard seems to have favoured this option. Without revealing the grounds on which the marriage could be nullified, 'it was said by many' (states Crowland) that Richard was considering 'a divorce for which he believed he had sufficient grounds'.[5] That Crowland himself did not know the grounds that have been uncovered by modern research makes his account more credible. Actually no divorce was needed because Queen Anne died on 16 March 1485. However politically convenient, Richard may well have been 'as sorye & in hert as hevye as man myght be' at her demise.[6]

Richard did not allow his sorrow and mourning to impede his imperative to father an heir and hence to remarry as soon as possible. It was a political necessity. He was already seeking a spouse within a week of Anne's death.[7] The prerequisite for this strategy, a nubile queen, had been located before Anne's death in Elizabeth of York, the senior of the bastardised daughters of Edward IV and Richard's niece. That Richard planned to marry her cannot really be doubted since Polydore Vergil, the official Tudor historian, admitted it, while claiming that the match was against Elizabeth's will.[8] To write otherwise would have damaged the reputation of the ancestress of all future Tudors. Elizabeth attended the Christmas festivities at court in 1484, was attired like Queen Anne whom she resembled

[5] For the fullest discussion, see Hicks, *Anne Neville*, pp. 194–211, and sources there cited; *Crowland*, pp. 174–7.

[6] *Acts of Court of the Mercers' Company*, eds L. Lyell and C.D. Watney (Cambridge University Press, 1936), pp. 173–4.

[7] J. Ashdown-Hill, *The Last Days of Richard III* (The History Press, 2010), p. 26.

[8] *The Anglica Historia of Polydore Vergil, AD 1485–1537*, ed. D. Hay, Camden 3rd series 64 (London Historical Society, 1950), pp. 2–3. The best discussion of this topic is now Hicks, *Anne Neville*, pp. 194–210.

physically, and may therefore have appealed sexually to the king. Most probably she danced with him. Already she was rumoured to be Richard's preferred spouse. The story leaked into the public domain. To marry Elizabeth would strengthen Richard's own title with those who disputed his right and would also have deprived Henry Tudor of the bride he needed to retain the support of the rebel Yorkist establishment. The Jacobean historian Sir George Buck quoted a letter showing that Elizabeth approved of the match although, reports Vergil after the king's death, she declared 'a singular aversion' to being 'united to a man who is the enemy of my family'.[9] If she approved, the implication is that her mother Queen Elizabeth and her Wydeville relatives also did so too. The approval of neither the princess nor the queen was necessary for such a marriage to take place, since the younger Elizabeth was a royal ward whose hand was in the king's gift. Political pragmatism demanded that Richard overlooked her bastardy and her Wydeville ancestry. Additionally he had to engage in incest with his niece, an extremely sinful practice that was far within the prohibited degrees and was strictly forbidden. Yet both Crowland and the official Tudor historian Polydore Vergil believed the match to have been Richard's intent.

While the Bible does not specifically mention uncle–niece marriage, it was so interpreted by many canon lawyers; hence a dozen doctors of theology objected: 'the Pope had no power of dispensation over that degree of consanguinity'.[10] Richard was not sensitive to such considerations. Witness the invalidity of his first marriage. He had a track record, moreover, of overcoming impossible obstacles, both in securing the Warwick inheritance on his own terms and in framing a title to the crown. He knew that the canon lawyers, who mattered more in such cases than the theologians, could bend the law of the Church, find exceptions to it and precedents, and as a matter of course had often to reconcile contradictory passages in the Bible. The pope could make incest acceptable not just to both parties, but to everyone else. Popes had indeed allowed such exceptions to canon law before, for instance for Henry IV's son Thomas Duke of Clarence

<hr />

[9] Ibid.
[10] *Crowland*, pp. 176–7.

(d. 1421) and his aunt by marriage Margaret Holland, and popes were to permit others in the 1490s. To seek papal permission of course necessitated delaying the wedding, although a retrospective dispensation after marriage was conceivable. Richard may have calculated that the pope could be induced to remove any objections retrospectively. English revulsion at his incestuous proposal might not have been dissipated so easily. The rejection by the English, in contradiction to the rest of Catholic Christendom, of the legitimation of bastards whose parents had married, and especially of the Beauforts, is instructive here. Legality might not be enough to sway public opinion.

For the scheme to achieve all its political objectives, of course, it was necessary for such a marriage to be public and recognised as valid. Actually, however, some of those loyal to Queen Anne and fearful of Elizabeth's vengeance for the deaths of her uncle Earl Rivers and brother Lord Richard Grey, objected decisively. They had the matter discussed at the royal council. Ratcliffe and Catesby threatened the king with the loss of the Northerners, his principal supporters, although one might suppose that by this date the king had generated much loyalty to himself. The opinion of the theologians was paraded. Richard yielded. He withdrew the proposal, at least for the moment, and was obliged to declare in public on 30 March 1485 at St John's Hall in Clerkenwell to the mayor and citizens of London that no such match was proposed and also that he had not poisoned his queen. This was a necessary humiliation. His declaration was not credited, Crowland writes, since it was made 'as many people believed, more by the will of these counsellors than his own'.[11] Richard had Elizabeth removed to Sheriff Hutton. Apart from secreting her from his Tudor enemies, he had not yet decided conclusively what to do with her. As on previous occasions, would he try again?

Yet Elizabeth of York was never Richard's only potential spouse. Elizabeth offered particular advantages, but Richard could not afford to wait. He looked therefore to the foreign princesses who were the normal consorts of English kings and to whom marriage implied the international recognition for him that he also needed and his integration into European

[11] *Crowland*, pp. 176–7; *Acts of Court*, eds Lyell and Watney, pp. 173–4.

royalty. Both proposals are wholly unnoticed in the English records and narratives, but there is some quite circumstantial and convincing evidence for them in Portugal. The second scheme pursued simultaneously with Portuguese approval was a double marriage with Portugal, which would have delivered Richard a potentially childbearing consort in Joan, sister of King John II (1481–95) and would also have disposed of Elizabeth in matrimony to the Duke of Beja, later King Manuel I (1495–1521). Princess Joan was religious and preferred not to marry anyone, but her wishes were overruled by John II. A 32-year-old queen who preferred chastity was not the ideal mate for a sensual king urgently in need of children. Unlike the English, foreigners accepted all children of married parents as legitimate and therefore rated Elizabeth of York as a princess. Such a diplomatic marriage would ensure that Elizabeth, like her sister Cecily, could not wed Henry Tudor. Any offspring born to her overseas would be disqualified by statute from the English crown. Less important was the vestigial Lancastrian claim of the Portuguese princess to the English throne, unrecognised in England but superior to Henry Tudor's, via Philippa eldest daughter of John of Gaunt by Blanche of Lancaster.[12]

A third option under consideration by Richard was to match himself with the Infanta Princess Isabella (b. 1470), the eldest daughter of King Ferdinand and Queen Isabella of Spain. She too had superior Lancastrian descent. 'It suits the king of England to marry straight away.'[13] Neither Joan nor Isabella were known in person to King Richard. While the Portuguese match was apparently favoured by the Portuguese council and in principle by Princess Joan herself,[14] it is uncertain where each stood in Richard's pecking order or indeed whether the proposals originated abroad and were known to Richard. There was certainly no agreement on such key details as the potential brides' dowries and dowerlands and no dispensations of their distant consanguinity. None of these deals could be clinched before the battle of Bosworth.

[12] Those born abroad were ineligible to inherit in England.

[13] Ashdown-Hill, *Last Days*, pp. 26–9. There are no English sources; the information is from Portugal.

[14] B. Williams, 'The Portuguese Connection and the Significance of "the Holy Princess" ', *Ricardian*, 80 (1980), pp. 139–42; D. Court, 'The Portuguese Connection – A Communication', *Ricardian*, 81 (1983), pp. 191–2.

The loss of his queen and son and the delay in remarrying weakened King Richard, who was no longer head of a dynasty, but an individual whose personal character, reputation, and notoriety became stronger factors in attracting or deterring support.

III

Up to his usurpation Richard had managed public opinion very effectively and had easily defeated the alternative versions and interpretations offered by the Wydevilles. He was, wrote Ross, 'the first English king to use character-assassination as a deliberate instrument of policy'.[15]

Richard realised that it was not just the royal council and the aristocracy that he needed to convince, neuter, or defeat, but also the local political elites, especially of London and its populace. It had been the populace beyond numbering that had swept away governments in 1460 and 1470. Richard had scrupulously informed and regularly updated not just Edward V's council, but also the London corporation, livery companies, and populace. Plausible explanations and justifications were offered at every point. Then the case for his kingship that was *Titulus Regulus* was proclaimed and republished to audiences of the London elite and mob, to the Calais garrison, to parliament, and perhaps also to those of whatever rank and locality to whom his oath of allegiance was tendered. Once he was king, Richard was entitled to everybody's obedience, loyalty, and service. He repeatedly declared his commitment to good rule and justice to all, to the commons as well as the political elite. An economic upturn may have generated greater contentment and thus removed any impulse among the people to explode into rebellion. His proclamations warned the commons against being 'abused and blynded' and encouraged defections from the rebels.

Richard addressed other more limited audiences and told them what they wanted to hear. He thanked James Earl of Desmond for the valuable service of his father Earl Thomas to Richard's own father Richard Duke of York. King Richard had been too young to be implicated in the execution in 1468 of Earl Thomas by the English Lord Deputy. He commiserated

[15] Ross, *Richard III*, p. 138.

now with Earl James and recalled how his own brother Clarence had also been 'extorciously slayne and murdred'.[16] He did not mention his own compliance in that event. His honourable reinterment of Henry VI at Windsor may have been designed to deflect criticism from his own role in the sainted king's murder. To the Hungarian visitor Niclas von Popplau he declared his desire to fight the Turks: at best a very distant prospect backed up at this stage with no practical support.[17]

Richard's rival Henry Tudor deployed different aspects of his title to different audiences. To the Yorkists in Brittany and France, it was his betrothal to Elizabeth of York that mattered. They committed themselves by oath to him in her right at Rennes Cathedral at Christmas 1483.[18] He was content to allow the French to suppose him to be a son of Henry VI – indeed they must have been so informed – which nobody English could credit. And his English correspondents, it seems, were told simply that he was rightful heir without further explanation. In his letters to England Henry even adopted the royal style, that he was already king, and therefore that Richard was the traitor.[19] Perhaps Richard's greatest strength was that Tudor's title was so weak. He made the most of it. 'Henry Tydder' was declared to be 'of bastard bloode both of ffather side and mother side'.[20] In the fifteenth century the English took legitimate birth exceptionally seriously and were less willing to credit the legitimation of Tudor's great-grandfather John Beaufort, earl of Somerset than his base birth. It remains uncertain whether Tudor's own father Edmund Earl of Richmond was the product of a marriage between Queen Katherine and Owen Tudor or a mere liaison. Surely nobody in England believed Henry was son to Henry VI and Lancastrians, if any, knew that others had better Lancastrian titles than him. There was an illogicality in a title derived via a female, his mother Margaret Beaufort who was still living, from the Beauforts whose claim if

[16] *Letters and Papers*, ed. Gairdner (London, 1861–3), vol. 1, p. 68.

[17] L. Visser-Fuchs, 'What Niclas von Popplau Really Wrote About Richard III', *Ricardian*, 145 (1999), pp. 527–8.

[18] Griffiths and Thomas, *Tudor Dynasty* (History Press, 1985), pp. 102–3.

[19] Ibid., pp. 125–6; R.E. Horrox, 'Henry Tudor's Letters to England during Richard's Reign', *Ricardian*, 80 (1983), pp. 155–7; Hicks, *Richard III*, pp. 173–82; M.K. Jones, *Bosworth 1485* (Tempus, 2002), p. 123.

[20] *Paston Letters*, ed. J. Gairdner, 6 vols (Chatto & Windus, 1904), vol. 6, p. 82.

any was as male heirs. Henry relied on coupling himself to Elizabeth of York, whose hand in marriage could become available only after victory. But it was the fact that Henry was not Richard that was his strongest suit.

Richard's proclamations also exposed his enemies as traitors, allies of the king's foreign enemies. Many of them stood attainted by parliament for past treasons and all now, having 'forsakyn there naturall countrey', aligned themselves first with Brittany and then with France. They updated Richard's charges of sexual immorality to cover the illegitimate descent of Henry Tudor on both sides. Such smears appealed to universal values and may have deterred potential rebels. So Richard apparently judged when he recycled them in 1484–5.[21]

Since there survive none of the opposition's proclamations, manifestos, bills, and placards that are known once to have existed, still less the slanders, rumours, and 'fake news' that definitely circulated, it is not possible to assess the thrust of Tudor propaganda, although Richard was so fearful that he wanted it not only torn down and sent to him, but also forbade it to be read. How was Henry's title promoted? The three letters he wrote when claiming already to be king in 1485 refer without explanation to 'my rightful claim due and lineall inheritance' and 'to us of right appertaining'. Richard is labelled a usurper, which he certainly was, a 'homicide and unnatural tyrant'. Was any appeal made to the common good or to good governance? One of these letters refers to Welsh liberties and the relief of the Welsh from servitude and to England's restoration to its 'ancient estate, honour, and property and prosperities'.[22] If there is little explicit here, it should be remembered that these are directed to a local audience of committed supporters and may well be reminders of larger promises made elsewhere.

Also recorded is Collingborne's humorous couplet:

The Catte the Ratte and Lovell owre dogge
Rulen all Engeland, undyr an hogge.[23]

[21] Ibid., vol. 6, pp. 81–4.
[22] Horrox, 'Henry Tudor's Letters', pp. 155–8.
[23] *Great Chronicle of London*, eds A.H. Thomas and I.D. Thornley (Guildhall Library, 1938), p. 236.

The cat and rat of course were Catesby and Ratcliffe; Richard's badge was the white boar – the hog. Lovell's emblem was actually a white lion rampant. Read in isolation, this couplet transmits little meaning, and needs supplementing by other knowledge, documentation, or by popular tradition. Are these the opening lines of a larger poem, now lost? The two lines ridicule three of Richard's most prominent adherents, who may perhaps be equated with the longer lists of evil councillors denounced in the first and second wars. By implication these three exerted undue influence. Catesby was a mere esquire and a Midlander; only Ratcliffe was a Northerner. The bestial imagery perhaps mirrors bestial government. Even if the couplet had wider currency than the single surviving reference, Richard surely cannot have been much concerned.

What the Tudor propagandists did far more successfully was to disparage Richard's character: not just from his death for all eternity, but during his life and reign. Richard was believed to have killed the two little Princes in the Tower, Edward V and his brother Richard Duke of York. While undoubtedly sinful and answerable to God, such an action had many precedents in the murder of Prince Arthur by King John and the violent deaths of three deposed kings – Edward II, Richard II, and Henry VI. While those earlier culprits had concealed what actually happened – wild speculation seems to have become rife – the despatch of their predecessors had not prevented Edward III, Henry IV, and Edward IV from having successful reigns. The princes, however, were different. An anonymous Tudor propagandist made brilliant capital of their disappearance. Although their bodies were not found and their fate never substantiated, the allegation that they were murdered by King Richard seems universally to have become believed. It was made the more heinous and aggravated because they were innocent children, infants, babes, helpless, and in his care as protector. All these were loaded terms. 'Innocent' in particular prompted comparison with King Herod, that most wicked of biblical rulers, who massacred the Holy Innocents in an attempt to slay the infant Jesus. Hence the casual references by Henry Tudor to Richard as a 'homicide' and to the 'shedding of innocent blood' on King Henry's first parliament roll.[24]

---

[24] Hicks, *Richard III*, p. 178; Horrox, 'Henry Tudor's Letters', p. 155; *PROME*, vol. 15.

There was no need to prove what was notorious and regarded as uncontentious, indeed unquestionable.

Richard was blamed also for the 'boocherly' death of the simple and even saintly king Henry VI, an act comparable in cruelty to the actions of the notorious John Tiptoft, Earl of Worcester, the 'Butcher of England'.[25] That Richard reinterred King Henry at Windsor may have stilled some criticism, but the allegation lingered on. And finally Richard's proposal to marry Elizabeth of York not only failed, but was exploited as incestuous and compounded by the poisoning attributed to him of his consort Queen Anne. Richard's public statements, so effective in the weeks before his accession, were discredited afterwards. Queen Elizabeth, who had rejected his promises in May and June 1483, insisted on the most explicit public guarantees when quitting sanctuary. The rumours that circulated that Richard intended an incestuous marriage with his niece and that he had poisoned his queen were so widely credited that Richard was obliged to deny them publicly. Most likely the poisoning story was untrue – unnecessary both because divorce was feasible and because his queen died naturally – but his denial, so Crowland reports, was not believed and recurs as fact in 1512 in Robert Fabyan's *Great Chronicle of London*. Although writing almost 30 years later, Fabyan recalled after Easter 1485 that 'much whispering was among the people' about the deaths of the princes and his queen, 'which Rumours & sayyngys cawsid hym wyth other thyngys beffore doon to ffall In grete hatered of his subgectys as well of men of [good be]havour as of othir'. They would even prefer to be French to being subject to Richard.[26] A king whose word was no longer believed had lost the automatic allegiance and obedience that gave all kings their preeminence. Londoners at least therefore may have been unwilling to fight for him, if not perhaps to back his rival.

Tudor propaganda does not appear greatly to have increased the numbers to fight for Henry Tudor, but it may have deterred subjects from

[25] More, *Richard III*, p. 8. The term 'carnifex' was applied to Worcester during in Richard's lifetime, see *Chronicle of the First Thirteen Years of the Reign of King Edward the Fourth*, ed. J.O. Halliwell (Camden Society, 1839), p. 63.

[26] Lyell and Watney, *Acts of Court*, pp. 173–4; *Crowland*, pp. 176–7; *Great Chronicle*, pp. 234–6.

mustering for Richard and from fighting for him. None of this would have
mattered had Richard not had a rival beyond his reach and protected by
his foreign neighbours.

IV

Richard took a more aggressive line than Edward IV towards Brittany,
France, and Scotland. From his accession he supported English privateers.
He wanted to compel foreign powers to recognise his legitimacy and to
assist in the extradition of Henry Tudor. This strategy failed completely.
Far from submitting, his neighbours looked for allies, sought to destabilise
his regime, and/or used such threats to extract concessions from him. The
death of Louis XI and the succession of the child Charles VIII in August
1483 should have removed any threat from France, but Richard's aggression prompted the regency to revive their alliance with the Scots and to
back Richard's enemies, both in exile and for an attack on England. The
French feared another English invasion, a revival of the English claim to
France and the resumption of the Hundred Years War. Richard's long-
term intentions were (and are) not known and overseas adventures were
certainly not imminent. The Bretons, Archduke Maximilian and the
Burgundians, and Queen Isabella of Spain, who all had their own reasons
to be hostile to the French, offered military support in such an eventuality.[27] Threatened by King Richard, Duke Francis II of Brittany did not
surrender the Tudors and other English exiles, preferring instead to retain
them as bargaining tools. If he secured what he wanted, Duke Francis
might then have arrested or even extradited Henry Tudor – although the
English exiles constituted a substantial military force – but instead about
September 1484 first Henry and then the other English crossed into France
to the protection of the regency government.[28] Tudor's capacity to foment
disorder in England was attractive to the French, who duly provided the
necessary resources for the invasion that ended at Bosworth.

Far from accepting Richard's overlordship, Scotland resisted at prohibitive cost to him and instead aligned with his enemies. Following Edward

[27] *Letters and Papers*, ed. Gairdner, vol. 1, pp. 31–2, vol. 2, p. 24.
[28] Ross, *Richard III*, pp. 196–200.

IV's death, Richard had fanned the outbreak of piracy in the Channel in order to put pressure on the Bretons and the French. Richard sought to deter the Bretons from harbouring Edward Wydeville and later to desert and ideally extradite Henry Tudor. Duke Francis was politically weak and the minority regime of King Charles VIII should also have been ineffective. However, both parties refused and became England's enemies. Duke Francis allowed and financed the ships and troops needed for Tudor's participation in Buckingham's Rebellion. When Tudor and many discomfited southern gentry returned before Christmas 1483, the Bretons received them and resourced them. Eventually they numbered about 500. Breton privateers joined up with the French, whose admiral in 1484 defeated a privateering squadron from Bristol and may indeed have pillaged Bristol itself. The privateering of the English may also have pressured Brittany towards accommodation with England. Richard did have a useful bargaining chip in Brittany's demand for English archers as defence against the French, but he consistently offered less than were needed and supplied in June 1484 only a thousand bowmen under the command of John Lord Grey of Powis.[29] Richard can hardly be blamed for this, however, since a mere thousand archers paid 6d per day cost £9,125 a year – significantly more than the Berwick garrison (£7,625) that was so hard to finance – and the 4,000 archers requested at £36,500 a year were quite beyond England's means.[30] Finally Richard persuaded Pierre de Landais, leader of the dominant Breton faction, that it was in his interests to detain the English exiles, but before he could act Henry Tudor escaped to France, where the dominant faction of Anne of Beaujeu not only harboured him, but proved much more dangerous backers than the Bretons had been. Four times previously – in 1460, 1469, 1470, and 1471 – foreign-backed expeditions had dislodged English governments: none had started with so many foreign troops as in 1485.

The French gave Tudor at least 40,000 livres tournois and lent him more, which he was able to use to secure 15 ships and perhaps as many as

---

[29] Ibid., pp. 194–7, 199.
[30] For the rate per day, excluding rewards and other expenses, see Barnard, *Edward IV's French Expedition* (Clarendon Press, 1925), p. 8.

4,000 men.[31] This was much more than the tiny force supplied to Jasper
Tudor in the 1460s, to Edward IV in 1471, to Oxford in 1473–4, even to
Warwick in 1470, and probably more than any of the previous expeditionary forces during the Wars of the Roses. Apart from about 500 English
exiles, Tudor may have commanded 1,500 French troops led by the
Savoyard Philibert de Chandée and 1,000 Scots under Sir Alexander
Bruce. All were professionals, trained and presumably equipped to continental standards. Whether they were equipped with 16-foot pikes, as
suggested by Michael Jones, or accompanied by significant artillery remains
uncertain and perhaps unlikely. There were enough of them to brush aside
any defenders at Milford Haven: the escort of the admiral of France
ensured their safe arrival there. There was no popular component to
Henry's forces.

V

Henry chose not to build his invasion on supporters within England, but it
may well be that treasons among such men significantly weakened Richard's
authority. A series of conspiracies, none of them particularly extensive,
suborned local gentry who urged Henry's return and sent him money.
Perhaps most of those who had submitted earlier, who had paid fines and
sealed recognisances, declined to plot further, but some were undeterred.
Not all those who submitted were truly reconciled. Some continued to
conspire, such as Richard Edgecombe of Cotehele in Cornwall and
William Collingbourne, or defected abroad, like William Berkeley by
October 1484, and Robert Skerne of Kingston-on-Thames.[32] There was a
trickle of deserters, most notably Sir James Blount with a chunk of the
Calais garrison from Hammes Castle, Sir William Berkeley of Beverstone
whom Richard had pardoned and, on the eve of Bosworth, Walter
Hungerford and Sir Thomas Bourchier.[33] 'Soom man of name passyd over
dayly unto Henry',[34] wrote Polydore Vergil much later, with considerable

---

[31] This is a maximum. The 2,000 proposed by Foard and Curry seems on the low side,
Bosworth 1485 (Oxbow Books, 2013), p. 26.

[32] Horrox, *Richard III*, p. 324.

[33] Ibid.; C. Skidmore, *Bosworth* (Weidenfeld & Nicolson, 2013), p. 206.

[34] Vergil, *English History*, p. 212.

exaggeration. Undoubtedly Berkeley hoped for the overthrow of Richard's regime that did eventually come to pass. Recognisances could not bind those committed to the other side, who were prepared to take the risk, to embarrass their sureties, and/or who were otherwise frightened by the regime. Certainly Richard mistrusted the sincerity of these submissions so much that he did not restore any such men to responsible local government office before his own demise.

Richard's patronage was designed not just to underpin his plantation of trustworthy rulers in the South and elsewhere, but also to reward his adherents for services done and to be done and to commit them by self-interest to his continued rule and to risk their lives for his cause. He created vested interests in his success. Actually, however, he may have viewed these measures as temporary. The defeat of Henry Tudor would ideally involve the submission of his adherents, who could then be restored to their property and resume the county offices from which they had been dismissed, obviously in lieu of the Northerners that Richard had inserted in their places. Some of Richard's supporters recognised this reality and chose therefore to reach private (and permanent) agreements with offenders for portions of their estates. While Northumberland was providing for his son Alan when securing the grant of Holderness to them jointly, most probably he was also recognising that Percy tenure of the lordship was likely to be brief and that this great lordship could never be incorporated in his estate. That some pardons and restorations had already happened before Bosworth may have weakened the call of self-interest. All recipients of such patronage lost their grants after Bosworth: how many decided such uncertain gains not to be worth the risk?

Obviously for those who did take the decisive steps of treason, conspiracy, or rebellion, all of which entailed forfeiture, the exaction of their bond was no additional deterrent. Dire threats for not turning out were probably bluff and anyway enforceable only if the king won. Richard also took hostages, notably the sons of Rhys ap Thomas and Lord Stanley, whose lives were hazarded by the acts of treason of their fathers. Both fathers nevertheless joined Henry Tudor. Richard ordered the execution of Stanley's son George Lord Strange, but his men deferred action pending the verdict of the battle. They feared Henry Tudor's punishment more than Richard's. Characteristically Stanley postponed committing himself until the result was clear. Such expedients were more effective in reinforcing existing loyalties than in creating new ones. Their effects in 1485 are not calculable.

VI

Three other sources of support demand discussion. Crowland reports that Catesby and Ratcliffe threatened Richard with the loss of Queen Anne's northern retainers if he remarried. After Anne's death, Richard's tenure of her estate and call on the fidelity of her retainers was reduced to his own life. Reversionary interests were created: her cousin Richard Lord Latimer was next heir of the northern Neville lands and her other cousin Edward Earl of Warwick to the rest. While some loss in devotion was surely inevitable, Richard as duke and king was so good a lord to Northerners that it seems unlikely that he had failed to add any value to his northern following beyond the loyalty due to Queen Anne. Some did desert his army at Bosworth, so Crowland reports.[35] Once king, Richard ceased to be such a committed defender and indeed expander of Anne's inheritance. Anne was licensed to alienate property to Queen' College, Cambridge. Disputed fragments of the Warwick inheritance that the kingmaker and his sons-in-law had withheld to were conceded to Lords Lisle and Bergavenny. Most important – and instantly – he allowed his retainer Sir Humphrey Stafford of Grafton to buy Latimer's marriage and hence in due course the northern Neville estate for his daughter Anne.

A second imponderable was the Earl of Northumberland. He had despatched the Wydevilles at Pontefract and had commanded the northern army that provided Richard with the brute force to usurp. He offered good service on the Scottish border and against Buckingham's rebels and was rewarded with the great chamberlainship of England, wardenship general of the marches, the lordship of Holderness, and livery of his mother's de Brian and Poynings inheritances in southern England. He diverted Holderness to a younger son rather than adding it to his patrimonial estate. However, what he did not obtain perhaps matters more. He remained

[35] *Crowland*, pp. 178–9.

excluded from the West March, where he was the greatest landowner and he was subjected to the council of the North in Yorkshire. King Richard retained possession of his own northern estates and treated Percy retainers as though they were his own. Lincoln and Ratcliffe were new powers in the North. It would be surprising therefore if Northumberland was not disgruntled. Richard does not seem to have doubted Northumberland's fidelity, but Tudor apparently had hopes of him and put out feelers to him. The story is feasible.[36] That Northumberland did not fight at Bosworth may be for this reason –he may have sat still and kept his troops still as in 1471[37] – but it may have been because of Richard's mismanagement of the battle.

The third imponderable is Thomas Lord Stanley. Although stepfather to Henry Tudor, he was retained as steward of Richard's household. He had not rebelled with his consort Margaret Beaufort and her son Henry Tudor in 1483 and had been rewarded with the constableship of England and custody of Margaret's lands. These included the honour of Kendal that usefully complemented his own estates. That this addition was temporary, however, was stressed repeatedly when grants were made from it to others in reversion, which must have been irritating. Richard acted like his own constable and appointed commissions to do what Stanley might have undertaken himself. The earl may well have expected a freer hand in the North-West, where Richard maintained his iron grip. Stanley did not stop Margaret's scheming. That Richard distrusted him is shown by his use of the earl's son George Lord Strange as a hostage to guarantee Stanley's good behaviour. This may be one reason why Stanley did not commit himself, which was his customary stance, but Strange's plight failed to keep his father loyal.[38]

[36] Hicks, 'Career of Henry Percy', MA thesis (Southampton University, 1971), pp. 60–1.

[37] *Arrivall*, p. 6.

[38] Vergil, *English History*, pp. 212, 218; *Crowland*, pp. 178–81. Stanley had a spare son.

Chapter Sixteen

DEFEAT, DISASTER, AND DEATH
THE BATTLE OF BOSWORTH

I

For most of his reign King Richard was on the defensive. Henry Tudor was a formidable rival, backed by an impressive group of exiles, protected and financed by first Brittany and then France. Henry was bound to invade England again and did so in August 1485. Richard could not know when or where the blow was to fall and wasted much energy and substance in defence against a threat that took 18 months to materialise.

Richard had a threefold defensive strategy. First of all he wished to prevent the invasion altogether, by securing Tudor's extradition. Although this was never achieved, there were moments – about August 1484 and the following summer – when he was close to success. Failing extradition, it was preferable to intercept the invasion before it arrived and to defeat the attackers at sea, and Richard did indeed maintain a modest naval force for most of his reign, albeit all-purpose and used also against the Scots. The squadron mustered by Lord Bergavenny in April 1485 was presumably that directed from Southampton by Viscount Lovell to patrol the southern ports.[1] Not just the south coast but the whole coastline of England and

---

[1] *Crowland*, pp. 176–7; *CPR 1476–85*, p. 545.

Wales, west, south, and east, was exposed to attack. Interception at sea was highly unlikely – home governments had already failed to block a dozen invaders in the Wars of the Roses – and in 1485 Tudor's squadron was shielded additionally by the admiral of France. This time the wind behaved.

Second, Richard hoped to repel any landing or to crush the invaders before they could unite and recruit locally. He wanted 'not to miss the chance of engaging the enemy with the united forces of the whole neighbourhood if they tried to land there'.[2] Preparations in March/April 1484 came to nothing, but in August 1485 the Tudor invasion did at last materialise. For all these 18 months Richard had to maintain and resource his defences along the whole coast of England and Wales, altogether to no effect, as Crowland pointed out.[3] Richard could not afford to keep his navy or his army constantly in the field. His army indeed consisted principally of men pressed from agriculture and obliged to serve for only 30 days. The previous chapter suggests reasons why Richard's store of loyal partisans may not have grown. In place of fervent commitment, Richard emphasised order and organisation. He distributed his patronage systematically, deployed his most reliable followers where best needed, maximised the size and quality of his retainers' companies, and reformed the militia to make it more militarily effective. The troops who were arrayed had no choice but to fight. Richard expected his regional commanders to deter or defeat any landings in their sectors: the duke of Norfolk in East Anglia and the South-East, Viscount Lovell along the south-coast, the earl of Huntingdon in Wales, and the earls of Lincoln and Northumberland in the North. Richard did not know where Tudor would disembark, nor indeed whether there were to be other uprisings timed to coincide with the main assault as in 1469, 1470, and 1471. He had to guard against all possibilities.

Third, failing victory on the coast, Richard determined on a battle: 'that therby he might ether make a beginning or ende of his raigne'.[4] He could not afford a prolonged campaign; he feared that Tudor's force would grow with time and a complete triumph offered him the best security. 'The king rejoiced', reports Crowland, 'or pretended to rejoice, sending his letters

[2] *Crowland*, pp. 176–7.
[3] Ibid.
[4] Vergil, *English History*, pp. 225–6.

everywhere to say that the day he had longed for had now arrived when he would easily triumph over such a wretched company and thereafter restore . . . the blessings of certain peac'.[5]

Richard based himself at Nottingham in the East Midlands, well-placed as in 1483 to move in any direction should Henry manage to pass the seaward defences. At Nottingham on 1 August, as in 1483, he consigned the great seal to the custody of the trusted Thomas Barrow, his chancellor as duke.[6] Routine chancery enrolments had already ceased.[7] Although unrecorded, it was probably there that Richard assembled his formidable ordnance train.[8] It was from his hunting lodge in nearby Beskwood Park on 11 August that the king summoned support from Staffordshire, York, and most probably all the other sectors that made up his army. His summons to Henry Vernon survives.[9] If there are no further records that particular arrays or retinues joined him, such data is also lacking for all other campaigns of the Wars of the Roses and does not indicate that such documents never existed. Although many stalwarts such as Tyrell and the York city contingent may have had insufficient time to arrive, King Richard appears to have assembled much the larger army: 'a greater number of fighting men than had ever been seen before one side, in England'. Vergil reports 'an host innumerable . . . twyse so many and more'.[10] His strategy changed when he learnt that Tudor intended seeking him out (and not, for example, marching on London). While Richard could expect more levies to join him if battle was deferred, he feared that Tudor would gain in strength too, and chose therefore not to avoid battle as Warwick had done in 1471.

II

Henry Tudor feared that Richard's strength would grow with time and he too therefore resolved on battle as soon as possible and sought to confront

---

[5] *Crowland*, pp. 176–7.

[6] *CCR 1476–85*, pp. 431, 433.

[7] Documents must have continued to be sealed, but the additional membranes were never returned to Westminster and appended to the rolls.

[8] The evidence is usefully collected in C. Skidmore, *Bosworth* (Weidenfeld & Nicolson, 2013), pp. 172–3.

[9] A. Goodman, *The Wars of the Roses: The Soldiers, Experience* (History Press, 2003), p. 134.

[10] *Crowland*, pp. 178–9; Vergil, *English History*, pp. 220, 223. Both surely exaggerated.

the king. Landing on 7 August 1485, he fought the decisive battle on the 22nd only a fortnight later.

Tudor's campaign was planned with some care. Five hundred exiles were the core of his force; perhaps 1,500 French and 1,000 Scottish mercenaries made up the rest. Apparently he decided not to invade the South, from whence most of the exiles came, nor Oxford's country in the east, which was perhaps testimony to the effectiveness of Richard's home guard. Yet Richard had to commit many of his best men to these localities and in particular around Milford in the New Forest, which was identified as a potential landfall and where Lovell was in command. This time the weather behaved and Henry was able to disembark all his troops without opposition at Milford Haven in Pembrokeshire in south-western Wales. His force was too big to be quashed by any local levies. Here supposedly Jasper Tudor, the former earl of Pembroke, still carried some weight; so, too, perhaps did the Wydeville-dominated council of the Yorkist Prince of Wales Edward V. Henry wrote to those Welshmen and others whom he thought potential supporters: certainly to Rhys ap Thomas, who responded favourably, to John ap Meredith and to Sir Walter Herbert whose reaction is uncertain, to Roger Kynaston who declined to help, and to the Stanleys and Northumberland, whose response was ambiguous.[11] Herbert and Northumberland were two of the very few who had known Henry Tudor: in the late 1460s all three had lived in the Herbert household.[12] Some Welshmen, but not many, joined him.[13] With Rhys ap Thomas's support, Henry bypassed South Wales – where Richard's great lordship of Glamorgan was held against him – via 'wild and twisting tracks',[14] and erupted at Shrewsbury in the Welsh borders. Such a difficult route may have limited the artillery that he could bring with him and prevented him from picking up significant reinforcements along the way. Thereafter he gained manpower: Sir William Stanley, chamberlain of North Wales; five hundred men under Sir Gilbert Talbot, uncle of the young George Talbot,

[11] R. Horrox, 'Henry Tudor's Letters to England', *Ricardian*, 80 (1983), pp. 155–8; Griffiths and Thomas, *Tudor Dynasty* (History Press, 1985), pp. 144–8; R.A. Griffiths, *Sir Rhys ap Thomas and his Family* (University of Wales Press, 1993), pp. 40–2.

[12] Hicks, *Clarence*, p. 56.

[13] Skidmore, *Bosworth*, pp. 234–40.

[14] *Crowland*, pp. 178–9.

earl of Shrewsbury, who himself served with King Richard; the Cheshireman Sir John Savage; the Midlanders Simon Digby and Brian Sanford who had deserted Richard; the Wiltshireman Walter Hungerford; and from Surrey Sir Thomas Bourchier of Barnes, who defected from Sir Robert Brackenbury at Stony Stratford en route to Richard. Presumably each brought his immediate entourage: perhaps also any local arrays that they commanded. Doughty though such recruits were, it may have been the weakening of Richard's force rather than the strengthening of Tudor's that mattered most. Unlike 1460 and 1470, there was no outburst of popular indignation to swell the invading army, yet Henry had no alternative to committing his forces to battle against King Richard.

Unsubstantiated legends rather than records chart Tudor's progress from Milford to Bosworth.[15] He proceeded via Shrewsbury (17 August), the cathedral city of Lichfield where he arrived on the 20th, and Tamworth to the fields around Merivale Abbey in Warwickshire, where his troops trampled the crops.[16] Richard had news of his disembarkation as early as 11 August and at once set about summoning and redeploying his forces. As in 1483, Richard determined to intercept and engage Tudor himself, 'towardes whose rencontring, God being our guide, we be utterly determined in our owne persone to remove in all hast goodly that we can or may'.[17] Once Tudor's aggressive plan was identified, the king decided instead to remain in the East Midlands and await his arrival. Not all his forces were able to join him before he had to emerge from Nottingham and to proceed to Leicester. Wearing his crown, he was accompanied by Norfolk and Northumberland, 'and other great lords, knights, and esquires and a countless multitude of commoners'.[18] Richard was maximising his impact on bystanders.

King Richard knew where the Tudor army was located when, on the evening of 21 August, he bivouacked facing his battlefield of choice. This was in open gently undulating and thinly populated country – hence the

[15] See W. Hutton, *The Battle of Bosworth Field* (London, 1788); Griffiths and Thomas, *Tudor Dynasty*, pp. 133–55; Skidmore, *Bosworth*, pp. 252–64.

[16] *Richard III: A Royal Enigma*, ed. S. Cunningham (National Archives, 2003), no. 12.

[17] Historic Manuscripts Commission *78, Manuscripts of His Grace the Duke of Rutland*, I (1888), pp, 7–8.

[18] *Crowland*, pp. 178–9.

names such as Sandford and Redemoor now forgotten that were attached to the battle. It was to the south of the small town of Market Bosworth, 13 miles east of Leicester, and was not fought at the traditional site on Ambion Hill where Leicestershire County Council have their battlefield centre, but on the plain beneath. A substantial area – Atherstone, Atterton, Fenny Drayton, Mancetter, Stoke Golding, Sutton Cheney, and Witherley – were wasted by the activities of the two armies.[19] Firing cannon did little damage, but, Molinet reports, revealed where Richard's troops were located.[20] It is probably Tudor propaganda that Richard suffered guilty nightmares and could neither break his fast nor attend mass on the day of battle itself.[21] A note attached to Norfolk's tent warning of treason,[22] if not apocryphal, did not deflect the duke, nor indeed the king, from fighting.

Bosworth is almost the worst recorded of the major engagements of the Wars of the Roses. There are no eyewitness reports of the battle. Most useful are the brief summary of Crowland who was not there and the lengthier account of Polydore Vergil, written 30 years later and at second hand. Neither was present or had visited the site. There is an almost contemporary Spanish account by Diego Valera that draws on the mercenary Juan de Salazar who was actually present, but even his version is somewhat garbled, because personal names were mistranslated and because combatants had no overview of what happened elsewhere on the battlefield. Much the most confident account is that of another absentee, the Frenchman Jean de Molinet, who does not state his source.[23] There are no muster rolls for either side, no reliable numbers for either force, and no heralds' lists of casualties.[24] Survivors from the losing side were anxious to conceal their presence, while adherents of Tudor and the Stanleys wanted to prove their participation, to

[19] Cunningham, *Richard III*, no. 12.

[20] *Richard III: A Source Book*, ed. K. Dockray (Sutton, 1997), p. 124.

[21] *Crowland*, pp. 180–1; see also M. Bennett, *The Battle of Bosworth* (Sutton, 1985), p. 100.

[22] Jack of Norfolk be not too bold/for Dickon thy master is bought and sold.

[23] A. Goodman and A. Mackay, 'A Castilian Report on English Affairs, 1486', *EHR*, 88 (1973), pp. 92–9. Most of the primary sources are collected in Dockray, *Richard III*, pp. 120–31. The fullest analyses are now *Bosworth 1485: A Battlefield Rediscovered*, eds G. Foard and A. Curry (Oxbow Books, 2013); P. Hammond, *Richard III and the Bosworth Campaign* (Pen & Sword Books, 2010). These are the main sources for what follows.

[24] The closely reasoned estimates of Foard and Curry build on insubstantial evidence, *Bosworth 1485*, pp. 38–40. Probably they seriously underestimate Richard's army.

claim the new king's rewards and a share of the glory, and their roles were often exaggerated or even invented in their petitions for rewards and the somewhat later Stanley ballads.[25] Apart from the royal household, Richard's army probably consisted of his household, shire levies, and noble retinues, all commanded by aristocrats. The 'many commoners' who bulked out the numbers mentioned by Crowland were not mobilised in overwhelming force by popular enthusiasm as in 1460 and 1470, but were rather pressed men from the shires, perhaps better drilled and equipped than hitherto, perhaps also reluctant to be distracted from the harvest.[26] Relatively few participants are identifiable. Only 32 of Richard's men including five peers were attainted. It was presumably while commanding their shire levies that the 29 commissioners of array died on or about 22 August. Of the 10 whose date of death was definitely 20–22 August, eight hailed from the East Midlands or Essex and presumably therefore fought with Norfolk and the king. The only two Northerners among them, Thomas Gower knight of the body and Robert Percy controller of the household, were courtiers who perished beside the king.[27] All other Northerners, including Richard's own men, presumably served with Northumberland, whose will of 27 July surely anticipated his participation in the fighting and the possibility that he might be killed. Two other wills, of Robert Morton and Thomas Long, more explicitly anticipated death in battle. Neither individual features in any narrative or record. The brass of John Sachaverell, who was killed on Richard's side, is another isolated indicator.[28]

The bodies were cleared and interred, everything of value was pillaged, perishable detritus decayed, and any oddments trampled into the ground

---

[25] The present author is more persuaded than in 1986 by Richmond's scepticism about their value, C. Richmond, '1485 And All That', in *Richard III: Loyalty, Lordship and Law*, ed P.W. Hammond (Richard III and Yorkist History Trust, 1986), pp. 172–3.

[26] As suggested in A. Goodman, *The Wars of the Roses*, p. 188.

[27] L. Boatwright, 'The Buckinghamshire Six at Bosworth', *Ricardian*, 13 (2003), p. 65.

[28] *PROME*, vol. 15, pp. 107–8; *Testamenta Eboracensia*, ed. J. Raine, vol. 45 (Surtees Society, 1864), vol. 3, p. 305; Foard & Curry, *Bosworth 1485*, p. 20; M.K. Jones, *Bosworth 1485: Psychology of a Battle* (Tempus, 2002), pl. 58; J. Alban, 'The Will of a Norfolk Soldier at Bosworth', *Ricardian*, 22 (2012), p. 7. The attainted peers (Norfolk, Surrey, Lovell, Ferrers, and Zouche) probably served in Richard's vanguard and centre, so the others listed by the 'Ballad of Bosworth Field' were conceivably unengaged in the wings, 'The Ballad of Bosworth Field', in *Bishop Percy's Folio Manuscript*, vol. 3, eds J.W. Hales and F.J. Furnivall (N. Trubner, 1868); but see Richmond, '1485 And All That', p. 173.

have been unearthed by centuries of ploughing and more modern mecha-
nised cultivation and removed. Past collections of artefacts have disappeared and minute fragments were what remained. Since the battlefield has
traditionally been located on Ambion Hill, historical narratives and battlefield centre were tailored to fit it, but the realisation by Peter Foss and others
that the battle was fought on the plain below has outdated all the past
discussions from Hutton in 1788 to Ross in 1981 and his immediate successors. A thorough archaeological investigation has revealed much about the
local landscape, which has changed over five centuries, the marsh especially
having been drained. The parish of Upton regrettably was not surveyed.[29]
Fragments of chain mail and badges and 33 projectiles (some definitely
fired) are among the tiny artefacts that were retrieved across several parishes.
No war graves have been found and only the reputed bones of King Richard
have been analysed. The battle itself was fought just to the west of the site
investigated. What the survey did not reveal and what archaeology probably cannot answer are the key historical questions: how large were the
opposing forces, where were the divisions located, who commanded them,
how did the battle unfold, what were the decisive factors, and how important were deficient morale, treachery, disloyalty, desertion, and other intel-
lectual factors in incapacitating Richard's troops? What is needed and is
unfortunately lacking is a contemporary eyewitness account.

Richard had much the larger force, which he strung out in long lines
facing northwards or north-westwards with the sun on their backs. His
left wing was fronted and partially protected (and also impeded) by a marsh
(the Redemoor). John Howard, duke of Norfolk, commanded his vanguard,
the king himself the central battle, the earl of Northumberland one wing
with the Northerners, including Richard's own Northerners; someone else
commanded the other wing. Which wing was which is unclear. Henry Tudor
could not match the whole line in force. Conceivably his wings commanded
by Talbot and Savage numbered only 500 men apiece: they never attacked
and thus never engaged the stronger forces that faced them. Talbot on his
right was protected by the marsh. There was 'a slender vanward' and a

[29] Foard & Curry, *Bosworth 1485*, ch 4. 'The terrain work provided a more detailed picture
than ever before of the medieval landscape of the five townships within which, somewhere,
we knew the battle must have been fought'; ibid., p. 96.

modest force around Henry himself in the rear. This risky distribution of his troops enabled Henry to mass his main force of elite gentry and foreign professionals under the earl of Oxford against the flank of Richard's centre.[30] The foreigners were a professional elite that were perhaps the best troops on either side. Deployed in this way, the invaders were no longer outnumbered. It was in the centre that the battle was fought and won. Henry's bold calculation paid off. Perhaps it was Oxford's plan. It is reminiscent of Robert E. Lee's brilliant deployment at Chancellorsville in 1863.

Finally it was the intervention of the Stanleys, Thomas Lord Stanley and his brother Sir William, that swung the battle. They may have brought with them as many as 3,000 troops. Still steward of Richard's household and constable of England, Lord Stanley was not reliable. Presumably it was in Richard's name that his men were arrayed from the palatine counties of Cheshire and Lancashire. Sir William's came from North Wales. The two Stanley contingents lurked nearby, initially committed to neither side and even wandered around the battlefield, for Stanley wished to ensure that he backed the winner. Eventually they were committed where he cast his vote. Stanley's force, recruited for Richard and apparently promised to Tudor, was an imponderable annoyance to both sides. Stanley may have been ambiguous about his intentions also because he wanted to save his son George Lord Strange, whom Richard had taken as hostage. When Stanley's treachery became obvious, one of Richard's last acts was to command Strange's execution, but his order was not fulfilled. It was Sir William who placed Richard's fallen crown on Henry's head, traditionally on Crown Hill, and claimed the credit for the victory.

Like Warwick the Kingmaker, Richard was a strategist and a logistician, not a tactician. At this only battle where he ever commanded, Richard seems to have mismanaged his forces. Most of them were never engaged. In particular the wing commanded by Northumberland awaited an enemy attack that never came. By advancing, Richard's wings could have overwhelmed Talbot and Savage's insubstantial forces and could have outflanked Tudor's centre. Perhaps the marsh that protected Richard's right wing actually barred any such advance. In the centre Richard's men left their

---

[30] Dockray, *Richard III*, p. 124.

defensive positions. Richard deployed his archers at the front and most probably his ordnance in the centre.[31] Both would have been most effective when attacked, as in the major English victories of the Hundred Years War and in the English defeat at Castillon (1453), but it was Richard who was the aggressor. The artillery had been bogged down at Northampton (1460), outmanoeuvred at the second battle of St Albans (1461), and negated by dead ground and fog at Barnet (1471). Instead of holding back and relying on such firepower, Richard's vanguard closed quickly to hand-to-hand combat where he may have expected his superior numbers to prevail. After unleashing a volley of arrows, Norfolk in the van pushed Tudor's forward back beyond the marsh, thus exposing itself to flank attack by Oxford and Philibert de Chandée. At some point the duke was slain. Perceiving Tudor's standard isolated to the rear, Richard determined to take his rival out, calculating perhaps correctly that Henry's death would decide the battle in his favour. Richard need not have charged in person – he could have delegated the command – but of course there was nobody better to be trusted to execute his wishes than himself. So it was King Richard himself with his crown on his head who led his central division into a headlong attack that nearly succeeded. The last of his many gambles, this assault was a rash and ill-considered forlorn hope that denied the king his coordination of his army, his capacity to direct the other wings and, in retrospect, the chance to escape and fight another day. Tudor's standard was knocked down, King Richard himself killed Tudor's standard bearer William Brandon and felled Sir John Cheyne, 'a man of muche fortytude far exceeding the common sort',[32] but he was held up, outflanked by Sir William Stanley, and repulsed. At this point Lord Stanley intervened on the Tudor side. King Richard himself may have become enmired and was unhorsed. Remounted, he could still have escaped, it was later reported by the Portuguese professional Juan de Salazar, but declined to do so. 'Salazar', he said, 'God forbid [that] I yield one step. This day I will die a king or win.' Crowland, Rows, Molinet, and Vergil report that he died fighting.[33] Conceivably he could have

[31] Hammond, *Richard III and the Bosworth Campaign*, p. 83.

[32] Vergil, *English History*, p. 224.

[33] Dockray, *Richard III*, pp. 123, 125–6, 130. It is difficult to believe he had the leisure for the reported debate at this juncture.

withdrawn with much of his army intact and certainly he could have continued his struggle. Apparently he was unwilling to become a rival contender or a former king and preferred to die rather than to lose his throne. Fighting courageously in the press and indeed desperately, he was slain, perhaps, as Molinet states, by a Welsh halberdier.[34] Richard's death ended his cause and decided the battle. His army submitted to the victor.

The thousand men who fell included several notables on Richard's side: Lord Ferrers of Chartley, Ratcliffe, Brackenbury, Kendal and Robert Percy; Catesby was beheaded after the battle and the two Brachers were hanged. Stripped naked, Richard's body was carted to Leicester Greyfriars and buried there.

III

Richard's reign thus ended in disaster and defeat. He left behind no heir and no cause. To the Tudor historians who wrote up the story, Richard's deficiencies and unpopularity were important factors in his defeat. 'The most part', Vergil reports so much later, would have deserted at the start.[35] It suited Tudor historians that few backed such a wicked tyrant, but the incidence of treachery and faint-heartedness on the battlefield, truancy, and desertion cannot be substantiated. Did the fighting take place away from Northumberland's wing or did he 'sit still' as in 1471 and thus deny his king the support of his Northerners on whom his power rested? It was Richard's mismanagement that allowed a much smaller force to overwhelm merely part of his army. It was typical of the man to go for broke – to throw his own life onto the scales – but whether he did so because he could not count on his troops (as the Tudors later argued) is impossible to say. Certainly he chose not to escape. Yet Richard's supreme gamble – his charge – came very close to success. He could have won the battle of Bosworth, which would certainly have prolonged his history. However badly or however well he reigned, the fate of King Richard and his regime remained open until 22 August 1485 and was decided on the battlefield of Bosworth.

[34] Ibid., p. 125. A halberd could have inflicted the head injury on the Leicester bones, but the wounds indicate the victim to have been without helmet and armour and thus more likely captured and despatched, rather than slain fighting as Richard certainly was.

[35] Vergil, *English History*, pp. 224–5.

Richard created his own fortune. To be born into the highest nobility and to have a brother for his king were of course indispensable, but Richard certainly maximised his opportunities in his preregnal career culminating in his victory against the Scots and then in taking the throne. Richard's early career as a great nobleman forged his character and prepared him well for the business of government. Determination, sheer force of personality, and a refusal to compromise made up for any physical defects. There is a consistency to his character and to his whole career. He always looked and planned ahead both as duke and king and made detailed planning, organisation, and discipline into substitutes for charm and charisma. He was pious and exceptionally generous to the Church. He shared the values and expectations of his age, operated by contemporary conventions, and framed his public image accordingly. He presented himself in turn as an outsider, a war hero, and an exemplar of personal morality and good governance, although he excepted himself whenever desirable from the rules. Mere capacity to rule did not, however, entitle him to the crown. Usurping the throne proved the step too far. He believed in himself and his right, but unfortunately others did not. That he had acceded and could do the job failed to earn him the overriding respect and allegiance that kings expected as sovereigns. Ruling proved much more difficult than he had expected. His dubious route to the throne was held against him and he encountered for the first time hostile propaganda and opponents who did not give way. His own fate demonstrates that the Wars of the Roses were not, in fact, a time when anybody could make himself king. Richard trusted in his own powers of presentation, his ability to persuade and to overawe, in his obvious capacity to rule, and in his self-evident commitment to the public good, yet his usurpation decisively breached the standards of conduct expected of the aristocracy and of a king. Usurpation overstepped the invisible line that subjects could accept and created the opposition that brought him down. The crimes with which he was slandered denied him the allegiance owed by every subject. No wonder Richard gambled on trial by battle – indeed on his own martial prowess – and lost as he could have won. He was a remarkable man who made more of himself by sheer determination and assertion than his physical limitations should have permitted. He was not perfect: nobody ever is. What changed a successful (but historically obscure career) into a notorious reign was the supreme gamble of his usurpation. Had he not usurped the throne, right or wrong, Bosworth could not have been fought, nor Richard slain there, nor could there have been a ruling dynasty of Tudors, nor would Duke Richard have remained memorable, a household name and byword. Kingship was the pinnacle of his career and also his ruin.

SELECT BIBLIOGRAPHY

PRIMARY SOURCES

Principal classes of documents in The National Archives, Kew, London:

C1	Early Chancery Proceedings
C 53	Charter Rolls
C 60	Chancery, Fine Rolls
C 66	Chancery, Patent Rolls
C 67	Pardon Rolls
C 76	Treaty Rolls
C 81	Warrants for the Great Seal
CP 25	Common Pleas, Feet of Fines
DL 26	Duchy of Lancaster, Ancient Deeds, Series LL
DL 29	Duchy of Lancaster, Ministers' Accounts
DL 37	Duchy of Lancaster, Chancery Rolls
DL 42	Duchy of Lancaster, Miscellaneous Books
DL 43	Duchy of Lancaster, Rentals and Surveys
DURH 3	Palatinate of Durham, Chancery Court, Cursitors Rolls
E 28	Exchequer, Treasury of Receipt, Council and Parliamentary Proceedings
E 36	Exchequer: Treasury of the Receipt: Miscellaneous Books
E 101	King's Remembrancer, Various Accounts
E 159	KR, Memoranda Rolls
E 315	Court of Augmentations, Miscellaneous Books
E 401	TR, Receipt Rolls
E 404	TR, Warrants for Issue
E 405	TR, Tellers' Rolls
KB 9	King's Bench, Ancient Indictments
KB 27	Coram Rege Rolls
KB 29	Controlment Rolls
PSO 1	Privy Seal Office, Warrants for the Privy Seal, Series 1

SC 1   Special Collections, Ancient Correspondence of the Chancery and the Exchequer
SC 6   Special Collections, Ministers' Accounts
SC11   Special Collections: Rentals and Surveys, Rolls
SP 46   State Papers Domestic, Supplementary

Collections of Manuscripts at the British Library, London:
Additional, Cottonian, Egerton, Harleian, Royal and Sloane MSS, Charters, and Rolls.

Other Repositories Consulted:
Bodleian Library, Oxford
Borthwick Institute, University of York
Cambridge, Queens' College
Carlisle Archive Centre
Cumbria Record Office
Devon Heritage Centre, Exeter City Archives
Durham Cathedral Archives
Durham University Archives
Essex Record Office
Greater London Record Office
Hull University Archives
Northamptonshire Record Office
North Yorkshire Record Office
Northumberland Record Office
Nottingham Archives
Nottingham University Library
St George's Chapel, Windsor
Westminster Abbey
West Yorkshire Archives, Leeds and Wakefield

PRINTED BOOKS

Accounts of the Lord High Treasurer of Scotland, vol. I, 1473–98, ed. R. Dickson (Edinburgh, 1877).

Acts of Court of the Mercers' Company 1453–1527, eds L. Lyell and C.D. Watney (Cambridge University Press, 1936).

André, B., *Historia Regis Henrici Septimi*, ed. J. Gairdner, Rolls Series (London, Longmans, 1858).

The Anglica Historia of Polydore Vergil, AD 1485–1537, ed. D. Hay, Camden 3rd series 64 (London, Royal Historical Society, 1950).

'Annales Rerum Anglicarum', in *Letters and Papers Illustrative of the Wars of the English in France*, ed. J. Stevenson, Rolls Series, vol. 2, part 2 (London, 1864).

The Antient Kalendars and Inventories of the Treasury of His Majesty's Exchequer, Together with Other Documents Illustrating the History of that Repository, ed. F.C. Palgrave, 3 vols (London, Record Commission, 1836).

'The Ballad of Bosworth Field', in *Bishop Percy's Folio Manuscript*, eds J.W. Hales and F.J. Furnivall, vol. 3 (London, N. Trubner, 1868), pp. 233–59.

British Library Harleian Manuscript 433, eds P.W. Hammond and R.E. Horrox, 4 vols (Gloucester, A. Sutton, 1979–83).

The Calais Letterbook of William Lord Hastings (1477) and Late Medieval Crisis Diplomacy 1477–83, ed. E.L. Meek (Donington, Richard III and Yorkist History Trust, 2017).

Calendar of the Charter Rolls, 6, *1427–1516* (London, HMSO, 1927).

Calendar of the Close Rolls, 1461–1509 (London, HMSO, 1949–53).

Calendar of Documents Relating to Scotland, ed. J. Bain, vol. 4 (Edinburgh, HM General Register House, 1888).

Calendar of Entries in the Papal Registers relating to Great Britain and Ireland, eds W.H. Bliss, J.A. Twemlow, et al., 20 vols (London, HMSO, 1893–).

Calendar of the Fine Rolls, 1461–1509 (London, HMSO, 1949–63).

Calendar of Inquisitions Miscellaneous (Chancery), 1422–85 (Woodbridge, Boydell Press, 2003).

Calendar of Inquisitions Post Mortem and Other Analogous Documents, vol. 26 (Woodbridge, Boydell Press, 2009).

Calendar of the Patent Rolls 1461–1509 (1897–1910).

Calendar of State Papers and Manuscripts Relating to English Affairs in the Archives and Collections of Milan, ed. A.B. Hinds (London, HMSO, 1913).

Calendar of State Papers Relating to English Affairs in the Archives of Venice, ed. R. Brown (London, HMSO, 1864).

Cartae et alia munimenta quae ad dominium de Glamorgancie pertinent, ed. G.T. Clark, 6 vols (Cardiff, 1910).

The Cely Letters 1472–88, ed. A. Hanham (London, Early English Text Society, 1975).

The Certificate of the Commissioners Appointed to Survey the Chantries, Guilds, Hospitals etc in the County of York, I, ed. W. Page (Durham, Surtees Society, 1894).

Christ Church Letters, ed. J.B. Sheppard, new series (London, Camden Society, 1877).

Chronicle of the First Thirteen Years of the Reign of King Edward the Fourth, ed. J.O. Halliwell (London, Camden Society, 1839).

'Chronicle of the Rebellion in Lincolnshire, in 1470', ed. J.G. Nichols, *Camden Miscellany*, vol. 1 (London, Camden Society, 1847).

Chronicles of London, ed. C.L. Kingsford (Oxford, Clarendon Press, 1905).

Commines, P. de, *Mémoires*, eds J. Calmette and G. Durville, 3 vols (Paris, 1923–5).

The Coronation of Richard III: The Extant Documents, eds A.F. Sutton and P.W. Hammond (Gloucester, A. Sutton, 1983).

The Coventry Leet Book and Mayor's Register, ed. M.D. Harris, Early English Text Book 134–5, 138, 146 (London, Kegan Paul, 1907–13).

The Crowland Chronicle Continuations 1459–86, eds N. Pronay and J. Cox (Gloucester, Sutton, 1986).

Death and Dissent. Two Fifteenth-Century Chronicles, ed. L.M. Matheson (Woodbridge, Boydell & Brewer, 1999).

A Descriptive Catalogue of Ancient Deeds in the Public Record Office, 6 vols (London, HMSO, 1890–1915).

Documents relating to the Foundation and Antiquities of the Collegiate Church of Middleham, ed. W. Atthill (London, Camden Society, 1847).

Dugdale, W., *Monasticon Anglicanum*, eds J. Caley, et al., 8 vols (London, 1846).

English Historical Documents, iv, *1327–1485*, ed. A.R. Myers (London, Eyre & Spottiswood, 1969).

English Wills Proved in the Prerogative Court of York 1477–99, eds H. Falvey, L. Boatwright, and P. Hammond (London, Richard III Society, 2013).

Excerpta Historica, ed. S. Bentley (London, 1831).

The Fabric Rolls of York Minster, ed. J. Raine (Durham, Surtees Society, 1859).

'Financial Memoranda of the Reign of Edward V', ed. R.E. Horrox, *Camden Miscellany* 29 (1987), pp. 200–44.

Foedera et cujuscunque Acta Publica, T. Rymer, eds J. Caley et al., 18 vols (London, Record Commission, 1827).

'Grant from Richard, Duke of Gloucester to Reginald Vaughan, 10 Edward IV', *Archaeologia Cambrensis*, 3rd ser, vol. 33 (1863), p. 55.

Great Chronicle of London, eds A.H. Thomas and I.D. Thornley (London, Guildhall Library, 1938).

Hall's Chronicle, ed. H. Ellis (London, 1809).

Historia Dunelmensis Scriptores Tres, ed. J. Raine, vol. 9 (Durham, Surtees Society, 1839).

Historic Manuscripts Commission Reports.

The Historie of the Arrivall of Edward IV and the Finall Recouerye of his Kingdomes from Henry VI, ed. J. Bruce (London, Camden Society, 1838).

Household Books of John of Norfolk and Thomas Earl of Surrey 1481–90, ed. J.P. Collier (London, Roxburghe Club, 1844).

Issues of the Exchequer, ed. F. Devon (London, J. Murray, 1837).

John Leland's Itinerary, ed. J. Chandler (Stroud, Sutton, 1993).

John Stone's Chronicle. Christ Church Priory, Canterbury, 1417–72, ed. M. Connor (Kalamazoo, MI, Medieval Institute Publications, 2010).

Letters and Papers Illustrative of the Reigns of Richard III and Henry VII, ed. J. Gairdner, Rolls Series, 2 vols (London, Longman, Green, 1861–3).

Letters of the Kings of England, ed. J.O. Halliwell-Phillips (London, H. Colburn, 1848).

The Logge Register of Prerogative Court of Canterbury Wills 1479–86, eds L. Boatwright, M. Habberjam and P. Hammond, 2 vols (Knaphill, Richard III Society, 2008).

London and Middlesex Chantry Certificate 1548, ed. C.J. Kitching (London Record Society, 1980).

Mancini, D., *The Usurpation of Richard III*, ed. C.A.J. Armstrong, 2nd edn (Oxford University Press, 1969).

Medieval Pageant. Writhe's Garter Book, eds A.R. Wagner, N. Barker, and A. Payne (London, Roxburghe Club, 1993).

Memorials of Henry VII, ed. J. Gairdner, Rolls Series (London, Longman, 1858).

More, T., *History of King Richard III*, ed. R.S. Sylvester (New Haven, CT, Yale University Press, 1963).

'Narrative of the Marriage of Richard Duke of York and Ann of Norfolk, the "Matrimonial Feast", and the Grand Justing', in *Illustrations of Ancient State and Chivalry*, ed. W.H. Black (London, Shakespeare Press, 1840), pp. 25–40.

Original Letters Illustrative of English History, ed. H. Ellis, 11 vols (London, Harding, Triphook and Leonard, 1822–46).

Palatine Anthology: A Collection of Ancient Poems and Ballads, ed. J.O. Halliwell-Phillips (London, 1850).

The Parliament Rolls of England 1275–1504, ed. C. Given-Wilson, 16 vols (Woodbridge, Boydell Press, 2005).

The Paston Letters, ed. J. Gairdner, 6 vols (London, Chatto & Windus, 1904).

Paston Letters and Papers of the Fifteenth Century, eds R. Beadle, N. Davis, and C. Richmond, 3 vols, Early English Text Society supplementary series 20–2 (Oxford University Press, 2004–5).

Pitcairn, R., *Ancient Criminal Trials in Scotland* (Edinburgh, Bannatyne Club, 1833).

The Plumpton Correspondence, ed. T. Stapleton (London, Camden Society, 1839).

The Plumpton Letters and Papers, ed. J. Kirby (London, Camden Society, 1996).

Political Poems and Songs, ed. T. Wright, Rolls Series, vol. 2 (London, Camden Society, 1861).

The Politics of Fifteenth-Century England: John Vale's Book, eds M.L. Kekewich, C. Richmond, A.F. Sutton, L. Visser-Fuchs, and J.L. Watts (Stroud, A. Sutton, 1995).

'Private Indentures for Life Service in Peace and War', eds M. Jones and S. Walker, *Camden Miscellany*, 32 (1994), pp. 1–190.

The Reburial of Richard Duke of York 21–30 July 1476, eds A.F. Sutton and L. Visser-Fuchs with P.W. Hammond (London, Richard III Society, 1996).

Register of Archbishop Rotherham, ed. E.E. Barker, vol. 1, Canterbury and York Society, 69 (1976).

Register of the Guild of Corpus Christi in the City of York, ed. R.H. Scaife (Durham, Surtees Society, 1872).

Register of John Blyth, Bishop of Salisbury, 1493–1499, ed. D. Wright, Wiltshire Record Society, 68 (2015).

Register of the Most Noble Order of the Garter, ed. J. Anstis, 2 vols (London, 1724).

Registrum Thome Bourgchier Cantuaroensis Archiepiscopi AD 1454–86, ed. F.R.H. Du Boulay, Canterbury and York Society, vol. 54 (Oxford University Press, 1957).

Report of the Lords' Committee on the Dignity of a Peer, vol. 5 (London, 1820–9).

Richard III: A Royal Enigma, ed. S. Cunningham (Kew, National Archives, 2003).

Richard III: A Source Book, ed. K. Dockray (Stroud, Sutton, 1997).

Richard III: The Road to Bosworth Fields, eds P.W. Hammond and A.F. Sutton (London, Constable, 1985).

Rolls of Parliament, 6 vols (London, 1783).

Rotuli Scotiae, eds D. MacPherson, J. Caley, and W. Illingworth, 2 vols (London, Record Commission, 1814–19).

The Rous Roll, ed. W.H. Courthope (London, 1859).

The Royal Funerals of the House of York at Windsor, eds A.F. Sutton and L. Visser-Fuchs with R.A. Griffiths (London, Richard III Society, 2005).

'The Statutes Ordained by Richard Duke of Gloucester, for the College of Middleham. Dated July 4, 18 Edw. IV, (1478)', ed. J. Raine, *Archaeological Journal*, 14 (1857), pp. 160–70.

Stonor Letters and Papers of the Fifteenth Century, ed. C.L. Kingsford, 2 vols, Camden 3rd series 24, 30 (London, 1919); *Camden Miscellany* 13 (1924).

A Summarie of the Chronicles of England . . . by John Stow, ed. B.L. Beer (Lewiston, NY, Mellen, 2007).

Testamenta Eboracensia, ed. J. Raine (York, Surtees Society, 1864).

Testamenta Vetusta, ed. N.H. Nicolas (London, 1826).

Thirty-Fifth Report of the Deputy Keeper of the Public Record Office (London, HMSO, 1874).

Three Books of Polydore Vergil's English History, ed. H. Ellis (London, Camden Society 1844).

Transactions of the Cumberland and Westmorland Archaeological Society, Tract series (Kendal, 1887).

Valor Ecclesiasticus, eds J. Caley, et al., 7 vols (London, Record Commission, 1810–34).

Visser-Fuchs, L. (ed.), 'Edward IV's *Mémoire* on Paper to Charles Duke of Burgundy: the so-called "Short Version of *The Arrivall*" ', *Nottingham Medieval Studies*, 36 (1992), pp. 167–267.

Waurin, J. de, *Recueil des Croniques et anciennes istoires de la Grant Bretaigne*, eds W. Hardy and E.L.C.P. Hardy, Rolls Series 5 (London, 1891).

York City Chamberlains' Account Rolls 1396–1500, ed. R.B. Dobson (York, Surtees Society, 1980).

York House Books 1461–90, ed. L.C. Attreed, 2 vols (Stroud, A. Sutton, 1991).

York Memorandum Book, 2, ed. M. Sellars (York, Surtees Society, 1914).

York Memorandum Book, 3, ed. J.W. Percy (York, Surtees Society, 1973).

SECONDARY SOURCES

Alban, J., 'The Will of a Norfolk Soldier at Bosworth', *Ricardian*, 22 (2012), pp. 1–8.

Anonymous, 'Richard III: Chantry Founder', *Notes and Queries*, clxvii (1934).

Antonovics, A.V., 'Henry VII, King of England, "By the Grace of Charles VIII of France" ', in *Kings and Nobles*, eds R.A. Griffiths and J.W. Sherborne (Gloucester, A. Sutton, 1986), pp. 169–84.

Armstrong, C.A.J., *England, France and Burgundy in the Fifteenth Century* (London, Hambledon Press, 1983).

Arthurson, I., *The Perkin Warbeck Conspiracy 1491–1499* (Stroud, Sutton, 1994).

Arthurson, I. and Kingwell, N., 'The Proclamation of Henry Tudor as King of England, 3 November 1483', *Historical Research*, 63 (1990), pp. 100–6.

Ashdown-Hill, J., *The Last Days of Richard III* (Stroud, The History Press, 2010).

Attreed, L.C., 'An Indenture between Richard Duke of Gloucester and the Scrope Family of Masham, and Upsall', *Speculum*, 58 (1983), pp. 1018–25.

Attreed, L.C., 'The King's Interest: York's Fee Farm and the Central Government, 1482–92', *Northern History*, 17 (1981), pp. 24–33.

Barnard, F.P., *Edward IV's French Expedition of 1475. The Leaders and their Badges* (Oxford, Clarendon Press, 1925).

Barnes, P.M., 'The Chancery *corpus cum causa* Files', in *Medieval Legal Records*, eds R.F. Hunnisett and J. Post (London, HMSO, 1978), pp. 430–45.

Barnfield, M., 'Diriment Impediments, Dispensations and Divorce: Richard III and Matrimony', *Ricardian*, 17 (2007), pp. 84–98.

Barron, C.M. and Davies, M. (eds), *The Religious Houses of London and Middlesex* (London, Institute of Historical Research, 2007).

Bateson, E. et al., *A History of Northumberland*, 15 vols (Newcastle, A. Reid, 1893–1940).

Bean, J.M.W., *The Estates of the Percy Family 1416–1537* (London, Oxford University Press, 1958).

Bennett, M., *The Battle of Bosworth* (Gloucester, Sutton, 1985).

Bennett, M., 'Edward III's Entail and the Succession to the Crown', *English Historical Review*, 113 (1998), pp. 580–609.

Bennett, M., *Lambert Simnel and the Battle of Stoke* (Gloucester, Sutton, 1987).

Blair, C. and Hunter, H., 'Two Letters Patent from Hutton John near Penrith, Cumberland', *Archaeologia Aeliana*, 4th series, 39 (1961), pp. 367–70.

Boatwright, L., 'The Buckinghamshire Six at Bosworth', *Ricardian*, 13 (2003), pp. 54–66.

Bolden, E.J., 'Richard III: Central Government and Administration', *Ricardian*, 149 (2000), pp. 71–81.

Booth, P., 'Richard, Duke of Gloucester and the West March towards Scotland, 1470–1483', *Northern History*, 36 (2000), pp. 233–46.

Brondarbit A., 'The Allocation of Power: The Ruling Elite of Edward IV, 1461–1483', PhD thesis (Winchester University, 2015).

Buck, G., *History of King Richard III*, ed. A.N. Kincaid (Gloucester, A. Sutton, 1979).

Calmette, J. and Périnelle, G., *Louis XI et l'Angleterre 1461–83* (Paris, Auguste Picard, 1930).

Carpenter, C., *The Wars of the Roses. Politics and the Constitution in England, c. 1437–1509* (Cambridge University Press, 1997).

Carson, A.J. (ed.), *Finding Richard III: The Official Account* (Horstead, Imprimis Imprimatur, 2014).

Chrimes, S.B, *English Constitutional Ideas in the Fifteenth Century* (Cambridge University Press, 1936).

Chrimes, S.B, *Henry VII* (London, 1970).

Chrimes, S.B, *Lancastrians, Yorkists and Henry VII* (London, Macmillan, 1964).

Chrimes, S.B., Ross, C.D., and Griffiths, R.A. (eds), *Fifteenth-century England, 1399–1609: Politics and Society* (Manchester University Press, 1972).

Clarke, P., 'English Royal Marriages and the Papal Penitentiary in the Fifteenth Century', *English Historical Review*, 120 (2005), pp. 1014–29.

Clay, J.W., *Extinct and Dormant Peerages of the Northern Counties of England* (London, J. Nisbet, 1913).

Cobban, A.B., *The King's Hall Within the University of Cambridge in the Later Middle Ages* (Cambridge University Press, 1969).

Cokayne, G.E., *Complete Peerage of England, Scotland, Ireland, Great Britain and the United Kingdom*, eds H.V. Gibbs, et al., 13 vols (London, St Catherine Press, 1910–59).

Coles, G.M., 'The Lordship of Middleham', unpublished MA thesis (Liverpool University, 1961).

Condon, M., 'Bosworth Field: A Footnote to a Controversy', *Ricardian*, 96 (1987), pp. 363–5.

Court, D., 'The Portuguese Connection – A Communication', *Ricardian*, 81 (1983), pp. 190–3.

Crawford, A., *Yorkist Lord: John Howard, Duke of Norfolk, c.1425–1485* (London, Bloomsbury, 2010).

Crawford, A., *The Yorkists. The History of a Dynasty* (London, Continuum, 2007).

Cunningham, S., *Henry VII* (London, Routledge, 2007).

Cunningham, S., 'Henry VII and Rebellion in North-Eastern England, 1485–92: Bonds of Allegiance and the Establishment of Tudor Authority', *Northern History*, 32 (1996), pp. 42–74.

Currin, J.M., 'Henry VII and the Treaty of Redon (1489): Plantagenet Ambitions and Early Tudor Foreign Policy', *History*, 81 (1996), pp. 343–58.

Delany, S., *Impolitic Bodies. Poetry, Saints and Society in Fifteenth-Century England. The Work of Osbern Bokenham* (Oxford University Press, 1998).

Dobson, R.B., *Church and Society in the Medieval North of England* (London, Continuum, 1996).

Dockray, K., 'The Political Legacy of Richard III in Northern England', in *Kings and Nobles*, eds R.A. Griffiths and J.W. Sherborne (Gloucester, A. Sutton, 1986), pp. 205–27.

Dockray, K., 'Richard III and the Yorkshire Gentry' in *Richard III: Loyalty, Lordship and Law*, ed. P.W. Hammond (London, Richard III and Yorkist History Trust, 1986), pp. 38–57.

Donmall, M. and Morris, R.K. 'The Bones in the Clarence Vault', in *Tewkesbury Abbey: History, Art and Architecture*, eds R.K. Morris and R. Shoesmith (Hereford, Logaston Press, 2003), pp. 31–40.

Drewett, R. and Redhead, M., *Trial of Richard III* (Gloucester, A. Sutton, 1984).

Dunham, W.H., 'The "Books of Parliament" and the "Old Record" 1396–1504', *Speculum*, 51 (1976), pp. 694–712.

Dunham, W.H., 'Lord Hastings' Indentured Retainers 1461–83', *Transactions of the Connecticut Academy of Arts and Sciences*, 39 (1955), pp. 1–175.

Dunlop, D., 'The "Redresses and Reparacons of Attemptates": Alexander Legh's Instructions from Edward IV, March–April 1475', *Historical Research*, 63 (1990), pp. 341–53.

Dunning, R.W., 'Thomas, Lord Dacre and the West March towards Scotland? 1435', *Bulletin of the Institute of Historical Research*, 41 (1968), pp. 95–9.

Edwards, R., *The Itinerary of Richard III 1483–5* (London, Richard III Society, 1985).

Emden, A.B., *Biographical Register of the University of Oxford to AD 1500*, 3 vols (Oxford, Clarendon Press, 1957–9).

Emden, A.B., *Biographical Register of the University of Cambridge to AD 1500* (Cambridge University Press, 1963).

Foard, G. and Curry, A., *Bosworth 1485: A Battlefield Rediscovered* (Oxford, Oxbow Books, 2013).

Gairdner, J., *History of the Life and Reign of Richard the Third* (Cambridge University Press, 1898).

Gill, L., *Richard III and Buckingham's Rebellion* (Stroud, Sutton, 1999).

Gillingham, J. (ed.), *Richard III: A Medieval Kingship* (London, Collins & Brown, 1993).

Given-Wilson, C., 'Chronicles of the Mortimer Family, c.1250–1450', in *Family and Dynasty in Late Medieval England*, eds R. Eales and S. Tyas (Donington, Harlaxton Symposium, 2003), pp. 67–86.

Goodman, A., 'The Impact of Warfare on the Scottish Marches, c.1481–c.1513', in *The Fifteenth Century VII: Conflicts, Consequences and the Crown in the Late Middle Ages*, ed. L. Clark (Woodbridge, Boydell, 2007), pp. 195–212.

Goodman, A. *The Wars of the Roses: Military Activity and English Society, 1452–97* (London, Routledge & Kegan Paul, 1981).

Goodman, A., *The Wars of the Roses: The Soldiers' Experience* (Stroud, History Press, 2003).

Goodman, A. and Mackay, A. 'A Castilian Report on English Affairs, 1486', *English Historical Review*, 88 (1973), pp. 92–9.

Goodman, A. and Morgan, D.A.L., 'The Yorkist Claim to the Throne of Castile', *Journal of Medieval History*, 12 (1985), pp. 61–9.

Green, R.F., 'The Historical Notes of a London Citizen 1483–88', *English Historical Review*, 96 (1981), pp. 585–90.

Gregory, P., *The Kingmaker's Daughter* (London, Simon & Schuster, 2012).

Gregory, P., *The White Queen* (London, Simon & Schuster, 2009).

Grey Friars Research Team, *The Bones of a King Richard III Rediscovered* (Chichester, Wiley, 2015).

Griffiths, R.A. 'Gentlemen and Rebels in Later Medieval Cardiganshire', in *Conquerors and Conquered in Medieval Wales* (Gloucester, Sutton, 1994), pp. 49–66.

Griffiths, R.A., *King and Country: England and Wales in the Fifteenth Century* (Hambledon, 1991).

Griffiths, R.A., *The Principality of Wales in the Later Middle Ages*, I, *South Wales 1277–1536* (Cardiff, University of Wales Press, 1977).

Griffiths, R.A., *Sir Rhys ap Thomas and his Family: A Study in the Wars of the Roses and Early Tudor Politics* (Cardiff, University of Wales Press, 1993).

Griffiths, R.A. and Sherborne, J.W. (eds), *Kings and Nobles in the Later Middle Ages* (Gloucester, A. Sutton, 1986).

Griffiths, R.A., and Thomas, R.S., *The Making of the Tudor Dynasty* (Gloucester, History Press, 1985).

Grummitt, D., *The Calais Garrison. War and Military Service in England, 1436–1558* (Woodbridge, Boydell & Brewer, 2008).

Grummitt, D., *The Wars of the Roses* (London, I.B. Tauris, 2013).

Grummitt, D., 'William, Lord Hastings, the Calais Garrison, and the Politics of Yorkist England', *Ricardian*, 12 (2001), pp. 262–74.

Halstead, C., *Richard III as Duke of Gloucester and King of England*, 2 vols (London, Longman, Brown, Green, 1844).

Hammond, P.W., *The Battles of Barnet and Tewkesbury* (Gloucester, Sutton, 1990).

Hammond, P.W., *Richard III and the Bosworth Campaign* (Barnsley, Pen & Sword Books, 2010).

Hammond, P.W. (ed.), *Richard III. Loyalty, Lordship and Law* (London, Richard III and Yorkist History Trust, 1986).

Hampton, W.E., *Memorials of the Wars of the Roses* (Upminster, Richard III Society, 1979).

Hanham, A., *Richard III and His Early Historians 1483–1535* (Oxford, Clarendon Press, 1975).

Harrison, F., *Life in a Medieval College: The Vicars Choral of York Minster* (London, John Murray, 1952).

Harriss, G.L., *Shaping the Nation. England 1360–1461* (Oxford University Press, 2005).

Hatcher, H., *History of Modern Wiltshire: Old and New Sarum*, ed. R.C. Hoare (J. Nichols, 1822–44).

Hicks, M.A., *Anne Neville, Queen to Richard III* (Stroud, History Press, 2005).

Hicks, M.A. *Bastard Feudalism* (Harlow, Longman, 1995).

Hicks, M.A., 'The Career of George Plantagenet, Duke of Clarence, 1449–78', D.Phil. thesis (Oxford University, 1975).

Hicks, M.A., 'The Career of Henry Percy, Fourth Earl of Northumberland (c.1448–89), with Special Reference to his Retinue', MA thesis (Southampton University, 1971).

Hicks, M.A., 'Crowland's World: A Westminster View of the Yorkist Age', *History*, 90 (2005), pp. 172–90.

Hicks, M.A., 'Did Edward V Outlive his Reign or did he Outreign His Life?', *Ricardian*, 108 (1990), pp. 342–5.

Hicks, M.A. 'Dynastic Change and Northern Society: The Career of the Fourth Earl of Northumberland, 1470–1489', *Northern History*, 14 (1978), pp. 78–107.

Hicks, M.A., 'Edward IV's *Brief Treatise* and the Treaty of Picquigny 1475', *Historical Research*, 83 (2010), pp. 253–65.

Hicks, M.A., *Edward V. The Prince in the Tower* (Stroud, History Press, 2003).

Hicks, M.A. 'English Monasteries as Repositories of Ancestral Memory', in *Monuments and Monumentality Across Medieval and Early Modern Europe*, ed. M. Penman (Donington, Shaun Tyas, 2013), pp. 224–38.

Hicks, M.A., *English Political Culture in the Fifteenth Century* (London, Routledge, 2002).

Hicks, M.A., *False, Fleeting, Perjur'd Clarence. George Duke of Clarence 1449–78* (Gloucester, A. Sutton, 1980).

Hicks, M.A., *The Family of Richard III* (Stroud, Amberley Publishing, 2015).

Hicks, M.A. 'The 1469 Statute of Livery', *Historical Research*, 64 (1991), pp. 16–20.

Hicks, 'Retainers, Monks and Wine: Three Insights into Everyday Life', in *The Later Medieval Inquisitions Post Mortem: Mapping the Medieval Countryside and Rural Society*, ed. M. Hicks (Woodbridge, Boydell Press, 2016), pp. 174–92.

Hicks, M.A., *Richard III* (Stroud, Tempus, 2000).

Hicks, M.A., *Richard III: The Man Behind the Myth* (London, Collins & Brown, 1991).

Hicks, M.A., *Richard III and his Rivals. Magnates and their Motives in the Wars of the Roses* (London, Hambledon Press, 1991).

Hicks, M.A., 'Richard Lord Latimer, Richard III, and the "Warwick Inheritance" ', *Ricardian*, 154 (2001), pp. 314–20.

Hicks, M.A. 'The Royal Bastards of Late Medieval England', in *La Bâtardise et l'Exercice du Pouvoir en Europe du XIIIe au début du XVIe siècle*, eds E. Bousmar, A. Marchandisse, C. Masson, and B. Schnerb, Revue du Nord (Université Lille, 2015), pp. 369–86.

Hicks, M.A., 'The Second Anonymous Continuation of the Crowland Abbey Chronicles 1459–1486 Revisited', *English Historical Review*, 122 (2007), pp. 351–70.

Hicks, M.A., 'A Study of Failure: The Minority of Edward V', in *Royal Minorities of Medieval and Early Medieval England*, ed. C. Beem (Basingstoke, Palgrave Macmillan, 2008), pp. 195–210.

Hicks, M.A., 'Unweaving the Web: The Plot of July 1483 against Richard III and its Wider Significance', *Ricardian*, 114 (1991), pp. 106–9.

Hicks, M.A., *The Wars of the Roses 1455–85* (Oxford, Osprey, 2003).

Hicks, M.A., *Warwick the Kingmaker* (Oxford, Blackwell, 1998).

Hipshon, D., *Richard III* (London, Routledge, 2011).

Holmes, G.A., *The Estates of the Higher Nobility in Fourteenth-Century England* (Cambridge University Press, 1957).

Horowitz, M.R. (ed.), *Who Was Henry VII? Historical Research*, special issue (London, Institute of Historical Research, 2009).

Horrox, R.E. (ed.), *Fifteenth-Century Attitudes: Perceptions of Society in Late Medieval England* (Cambridge University Press, 1994).

Horrox, R.E., 'Henry Tudor's Letters to England during Richard's Reign', *Ricardian*, 80 (1983), pp. 155–8.

Horrox, R.E., 'An Invisible Man: John Prince and the Dispute over Gregories Manor', in *Much Heaving and Shoving. Essays for Colin Richmond*, ed. M. Aston and R. Horrox (Lavenham, Aston & Horrox, 2005), pp. 67–75.

Horrox, R.E., 'Richard III', *Oxford Dictionary of National Biography* (Oxford University Press, 2004), 46, p. 739.

Horrox, R.E., 'Richard III and All Hallows Barking by the Tower', *Ricardian*, 77 (1982), pp. 38–40.

Horrox, R.E., 'Richard III and London', *Ricardian*, 85 (1984), pp. 322–9.

Horrox, R.E. (ed.), *Richard III and the North* (Hull University, 1986).

Horrox, R.E., *Richard III. A Study of Service* (Cambridge University Press, 1989).

Horrox, R.E. and A.F. Sutton, 'Some Expenses of Richard Duke of Gloucester 1475–7', *Ricardian*, 83 (1983), pp. 266–9.

Hughes, J., ' "True Ornaments to Know a Holy Man": Northern Religious Life and the Piety of Richard III', in *The North of England in the Age of Richard III*, ed. A.J. Pollard (Stroud, Sutton, 1996), pp. 149–90.

Hutton, W., *The Battle of Bosworth Field* (London, 1788).

Ives, E.W., 'Andrew Dymmock and the Papers of Antony Earl Rivers 1482–3', *Bulletin of the Institute of Historical Research*, 41 (1968), pp. 216–29.

Johnson, P.A., *Duke Richard of York 1411–60* (Oxford University Press, 1988).

Jones, M.K., *Bosworth 1485: Psychology of a Battle* (Stroud, Tempus, 2002).

Jones, M.K., 'Sir William Stanley of Holt: Politics and Family Allegiance in the Late Fifteenth Century', *Welsh History Review*, 14 (1988), pp. 1–22.

Jones, M.K. and Underwood, M.G., *The King's Mother. Lady Margaret Beaufort, Countess of Richmond and Derby* (Cambridge University Press, 1992).

Jurkowski, J., Smith, C.L. and Crook, D., *Lay Taxes in England and Wales 1188–1688* (Kew, Public Record Office, 1998).

Kendall, P.M., *Richard III* (New York, W.W. Norton, 1955).

King, T.E. et al., 'Identification of the Remains of King Richard III', *New Communications*, 5 (2014), pp. 1–8.

Kingsford, C.L., *English Historical Literature of the Fifteenth Century* (Oxford, Clarendon Press, 1913).

Kleineke, H., *Edward IV* (Abingdon, Routledge, 2009).

Kleineke, H., 'Gerhard von Wesel's Newsletter from England, 17 April 1471', *Ricardian*, 16 (2006), pp. 66–83.

Kleineke, H., ' "The Kynges Cite": Exeter in the Wars of the Roses', in *The Fifteenth Century VII: Conflicts, Consequences and the Crown in the Late Middle Ages*, ed. L. Clark (Woodbridge, Boydell, 2007), pp. 137–56.

Kleineke, H., 'Why the West was Wild: Law and Disorder in Fifteenth-Century Cornwall and Devon', in *The Fifteenth Century III: Authority and Subversion*, ed. L. Clark (Woodbridge, Boydell, 2003), pp. 75–93.

Kleineke, H. and C. Steer (eds), *The Yorkist Age* (Donington, Shaun Tyas, 2013).

Kleyn, Diana, *Richard of England* (Oxford, Kensal Press, 1990).

Lander, J.R., *Crown and Nobility 1450–1509* (London, Hodder & Stoughton, 1976).

Langley, P. and Jones, M., *The Search for Richard III: The King's Grave* (London, Hodder & Stoughton, 2013).

Laynesmith, J.L., *Cecily Duchess of York* (London, Bloomsbury, 2018).

Laynesmith, J.L., *The Last Medieval Queens* (Oxford University Press, 2004).

Levine, M., 'Richard III: Usurper or Lawful King?', *Speculum*, 34 (1959), pp. 391–401.

Levy, F.J., *Tudor Historical Thought* (San Marino, CA, Huntington Library, 1967).

Macdougall, N., *James III. A Political Study* (Edinburgh, John Donald, 1982).

Macdougall, N., 'Richard III and James III. Contemporary Monarchs, Parallel Mythologies', in P.W. Hammond, *Richard III: Loyalty, Lordship and Law* (London: Richard III and Yorkist History Trust, 1986), pp. 148–71.

McFarlane, K.B., *England in the Fifteenth Century* (London, Bloomsbury, 1981).

McFarlane, K.B., *The Nobility of Later Medieval England* (Oxford, Clarendon Press, 1973).

McKelvie, G., 'The Bastardy of Edward V in 1484: New Evidence of its Reception in the Inquisitions Post Mortem of William, Lord Hastings', *Royal Studies Journal*, 3(1) (2017), pp. 71–9.

McKelvie, G., 'The Legality of Bastard Feudalism: The Statutes of Livery, 1390 to c.1520', PhD thesis (Winchester University, 2012).

Meek, E., 'The Career of Sir Thomas Everingham, "Knight of the North" in the Service of Maximilian, Duke of Austria 1477–81', *Historical Research*, 74 (2001), pp. 238–48.

Mertes, K., *The English Noble Household 1250–1600* (Oxford, Blackwell, 1988).

Metcalfe, W.C., *Book of Knights* (London, Mitchell & Hughes, 1885).

Molleson, T., 'Anne Mowbray and the Princes in the Tower', *London Archaeologist*, 5(10) (1987), pp. 258–62.

Moreton, C., 'A Local Dispute and the Politics of 1483: Roger Townshend, Earl Rivers and the Duke of Gloucester', *Ricardian*, 107 (1989), pp. 305–7.

Morgan, D.A.L., 'The King's Affinity in the Polity of Yorkist England', *Transactions of the Royal Historical Society*, 23 (1973), pp. 1–25.

Morgan, P., ' "Those Were the Days": A Yorkist Pedigree Roll', in *Estrangement, Enterprise and Education in Fifteenth Century England*, eds S. Michalove and A. Compton Reeves (Stroud, Sutton, 1998), pp. 107–16.

Morris, M. and Buckley, R., *Richard III: The King Under the Car Park* (University of Leicester, 2014).

Musson, A. and Ramsay, N. (eds), *The Courts of Chivalry and Admiralty in Late Medieval Europe* (Woodbridge, Boydell Press, 2018).

Myers, A.R., 'The Character of Richard III', in *English Society and Government*, ed. C.M.D. Crowder (London, Oliver & Boyd, 1967), pp. 112–33.

Myers, A.R., *Crown, Household and Parliament in Fifteenth Century England*, ed. C.H. Clough (London, Hambledon Press, 1985).

Myers, A.R., *The Household of Edward IV* (Manchester University Press, 1959).

Myers, A.R., 'Richard III and the Historical Tradition', *History*, 53 (1968), pp. 182–3.

Noble, E. *The World of the Stonors: A Gentry Society* (Woodbridge, Boydell, 2009).

Orme, N., *From Childhood to Chivalry. The Education of English Kings and Aristocracy 1066–1530* (London, Routledge, 1984).

Oxford Dictionary of National Biography, 60 vols (Oxford University Press, 2004).

Palliser, D.M., *Medieval York 600–1540* (Oxford University Press, 2014).

Petre, J. (ed.), *Richard III: Crown and People* (Gloucester, Sutton, 1985).

Pitts, M., *Digging for Richard III: How Archaeology Found the King* (London, Thames & Hudson, 2014).

Pollard, A.J., *Edward IV. 'The Summer King'* (London, Allen Lane, 2016).

Pollard, A.J., *Late Medieval England 1399–1509* (Harlow, Longman, 2000).

Pollard, A.J., 'Lord FitzHugh's Rising in 1470', *Bulletin of the Institute of Historical Research*, 52 (1979), pp. 170–5.

Pollard, A.J. (ed.), *The North of England in the Age of Richard III* (Stroud, Sutton, 1996).

Pollard, A.J., *North-Eastern England during the Wars of the Roses: Lay Society, War, and Politics 1450–1500* (Oxford, Clarendon Press, 1990).

Pollard, A.J., 'The Northern Retainers of Richard Nevill, Earl of Salisbury', *Northern History*, 11 (1976), pp. 52–69.

Pollard, A.J., *Richard III and the Princes in the Tower* (Stroud, Sutton, 1991).

Pollard, A.J., *The Wars of the Roses*, 3rd edn (Basingstoke, Palgrave Macmillan, 2013).

Pollard, A.J. (ed.), *The Wars of the Roses* (Basingstoke, Macmillan, 1995).

Pollard, A.J., *Warwick the Kingmaker. Politics, Power and Fame* (London, Bloomsbury, 2007).

Pollard, A.J., *The Worlds of Richard III* (Stroud, Tempus Publishing, 2001).

Potter, J., *Good King Richard?* (London, Constable, 1985).

Prince, J. *The Worthies of Devon* (Plymouth, Rees & Curtis, 1810).

Pugh, T.B., 'The Estates, Finances and Regal Aspirations of Richard Plantagenet (1411–60), Duke of York', in *Revolution and Consumption in Late Medieval England*, ed. M. Hicks (Woodbridge, Boydell Press, 2001), pp. 71–88.

Pugh, T.B. (ed.), *Glamorgan County History, vol. 3, The Middle Ages* (Cardiff, University of Wales Press, 1971).

Pugh, T.B., 'Richard, Duke of York and the Rebellion of Henry Holland, Duke of Exeter, in May 1454', *Historical Review*, 63 (1990), pp. 248–62.

Pugh, T.B., 'Richard Plantagenet (1411–60), Duke of York, as the King's Lieutenant in France and Ireland', in *Aspects of Late Medieval Government and Society*, ed. J.G. Rowe (University of Toronto Press, 1986), pp. 107–42.

Raban, S., *Mortmain Legislation and the English Church 1279–1500* (Cambridge University Press, 1982).

Ramsay, N., 'Richard III and the Office of Arms', in *The Yorkist Age*, eds H. Kleineke and C. Steer (Donington, Harlaxton Medieval Studies, 2013), pp. 142–63.

Rawcliffe, C., 'Richard, Duke of York, the King's "Obeisant Liegeman": A New Source of the Protectorates of 1454 and 1455', *Historical Research*, 60(142) (1987), pp. 232–9.

Rawcliffe, C., *The Staffords, Earls of Stafford and Dukes of Buckingham, 1394–1521* (Cambridge University Press, 1978).

Reid, R.R., *The King's Council in the North* (London, Longman, 1921).

Richmond, C., 'Fauconberg's Kentish Rising of May 1471', *English Historical Review*, 85 (1970), pp. 682–9.

Richmond, C., *John Hopton: A Fifteenth Century Suffolk Gentleman* (Cambridge University Press, 1981).

Rose, S. *The Wealth of England* (Oxford, Oxbow Books, 2018).

Rosenthal, J.T., 'Other Victims: Peeresses as War Widows 1450–1500', *History*, 72 (1987), pp. 213–30.

Rosenthal, J.T., 'Richard, Duke of York: A Fifteenth-Century Layman and the Church', *Catholic Historical Review*, 50(2) (1964), pp. 171–87.

Roskell, J.S., 'The Office and Dignity of Lord Protector of England, with special reference to its origins', *English Historical Review*, 68 (1953), pp. 193–233.

Roskell, J.S., *Parliament and Politics in Late Medieval England*, 3 vols (London, Hambledon Press, 1981–3).

Ross, C.D., *Edward IV* (London, Eyre Methuen, 1974).

Ross, C.D. (ed.), *Patronage, Pedigree and Power in Later Medieval England* (Gloucester, A. Sutton, 1979).

Ross, C.D., *Richard III* (London, Eyre Methuen, 1981).

Ross, J.A., *John de Vere, Thirteenth Earl of Oxford, 1442–1513: 'The Foremost Man of the Kingdom'* (Woodbridge, Boydell Press, 2011).

Ross, J.A., 'Richard, Duke of Gloucester and the De Vere Estates', *Ricardian*, 15 (2005), pp. 20–32.

Ross, J.A., 'Richard Duke of Gloucester and the Purchase and Sale of Hooton Pagnell, Yorkshire, 1475–80', *Ricardian*, 22 (2012), pp. 47–54.

Rowse, A.L. *Bosworth Field and the Wars of the Roses* (London, Macmillan, 1966).

Royle, T., *The Road to Bosworth Field* (London, Little, Brown, 2009).

Sadler, J., *The Red Rose and the White: The Wars of the Roses 1453–87* (Harlow, Longman, 2010).

Santiuste, D., *Edward IV and the Wars of the Roses* (Barnsley, Pen and Sword, 2010).

Saul, N., *The Three Richards: Richard I, Richard II and Richard III* (London, Hambledon Continuum, 2005).

Scofield, C.L., *The Life and Reign of Edward the Fourth*, 2 vols (London, Longmans, Green, 1923).

Searle, W.G., *The History of the Queens' College of St Margaret and St Bernard, Cambridge* (Cambridge Antiquarian Society, 1867).

Sellar, W.C. and Yeatman, R.J., *1066 and All That* (London, Methuen, 1930).

Shakespeare, W., *Richard III*, ed. A. Hammond, Arden edn (London, Methuen, 1981).

Sharp, C., *The Rising in the North: The 1569 Rebellion* (Durham, Shotton, 1975).

Shaw, W.A., *The Knights of England* (London, Sherratt and Hughes, 1906).

Skidmore, C., *Bosworth. The Birth of the Tudors* (London, Weidenfeld & Nicolson, 2013).

Somerville, R., *History of the Duchy of Lancaster*, vol. 1 (Chancellor and Council of the Duchy of Lancaster, 1953).

Steel, A.B., *Receipt of the Exchequer 1377–1485* (Cambridge University Press, 1954).

Stone, L., *Family and Fortune: Studies in Aristocratic Finance in the Sixteenth and Seventeenth Century* (Oxford, Clarendon Press, 1973).

Storey, R.L., 'The Wardens of the Marches of England towards Scotland, 1377–1489', *English Historical Review*, 72 (1957), pp. 539–615.

Summerson, H., *Medieval Carlisle*, 2 vols (Kendal, Cumberland & Westmorland Antiquarian & Archaeological Society, 1993).

Surtees, R., *History and Antiquities of the County of Durham*, 4 vols (1816–40).

Sutton, A.F., 'Richard of Gloucester 1461–70: Income, Lands and Associates. His Whereabouts and Responsibilities', *Ricardian*, 26 (2016), pp. 43–53.

Sutton, A.F., 'Richard of Gloucester's Lands in East Anglia', in *Richard III and East Anglia: Magnates, Gilds and Learned Men*, ed. L. Visser-Fuchs (London, Richard III Society, 2010), pp. 5–10.

Sutton, A.F., 'Richard of Gloucester Visits Norwich, August 1471', *Ricardian*, 95 (1986), pp. 233–4.

Sutton, A.F., 'Sir John Skrene, Richard of Gloucester, and Queens' College, Cambridge', *Ricardian*, 21 (2011), pp. 38–45.

Sutton, A.F. and Visser-Fuchs, L., ' "Chevalerie in som partie is worthi forto be comendid, and in some part to ben amendid". Chivalry and the Yorkist Kings', in *St George's Chapel, Windsor, in the Late Middle Ages*, eds C. Richmond and E. Scarff (Dean and Canons of Windsor, 2001), pp. 107–33.

Sutton, A.F. and Visser-Fuchs, L., *Hours of Richard III* (Stroud, A. Sutton, 1990).

Sutton, A.F. and Visser-Fuchs, L., 'Laments for the Death of Edward IV', *Ricardian*, 145 (1999), pp. 506–24.

Sutton, A.F. and Visser-Fuchs, L., *Richard III's Books* (Stroud, A. Sutton, 1997).

Sutton, A.F. and Visser-Fuchs, L., 'Richard of Gloucester and *la grosse bombarde*', *Ricardian*, 134 (1996), p. 461.

Sutton, A.F., Visser-Fuchs, L. and Kleineke, H., 'The Children in the Care of Richard III: New References. A Lawsuit between Peter Courteys, Keeper of Richard III's Great Wardrobe, and Thomas Lynom, Solicitor of Richard III, 1495–1501', *Ricardian*, 24 (2014), pp. 31–62.

Sweetinburgh, S., 'Those who Marched with Faunt: Reconstructing the Canterbury Rebels of 1471', *Southern History*, 39 (2017), pp. 36–57.

Tanner, L.E. and Wright, W., 'Recent Investigations Regarding the Fate of the Princes in the Tower', *Archaeologia*, 34 (1934), pp. 1–26.

Tey, J., *The Daughter of Time* (Harmondsworth, Penguin, 1969).

Thomas, D.H., *The Herberts of Raglan and the Battle of Edgecote 1469* (Enfield, Freezywater Publications, 1994).

Thomson, J.A.F., 'Bishop Lionel Woodville and Richard III', *Bulletin of the Institute of Historical Research*, 59 (1986), pp. 130–5.

Tudor-Craig, P., *Richard III* (London, National Portrait Gallery, 1973).

Virgoe, R., *East Anglian Society and the Political Community of Late Medieval England*, eds Barron, C., Rawcliffe. C. and Rosenthal, J.T. (Norwich, University of East Anglia, 1997).

Visser-Fuchs, L. (ed.), *Richard III and East Anglia: Magnates, Gilds and Learned Men* (London, Richard III Society, 2010).

Visser-Fuchs, L., 'Richard in Holland 1461', *Ricardian*, 6 (1983), pp. 182–9.

Visser-Fuchs, L., 'Richard was Late', *Ricardian*, 147 (1999), pp. 616–18.

Visser-Fuchs, L. (ed.), 'Tant D'Emprises – So Many Undertakings. Essays in Honour of Anne F. Sutton', *Ricardian*, 13 (2003).

Visser-Fuchs, L., 'What Niclas von Popplau Really Wrote About Richard III', *Ricardian*, 145 (1999), pp. 525–30.

Walpole, H., *Historic Doubts on the Life and Reign of Richard III*, ed. P.W. Hammond (Gloucester, A. Sutton, 1987).

Ward, M., *The Livery Collar in Late Medieval England and Wales: Politics, Identity and Affinity* (Woodbridge, Boydell Press, 2016).

Wedgwood, J.C., *History of Parliament 1439–1509. Biographies of the Ministers and Members of Both Houses* (London, HMSO, 1936).

Wedgwood, J.C., *History of Parliament 1439–1509. Register of the Ministers and Members of Both Houses* (London, HMSO, 1938).

Weightman, C., *Margaret of York, Duchess of Burgundy 1446–1503* (New York, St Martin's Press, 1989).

Wilkinson, J., *Richard. The Young King to Be* (Stroud, Amberley Publishing, 2008).

Williams, B., 'The Portuguese Connection and the Significance of "the Holy Princess" ', *Ricardian*, 80 (1980), pp. 138–45.

Williams, M.E., 'Richard III: Chantry Founder', *Notes and Queries*, 167 (1934).

Wolffe, B.P., *The Crown Lands 1461–1536* (London, George Allen & Unwin, 1970).

Wolffe, B.P., *The Royal Demesne in English History* (London, George Allen & Unwin, 1971).

Wood, C., 'The Chantries and Chantry Chapels of St George's Chapel, Windsor Castle', *Southern History*, 31 (2010), pp. 48–74.

Woolgar, C. 'Fast and Feast: Conspicuous Consumption and the Diet of the Nobility in the Fifteenth Century', in *Revolution and Consumption in Late Medieval England*, ed. M. Hicks (Boydell Press, Woodbridge, 2001), pp. 7–25.

Yorath, D.M., 'Sir Christopher Moresby of Scaleby and Windermere, c.1441–99', *Northern History*, 53(2) (2016), pp. 173–88.

Yorath, D.M., '"There and back again": The Career of John Terranzeane (*c.* 1464–*c.* 1513)', *Northern History*, 55 (2), pp. 139–60.

INDEX